John Pilger

DISTANT VOICES

V

VINTAGE

FOR JANE AND DAVID

First published in Vintage 1992

10

This collection copyright © John Pilger 1994

The right of John Pilger to be identified as the author of this work has been asserted by him in accordance with the Copyright, Designs and Patents Act, 1988

This revised edition first published by Vintage, 1994

Vintage Books
Random House, 20 Vauxhall Bridge Road, London SW1V 2SA

Random House Australia (Pty) Limited
20 Alfred Street, Milsons Point, Sydney
New South Wales 2061, Australia

Random House New Zealand Limited
18 Poland Road, Glenfield
Auckland 10, New Zealand

Random House (Pty) Limited
Endulini, 5a Jubilee Road, Parktown 2193, South Africa

The Random House Group Limited Reg. No. 954009
www.randomhouse.co.uk

A CIP catalogue record for this book
is available from the British Library

Papers used by Random House are natural, recyclable products made from wood grown in sustainable forests. The manufacturing processes conform to the environmental regulations of the country of origin

ISBN 0 09 938721 2

Printed and bound in Great Britain by
Cox & Wyman Ltd, Reading, Berkshire

CONTENTS

CONTENTS

CONTENTS

PREFACE
by Martha Gellhorn

PUNCHING THROUGH TV channels, I found myself watching
a strange scene. A gang of literary lights was attacking a tall
lanky sunburned young man with curare-tipped words. It
was a very high-class panel book review programme. The
young man looked bewildered but dignified. I had never
heard of him, by name John Pilger, nor of his book, *The Last
Day*. It was apparently his first book, the record of an historic
event, the Retreat from the Embassy Roof, the suitably
shameful end of a vilely shameful war. The literary lights,
none of whom had attended that war (or probably any
other), were really attacking John Pilger's viewpoint, not his
facts or his prose. They seemed to think the Vietnam War
had been a good thing.

The next day, I bought and read the book and wrote to
the author, telling him how fine it was and that he should
not pay the slightest attention to his critics. That was in
1975. They've been attacking him ever since. Which proves
John's continuous success. ('Yeah,' John might say, a unique
drawled two-syllable sound that suggests he has been thinking it over calmly and almost agrees with you.)

After my fan letter, John came to see me. He said that
Hugh Cudlipp, then editor-in-chief of the *Mirror* (ah, the
golden past), read my 1966 Vietnam articles in the *Guardian*,
called him in, gave him the articles and said, that's the story,
go and get it. So began John's long devotion to the people of
Indo-China. I am always convinced that my writing is useless

xi

but it had done something very good if it got John to Vietnam. My 1966 articles appeared two years too early. I was repeatedly refused a visa to return to Vietnam. I had the painful honour of being the only journalist blacklisted out of that country and that war. Probably John did my work for me – though I must say I'd rather have been able to do it myself.

John is a compulsive worker, compulsive but not frenzied. He has plenty of material; he will never come to the end of it. Basically, it seems to me, he has taken on the great theme of justice and injustice. The misuse of power against the powerless. The myopic, stupid cruelty of governments. The bullying and lies that shroud *realpolitik*, a mad game played at the top, which is a curse to real people.

Conscience has made John a brave and invaluable witness to his time. In many circles, conscience is regarded as oafish; in periods of crisis, it is considered treasonable. During the Vietnam War, contempt for conscience produced the term 'bleeding hearts'. (Mrs Thatcher's 'wet' was of the same order of contempt.) It is tiring to own a conscience, and it does not endear the owner to our rulers. Not surprisingly, John opposed the use of force in the Gulf War, urging continued use of sanctions. Considering the miserable end of that war, with Saddam Hussein still firmly in place in Iraq, uncounted thousands of innocents dead, and millions uprooted, it looks as if his conscience was a first-rate guide.

I have not followed all of John's work; there is too much of it. More than 30 documentary films, five books, hundreds of thousands of words of reporting. But I do not forget the documentaries I have seen and probably no one who saw it will ever forget the great film *Year Zero*, made with David Munro, that showed the world what Pol Pot had done to the Cambodian people. Like John, I think that Nixon and Kissinger were father and mother to Pol Pot and that successive US governments, tirelessly punishing Vietnam for having won that war, have extended their vengeance to the Cambodians. John never hesitates to blame the powerful in the clearest language; they never fail to react with fury.

John's range is wide. He has done noble service to the Aborigines of Australia, and condemned his own government in the process. He made a film, dangerously and secretly, on the Charter 77 members in Czechoslovakia. He went to Japan and discovered the poor.

Whoever thought of Japanese as being poor? (To me, those black-clad hordes pouring out of bullet trains in Tokyo always looked like African soldier ants, which move in packed narrow streams and eat their way through everything, dead or alive.) Suddenly, like a revelation, the Japanese became human: a gently smiling giant, John bent to listen to tiny, wrinkled old people, and it turns out that Japanese can be poor, neglected and out of it, in rich Japan, as anywhere else. Steadily, John documents and proclaims the official lies that we are told and that most people accept or don't bother to think about. He is a terrible nuisance to Authority.

We agree on every political subject except Israel and the Palestinians. Thinking it over, I believe this has to do with age. John was born in October 1939, an infant in Australia during the Second World War. He was eight years old when the Jews of Palestine, who had accepted the UN Partition Plan, were forced to fight practically with their hands to survive the first combined Arab onslaught and declared their state. Perhaps nobody can understand Israel who does not remember the Second World War and how and why the nation came into being. Since we cannot change each other's views, John and I declare a truce, for I fear the Arab–Israel problem will not be solved in my lifetime.

It is lovely and comforting to have a friend who is as angry about the state of the world as you are yourself. It means you can give it a rest, have some drinks, go to the movies, talk about surfing and snorkelling – our different favourite occupations – make each other laugh. All the fame and fuss about John have not affected him. Off screen and off print, he is a modest, easy, somewhat shy man. He takes his work very seriously, but not himself. And that is, in itself, a remarkable quality.

Some years ago, John made an unnoted documentary series

called *The Outsiders*. He interviewed six or seven people, among them myself, dragooned by friendship into what I least like doing. I never saw the finished product and remember the names of only two of my fellow participants. I had never thought of myself as an outsider or an insider; the question did not arise. I wonder if Helen Suzman, at home in her own country saying 'No', thought of herself as an outsider. Or did Wilfred Burchett, an Australian, who said 'No' so much that the Australian Government peevishly took away his passport, think of himself that way?

It seems to me that John was simply interviewing people who had their own opinions and did their own work, whatever it was, as they saw fit. At most they could be called dissenters, but even that is rather grand, since we are used to dissenters paying with their life or liberty for their unpopular ideas. It occurred to me that this odd label had to do with the peculiar Aussie–Brit relationship and the way they regard each other. And, as a result, John saw himself as an outsider.

Of course he is not. He belongs to an old and unending worldwide company, the men and women of conscience. Some are as famous as Tom Paine and Wilberforce, some as unknown as a tiny group calling itself Grandmothers Against the Bomb, in an obscure small western American town, who have gone cheerfully to jail for their protests. There have always been such people and always will be. If they win, it is slowly; but they never entirely lose. To my mind, they are the blessed proof of the dignity of man. John has an assured place among them. I'd say he is a charter member for his generation.

July 12, 1991

ACKNOWLEDGEMENTS

I WOULD LIKE to express my appreciation to Frances Coady, who took up the idea for this book and shaped it and published it with such care and enthusiasm. While there are those like Frances publishing books, the threat to free information – one of the themes explored in these pages – faces formidable opposition.

I wish also to thank the following people who, in one way or another, have given me help and encouragement: Ron Beard, David Bowman, Mike Broderick, Carmel Budiardjo, Kevin Christanus, John Cody, Sue Crouch, Rachel Cugnoni, Gillian Curtis, Ana de Juan, Paul Donovan, Peter Dyer, Phyllis Few, John Garrett, Martha Gellhorn, Sue Griffin, Michelle Hartree, Tony Hewett, Barbara Hyik, Deborah Inman, Roger James, Jan Joyce, Ben Kiernan, Arnie Kohen, Jacqueline Korn, Stephen McEntee, Helen Martin, Bobby Muller, Chris Mullin, David Munro, Sue Nellis, Lorraine Nelson, Colin Nicholson, Carlos Otero, Donal Park, Sam Pilger, Zoë Pilger, Steve Platt, Chris Ramsey, Geoffrey Robertson, Chris Roffey, John Ross, Gil Scrine, Frances Shipsey, Bernie Simons, Val Simpson, Paul Vickers, Sarah Westcott, Sarah Wherry, Tracy Whitehouse.

I would like to add my special, loving thanks to Jane Hill, to whom this book is dedicated (with David Munro) and whose care for these pages, and for the author, made this work possible.

INTRODUCTION

THIS BOOK SETS out to offer a different way of seeing events of our day. I have tried to rescue from media oblivion uncomfortable facts which may serve as antidotes to the official truth; and in so doing, I hope to have given support to those 'distant voices' who understand how vital, yet fragile is the link between the right of people to know and to be heard, and the exercise of liberty and political democracy. This book is a tribute to them.

Written originally as essays for the *New Statesman and Society*, and the *Guardian* and the *Independent*, the collection draws on my previous books, notably *Heroes*.[1] Indeed, in some respects it is an extension of *Heroes*. I have rewritten and combined many of the pieces, adding new material as the dates at the end of each chapter indicate. This is especially true of the four long Cambodia chapters, which grew out of work published over a dozen years. Indeed, in this completely revised edition there is a great deal that is new, notably the chapters on East Timor, which formed the basis for my documentary film, *Death of a Nation*, broadcast in 1994.

I have used a range of styles, which I hope readers will regard as a strength. There are pieces written in response to unfolding events, as in the Gulf War, which have a contemporary feel rather than a linear narrative, and more reflective chapters such as those on East Timor, Cambodia and Australia. And there are pieces simply about people, which I enjoy writing, as in the opening chapters of 'Invisible Britain' and later, in 'Terminator in Bifocals'. There is also a shame-

1

lessly sentimental tribute to my typewriter, 'Baby Hermes', still going after 30 years and numerous close calls.

The title *Distant Voices* is taken from an essay I wrote in the wake of the disintegration of communist power in Eastern Europe and which argued that Western triumphalism and the 'new world order' had brought a renewed threat to many freedoms, such as diversity of expression.[2] The media, the arena in which I work, has been both a major victim of and a collaborator in the narrowing of information and ideas, although it is misrepresented as the very opposite. That's why the majority of these essays are about or touch upon the role of the media in controlling the way we see and in confining and isolating us in the present. This new power is perhaps best demonstrated in the section 'Mythmakers of the Gulf War'.

Long after the Gulf War, I remember vividly two surreal moments from television. The first was on the BBC's arts programme *The Late Show*, which devoted an edition to foreign correspondents talking about their adventures in the Gulf.[3] As each one spoke, the background filled with images from the war itself, mostly tanks and artillery and missiles flashing in the night. Then suddenly the scene changed to bulldozers at work; and the reporter's monologue was overwhelmed by shocking pictures behind him. Driven by Allied soldiers, the bulldozers were pushing thousands of bodies into mass graves. Many of the bodies were crushed, as if they had been run over. The memory reached back to similar scenes at Belsen, Dachau and Auschwitz where newsreel cameras recorded bulldozers pushing thousands of bodies into open pits.

To my knowledge the BBC's subversive blink was the only time the British public was allowed to see the *extent* of the slaughter in the Gulf. Certainly there were news reports of the 'turkey shoot' on the Basra road; and the famous *Observer* photograph of a man burnt to a skeletal monster, upright in the cabin of his truck.[4] But the dead generally were represented as looters, and the pathetic objects they had taken from Kuwait – toys, electric fans – were highlighted as evidence of their guilt. The crime of slaughtering people who were fleeing was passed off as an 'unfortunate' and 'tragic' postscript to a necessary war – a war in which precious few Allied lives were lost and Western technology had entertained the viewers at home. It had been both a good war and a clean war. That was the official truth.

The second memorable moment was Clive James reviewing 1991, again on BBC Television. In awarding Saddam Hussein the 'BBC's *Gardener's World* Award' as 'the person who's done most to transform the appearance of our planet in 1991', James made the war the joke of the year.[5] No bulldozers were shown, no bodies piled in open pits.

When these events next entered public consciousness, the process was complete: the unthinkable had been normalised. In May 1992 a coroner in Oxford handed down an 'unlawful killing' verdict on the deaths of nine British soldiers killed by American 'friendly fire'. Newspapers which had supported sending the troops to the Gulf and had colluded with the Ministry of Defence in obscuring the true nature of the war now attacked the government for 'covering up the truth' about the soldiers' deaths.

No irony was noted. Not a single reference was made to what the American writer Michael Albert has called 'one of the more wanton, cowardly massacres in modern military history', and which resulted in the deaths of as many as 200,000 men, women and children, none of them the subject of a British inquest or an international enquiry convened by the United Nations in whose name the slaughter was initiated. Most were almost certainly killed unlawfully: either by 'anti-personnel' weapons and 'weapons of mass destruction', whose legality has yet to be tested under the Geneva Convention; or by attacks on civilian centres, such as the RAF attack on the town of al-Nasiriyah; or while retreating and surrendering. Countless defenceless men were buried alive in the night beneath advancing American bulldozers, the same machines which were later used unlawfully to dump the dead in pits without respect for human identity and for the rights of their families to know the truth and to mourn.

The fact that the war continues today against the children of Iraq is of no interest to the Western media. Iraq is no longer 'a story'. There are more dramatic, more 'relevant' pictures to be had elsewhere. Thanks to a few – the voluntary aid agencies, the Harvard medical teams, Dr Eric Hoskins of the Gulf Peace Team, Victoria Brittain of the *Guardian* – careful readers will know that, as a direct result of American and British-led sanctions against Iraq, more than a million Iraqi children are seriously malnourished and more than 100,000 are seriously ill, and many of those are likely to die.[6] Iraqi doctors are struggling with a disease not seen for many years, *pica*, which babies contract by eating dirt.[7] In its latest study, the Harvard team describes Iraqi infants as 'the most traumatised children of war ever described'.[8] Like the slaughter that preceded it, the 'unthinkable has been normalised', as Edward S. Herman wrote in his fine essay, 'The Banality of Evil'.

Understanding this concept, in war and peace, is one of the aims of this book. As Herman pointed out: 'Doing terrible things in an organised and systematic way rests on "normalisation" . . . There is usually a division of labor in doing and rationalising the unthinkable, with the direct brutalising and killing done by one set of individuals . . . others working on improving technology (a better crematory gas, a longer burning and more adhesive Napalm, bomb fragments that penetrate flesh in hard-to-trace patterns). It is the function of the experts, and the mainstream media, to normalise the unthinkable for the general public.'[9]

Of course, 'normalising' can only be successful once 'distance' has been established. General Schwarzkopf's video game show during the Gulf War, which television dutifully transmitted at peak viewing times, was an outstanding example of this. Like the pilots who dropped the 'smart' bombs, politicians, journalists, bureaucrats and the public, all of us, were kept at a distance. In East Timor, the Suharto regime's murder of two television crews, its sealing of the country, and the collusive silence of Western governments, kept us all at a distance. What we could not see did not happen.

My own experience as a journalist, much of it spent in wartime and at places of upheaval, has taught me rudely about this process. The first time I saw and touched a victim of Napalm – her smouldering skin came away and stuck to my hand – I also saw the aircraft that had dropped the Napalm bomb on a village path. When, a few days later, I stood up at a press conference and asked an American briefer, a pleasant man just doing his job, if *he* had ever seen a victim of Napalm, he stared blankly at me, a beacon of incredulity. Earlier he had used the term 'collateral damage'. I asked him what this meant. He stared some more. Surely, I knew my 'ABC'. He finally asked me to 'rephrase' the question. I repeated it, twice, until he said the word 'people'. When I asked him if this meant 'civilian people', his affirmation was barely audible.

No doubt because I was young, this and other encounters of striking similarity left an impression upon me. I formed the view that journalism ought not to be a process that separated people from their actions, or itself an act of complicity. I became especially interested in the decision-making of those of apparently impeccable respectability, whose measured demeanour and 'greyness' contained not a hint of totalitarianism and yet who, at great remove in physical and cultural distance, executed and maimed people, destroying and dislocating their communities on a scale comparable with the accredited monsters of our time.

In the Cambodia and East Timor chapters I have described this synthesis – in Cambodia, between Nixon and Kissinger on the one hand and Pol Pot and his gang on the other. What the former began from afar, the latter completed. Only the method varied. To understand that is to begin to understand the true nature of the crime perpetrated in Cambodia and where the responsibility for it lies. And it helps to explain why every conceivable moral and intellectual contortion is currently being attempted to protect those who, in the 'division of labour', share the culpability either as accessories or apologists.

In the East Timor section I have drawn together my own experience as a reporter going undercover, with interviews conducted around the world with those who played a part in the cataclysmic events that have consumed that country beyond the reach of the TV camera and the satellite dish. In this way, with hillsides of crosses and faces of unsmiling, courageous people fresh in our memory, David Munro and I were able to reconstruct a largely forgotten history and lay before its culpable participants the enduring evidence of their work. For me, the brutal death of 200,000 East Timorese, a third of the population, says much about how the modern world is ordered and how most of us are pressed to believe otherwise.

The long 'silence' over the genocide in East Timor is indicative of how much of the modern media is ordered. In recent years a new version of an old ethos has arisen in the so-called 'free' media in the west. It was expressed succinctly in May 1992 by the director of programmes of the new British network television company, Carlton, which replaced Thames following the infamous auction of commercial franchises instigated by former prime minister Thatcher. Current affairs programmes 'that don't deliver', he said, 'will not survive in the new ITV'. To 'earn their way', they have to attract viewing audiences of at least six to eight million people, regardless of the subject matter. 'We have to be hard-headed and realistic,' he said.[10]

The departing editor of Thames's *This Week* series – which died with Thames – analysed this 'hard-headedness' and apparent failure to 'deliver'. He pointed out that the two ITV current affairs flag carriers, *This Week* and *World in Action*, represented 'the only area in commercial television that had not only maintained its popular audience, but improved it'; that current affairs audiences had increased by 60 per cent; and that *World in Action* with its thirty-five-year tradition of controversial, award-winning broadcast journalism, was set to *average* eight million viewers per programme. Moreover, current affairs drew larger audiences than even some 'light entertainment'.[11] Following the late-night screening of *Death of a Nation*, my film on East Timor, British Telecom reported calls to the advertised ITV 'helpline' number running at 4,000 a minute.

None of this ought to be surprising. What the public wants is so often not what the editor of the *Daily Beast* says they want. Year after year surveys of television trends demonstrate people's preference for strong, hard-hitting factual programmes. This and quality drama remain the strengths of British television while its listings show more and more anodyne sitcoms, the worst of Hollywood and soaps. In April 1994 Granada Television announced that it was dropping *World in Action* for two months to make way for a 'bumper episode' of *Coronation Street*. This will be the series' longest absence from the screen in its history.

Official truths are often powerful illusions, such as that of 'choice' in the media society. One of the principal arbiters of this is Rupert Murdoch. Having swallowed Times Newspapers and British Satellite Broadcasting with the help of his friend, Margaret Thatcher, Murdoch in 1992 added the television coverage of Britain's most popular game, football. In secret collusion with the BBC, Murdoch's BSkyB bought the rights to live coverage of all premier league games. As its cut of the deal, the BBC shows the highlights. Even those who already own a Murdoch satellite dish will almost certainly have to pay a monthly football charge, or be excluded from what millions regard as the high point of their week.

This is 'choice' at its most Orwellian, denying people not only programmes that are politically unpalatable but also their time-honoured pleasures. Murdoch's next 'buys' are reported to be the television coverage of the Grand National and the rugby union final. One wonders what the purpose is of such voracity. Profit, of course; and power of an explicit kind.

In an article entitled 'Britain's class war in a satellite dish', the London correspondent of Murdoch's *Australian*, Nicholas Rothwell, described Murdoch as a free-market Karl

Marx. 'Murdoch's empire has always shared one thing with the Marxist enterprise,' he wrote, 'it turns ideas into social and economic experiments . . . If BSkyB's swoop to seize control of televised soccer marks the climax of News Corporation's long-term plan for a self-reinforcing media system, it is also the culminating event in a social . . . and even ideological . . . transformation of Britain in the image of a radical philosophy: one which places the media corporation, as a promoter of information to the ordinary consumer, in direct opposition to the established elites'.[12]

This is presumably what Murdoch himself believes. As a principal backer of Thatcherism's 'radical philosophy', he can claim to have shaken the old order, helping to abolish the humanist wing of the Tory Party and to damage the royal family. As his London man implies, he intends to replace this with a Murdoch-approved elite which 'places the media corporation . . . in direct competition to the established elites'. In other words, so powerful are Murdoch and his fellow media corporatists that they hardly need governments any more.

For many people, this struggle between the elites means an accelerated erosion of real freedom. Under the old system the bias of the state operated through a 'consensus' that was broadly acceptable to the established order. Controversial television programmes could be kept off the air, or watered down, merely by applying arbitrary 'guidelines' that were accompanied by ritualistic nods and winks. In this way, *The War Game*, a brilliant dramatisation of the effects of a nuclear attack on Britain, was suppressed by the BBC for twenty years;[13] and during the same period more than fifty programmes critical of the war in Ireland were banned, delayed or doctored.[14]

As the influence of television has surpassed that of the press, perhaps in no other country has broadcasting held such a privileged position as an opinion leader. Possessing highly professional talent, and the illusion of impartiality (a venerable official truth, with its lexicon of 'balance', etc.), as well as occasionally dissenting programmes, 'public service broadcasting' developed into a finely crafted instrument of state propaganda. Witness the BBC's coverage of the Cold War, the wars in the Falklands and the Gulf, and the 1984–5 miners' strike.

One wonders why Thatcher wanted to change it. Of course paternalism and false consensus were not her way, neither was dissent in *any* effective form, albeit token. Thus, she never forgave Thames Television for showing *Death on the Rock* and exposing the activities of an SAS death squad in Gibraltar.

As for the BBC, most of its voices of dissent have long fallen silent. They are the broadcasters and producers who opposed the slaughter in the Gulf and the way it was represented to the British people, but who remained anonymous. Even before the last British election campaign had got under way, the BBC's principal current affairs programme, *Panorama*, felt the need to suppress a report that had made a few mildly critical observations of seasonal Tory back-stabbing over economic policy.[15]

Today BBC current affairs is seldom controversial as it is secured within a pyramid of 'directorates' that have little to do with free journalism and are designed to control: to shore up assumptions, not to challenge them. In any case, silence is no longer optional in the increasingly centralised, undemocratic state that is the other side of the media society. As the market has been 'freed' from state controls (i.e. nineteenth-century *laissez-faire* nostrums have been re-imposed), so information has been subjected to draconian new controls.

I have touched upon these restrictions in several chapters, believing that many people may be unaware that, behind the supermarket façade, certain state controls are now reminiscent of those in the old Soviet Union. As you drive south across Vauxhall Bridge in London you pass the most striking new building in the capital; it houses the domestic secret intelligence service, MI5, now expanding its role as a police and domestic surveillance force, its anonymity and unaccountability guaranteed by Parliament. How ironic that is, now that the KGB is no more. While John Major professes 'open government' and theatrically names Stella Rimington as the head of MI5, the secret state grows more powerful than ever.

As Tim Gopsill has pointed out, Britain is the only country in the world with a statutory bar on an elected member of Parliament addressing his constituents through the broadcast media.[16] There are now more than 100 laws in Britain that make disclosure of information a crime. Under the 'reformed' Official Secrets Act – 'reformed' being officialspeak for even more restriction – all the major revelations of official lying and venality in the 1980s would now be illegal. The *Sunday Telegraph* once likened investigative journalism to an offence against the state; it has become just that.[17]

Two examples: the 1981 Contempt of Court Act empowers judges and magistrates to ban the reporting of trials. Thus, hundreds of trials take place in secret every year, some of them deeply sensitive to the state. Under the 1984 Police and Criminal Evidence Act, broadcasters and journalists must surrender film and source material to the police; and an order against one media organisation automatically applies to the others.

In 1991 Central Television and I encountered the full sanction of government secrecy and intervention in the courts in a libel action brought against my film *Cambodia: The Betrayal*. 'Public Interest Immunity Certificates' – gagging orders – were used successfully against us before they were exposed in the Matrix Churchill trial. I have described this in the chapter 'Through the Looking Glass'. Britain has the most restrictive libel laws in the democratic world – a fact which Robert Maxwell exploited until the day he drowned.

The Director of Public Prosecutions has used the Prevention of Terrorism Act to force Channel 4 and an independent programme maker to reveal the identity of an informant whose life could be at risk. The case concerned a documentary film, *The Committee*, which alleged widespread collusion between members of the British security services, Loyalist paramilitaries and senior members of Northern

Ireland's business community in a secret terrorist campaign dedicated to sectarian and political assassination.[18]

This, and similar cases, receive scant attention compared with the sex lives of establishment politicians, and the marriage difficulties of the royal family. There are the perennial calls for protection of privacy legislation, but this has little to do with protecting the rights of ordinary people, and everything to do with protecting the reputations of establishment figures. There is no real desire to intervene in 'tabloid scandal-mongering' – which is duly reported in depth by the 'quality' press. The scandal mongers, after all, are important people. They can witchhunt dissenters when required; and every five years most of them can be relied upon to help elect a Tory government. For this, the Queen is instructed to honour their editors: a fine irony. The lost issue is the need to protect the public from the state, not the press.

I have devoted the final chapters to Australia, which in many ways offers a model for the future. In the 1960s Australians could boast the most equitable spread of personal income in the world. Since then the redistribution of wealth has been spectacular as the world's first Thatcherite Labor government has 'reformed' the fragile Australian economy and given it over to the world 'free market'. Bob Hawke's 'big mates' – the likes of Murdoch, Kerry Packer and Alan Bond – were able to borrow what they liked and pay minimal income tax.[19] In 1989 Bond's borrowing accounted for 10 per cent of the Australian national debt.[20] Today, Bond's empire has collapsed, Bond himself has been in and out of prison; unemployment is as high as 15 per cent and the rate of child poverty is the second highest in the developed world.[21] And Australia can now claim the most monopolised press in the Western world.

Of twelve metropolitan dailies, Murdoch controls seven and the Canadian Conrad Black three. Of ten Sunday papers Murdoch has seven, Black two. In Adelaide Murdoch has a complete monopoly. He owns all the daily, Sunday and local papers, and all the printing presses and printing premises. In Brisbane he owns all but a few suburban papers. He controls more than 66 per cent of daily newspapers in the capital cities, where the great majority of the population lives. He owns almost 75 per cent of all Sunday papers. And Black controls most of the rest.[22]

Both are conservative ideologues. Another arch conservative, Kerry Packer, owns most of the magazines Australians read and the only truly national commercial TV network. None of this could have happened without government collusion: the bending of regulations and legislation advantageous to a few 'big mates'.[23] In the East Timor section I have documented how the interests of the Keating government and its principal media 'mate' converge in the promotion of the Suharto dictatorship in Indonesia as 'stable' and 'moderate' while the truth of the regime's genocide in East Timor is suppressed and obfuscated.

This presents good journalists in Australia and all over the world with an increasingly familiar dilemma. How can they pursue their craft without serving such concentrated power? And once having enlisted and taken on the day-to-day constraints of career and mortgage, how do they remain true to a distant notion of an 'independent' press?

Some journalists try their hardest, maintaining high standards in mostly uncontroversial fields. Others believe they can change the system from within, and are forced out. Others are unaware of their own malleability (I was), or they become profoundly cynical about their craft. Echoing the fellow travellers of Stalin's communist party, they insist, as one Murdoch editor once told me, 'I can honestly say I have never been told what to put in the paper and what to take out of it'.[24] The point was that no one *had* to tell him, and his paper reflected the unshakeable set of assumptions that underpin Western power and prejudice, including those that would lead us, to quote Nicholas Rothwell, into 'a social and even ideological transformation . . . in the image of a radical philosophy'.

I have attempted throughout the book, to show how closely censorship in the old communist world compares with that in the West today and that only the methods of enforcement differ. I am reminded of a story recounted by the writer Simon Louvish. A group of Russians touring the United States before the age of *glasnost* were astonished to find, after reading the newspapers and watching television, that all the opinions on the vital issues were the same. 'In our country', they said, 'to get that result we have a dictatorship, we imprison people, we tear out their fingernails. Here you have none of that. So what's your secret – how do you do it?'[25]

In the section 'Tributes' I express my admiration for Noam Chomsky, whose formidable analysis has helped many of us to identify how they do it. It was Chomsky who understood the nature of the 'delusional system' of one-doctrine democracy and the sophisticated manipulation of public opinion, using the 'free' media.

The results of this manipulation are often historic. When President Kennedy declared in the early 1960s that there was a 'missile gap' with the Soviet Union, his message was carried without question by the Western media, and the nuclear arms race accelerated. In fact, the opposite was true: America was well ahead in missile development.[26] When President Johnson unleashed American bombers on North Vietnam in 1964, he did so after the media had helped him sell to Congress a story that communist gunboats had 'attacked' US warships in the 'Gulf of Tonkin Incident'. There was no attack, no 'incident'. 'Hell,' Johnson is reported to have said in private, 'those dumb stupid sailors were just shooting at flying fish.'[27] Thereafter the American invasion was legitimised, millions of people were killed and a once bountiful land was petrified.

In manipulation on such a scale, a vital part is played by an Orwellian abuse of conceptual thought, logic and language. In Vietnam, the indigenous forces resisting a foreign invasion were guilty of 'internal aggression'.[28] In the Gulf the slaughter was described as one in which 'a miraculously small number of casualties' was sustained.[29] In Russia today, anti-Yeltsin democrats opposing 'free market reforms' – 'reforms' that are likely to reduce some 60 million pensioners to near starvation – are dismissed as 'hardliners' and 'crypto communists'.[30]

The unerring message is that there is only one way now. It booms out to all of humanity, growing louder and more insistent in the media echo chamber. Those who challenge this sectarianism, and believe in real choice in public life and the media, are likely to be given the treatment. They are 'outside the mainstream'. They are 'committed' and 'lacking balance'. If the criticism is aimed at American power, the critics are 'anti-American' – a revealing charge for it evokes the 'un-German' abuse used effectively by the Nazis and the 'anti-Soviet' provisions of the old Soviet criminal code.

These attacks come not only from the Murdoch camp, but also from a liberal elite which sees itself as the fulcrum of society, striking a 'sensible balance' between opposing extremes. This is often translated into evenhandedness between oppressor and oppressed. Faithful to the deity of 'impartiality', it rejects the passion and moral imagination that discern and define the nature of criminality and make honest the writing of narrative history.

In Britain and the United States members of this liberal group can be relied upon to guard the conservative flame during difficult times, such as when established forces go to war, or feel themselves threatened by civil disturbance or a surfeit of political activity and discussion outside the confines of Parliament. This is especially true of the 'modernised' Labour Opposition which, in moulding itself to what 'market research' tells it, serves to muffle any suggestion of mass resistance. What it says, in effect, is that society is static and people's consciousness cannot be raised. Of course this is a role that goes back a long way, perhaps as far as the reaction to the seventeenth-century revolution when John Locke thought that ordinary people should not even be allowed to discuss affairs of state.

In the BBC Locke's views have also been modernised; people *are* allowed to discuss the affairs of state, though within a certain framework, as represented by *Question Time* on television and the *Today* programme on radio, where 'politics' is defined as that which takes place inside, or within a short cab journey of, the Palace of Westminster. In this way journalists, politicians and other establishment representatives promote each other's agendas and set the limits of political 'debate'. This is known as 'the mainstream'.

In *Distant Voices* I have set out to identify some of the principal agendas. The most important is that of the 'new world order', which is promoted as having been approved by the United Nations and the 'world community'. In his State of the Union address following the 'victory' in the Gulf, President Bush spoke of his 'big idea, a new world order, where diverse nations are drawn together in common cause [but] only the United States has both the moral standing and the means to back it'.[31]

In the chapter 'How the world was won over', I have set out how 'diverse nations' were given the biggest bribes in history to join the 'common cause' – bribes based upon their indebtedness to the World Bank and the International Monetary Fund, many of them funded by the oil sheikhs. Far from upholding international law, the 'new world order' (a term used by Benito Mussolini) ordains American military and economic power and law breaking.

We used to be reminded constantly of the illegal Soviet invasions of Hungary and Czechoslovakia. We are not reminded of the illegal American invasions, such as the assault on Panama, when thousands of civilians were killed on the pretext of arresting a drug dealer, the former American client, General Noriega. (The real reason was US control over the Panama Canal.) Today Panama is forgotten, occupied and ruined. Neither are we reminded of the genocidal violence of Washington-sponsored regimes, such as that of the 'moderate' regime in Indonesia. As the Guatemalan journalist Julio Godoy has pointed out, Europeans under the Soviet heel were 'in a way luckier than Central Americans . . . while the Moscow-imposed government in Prague would degrade and humiliate reformers, the Washington-made government in Guatemala would kill them. It still does [and] has taken more than 150,000 victims'.[32] Under the 'liberal' presidency of Bill Clinton, nothing in essence has changed.

Since the birth of the 'new world order', power at the United Nations has shifted from that of peacemaker to war-maker: from the General Assembly to the US-dominated Security Council. Instead of a 'peace dividend' there is rearmament; in the year of the collapse of the Soviet 'enemy', US arms sales rose by 64 per cent, the greatest increase ever; and there are serious proposals for a Nuclear Expeditionary Force 'primarily for use against Third World targets'.[33] By 1994 the British arms industry controlled 20 per cent of the world market, much of it linked to 'aid' sweeteners, notably in Malaysia and Indonesia.

The agenda of the 'free market' ruled the 1980s, allowing millions to break the bonds of the state, so it was said. In fact, the 1980s was the decade of global impoverishment, producing the greatest division between rich and poor in the history of humankind. In the section 'War by other means', I have described how unrepayable interest has become the means of controlling much of humanity, its natural resources, commodities and labour, without sending in a single marine. In many countries, an era of social Darwinism has begun, imposed and policed by the financial institutions of the rich world. According to the United Nations' *State of the World's Children*, more than half a million children die every year as a direct result of the burdens of debt repayment.[34] Debt has normalised the unthinkable.

'A prolonged and ferocious class war is under way', writes the author of a UN Development Programme study, adding, 'You cannot hide the poorest behind national boundaries'.[35] Indeed, in developed countries, this war is heard now as distant gunfire. It will grow louder as social Darwinism is applied at home, ensuring that Los Angeles and London become extensions of the Third World. Britain now has a quarter of Europe's poor; one British child in four now lives in poverty.[36]

The political prescriptions agreed by elites in the developed countries offer no solutions. In Britain there is 'convergence' between the policies of the main political parties – policies that declare people expendable and the notion of common obligation heresy, eroding the premises upon which a modest civilisation rested. In a new section, 'The Quiet Death of the Labour Party', I have described how Britain has become a 'democratic' one-party state where power is exercised by an increasing number of unaccountable 'quangos' and access to power depends on connections to an ideological elite unchallenged by a 'modernised', supine Labour Party.

Elsewhere voices remain muted. In the West almost no writers of renown have emerged to make literature of the struggles of ordinary people. In America there is no Upton Sinclair; no *The Jungle* and *It Can't Happen Here*, no Steinbeck, just the flatulence of Mailer. In Europe there is no Orwell, no Tressell, no Kafka. In his *Guardian* essay 'While the pen sleeps', D. J. Taylor invited us to 'read the review pages of a Sunday newspaper or one of the right-wing weeklies and note their languid air of complacency, the unspoken assumption that a book should consist of drawing room twitter, gentle mockery, "fine writing" ... Given the radical agenda of the last nine years, given the Falklands, Ireland, the Bomb, could any age be more political than our own? [and yet] writers have lost the ability to describe and define the society of which they are a part.'[37] Taylor's piece was as memorable for its rarity as its insights.

We are left with publications not unlike *samidzat*. In America there is a group of them, like *Z Magazine* and *Covert Action*, that publish documented unofficial truth. The enduring popularity of the great journalist Studs Terkel, incorrigible behind his microphone in Chicago, provides a glimpse.

'I hate to use the word yuppie', he said recently, 'because yuppie is not what most of the young are. Most are bewildered and lost ... but I'm waiting for a bus where I live in uptown and I bump into this couple who really are yuppies, the ones you see in the suds-sex-beer commercials. So I talk while we're waiting for the bus. It's a few days before Labor Day, so I say Labor Day is coming up, a celebration of

American trade unions. Unions! they say. God, we despise unions! I ask: "How many hours a day do you work?" Eight hours. "Why don't you work 18 hours like your grandparents or your great-grandparents did?" They don't know. I say: "You know why? Because four guys hanged so you could work eight hours a day [the Haymarket Martyrs in 1886]. Don't you know that people got their heads busted in the 1930s fighting for the 40-hour week?" They just don't know. The point is that we have no sense of history. There's just the sound bite.'[38]

In Britain there are outstanding independent journalists who are published in the 'mainstream' and those, like Jeremy Seabrook, who are not. In commercial television there is still a clutch of fine broadcasters and directors, the products of a British documentary tradition which began with John Grierson, Norman Swallow and Denis Mitchell and owes nothing to bogus 'balance'. They were film makers – film *journalists* – who presented people and places as they saw them; and their work was rich and moving. They understood broadcasting as a medium in which experience could be shared. They illuminated those areas in society which had long remained in shadow. Today they would be called 'campaigning' and 'committed', and perhaps they were. They dared to put microphones and cameras in front of ordinary people and let them talk. And what they revealed was the blood, sweat and tears of another nation.

Their heirs are not yet 'distant voices', though their future depends on the strength of their backing against specious 'realism'. They are part of a great constituency of public resistance, which has little to do with 'mainstream' political forces and whose achievements are remarkable: the exposure of a deeply corrupt criminal justice system and a mobilised popular revolt against a vicious tax. It was the British peace movement that made universal the principle that the nuclear arms race could be stopped only by bold unilateral acts – a principle embraced by Gorbachev and eventually by others.

The most courageous 'distant voices' are in the Third World, and this book pays special tribute to them. They produce literature and journalism that have no equivalent in the developed world (like the analyses in *Third World Resurgence*, published in Malaysia), and often in conditions of great personal danger. Every year hundreds of journalists pay for their outspokenness with their health and their lives. The wider resistance they represent, much of it underground, is barely acknowledged in the West. In the section 'Under the Volcano' I have described the stamina and sophistication of the 'popular organisations' in the Philippines, a country so often reported as a place of disasters and freaks.

The millennium may have to end before, like Milton's Satan, they 'soon rise up and resume their defiance'. But rise up they will, as people did in this century and others. For although 'normalised' to the foreign eye, they are never still. 'Half of humanity', says Susan George, author of *A Fate Worse Than Debt*, 'are young, frustrated and angry, and they are going to become more so.'[39] The uprising of the Zapatistas in Mexico against unemployment, debt and trade deals that enrich the powerful is just a beginning. All over Latin America, and elsewhere, other Zapatistas are stirring. We should watch them.

'I sometimes feel', wrote the Uruguayan poet Eduardo Galeano in 1990, 'as if they have stolen even our words. The term "socialist" is applied in the West as the false face of injustice; in the West, it evokes purgatory or perhaps hell. The word "imperialism" is no longer to be found in the dominant lexicon, even though imperialism is present and does pillage and kill. In a few months we have witnessed the turbulent shipwreck of a system that usurped socialism. Now we must begin all over again. Step by step, with no shields but those born of our own bodies. It is necessary to discover, create, imagine. And today, more than ever, it is necessary to dream. To dream, together . . .'[40]

London, May 1994

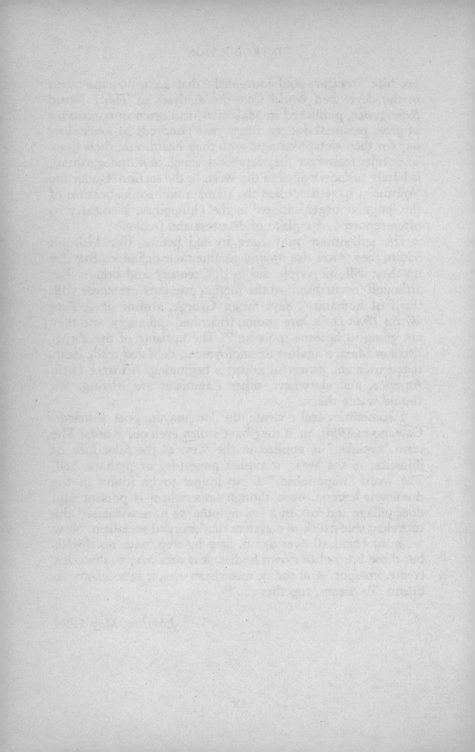

I
INVISIBLE BRITAIN

THE MAN WITH NO NAME

WHEN IT WAS raining hard the other day, a familiar silhouette appeared at my front door. I knew it was him, because, having rung the bell, he retreated to the gate: a defensive habit gained on the streets. 'It's the man', said my young daughter, 'with no name.'

He had on his usual tie and tweed jacket and was leaning against the hedge, though he said he hadn't had a drink. 'Just passing through,' he said as usual, and money passed between us with the customary clumsy handshake. 'I'd better give that a trim,' he said, as he always did, pointing at the hedge, and again I thanked him and said no; he was too unsteady for that. Collar up, he turned back into the rain.

I have known him for about three years. He comes to my door at least every week, and I see him out on the common in all weathers, asleep or reading or looking at the traffic. I see him nodding as if in silent discussion with himself on a weighty matter; or waving and smiling at a procession of women with small children in buggies. Understandably, women hurry away from him; others look through him.

He has no home, though he once told me he lived 'just around the corner'. That turned out to be a hostel. From what I can gather, he sleeps rough most of the time, often on a bench in front of a small powerboats clubhouse, or in a clump of large trees where sick and alcoholic men go and where there was a murder some years back. In winter, he has newspapers tucked inside his jacket. Perhaps he is fifty, or more; it's difficult to tell.

He vanishes from time to time, as the homeless tend to do;

and when I last asked him about this, he said he went to 'visit my sister'. I very much doubted this; I know he goes to one of several seaside towns for a few weeks at a time. There he scans the local newspaper small ads for 'unemployed guests wanted'. These are inserted by the owners of bed-and-breakfast hotels and hostels, where homeless people are sent by local authorities and by the Department of Health and Social Security.

I can imagine a little of what it must be like for him. As a reporter I once ended up in one of these 'hotels'. When I couldn't produce the Social Security form that would allow the owner to collect every penny of his 'guest's' state benefit, I was thrown out. This wholesale diversion of public money is acknowledged as one of the fastest ways of getting rich in Britain since the Thatcher Government stopped councils spending on housing more than ten years ago. Hotel owners are said to make about £120 million a year. In the Enterprise Society, homelessness, like drinking water, has been 'privatised'; or is it 'restructured'?

My friend is one of 80,000 people who are officially homeless in London. This is the equivalent of the population of Stevenage, in Hertfordshire; the true figure is greater, of course. The national figure for homeless households is 169,000, ten times higher than a decade ago. The homeless are now a nation within a nation, whose suffering makes a good television story at Christmas or when there is snow and ice.

I have never been made homeless. To have nowhere to go, perhaps for the rest of my life, to face every day the uncertainty of the night and fear of the elements, is almost unimaginable. I say 'almost', because in writing about the homeless I have gleaned something of their powerlessness once they are snared in what used to be known as the 'welfare state'. This was true before Thatcher.

The difference these days is that there are no 'typical' homeless any more. They are also from the middle classes and the new software classes. They are both old and young – an estimated 35,000 children are homeless in London

24

alone. My friend is typical in that he bears the familiar scars of homelessness: such as a furtiveness that gives the impression of a person being followed; a sporadic, shallow joviality that fails to mask his anxiety; and a deferential way that does not necessarily reflect his true self. The latter, because it is out of character, is occasionally overtaken by melodramatic declarations of independence. When he told me he had to go to hospital one day for a stomach operation and I offered to take him, he said, 'No! I can walk! Of course I can!' And he did.

I didn't know who or what he was until recently. It seemed an intrusion to ask. My place in his life was simply as a source of a few quid from time to time. Then one day he was telling me about a television programme about Asia he had seen, and it was clear he had been there in the Army. And that led to a statement of pride about what he had done with his life on leaving the Army. He had worked in a garage, training apprentice mechanics, until this was thwarted by a string of personal tragedies: a divorce and finally his 'redundancy': that wonderful expression of the Enterprise Society. He was then too old to start again; and he was taking to drink.

He has turned up with cuts and bruises, and blood caked on his cheek. Once, when I said I would go and call a doctor, I returned to the door to find him gone. On the common and in the streets, he is prey to thugs and to the police. He has little of the protection the rest of us assume as a right, provided by a civilised society. The defences that have been built up for the likes of him since the great Depression of sixty years ago continue to be dismantled with platitudes that are spoken, unchallenged, on the news almost every night.

Recently it was National Housing Week. The junior housing minister, Tim Yeo, said the government's 'rough sleepers initiative', which was launched during the freezing conditions of last winter, had halved the numbers of homeless sleeping out in London.

Anyone driving through London's West End knows this to

be untrue. The homeless in the capital have become a tourist curiosity. Europeans are incredulous at having to step over so many human bundles on the pavement, in the Underground, on the steps of galleries and museums. Eavesdrop on a French tour guide describing the sights in the shopfronts of the Strand. 'They were hosed away,' she says, 'but they have come back.'

With the maximum publicity, the government allocated £300 million for 'rough sleepers'. As the London Housing Unit has pointed out, this has been wiped out by the £138 million in cuts in long-term housing investment by councils and by the abolition of £100 million-worth of special allowances for London boroughs.[1] The minister, Tim Yeo, said: 'You will see a similar priority given to housing as to education and health between now and the general election.'[2] In the circumstances this had to be irony; but it was not.

June 14, 1991

ABSOLUTELY NO EXCUSE

I SOMETIMES DELIVER a friend of my small daughter to her grandmother's home on a housing estate in south London. It is not the worst of the estates put up in the early 1960s, yet it takes just a dozen steps to cross into another world, inhabited by a nation long declared expendable, if not invisible.

The child in my brief care is terribly thin; and when the door opens, the nodding faces display the same ghostly pallor. The older faces are skeined grey: the indelible mark of white poverty. The view from their door is of asphalt and cracked concrete, broken glass and broken swings, crisp bags and dogshit; and a rusting banger on which teenage boys gather in their cheap jeans and trainers. The pent-up energy of these boys is like a presence; to an old person or a young child it must be menacing. I have watched them expend some of it by riding a bike in slalom course through the glass and dogshit, back and forth, back and forth.

Whenever I ask them what they 'do', their reaction is incredulity. One of them laughs. They do nothing of course! Even those still at school do nothing; and leaving school will mean more nothing. That, they seem to say, is what they are for. They are the literal opposite of nihilists; for it is *they* who have been rejected.

It is likely they knew about this state of nothingness as far back as the age of seven. That is when the ego expands and children get a pretty good idea of where they are heading, especially those in a class-based society. Modernised poverty adds another dimension. There is the beginning of conflict between popular, illusory expectations and the inability of many young people to grasp that these are illusions and not for them. By the time they reach their teens, they will be blamed for not living up to inspirational images that are almost all of wealth and acquisition. The resulting frustration will produce violence, most of it of no direct threat to others; it is inward violence manifest in failure at school, the disintegration of relationships, and in general ill-health.

In 1989, the chief medical officer at the Department of Health reported that the death rates for British men and women between the ages of fifteen and forty-five had risen every year since 1985. This was unprecedented.[3] In the same year, the results of a study by one of the leading authorities on poverty, Professor Peter Townsend, shocked even its author. The study showed that in the five poorest wards of Manchester there were 1,446 more deaths every year than the national average; and that the process begins in the cradle. Whereas in the affluent parts of Manchester only 3 per cent of babies were born underweight, in the poor estates the figure was 14 per cent. 'I find the severity of the findings somewhat awesome,' Professor Townsend said. 'I've been taken aback by the extent of hardship in a concentrated form in our inner cities.'[4]

This means that most of the violence in the other nation is a quiet destroyer. 'Poverty kills,' says Peter Townsend, 'that is not a political or a social comment, but a scientific fact.'[5] Heart disease, cancer, mental illness, not petrol bombs, kill and maim; and in recent years the violent assault on the spirit of the young has been unrelenting. A quarter of Europe's poor now live in Britain. One in five of the very young now live in poverty.

In estates all over the country youth unemployment is more than 80 per cent. During the Thatcher decade economic inequality rose more sharply than at any time since modern records were kept: a fact that alone puts paid to her ridiculous posturing about 'democracy' and 'choice'.[6] The decimation of industry, schools, clinics and public services, the extinction of a national housing programme, have been violent acts of historic proportions.

A new poverty has arisen in the space of less than two decades, as British manufacturing has abandoned more than two-thirds of its workforce. Men with absolute skills have been marooned. Women and the unskilled are employed in 'service industries' for wages that have no minimum. Working conditions, including safety provisions, have deteriorated, as the unions are routed and almost every net is taken away. For the working-class young, there is no longer the prospect of apprenticeship and the pride that went with it; at best they must accept training schemes that are fraudulent. In the meantime, the social landscape has changed.

The solidarity that once held working people together and helped them mobilise and build their organisations has been undermined by the isolation of one-parent life on the estates, of Brave New Britain, now secret, obsolescent Britain. And who speaks for these people? Labour says it does, but the new poor don't believe them, or anyone, any more. When Neil Kinnock was asked for his response to the riot at Meadow Well estate in North Shields – where almost all the young people are jobless and all the children at the local primary school are on clothing grants – he said there was 'absolutely no excuse' for it.[7]

Roy Hattersley did refer briefly to unemployment. Unless I missed something, the distinct impression was that Labour was most concerned that Murdoch's and Maxwell's yob-hunters were watching them. The *Daily Mirror* attacked the Bishop of Newcastle, Alec Graham, for saying: 'There comes a time when the feeling of helplessness and hopelessness overcomes people and they act in a wild way.'[8] The Bishop, said the *Mirror*, was talking 'twaddle through his episcopal hat'. It says much about the melancholy state of British politics that such an understatement of the obvious is routinely belittled. So narrow is the political debate now, so collaborative or cynical or cowed are those who claim to oppose the true enemies of the people, that a rare eruption of violence in the streets has the barkers of authority in full panic.

As for the liberal establishment, which a dozen years ago was still reputed to be applying the principles of R. H. Tawney, there is now silence, broken by the drawing-room twitter of people of letters and the apologia of the old middle-aged on sterile television programmes or in the 'quality' press. Thatcher's children, the old young men, have seen them off.

A dozen years ago there would have been efforts by the caring services to negotiate short-term solutions in places of poverty like Meadow Well, and sustained attempts to understand the reasons why; to explain the past and the nature of the betrayal of at least two post-war generations; and the smashing of so much of the community life that was this country's strength.

In the 1970s, I walked along Peel Street and Gladstone Terrace that overlooked the green vales of County Durham. The view from the houses with teefall roofs was of Friesian dairy cows and Hereford crosses and of hawthorn bramble and wild rose that smothered the cuttings and embankments of disused railway lines. These were village streets with pubs and clubs, pigeon crees and football teams and the warmth of the inhabitants for each other. They became known as 'D villages' and, along with so many industrial communities on the edge of the countryside, they were smashed: no, 'phased out' was the term insisted upon at the time.

The people were 'phased' into estates, high- and low-rise, with Western Ways and Central Avenues and without pubs and clubs and football teams. The restoration of their old fine terraces and the inception of a few bus routes would have saved these communities. Instead, they were dumped – the word is precise – in jerry-built boxes whose window frames had already burst free and where damp had already risen and the rats arrived by the time the first key had turned in the door. To isolated women and the young, they were sort of concentration camps. Getting a youth club, staffed by experts who gave a damn, was a Herculean achievement. I recall that in the desolate River Streets area of Birkenhead the campaign for the funding of a youth and community hall ran for years.

These struggles again come to mind with the news that youth services in Newcastle upon Tyne are to be cut by £8 million. Youth clubs are to be closed where there is nothing else. This, says Newcastle council leader Jeremy Beecham, is 'a bitter paradox' that can 'only further weaken a social fabric already strained by years of unemployment, poverty and absence of hope'.

There was no paradox when Thatcher and her ideologues invented the 'two thirds society', in which a few got very rich and many did all right on credit and a large minority were dispossessed in the American way. That is, the poor were declared an 'underclass' to be contained on ghetto-estates and forgotten about or blamed, whichever was politically appropriate.

Shortly after Thatcher won a second term in 1983 (when her fortunes soared from a 17 per cent popularity rating due to her victory over General Galtieri) a senior Department of Education official warned in a secret report that legislative powers might be necessary to 'rationalise' the schools' curricula. 'We are in a period of considerable social change,' he wrote. 'There may be social unrest, but we can cope with the Toxteths ... but if we have a highly educated and idle population we may possibly anticipate more serious conflict. *People must be educated once more to know their place.*'[9]

Complementing this was propaganda that presented the working-class young as 'spongers'. Although this was false, legislation was passed to prevent the 'work-shy' who left home from claiming state benefits. They were to 'return to their families' and make 'genuine efforts to look for employment'. Following years of campaigning by Shelter and other organisations, the government finally commissioned research last year. MORI interviewed 551 young people with no income who had applied for severe hardship payments. The report showed that more than 70 per cent had tried Youth Training, 66 per cent had worked previously and 80 per cent visited their careers offices. MORI also found that 65 per cent of young people who had 'left home' had been thrown out. Almost a quarter had been physically or sexually abused by a member of their family or by staff at a children's home.[10]

The betrayal of the young began with both Tory and Labour governments; but of course Thatcher went much further. For all its pretensions to be a modern European state, Britain is unique in making changes to its social benefits and tax system that have taken most from the poor and given most to the rich. During the Thatcher decade, the bottom half of the population lost £4,800 million in tax and benefits to the top 5 per cent. A single pensioner, whose pension in 1991 is £52 a week, is getting £14 a week less in real terms than he or she would have received in 1979. No other country in the European Community has seen such a large increase in the number of people who are in poverty.[11]

Michael Heseltine's theatrical promises of support for the inner cities following the Toxteth uprising in 1982 were little more than a hoax. No one likes 'yobs'; and the young who exercise briefly, as Melanie Phillips wrote in the *Guardian*, 'the feeling they could do anything, a feeling of power', are the perfect scapegoats.[12] The hope is in the volatility their actions, at the very least, represent: that there are many others who do not 'ram raid' or burn down the chippie but who, like those who fought the poll tax, will refuse to be educated once more to know their place, and will resist.

September 20, 1991

RACE AND PINSTRIPES

FOR MOST WHITE people racism is an abstraction that does not touch their lives. Drive past a group of white policemen standing around a black driver at the kerbside and you glimpse it, though you cannot be sure. Walk past an Asian estate on these dark afternoons and watch how carefully the children are shepherded, then talk to the brothers and uncles who guard them. You will hear described attacks even on infants, and excrement pushed through letter boxes and fire-bombing as a matter of routine. To gain their confidence, you will have to establish first that you are not in authority; policemen ask for passports.

This may not be universally true, but it is the unerring experience of the Asian families I have known and who have been attacked. I think I first understood the real meaning of racism in Britain when, huddled inside a house in an East End cul-de-sac, I listened to bricks crashing against the door and heard bellowed abuse that was not interrupted by the arrival of the police, even though they had been called. So certain were the attackers of their own authority that they ambled away only when they grew tired, each booting the door as he went.

The teenage daughter of the Asian family whose home that was kept a diary, often written by candle-light because she dared not turn on the light. This was a typical entry: 'When the trouble started, we phoned the police, but they never came. Then my father went to the police station to get the police . . . we had a witness. The police said they didn't need a witness.' She wrote to her Labour MP, then Arthur Lewis:

'Dear Mr Lewis, We are an Asian family under attack . . . My mother has not slept for two months and has had to go to hospital for several days. We cannot furnish or decorate our home because we are too busy looking out through the window day and night, ensuring nobody attacks our house . . . '

Arthur Lewis quoted the letter during question time in the House of Commons and was told by Margaret Thatcher that the matter would be 'taken up'.[13] It wasn't. So the girl wrote to Thatcher: 'Dear Margaret, I am sorry to tell you you do not understand our problem. You don't care if we get beaten up, do you? . . . We are asking for your help, not your money . . . ' She received a reply not from Thatcher but from a Home Office official, C. D. Inge. 'I am sorry I am not able to give you a more helpful reply,' wrote Inge, 'but let me take this opportunity to assure you that the Government is committed to a multi-racial society . . . '

This 'commitment' has yet to take effect, which is not surprising. Those who generate, collude with and ultimately run racism in Britain are the moral heirs of the Christian gentlemen who carried it in their bags to all points of the Empire. Many, like Enoch Powell, who never forgave India for turfing out the Raj, brought it back home again. Until Thatcher, extravagant 'mavericks' like Powell were kept at a safe distance and were disavowed. When Thatcher said on national television in 1978 that 'the people are really rather afraid of being swamped by an alien culture', the sum of her message was that racism was safe with her.[14] Her omissions were just as effective. She had nothing good to say about these 'aliens'. They were, well, aliens, and frightening. They did not enrich society. The multiculturalism they represented was not something to be proud of, rather a disease like rabies, from which the nation had a duty to protect itself.

Two years later, a study concluded that Asian people were fifty times more likely to be attacked than any other racial group.[15] When the Home Office published this, I tried and failed to find a single case of an attacker being convicted. The police called them 'delinquents' and did not recognise 'racially motivated' crimes. Thatcher, of course, would never condone fire-bombings, stabbings and the like or even negligent and indifferent policemen. What she and her acolytes gave them, to borrow from her, was the 'oxygen' of her own public position, which amounted to silent approval. When those on the extreme right point out that Britain has no neo-fascist party on the scale of Le Pen's National Front in France, because it has had Thatcher, they appear to do so with straight faces. According to the Thatcherite weathervane, Paul Johnson, it was enough for Thatcher to make 'the right noises'.[16] In Britain, the 'right noises' make fascist parties redundant; the Tories offer quite enough to the fascists, who are apparently not bothered by the code and euphemisms in which respectable racism speaks.

The Asylum Bill offers these 'right noises'. It will give the government the power to get rid of people on a 'fast track' procedure; to send desperate people back unless they claim asylum in the first country they reach; to refuse legal aid; to fingerprint refugees; to penalise refugees if anyone mounts a campaign on their behalf; and to discriminate against students who criticise the very government from whom they are taking refuge. For refugees read black/brown people. The issue is race.

The way the press has been used to prepare the ground for this legislation is virtually affirmation of its real meaning. Since the summer, Home Office briefings and tip-offs to selected journalists have produced a harvest of scare stories. The *Daily Telegraph* 'examined Home Office records for one sample week' and found a 'flood of asylum pleas'.[17] 'Bogus refugee crackdown' was the *Daily Mail*'s headline over a story about the 'flood of immigrants'. This was accompanied by a leader headlined 'How to stop them tricking Britain', which spoke of 'tidal waves of refugees'.[18] Following a series in the *Daily Star*, Home Secretary Kenneth Baker was quoted as being deeply concerned about the paper's revelations and reported that he had ordered the recruitment of 350 extra immigration officers.[19]

As the Tory Party conference approached, the campaign

intensified. On October 3, the *Daily Mail* published, under the headline 'Labour's migrant masses', Baker's proposals for the new bill, which was essential, said the *Mail*, because 'Britain is besieged by bogus asylum seekers'.[20] The *Sun* did similar work, but went further. 'Figures obtained by the *Sun*', it said, 'show that two thirds of our immigrants come from Africa and Asia.'[21]

When Baker made his speech to the Tory conference the press response was a crescendo of indignation. The *Mail* published a three-part series called 'The invasion of Britain' in which, yet again, a 'flood' was conjured up, this time of people who claimed 'utterly fraudulently that they are political refugees'. The writer was careful to counter-balance 'the influx of phoney third world refugees' with 'the invasion from eastern Europe' – a precaution that was neatly negated by a headline on 7 October: 'Out of Africa and on to our doorsteps'.

Using the press to play 'the race card' is an old tactic. In an important essay, 'Unleashing an Uncritical Press', published in the *Guardian* in 1982, the solicitor Gareth Pierce demonstrated how the police were able to use the press in order to distort figures about 'black crime' and so pave the way for legislation giving the police greater powers.[22]

When Baker was convicted of contempt of court recently, he and his bill were largely protected by the press. The disgrace of a home secretary having been found guilty of breaking a law he was meant to uphold was softened by those whose first allegiance always seems to be to politicians, rather than to journalism. Baker was 'unlucky'; it had been a 'rough year' for him. He had 'all that business with vicious dogs', then the Brixton break-out: a bad year, indeed, though not as bad as that suffered by the Zairean refugee who was sent back on Baker's personal order and may have been lucky to escape with his life. He was hardly mentioned.[23]

The United Nations has condemned Baker's bill as 'in conflict' with internationally accepted principles. The UN High Commission for Refugees (UNHCR) said that one of the bill's main provisions – to deport refugees back to countries where they faced persecution – was illegal under the 1951 UN Convention on Refugees, to which Britain is a signatory. And it was illogical, said the UNHCR, not to regard someone as a refugee merely because they fail to say straight away that they are seeking asylum. An asylum seeker may well be traumatised and the last person he or she wishes to confide in is an official. As for the 'liars', whom the press have made much of, the UNHCR pointed out that inconsistent and muddled statements are inevitable, given language difficulties, fear of officialdom and stress.[24]

Newspaper readers are almost never reminded that all primary immigration to Britain has stopped; that as many leave the country as enter it; that in 1990, the last full year for which figures are available, some 25,000 people sought refugee status or asylum and of these, by the end of the year, 5,524 had been allowed to stay on – most of them only temporarily.

During the election campaign the press returned to its racist theme with renewed heart, reminding its readers that the Tories were the ones that would 'stand firm' on immigration. Only the Tories would enact an Asylum Bill, so necessary to 'stem the tide' of immigrants who were out to 'defraud Europe's generous social and welfare system'.[25] Labour was given the full treatment on race, such as 'Kinnock won't curb flood of bogus refugees' (*Evening Standard*) and 'Labour's madness on migrants' (*Daily Mail*).[26] Here mendacity was ironic; shortly before the election campaign got under way, Roy Hattersley, the shadow home secretary, offered to do a deal with Baker to see the Asylum Bill through the last session of Parliament.

John Major could be telling the truth and putting the 'problem' in its true perspective, but he has clearly chosen not to. There is too much to be gained by making the 'right noises'. Or so he and his advisers may think. He wants it both ways. He wants to be Mr Ordinary who grew up in Brixton and knows what it's like to be out of work. Major has done well to have cultivated this highly dubious image of himself, for he is, above all, both a Thatcherite and Thatcher's choice; and he is not at all 'grey' in his own political choices, which, if you examine his record, are old-fashioned reactionary. Witness his view that the neo-Nazi attacks across Europe could be countered only by stricter immigration controls and the reduction of asylum rights. By keeping out or kicking out the victims of fascist violence, you stop the fascists. This message has become something of a new orthodoxy, recycling old racist arguments in pseudo anti-fascist language.

Two days before the election Kenneth Baker refined this tactic even further. Because fascists had made gains in the European elections, he argued, the case against proportional representation was made. 'Nazi riots will hit Britain – PR aids Fascists, claims Baker', warned that bastion of anti-Nazism, the *Sun*.[27]

It's an unhappy fact that, on race, politicians, spurred on by the press, seldom appeal to the better side of the British: to people's innate sense of decency and natural justice. Even in reply to one of those loaded questionnaires in the *Sun*, 49 per cent said they did not want the government 'to turn its back on our tradition of giving a haven to refugees'.[28] But these are hard times, and dangerous times. Scapegoats are required.

I have heard it argued that racism and fascism are not necessarily complementary. Mussolini is given as an example. And while it is true that Mussolini represented no threat to Italian Jews and other minorities, his racism was expressed ferociously in his slaughter of the peoples of the Horn of Africa. Everything in my experience tells me that fascism and racism are indivisible: that one grows out of the other and feeds off the other. There is usually a relatively mild, even mundane, initiation; and the promoters may regard themselves as men of the sensible middle ground, of 'moderation' and right-thinking. They will not wear brown or black shirts. Pinstripes will do.

December 20, 1991 to April 1992

CASUALTY WARD

THERE IS A grainy, almost Gothic atmosphere in the casualty department of King's College Hospital, south London. The people sitting waiting, lying, waiting, occasionally screaming and dying without dignity, are from an album of working-class life that was meant to have closed. Perhaps it is generally true that poverty has been modernised, its icons superseded by shapeless, mostly internalised despair; but not here. This is the 1940s, when the word 'Dickensian' still applied.

This is not to say that medical science and nursing care are wanting. Indeed, King's College is a microcosm of the National Health Service. On the one hand, it is one of Britain's finest teaching hospitals, whose speciality of haematology is world-renowned, and whose standard of general care is remarkable in the circumstances. The circumstances, however, are notorious. Ed Glucksman, an American inner-city doctor who runs casualty, told me, 'We often have no choice but to Dunkirk it here.'

The analogy with war crops up in casual conversation. In reply to my question about who suffered most, the nursing sister on duty in casualty said, 'The elderly. This is a war zone, and you can't have elderly people lying about near the front line, now can you? You can't have them occupying a trolley when an emergency comes in; anyway, the trolleys play havoc on the delicate skin of the old. And you can never be sure when something's going to go wrong with them.'

Julia Branch, aged 79, a cancer patient, strayed on to the front line and spent nine hours dying and in pain on a hard trolley before being transferred to Dulwich Hospital, where she died. She was put 'on hold' during a 'red alert', which is a period when only emergencies have priority, and planned admissions are cancelled without notice because no beds are available. Michael Mulhall, aged 52, with life-threatening heart disease, was turned away from King's College on the day he was due to be admitted. He died at home in the early hours of the morning, while his daughter Maria and son Gary struggled to resuscitate him.

'It is a matter of deep regret', wrote the hospital's general manager, Julian Nettel, 'that before we were able to make new arrangements for his admission, Mr Mulhall collapsed and died.'[29] Said Maria, 'Although they made clear my father died because the hospital had been starved of resources, they tried to cover themselves by saying he might have died on the operating table anyway. The point is, he was never given the chance. And, the pity is, he could've gone private: but he said doing that would only help to undermine the National Health Service. "I'll support the NHS," he used to say, "until the day I die." '[30]

This is reminiscent of *triage*, the French military policy during the First World War of deciding who among the wounded should be helped and saved, and who should wait and die. In the Health Service, a modified version of *triage* has been operating in certain British hospitals, especially during the winter months when the old are brought in, often as a last resort. 'If you have one bed and two customers', said Dr Glucksman, 'and one of them is middle class, has a hernia and can be sent home in twenty-four hours, while the other has pneumonia and lives alone, the temptation is to give it to the first.' That way the hospital makes more money. 'Financial incentives', he said, 'can overwhelm the quality levers. There are no longer enough safeguards to protect the patients.'[31]

Malcolm Alexander, secretary of Camberwell Community Health Council, which covers King's College, is in no doubt. 'We believe that the concept of "institutional negligence" could be applied to this situation,' he said, 'because when the district health authority closed 100 beds last year in order to save £8 million, the managers either knew that their action would lead to 20- or 30-hour waits on trolleys in casualty, or they did not.'[32]

The point is that managers follow political orders, some more enthusiastically than others; and the assault on the Health Service, which began under the Callaghan Government of the late 1970s, has reached such a stage where the Major Government is vulnerable on that issue alone. Having written a great deal about the National Health Service during my time on the *Daily Mirror*, I am struck by the conspicuous absence of a coherent Opposition campaign.

This is not to underrate the interventions of Robin Cook and the hard work of Harriet Harman, Labour's spokeswoman on health whose constituency covers King's College; but something is clearly wrong when the National Health Service, an institution valued across class lines (and used mostly by the middle class), is being effectively dismantled by a government that could be re-elected in spite of its destructive agenda. Why is this so?

The question demands attention on arrival at King's College casualty. Near the entrance there is, or was, a pigeon's nest and pigeon droppings. 'We feel it is inappropriate', says a Community Health Council report with fine understatement, 'for debilitated patients to be exposed to this on the way into casualty.'[33] The same report described filthy lavatories, overflowing dustbins, an out-of-order drinks machine and the humiliation of sick and troubled people. These people sit or lie so close to each other that, as you enter, there is a perspective that they are actually on top of each other. Some, slumped near the door, smoke and clutch a can of strong lager; the nurses are wise to let them be. Where medical treatment is unattainable within a decent length of time, and a hospital bed out of the question, a can of Tennent's and a fag is just the job.

There was an old man who came in the other night and who already had had quite a few Tennent's, or suchlike. His head was gashed open and blood spilled on to the floor. He shouted; and the children waiting looked at him in apprehension; and he paced and shouted some more; and he finally left, only to return with another gash on his head. On the same night – which wasn't 'too bad', said a nurse – Lillian Cornford lay on her metal-hard trolley, her eyes held tightly shut from the severe pain in her chest. She is 86. She had been there since eight o'clock that morning; after twelve hours she was found a bed.

On another night the main area and corridors of casualty were filled with people lying on seventeen trolleys. There were no beds available, because beds had been cut so that the hospital management could achieve 'cost effectiveness'. On several of the trolleys were people suffering sickle cell disease, an hereditary ailment. Their screams expressed the degree of their pain. Others held their heads down and said nothing. During a crisis they need Pethidine administered to them every hour. The nurses in casualty, whose numbers are down because of their own ill-health, have the responsibility of keeping this up, knowing that a sickle cell sufferer can die during a crisis. Some of these people have lain on trolleys, side by side, nine inches apart, with the elderly and the inebriated and the bloodied, for up to thirty hours.

One of the nights I was there Jim Armfield, a 74-year-old retired postman, was admitted with a stroke after waiting more than two hours for an ambulance. He lay six hours on a trolley before he fell to the floor and fractured his skull. He later died from his injury. At the inquest the Coroner criticised the bed shortage, and the doctor who tried to save him said, 'People don't go to hospital to fall off trolleys.'[34]

When people are brought into casualty at King's College one of their first sights is the padlocked doors of the children's casualty ward. For something to do, those waiting the hours peer through the glass at the empty beds, and the toys, and cheering pictures. 'Two years ago we were told to balance our books,' said Dr Glucksman. 'If we didn't balance them, we had to sacrifice the quality of treatment for 20 per cent of our patients in order to keep the quality for the remainder. The 20 per cent were the children. This was a real pity, because the ward allowed us to keep the kids away from the sights of casualty; and for nurses to observe children in a small environment with their families and for us to be able to identify clinical problems that are more difficult to under-stand when kids are part of . . . well, you've seen it out there.'[35] Camberwell has a high incidence of child abuse; for junior doctors and nurses to spot certain types of child abuse in the conditions that exist in the war zone would be, it seemed to me, quite impossible.

The casualty department was built in 1912 to accommodate 30,000 patients a year. It now sees 80,000 a year. Forty per cent of these are people who either cannot get on a general practitioner's list, or are transient, or homeless, or desperate in some way. King's College stands at the epicentre of the Britain of the nineties, in which structures of civilisation, long taken for granted, have been and are being torn down. The doctors and nurses know this. Several have left because, they say, professional standards will not allow them to continue.

The nurses who run casualty are a marvellous mixture of professional carer and brilliant make-doer. They speak out with nothing to lose; and they encourage the patients to do the same. 'I tell them,' said one, "You have rights. Don't let yourself be treated like this. Write and write again." I think we've got through to them. People are funny; they take it all, then suddenly they don't. It's difficult to describe the aggression we feel here, not directed at *us*, but at what they feel is being done to them.'[36]

King's College's management is probably like most post-Thatcher National Health Service regimes. Terms such as 'purchasing services' and 'customers' are the ingrained jargon now. When I asked Dr Glucksman if his use of 'customers' instead of patients was ironic, he smiled and said, 'No, unfortunately, I've got used to it. All those meetings have done it.' The top managers in health authorities are paid more than £60,000. The pay of most administrators is 'performance-related', so that if they can balance the books – that is, close a children's ward – it's likely they will be marked for promotion, or get a 'discretionary lump sum'.

Some of the managers are excellent professional administrators; yet the system has its way with them. The medical staff describe an authoritarianism that, they say, compounds the conditions under which they have to work. Some of the letters I was shown demonstrate this, demanding that doctors make cuts. In the haematology department the number of beds has been cut by half to four; and if a consultant wants to treat a leukaemia patient from outside the hospital's district, he must get permission. So whether the patient becomes a 'customer' and is given a bone-marrow transplant, and lives or dies, can hinge on the decision not of a doctor, but of an administrator.

'We have been threatened', said one doctor, 'that if we go against these diktats – if we decide to treat people purely on medical and ethical grounds – our admitting rights will be taken away. We shall be allowed to teach, but not to treat sick people.'[37] When doctors 'sneaked in' sixty-one seriously ill patients, they were threatened with disciplinary action. When consultant Linda Cardoza spoke out in the national press about conditions at King's College, she was publicly upbraided by officials for 'behaving in this way' and 'damaging morale'.[38] Yet one official told me he regarded much of the bad publicity as 'important in the circumstances . . . but don't quote me'.

Secrecy is reinforced by the new order. Should King's College be allowed to opt out, as its management wants, the legal right of the Community Health Council to act as the public's watchdog may be withdrawn. According to a confidential Health Department document, trust hospitals need to be freed from 'petty consultation', and there should be rules that 'diminished the ability of CHCs to obstruct'.[39] As a trust hospital, King's College would regard certain 'customers', like those suffering from leukaemia, as 'assets or liabilities'. 'The system', said a consultant, 'says that we take on certain surgery because it brings in more revenue, and that we neglect the Cinderellas.'

The managers deny this, and say they have fought for the well-being of patients along with the medical staff. They say the problems ought not to be minimised, but 'horror stories' are unusual. The chief executive, Derek Smith, told me that 'the casualty and out-patient departments would be completely rebuilt, beginning next summer'. He said that the South East Thames Regional Authority had agreed, in principle, to release £34 million after consultations.

This is good news. Unfortunately, it will not be paid for by new money from the Department of Health, but will be part of an 'acute services strategy' about which there is much scepticism. Although this has positive features such as the establishment of paramedical and trauma units, it will mean the closure of a number of London and near-London hospitals. As a result, people will have greater distances to travel to a casualty department, placing even greater strain upon the ambulance service. As the Community Health Council has pointed out, children suffering broken bones, head injuries and pneumonia sometimes have to travel more than an hour to Kent or Surrey before getting a bed. If this is the exception now, it could well become the rule with more closures.

During the general election campaign John Major showed us Brixton, his childhood home, from his chauffeur-driven, bullet-proof Daimler. As he drove along Denmark Hill the camera picked up King's College Hospital, over which the commentary extolled the government's record on the Health Service. It did not say that the previous October the health secretary, William Waldegrave, had announced more cuts to London's hospitals. Waldegrave was also in the area at that time and was asked by the Community Health Council to visit King's College. He did not acknowledge the invitation. 'The secretary of state', said an official, 'cannot possibly be everywhere at the same time.'[40] Nor could Julia Branch, Michael Mulhall and Jim Armfield before they died.

January 3 to March 25, 1992

THE MINERS

ON A DURHAM beach in the early morning a figure approaches, etched against a grey veined sky, buffeted by a freezing wind. The sea is so black that the breakers are incandescent. The beach is black, a quarry of polished black stones and scabrous mud. There is no colour. The whites of his eyes peer from beneath a sack of coal so heavy he is doubled.

'Coming back is worse than going,' wrote George Orwell of miners in *The Road to Wigan Pier*, 'not only because you are already tired out but because the journey back to the shaft is probably uphill. You try walking head down as miners do, and then you bang your backbone. Most of the miners have what they call "buttons down the back" – that is, a permanent scab on each vertebra.'[41]

The bent man with the sack is another kind of miner. It is likely he, too, has 'buttons down the back' from his yoke of coal. From dawn it takes him five hours to scavenge and load just three sacks of 'sea coal' and to carry them up a steep incline, past the Fair World Bingo Club; for this he gets £6. A few of the scavengers have bikes; most have nothing. In his ragged hat and enforced poverty, he is from another age, which has returned. 'Don't show m'face,' he says to my photographer friend John Garrett. 'They'll take away m'dole. Can't live on it; can't live without it.'

We are near Murton, Vane Tempest and Easington collieries. Murton, sunk in 1838, was closed just over a year ago. 'They told us on the Friday and closed it on the Monday,' says Dave Temple, a former Murton miner. Easington and

Vane Tempest are among the thirty-one pits which the President of the Board of Trade, Michael Heseltine, announced last October would close; following protests that almost brought down the Government, they were spared to await his 'review'. Vane Tempest is one of ten pits that have not been allowed to work on, in spite of a High Court ruling that Heseltine's action was illegal. Some 10,000 miners are now turning up for work and being sent home. The other day Arthur Scargill called at Newcastle-upon-Tyne police station to ask if the thousands of riot police who had forcibly kept open pits during the 1984–5 strike would now be available to go to Vane Tempest colliery to do the same thing. Such panache has helped to see the man through.

I have known these communities for almost twenty years, though my first encounter with Durham miners was as a boy in the coalfields of New South Wales where both my grandfathers and my father worked, and where there was a 'Durham pit'. The miners there had emigrated *en masse* from three villages and spoke a dialect that owed as much to Norway as England; I first heard the word 'marra' (friend) and 'crack', meaning everything from comradely talk to gossip. They are a remarkable people, preserving and expressing vividly that sense of community that is often spoken of, across class lines, as society's most abiding strength. I first went to Murton just before Christmas 1973, on the eve of only the second strike that the miners have 'won'. That is to say, they went from being very low paid workers to moderately low paid workers. (Today a miner's average weekly take home pay is £240. A third of miners take home less than £200. Just to earn a decent wage, many work the equivalent of seven days a week.) By 'winning' in 1974 the miners helped to bring down a Tory government, for which they were never forgiven and are now paying what is clearly the final instalment of the price.

Murton then was the archetypal pit village. With its Democratic Club, Colliery Inn, ribbons of allotments producing champion leeks and pigeons, there were relatively few 'travellers', as pitmen from closed mines are called. Everybody knew everybody in an easy freemasonry. John Cummings, then secretary of the Murton mechanics, was the sixth generation of his family to work at the pit. They had lived in the same house in Albion Street from 1839 to 1957 and John remembers the lavatories in the middle of the street and the three public water taps.

Long before governments thought seriously about providing social welfare, the miners of Murton were looking after their most vulnerable, building homes for the old, providing for pensions, convalescence, recreation. All this was paid for at the pit. There has always been an ambiguity among miners about the nature of their job, but there is none about their loyalty and pride. In the cemeteries the inscriptions speak much about 'respect' for those who died and who 'rest appreciated by all his friends'.

Standing at the heart of the town, the mine was both provider and enemy, a Hell's Kitchen into which men went like troops. This is not a romantic notion, as I learned in January 1974, when I joined a night shift at Murton. I went down a difficult seam called F32, a third of a mile beneath Murton, extending to the sea. This is how I described it at the time:

It was approaching midnight at the pithead, and the first hand I took was a claw. 'It's me ... Harry,' said its owner, knowing I had failed to recognise him in his helmet, lamp and overalls. His hand, with three fingers gone and a stump, was no guide; so many hands were like that, which helped to explain why so few were offered. Except for brief, muttered monosyllables and the catching of breath, there was silence as we filled water bottles and strapped on rubber knee-pads and the 'self-rescuer', which is a small metal box with gas mask designed to keep you alive until they reach you.

We walked to the cage. We each carried two numbered metal tokens, one to hand to the banksman on the pithead as we went down and one to surrender when we came up. A missing token means a missing man. The banksman frisked us for matches and cigarettes and slammed shut the cage, which rocked with the gale hitting the pithead at 70 miles an hour. There was total blackness now; no one spoke.

Just before one o'clock in the morning we reached 1,100 feet and the shift only now began; this was the time the Coal Board started paying, although most of the men had been at the pit, preparing to go down, for an hour or more.

Now we were walking downhill through the swirls of stone dust, judging the man in front from the beam of his lamp. Bill Williams, who had been doing this since he was 14, bit off some tobacco. 'Aye, that'll catch some of the muck,' he said. He also lifted his ribcage, as someone might hitch up his trousers, and attempted to clear his lungs of 'the muck', but without success.

Now suddenly the atmosphere was humid, almost tropical, and the pit's first sounds were the hissing of the compression pumps, pumping out 200 gallons of water every minute. At two o'clock we reached the coal-face. Joe Ganning and Doug Walton wore masks of white clay as they worked a drill at the stone; the noise was incessant and the sting from the dust and water was relieved only when I lay on my stomach in the slush and crawled into the tunnel beside the coal-face, which was three-and-a-half feet high and slightly wider than my shoulders.

This was the core of the mine and, except for the machinery, it might have been a scene from a Victorian etching; the men, their bodies contorted, 'titillating' the roof to test for a fall and moving the hydraulic chocks, as heavy as cannons, which propped up the roof. They reminded me of men bringing up artillery under fire. Our lives depended upon on how they worked; and in every sense – the clipped commands of the deputy, the tense, planned assault on a stubborn adversary, the degradation of a filthy wet trench and the spirit of comradeship, of watching out for each other – this was another kind of front line. 'Over there,' shouted a voice behind me, 'our last one was killed; Peart was his name. He was impaled by the machine. Just not quick enough, poor lad.'

It was now twenty past eight in the morning. The walk back seemed eternal, the breathing of the men in time with their long steps metallic. Then, at last, the cage! Now the Coal Board had stopped paying. In the lamp room Harry Mason, the man whose hand was a claw, said, 'This is where we keep the wounded.' Silhouetted behind the wire mesh Nick Gowland walked in pain with his smashed hip. He is 22 and, because he was too young at the time, received no compensation.

Now the young men sprinted for the baths, while the older men tried. Black faces and white bodies darted from lockers to showers, along aisles of steam, at the end of which were private showers 'for the lads with a bit missing'. I was conscious of a background noise of wheezing and hacking. The lung disease, pneumoconiosis, known as 'the Dust', often doesn't show up on X-ray for decades. 'It's been difficult to breathe for a long time,' said Ron Sugden. 'You know what the doctor said to me? He said I should keep out of 'the Dust'! The laughter at Ron's remark resounded in the baths, and when they laughed the hacking reached a crescendo.

I returned to Murton in July 1984 with the great strike under way. All around pits had closed, the Consett steel works had been levelled and the shipyards were empty. The miners' victory a decade earlier had led to seductive productivity deals, which provided their enemies with a new weapon of divisiveness. A spurious 'social contract' had seen a Labour government side squarely with capital. Now, with Thatcher in power, the miners' union was the target. To be in a village like Murton then was to understand just how little the rest of the country knew about the state's tactics during that strike. While the government and the media spoke virtually as one and incessantly highlighted the violence of miners, paramilitary police cut off the villages and assaulted almost anybody, including the old. As it was later revealed, most arrested miners had committed no offence and their arrests were illegal.

'You're bringing bloody revolution to the streets of Britain,' Robert Maxwell railed at Arthur Scargill in my presence. 'You are doing nothing less than attacking the sovereignty of this nation' – at which Scargill asked for a cup of tea.

An insidious violence was directed at miners' families through an increasingly politicised bureaucracy. The case of Patrick Warby's daughter, Marie, was fairly typical. Marie, aged five, suffered from a bowel deformity and needed a special diet. She was denied benefit by the Department of Social Security. After Patrick went to a tribunal I obtained records of the case showing that Marie had been turned down because her father was 'affected by a Trade dispute'.[42]

Murton remained solid until the end when, said John Cummings, 'The banks and finance companies turned the screws at once.' The trade union establishment had hoisted the white flag long before that. In February 1985 I happened to be in the Murton Miners' Institute when the television news showed the recently retired TUC leader Len Murray doffing his cap three times to Lord Hailsham, as 'Lord Murray of Epping Forest' took his seat in the unelected upper chamber. Before departing for the Lords, Murray had called for an attitude of 'reality' from the miners, as had Margaret Thatcher. Such a spectacle of ritual betrayal caused an embarrassed silence among the men I was with. Either they were too incredulous, too exhausted or too generous to say what was in their minds. 'There goes Len,' said one of them finally.

Today, yellow street lamps illuminate the town's dead heart. When the pit was closed in December 1991 it was levelled, leaving one listed building like a monument set in gravel. Even the swimming pool which the miners built, the only Olympic-sized pool on the coalfields, was demolished; the council didn't have the money to take it over. Tom Parry was the last man out. 'It was a Friday at about three in the afternoon,' he said. 'As I left, Mr Thomas the demolition expert blew up our workshops. I couldn't believe it. I couldn't believe they'd take away not just our jobs, but the lives we'd given to it.'

The closing of Murton Colliery followed a murky campaign that is not untypical of British Coal, whose incentive to destroy and prepare for privatisation has swept aside all vestiges of the old paternalism. A divisive 'review procedure' offering redundancy 'sweeteners' led to the interrogation of individual miners and a threat to withdraw bonuses and overtime, which represent up to 50 per cent of miners' pay. 'Look at what's happened in Germany,' said Dave Temple, who was secretary of the mechanics. 'Murton is twinned with Baersweiller. When the pit closes there the men will have had five years' notice, retraining and guarantees of new jobs. The town has been given grants for new industry. We've none of that.'

Murton's biggest employer now is the Co-op, employing women on a part-time basis: a microcosm of the post-modernist nation. Then there is the bakery. Then nothing. Unemployment is around 30 per cent. Emmanuel Shinwell, the Minister for Fuel and Power in the Attlee Government, openly discouraged post-war industry from going into the coalfields, and 'providing warm factories', so that the men would have no choice but to work in the mines. Ask why miners do it and there is part of your answer.

Youth unemployment in all the pit villages is up to 80 per cent. For them, the denial of choice is explicit. Wheel clamps in the streets indicate the rise of youth crime. Teenage pregnancies are more numerous than ever, it seems. Of all the subjects that provoke anger here, 'youth training schemes' lead the list. Dave Temple's daughter, Corina, was one of 50 on a scheme farmed out to a private agency. She is the only one to have found a job: as an audio-typist. The agency was not pleased. Her qualifications, her character and the health and safety conditions of the office of her future employer were questioned. Only when she demanded to be released, and threatened to take it further, was she allowed to take the job. Private agencies lose a substantial subsidy when they lose a 'trainee'. The more unemployed youngsters, the greater the profit.

Most of the Murton miners were transferred to Easington pit. Their brief sense of security ended with Heseltine's announcement last October. One British Coal executive broke ranks. Ian Day, the area production manager, wrote to the *Sunderland Echo*, describing the Government's action as 'criminal ... To talk now about measures to help the mining areas affected, to attract new jobs, is unbelievable. What new jobs and when? How can anyone replace 4,500 jobs in the north-east overnight?'[43]

In the north-east most local authorities have their own 'development unit'. Government policy has forced them to compete with their neighbours, no matter how close and common their interests. What matters is that they are seen to be vying for 'business', trying to catch the eye of a passing Nissan man, offering everything on the cheap, especially labour.

By any measure of economics, there is no logic to this: it is purely doctrinaire. This is demonstrated by the Government's refusal to allow £7,500,000 in European Community money to go to east Durham simply because it would break the ideological embargo on allowing local authorities to decide how to spend resources. Easington District Council has been allowed to spend just £600,000, about enough to fill in holes and paint the lamp posts.

There is no shortage of studies that conclude the obvious: that the cost of providing alternative employment is far greater than any subsidy to, or investment in, the mining industry. The coal reserves are there; British Coal continues to suppress the results of its bore-drilling off the Durham coast, having admitted that 'the information is commercially valuable'.[44] Reports by McCloskey Coal Information Services and experts at Durham and Newcastle universities show that the retention of both Easington and Vane Tempest pits makes economic sense.[45] In one of its own glossy brochures, British Coal describes Easington as 'one of the North-east's undersea super pits', which two years running produced a million tons of coal in record time.[46]

Of course, all this is irrelevant to the aims of privatisation, the spirit of which is expressed in a series of national newspaper advertisements. There is a photograph of a miner, Arnie Makinson, who is lauded as 'one of Britain's most successful businessmen'. The caption reads, 'Meet Arnie . . . a member of a workforce that's more than doubled productivity in just five years. He may not be Sir John Harvey-Jones but, as far as we're concerned, he's got as much to offer. We're tapping the richest seam of all – the hidden talents of our workforce.'[47]

Mr Makinson has his arms folded. So you cannot see that one hand is mutilated. Last year he lost the little and index fingers of his right hand in a terrible accident at Stillingfleet Colliery in Yorkshire during the week that Stillingfleet set out to break the European production record, and succeeded. Mr Makinson was working at the coal-face and his hand was so badly crushed that it seemed amputation might be necessary on the spot. Although he has to undergo more surgery, he has returned to work at the coal-face. If he joined other injured men at the pithead, he would be paid considerably less. 'One of Britain's most successful businessmen' is still awaiting compensation.

Under privatisation, the British coal industry is to be sold off in order to 'compete' in a home market that is about to be decimated by the importation of cheap foreign coal. In the meantime, pits that produce the cheapest coal in Europe are to be closed. Fewer pits will mean big profits – profits at the expense of the future. Some people are about to get very rich indeed.

Last July, the miners' parliamentary group – all of them ex-miners – met the board of British Coal. Their secretary, Dennis Skinner, asked each board member to answer one question: 'If this industry is privatised, will you give a guarantee that you personally will not benefit from the new set-up?'

'I got an immediate response from the deputy chairman, Ken Moses,' Skinner told me. 'He shouted that he wouldn't give any bloody guarantee. "Not me, Skinner!" he said. After that the chairman, Neil Clarke, said, "Nobody must answer that question," and he led them out the door.'

According to Arthur Scargill, if all the 31 pits eventually go, the number of unemployed in those industries tied to coal will be 70,000. 'If there is anyone who thinks that this is about the mining industry,' he has said repeatedly, 'then they don't understand the nature of the struggle.' But a great many people do understand now; and Scargill, who was right a long time ago, is respectfully listened to. His warning that the Government would reprieve enough pits to satisfy its rebellious backbenchers, then 'quietly' close them down one by one, when the public fire had faded, is proving correct.

In the Colliery Inn, the miners' pub, John Cummings, now the local MP, sits with his little dog Grit (who appeared in his campaign pictures). His aunt, Helen Abbott, wrote the pit's obituary before she died: 'The end of a pit; the end of a world; all too final in its premature end of a people.' Her *Requiem for a Dead Stalwart* appears as a preface to column upon column of names of miners killed in the pit, including one James Crewe and his four sons, who died in separate accidents. John has a nice turn of irony. 'To Thatcher,' he says, 'we were the enemy within.' He lists the establishment honours bestowed upon Murton, including a Victoria Cross, a Military Cross, Distinguished Flying Crosses and Medals, OBEs, MBEs, and so on.

Geordie Maitland, whom I met in 1974, seems as chipper as then. He tells me matter of factly that, days after I saw him, he was dragged along a conveyor belt into machinery and his foot was crushed. It has since been crushed again. 'Where's Bill Williams?' I asked. 'The bloke who took me down, who chewed tobacco.' Bill is dead. And Ron Sugden, who had the Dust? He is alive: indestructible is Ron. 'None of the lads you've known ever scabbed,' someone says. 'Good lads.' Scabs are not allowed in the Colliery Inn.

The mood in the town is strange and uneasy. Some call it apathy; others say it is tinged with guilt, because perhaps a third of the men who transferred to other pits, like Easington, want to take redundancy. They are exhausted. They also know that even if they wanted to fight openly, they would lose their redundancies. Above all, they know they cannot stand alone again; and neither should they be expected to do so.

The women put this well. Mary Parry, who with Jan Smith carried the banner on the return to work in 1985, says the rest of the country has to lead now. 'We'll be there,' she says, 'but it's only fair we're with others . . .' In their 24-hour vigils the Women Against Pit Closures exemplify the spirit that has seen scorned and brutalised working-class organisations re-establish basic liberties in Britain: from Peterloo in 1819 to the turn-of-the-century struggle against laws hostile to trade union rights.

On the bitter March morning in 1985 when the Murton miners went back to the pit, their prize brass band emerged from the mist with the women marching first. This had not happened before. What their long and heroic action meant, at the very least, was that ordinary men and women had once again stood and fought back. And that, for me, is Britain at its best. The shadow that has since lengthened over them – that of the centralised state progressively shorn of all countervailing power – is now the shadow over most of us.

January 30, 1993

WAITING FOR ARMAGEDDON

ON THE DAY Prince Charles made a speech on 'declining standards' in education, there was another news item. It was a report warning that nuclear warheads for British Polaris and Trident submarines and for RAF bombs were unsafe and could explode accidentally, dispersing radioactive material over a wide area, and putting cities at risk. Glasgow, especially, is vulnerable. The report's authors, the authoritative British American Security Information Council (BASIC), called on the Government to halt 'the handling and transportation of all UK nuclear weapons until a full safety review is carried out, overseen by an independent panel'.[48]

What is most alarming about the report's conclusions is that they are drawn mainly from an official study commissioned by the US House of Representatives Armed Services Committee. Known as the 'Drell Report', this warned that certain nuclear weapons could explode if involved in an accident or exposed to fire. 'For a while we were worried that these things might go off if they fell off the back of a truck,' a Pentagon official was quoted as saying in the *Washington Post*, whose investigation and disclosures triggered the committee's inquiry.[49]

The Pentagon has since hastily withdrawn two types of nuclear weapons from deployment. One is the SRAM-A air-launched missile, which was fitted to F111 and B52 bombers; the other is the W79 nuclear artillery shell, which has been in Europe since the mid-1980s and apparently could go off if struck 'in the wrong place'.

According to the BASIC report, the American concern

arose 'as a result of more powerful computer modelling techniques recently developed'. That is to say, computers are now able to simulate almost precisely the causes and conditions of nuclear accidents. This has led to enhanced safety provision in the United States; but there are no equivalent measures in this country, leaving certain British nuclear weapons without up-to-date safety features. The British WE177 'tactical freefall bomb', deployed by the RAF for the past twenty-five years, fails the new tests completely.

'These are not academic concerns,' says the BASIC report. These bombs are 'regularly transported around the UK'. The authors estimate that there is, on average, approximately one convoy carrying these warheads on Britain's roads every week; one left RAF Honington in Suffolk on Monday of last week. Convoys carrying WE177s have been involved in two known traffic accidents.

The British Polaris/Chevaline programme, a legacy of the Callaghan years, was developed in such secrecy that the Cabinet meetings at which it was discussed were not numbered. Drawing on an American design that, says the BASIC report, had 'serious corrosion problems', Chevaline was 'a system produced under pressure... that far outstretched British knowledge and technology'. Chevaline also fails to meet the new safety criteria. Chevaline's warheads are transported by road between Coulport in Scotland and the Atomic Weapons Establishment at Burghfield in Berkshire, a journey of more than 600 miles.

The American study is sharply critical of the warheads fitted to D5 Trident submarines. Britain has ordered four Tridents at a cost of more than £9 billion. Using the new computer techniques, it has been discovered that the design of the Trident missiles' W88 warheads – which are shaped to surround the propellant – makes them vulnerable to detonation if the missile is involved in collision or it literally falls off the back of a lorry.

The US Navy is now studying a complete redesign of the Trident warhead. Hitherto unpublished Ministry of Defence evidence to the Commons Defence Select Committee has confirmed that the British warhead is the same as the American, and that a redesign has been rejected as 'too expensive'.

The Ministry of Defence has 'dismissed Trident fears', according to the *Guardian*'s defence correspondent, David Fairhall. He wrote that officials 'point out that the [Trident] missiles are never moved around with the warheads inside, so the proximity of the propellant only affects their safety while on board the submarine'.[50]

This is not so. Polaris missiles are moved, with their warheads, from the jetty at Coulport up a winding road to their bunkers. Trident's missiles will be stored on top of the hill, for which special armoured carriers are being designed so that the missiles, with their warheads, do not slip off the back of their particular lorry. Glasgow is just thirty miles away as the wind blows.

The official 'dismissal' makes no mention of the other British weapons referred to in the report as unsafe. The armed services minister, Archie Hamilton, gave assurances to Parliament that British nuclear weapons were constantly safety-tested and scrutinised with 'the most sophisticated computer modelling'. William Peden, principal author of the BASIC report, told me, 'There are only certain ways you can use the computer. The question is: how could the minister *not* be aware of the American findings?'

There seem to be two pressing issues here. The first is the public's absolute right to know about potential catastrophe, no matter how 'infinitesimal' the danger. The widely held view in Whitehall, and the media, that people are not concerned with such matters was addressed in a Gallup poll commissioned by BASIC. The results were offered to several Sunday newspapers, but appeared in none. They are: 58 per cent of the British people believe all transporting of nuclear weapons should stop immediately; 79 per cent believe Parliament should have the same access to information on nuclear weapons as the US Congress.

The second issue is the policy of the Opposition. Rather, what Opposition? Labour is for Trident; but what is Trident for? It is not a defensive weapon. So at whom is it aimed?

Baghdad? Tripoli? The £10.5 billion cost is the 'official' figure. This takes no account of construction and operational costs, as well as the running of the weapons factory at Aldermaston. According to a Greenpeace study, the Government has underestimated the total cost of the Trident programme by £22,567 million.[51] What this money would otherwise buy requires just a little imagination. Here's a scribbled shopping list:

Ending homelessness and restoring a national housing programme: £3.8 billion

Restoring the transport system: £2.4 billion

Stopping the haemorrhage of teachers from our schools by raising salaries in education to a decent level: £1.5 billion

Paying every outstanding bill in the National Health Service and ensuring that people no longer die waiting for operations or because of the scarcity of equipment: £7 billion

Research and development that would catch up with the best in Europe: £3 billion[52]

Spread over twenty years, this would still leave billions of pounds in the Exchequer. No Labour leader, let alone a prime minister, has ever laid out these choices to the British people, who are constantly said to be 'pro-nuclear'. During the election campaign the 'peace dividend', like so much else, was not an issue and the Trident farce was hardly mentioned. Yet less than a third of the public say they want to keep Trident.[53]

'They who put out the people's eyes', wrote Milton, 'reproach them of their blindness'. Yes; but it's not the people who have been blinded.

April 1991 to May 1992

II

DISTANT VOICES OF DISSENT

ORGANISED FORGETTING

TRIUMPHANT CLICHÉS THAT the 'West has won' in Eastern Europe are incessant in the British media. They echo Margaret Thatcher's pronouncement that 'our values' have been adopted: a theme ordained by liberal commentators as received truth. With honourable exceptions, the coverage of Europe's upheaval has been so beset by jingoism, from the bellicose to the insidious, that the nature of change, and the emerging hopes and alternatives, have been obscured.

Czechoslovakia is a case in point. In 1977 I interviewed many of the Charter 77 people shortly after their organisation was forced underground. I was much moved by their political and intellectual courage in seeking democratic forms of their own. They were adamant in rejecting, as one of them put it, 'the way of Washington, Germany, London'.

They knew that, just as socialism had been subverted in their own country, so democracy had been devalued and often degraded in the West. I attended a secret meeting in Prague in which speaker after speaker warned of the dangers of adopting the 'values' embodied in NATO, an organisation which had legitimised the Brezhnev Doctrine and thereby reinforced their own oppression.

They also understood – unlike many of us in the West – that state power in the democracies is enforced not with tanks but with illusions, notably that of free expression: in which the voice of the people is heard but what it says is subject to a rich variety of controls. Writing in the 1920s, the American sage Walter Lippmann called this the 'manufacture of consent' (i.e. brainwashing). 'The common interests', he wrote, 'very largely elude public opinion entirely, and can be managed only by a specialised class'. The public is to be 'put in its place' as 'interested spectators'.[1] In this way, illusions of 'consensus' are created, rendering a free society passive and obedient.

In 1977 the banned Czech writer Zdener Urbanak told me, 'You in the West have a problem. You are unsure when you are being lied to, when you are being tricked. We do not suffer from this; and unlike you, we have acquired the skill of reading between the lines.'[2]

In Britain today we need to develop this skill urgently, for as freedom is gained in former communist Europe, it is being lost here. Our 'new age' is to be an information society, the product of a 'communications revolution', as Rupert Murdoch likes to call it. But this is a fraud. We are in danger of mistaking media for information, of being led into a media society in which unrestricted information is unwelcome, even a threat.

The narrowness of the British media, our primary source of information, is a national disgrace. This is not to say the *Sun*, the 'market leader', is a mere comic; on the contrary, it is intensely ideological with a coherent world view of our 'new age' society: one in which you stand on your own two feet, pull yourself up by your bootstraps and trust nobody; one in which money is what matters – the 'bottom line' – not to mention voyeurism: looking on at misfortune and violence. Objectors to this are 'loony'. Mrs Thatcher has said as much.

The damage runs deep. Racism, for example, is all but acceptable. 'The Press', says a Runnymede Trust report, 'plays a very significant role in maintaining and strengthening and justifying racism at all levels of society, providing a cover for racist activity, especially racist violence . . . '[3]

The 'quality press' is very different from the *Sun* and its pale shadows, but there are common strands. Censorship by omission is one; and I wonder if younger journalists on the serious newspapers are aware of the subtle influences of Murdochism on their own work, notably the cynicism. When in recent times have the now voluminous Sunday quality papers published anything that might pose a sustained challenge to the status quo? Salman Rushdie's brilliant defence of his work in the *Independent on Sunday* was an exception.[4]

Increasingly, languid commentary and tombstones of vacuous stylism, owing much to the language of advertising, occupy the space of keen writing and provocative journalism. In the *Observer* a recently hired columnist, who on his first day wondered who he was and what he stood for, still apparently wonders. In the same pages Clive James is brought back from television to continue his self-celebration and empty repertoire. Perhaps this is meant as parody; certainly it is a metaphor.[5]

Most of the quality press shares the same triumphalism as the *Sun*. The 'new age' corporate truth is upon us; there is nothing to challenge and scant need of a second opinion, except as a token, because everyone is agreed: 'we' have won.

On Eastern Europe, a genteel McCarthyism is evident. Communists are 'on the run' or slinking away from the 'irrefutable' truth that the free-market system 'works'. Such simplistic nonsense, however decorous in word and display, remains simplistic nonsense. Let there be a free-ranging critique of communism, whatever communism may mean, but let there also be an equally rigorous review of 'liberal capitalism'. For these days it is barely mentioned that a world war is being fought by 'the system that works' against the majority of humanity: a war over foreign debt which has interest as its main weapon, a war whose victims are millions of malnourished and dying children.

Television news, from which most people learn about the world, is a moving belt of headlines, caricatures and buzzwords, with pretensions that it is otherwise. In this way the Russian threat pervaded the nightly Cold War saga of good guys and bad guys; and the habit is hard to break. The bad guys may have slipped from view, but the principal good guys cannot be deserted.

'It's up to the United States,' we are told, 'to sort out its Central American backyard.' The coverage of the American invasion of Panama was not quite as bad as in the United States. There were dissenting voices in the British media, but they were not well-informed and so served to legitimise the Accredited Truth: that the whole fiasco was a cowboys-and- Indians pursuit of Old Pineapple Face.

Noriega, of course, had precious little to do with it. George Bush ran the CIA when Noriega was their man; and drugs have long been a CIA currency. The aim was to put Panama, its canal and its US base under direct American sovereignty, managed by other Noriegas. The Panamanian police chief appointed by Washington, Juan Guizado, is the same thug whose troops attacked the presidential candidates last May.

Consider how our perspective is shaped. It now seems certain that more than 2,000 Panamanians were killed in the American bombardment: more than died at the hands of the People's Liberation Army in Beijing last June. And which victims do we remember, I wonder, and the politicians honour? Not those in Panama, to be sure. Thus, our 'manu- factured consent' allows the British Government to give its obsequious support to the American invasion, having con- demned for a decade the Vietnamese expulsion of the geno- cidal Pol Pot.

In his book *McCarthy and the Press*, Edwin P. Baley, a distinguished American reporter of the 1950s, reveals how he and his colleagues became the tools of McCarthyism by reporting 'objectively' propaganda and seldom challenging its assumptions.[7]

In Britain today, the 'free market and a strong State' doc- trine belongs to another 'ism', but many of its effects are no less menacing and its dangers no less great, not least the process of indoctrination itself.

The Thatcher Government's secrets legislation is as sweep- ing as the notorious 'loyalty pledges' of the McCarthy period. Old-style civil servants, with a genuine sense of public service, are being replaced by the new 'privateers', who, as recent disclosures about the water industry demonstrate, are pre- pared to show their loyalty to government by misleading the public. This is a trend throughout the bureaucracy.

'Loyalists' are being introduced at every level of the health service to implement the White Paper, perhaps to dismantle the NHS by stealth. The doctors and nurses understand this 'hidden agenda'. But it is not the message reaching the public because the media, too, has its powerful loyalists.

When is there to be an effective opposition to a plethora of laws which give this country a distinction shared with no other Western democracy: that of legislated sycophancy, at virtually every level of current affairs journalism? Not a single broadcasting institution has challenged in court the government edict that makes criminals of television and radio journalists who interview certain Irish politicians, including those elected to Westminster.

Moreover, propaganda today bears little likeness to its historic models. Since 1979, the public relations and advertising industries have developed as powerful instruments of government propaganda. Consider the share-issue campaigns in which millions of pounds have been spent promoting the sale of public assets. Today, almost half of all advertising is originated by central government.

At the very least, a genuinely free society should forge the link between Macaulay's 'fourth estate of the realm' and the rights of liberty and political democracy for all. This is the heart of it. A gathering silence ensures that freedom, real freedom, is denied: that nine million British working people will continue to live on or below the Council of Europe's 'poverty threshold' and one in four British children will experience poverty, thousands of them incarcerated in bed and breakfast hotels and on crumbling estates. There are millions of Britons like that; another, unseen nation not far from the bijou doors and Roman blinds, and who are now so crushed they are probably unable to share a vision of anything.

And what if they did? Lech Walesa's revolution could not happen in Britain, where the right to strike and the right to assemble and associate have been virtually destroyed. Those rights being fought for and restored in Eastern Europe are those under review and in receivership here – Habeas Corpus, trial by jury, the right to silence, and so on. No other regime has been brought before the European Commission on Human Rights so often as that of the United Kingdom; and no other has so often been found guilty.

The Thatcher Government understands the importance of the media immeasurably more than its predecessors. That is why a 'reforming' Broadcasting Bill is being hurried through Parliament. 'Economic analysis', noted a Home Office study, 'tends to view broadcasting as an economic commodity – a service from which consumers derive satisfaction much as they might from a kitchen appliance and whose value to society should be assessed accordingly.'[8]

That is the doctrine of the British revolution in which the price of 'consumer satisfaction' is a state discarding its democratic veils. There is no counter revolution, of course; we have not yet learned to read between the lines. But there is a profound unease. So, when will Macaulay's link be forged? When will journalists and broadcasters reaffirm surely the most vital and noble obligation of their craft: that of warning people when their rights are being taken away, and of reminding them of the historic consequences of vigilance lost. 'The struggle of people against power', wrote Milan Kundera, 'is the struggle of memory against forgetting.'[9]

February 12, 1990

INFORMATION IS POWER

ON THE DAY Robert Maxwell died, an estimated 6,000 people were killed in a typhoon in the Philippines, most of them in one town. Maxwell's death consumed the British media. It made an intriguing story, with few facts. Speculation and offerings by former retainers were unrelenting. His yacht was described in all its opulent detail; there was the great bed the man had slept in and the crystal he and potentates had drunk from. It was said he consumed £60,000 worth of caviar in a year. And there was the man himself: in shorts, in shades, in a turban, with Elton John on the sports pages.

The death of the Filipinos, the equivalent of the sudden extinction of a Welsh mining village, with many more children killed than at Aberfan, was mentioned in passing, if at all. On the BBC's *Nine O'Clock News* Maxwell was the first item; the disaster in the Philippines was one of the last in a round-up of 'fillers'.[10]

In one sense, the two events were connected. Although promoted as an 'outsider', Maxwell embodied the new age of imperialist wealth: of triumphant rapacity based on asset-stripping, 'off-shore' secrecies, government collusion and, above all, debt. The people who were swept to their deaths at Ormoc on the island of Leyte were also part of the new age. In an area with no previous experience of natural calamity, most of them died in flooding and mud slides that may well have been the result of deforestation. 'It's a man-made disaster abetted by nature,' said Leyte's governor.

With almost half their national budget committed to

paying the interest on debt owed to the World Bank, the International Monetary Fund (IMF) and Western commercial banks, Filipinos are raping their beautiful country in order to export anything that brings in dollars and yen. Coral reefs are poisoned with cyanide to provide goldfish for the goldfish bowls of America. Forests are logged illegally to satisfy a Japan long ago stripped of trees.

This is not news, just as the deaths of the victims are, at most, 'slow' news. 'Small earthquake: not many dead' is not quite the joke it used to be. Natural disasters in the Third World *are* reported; it is the manner of the reporting, and the subtext, that helps to secure for the majority of humanity the marginal place allotted them by the world's media managers.

A typhoon, an earthquake, a war: and they are news of a fleeting kind, from which they emerge solely as victims, accepting passively their predicament as a precondition for Western acknowledgement and charity. That is one reason why independence movements are treated so negatively in the Western media: they smash the beloved stereotype of dependence.

Consider the strictly controlled Western perspective of Africa. The fact that Africa's recurring famines and extreme poverty – a poverty whose rapid increase is a feature of the 'new age' – have political causes rooted in the West is not regarded as news. How many of us were aware during 1985 – the year of the Ethiopian famine and of 'Live Aid' – that the hungriest countries in Africa gave twice as much money to *us* in the West as we gave to them: billions of dollars just in interest payments.[11]

We were shown terrible television pictures of children dying and we were not told of the part our financial institutions had played in their deaths. This also was not news. The camera was allowed to dictate a false neutrality, as is often the case, with the reporter playing the role of concerned innocent bystander and caption writer. Public attitudes flow from both perspectives and omissions. Unless prejudice is countered, it is reinforced. Unless misconceptions are cor-

70

rected, they become received truth. This 'neutrality' is commonly known, with unintended irony, as 'objectivity'. Indeed, it has been ordained a 'rule' and invested with a certain sanctity. There are many exceptions to this 'rule', especially when the pretence of 'objectivity' has to be suspended altogether. The Gulf War was a recent example.

Most of the British press is owned by oligarchies in the making: Murdoch, the Maxwells, Lord Stevens, Viscounts Rothermere and Blakenham, 'Tiny' Rowland. TV and radio news have been greatly influenced by Murdoch and now, increasingly, by the American Cable News Network (CNN). There are some excellent programmes on British television that challenge the partial, colonial view of the rest of the world – such as those made by Central Television and Channel 4's *South* series – but the imbalance is growing.

All the media oligarchies collaborated with Thatcher's media 'strategy', which was essential to her doctrine of a 'free market/centralised state'. 'News values' complement this. Whatever used to be said about him personally, one Maxwell is worth more than 6,000 Filipinos. One captured RAF pilot is worth more than tens of thousands of Iraqis killed, including those buried alive in their trenches by American bulldozers. One British child is worth more than countless Iraqi children, embargoed, traumatised and dying for want of essential services, food and drugs. When a group of London schoolchildren was asked for their view of the Third World, several of them wrote 'Hell'. None of them could provide a coherent picture of actual people.

The majority of humanity are not news, merely mute and incompetent stick figures that flit across the television screen. They do not argue or fight back. They are not brave. They do not have a vision. They do not conceive models of development that suit *them*. They do not form community and other grass-roots organisations that seek to surmount the obstacles to a better life.

'Never', wrote Jeremy Seabrook about the Western media, 'is there a celebration of the survival, the resourcefulness and humanity of those who live in the city slums; nowhere is there mention of the generosity of the poorest, of the capacity for altruism of those who have nothing, of the wisdom, endurance and tenacity of people displaced from forests, hills or pastures by western-inspired patterns of development.'[12]

Ninety per cent of international news published by the world's press comes from the 'big four' Western news agencies. They are United Press International (UPI), Associated Press (AP), Reuter and Agence France Presse (AFP). Two are American, one is British, one is French. Their output is supplemented by the transnational giants: from Murdoch to Times-Warner to CNN. Almost all of these are American. The largest news agency, UPI, gets 80 per cent of its funding from US newspapers. A survey in the mid 1980s found that UPI devoted 71 per cent of its coverage to the United States, 9.6 per cent to Europe, 5.9 per cent to Asia, 3.2 per cent to Latin America, 3 per cent to the Middle East and 1.8 per cent to Africa.[13]

'These figures', wrote the Grenadian writer Don Rojas in *Third World Resurgence*, 'give a clear picture of the phenomenon called information imperialism. In the total volume of UPI's information, news about the United States took up more space than that devoted to the whole African continent, where more than 50 countries are situated.' Former Tanzanian president Julius Nyerere once noted sarcastically, wrote Rojas, that 'the inhabitants of developing countries should be allowed to take part in the presidential elections of the United States because they are bombarded with as much information about the candidates as are North American citizens'.[14]

In the same issue of *Third World Resurgence*, the Zimbabwean journalist Dingaan Mpondah wrote that 'running against the fast current of this broad river of news from the West is a trickle of information from the Third World which barely manages to reach the doors of the readers in New York, London or Paris. The exchange of news between the West and Asia is typical of the imbalance. AP sends out from New York to Asia an average of 90,000 words a day. In return AP takes in 19,000 words ... '[15]

Old empires live on with the 'big four'. AFP is strongest in French-speaking Africa. AP and UPI are in the Americas and Japan, South Korea and the Philippines, which the United States dominated in the post-war period, and Reuter maintains its influence in the former Commonwealth. 'No other single factor', said Reuter chairman Roderick Jones in 1930, 'has contributed so much to the maintenance of British prestige ... ' These days Reuter makes huge profits from dispensing 'market information' to the world.[16]

The agencies produce much fine on-the-spot reporting, as well as critical analysis of events, individuals and policies. But these do not necessarily illuminate false assumptions and seldom challenge stereotypes. In the cataract of words that goes out every day, the jargon, euphemisms, acronyms and assorted inanities that comprise a deadening shorthand are rarely weeded out. Terrorism is almost never associated with the West, only with the Third World. It is not important that the US Government trains terrorist armies and its agents run death squads. The State of Israel is not described, like the Libyan regime, as a sponsor of terrorism: only Arabs are terrorists. As Dingaan Mpondah pointed out, 'The names of many independent-minded nationalist leaders – like Mossadeq or Allende – are invariably prefixed by terms like "leftist" or "communist". The effects of the constant use of terminology should not be underrated. Such a bias moulds public opinion to the point where Western military intervention in Vietnam or El Salvador is made quite acceptable.'[17]

During most of the Vietnam War the Vietcong, who were southern Vietnamese, were portrayed as 'communist aggressors'. The Americans, to my knowledge, were never referred to in the mainstream media as invaders. They were merely 'involved'. Thus the transition from news to Hollywood was smooth, with the emphasis on the angst of those 'involved', not the suffering and heroism of the defenders.[18]

Similarly, without a six-month media campaign that elevated Saddam Hussein to the status of a 'new Hitler', General Schwarzkopf might not have been able to conduct his 'media war', along with his slaughter of Iraqis, quite so expeditiously.

Yet even though the enemy had been thoroughly demonised and 'made ready', 75 per cent of the American public told pollsters they favoured negotiations, a 'diplomatic solution'. (The figure was about 56 per cent in Britain.) When war finally broke out, most people were unaware that the Iraqi dictator had made numerous attempts, through credible intermediaries like the Saudis, to extricate himself from Kuwait. These were not reported by most of the British and American media until after the war, and ignored by Washington and London. Not surprisingly, when 'our boys' went into action against an 'intransigent' foe, a majority supported them.[19]

This was not how most of the world saw it, of course. During the war you had only to take a sample of Third World newspapers to glimpse a worldwide opposition to the disproportionate violence and its real aims, together with a recognition of Western, and Iraqi militarism, that was unbeknown to us in the West.

Reading Third World commentators, I am struck by their informed fear of post-Cold War recolonisation, especially that which deploys information technology. 'The global news giants prescribe us information . . . ' wrote Shiraz Kissam. 'Like the explorers who preceded them, they are mapping the world on a principle of perpetual extension. Hence, the globe is seen in terms of the West's need for it.' People see and learn about each other, she says, 'only via this distorting mirror'.[20]

And yet there *is* awareness. In many Third World countries the seduction is not going well: many people know by their own experience that consumerism and democracy are not the same thing and that the so-called 'free market' is about the power of capital and not at all free. For example, the 1991 World Bank/IMF conference in Bangkok was reported very differently in many Third World countries from the way it was in the West. The World Bank was seen as responsible for, not a solver of, problems. The same was true of the meetings of the General Agreement on Tariffs and Trade (GATT), in which the United States sought to include as 'free trade' the resources of 'services, finance, tourism and intellectual property rights' in the developing countries.

The media labours under many restrictions in the Third World; yet much of it is bold and many of its journalists see themselves as allied not with the establishment but with the people. This can be frustrating work. In Britain, the situation is very different; and it is ironic that, as media technology advances, it is not only the traditional methods of journalism that have become obsolete, but the honourable traditions. It will be a further, shaming irony if these traditions are upheld in the 1990s by the very people who never make news.

November 15, 1991

A BETRAYAL OF PURPOSE

NEWSPAPERS, WROTE A. J. P. Taylor, 'serve their noblest purpose when they are popular newspapers. A newspaper which is read by just a few of the so-called influential figures of the establishment is like an inter-departmental memorandum of the élite. It is a bloodless thing. Newspapers are also about crusading. They are part of people's lives. That is what the great popular newspapers were in the past and should be now.'[21]

The man who popularised history got it right. He wrote those words in 1984 when Robert Maxwell bought the *Mirror*, a paper for which I worked for most of my adult life. His sentiments were, of course, nostalgic; by that time all mention of popular or tabloid journalism conjured little that was noble and much that was ignoble and cynical. The *Sun* had provided a new model in 1970; and today there is little to choose between Rupert Murdoch's moneymaker and its rivals, especially the *Mirror*. Take away Paul Foot's fine weekly column and an occasional defence of the National Health Service and the homeless and the difference is, says a *Mirror*-man of many years, 'about the width of a cigarette paper'.

The *Mirror*'s support for the Labour Party is spoken of as a significant difference; but this is confined to the uncritical underpinning of a leadership whose policies owe more to Thatcher's influence on British political life than to the needs of Labour's constituency. Moreover, it is a support that is prepared to go to the same lengths as the Tory papers in defence of the established order – such as the smear campaign

76

against Arthur Scargill, whose warning about the coal industry has been proven right, whose willingness to negotiate and compromise during the coal strike was suppressed and whose personal honesty bears striking comparison with that of the crook, Maxwell, who tried to crush him. It was a hatchet job the *Sun* and other tabloids could only admire. That the *Mirror*'s dogs barked after an honest man while they remained silent, presumably gulled, as their own master stole from them, describes the extent to which the 'noblest purpose' of popular journalism has been betrayed.

'The history of the *Daily Mirror* is the history of our times,' wrote Maurice Edelman in his book about the paper.[22] If that is so, Maxwell's coming was inevitable. He and Murdoch, their voraciousness feeding off relentless loans and secret deals, exemplified the Thatcher years. Between them, they hijacked popular journalism; yet even that truth is denied, no doubt because there remain so many acolytes to deny and distort it. Consider, for example, the now infamous headline, 'The man who saved the *Mirror*,' which was splashed across the *Mirror*'s front page the day after Maxwell's death.

To understand the falsity of this claim, one need only look at the period immediately before Maxwell took over in 1984.[23] After more than a decade of decline in the 1970s, during which the *Mirror* had tried and failed to compete with the *Sun*, the paper's fortunes began to improve in the early 1980s. For example, during the Falklands War the *Mirror*'s circulation rose when it countered the *Sun*'s racist hysteria ('Argies' and 'GOTCHA!') with calm, erudite leaders (written mostly by Joe Haines) that, while not opposing the war, expressed the misgivings of a large section of the British population. This was popular journalism at its best.

Not only did the circulation continue to recover, but there was the prospect of a new kind of ownership that had every chance of guaranteeing the independence of the paper for many years. The chief executive of the Abbey National Building Society, Clive Thornton, was appointed chairman of the Mirror Group with a brief from the owner, Reed International, to prepare the company for flotation on the stock market. Thornton was an interesting maverick who had grown up in poverty on Tyneside, left school at fourteen, and studied law the hard way. While at the Abbey National, he broke the building societies' cartel and financed inner-city housing. He drew up a 'protective structure' for the *Mirror* in which no single shareholder could own more than 15 per cent of the company; and he began to assemble a portfolio of solid, institutional capital. On top of this, he intended to give the workforce a substantial share of the company. He had no airs. He shunned the executive lift. He ate in the office canteen.

Reed was taken aback: it had hired Thornton on the implicit understanding that he would 'cut the unions down to size' and instead he was winning them over. He found the unions co-operative and the real canker in the management. He also proposed that the company launch a 'serious left-wing tabloid' in addition to the *Mirror*, with a second London evening paper. For all of this, he was criticised as 'naive' by managers and journalists alike. When Reed chairman Alex Jarratt broke his public pledge not to sell to 'a single individual' and looked like selling to Maxwell, the unions, including the journalists, gave Thornton a pledge of industrial peace for a year: a commitment unprecedented in newspapers.

I well remember the passion expressed at the *Mirror* chapel meeting at which we voted for Thornton. A red-faced Joe Haines said he would have to be 'dragged through the door to work for a crook and a monster like Robert Maxwell'. Indeed, Haines was one of those who all that week had been warning us that Maxwell might plunder the pension fund. Within 48 hours, Thornton was virtually thrown out of the *Mirror* building by Maxwell, and Haines was Maxwell's man.

One year later the leader of the Labour Party was guest of honour at a lavish party which Maxwell held to celebrate the first anniversary of his takeover of the *Mirror*. Neil Kinnock, it was said, did not approve of Maxwell, but Roy Hattersley ensured they kept smiling. Of those who now controlled Britain's press, Maxwell was all they had. Seen from the point of view of *Mirror* readers and Labour voters, the scale of the tragedy became clear. And if the journalists could not spot the con man, the readers could. They resented their paper being turned into a Maxwell family album; and they stopped buying it in their droves. In June 1984 the *Mirror* under Thornton was selling 3,487,721 copies daily. After eighteen months under Maxwell, this had dropped to an all-time low of 2,900,000 and falling.[24] Calculating readership figures, at least a million people stopped reading the *Daily Mirror* in the wake of Maxwell's takeover. 'It takes something close to genius', according to an observer quoted by *Marketing Week*, 'to lose so much circulation so quickly.'[25]

The Murdoch press have had wonderful sport at the expense of the *Mirror*, and who can blame them? But surely we can now expect the Insight team of the *Sunday Times* to dig into Murdoch's own, huge indebtedness and the allegations regarding his business practices made by Christopher Hird in his book on Murdoch and his Channel 4 investigation?[26] And will they now ask how Murdoch ended up controlling 70 per cent of the press in his native Australia when the Foreign Investment Review Board opposed his acquisition of the *Herald* and *Weekly Times* empire?

In Britain, the Murdoch and Maxwell papers between them have the biggest single share of the daily tabloid market. On Sundays, their papers are the majority. Such is the influence of Murdoch that a whole generation of journalists have come to the craft believing that Murdochism is an immutable tabloid tradition: that sexism, racism, voyeurism, the pillorying of people and fabrications are 'what the British public wants'. This means, at best, patronising the readers. For journalists on the *Mirror* it meant – and still means – a breathless wait on the editorial floor for the arrival of the first edition of the *Sun*. It means a vocabulary of justification and self-deceit. 'The readers', that strange amorphous body, are constantly evoked. 'The readers' are no longer interested in real news and serious issues; 'the readers' are interested mainly in royalty scrapings, and handouts from those who hustle television soaps and pop music business.

In last week's *Sunday Mirror*, under a front-page headline 'Bedded and Fired', a secretary claiming to have been 'seduced' by Maxwell, a man she found 'repulsive', complained that he 'made' her go home on a bus and did not keep a 'promise' to give her a flat and a car. As part of the *Mirror*'s current spasm of contrition, the aim of this story was no doubt to show what a rat Maxwell was. It didn't work. Instead, it provided yet another example of how deep the rot in popular journalism is. Over the page was some self-serving nonsense about how the paper had had 'an awful week' and it promised 'at all costs, to continue to expose corruption WHEREVER we find it . . . ' The reference to 'continue' will puzzle those *Mirror* pensioners embezzled by the publisher of the *Mirror*. The rest was oddly familiar. 'Our rivals in Fleet Street', it complained, 'are trying to talk us down because they can't beat us down. Jackals and reptiles in harness!' Did Cap'n Bob dictate this from the grave? 'Our heart', it finished up, 'beats strongly because we and you, our readers, care for each other . . . '[27]

The last line has become something of a refrain lately as the rudderless *Mirror* papers lay claim to a legacy that is no longer theirs. The years of Murdoch and of Maxwell show. The obsequiousness of yesterday has been replaced by abuse of Maxwell that abuses too much and protests too much. Meanwhile, the newspapers of the ordinary man and woman are, on many days, hardly newspapers at all. It is almost as if there is a missing generation of journalists. As young journalists are often told that the standards of Hugh Cudlipp's *Mirror* are 'not what the readers want', many are unaware that a popular tabloid, the *Mirror*, brought the world to a quarter of the British people every day, and did so with humanity, intelligence and a flair that never patronised readers; and that such a paper encouraged its writers to abandon what Dr Johnson called 'the tyranny of the stock response' and, above all, to warn their readers when they were conned – conned by governments or by vested interests or by powerful individuals. Mawkish tracts about 'caring for each other' were never necessary; care was evident.

Since popular journalism was redefined by the *Sun*, the effect on young journalists has, in my observation, been phenomenal. Denied a popular paper that allows them to express their natural idealism and curiosity, many instead affect a mock cynicism that they believe ordains them as journalists. And what they gain in cynicism they lose in heart by having to pursue a debased version of their craft. This applies to the young both on tabloids and the 'quality' papers.

This need no longer be so. The demise of Maxwell offers an opportunity to journalists to confront not only the truth of proprietorial crookedness but the corruption of journalism itself and to purge it with a paper that is truly on the side of its readers. The *Mirror* could be this paper again – as long as the residue of Maxwell's influence is cleared away completely. Or another could take its place.

It is significant that, of all the discussion about Europe, none has been about the press. In France, anti-trust media laws prohibit any individual or group from owning newspapers with more than 30 per cent of combined national and regional sales. In Germany, a cartel office sees that minority shareholders in newspapers have rights to veto the decision of a block majority. In Sweden, a Press Support Board ensures, independent of government, the health of a wide range of papers. In none of these countries does the existence of specific legislation restrict the freedom of the press. Rather, freedom and independence are enhanced.

My source for this is a Labour Party discussion document, 'Freeing the Press', published in 1988. It proposed a Media Enterprise Board similar to the Swedish board that provides 'seed' funds for new newspapers. It calls for a right of reply and legal aid on libel cases. It recommends a Right to Distribution, similar to that in France which allows small imprints to reach the bookstalls; and, most important, it says it is time for an anti-trust legislation and a legally binding obligation on owners to ensure editorial independence.

Are Labour still serious about this? If they are, they should say so now before their enemies catch them for having consorted with Maxwell. Of course, there is much to add to these reforms, notably that aspiring young journalists are taught and encouraged to believe that achievement of that 'noblest purpose' is indeed possible, and that in the end it depends on them.

December 13, 1991

A CODE FOR CHARLATANS

THE NATIONAL FILM Theatre is to hold a series of debates and films about censorship. I hope the discussions about television are not too late to galvanise real opposition to one of the most blatant, audacious attempts to impose direct state censorship on our most popular medium.

The arts minister, David Mellor, has described a proposed amendment to clause six of the Broadcasting Bill – due to be published this week – as 'British and sensible'. Mellor is a lawyer; he will understand that the corruption of language is the starting point. Indeed, there is something exquisitely specious about the conduct of this affair. Censorship is never mentioned. The code words are 'impartiality' and 'balance'; words sacred in the wordstock of British broadcasting, resonant with fair play and moderation: words long abused. Now they are to provide a gloss of respectability to an amended bill that is a political censor's mandate and dream.

Until recently, lobbyists within the industry believed they had secured from David Mellor 'safeguards' to protect quality programming from commercial domination as ITV was 'de-regulated'. Mellor was duly anointed 'civilised'; and the lobbyists did not watch their backs, or the House of Lords.

In July, the home office minister in the Lords, Earl Ferrers, announced that the Government wanted to amend the Broadcasting Bill with, in effect, a code of 'impartiality' that would legally require the television companies to 'balance' programmes deemed 'one-sided'. Moreover, the amendment

83

would 'include the ways in which impartiality could be achieved within a specific context . . . '

The point about this amendment is that it has nothing to do with truth and fairness. Charlatans and child abusers, Saddam Hussein and Pol Pot, all will have the legal right to airtime should they be the objects of 'one-sided' journalistic scrutiny. But control is the real aim. The amended bill will tame and, where possible, prevent the type of current affairs and documentary programmes that have exposed the secret pressures and corruption of establishment vested interests, the lies and duplicity of Government ministers and officials.

Thames TV's *Death on the Rock* exemplified such a programme. Unable to lie its way to political safety, the government tried unsuccessfully to smear both the producers of *Death on the Rock* and the former Tory minister whose inquiry vindicated them.[28] The amendment is designed to stop such programmes being made.

All this has clearly come from Thatcher herself, who, the record is clear, has done more than any modern British leader to use the law to limit basic freedoms, notably freedom and diversity of expression. She achieved this distinction (the Official Secrets Act, the Interception of Communications Act, the Contempt of Court Act, the Criminal Justice Act, etc.) while protecting and honouring those who have done most to damage and devalue modern journalism.

It is hardly surprising that a Government majority in the Lords saw off a very different kind of amendment to the Broadcasting Bill. This would have forced Rupert Murdoch to have relinquished control of Sky Television in 1992. It would have brought him into line with proposed rules that prevent any national newspaper owner from taking more than a 20 per cent stake in Sky's rival, BSB, and in any new domestic satellite broadcasting service.

A skilful political game has been played. Thatcher's stalking horse in the Lords has been Woodrow Wyatt, whose brief career on BBC's *Panorama* was marked by his obsequious interviews with Government ministers. Mostly, he is remembered for his red-baiting in the electricians' union. His prejudices are now published in Murdoch's *News of the World* and *The Times*.

Wyatt's refrain has been that broadcasting in Britain is a quivering red plot: 'left-wing bias' he calls it. In the Lords, he tabled an amendment to the Broadcasting Bill that would 'define impartiality'. He and Thatcher agreed this at a meeting in Downing Street. When Earl Ferrers picked up the scent and replied that the Government would table its own amendment, Wyatt and his backers withdrew theirs.

At last month's Royal Television Society dinner David Mellor went out of his way to describe the Wyatt proposal as 'unworkable'.[29] For this he received appreciative applause from television's liberal establishment. However, the publication last week of the amendment shows that Mellor's speech was massage and misleading.

The amendment gives Thatcher and Wyatt much of what they want, and is to be rushed through Parliament. The haste is likely to intimidate broadcasters in time for the next election; or that is the hope. Such obsession with political control stems mainly from a significant shift in how the establishment and the public regard the media. In many eyes television has replaced the press as a 'fourth estate' in Britain. This alarms those who believe television is there to present them, their ideology and their manipulations in the best possible light.

In contrast, much of the public now looks to television current affairs, documentaries and drama documentaries to probe the secrets of an increasingly unaccountable state. Every survey shows public approval of television current affairs, and offers not the slightest justification for new restrictions. Television's successes have been notable. The Guildford Four might not be free now had Yorkshire Television's *First Tuesday* not mounted its original investigation. For more than a quarter of a century Granada's *World in Action* has exposed injustices, great and small, and made the sort of enemies of whom serious journalists ought to be proud.

Not surprisingly, the series has borne the brunt of the

Thatcher/Wyatt wrath. This has come lately from the 'Media Monitoring Unit'. Last March the MMU was exposed by the *Independent on Sunday* as little more than a propaganda shopfront following a series of well-publicised attacks on Radio 4's *Today* programme for its 'anti-government bias'.[30] The MMU's founder is Lord Chalfont, a pal of Thatcher, who appointed him IBA deputy chairman. Chalfont is also a pal of Wyatt, whom he supported in the Lords debate.

Factual programmes are expensive, particularly investigations that require time and patience. Under the new bill, how many companies will now risk controversy if it means having to make two or more 'balancing' programmes? What happened to Ken Loach's *Questions of Leadership* in 1983, to be shown this week at the NFT, is salutary. Loach's four films demonstrated how the trade union leadership often collaborated with government against the interests of millions of working people. After months of circuitous delay and decisions taken in secret, the IBA decided that each of the four films would need 'balancing' and that another longer programme would be made to 'balance' that which had already been balanced. Arguing against this absurdity, Loach maintained that because his films provided a view of trade unions rarely seen on television, they themselves 'were the balance'. They were never shown.[31]

In 1983, David Munro and I made *The Truth Game*, which sought to decode the language of nuclear inevitability and to illuminate the history of nuclear weapons as an exercise in keeping information from the people the weapons were meant to 'defend'. The IBA decided that *The Truth Game* could not be shown until a 'balancing programme' was made. Central Television approached several 'pro-bomb' names but they refused. Finally, Max Hastings agreed to make a separate programme but not to do as the IBA wanted: to rebut our film virtually frame by frame. *The Truth Game* was made when television reflected the bellicose establishment view of the 'Russian threat'; this was a time when Washington's 'first strike' strategy included the possibility of a 'limited' nuclear war. Thus, like *Questions of Leadership*, our film provided modest 'balance' to an overriding 'imbalance' in the coverage of the nuclear arms race. Under the new amendment, it probably would not have been made.[32]

That Britain already has television censorship ought to be enough to alert us to the nature of the demands of Wyatt and Co. This is known as 'prior restraint', a nod-and-wink system instituted in the name of Lord Reith, founder of the BBC. In 1937 Reith boasted that he had 'fixed up a contract between Broadcasting House and the Home Office', and had 'made it clear that we must be told ahead of things that might cause trouble'.[33] When in 1988 Home Secretary Douglas Hurd decided to make criminals of TV and radio journalists who interviewed members of certain Irish organisations, including those elected to Parliament, he first informed the BBC as was customary. 'Impartiality' is spoken about at the BBC as a 'Reithian principle'. The irony is usually unintended.

Anti-bill lobbyists have argued that British television is among the best in the world. Yes, but this reputation derives, in great part, from those very 'dissenters' who are the amendment's target. Wyatt and Co. would certainly have wanted to 'balance' John Grierson, Denis Mitchell and Norman Swallow. And great journalists like Ed Murrow and James Cameron would have been seen off, along with the likes of Cobbett, Swift and Dickens.

The Thatcher Government is not 'misguided', as some have suggested. Its assault on free journalism has got this far because Thatcher and her acolytes have encountered only polite and confused opposition. The politeness should end. If broadcasters and the public do not defend the public's right to know, who will?

October 8, 1990

87

THE CORRECT IDEAS

AT A TIME when modern imperialism is producing a new obfuscating vocabulary, and the narrative of recent history is being murdered, I am grateful to Edward Said, Noam Chomsky and Susan George for their new books.

In *Culture and Imperialism*[34] Edward Said provides a rich historical guide to imperialism in its most insidious form: that is, western culture from Joseph Conrad's *Heart of Darkness* to present-day, ubiquitous 'media culture'. Said shows how the perceptions of colonisers and colonised are entwined by the assumptions that drove imperialism 100 years ago and drive it today. He connects William Blake ('The Foundation of Empire is Art and Science . . .') with Walter Lippmann, who devoted his writings to preparing Americans for the 'reality' of their imperial role, to George Kennan, a principal author of the theory of 'containing communism' and the cold war, who believed his country to be 'the guardian of civilisation'.

Edward Said is especially telling when he describes the effects of modern 'media culture' on American attitudes towards the rest of the world. There is, he says, 'an almost perfect correspondence between prevailing government policy and the ideology ruling news presentation and selection [which] keeps the United States' imperial perspective towards the non-western world consistent.' This reinforces American support for dictatorial regimes and for 'a scale of violence out of all proportion to the violence of native insurgency'. It also fits exactly a contemptuous media 'world view' that regards 'the history of other cultures [as] non-existent until it erupts in confrontation with the United States', and believes that 'most of what counts about foreign societies [can be] compressed into 30-second items, "sound bites", and into the question of whether they are pro- or anti-America . . .'

As Said points out, the essential difference between cultural indoctrination in the nineteenth century and during the American imperium is 'the epic scale of United States global power and the corresponding power of the national domestic consensus created by the electronic media'. Thus, in *Heart of Darkness*, Conrad saw his central character 'as a European in the African jungle and Gould as an enlightened westerner in the South American mountains, capable of both civilising and obliterating the natives'. Said also invites us to imagine the same power, on a world scale, which 'is true of the United States today'.

The point is made constantly by Hollywood, which produces the great majority of films shown in this and many other countries. Francis Ford Coppola's movie *Apocalypse Now* was the Hollywood version of *Heart of Darkness*. Seen by millions in the cinema and on television and video, it has been called 'a classic, definitive portrayal' of the Vietnam war. That Coppola reduced the Vietnamese and Montenard peoples to stereotypes of Oriental viciousness was generally passed over by the admiring critics. The film claimed that Vietcong soldiers hacked off the arms of children to discourage a vaccination programme, implying this was one of the reasons why the United States had invaded Vietnam. When an American journalist wrote to the screenwriter, John Milius, asking where the severed arms story had originated, Milius returned her letter with a US Special Forces' death's head drawing on it, together with the words:

We must burn them,
We must incinerate them,
Press after press,
Pen after pen,

Pencil after pencil,
No dialogue with communist criminals.[35]

In its crude way, this said a great deal about Hollywood's treatment of the longest colonial war this century, a war that left more than two million people dead and Indochina in ruins. Films like *Apocalypse Now, The Deer Hunter, Platoon,* and even the *Rambo* series became the popular historical and cultural reference points. In all of them, self-pity, the angst of the American invader, is celebrated while the Vietnamese flit across the screen as stick figures of no consequence, or as monsters, or as noble savages, or as child-like objects of patronising sentiment. Truth was not just turned on its head, but all irony was lost. Far from being vanquished in South East Asia, the United States devastated, blockaded and isolated Vietnam and its 'communist virus', while subordinating to American interests almost every regime in the region.

Noam Chomsky returns to this theme in *Year 501: The Conquest Continues.*[36] Chomsky uses the 500th anniversary of Columbus's 'discovery' of America to follow the unerring line of western domination from the earliest conquests of the American indigenous peoples to the slaughters in Vietnam and the Gulf. Like Edward Said, he compares the role played by imperial elites through the centuries.

The similarities are striking. While eighteenth- and nineteenth-century liberals often expressed anti-colonial views, they were not against imperialism, arguing for its more humane application and thus legitimising and reinforcing it. This is true of contemporary liberal moralists, who frequently see themselves as striking a 'decent, sensible balance' between oppressed and oppressor. They, too, are not against imperialism; indeed, their support for colonial wars can be counted upon.

Chomsky compares the weight of historical importance given to the 'politically correct' fiftieth anniversary of Pearl Harbor, the 'day of infamy', with other days of infamy declared unfit for public commemoration. For example, on October 11, 1961, President Kennedy ordered the escalation of the Vietnam conflict 'from large-scale international terrorism to outright aggression'. Thirty years later, almost to the day, President Bush blocked the admission of Vietnam to the world community. And yet, writes Chomsky: 'It is a staple of the media, and the culture generally, that we were the injured party in Vietnam.'

Although the Nazis remain the twentieth century's arch demons, it was, as Chomsky points out, Nazi models that determined United States 'counter-insurgency' doctrine in Indo-China and around the world. This was never reported in the 'mainstream' media, and ignored by Hollywood and other historical and cultural managers, just as genocidal atrocities were never reported. In neighbouring Laos, on which the Americans dropped the greatest tonnage of bombs in the history of war, there is no commemorative date at all, although it is thought that up to a million people may have perished.

Imperial history has many such silences, as Hugh Cudlipp reminded us in 1989, on the eve of the fiftieth anniversary of Chamberlain's declaration of war, when he wrote, 'There will not be nostalgic features in the *Times*, the *Observer*, the *Daily Mail* and the *Daily Express* recalling "What we said in the six years that led to the second world war".'[37] What they had said, of course, amounted to a cover-up and apology for Hitler and his ambitions.

Will we look back with comparable insight, and perhaps even shame, on the 'coverage' of the Cold War? In 1987, the celebrated establishment historian, Michael Howard, wrote, 'Few historians now believe that Stalin ever intended to advance his frontiers beyond the territories occupied by his forces in 1945.'[38] Two generations in the west were instructed to believe that the opposite was true, that the 'Russians were coming', that communism was taking over the world, that God and Coca-Cola were in danger. As a result, millions of innocent people, in most poor societies, were killed, maimed, dislocated and isolated in the 'noble cause' (Reagan) of 'stopping communism in its tracks' (Bush).[39]

Yet the attitudes of the Cold War still dictate the way we

live now and in the next century. Following the collapse of the European tyranny known as 'communism', monopoly capitalism declared itself the victor. Once again, truth was turned inside out. The 'victory' was marked by irrefutable evidence of capitalism's failure even in its own terms, and of its most enduring disaster since the Second World War. A quarter of Europe's poor now live in Britain; bankruptcies occur every few minutes. In the developing world, the gap between rich and poor is greater than at any time since records were kept.

In her book, *The Debt Boomerang*,[40] Susan George asks why all this should be regarded as the 'natural order of things', and why 'free-market' dogmas like privatisation have gained such momentum. 'You fund people', she explained, 'to create an ideological climate which becomes the life-support system for the doctrine. It becomes the water for the fish – the fish doesn't even know he's swimming. You put enough people with the "correct" ideas in universities. You create the institutes and the foundations. All these people come together in the colloquia and symposia, open to the press, that you sponsor. And they all write in the journals that you also fund, and from there they get on the editorial pages and on the air. Pretty soon, you have those three-man (they almost always are men) pseudo debates on television between the raving radical right, the extreme-right and the right of centre. Anyone who thinks differently soon begins to seem a pariah, or someone who at the very least must make apologies for his or her beliefs.'

Much of this pseudo debate, which equates imperial aims with democracy and the 'free market' with freedom, is to stifle dissent. This is true of the current 'debate' about 'free trade', following President Clinton's announcement that US trade and foreign policies are to be linked. They always were, of course. To the great powers, especially the US, 'free trade' is the freedom to control commodities that are the staples of poor, non-industrial countries, along with their resources of services, tourism, finance and intellectual property rights. This is, and always has been, the essence of imperialism.

And, like debt, 'free trade' is much more effective than a gunboat or a Rockeye cluster bomb.

Simply being aware of this can be almost as effective as opposing it. For once awareness spreads, it becomes an antidote to propaganda that seeks to make invisible the lives and culture, and fate, of millions. Without awareness, there can be no understanding, and no resistance. Some things never change.

March 12, 1993

III

THE QUIET DEATH OF THE LABOUR PARTY

A PALER SHADE OF BLUE

THERE IS TALK in the press, following the Labour Party's defeat in a general election it ought to have won, about a 'struggle' for the party leadership. Candidates are said to be 'embittered' at a 'stitch-up' and one of them, Bryan Gould, is reported to have 'unleashed his pent-up fury'. Such passion between those whose political differences are about as wide as this page provides the final post-election Mogadon.

Some people apparently believe this is 'politics'. Swathes of newspaper are devoted to it and to similar institutional games, whose rules insist that journalists, politicians and assorted 'experts' promote each other's agendas. This is known as the 'mainstream'.

Anything that intrudes from outside this 'mainstream' is likely to be blocked or suppressed. Take the sacred cow of 'defence'. To my knowledge, only one newspaper commentator (Ian Aitken) pointed out that John Smith's tax proposals could have been funded from Britain's annual military budget of £24 billion, without dismantling the country's defences or frightening away voters. Aitken's revelation was published *after* the election.

The election 'image' over which Labour's general secretary agonised last week was, in fact, just right. The party looked and sounded conservative in every way. The language was right, too. 'Modernising' and 'choice' and other Tory euphemisms so limited the national political debate that the perversity of their impact was minimal. Moreover, during the election campaign, it was widely agreed that 'convergence' had taken place between the principal policies of the parties. These policies reaffirmed the elevation of profit above people in almost all areas of life and derided the notion of common obligation as heresy. Labour differed from the official Conservatives only in tone. There was no suggestion that a Labour government would take away from the politicised bureaucracy its incentives to undermine the premises upon which a modest civilisation is based.

For example, it was made clear that pay beds in National Health Service hospitals were no longer a Labour concern; and there was no commitment to repeal the NHS and Community Care Act (1990) whose 'reforms' are privatisation by another name. Labour's manifesto referred to 'incentives to improve performance', which is the language of the Tories. In education, Labour said it would 'modernise', not throw out, the hated national curriculum and that schools would be 'free to manage their day to day budgets', which the government has already decreed and which had driven out teachers and brought schools close to bankruptcy.

The success of Labour's emergence as a conservative party has been much lauded. To date, this success has been expressed not at the polls, but in stirring victories over dissenters within the party. Something called 'electability', which Labour's leading conservatives maintained would be the party's reward for its conversion, has not materialised. Not surprisingly, the voters prefer the original, true blue to a paler shade.

Those who still mourn Labour's defeat might consider their degree of disillusionment had Labour won. I recommend they cast an eye over the experience of the 'modernised' Australian Labor Party, which, in many ways, provides a model. Within days of taking office in 1983, Labor embraced a version of the City, known locally as 'the big end of town'. Its complete conversion took about six months. Thereafter the Hawke Government oversaw the most dramatic redistribution of wealth in the nation's history (from the wage-earning majority to a new group of rich spivs), the highest unemployment since 1930, the greatest number of bankruptcies since

records were kept and the establishment of the most monopolised press in the democratic world.

Because Labour in this country has abandoned the policies
that distinguished it, good political sense dictates that it, too,
should be abandoned by those who last April gave it 'one
last chance'. This is not negativism. It is Labour that is
negative. It is Labour that has given up trying to persuade,
while moulding itself to what the opinion polls tell it. It is
Labour that declares in effect that society is static and
people's consciousness cannot be raised. The party's claim on
many people's loyalty is no longer tenable; for it is no longer
a great mass movement, but a force of reaction that muffles
any tentative suggestion of mass resistance. It is almost as if,
by its very institutional aspirations, Labour exists to blunt
people's radical instincts.

There is a striking parallel with America in the 1950s. The
great unspoken among the Labour leadership is its terror of
the media. For all its sport with the Windsor family and the
'morals' of Tory ministers, the media lie in wait for Labour
to deviate from its role as a reconstituted SDP. In America
forty years ago, the media's reaction to Franklin Roosevelt's
limited social reforms – which introduced measures hitherto
unheard of in a capitalist society: graduated income tax,
wealth tax, public housing and a welfare state – was almost
uniform. The equivalent reforms in Britain – those of the
Attlee Government – produced a more delayed, though similar, reaction, in the 1980s and today.

Both the Roosevelt and Attlee 'new deals' were at the core
of an historic contract that allowed the powerless to consent
to be governed. Of course, the deception that *radical* change
was on the way was smothered in what became known in
Britain as 'consensus', and which made genuine, popular
democracy *seem* possible. In America in the 1950s, those
who supported the legacy of the Roosevelt reforms were
ostracised as dogmatists, sometimes as 'communists'. Civil
servants, teachers, broadcasters, trade unionists and others
were cast aside. The media – newspapers and radio – became

the means of hijacking 'freedom' on behalf of those who would suppress it.

This is broadly the pattern of events in Britain today. T. S. Eliot's truth, that 'the historical truth involves a perception, not only of the pastness of the past, but of its presence', has no place among the 'modernists' of the Labour Party. For them, there is no struggle to continue, no gains to be defended. Like Henry Ford, they believe history is 'bunk'.

Fortunately, Henry Ford was wrong. And by letting Labour go its conservative way, and by ending the ambivalence and guilt that ties many to Labour, the great constituency of political activism in Britain is released to build upon the historic successes it has already achieved *outside* Parliament.

The point is people should not lose heart, or be defensive. It was the peace movement in Britain and Germany that made universal the principle that the nuclear arms race could be stopped only by bold unilateral acts. Mikhail Gorbachev embraced the principle. That Labour should lack the political and moral imagination to make capital of such an achievement, even to disavow it, says much about its new values. As we are entering a period of re-armament, the same movement is needed urgently.

Another popular force outside Parliament and the Labour Party was that which defeated the poll tax. In the field of criminal justice, a small, informed, vociferous coalition exposed a corrupt system. Some 800 miscarriages of justice have been brought to the surface. Independent journalists and lawyers, MPs and tenacious public committees have done this. The state honoured Terry Waite and the Beirut hostages for their undoubted courage in captivity, while the resistance of Mark Braithwaite, Engin Raghip, the Maguires and the Birmingham Six – victims closer to home – went unrecognised. They, and those who fought for them, ought to be among our heroes.

Addressing other issues of little interest to the 'mainstream' – poverty and race attacks – is a movement comprising those who have demonstrated their power to be heard, despite the media's echo chamber. One thinks of battles waged with the analytical weaponry of the Child Poverty Action Group, the Runnymede Trust and the Campaign Against Racism and Fascism.

It is true that many people remain isolated and immobilised by the lack of a *mass* opposition. But as social Darwinism becomes government policy, resistance will grow. Nothing is surer. The riots in Los Angeles were distant gunfire in Britain. Before the next millennium, the noise will grow louder here and all over the world. Shortly after he left the Labour Party recently, the veteran black socialist Ben Bousquet said, 'Ideas don't die. What happens is that people corrupt the ideas, but sooner or later those people go and we have to start to rebuild all over again.'

June 1992 – February 1993

THE WITCHHUNTERS

IN RECENT WEEKS, a BBC series, *The Un-Americans,* has provided reminders of how Senator Joseph McCarthy and his House Un-American Activities Committee witchhunted thousands of Americans for their political views or because they were 'suspect'. I hope those who run the Labour Party were watching and heard the echo of their own actions.

Witchhunting is not on the agenda of next week's party conference, though it ought to be. Of course, there is not the hysteria of the McCarthy period. This is Britain; the witchhunting is muted and conducted by the kind of sub-managerial apparatchik who now polices the party's 'modern', sub-managerial values. But the parallels are there. Guilt by suspicion and association are pronounced upon or implied, denying natural justice with a shabbiness reminiscent of the demagoguery of the McCarthy inquisitors who demanded, 'Are you or have you ever been a member of . . .?'

Some of those who come before the 'court' of the modern Labour Party are asked such a direct question. Their offence may be 'evidenced by' . . . 'involvement in anti-poll tax unions' or links with Militant, which is proscribed, or with other organisations that are not. Others are less certain of their 'crime' and find themselves facing a catch-all charge of 'bringing the party into disrepute evidenced by involvement in public activity designed to discredit the party'.[1]

Absurdity is, of course, close at hand. Dave Boardman was suspended from the party more than a year ago. The 'evidence' against him included an informer's statement that he was seen in a pub in Walton, near Liverpool, where a Militant

102

candidate was standing. He was not canvassing; he was there with a team of youngsters to play football. His local party, Oldham, conducted an enquiry and cleared him. However, the 'allegation' was apparently enough for Labour head-quarters in Walworth Road, London, which sent him a one-sentence letter suspending him and effectively ending his membership.

This is not uncommon. In Coventry, 127 members have been suspended, many of them for their 'suspected support' of Dave Nellist MP. No more than a dozen are, incidentally, Militant members. In Manchester, two councillors were sus-pended for visiting a friend jailed for poll tax non-payment. In Lambeth, thirteen councillors have been suspended for opposing the poll tax and the Gulf war. In Bedford, several councillors have been threatened with expulsion for opposing a pact with the Liberal Democrats.

These are but random examples. When I telephoned the Labour Party and asked if there was a nationwide figure for suspensions, I was told there was none. This seems strange in such a bureaucracy. What is clear is that many local party branches are falling apart as the most energetic activists face discipline from Walworth Road, and entire constituency parties are being suspended for years on end.

For those members brought to 'trial', a Kafka quality is present. First, there is the preliminary 'investigation' con-ducted by the party's Directorate of Organisation – a name with unfortunate overtones of Big Brother. The potential 'defendant' often has no idea of what he or she may be accused of, and is therefore ill-prepared to respond and likely to make incriminating statements. Questions to the 'investi-gator' often bring forth the reply, 'I am only here to listen to you.'

A former Brighton councillor, Jean Calder, herself awaiting 'trial', described the process of investigation in a letter to John Smith. 'There are no sworn statements,' she wrote, 'and unsupported hearsay evidence and rumours are accepted and "secret" evidence is made available to the "prosecution" which the defence is not permitted to see.'[2]

A 'trial' is run by a 'prosecutor' from Walworth Road, with the 'judges' drawn from Labour's Constitutional Committee. The committee was given extraordinary and secretive powers in the early 1980s when the Labour leadership decided to reactivate proscription, which had been abandoned in 1974.

The 'judges' have virtually limitless powers, thanks to an amendment to the party's constitution that reads, 'Where appropriate, the NEC shall have regard to involvement in financial support for and/or the organisation of and/or the activities of any organisation declared ineligible for affiliation'. In other words, membership of *any* political group can be called a crime against the party. These include broad-based organisations and the newspaper *Labour Briefing*, as well as local support groups such as the Friends of the Brighton Labour Party.[3]

During the 'trial', the prosecutor can call witnesses without forewarning the defendant, yet rules require that the defendant give two weeks' notice if he or she intends to do the same. A subsequent report to the NEC – described as 'about half the size of a telephone book' – is marked 'confidential'. The defendant has no right of access to it and no guarantee that the information it contains is accurate, or that it is not held on computer in contravention of the Data Protection Act.

Loyal party members have been suspended for actions which, at the time they took place, were not against the rules, and for misdemeanours for which they have already been punished. Disproportionate weight may be given to the submissions of those who support disciplinary action while others, even if they represent a large majority, are ignored or suppressed.

Ray Apps is a 62-year-old, working-class man. He is well known in Brighton for his support for what used to be known as 'basic Labour Party principles'. This has earned him the respect even of his opponents. He joined the party in 1945 when Labour was 'building Jerusalem', and has since held numerous senior positions in the local party, including chairperson, election organiser and conference delegate. As a dedicated socialist, he sees no contradiction in his support for Militant and in maintaining an honourable tradition of dissent that refuses to recant in the face of established authority. As one who joined the party forty-seven years ago, he can hardly be accused of 'entryism'.

Apps's trial took place on September 12 at the Old Ship Inn in Brighton. The defendant appeared to many who attended as the embodiment of the struggle of ordinary people during the past half-century. Speaking quietly, with some of the self-deprecation for which he is known, he said he had 'always fought for reconciliation within the party'. Later he reflected, 'It comes hard after a lifetime of work helping to build the Labour Party to have to face this. I can't deny there's a feeling of hurt and injustice. With other members of my generation, I worked for the party from the time we had only seven councillors, right through until Labour took control. It seems ironic that I am not wanted now.'

At Apps's trial one of his friends wept; and both 'prosecutor' and 'judges' looked decidedly uncomfortable. 'But Ray,' said one of them, 'we never suggested you had not worked hard for the party.' He was expelled.

The treatment of Ray Apps is part of a witchhunt that began in earnest in 1990, when Brighton Labour Party called for the reinstatement of six councillors who had been suspended from the Labour Group. In line with local party policy, the councillors had refused to support the use of the courts against poll tax non-payers. 'We undertook', wrote Jean Calder to John Smith, 'to stand alongside the 30,000 Brighton residents who could not afford to pay the tax. Though we expected punishment for breaking the Labour Group whip, we were unprepared for the draconian response of the party leadership. We were suspended indefinitely, and when the local party protested, it too was suspended for "investigation". Small wonder that, with dissident councillors barred from standing for re-election, the Labour vote reduced by 6,000 in 1991 and by a further 4,000 in 1992 with a loss of eight Labour seats.'

Of the twenty members suspended in Brighton, only six belong to Militant; and this is not untypical throughout the country. Jean Calder is a Christian Socialist. In her letter to John Smith, she reminded him of his own 'dual allegiance, not just to socialist principles but to our faith as well'. She wrote, 'A system has been set up which penalises honesty, and encourages sneaks, bureaucrats and informers. Aided by the ambitious, the corrupt and the naïve, they have taken over our party. Now the witchhunt has acquired a terrible life of its own. With the national membership scheme and the party's finances in crisis, recruitment is at an all-time low . . . and a climate of fear has been created. Last week I was shocked when a very elderly and frail member, who I had always thought supported the witchhunt, apologised to me, saying, "I should have done more to help you, but I was frightened I'd get on a list. I've been a member for years. I didn't want to get expelled too".'⁴

Labour is said to spend hundreds of thousands of pounds on its 'investigations' and 'trials'. To what end? The 'modernisation' of the party has failed; Labour distinguished itself by being defeated in a general election at the depth of an economic depression.

If the aim of the witchhunters is to destroy the party of the rank and file, leaving a rump to provide for the new conservatism, they have not succeeded, not yet. There are still a great many people in the Labour Party who cling tenaciously to the reason they joined. In Blackpool next week their voices should be heard.

September 22, 1992

LAUGHING NINE TIMES

THIS WEEK, A secret Labour Party report will admit that the party is dying as a mass movement. The report, by the finance working party, will tell the national executive that individual membership will fall below 200,000 and union-affiliated membership will drop by a million within the next four years, unless there is 'a new spirit both to attract and retain members and to mobilise support in the community'. In many areas, says the report, 'the party on the ground has deteriorated . . .'[5]

There is a call for 'new ideas', one of which is a recruitment campaign that includes 'new techniques' such as telephone canvassing and subscription fees linked to income. The irrelevance of this when set against the unstated causes of the 'deterioration on the ground' is striking, though not surprising. There is no mention of the principal cause: that tens of thousands of Labour Party members and activists have been driven away from the party by years of executive thuggery and witchhunting and, above all, by the abandonment of the pretence of *opposing* the now rampant reactionary forces in Britain.

At the end of two extraordinary months in politics, during which the Conservative government has shown itself to be corrupt and run by liars – a government more deeply unpopular than any since the Second World War – Labour has proved itself to be an enfeebled component of a rotting system, further disenfranchising those millions of people who still look to it as the constituted opposition.

John Smith and his people are not wholly to blame. This

107

is an historic process at work, perhaps in its final stages. Modern labourism based its postwar credibility on the reforms of the Attlee Government. 'Social justice' and 'welfare rights' were not seen by the public as a new form of charity. They were at the core of a contract that made it possible for the powerless and the poor to consent to be governed. They made popular democracy *seem* possible, even though its premises – employment, state education, a national health service, decent housing – were always more tenuous than was widely realised. 'Gentling the masses', rather than liberating them, was the aim of a 'consensus' which masked the collusion between capital and the defenders of labour, between the imperial state and those claiming to speak for democracy.

In fairness to the Labour hierarchy, be it in the party or the Trades Union Congress, its history was there to be read. From the 1926 general strike to the 1984–85 miners' strike, the trend was an unerring one of surrender and collaboration. From the British occupation of Ireland to the slaughter in the Gulf, Labour's leaders have not been equivocal. 'During the long period of collusive silence,' wrote Jeremy Seabrook a few years ago, 'a majority of us became accustomed to what we had gained, so *dependent* upon it continuing that way, that we were prepared to accept all kinds of repugnant social by-products of so fortunate a state of affairs, as long as it seemed that nothing would impair our rising standards of living. This is how new forms of ugliness and violence came to be assimilated into our daily lives . . .'[6]

In Labour's municipal bastions a flatcappery that depended upon apathy condoned corruption and failed to root out slumlords. Margaret Thatcher may have spoken out about Britain being 'swamped' by immigrants, but it was a Labour home secretary, James Callaghan, who introduced the most racist immigration bill more than a decade earlier. Attacks on the gains of the 'consensus' – on the health service, education and welfare rights – began under Labour, not Thatcher. The doctrine of a 'free market and a strong state' – with its high secrecy and 'privateers' within the bureaucracy

– owes as much to Labour as it does to Thatcher. Thatcherism, it is fair to say, began under Labour.

The behaviour of the Labour leadership during most of
the 1980s, as it tried to catch up with Thatcher, while witchhunting those who were often Labour's most committed
defenders, all but destroyed the party as a great popular
movement; the collapsing membership now tells us that.
Should further proof be required, I recommend the book
Defeat from the Jaws of Victory, whose authors, the Labour
historian Richard Heffernan and Mike Marqusee, editor of
Labour Briefing, take us behind the closed doors of the
'modernised' party to witness the Labour hierarchy in action.
It is a chronicle of rigged voting, stage-managed meetings,
patronage dispensed to favourites, score-settling and McCarthyism.[7]

'By the end of Neil Kinnock's tenure as leader,' they write,
'investigations of local parties and disciplinary action of one
kind or another had directly affected party members in over
80 constituencies in all regions of the country.' Although
Militant was singled out for attack, the real target was always
wider; in many areas, the majority of members expelled had
nothing to do with Militant. An official register of unaffili-
ated Labour Party groups was drawn up in 1982, leading to
the expulsion of any group and anyone espousing ideas on the
left – be they socialist, Christian, anti-war, whatever – who
were deemed to 'bring the party into disrepute'.

'Violations of natural justice were legion,' write Heffernan
and Marqusee. 'The presumption of innocence was hope-
lessly subverted. Guilt by association became commonplace.
Smears, innuendo and catch-all charges proliferated. Hearsay
and other forms of uncorroborated evidence were uncritically
accepted. Judgments were made on the basis of secret dossiers
compiled by anonymous figures whom the accused could
never confront . . .'

Although a special body, the national constituency committee, elected by party conference and independent of the NEC,
was set up to adjudicate on expulsions, only one case was
ever heard by the full NCC. This was the case of Sharon

Atkins, who had been removed as the candidate for Nottingham East before the 1987 general election because of remarks she had made at a black sections public meeting.

General Secretary Larry Whitty presented the NEC's case against Atkins, who was defended by Lord Gifford QC. As Heffernan and Marqusee show, Gifford tore Whitty's case to shreds, pointing out legal, logical and factual errors in charges he described as 'fundamentally misconceived'. He expressed 'utter astonishment that they are being seriously put forward'. The NCC was forced to recognise that no grounds could be found for expulsion.[8]

All other cases were heard by panels of three NCC members, the majority always on the right. The kangaroo 'investigations' of Terry Fields and Dave Nellist are told in shaming detail. As the authors point out, one of the main reasons the Labour Party is now deeply in debt, with little hope of making up the losses, is the squandering of the party's finances on 'discipline'.

The value of this book is that it helps to dispel myths. For example, the British people did not overwhelmingly support the Gulf slaughter, yet the Labour leadership was at times even more committed to war than the Government, even rejecting Edward Heath's attempts at a diplomatic solution. The *Sun*'s evaluation of ordinary people became Labour's; the popular consciousness, according to Walworth Road, could never be raised above ignorant certainties.

This almost total failure of political imagination – if that is not being too charitable – ensured that the issue of the 'peace dividend' remained outside the public arena. The enormous savings to be had from reducing Britain's defence spending to that of Germany were never mentioned. All discussion about Trident was suppressed.

To many people, the consequences of such 'collusive silence' are now provided daily by the demolition of industry, training schemes, social services and of lives once remote from the fear of poverty. Today, the bodies of 'redundant' people found on the railway lines wear cheap copies of designer jeans and trainers. Scan the reports of coroners'

inquests in the local press and you will get an idea of the
number now taking their own lives. They are the victims of
a revolution no modern Orwell has yet described.

Perhaps the real tragedy of the Labour Party is the time
its wilful distractions have lost. The 'market' revolution has
begun and there is now the popular will to resist it; but
where is the mass-movement banner? Soon, capital will no
longer need living labour, except as minor disposable servants. With an entire workforce being de-skilled and their
communities destroyed, the balance of dependency between
capital and labour is being altered as never before – so much
so that capital will soon be able to free itself of labour, while
still holding labour captive. That is, unless people fight.

The lessons of how not to fight were demonstrated on
December 9. The defenders of labour, led by Norman Willis,
the staunch royalist, called a National Day of Recovery. This
was the TUC's response to the two great demonstrations in
October that followed the Government's proclamation that
it was virtually closing down the coal industry. The TUC
general council first sought the views of employers, while
'ruling out a general strike'. In other words, all that the
defenders of labour can offer is a call to working people to
consummate a union of shop-floor, boardroom and government while their only power – their labour – is emasculated
by their new conjugal partners.

Willis's successor, John Monks, has been rewarded for
his modernist thinking with a promise of two confidential
meetings a year with the Chancellor of the Exchequer, Kenneth Clarke. 'I think', said Monks, 'there is a recognition
that things are going to go in a direction inimical to the
traditional values that the prime minister claims to espouse,
and that the world of work may be connected with this
development.'[9] Although the TUC denies it, the model
appears to be the American system, where one in five of all
workers, and nearly half of all young workers, earn poverty-
line wages; where working hours are longer and holidays
shorter than in most advanced industrial countries; where

the rate of accidents in the workplace doubled in the 1980s as a result of deregulation and imposed overtime.

And what of Labour? John Smith did turn up at the great rally in Hyde Park in October 1992. His absence would have been embarrassing; this was a time when even the *Daily Mail* was discovering the 'nobility' of Britain's miners. When Smith spoke, he urged the 'public' to keep up the pressure. As mining communities were attacked during the winter and spring, he said nothing. He did not even reply to the NUM's appeal for support for a one-day strike. He went on to address the Confederation of British Industry's conference and, according to the *Daily Mirror*, caused his audience to laugh nine times.

While many Labour Party members despair at this, they remain fixed in the belief that there is no alternative to Labour. They should look to New Zealand. During the 1980s the New Zealand Labour Party and the conservative Nationals became indistinguishable as the 'New Right'. At the general election in November 1993 the breakaway Alliance, representing Labour's activists, took 18.3 per cent of the vote. Alliance leader Matt McCarten has refused to join a coalition with Labour. 'The main arena is now going to be in Parliament', he said, 'because Parliament is going to be democratic, at last. We will vote for laws that move towards our manifesto and against laws that go against it. We are a mass movement, and we shall address issues of class and race and gender. It's a beginning.'[10]

December 1992 – December 1993

THE COUP

BORIS YELTSIN'S 'REFORMS', said President Clinton last week, 'must be protected because they represent our way of life.' John Major echoed that Britain's support for Yeltsin's 'democracy' was 'unambiguously clear'. Yeltsin, meanwhile, had just issued his umpteenth decree, suspending the constitution and taking control of the media 'in order to guard its independence'.

This, of course, is normal behaviour in many countries 'protected' by the west. Should democracy break out in these places – that is, democracy in the dictionary, rather than the Orwellian, sense – it is quickly discouraged or crushed. Haiti, Angola and Zaire are recent examples. There is a western Newspeak that complements this process. Yeltsin's opponents are 'hardliners' or 'former communists', regardless of their democratic credentials. Widespread public opposition to his 'reforms' is unmentionable; the fact that 60 million pensioners stand on the brink of starvation is irrelevant.

Our controlled perspective of events in Russia, which owes much to a perverse use of language that is the currency of news, mirrors the way we are directed to see events at home. Here, 'reforms' that are similar in nature and purpose, if not in scale, are at a critical stage. The destruction of the value of pensions in Russia and the economic warfare being waged against millions of people in Britain come from the same ideological source, which is the antithesis of democracy. When Margaret Thatcher said there was 'no such thing as society', she was defining the ideology that bears her name worldwide.

As Thatcher knew, society is something that can only be organised collectively and through the public and community sphere; and every day that society cedes its countervailing power to the absolute claims of 'the market' it dies. It dies not only in socialist terms, but in liberal terms. The great wave of unemployment and insecurity has now broken over the middle class; and those liberal commentators who insist that Thatcherism is discredited deny the evidence of their eyes. Thatcherism remains in safe hands. Indeed, it is unlikely Thatcher herself would have done all that Major is doing, such as privatising the railways and preparing to sell off the Post Office. Major's media persona as a decent, if incompetent, drone has been, for him, a godsend.

The coup against democracy in Britain has been a silent one. Here there is no Yeltsin and no constitutional difficulty; the coupmasters are a coalition of accredited factions. There is the government faction and the 'opposition' faction. Should their alliance be doubted, I recommend a reading of last month's anthem to 'the market' by Gordon Brown, and the recent speeches of Tony Blair on crime and punishment. 'Blair', said Kenneth Clarke, then Home Secretary, 'is the best opponent I've had. We're trying hard to find differences on law and order.' In its quest to out-Tory the Tories, Labour has become the New Right in what is, in effect, a one-party state.

In the meantime, and with virtually unlimited prerogative powers provided by the British Crown, the Thatcherite executive has appointed an unelected, secret nomenclature. This bureaucracy is in charge of the 'reforms' that are destroying democratic accountability in Britain. For example, the National Health Service is now run entirely by the Government's placemen. The one small local democracy component was scrapped under the legislation that gave the NHS over to the 'internal market' – the system that causes death after death among patients denied treatment by the 'logic' of the market.[11]

In education, the Schools Examination and Assessment Council now dictates directly to schools 'on anything from the age at which children should use commas to when they should learn to swim'. Following the abolition of the elected Greater London Council, its £7.5 billion budget went to unelected and unaccountable bodies such as the London Docklands Development Corporation. Thus, millions in state aid were 'invested' in the bankrupt Canary Wharf and other disasters.[12]

The list of undemocratic bodies embraces every area of public control, from the Training and Enterprise Councils to the Teachers' Pay Review Body. Whereas in the days of 'consensus' some effort was made to include trade unionists and 'ordinary people' on quangos, today's secretive committees are packed with right-wing sectarians, of whom the principals are approved by the Policy Unit at Downing Street. And many such 'loyalists', as Thatcher called them, skip from one quango to another. (This is not to suggest they would be different if replaced by Labour nominees, as the singular voice of the bi-party parliamentary select committees demonstrates.)[13]

At the same time the Crown prerogative (this active, *political* power of the monarchy is almost never mentioned in the British press) gives government ministers undefined discretionary powers to abolish any level of sub-national government. These powers were used in abolishing the Greater London Council and metropolitan counties in the mid-1980s. The executive even drafted a bill to abolish elections to speed up the counties' demise.[14]

Of course, a 'free market and a centralised state' were the essence of Thatcherism. The 'logic' of this is expressed in exquisite doublespeak. As the market was 'freed' (that is, rigged), so democracy was 'freed' (more tightly controlled than ever). The Yeltsin Russians and the Li Peng Chinese understand this well, and that their own anti-democracy can flourish behind a façade of 'new economic zones', run on cheap labour and environmental vandalism.

However, they can learn from Britain. Take the rigged energy 'market', the jewel in the crown. The privatising of coal, and the decimation of pits, will make wealthy the placemen who run electricity, gas and coal. The final destruction of the miners' union is a bonus. The scrapping of some 50,000 working lives is irrelevant to the 'dynamics' of the market.

The coupmasters depend on the media to spread the exciting word and to silence those who understand its truth. However, it is too easy to believe that political reality is fabricated by the media. In fact, there is a kind of critical intelligence and common sense inherent in ordinary language, in the way people arrive at their values. According to *Social Trends*, most of the British have dangerous thoughts about 'market' ideology. More than three-quarters of them believe profit is something that should be invested and go to the benefit of working people. Barely three per cent believe that shareholders and managers should benefit.

Increasingly, the British middle class understands that the destruction of the trade union movement and the public sector is a threat to *their* security. The concerted action that is now building among teachers, health workers, railway workers, miners and other public employees is likely to receive wide support. If eight million can take part in a general strike in Italy, often in defiance of their trade union aristocracy, something similar can happen here. If direct action can prevent France from dismissing thousands of employees, the same can happen here. The problem is one of national leadership, not impact. A secret Ford management document says, 'A British truck fleet dispute would probably result in the progressive closure of all Ford European manufacturing plants within three days.'

Such is the power that working people have within their grasp. Once again, *they* are the countervailing power. There is no other.

April – December 1993

THE ITALIAN FACTOR

WATCHING THE POLITICAL caricatures at the Tory Party conference in Blackpool last week, I recalled Edward Thompson's lament that he belonged to 'an emaciated political tradition, encapsulated within a hostile national culture'. Thompson described this country as his 'reluctant host', suggesting that those who oppose Toryism are a beleaguered minority.

I can well understand his sense of despair; millions of people all over Britain will have felt the same as they watched the precocious Peter Lilley and the unctuous Michael Howard competing for Armband of the Week. Their targets were the vulnerable: the old, the young, the disabled, single parents and those men and women who exercise and defend the right to work for more than a pittance, and in safety.

Under Margaret Thatcher and John Major much has been achieved in these areas. More than ten million British workers now live in poverty. A quarter of all British children are growing up in poverty. As in the early nineteenth century, new prisons are to be built to meet the predictable boom in petty crime.

Of course, there will be no new prisons for those who owe £23,000 million in unpaid corporation tax and £1,600 million in unpaid Value Added Tax; and for those who engage in City fraud amounting to £5,300 million every year. Lilley and Howard said nothing about the £12,000 million in public money lost in the privatising of the water, gas and electricity industries; and the decimation of the pits that means that foreign coal has to be imported; and the acceptable corruption.

Tory Britain is not a long way from corrupt Italy. *Lo stile è diverso*. Indeed, acceptable corruption is evident at every level of the Tory pyramid, from the selling of knighthoods (£500,000 in party 'donations'; individuals usually no less than £50,000), to the 'packing' of health trusts with the acolytes and funders of the Tory Party, to the manipulation of official statistics, to the lying that is now part of ministerial duty, as the enquiry under the judge, Lord Justice Scott, has shown.

The Scott inquiry is an aberration. Meant as a device to silence parliamentary debate following the scandalous behaviour of ministers in the Matrix Churchill affair, it has provided a glimpse, no more, of the rottenness of state power in Britain, or how the system works. It has shown how the Government embarked on a cover-up in which it was ready to see innocent businessmen go to prison rather than admit that it had deceived Parliament.

In the witness box ministers have blamed their officials, and the officials have charted the extent of the lying. Margaret Thatcher has been directly implicated in approving arms exports to Saddam Hussein, while denying everything. John Major has also denied everything, in spite of the fact that he was the chief secretary to the Treasury who increased export credits to Iraq, and foreign secretary when the guidelines for trade with Iraq were being administered by William Waldegrave, his minister of state, and chancellor when Customs and Excise reported to his private office that it had begun investigating Matrix Churchill, and prime minister when he discussed with Alan Clark, a defence minister, the export of arms to Iraq. Appearing before the enquiry, Major uttered this gem: 'One of the charges at the time was that in some way, because I had been foreign secretary, chancellor of the exchequer and prime minister, I must have known what was going on.'[15]

There may at times be a farcical 'carry on' element to Tory corruption, but corruption it is. And ordinary Tories apparently believe it is. In a poll taken by the *Daily Telegraph*, 64 per cent of its readers found the government most of them had voted for 'disreputable' and 'sleazy'.[16]

Here, I disagree with Edward Thompson: I believe that Toryism as the 'host culture' is an illusion, albeit a powerful one. What it has, above all, is an unchallenged voice. For example, Thatcher was not a 'unique political force', as her mythmakers contend. What she did was to popularise *petit-bourgeois* reaction and to silence any opposing voice. Indeed, her greatest single achievement was the co-opting of British liberalism: from the liberal media to the Labour Party.

The liberal intelligentsia, in the press and academia, never seriously exposed Thatcherism by denouncing its tactics and decoding its language. Fraudulent notions of 'freedom', 'choice', 'enterprise', 'modernising' (as in Cruise missiles and the Labour Party), 'family values' and 'reform' were not only allowed to become common usage, but were adopted by those once proud of their liberal credentials.

Moreover, liberal celebration of the rigged 'market' was always assured; count the number of times the BBC refers to 'economic reforms', a propaganda term. In a recent *Panorama*, the falsehoods of the Government's current assault on single mothers were reinforced with some of the most reactionary voices in Britain, dubious statistics from America and the reporter's judgmental question: 'Should *we* accept single mothers as the norm?'[17]

Who are 'we'? 'We' are those who work to and speak for a Tory agenda while pretending otherwise. 'We' are the New Right. The present Labour Party leadership, who are Thatcher's greatest triumph, are every bit as effective as Lilley and Howard. 'We are the party of law and order,' announced Tony Blair in Brighton, no doubt prompting Michael Howard to up the ante one week later.[18] This is the essence of the relationship between the two party leaderships. Gordon Brown says he will not take Value Added Tax off fuel; Kenneth Clarke concurs. David Blunkett says there is 'not enough productivity' in certain London hospitals; Virginia Bottomley agrees and promises to close them. Barry Sheerman, from

Labour's front bench, urges the minister for defence procurement to sell more British arms to tyrants like the Emir of Kuwait; the minister assures him he will do his best. And so the pattern proceeds, with each side pushing the other along the same sectarian path.

For this reason the Labour Party conference was significant. The 'broad church' was finally demolished, and John Smith's 'triumph' had nothing to do with the 'democratic principles enshrined in one man, one vote', but in the historic fact that Labour's New Right is finally accepted by the media.

The official Tory, as well as the liberal, media understand the scale of the New Right's achievement: that Labour has finally rejected Anthony Crosland's argument, which spoke for the party's once dominant old right, that 'a concerted attack on the maldistribution of wealth should be part of Labour's policy'. That last veil has now been dropped. At Brighton, the term 'one member, one vote' represented an attack not on the trade union establishment, but on the party's remaining egalitarian values. In order to give John Smith his media triumph, trade union leaders reversed the democratic decisions of their rank and file. For example, 750 delegates of the Union of Communication Workers voted against Smith's proposals. At Brighton, just nineteen delegates went against them.

It is this kind of collaboration that has served to blunt real political opposition in Britain. When the party conference voted democratically against the nonsense of keeping Trident, the leadership demonstrated its commitment to 'democracy' by ignoring it.

In my experience, Britain's 'host culture' is a rich mosaic of multicultural life: of people who enjoy both their differences and their sense of community and owe no allegiance to an *ancien régime* or Toryism's 'modernised' successor. Like *Social Trends*, a *Guardian* poll has found that Britons are now well to the left of all the 'mainstream' parties. Clear majorities believe that there is 'one law for the rich and one for the poor'; that privatisation should be stopped; that there should be higher taxes; that it is more important to reduce unemployment than to control inflation.[19] In other words, those who have 'put out the people's eyes', to paraphrase Milton, have not blinded them.

October 1993 – January 1994

IV

MYTHMAKERS OF THE GULF WAR

SINS OF OMISSION

AT THE HEIGHT of the First World War Lloyd George, the prime minister, confided to C. P. Scott, the editor of the *Manchester Guardian*: 'If people really knew, the war would be stopped tomorrow. But of course they don't know, and they can't know.'[1]

His words may soon apply to a modern equivalent of that slaughter. Like events in the Gulf, current and beckoning, the First World War was distinguished by a 'drift to war' – a specious notion that allowed for war preparation – and by an inferno of which there was little public comprehension or warning, and by the theatrical distortions and lies of the warlords and their mouthpieces in the press.

'There is no need of censorship,' wrote Philip Gibbs, a leading journalist of the time, later knighted for his services. 'We were our own censors . . . some of us wrote the truth . . . apart from the naked realism of horrors and losses, and criticism of the facts which did not come within the liberty of our pen.'[2] Max Hastings, a former Falklands War correspondent and now editor-in-chief of the *Daily* and *Sunday Telegraph*, said something strikingly similar on BBC Radio the other day: that it was the duty of a journalist in effect to gloss over during wartime, because 'one should recognise the national interests of the nation of which one is a part . . . '[3]

That 'national interests' include going to war when one's nation is not in any way threatened is rarely mentioned these days. Hastings's view is widely shared: if not openly, then subliminally. My own experience of war reporting is that journalists – bar the few 'mavericks' – seldom question the assumptions behind 'our wars'. An almost secular myth about the Vietnam War was that the media was against it. This was never the case; most were against the fact that the war was fought inefficiently, and that the Americans were losing it. Equally, some of the journalists in the Falklands who had previously defended their objectivity were unabashed in praising their own *subjectivity* in the cause of Queen and country. Their main complaint was about access, being denied the facility to be on 'our side' and help win the propaganda war.

If war breaks out in the Gulf the British media – which, unlike Iraq's, is said to be 'free' – will bear much of the responsibility for a 'patriotic' and culpable silence that has ensured that people don't know and can't know.

It is as if the very notion of the journalist as a teller of truths unpalatable to ruling elites, as whistle-blower in the *public* interest, has been fatally eroded. This is in part the result of the 'communications revolution' or 'total television', in which vast amounts of repetitive information are confined to a narrow spectrum of 'thinkable thought', and the vocabulary of state and vested-interest manipulation is elevated above that of free journalism. In the Gulf coverage, the effect is that many people are overwhelmed and immobilised, their misgivings not reflected in the opinion polls, only their compliance.

From tabloids to television, radio to 'qualities', the war drums are heard, their beat perhaps made all the more acceptable by the work of honourable sceptics, humanitarians and professionals, journalists like John Simpson and Robert Fisk. Otherwise we have the 'ugly momentum that is driving Bush steadily towards war' (*Observer*); a war that is 'necessary to protect civilised values' (*The Times*); a war for which 'no price is too heavy to pay' (Bush, reported uncritically almost everywhere). And anyone who gets in the way is a 'yellow-belly' (*Sun*); or 'an eccentric with a lust for publicity . . . a very British kind of nut' (*The Times* on Tam Dalyell); or using 'weasel words' (*Guardian*).[4]

And, of course, war is fun! Every night there is Peter Snow's bloodless sandpit to play in, and sexy shots of Hornets and Tornadoes, with a camel left of frame and the sun rising over the cockpit. Cue the bagpipes; cue the British major who wants to 'get in there now!'[5]

Military minders attached to the Joint Information Bureau manipulate most of what you see from the Gulf. A well-known broadcaster, who does not wish to be named, says: 'The cocoon is such that you end up being gung-ho and unquestioning. It's a bit much when you know things that you can't say: for instance, that many of our lads will almost certainly be killed by friendly fire, from the Allied side.'

The military's ability to distort and the media's malleability were demonstrated in August when television showed images of what appeared to be a highly efficient US military machine moving into the desert. This was a bluff: many aircraft arrived half full, the 'machine' was unprepared. Most of the media accepted what they were told.

We are told the use of nuclear weapons has 'not been ruled out'. Yet a study on the effects of a nuclear war in the Gulf has been virtually ignored.[6] Nik Gowing, diplomatic editor of Channel 4 News, describes the narrowness of the debate thus: 'It's quite shocking. I am thunderstruck that the British public know so little about the potential nightmare of this war. Naively, people are unaware that even if Iraq is defeated, the war may come to them: in acts of reprisal and terrorism in the centre of London, as the director of the CIA has warned.'[7]

Stewart Purvis, editor of ITN, gives an interesting reply to this issue: 'The line which the Opposition takes in Parliament is important to the level of news coverage of political debate. On the Gulf, Labour is synchronised with Government policy, so there is less news arising from the political debate.'[8] Few other broadcasters and senior press reporters will go on the record. 'My access to the MoD and the Foreign Office is a lifeline,' said one of them. 'I can't jeopardise it.'[9]

The *Independent*'s correspondent in the Gulf has written, 'Second guessing President Saddam's intentions has not proved a precise science Who predicted that he would invade

Kuwait on August 2?'[10] The answer is that the United States predicted it; and it is in this area of America's war aims and strategic purpose that the suppression of vital facts has been most evident.

According to George Bush, John Major, Douglas Hurd *et al.*, the sole aim of the war is 'the liberation of Kuwait'. The truth is to be found in events notably excluded from the present 'coverage'. In May 1990 the president's most senior advisory body, the National Security Council, submitted to Bush a White Paper in which Iraq and Saddam Hussein are described as 'the optimum contenders to replace the Warsaw Pact' as the rationale for continued Cold War military spending and for putting an end to the 'peace dividend'.[11]

On July 25 – a week before the Iraqi invasion – the US ambassador to Iraq, April Glaspie, told Saddam Hussein that she had 'instructions from the President' that the United States would have 'no opinion on your border conflicts with Kuwait'. She repeated this several times, adding, 'Secretary of State James Baker has directed our official spokesman to emphasise this instruction from the President.'[12] It was clear, wrote the syndicated American columnist James McCartney, one of the few journalists to study the leaked transcript, that the United States had given Saddam Hussein 'a green light for invasion'.[13] Moreover, two days before the invasion, Assistant Secretary of State John Kelly told a Congressional hearing that the United States was not committed to defend Kuwait.[14] Four days before the invasion, according to the chairman of the Senate Intelligence Committee, the CIA predicted that the invasion would happen when it did.[15] And did the CIA tip off the Kuwaitis?

Then there are the actions of General Norman Schwarzkopf, head of US Central Command, during the same period. At the time April Glaspie was reassuring Saddam Hussein in Baghdad, Schwarzkopf convened his top commanders for an exercise which, according to the *New York Daily News*, simulated 'exactly the contingency' of an Iraqi drive into Kuwait. 'The similarities were eerie,' said the paper's source, adding that: 'When the real thing came, the one way they could tell real intelligence from the practice intelligence was the little *t* in the corner of the paper – *t* for training.'[16]

There is other evidence that Saddam Hussein was deliberately squeezed or 'entrapped' into invading Kuwait. As a US client, he had become too powerful, too cocky and so – rather like Noriega – he had to go. And, like its strategic plans for Panama, the United States has long had a secret contingency for a permanent military presence in the Gulf, notably for the air force.

The timing of the Iraqi invasion could not have been better. Today, the US arms industry no longer faces the cuts of a 'peace dividend' and the recession no longer threatens America's 'world leadership'. 'In the future,' said the chairman of the House Armed Services Committee, Les Aspin, 'we are more likely to be involved in Iraq-type things, Panama-type things, Grenada-type things . . . ' But what of Kuwait, whose 'liberation' is the reason for the war? 'Our position,' said Aspin, 'should be the protection of the oilfields. Now whether Kuwait gets put back, that's subsidiary stuff.'[17]

According to Bush, Saddam Hussein has refused to get out of Kuwait 'at any price' and that 'extraordinary diplomatic efforts have been exhausted'. When the war started, the *New York Times* reported that the administration feared 'a diplomatic track' that might 'defuse the crisis' at the cost of 'a few token gains' for Iraq, perhaps 'a Kuwait island or minor border adjustments'.

In fact, Washington received an Iraqi proposal along these lines and, although described by a US official as 'serious' and 'negotiable', it was dismissed. Indeed, on January 3, the Iraqis put forward an offer to withdraw, which, again, State Department sources described as a 'serious pre-negotiating offer' that 'indicated the intention of Iraq to withdraw'; and, again, it was dismissed.[18]

Put these events together, add the absence of any US effort to create an international opposition while there was time, and urgent questions are raised. But who is to raise them if there is general agreement among the opinion-leaders that this is a matter of good versus evil and that the 'national interest' is at stake? Who is to say: this crisis *can* be settled diplomatically and a war that merely legitimises militarism is not a just war.

In a genuinely free society, there needs to be unrestricted debate, drawing on a diversity of sources that reflect the complexion of a society that is not one nation. As the *Daily Mirror* has pointed out, it will be the sick and old who will pay the bill for this war. So whose 'national interest' is at stake?

Is the build-up to war really a demonstration of America's world 'leadership' at a time of deepening recession and diminishing sources of raw materials and opportunities for 'free trade'? Why have sanctions not been allowed time to succeed? We all, it seems, live by the January 15 deadline. Saddam must leave Kuwait by that date. But the facts are not as they have been represented. At his news conference on November 30, Bush actually hoped Saddam would meet James Baker 'at a mutually convenient time' between December 15 and January 15. He did not name a specific date. The Iraqis may be awkward about the date, but so is Bush; and why should life and death for thousands of innocent people, who do not appreciate the 'values' of *High Noon*, hang upon it?

The *Observer* recently illustrated an article about the British Army in the Gulf, with a picture of a Colonel Denaro blowing a hunting horn to summon his driver. The colonel was described as 'an extravagant character with an attractive swashbuckling manner'. His regiment, the Hussars, 'are sometimes to be found wearing their big Browning automatics in shoulder holsters over tank crew's overalls, which gives them a rakish appearance'. Some of the officers come from 'the same stock as Wellington', and are heirs to the Light Brigade, 'the same gallant six hundred . . . '[19] The Charge of the Light Brigade was one of the most pointless imperial disasters in history.

The national newspaper editors being called to discuss war coverage at the Ministry of Defence should read the Crimea diaries of perhaps the greatest of all British war reporters,

William Howard Russell, of *The Times*. Not for him propaganda in the 'national interest'. He reported the sacrificial battles, the waste, the blunders. 'Am I to tell these things?' he wrote to his editor, John Delane, 'or am I to hold my tongue?' To which Delane replied: 'Continue as you have done, to tell the truth, as much of it as you can.'[20] Both were described as 'treasonous', having incurred the wrath of the monarch, the prime minister and the rest of the establishment. This, of course, ought to be no more than an occupational hazard.

January 7, 1991

VIDEO NASTIES

IN 1972, I watched American B52s bombing southern Vietnam, near the ashes of a town called An Loc. From a distance of two miles, I could see three ladders of bombs curved in the sky; and, as each rung reached the ground, there was a plume of fire and a sound that welled and rippled, then quaked the ground beneath me.

This was Operation Arc Light, described by the Pentagon as 'high performance denial interdiction, with minimised collateral damage': jargon that echoes today. The B52s were unseen above the clouds; between them they dropped seventy tons of explosives in a 'long-box' pattern that extended several miles. Almost everything that moved inside the box was deemed 'redundant'.

On inspection, a road that connected two villages had been replaced by craters, one of them almost a quarter of a mile wide. Houses had vanished. There was no life; cooking pots lay strewn in a ditch, no doubt dropped in haste. People a hundred yards from the point of contact had not left even their scorched shadows, which the dead had left at Hiroshima. Visitors to Indo-China today are shocked by the moonscape of craters in Vietnam, Laos and Cambodia, where people lived.

The B52s now operating over Iraq are the same type of thirty-year-old aircraft. We are told they are bombing Saddam Hussein's Republican Guard, and the 'outskirts' of Baghdad. Before the introduction in Vietnam of military euphemisms designed to make palatable to Congress new hi-tech 'anti-people' weapons, the term used was carpet-bombing. This was vivid and accurate, for these aircraft lay carpets of death, killing and destroying comprehensively and indiscriminately. This is what they were built to do; and that is what they are no doubt doing in a country where most people neither have shelters nor are 'dug in'.

The other night, on television, a senior ex-RAF officer included the current B52 raids in his description of 'pinpoint strikes . . . part of the extraordinary precision work of the Allies'. John Major and Tom King constantly refer to this 'remarkable precision' and, by clear implication, the equally remarkable humanitarian benefits this brings to the innocent people of Iraq, although further information about these benefits is curiously unforthcoming.

The British media amplify this. Indeed, so zealously have the London-based 'media response teams' spread the authorised word that the controllers of information in Whitehall have had to rein them in, rather like the sorcerer and his apprentice. George Bush has wagged his finger. Come on guys, let's not be 'overly euphoric'. John Major's autocue has said as much.

The first authorised version of the war was the Euphoria Version, put out by Bush himself and the Major autocue. This has now been replaced by the It Won't Be Easy Version. According to the Controllers of Information, the 'phenomenal surgery' of Allied technology, alas, failed to 'take out' most of the Iraqi Air Force and the Scud missiles. The echoes from Vietnam grow louder. The fabled 'tunnel' has returned. Wait now for the 'light'.

Protesting far too much, Bush says comparisons with the Vietnam War are inappropriate. Listen carefully to General Colin Powell, the chairman of the Joint Chiefs of Staff and himself a product of the Vietnam War, and the vocabulary and attitude are the same. The principal weapons used against Iraq, such as the Tomahawk cruise missile, have a 'circular error probability'. This means they are targeted to fall within a circle, like a dart landing anywhere on a dart board. They do not have to hit, or even damage, the bull's-eye to be considered 'effective' or 'successful'. Some have hit the bull's-eye – the Tomahawk that demolished the Ministry of Defence building in Baghdad is the most famous – but many, if not most, clearly have not. What else have they hit? What else is within the circle? People, maybe? The numerous autocues say nothing.

General Powell has also referred to 'minimised collateral damage'. Like 'circular error probability', this term was invented in Vietnam. It means dead civilians: men, women and children. Their number is 'minimised', of course, although we are not told against what benchmark this is measured. Of course, the Iraqis have no wish to admit they are bleeding badly, preferring to exaggerate the numbers of enemy planes brought down: just as the British did during the Battle of Britain.

The common feature of the Euphoria Version and the It Won't Be Easy Version is manipulation. What is distinctive about this war, compared with even the Falklands War, is that media scepticism has been surrendered without a whimper. There are rare exceptions, notably in the *Guardian*. Lies dished out are lies swallowed whole. Video-game pictures are believed by intelligent people; no context is called for. John Major's congratulatory message to the BBC was affirmation of the public broadcaster's role.

Television's satellite and video-game wizardry merely reinforces our illusions. The system of 'sound bites', perfected by the Cable News Network (CNN), means that if truth intrudes, it is quickly rendered obsolete. Genuine, informed analysis is out of the question. There is no blood. An emotional screen is erected between us and reality, and our sensibilities are adjusted accordingly.

Pilots are represented as heroic, as heirs of 'the few' who faced the *Luftwaffe*. Truth is turned on its head. No one doubts the pilots' courage; but the original 'few' were up against equals, not those of a Third World country – regardless of propaganda about a 'massive Iraqi machine'. The Israelis are also described as showing 'extraordinary courage' in the face of 'this outrageous attack' on them, while the people of Iraq are devoid of human form, let alone courage.

Unlike the Vietnamese, they are not even stick figures allowed to flit like phantoms across the screen.

Long before the war started, in order to prepare them, the British people were denied an understanding of the complexity of reasons behind the crisis in the Gulf. It was not mentioned that Britain virtually invented Iraq and divested it of Kuwait in order to divide and rule the region, laying the roots of this war. That the Americans had helped to put Saddam Hussein in power, providing him with a hit list of his opponents, was regarded as irrelevant. That Britain, America and other 'allies' sustained his murderous regime was relegated to the letters pages.

Remember the United Nations? The UN role is now hardly mentioned. Once the countdown to January 15 had begun, sanctions, the fraudulence of the American deadline and the dubious legality of Resolution 678, in relation to the UN Charter, were issues apparently unworthy of impartial scrutiny by those who wear their impartiality where others are said to wear their heart.

Beware, wrote Robert Louis Stevenson, of 'your sham impartialists, wolves in sheep's clothing, simpering honestly as they suppress'.

January 25, 1991

SALESMAN HURD

I ONCE GLIMPSED Henry Kissinger in Bangladesh when he was Richard Nixon's secretary of state. His visit was described by the American Embassy as a 'hardship stopover'; and he was driven in haste to the ambassador's residence, where he spent the night before being delivered back to the airport.

Bangladesh was then in the grip of flood and famine; and I, and other reporters, enquired if Kissinger's motorcade might be diverted a few miles to a camp where tens of thousands of desperate people had been herded. This seemed especially relevant, as Kissinger had earlier dismissed Bangladesh as a 'basket-case' and had established in the State Department the Office of Multilateral Diplomacy, better known as the 'Zap Office'. It was here that the voting patterns of Third World members of the United Nations were scrutinised so that those countries which voted against US motions could be identified and warned and, if need be, 'zapped' – that is, their US food 'concessions' would be cut off.

In a land of starving people, Kissinger probably saw not one. I mention this because Kissinger has always exemplified for me those who exercise imperial power and seldom see the consequences of their actions. There is also the ingredient of hypocrisy.

Latter-day Kissingers, 'statesmanlike' men of equally impeccable manner if not repute, are prosecuting the colonial war in the Gulf without the slightest risk of confronting the consequences of their actions, such as human beings 'zapped' by British and American cluster bombs. I once saw a rare survivor of a cluster attack; minute shrapnel, like needles, were 'swimming' through her organs, according to a doctor, torturing her to death.

Latter-day Kissingers often use a language few people speak: a semantic syrup that reveals nothing, omits a great deal and dispenses words like 'principles'. In an article in the *Guardian* last week, Douglas Hurd managed to mention 'principle' and 'oil' in the same column. Addressing critics of the war, and those he described as 'cynics', Hurd wrote, 'What of the charge that the problem of Saddam Hussein is of the West's own creating? Critics claim we supported and armed him during the Iran–Iraq War. But . . . we refused to sell armaments to either side'.[21]

In July 1981 Hurd, then a foreign office minister, flew to Baghdad as a 'high level salesman' (*Guardian*, July 17, 1981). His mission was to court Saddam; what he was hoping to sell, once the Iran–Iraq War was over, was a British Aerospace air defence system: a sale that 'would be the biggest of its kind ever achieved'. Ostensibly, Hurd was in Baghdad to 'celebrate' with Saddam the coming to power of the Iraqi Ba'athists in 1968, one of the bloodiest episodes in modern Middle Eastern history, which, with Washington's help, extinguished all hope of a pluralistic Iraq. Hurd would have known that the man whose hand he shook, the man to whom he came as a 'super salesman' of British technology, was renowned as an interrogator and torturer of Qasr-al-Nihayyah, the 'Palace of the End'.

Far from 'refusing to sell armaments' to Iraq, the British Government has played a critical role in building what Hurd now constantly refers to as 'the massive Iraqi military machine'. This has been done by subterfuge and sleight of hand. According to a report soon to be released by the Campaign Against the Arms Trade, at least 20 British companies have been allowed to supply Saddam Hussein with missile technology, radar and computerised machine tools. Although 'lethal defence equipment' to Iraq has been banned, 'existing contracts' have been honoured. A number of British

137

companies, including at least one owned outright by Iraqis tied to the Iraqi military, have exported equipment that has gone straight to weapons and ammunition factories. The 'super gun' is the most famous example. Others have exported machine tools said to have been designed for civilian production, which have 'dual use'. Indeed, 'lethal defence equipment' apparently does not include British-machined shells, British-designed bomb shelters, British-made anti-gas kits, British uniforms and the training of Iraqi fighter pilots in the Lake District.[22]

Following Saddam Hussein's genocidal gassing of Iraqi Kurds in 1988, Trade Minister Tony Newton flew out with 20 British officials and offered 'the Butcher of Baghdad' £340 million worth of British trade credit – more than double that of the previous year. The flow of British largesse was not interrupted by Saddam Hussein's murder of the *Observer* journalist Farzad Bazoft.

'Some people,' wrote Douglas Hurd, 'ask why if principle is involved, the West or the UN did not try to reverse Israel's occupation of Arab territories? Again, the parallel is partial and false. Israel occupied the territories as a result of war in which her neighbours were clamouring for an end to Israel's existence.'[23]

No, it is Hurd's reply that is partial and false. He makes no mention that the West has blocked all attempts to legally enforce Resolution 242 and most of the other UN resolutions on the Middle East. Only last October the United States blocked the Security Council from imposing sanctions on Israel after the massacre of unarmed Palestinians in Jerusalem. Similarly, Israel was able to invade and effectively carve off a piece of Lebanon, causing untold civilian deaths, without a single American or British bomb 'taking out' with 'surgical precision' the sources of this outrage.

George Bush also refers incessantly to the 'principle' of the 'Allied' cause. As a former director of the CIA, Bush will know the facts. He will know that the CIA helped put Saddam and his Ba'athist fascists in power. He will know that Saddam and his gang competed for CIA favours; that a

CIA-directed campaign oversaw the slaughter of the Iraqi opposition: socialists, trade unionists, teachers, journalists.[24]

Like other American-sponsored tyrants before him – Diem in Vietnam, Noriega in Panama – Saddam Hussein outlived his usefulness, especially when he had the temerity to challenge America's divine right to the resources of the Gulf. And for this 'principle' many thousands of people are about to be zapped.

February 1, 1991

TURKEY SHOOTS

LAST WEEK, AN American fighter pilot, Colonel Richard 'Snake' White, described his bombing missions over Iraq as a 'turkey shoot'. He elaborated: 'It's almost like you flipped on the light in the kitchen at night and the cockroaches start scurrying, and we're killing them.'[25]

At the time of writing, some 60,000 'sorties' have been flown against Iraq: that is, 30,000 more missions than were mounted against Japan during the last year of the Second World War. The target has been a country of mostly impoverished people, who live not in 'hardened shelters' but in the most fragile of structures. Indeed, as in most of the Third World, they are out in the open most of their lives, trudging along roads, spilling out of overcrowded transport, crossing and lingering on bridges.

Last week, a 'sortie' against the bridge in al-Nasiriyeh city killed forty-seven civilians and wounded 102. One of the wounded was a thirteen-year-old boy, Quaser Said, whose leg was amputated. He was crossing the bridge with his uncle and aunt, both of whom were killed; no doubt they were scurrying for shelter, as cockroaches do.

According to Patrick Cockburn, the *Independent*'s correspondent in Baghdad, there was 'no reason to doubt [the number of casualties] since the accounts of survivors, doctors and witnesses all tally'. We owe much to the few like Cockburn who have dared to lift the stone off this war and allowed us to observe its true nature: the slaughter of people with whom we have no quarrel.[26]

The killing of civilians is the story that, above all others, the warlords in Washington and London and their 'media contractors' (John Naughton's concise description in the *Observer*) have sought to suppress.[27] Witness the speed with which they moved to discredit Cockburn's report of the bridge. The BBC even produced a cameraman to say that there were wounded in the hospital wearing military uniforms; no interviews with survivors and witnesses were broadcast. That the International Red Cross now believes that the civilian casualties are considerably higher than reported was mentioned briefly, but unexplored and lost. For the BBC, the priority seemed clear: to get over that the civilian horror at al-Nasiriyeh was a con.[28] Not to do so would, of course, negate the nightly propaganda that Western technology discriminates between the 'evil' and the innocent.

Nevertheless, the truth *is* getting out. On Monday night, the BBC demonstrated a scepticism it seldom applies to Allied claims when it broadcast the figure of 6,000 to 7,000 civilian deaths.[29] This is the estimate of the Iraqi Red Crescent, quoted by the former US attorney general, Ramsey Clark. Although ignored at first, Clark has been in Iraq, picking his way through the rubble of Basra, which he described as 'a human and civilian tragedy' and 'staggering in its expanse'. The relentless Allied bombardment of Iraq's second city, he said, had destroyed residential areas, night clubs, hospitals, coffee shops, clinics and law offices. 'You don't have to bomb cities,' he said. 'It has nothing to do with Resolution 678.'[30]

A Vietnamese civil engineer working in Basra, Nguyen Hai Xuan, said the raids on Basra reminded him of the bombing by American B52s which devastated his home city, Haiphong. 'I thought I was back in Vietnam,' he said.[31]

I saw Haiphong following the bombing of which he spoke. B52s had laid their 'carpets' with extraordinary accuracy: down one street, then down the next, then the next, leaving the shells of churches, hospitals, clinics, blocks of flats. When James Cameron and cameraman Malcolm Aird brought back exclusive film of earlier American raids on North Vietnam, a memo was circulated in the BBC instructing producers to have nothing to do with them. Cameron was castigated as a 'dupe': a charge, he later told me, he relished. 'Only when they called you a dupe,' he said, 'did you know you'd broken the great mould that covered the reporting of the war and that maybe you'd got it right.'[32]

The 'great mould', the cover-up, is similar today, though on a larger scale. One got a sense of this when President Mitterrand warned the Allies against employing weapons 'whose use would mark a retreat into barbarity'; and his defence minister, Pierre Joxe, said that Allied bombing had 'certainly' killed 'thousands' of civilians. The *Daily Mirror* reported Joxe as 'blowing the gaffe' because many observers believe the top brass are keeping quiet about what they *do* know. 'Allied chiefs are believed reluctant to reveal numbers because they know public opinion will turn against the war if a high death toll is shown on *either* side.'[33]

On the rare occasions he has been asked about this, General Schwarzkopf has displayed irritation and discomfort. 'I have absolutely no idea what the Iraqi casualties are,' he said recently, 'and I tell you, if I have anything to say about it, we're never going to get into a body-counting business.'[34]

Only the congenitally naive would believe this. The Schwarzkopf strategy of 'denying the enemy an infrastructure' means bombing water, fuel and electrical supplies. It also means 'denying' transport used by the emergency services and for food distribution, as well as killing the civilians who provide, live near and depend upon these supplies and services. The result has been amputations performed by candlelight, and shortages of blood for transfusions and of antibiotics and painkillers, even of water for doctors to scrub up in before operations.

One of the thousands of videos never shown on the nightly Schwarzkopf Show, live from Riyadh, showed the look of horror on an Iraqi lorry driver's face as a missile flew through the window of his cab. This is 'classified', of course. Likewise, when was it last explained in detail what the 'heroic' Allied air forces actually drop on Iraq? One of the most commonly used bombs is the Rockeye cluster bomb (Mark 20). This comprises 247 bomblets, each an 'anti-personnel' grenade

that explodes into 2,000 high-velocity, needle-sharp fragments. According to Dr Paul Rogers of Bradford University,
one bomb 'wipes out anything that stands or moves over an
acre . . . it shreds people'.[35]

Equally, during the recent celebration of the 'phenomenal'
precision and humanitarian effects of the Tomahawk cruise
missile, we were not told that the Tomahawk delivers three
'packages' of 'grenade sub-munitions' that spray tens of thousands of small pieces of shrapnel aimed at 'soft targets': that
is, people. Most of these cluster bombs were developed and
tested in Vietnam, often against civilians, who made up 75
per cent of casualties. Little of this has emerged from the so-
called 'coverage'.

The British have not yet begun to die in this war, but, as
in the early summer of 1914, the 'enemy', that is, a large
human community, has already been dehumanised and cari-
catured in the third person singular of 'he' or 'Saddam Hussein': the tyrant equipped and sustained by the West is now,
as Edward Said has written, 'transformed into a worldwide
metaphysical threat'.[36]

In Britain, the media and the opinion polls reflect each
other's distortion. When the question is put, 'Do you support
the Government on the war?' no real alternative is offered,
just as no alternative to the Authorised View is available on
the television news, the nation's principal source of information. When an alternative *is* offered, the difference is striking. At the start of the war a *Washington Post* poll found
that 63 per cent of those polled supported the war. However,
when people were asked what their attitude would be if 1,000
Americans were killed, the support dropped by a third.[37] So
we can understand why the Pentagon has banned, for the
first time since Vietnam, the filming of flag-draped coffins
arriving at Dover air force base, and why estimates of American casualties have been classified Top Secret; and why 'body
bags', now in the American lexicon along with Coca-Cola,
have been renamed 'human remains pouches'.

The other day, a leading item on the television news told
us much about the corrupting effects of this war on its

bystanders. The verbose Schwarzkopf produced his latest video and invited his captive audience of journalists, many of them in uniform, many of them young and reporting on their first war, to observe 'the luckiest guy in Iraq'.

We saw the outline of a lorry on a bridge, then the bridge between the cross hairs, then the bridge blown away by a cluster bomb; and the 'lucky' lorry scurrying away. No mention here of the other 'unlucky' lorry driver. We heard no explosion, no screams; what we heard was the belly laughter of the journalists in the 'briefing room'. In every metaphorical sense, their laughter drowned the cries of the people of Iraq.

Bush speaks of war crimes as if the Geneva Convention was designed for 'us', never for 'them'. International law prohibits the use of all indiscriminate weapons, including those that cause unnecessary suffering or superfluous injury. Exploding dum-dum bullets are specifically banned. Cluster bombs are hi-tech dum-dums, designed deliberately as terror weapons, to cause unnecessary suffering and superfluous injury. The use of B52s laying 'carpets' of bombs a mile long – by any definition indiscriminate – is also unlawful. 'These are violations', said Ramsey Clark, America's former chief law officer, 'of the Hague Conventions, the Geneva Conventions and Nuremberg; they are war crimes.'[38]

The Vietnam War was a war of such atrocities. For all the protestations to the contrary, it is in many ways the model for this war. Like the Gulf now, Vietnam was a war of rampant technology directed against a Third World people. It was a war in which the United States dispatched its greatest ever land army, dropped the greatest tonnage of bombs in the history of warfare, pursued a military strategy deliberately aimed at forcing millions of people to abandon their homes and used chemicals in a manner that profoundly changed the environment and genetic order. Some two-and-a-half million people were killed, and many more maimed and otherwise ruined.

These truths are the truths of history, not of Hollywood or the version studiously recast during the Reagan years. Nor are they the 'old slogans' of 'ageing radicals' now derided by liberal commentators who seem proud of their glib ignorance and their effete ability to adopt mutually contradictory positions without feeling their feet squirm underneath them. Every 'noble cause' has had such apologists far from the bloodshed. Let Michael Ignatieff of the *Observer* stand beside an Iraqi doctor amputating the limb of a child without anaesthetic and still declare that we should 'press on until the bitter end'.[39]

It is often said disingenuously of the Vietnam War that the United States fought 'with one hand tied behind its back'. If seven-and-a-half million tons of bombs dropped on a peasant land and two-and-a-half million people killed is the result of such constraint, the prospect of both hands free ought to bring pause to those who believe the end justifies the means. Echoing his president, an American pilot said, 'Listen, we don't have the manacles on us this time.'[40]

How long must the present silence be contrived? How long will the outspokenness of a former Tory prime minister, Edward Heath, continue to shame the Labour Party? How long will the Labour leadership acquiesce in bombing which, according to the British commander in the Gulf, is 'minor compared with what's coming'? Or is the question disingenuous?

February 15, 1991

145

NEW AGE IMPERIALISM

I NEVER MET Bobby Muller during his time in Vietnam. I first saw him at the Republican Party convention in 1972. From the floor, his booming eloquence reached the candidate for president, Richard Nixon, over the cat-calls of the Nixon faithful. He described Nixon accurately as a liar and the perpetrator of an unnecessary and atrocious war. For that, he and other disabled Vietnam veterans were thrown out, in their wheelchairs.

Five years later I saw him again, out in the sun on the steps of City Hall, New York. It was Memorial Day, the day America remembers its 'foreign wars'. There were flags and medals and dignitaries; then former Lieutenant Robert O. Muller of the US Marines, a much decorated American hero of the kind Ronald Reagan and John Wayne never were, whose legacy of that 'unnecessary and atrocious war' was never to walk again, took the microphone and caused even the construction site beyond the crowd to fall silent.

He spoke about the killing of Vietnamese civilians. He described how half of those who had carried America's battle colours were now unemployed or beset by alcohol and drugs; and he said that as many Americans who had died in the war had since taken their own lives. Finally, he proposed that such an adventure should never happen again. 'Wake up, America!' he said and wheeled himself away.[41]

Bobby Muller and his comrades founded the Vietnam Veterans of America Foundation in 1976 and have devoted themselves to preventing a repeat of their war. They have travelled frequently to Indo-China, to promote reconciliation with a people who remain fixed in America's demonology. They have initiated and sustained projects for Asian children orphaned and handicapped by the war, and for the victims of US foreign policy in Central America. At home, they have financed a curriculum for schools and colleges on the Vietnam War, seeking to end the 'historical amnesia' that has allowed the same gang in Washington to prosecute 'other Vietnams' in Latin America, Asia, the Caribbean and now in the Middle East.

They are only too aware of the enormity of the task they have set themselves. When Bobby Muller was invited to the White House one Veterans Day, he heard Ronald Reagan mention every American war since 1776 – except Vietnam. As Reagan was leaving, he found his way blocked by Bobby Muller's wheelchair. 'I said to him, "Mr President, when are you going to listen to *us*?" His reply was unbelievable. He said, "Bob, the trouble with Vietnam was that we never let you guys fight the war the way you could have done, so we denied you the victory all the other veterans enjoyed. It won't happen like that again, Bob . . . " '[42]

'Victory' in the Gulf will no doubt remove the canker of Vietnam from the American establishment – Hollywood has almost completed its first Gulf movie. At the same time America's 'historical amnesia' will deepen, the obsolescence of truth will quicken and the mendacity of state propaganda will be transmuted into history for the majority. The Gulf War will be promoted as a 'noble cause' triumphant; and this will justify 'other Gulfs' and form the basis for the 'new world order'.

I mention Bobby Muller because he is coming to London this week and because he represents those whom Martha Gellhorn once described as 'that life-saving minority of Americans who judge their government in moral terms, who are the people with a wakeful conscience and can be counted on . . . they are always there'.[43] They are not a political grouping – the left died long ago in the United States – and those like Richard Falk, Noam Chomsky, Bobby Muller and others are now classified as 'dissidents'. Certainly, their notions of ecency, of democracy as more than an exchange of power between elites, have long been manipulated by fundamentalists whose belligerent sense of moral superiority, not to say paranoia, spawned the fatuous term 'anti-American'.

I have known and admired many of them: from freedom riders who braved the segregated South, to Bobby Muller and his heretics who have analysed the militarism that demands more than half of every tax dollar. These Americans believe that their Government ought to behave abroad according to the democracy its leaders claim for it at home. They reject the divine right of intervention that is the essence of the American empire, from the Monroe Doctrine, to Vietnam, to the Gulf. Their warnings, therefore, are critical today.

These warnings – paraphrased here – are as follows: the 'new world order' is a new age of imperialism. Wearing the UN figleaf, Washington's divine rightists will now do virtually as they like. They will continue with the old system: that is, to discipline the US global network with a phalanx of local servants and thugs, many of whom will be installed and replaced at will. But should a 'regional dispute', such as that in the Gulf, threaten US imperial interests or Washington's current, obsessive need to be seen as 'world leader', the USS *Wisconsin* can now be brought up to fire Tomahawk cruise missiles.

In this new age, territorial acquisition by force will not necessarily be outlawed. Rather, the world policemen in Washington will decide which aggressors are to be punished and which encouraged. In the case of another Saddam Hussein – installed and equipped by Washington, even given the benefit of American chemical warfare technology – he will be encouraged. However, if he gets too cocky and intrudes elsewhere in the empire for whatever reason, he will be judged an 'Unacceptable Aggressor' and expelled forcibly. As in the Gulf, a 'coalition' may be formed with large bribes and the false promise that an economic blockade is the goal.

There are exceptions to this, of course. Another US client, Israel – which has invaded, occupied and terrorised Palestinian, Jordanian and Lebanese territories and has been con-

demned by almost every government on earth in a series
UN resolutions – has permanent status as an Acceptabl
Aggressor. As America's moored gunboat in the Middle East,
as well as an agent of American policy and terror far from the
region, Israel is to be encouraged in almost all circumstances.

Should this be doubted, it is necessary only to recall that
Iraqis were recently slaughtered for the unacceptable
aggression of their leader, while Israel, whose record of
aggression in the Middle East is unequalled, was praised for
its 'restraint' and promised more weapons and dollars.
Indeed, at the very moment the Unacceptable Aggressor was
being punished with American bombs, the Acceptable
Aggressor was moving its citizens on to Palestinian land and
deporting more Palestinians from their homes.

In the new age, the red menace will no longer provide a
cover for intervention. Instead, new ideas will be market-
tested, such as the 'War on Drugs'; and new Hitlers will be
invented. Saddam Hussein has been quite brilliant in this
role: so much so that those currently concerned with his
atrocities in Kuwait are those who for years ignored his
atrocities against the Kurds, the Iranians and his own
people. But of course he was an Acceptable Aggressor in
those days.

In the new age, there is a new world vocabulary. The
imposition of the imperial will is known as a 'peace plan' –
as in Cambodia, where Pol Pot, an Acceptable Aggressor, is
given new opportunities to terrorise and regain power. Genuine peace plans and genuine attempts to resolve regional
differences will be described as 'nightmare scenarios' and
'muddying the diplomatic waters'. Regardless of successful
diplomatic overtures, an Unacceptable Aggressor will be
given until high noon to get out of town, while an Acceptable
Aggressor – Israel – will get twenty-four years to think it over.

In the new age the word imperialism will be, as A. Sivanan-
dan wrote, 'a non word, an unfashionable word, a word
that has gone out with the Cold War, as though it was a
counterweight to "actually existing socialism", its antonym.
And with the writing off of the word, in an age where the

ord is deemed to be "as material as the world" and discourse the currency of power, the Third World has been written off . . . except as an occasion for grieving, an object of charity, a virtuous venue for righteous wars.'[44]

In the new age, the poor will revert to their traditional role of providing resources and products for markets in the rich world. This will be better organised than before, now that technology allows capital to be truly 'multi-national' and usurps labour's power of denial. This will progress beneath an apparently calm surface, as if control is complete and history has ended; then people, and their popular movements, will do as they have always done, and the phenomenon of great change and renewal will begin again. This is already happening: in Latin America it is well advanced in Mexico, Brazil, Nicaragua, El Salvador, Chile and Uruguay.[45]

As for Britain in the new age, the numbers of unemployed and disaffected will grow. This will not necessarily disturb those in comfort, until those on the other side of prosperity realign, which they will. Meanwhile, as in a previous age, the British elite is back on the world beat, with violent solutions for political problems, wielding a highly efficient, go-anywhere military force: Desert Rats, Tornadoes, SAS, nukes. They, at least, have found the role they lost, doing what they do best.

March 1, 1991

150

A BLOODFEST

WHAT OUGHT TO have been the main news event of the past week was that as many as 200,000 Iraqis may have been killed in the war in the Gulf, compared with an estimated 2,000 killed in Kuwait and 131 Allied dead. The war was a one-sided bloodfest, won at a distance with the power of money and superior technology pitted against a small Third World nation.

Moreover, it now appears that a large number of the Iraqi dead were slaughtered – and the word is precisely meant – during the brief land war launched by Washington after Iraq had agreed in Moscow to an unconditional withdrawal from Kuwait. And most of these were in retreat, ordered to withdraw, trying to get home. They were, as Colin Hughes wrote in the *Independent*, 'shot in the back'.[46]

So 'ring your churchbells' and 'rejoice' in such a 'great victory': a military operation of 'almost aesthetic beauty' . . . and so on, and on, *ad nauseam*.

'The glee', wrote Colin Hughes, 'with which American pilots returning to their carriers spoke of the "duck shoot" presented by columns of Iraqis retreating from Kuwait City [has] troubled many humanitarians who otherwise supported the Allied objectives. Naturally, it is sickening to witness a routed army being shot in the back.' This 'duck shoot', suggested Hughes, 'risked staining the Allied clean-fighting war record'. But no; it seems the Iraqis were to blame for being shot in the back; an Oxford don, Professor Adam Roberts, told the paper that the Allies 'were well within the rules of international conduct'.[47] The *Independent* reported the deaths of tens of thousands of Iraqis on its front page, while inside a leading article referred to 'miraculously light casualties'.[48]

Yet the *Independent* was the only British newspaper to give consistent, substantial coverage to this slaughter. 'The retreating forces huddling on the Basra beachhead', reported Karl Waldron, 'were under permanent attack yesterday from the air. Iranian pilots, patrolling their border 10 miles away, described the rout as a "rat shoot", with roaming Allied jets strafing both banks.'[49] Waldron described the scene as 'Iraq's Dunkirk'.

The Iraqi casualty figures are critical to the 'great victory'. Leave them out and the Murdoch comic version applies: Western technology, and Western heroism, has triumphed. Put them in and the picture bleeds and darkens; and questions are raised, or ought to be, about the 'civilised values' for which 'we' fought. The *Guardian* announced the death of 150,000 Iraqis in the body of a piece on page three. *The Times* and *Telegraph* performed a similar burial.[50] The next day, the *Telegraph* referred to a 'massacre' on the road to Basra. American pilots were said to have likened their attack on the convoy to 'shooting fish in a barrel'. Ducks, rats and now fish were massacred. No blame was apportioned.[51]

On the contrary, most newspapers carried prominently a photograph of a US Army medic attending a wounded Iraqi soldier. Here was the supreme image of tenderness and magnanimity, a 'lifeline' as the *Mirror* called it: the antithesis of what had actually happened.[52] Such a consensus was, to my knowledge, interrupted only once.

During a discussion about the rehabilitation of wounded soldiers, the BBC's Radio Four delivered a remarkable live report from Stephen Sackur on the road to Basra. Clearly moved and perhaps angered by what he had seen, this one reporter did as few have done or been allowed to do. He dropped the 'we' and 'them'. He separated ordinary Iraqis from the tyrant oppressing them. He converted the ducks, rats and fish into human beings. The incinerated figures had been trying to get home, he said. Among them were civilians, including contract workers from the Indian subcontinent; he saw the labels on their suitcases.[53]

However, on the evening television news bulletins there was no Stephen Sackur. Kate Adie described the 'evidence of the horrible confusion' that was both 'devastating' and 'pathetic'. The camera panned across the 'loot' – toys, bottles of perfume, hair curlers: pathetic indeed – strewn among the blackened dead. There had first been a 'battle', we were told. Battle? A US Marine lieutenant looked distressed. They had no air cover, he said: nothing with which to defend themselves. 'It was not very professional at all,' he said, ambiguously; and he was not asked to clarify that.[54]

Apart from his words, I could find none, written or spoken, that expressed clearly the nature of this crime, this mass murder that was there for all eyes to see, and without the Iraqi Ministry of Information to 'supervise' those eyes. One recalls the interrogation by satellite that the BBC's man in Baghdad, Jeremy Bowen, had to endure following his harrowing and personally courageous report of the bombing of the air-raid bunker in which hundreds of women and children died. 'Are you absolutely *certain* it wasn't a military bunker?' he was asked:[55] or words to that effect. No such interrogation inconvenienced his colleagues on the road to Basra. The question, 'Are you *absolutely certain* that Allied planes did this *deliberately to people running away?*' was never put.

Thus, self-censorship remains the most virulent form. At the time of writing, the message of a war with 'miraculously light casualties' drones on and on. There is a radio report of the trauma suffered by British troops who had to bury the victims of the atrocity on the Basra road. In the commentary, there is no recognition of the victims' human rights even in death; and no acknowledgement of the trauma awaiting tens of thousands of Iraqi families for whom there will be no proper process of grief, not even a dog-tag.

Like the bulldozers that cleared the evidence on the Basra road, the propagandists here now attempt to clear away the debris of our memories. They hope that glimpses we had of the human consequences of the greatest aerial bombardment in history (a record announced with obvious pride) will not form the basis for a retrospective of the criminal nature of the relentless assault on populated areas as part of the application of criminal solutions to political problems. These must be struck from the record, in the manner of modern Stalinism, or blurred in our consciences, or immersed in celebration and justification.

Celebration, of course, is a relatively simple affair. For those of us lacking churchbells, David Dimbleby will have to do. However, justification is quite another matter, especially for those who seem incessantly to describe themselves as 'liberals', as if they are well aware that their uncertainty, selectivity and hypocrisy on humanitarian matters is showing. Bereft of reasoned argument, they fall back on labels, such as 'far left', to describe those with humanitarian concern.

According to Simon Hoggart of the *Observer*, one of the myths spread by this 'far left' is that 'the Allies were unnecessarily brutal to the Iraqi forces ... Of course the death of thousands of innocent conscripts is unspeakable. But you cannot fight half a war.' The basis for Hoggart's approval of the 'unspeakable' is apparently that his sisters are married to soldiers who went to the Gulf, where they would have been killed had not retreating Iraqi soldiers been shot in the back and Iraqi women and children obliterated by carpet-bombing.[56]

Robert Harris, the *Sunday Times* man, is even more defensive. He writes that Rupert Murdoch did not tell him to support the war: a familiar refrain. Murdoch, of course, didn't have to. But Harris adds another dimension. Disgracefully, he insults Bobby Muller, the former decorated US Marine who lost the use of his legs in Vietnam, as a 'cripple' and a 'cardboard figure' whom I 'manipulate'.[57]

Even Muller, who is a strong personality, was shocked by this; and at a large meeting in central London last Monday night invoked Harris's name in the appropriate manner. Unlike Harris, he has fought and suffered both in war and for his convictions. Harris's main complaint, it seems, is that those against the war have neglected to mention Saddam Hussein's atrocities in Kuwait – which apparently justify slaughtering tens of thousands of Iraqi conscripts and civilians.

The intellectual and moral bankruptcy of this is clear. First, as children we are told that two wrongs do not make a right. Second, those actively opposed to the war are the same people who have tried to alert the world to Saddam Hussein's crimes. In 1988, 30 MPs signed Ann Clwyd's motion condemning Saddam Hussein's gassing of 5,000 Iraqi Kurds. All but one of these MPs have been steadfastly against the war.

In contrast, those who have prosecuted and promoted the war include those who *supported* Saddam Hussein, who armed and sustained him and sought to cover up the gravity of his crimes. I recommend the current newspaper advertisement for Amnesty International, which describes the moving plea of an Iraqi Kurdish leader to Thatcher following Saddam Hussein's gassing of the Kurds.[58]

'One of our few remaining hopes', he wrote, 'is that democrats and those who cherish values of justice, peace and freedom will voice their concern for the plight of the Kurds. That is why I am making this direct appeal to you . . . ' The letter was dated September 16, 1988. There was no reply. On October 5, the Thatcher Government gave Iraq more than £340 million in export credits.

March 8, 1991

LIBERAL TRIUMPHALISM

WHILE AN ESTIMATED fifty children die each day as a result of the deliberate bombing of Iraq's water, power and sewage systems, the triumphalists claim their place in the victory parade. Some do not want to be seen in the streets shoulder to shoulder with the 'boys'. This is understandable. They prefer to march gently in print, not as Worsthornes and other Kitcheners reincarnate, but as the liberal shareholders of Just War PLC (shortly to display its 'combat-proven' wares at the Dubai Arms Fair).

So they are triumphant, yes, but confused, alas. They describe as a 'famous victory' the crushing of a small Third World country and the killing of the equivalent of the population of Norwich: mostly conscripted soldiers running away, and civilians. But their use of the term 'victory' is puzzling, though it is not as mysterious as their correlation of a triumphant moral and intellectual position with triumphant onesided slaughter. So there is a nervousness about their triumphalism, as if they are concerned that the 'famous victory' will not endure and their supporting role will be fully acknowledged.

Liberal triumphalism is as important after this war as liberal defeatism was after Vietnam. Both serve to protect the nobility of the cause and the rightness of the war aims, and especially to state repeatedly the purity of 'our civilised values'. Following the Vietnam War, the United States' 'honest mistake' and 'tragic innocence' were promoted in the liberal media. There are many examples. For me, the finest is Stanley Karnow's 700-page *Vietnam: A History*, which

156

describes the war as a 'failed crusade' fought for the 'loftiest of intentions'. To Karnow, the Vietnamese were 'terrorists' who were 'merciless' and 'brutal' in contrast to the Americans, who were 'sincere' and 'earnest' and whose 'instincts were liberal'. Good guy Lyndon Johnson 'mistakenly imputed [American] values to the communists', believing 'they would respond like reasonable people' (to US threats to destroy their towns) but they were 'rarely troubled by heavy human tolls'. Karnow gives the My Lai massacre one line, and other atrocities not a word. His book is one of the most widely read histories of the war.[59]

The protection of the West's 'civilised values', as expressed in the conduct of the Gulf War, is well in hand. Reading the liberal press on both sides of the Atlantic, John Bunyan's Mister Facing-Both-Ways seems to be everywhere. The war was horrible, the massacre on the Basra road especially so, yet we are assured the West is growing 'more squeamish' about this sort of thing. One of the reasons for the ceasefire on February 28 was 'the genuine panic of Western political leaders at the scale of the killing. They had caused it, even willed it. But they had not imagined what it would be like.' It was the 'stain' on their otherwise 'clean fighting record'.[60] When Phillip Knightley was asked on BBC Radio about the 'news blackout' at the start of the land war, he replied that its aim was clearly to prevent the outside world knowing the ferocious nature of the Allied assault. The BBC dropped the programme. Not 'imagining' what 500-pound bombs do in populated areas, what B52s do, what 'daisy cutters' do, what 'fuel air explosion' bombs do, what Rockeye clusters do (used to great effect on the Basra highway) is akin to not imagining what a bullet does when it is fired point blank at the human brain.

Without a hint of irony, Adrian Hamilton wrote in last week's *Observer*, 'To accept that US intentions in the Gulf may be well meant is not to say they are innocent . . . ' As part of these 'well-meant intentions' America's 'domestic political aim' in the war was 'to win a decisive victory that would erase the memory of Vietnam, with the lowest possible Allied casualties'. Thus, tens of thousands of Iraqi men, women and children were obliterated in order to 'erase the memory of Vietnam'.[61]

What is so horrific about this is that the 'memory of Vietnam' – that of defeat and a 'failed crusade', as reflected in the angst-ridden Hollywood movies – is a Big Lie. Central to this Big Lie is that the war was a 'quagmire' into which the United States 'stumbled', for which there are not so faint echoes in current assessments of the Gulf War. In truth, the Vietnam War was waged by America *against* Vietnam, North and South. The massive official documentation of the *Pentagon Papers*, leaked in the early 1970s, alone confirms this. Far from being vanquished, the United States succeeded in devastating, blockading and isolating Vietnam and its 'virus' and subordinating to American interests most regimes in the region. In fact, Washington had a significant victory. Not even Hollywood has understood the scope of this achievement.

The logic follows that the slaughter of people in the Gulf War – people who had nothing to do with the American adventure in Vietnam or its 'memory' – was entirely unnecessary as a 'domestic political aim'. Indeed, their deaths have merely allowed one Big Lie to follow another.

The new Big Lie has many components. For example, it is said to be the first war of 'smart' weapons whose 'precision' and 'reliability' make possible 'short, sharp wars of the future'. One story never published in the British press was reported recently in the *International Herald Tribune*. It said that 'estimates of the accuracy of US bombs dropped on military targets in Iraq and Kuwait suggest that hundreds of precision-guided munitions as well as thousands of "dumb bombs" have missed their targets and in some cases struck unintended sites, according to US officials.' The report described these 'dumb bombs' as 'simple shell-encased explosives, including some with designs dating back to World War II that follow unguided trajectories to their targets, usually hitting within 50 to 100 feet but sometimes missing by much greater distances.' 'Dumb bombs' were used against targets in populated areas.[62]

Perhaps the most important element in the new Big Lie concerns sanctions – the preferred alternative to killing tens of thousands of Iraqis. In a new study, the Glasgow University Media Group has found that 'ironically, as the war drew nearer, evidence of the power of sanctions was just beginning to emerge', but at the same time the option of sanctions 'effectively disappeared as a news story'.[63]

During this critical period, found the researchers, clear evidence was available that the effect of sanctions was 'devastating'; but only the *Guardian* and the *Morning Star* argued against force; the *Guardian* quoted a CIA report that sanctions had stopped 97 per cent of Iraqi exports. The rest of the press associated sanctions with 'appeasement' ('Spineless appeasers' – the *Sun*). Television news contributed: 'All efforts to find a peaceful solution to the Gulf crisis seemed to have ended in failure tonight' (BBC, January 15) and 'War in the Gulf looks unavoidable . . . ' (ITN).[64]

Under the new Big Lie, Iraqis, Palestinians and Arabs in general are to be demonised by Hollywood, as the Vietnamese were. Gulf War movies on the way include: *Desert Shield*, in which the US Navy heroically destroys chemical warheads in Iraq (no mention, of course, that the United States gave Iraq much of its chemical warfare technology); *Desert Storm*, in which Iraqis plot to wipe out Israel (originally this one was called *Shield of Honour* and the forces of evil were Libyan); *The Human Shield*, which depicts an Iraqi officer attempting to murder an old woman and child and kidnapping the brother of a US colonel; and *Target USA*, in which US heroes unravel an Iraqi terrorist plot . . .

In his speech to Congress last week President Bush said the United States would maintain forces in the Gulf for years. This was not envisaged by those who believed, with invincible naivety, the yarns about 'defending Saudi Arabia' and 'liberating Kuwait'. Perhaps they should have listened to authentic establishment voices.

Interviewing the American ambassador to Britain at the

outbreak of the war, David Dimbleby said, 'Isn't it in fact true that America, by dint of the very accuracy of the weapons we've seen, is the only potential world policeman? You may have to operate under the United Nations, but it's beginning to look as though you're going to have to be in the Middle East just as, in the previous part of this century, we and the French were in the Middle East.'[65]

Quite so.

March 15, 1991

NORMALITY IS RESUMED

THE PARADE HAS not yet begun, but the triumphalists are falling silent, their angst on show. It was not meant to be thus. Kuwait is free, yes – free to kill and torture Palestinians and to dispossess a million of its citizens. The Iraqi Army was pounded to bits as it cut and ran; alas, in contravention of the Geneva Convention, the dead of war were not 'honourably interred' but shovelled and bulldozed into open pits.

The 'famous victory' is not what it was. Instead, normality is reasserting itself, bringing a truth so obvious that even those celebrants who called on us to go to the 'bitter end' in the cause of a 'just war' appear to be having difficulty remaining in the one spot, rather like weathervanes during a high wind. 'The victory is being turned into a defeat,' laments an *Observer* headline, while, beneath, its columnist calls on the Allies 'to commit themselves to a democratic and demilitarised Iraq . . . ' (And earlier: 'But it is wishful thinking to suppose a post-sanctions Iraq would have been much better.' Does the saving of as many as 200,000 lives qualify for the 'much better' category?)[66]

Normality in much of the world's affairs is determined by an imperialist logic. This has been the case for a very long time, and there is nothing in current developments to suggest that the historical pattern is about to be broken. On the contrary, unparalleled and unchallenged power, concentrated now in a single imperial source, ensures that the trend is reinforced.

Indeed, editorial writers are wrong to criticise President Bush for 'prevaricating' over the present turmoil in Iraq. Bush is conducting US policy in an entirely consistent manner, doing no more or less than Presidents Reagan, Carter, Ford and Nixon did in the region and much of the world. He is ensuring that a substantial minority – in this case, the Kurds – are crushed so that a reigning tyranny can retain control of a strategically important country and, presumably with the usual help from the CIA, replace the present tyrant with one considerably less uppity and more amenable to Washington's demands.

As for the anguished call for a 'democratic and demilitarised Iraq', contemporary history blows a raspberry at that. The Iraqi opposition say they will support Kurdish autonomy if a democratic regime is installed in Baghdad. The Kurds themselves include democratic and socialist elements. Thus, they are doomed. When the Ba'ath Party – Saddam Hussein included – seized power in Iraq in 1968, it was able to do so thanks in large part to the lists of opponents supplied by the CIA: trade unionists, socialists and assorted dangerous pluralists, many of whom were murdered.

When another tyrant, an 'acceptable Saddam Hussein', is duly installed, and thousands of Kurdish and Shi'a dead are added to the 200,000 said to have been slaughtered during 'Hannibal' Schwarzkopf's 'march', normality will be resumed. This is already past the planning stage. The *Independent* last week reported from the United Nations: 'Fearing the Kurdish rebellion will cause the break-up of Iraq and further destabilise the oil-rich region, the US and other permanent members of the UN Security Council have determined that Baghdad should be permitted to use its fighter and ground attack aircraft to quell internal dissent once it has accepted the Security Council's plan for a formal ceasefire in the Gulf.'[67]

While accepting the imperialist logic of this, one might pause to reflect on the recent months of sanctimonious waffle about the 'new role' of the United Nations. One wonders what decisions imposed by the Security Council have to do with the spirit of the UN Charter. 'We, the peoples . . .' begins the Charter. Tell that to the Kurds, the Palestinians, the Khmer, the Panamanians, the Guatemalans, the Timorese and the Iraqi children now dying from disease in cities and towns bombed by the Allies. 'We, the powerful regimes . . . ' the preamble should read, 'We, the underwriters and keepers of the new imperialist order . . . '

Although fighting like lions, the Kurds must be under no illusions. Betrayed by the colonial powers in the 1920s, bombed by the RAF, they have tested the faith of every imperialist 'saviour' only to become its victims. In 1975, having been led to believe that Washington looked favourably on their hopes for nationhood, they were told by the CIA to fight on, and given $16 million worth of secret American military aid. But this was a double-cross.

As the Pike Congressional Committee investigating the CIA later revealed, America's support for the Kurds was not intended in any way to help them, but to strengthen the Shah of Iran's hand in finalising an oil deal with Iraq. Washington's true policy, reported the Pike Committee, 'was not imparted to our clients, who were encouraged to continue fighting. Even in the context of covert action, ours was a cynical exercise.'

Unaware of this, the Kurds appealed to Henry Kissinger, then secretary of state: 'Your Excellency . . . our movement and people are being destroyed in an unbelievable way with silence from everyone. We feel, your Excellency, that the US has a moral and political responsibility towards our people who have committed themselves to your country's policy.'[68] The Shah got his deal; the Kurds were abandoned.

Today, while the killing goes on in Iraq, normality is being re-established elsewhere in the region. President Bush has said he wants 'a slowdown in the proliferation of weapons of all kinds' because 'it would be tragic if the nations of the Middle East and the Persian Gulf were now to embark on a new arms race'.[69] Within three days of his making that announcement, the *New York Times* reported, 'The US has emerged from the war as the Gulf's premier arms seller. The White House has told Congress in a classified report it wanted five Middle East allies to buy an $18 billion package of top drawer weapons.'[70] This will be the biggest arms sale in history.

When he resigned at the end of January the head of Italian naval forces in the Gulf said, 'I wondered if, in a certain sense, we hadn't all been made fools of . . . if they [the United States] hadn't drawn us into a much larger game. I still wonder about that.'

April 5, 1991

WHO KILLED THE KURDS?

PRESIDENT BUSH described the Gulf War to David Frost as 'the greatest moral crusade since World War II'. To date, the war has virtually destroyed the infrastructure of two countries, caused the violent death of as many as 200,000 people, triggered an ecological disaster, ensured that a fascist regime retains power in Iraq and stimulated the world arms trade. (Reviewing its war budget, the Pentagon reports a 'profit' of several billion dollars.)

It is now clear to many people who honestly defended the war on the basis of George Bush's word and John Major's word that they were misled. It is the Kurds' struggle for life that has opened eyes and allowed people to perceive the 'moral crusade' as one whose aim was never to 'liberate' anyone, but to weaken Iraq's position in relation to other US clients in the Gulf and Israel, and to demonstrate America's unchallenged military power in the 'post-Cold War era'.

The propaganda was always fragile; hence the ferocious attacks on those who identified and resisted it. What has given the game away is the suffering of the minority peoples of Iraq, especially the Kurds and the Shi'a. Why, people now ask, if the war was a matter of right against wrong, of good against evil, as its salesmen pitched it, was the regime of the 'new Hitler' preserved, deliberately and legalistically, and his victims left to their fate? Why did Bush, who saluted before Congress 'the triumph of democracy', refuse to meet Iraq's democratic opposition until Saddam Hussein's terror apparatus had been restored?

To people in Britain watching the news, who live their

165

lives by the rules of common decency, none of this makes sense – unless they have been lied to. In undermining Iraq, then watching the Kurds perish, the Americans are doing what the British, French, Spanish, Dutch and Portuguese in their time did elsewhere. Imperialism has no use for democracy, which may be difficult to control, or for troublesome minorities, which threaten to upset the imperialist board game with its frontiers intended to divide ethnic nations. History provides no evidence that imperialist wars have anything to do with 'morality'. Rather, they are about power and naked self-interest, and are fought accordingly with the utmost ruthlessness.

If further evidence is required to demonstrate this, the massacre of the Iraqi minorities *during* as well as since the Gulf War is a testament. I am not referring here to the actions of Saddam Hussein, whose barbarism towards the Kurds has been graphically documented (notably by Martin Woollacott in the *Guardian*). What has been overlooked is that the Allies have been more successful in killing, maiming and terrorising the Kurds and other minorities than Saddam Hussein: a considerable achievement.

During the war little attention was paid to the fact that Iraq was not a homogeneous nation. Little mention was made of the Kurds and Shi'a as the Allied bombs fell on populated areas. Certainly 'Hannibal' Schwarzkopf did not say he was bombing Kurdistan or Shi'a communities. Anyway, where *was* Kurdistan? Was it marked on the war-room map at Rupert Murdoch's Wapping HQ?

And why were the Iraqi prisoners-of-war so pleased to see their captors? Only a careful scrutiny of the media coverage will suggest why. Reporting from the carnage on the Basra road, where American pilots conducted their famous 'turkey shoot' on a retreating convoy, Kate Adie said: 'Those who fought and died for Iraq here turned out to be from the north of the country, from minority communities, persecuted by Saddam Hussein – the Kurds and the Turks.' Shortly afterwards, Jeffrey Archer reported for ITN: 'The Shi'as have a powerful incentive for opposing Saddam Hussein. Most of the thousands of conscripts who died in the trenches of Kuwait were Shi'as.'[71]

In other words, those sections of the Iraqi Army least loyal to Saddam Hussein and most likely to rise up against him – the very people to whom Bush issued his call to rise up – were massacred by the Allies. They were conscripts, positioned on the southern frontline while the loyalists were held further north. Schwarzkopf knew this; Bush must have known it. So for those of us now grieving for the Kurds struggling towards the Turkish border and pursued by Saddam's gunships, let us also grieve for the tens of thousands of Kurds and Shi'a slaughtered as the price of Schwarzkopf's 'famous victory'.

Much of the media 'coverage' that galvanised support for the war concentrated on Saddam Hussein's mistreatment of the environment – an issue close to the hearts of many in the West. When, shortly after the outbreak of war, two tankers off Kuwait started pouring oil into the Gulf at a rate of four million gallons a day, Bush claimed that the Iraqis deliberately caused the spill. For this 'crime', he said, Saddam Hussein was 'kind of sick'. It now appears that Iraqi claims at the time – that American bombers had hit the tankers – were correct. An American scientist, Richard Golob, a world authority on oil spills, told the *Boston Globe* that the 10.9 million gallons discharged by the *Exxon Valdez* tanker could turn out to be a 'small fraction' of the damage caused by Allied bombing in Iraq and Kuwait.[72]

The propaganda also misled people on the nature of the bombing itself. Pentagon sources now say that only 7 per cent of American explosives dropped during the war were high-tech 'smart' bombs: that is, bombs programmed to hit their targets; and shown around the world doing so.[73] How convincing this made the military boast, of the kind heard frequently in Peter Snow's sandpit, that war, at last, had become a science. The truth was the diametric opposite. Seventy per cent of the 88,500 tons of bombs dropped on Iraq and Kuwait missed their targets completely. The fact that most of these found other 'targets' in populated areas ought to be enough for us to conjure up the human conse-quences.[74]

In Britain, the drum beaters are still mostly silent on this carnage and the reasons for it. Instead they are 'disappointed' in Bush, who goes fishing and plays golf while Kurdish children freeze on the Turkish border. Bush, they say, is 'remarkably insensitive', even 'uncaring'. Oddly, none of this indignation was directed at Bush while his planes were shred-ding Kurds on the Basra road and incinerating Shi'a con-scripts in their Kuwaiti trenches. But those were the days when such people were designated 'turkeys'; only recently have they become news-fashionable.

These same moral crusaders used to tell us that the old Cold War was a war of attrition between the two super-powers, between East and West. But this was only partly true. Most of the Cold War was fought in faraway, impover-ished lands with the blood of expendable brown- and black-skinned people. The Cold War was an imperialist quest for natural resources, markets, labour and strategic position. It was not so much a war between East and West as one between North and South, rich and poor, big and small. And the smaller the adversary the greater the threat, because a triumph of the weak would produce such a successful example as to be contagious.[75]

As we now know, the 'new world order' is the old Cold War by way of Saatchi and Saatchi. The enemy, for imperial-ist Washington, remains nationalist, reformist and liberation movements, as well as irrepressible minorities. A leading US defence journal has called them 'that swirling pot of poison made up of zealots, crazies, drug-runners and terrorists'.[76] The means of combating them is currently a matter of conjec-ture and competition within the US war establishment. According to a classified study for the Pentagon, the US Air Force wants to send its Stealth bombers against the Third World (they can fly 14,000 miles non-stop), and the US Navy wants to send its carriers and cruise missiles.[77]

In the end, the means of 'keeping the violent peace', as they say in Washington, will almost certainly be the usual, reliable client regimes and their revolving-door tyrants, who are encouraged to use all forms of violence and are equipped and trained accordingly. The crimes committed against the Kurdish and Iraqi peoples by Saddam Hussein and George Bush are but current examples.

April 12, 1991 to June 1992

ANOTHER REALITY

THERE IS AN epic shamelessness about the symmetry of current, imperial events. An honorary knighthood is hand-delivered by the Queen to General Schwarzkopf, while his victims, mostly young children, continue to die in Iraq, in conditions described by the United Nations as 'near apocalyptic'.[78]

Certainly, the general's most enduring accomplishment ought not to go unrecognised. On May 11, the former US attorney general, Ramsey Clark, set up an international commission of enquiry and war crimes tribunal, which will investigate what was really done in the Gulf, as opposed to the version represented by the artifices of media images and the measured cant of both government and opposition politicians. Not surprisingly, the Clark Commission has been all but ignored by the media. Ramsey Clark distinguished himself as America's chief law officer under President Johnson. He is an authority on the prosecution of war crimes and believes the law is not as equivocal in that area as it is often presumed.

The Clark Commission will concentrate on the body of international law codified in the 1977 Geneva Protocols subjoined to the Geneva Convention of August 12, 1949, which expressly prohibits attacks on 'objects indispensable to the survival of the civilian population, such as foodstuffs, agricultural areas ... crops, livestock, drinking water installations and supplies and irrigation works'. Article 56 states that 'dams, dykes and nuclear electrical generating stations shall not be made the object of attack, even where these objects are military objectives, if such an attack may cause the release

170

of dangerous forces and consequent severe losses among the civilian population . . . '

In the announcement of its formation the commission noted that there is 'abundant *prima facie* evidence to support their allegation of war crimes . . . the US Air Force between January 16 and February 27 carried out the most sophisticated and violent air assault in history against a virtually defenseless people. A deliberate policy of bombing civilians and civilian life-sustaining facilities has resulted in the destruction of the Iraqi economy and urban infrastructure'.[79] The evidence will draw on a range of sources, including the report of an investigating team commissioned by the UN Secretary General which says that, due to the bombing, 'Iraq has, for some time to come, been relegated to a pre-industrial age' and left in a 'near apocalyptic state' with 'even sewage treatment and purifying plants brought to a virtual standstill'.[80]

We have had only glimpses of this, notably in the *New Statesman and Society* and the *Guardian*. There has been just one indelible image of the war's horror: a photograph published in the *Observer* of an Iraqi petrified in death on the Basra road.[81] According to the Clark Commission, between 150,000 and 300,000 Iraqis were killed; yet we are left with just this one icon. Why?

Why have we not seen a single frame of film of the Iraqi trenches after they were cluster-bombed and Napalmed? Why have we not seen the bulldozing of bodies into mass graves? This image is the one that those who prosecuted the war fear most. They know it will evoke the memory of bodies bulldozed into pits in the Nazi concentration camps. Official film exists. Will it go the way of the visual record of what was done to the people of Hiroshima and which was classified 'secret' for 23 years?

'Do we even care', wrote Linda Schabedly, in a letter to the *Guardian*, 'about the other version of reality that exists beyond the media?'[82] It is a central question, to which the answer is that a great many people do care but are denied the 'other version of reality', just as they were denied it during the war itself. Through the narrow focus of those supportive and protective of the state, the misgivings of the public are trivialised or silenced.

Maintaining this one version is essential to British policy in the region, with its sub-imperial posturing by the latter-day Lord Palmerston, Douglas Hurd, who began his ministerial life at the Foreign Office by travelling to Baghdad as a 'high-level salesman' of weapons to Saddam Hussein. Many people must now wonder if they can believe a government that cannot even tell the truth about the 'friendly fire' deaths of nine British servicemen.[83] Yet the Ministry of Defence used the 'feelings of families' to justify much of its exaggerated censorship during the war. Where truth has emerged, it has come from those who are driven by humanitarian concerns, who assume no obligation to side with the state. This is especially true of the voluntary aid organisations, like Oxfam.

In September 1990 Oxfam was threatened by the Department of Trade and Industry that 'breaching sanctions is a serious offence' for which 'the maximum penalty is up to seven years' imprisonment or an unlimited fine or both'. The threat was repeated just before Oxfam's team – led by Jim Howard – left for Iraq in March 1991.[84] It was immediately clear to Howard and his colleagues, on arrival in Iraq, that sanctions must at least be partially lifted if tens of thousands of people were to survive; contamination of water alone is decimating young children. With the Save the Children Fund, Oxfam reported that Baghdad had no uncontaminated running water, no refrigeration, no fuel and no food-processing capacity. 'The unavailability of powdered milk', says the report, 'spells nutritional and health disaster for children . . . the spread of diseases such as cholera and typhoid in the present conditions is inevitable.'[85]

UN Resolution 661, passed on August 6 last year, stated that the following items are exempt from sanctions: 'Supplies considered strictly for medical purposes and humanitarian food stuffs.' As Dr Eric Hoskins of the Gulf Peace Team has graphically pointed out, this Resolution has been disregarded and 'Iraqi civilians have been dying of starvation and disease in their thousands ... because of lack of basic food and medicines ... Never before in history has a government been prohibited from purchasing and importing food and medicine for its own people.'[86]

The silence over Iraq is even greater over those countries directly and indirectly affected by the Gulf War. The people of the developing world, according to US Secretary of State James Baker, live in 'an era full of promise ... one of those rare transforming moments in history'.[87] The people themselves will have grave doubts about the word 'promise' – except of course in an ironic sense – but they will not argue that their lives are undergoing 'one of those rare transforming moments'.

The scale of this transformation is comprehensively documented in a remarkable study submitted to the House of Commons Foreign Affairs Select Committee in March 1991. Entitled *The Economic Impact of the Gulf Crisis on Third World Countries*, it was sponsored by Britain's principal non-government development agencies, such as Oxfam, Save the Children Fund and Christian Aid.[88] In stark, prosaic terms it describes a vision of the poor world in the wake of the Gulf War. 'At least 40 developing countries are facing the equivalent of a natural disaster,' it says. 'Fourteen of these countries are deeply impoverished sub-Saharan African countries, which were suffering famine before the war started.' They include Ethiopia, Sudan, Liberia and Mozambique. Moreover, the effect of the war is being felt in countries as distant as Jamaica and Paraguay, countries which are already suffering the consequences of the recession in the developed north, the debt crisis and falling prices for many commodities.

The war delivered two body blows to the poor. In the region itself hundreds of thousands of workers from developing countries were trapped or had to flee for their lives; their savings, possessions and livelihoods were destroyed or abandoned. Millions of people were dependent on receiving support from relatives working in the Gulf. Many more

173

millions, says the report, 'have seen their poverty deepened and their opportunities curtailed by the wider effects of the crisis'. For example, between August 1990 and January 1991, when war seemed imminent, the price of oil averaged $30 a barrel, almost twice its previously stable price. In Uganda, public transport has been severely curtailed or become so expensive that thousands of people now have to walk great distances to work, schools and hospitals.

In countries as far apart as Bangladesh and Botswana, the sudden rise in kerosene prices means that many poor families can no longer afford fuel for their lamps. The poor, who tend to cook with kerosene, thus bear a disproportionate share of the oil price increase. In Pakistan, fuel is being rationed and petrol prices have risen by 40 per cent; travel costs in all major cities have doubled and now amount to about a quarter of a worker's monthly earnings.

In addition, demand for developing countries' exports has been seriously affected, in some countries almost wiped out. Jordan has suffered a total loss of exports to Kuwait and Iraq. Other countries have suffered a loss of aid as rich states, such as Saudi Arabia, bear much of the cost of the war and of 'compensatory payments' to affected countries such as Egypt.

In those countries that did not join the coalition, or opposed the American-led war, the effects have been catastrophic. Yemen has lost 10 per cent of its Gross National Product; a 1 per cent loss is the United Nations' economic criterion for defining a natural disaster. On top of this, Yemen has lost 75 per cent of its exports and services.

Jordan has borne the greatest relative cost, estimated at a quarter of its Gross National Product: a 'natural disaster' twenty-five times over. Jordan has also lost 75 per cent of its exported goods and services. According to a UNICEF report last December:

Typically, families are poor because the father works in erratic, menial jobs for very low wages, and cannot rely on a regular monthly income. In the last three months [during the build-up to the war], many families have slipped into poverty because the main breadwinner suddenly found himself unemployed due to the impact of the Gulf crisis, especially in tourism, transit trade, shipping and construction.

Like Jordan, Sudan 'backed the wrong side', according to Washington; and with nine million people now at risk from famine, the Sudanese 'haven't seen anything yet', in the words of one Western ambassador in sub-Saharan Africa.[89] Since August last year, the rising cost of fuel has added 46 per cent to the cost of air-lifting food to stricken southern Sudan. In Sri Lanka, which before the war sent 100,000 migrant workers to the Gulf, along with much of its tea exports, the poverty that was always present has taken on a 'new dimension', according to a Sri Lankan friend just returned. The development agencies say that the cost of compensating these countries is 'manageable for the world community'. They point out that the Overseas Development Institute in London estimates that $12 billion is needed to compensate the most seriously affected countries; and that this figure is considerably less than the debt that the Americans 'forgave' Egypt in return for its support.

This year the World Bank will mark a record net income: the kind of mammoth money that could alleviate both the effects of the Gulf War *and* the famine in Africa. The Bank is run from Washington by the developed countries under the constant influence and manipulation of the United States. It is said to be the banking version of the United Nations. Article 50 of the UN Charter provides for compensation to member states affected by Security Council decisions.

The money is there. More than $62 million was found to pay for bombs dropped by American B52 aircraft on Iraq. This was the equivalent of Oxfam's entire budget for 1990. And £105 million was found to replace five British Tornado aircraft which crashed or were shot down during the war. This would have bought enough grain to feed for one month all the twenty million people likely to starve in Africa this year. And £3 million was found to train one Tornado pilot. This would have provided 25,000 Eritrean families with enough seeds and tools to recover from the current drought.[90]

Perhaps only those who can trigger such misery while expressing pride in their actions can then ascend to the moral high ground. Douglas Hurd said recently that there was 'more to gain' than the just cause of Kuwait. 'It is about the sort of world in which we wish to live,' he said. 'In the late twentieth century, nations must be able to conduct affairs by a code more worthy of rational human beings than the law of the jungle . . . '

In 1990 the British Government gave to famine relief in Africa about the equivalent of two days' British military operations in the Gulf War.[91] In 1991 the figure was less. At the same time the British arms industry has been stimulated by the war and secretly encouraged by the Government. The Ferranti company, for example, has negotiated a secret deal to supply 'smart' missiles to Gulf states. Such is the 'sort of world in which we wish to live'.

April to June 1991

HOW THE WORLD WAS WON OVER

IT IS ONE year since the United States and its 'coalition' allies attacked Iraq. The full cost had now been summarised in a report published by the Medical Educational Trust in London.[92] Up to a quarter of a million people were killed or died during and immediately after the attack. As a direct result, child mortality in Iraq has doubled; 170,000 under-fives are expected to die in the coming months. This estimate is described as 'conservative'; UNICEF says five million children could die in the region.

More than 1.8 million people have been forced from their homes, and Iraq's electricity, water, sewage, communications, health, agriculture and industrial infrastructure have been 'substantially destroyed', producing 'conditions for famine and epidemics'. Add to this the equivalent of a natural disaster in 40 low- and middle-income countries.[93]

How were these historic events set in train? Forgotten facts tell us much. On October 29, 1990, US Secretary of State James Baker declared, 'After a long period of stagnation, the United Nations is becoming a more effective organisation. The ideals of the United Nations Charter are becoming realities.' Within a month Baker had tailored the ideals of the UN Charter entirely to suit American interests. He had met the foreign minister of each of the 14 member countries of the UN Security Council and persuaded the large majority to vote for the 'war resolution' – 678 – which had no basis in the UN Charter. Such a vote, remarked Yemen's UN ambassador Abdallah al-Ashtal, was inconceivable without 'all kinds of pressures – and inducements'.[94]

So came about the dawn of what is celebrated by Western commentators as the United Nations' 'new age'. In fact, it was one of the most shameful chapters in the organisation's history. For the first time, the full UN Security Council capitulated to the War Party and abandoned its commitment to advancing peaceful and diplomatic solutions. Throughout the crisis, the UN Security Council ignored and contravened its own charter; it merely served up the *appearance* of international legality, a truth that became spectacularly clear when the bombing began in January. It was then that the United States withdrew its embrace of the United Nations and actively, and illegally, prevented the Security Council from meeting.

But this degree of control was possible only through a campaign of bribery, blackmail and threats. It is no secret that rewards were provided to certain Arab states for their participation in the 'coalition'. *US News and World Report*, in an article entitled 'Counting on New Friends', described how James Baker had 'cajoled, bullied and horse-traded his way' to get Resolution 678 through the Security Council. Several of the larger deals – for example, the 'inducements' to Egypt and China – were widely publicised.[95]

Some commentators even expressed moral qualms about 'distasteful bargains' with the 'butchers of Beijing', the 'loathsome Assad' and other unsavoury clients, although the concern was clearly that such deals might impede the course of US war policy; the tactics themselves were barely questioned. Thus, the full extent of the deals has remained secret. For the record, I offer here a beginner's guide to the greatest bribes in history.

Turkey. Right from the beginning the Turkish regime knew that it was on to a winner. Based just across the border, American planes could bomb Iraq with impunity. By November 3, 1990, the promised booty was pouring in and President Turgut Ozal celebrated in a public address. 'In a way,' he said, 'we have benefited from this crisis and made very significant progress towards our goal of modernising and strengthening our armed forces.'[96]

Ozal boasted that Turkey received at least $8 billion worth of military gifts from the United States, including tanks, planes, helicopters and ships. According to Steve Sherman of *Middle East International*, the United States also pledged to speed up the delivery of Phantom bombers delayed by the pro-Greek lobby in Washington; and the US Export Import Bank agreed to underwrite the construction of a Sikorsky helicopter factory in Turkey: itself worth about a billion dollars to the Turkish regime.[97]

In his November 3 speech President Ozal said: 'We are on the brink of finding new markets for Turkish goods and Turkish industry.' Five days later Turkey was told that its quota of US textile exports would increase by 50 per cent. At Washington's urging, the World Bank and International Monetary Fund (IMF) 'freed-up' some $1.5 billion in low-cost loans to Turkey and dropped the initial condition that the government would have to cut subsidies. George Bush personally promised to back Turkey's application to join the European Community, which still has questions about Turkey's human rights record.[98]

There were 'human rights pay-offs' too. Just because Bush and Major suddenly adopted, and almost as quickly dropped, the Iraqi-battered Kurds did not mean they would show concern for the treatment of Turkish Kurds. The routine persecutions carried out by the Turkish regime continued unnoticed; and continue today.

Egypt. In 1990, Egypt was the most indebted country in Africa and the Middle East. According to the World Bank, the government of President Mubarak owed nearly $50 billion.[99] Baker offered a bribe, or 'forgiveness' of $14 billion. Under pressure from the United States, other governments – Saudi Arabia and Canada among them – 'forgave' or postponed most of the balance of Egypt's debt.[100]

Syria. The main exchange in the deal with President Hafez Assad was Washington's go-ahead for him to wipe out all opposition to Syria's rule in Lebanon. To help him achieve this, a billion dollars' worth of arms aid was made available through a variety of back doors, mostly Gulf states.[101] Although on America's list of 'sponsors of terrorism', Assad and his Ba'athist fascists – not dissimilar to Saddam Hussein's fascists – were given a quick paint job in time to support America's war. 'Photo opportunities' were arranged with Baker and Bush; the locked smiles told all, as 'old friends' were reunited.[102]

Israel. The 'pacification' of Israel was vital if the United States was to preserve its Arab 'coalition'. The regular $5 billion America gives to Israel clearly was not going to be enough; and Israeli Finance Minister Yitzhak Modai told US Deputy Secretary of State Lawrence Eagleburger that Israel wanted at least another $13 billion. Israel agreed to a down-payment of $650 million in cash, and to wait for the $10 billion loan guarantees until later. This partly explains why the Israelis appear not to give a damn about current American 'warnings' as they expel still more Palestinians and build still more homes for Russian Jews in the occupied territories.[103]

Iran. In return for Iran's support in the blockade of Iraq, America dropped its opposition to World Bank loans. On January 9, Reuter reported that Iran was expected 'to be rewarded for its support of the US . . . with its first loan from the World Bank since the 1979 Islamic revolution'. The Bank approved $250 million the day before the ground attack was launched against Iraq.

Last November, Britain restored diplomatic ties with Iran, in spite of the fact that the death sentence on Salman Rushdie, a British citizen, had just been reaffirmed.

Soviet Union. With its wrecked economy, the Soviet Union was easy prey for a bribe – even though President Gorbachev strongly preferred sanctions. The Bush administration persuaded the Saudi Foreign Minister, Sa'ud al-Faysalwe, to go to Moscow and offer a billion dollar bribe before the Russian winter set in.[104] Once Gorbachev had agreed to Resolution 678, another $3 billion materialised from other Gulf states. The day after the UN vote, Bush announced that the United

States would review its policy on food aid and agricultural credits to the Soviet Union.[105]

The Soviet Union's impotence in the face of this degree of American pressure was illustrated when an American reporter, Phyllis Bennis, cornered the Soviet ambassador to the United Nations, Yuli Vorontsov, in a lift the night the American bombing started. She asked him if he was concerned that a war was being fought in his government's name. He replied with a sigh: 'Who are we to say they should not?'[106]

China. In exchange for China's vote on Resolution 678, the United States arranged China's return to diplomatic legitimacy. The first World Bank loan since the Tiananmen Square massacre was approved. On November 30, the day after the UN vote, Foreign Minister Qian Qichen arrived in Washington for a 'high profile' meeting with Bush and Baker. More photo opportunities; more frozen smiles. Within a week, more than $114 million of World Bank money was deposited in Beijing.[107]

The impact of the bribes inside China was explained by the scholar Liu Binyan. 'For quite some time', he said, 'there has been much talk of formal charges and trials being brought against the dissidents, but the pressure from abroad prevented it. Since August, however, Beijing has skilfully manipulated the Iraqi crisis to its advantage and rescued itself from being the pariah of the world.'[108]

The vote of the non-permanent members of the Security Council was crucial; and the following bribes and threats were successful. Within a fortnight of the UN vote, Ethiopia and the United States signed their first investment deal for years; and talks began with the World Bank and the IMF. Zaire was offered US military aid and debt 'forgiveness' and in return acted for the United States in silencing the Security Council after the war began. Occupying the rotating presidency of the council, Zaire refused requests from Cuba, Yemen and India to convene the Security Council, even though it had no power to refuse them under the UN Charter.[109]

Only Cuba and Yemen held out. Minutes after Yemen voted against the resolution, a senior American diplomat was instructed to tell the Yemeni ambassador, 'That was the most expensive "no" vote you ever cast.' Within three days, a US aid programme of $70 million to one of the world's poorest countries was stopped. There were suddenly problems with the World Bank and the IMF; and 800,000 Yemeni workers were expelled from Saudi Arabia. The 'no' vote probably cost Yemen about a billion dollars, which meant inestimable suffering for its people.[110]

The ferocity of the American-led attack far exceeded the mandate of Resolution 678, which did not allow for the destruction of Iraq's infrastructure and economy. The lawlessness did not end there. Five days after 678 was passed, the General Assembly voted 141 to 1 reaffirming the ban on attacks on nuclear facilities. On January 17, the United States bombed nuclear facilities in Iraq, including two reactors twelve miles from Baghdad.

When the Security Council finally convened a meeting in February, the United States and its allies forced it to be held in secret, one of the few times this has ever happened. And when the United States turned back to the United Nations, seeking another resolution to blockade Iraq, the two new members of the Security Council were duly coerced. Ecuador was warned – by the US ambassador in Quito – about the 'devastating economic consequences' of a no vote. Zimbabwe, whose foreign minister had earlier described the resolution as 'a violation of the sovereignty of Iraq', finally voted in favour after he was reminded that in a few weeks' time he was due to meet potential IMF donors in Paris. Neighbouring Zambia has had great difficulty negotiating IMF loans – in spite of democratic reforms. Zambia opposed the resolution.[111] The punishment was most severe against those impoverished countries that supported Iraq; Sudan, though in the grip of a famine, was denied a shipment of food aid.[112]

The other day I interviewed Ramsey Clark, whose war crimes commission has sought to establish the illegality of the Gulf War. 'Not only were the articles of the United Nations disregarded,' he said,

but every article of the Geneva Convention was broken. Of course it is not easy to persuade people to stand up against power: but when they do, there are successes. During the Vietnam War the issue of legality prevented military personnel going who did want to go, and defended the publication of the *Pentagon Papers*, which gave us much of the truth about the war. What we need urgently is a permanent international tribunal, independent of the UN and similar to the International Court of Justice. Without that, we shall always have victor's justice, the perpetrators of crimes will never be called to account and there will be more and more illegal wars.

None of these issues was widely debated before, during or after the Gulf War. Getting Saddam Hussein out of Kuwait skilfully and without putting to death thousands of people – the same people who were oppressed by him – was only of marginal interest to the Western media. Censorship was, always, less by commission than omission. As Peter Lennon later wrote in the *Guardian*:

War engenders corruption in all directions. As the broadcasters were arranging the terms of the stay in Saudi Arabia, Amnesty published an account of torture, detention and arbitrary arrests by the Saudis. Twenty thousand Yemenis were being deported every day and up to 800 had been tortured or ill-treated. Neither the BBC nor ITV reported this ... It is common knowledge in television that fear of not being granted visas was the only consideration in withholding coverage of that embarrassing story.[113]

Other media people who sat red-eyed in studios dropped

the last veil of their 'impartiality'. Who can forget, on the first day of the bombing, the Sir Michael and David Show on BBC Television? There sat David Dimbleby with Sir Michael Armitage, former head of Defence Intelligence, as if they were in their club. Sir Michael's distinguished career made him an expert on black propaganda in the cause of Queen and Country; and here he was being offered up as source of information to the British people. The British, opined Sir Michael, were super and brave, while the Iraqis were 'fanatics holding out'.

For his part, Dimbleby could barely contain himself. He lauded the 'accuracy' of the bombing as 'quite phenomenal', which was nonsense, as we now know. Only a fraction of the bombs dropped on Iraq hit their target. Where was the broadcaster's professional scepticism?

Growing ever more excited, Dimbleby interviewed the American ambassador to Britain and declared that the 'success' of the bombing 'suggests that America's ability to react militarily has really become *quite extraordinary*, despite all the critics beforehand who said it will never work out like that. You are now able to claim that you can act *precisely* and therefore – to use that hideous word about warfare – *surgically*!' Thereupon Dimbleby pronounced himself 'relieved at the amazing success' of it all.[114]

Fortunately, there are some journalists who see their craft very differently. Thanks to Richard Norton-Taylor, David Pallister, Paul Foot, David Hellier, Rosie Waterhouse, David Rose and others, we can now comprehend the scale of the duplicity and hypocrisy that underpinned the 'famous victory'.

We now know that the British Government allowed British firms to break the embargo against Iraq: to continue producing vital parts for the famed 'supergun' and other weapons supplied to Iraq only months before Saddam Hussein invaded Kuwait. We now know that shells for the guns that were trained on British troops came from British-made machines. We now know that, in spite of an investigation by a House of Commons Select Committee, there was and remains a cover-up of ministerial wrong-doing.[115]

This no more than mirrors the cover-up by those who ran the war in Washington. Thanks mostly to one maverick Congressman, Henry Gonzalez, chairman of the House Banking Committee, we now have detail of how George Bush, as president and vice-president, secretly and illegally set out to support and placate Saddam Hussein right up to the invasion. According to classified documents, Bush personally directed the appeasement of Saddam and misled Congress, and US intelligence was secretly fed to Saddam. 'Behind closed doors,' says the Gonzalez indictment,

> Bush courted Saddam Hussein with a reckless abandon that ended in war and the deaths of dozens of our brave soldiers and over 200,000 Muslims, Iraqis and others. With the backing of the President, the State Department and National Security Council staff conspired in 1989 and 1990 to keep the flow of US credit, technology and intelligence information flowing to Iraq despite repeated warnings by several other agencies and the availability of abundant evidence that Iraq used [US bank] loans to pay for US technology destined for Iraq's missile, nuclear, chemical and biological weapons programmes.[116]

It is clear that in the summer of 1990 George Bush believed that Saddam Hussein – his 'man', the dictator he backed against the mullahs in Iran and trusted to guard America's interests – had betrayed him. It also seems clear Bush believed that if his appeasement of Saddam ever got out, the invasion of Kuwait might be blamed on him personally – hence the magnitude of his military response. To cover himself, the price was carnage, which he described as 'the greatest moral crusade since World War Two'.

January 17, 1992 to May 1992

WHAT IS PARLIAMENT FOR?

DURING THE FIRST session of Parliament following the 1992 general election Britain is threatening to take part in an attack on two countries with which it is not at war. This has provoked almost no interest at Westminster, prompting the serious question: What is Parliament for? It is a question I shall return to. Meanwhile, some background:

Prime Minister Major has told President Bush that the United States is free to use British air bases to attack Libya, and that Britain will take part in a renewed American assault on Iraq 'if necessary'.[117] The contingency for these attacks is justified with a UN resolution whose legitimacy rests on Article 51 of the UN Charter. This says that a member can defend itself, but in no sense does it endorse a prolonged campaign of counter-attack. Since the Gulf War, the United States and Britain have used the United Nations to conduct a campaign of attrition against Iraq, bleeding it; the sufferers have been primarily children, whose death-rate is said to have increased by an estimated 400 per cent.[118]

Now the United States and Britain are on the verge of bombing Iraq on the pretext that Iraq refuses to destroy its 'weapons of mass destruction' – when, in fact, Iraq has asked that some of its military industry be converted to civilian production laid waste by Allied bombing. The bombing would probably finish off Iraq's industrial base.

A similar attack is likely against Libya. American and British domination of the United Nations on this issue has produced yet another 'high noon' deadline by which Libya must surrender two men accused of the Lockerbie bombing, or face sanctions and worse. That the evidence against the two is, at best, circumstantial, and their prospects of a fair trial in Scotland or the United States remote, are not considered relevant factors.

The Scottish Prime Minister (John Major) has told Parliament that the accused Libyans are 'the perpetrators' of the outrage. Alex Carlile, MP has similarly described them as 'these two mass murderers', who should be brought here for 'a fair trial'.[119] As numerous fitted-up Irishmen can bear witness, the fairness of British justice can no longer be guaranteed.

The American campaign against Libya, like its counterpart against Iraq, relies on the obsolescence of history. In the United States this is guaranteed by a standard assumption that the Libyans are guilty, thus providing the Bush administration with the kind of support it needs in an uncertain election year.

Few can doubt that Colonel Gaddafi runs an odious autocracy. However, if this was justification for blockading and bombing his country, most of the regimes propped up by the United States would be awaiting a similar fate. The truth is that Libya has been stitched up on several occasions since Libyan oil was nationalised in 1969 and Gaddafi refused to behave like the American client his predecessors used to be. In 1981, he was accused of sending a team of assassins to America, armed with surface-to-air missiles and led by 'East German terror experts' under orders from the colonel to kill Ronald Reagan, the secretary of state and secretary of defence. The Soviet Union was said to be behind it. Comicbook sketches of the would-be assassins were published.[120]

None of it was true. In 1986, *TV Guide* published a cover story entitled 'Why American TV is So Vulnerable to Foreign Propaganda', in which it claimed that the Libyan hit team story was really a figment of a KGB campaign to spread alarm and 'to destabilise public opinion in the West'.[121] The admission came shortly after American warplanes had bombed Libyan civilians from British bases. Libya's 'crime' then was a terrorist bombing in Berlin that was later traced to the Assad regime in Syria. In 1990, the same Syrian regime was rewarded with millions of dollars' worth of arms credits.[122] 'We have problems with their support of terrorism,' said Secretary of State James Baker, 'but we share a common goal.'[123] The goal was the destruction of Syria's old foe, Iraq.

That goal is now drawing closer, along with the goal of finishing off the uppity Gaddafi, a perfect hate figure in an election year. The United Nations will provide legitimacy for what are little more than acts of international piracy. As Francis Boyle, the distinguished American authority on international law, has pointed out, the US and Britain have violated both the Montreal Sabotage Convention and the UN Charter. 'The conclusion is unescapable', he wrote, 'that the reason why the US and UK have illegally rejected all means for the peaceful resolution of this dispute with Libya is that both states know full well that Libya was not responsible for the Lockerbie bombing.'[124]

The 'new world order' strategists may, however, come unstuck in Libya. Arab hostility towards American dominance in Middle Eastern affairs has sharpened since the destruction of Iraq. The ripple effect on economic and political life in the region has reinforced fundamentalism, as recent events in Algeria demonstrate. The Arab world has identified the essential hypocrisy of UN pressure on Iraq and Libya. Israel, having repeatedly thumbed its nose at UN resolutions, is under no such pressure.

As for Britain, it is the tenth anniversary of the Falklands War and the British foreign policy establishment is reminding itself of the debt it owes to Washington, without whose satellite intelligence Margaret Thatcher might not have been able to call upon us to 'rejoice'. However, Britain's role during the past decade has been more active than that of indebted loyal lieutenant. As John Gittings has pointed out, the British have 'exalted the values of war over peace, of unilateral settling of scores rather than multilateral negotiations of differences'.[125] It was Thatcher who promoted these values more than Reagan or Bush. In accepting cruise missiles in Britain, she single-handedly accelerated the nuclear arms race.

Great power nostalgia and pretensions are always close at hand in Britain. The Conservative election manifesto emphasised the need for Britain 'to regain . . . rightful influence' and to 'lead the world'. Labour wanted to 'partner' the United States in reducing nuclear weapons. Instead of calling for a total moratorium on arms sales to the Middle East, Labour wanted to 'control' the arms bazaar. Like John Major's 'arms register', this would have merely screened the scandals and corruption of the British arms industry. So the question is put: What is Parliament for?

In supporting the slaughter during the Gulf War – Tory and Labour together – Parliament failed in one of its primary obligations: to represent and articulate the misgivings of a large section of the population. Since then, Parliament has been instrumental in the covering up of a report into Britain's biggest arms contract with one of the beneficiaries of the war and the principal Western client in the Gulf, Saudi Arabia.

Parliament's public-spending 'watchdog', the Public Accounts Committee, has refused to publish the results of a three-year enquiry into the Saudi deal, which is for British Tornado aircraft worth £20 billion. The chairman, Robert Sheldon, a Labour MP, says that he has spent 'many hours worrying about this decision, but there really are enormous amounts of jobs at stake'.[126] He says that there is 'no evidence of corruption or of public money being used improperly'.[127] If this is true, why can't the report be released? What are parliamentary committees for if not to shed light on that which officialdom wishes to conceal?

In the case of the Saudi deal, like so much to do with British 'interests' in the Gulf, secrecy and stink go together. The National Audit Office, which refused to show its own report to Sheldon's committee, has found that the Saudi contract was written in such a way that huge 'commissions' running into hundreds of millions of pounds may have been paid by British Aerospace to Saudi and British middlemen.[128] How does this square with Sheldon's statement that there is 'no evidence of corruption'? And is it not true that when the National Audit Office announced that it was to hold an enquiry, the Saudis threatened to pull out of the Tornado deal?[129]

According to the *Observer*, Mark Thatcher may have received as much as £10 million from one of the main British Aerospace agents involved in the Saudi deal, which was negotiated while his mother was prime minister.[130] He has been named in a civil action in the United States as having helped British Aerospace and Rolls-Royce to win a helicopter defence contract in Saudi Arabia. A confidential memorandum refers to $4 billion 'mentioned in connection with M. Thatcher's son'.[131] If none of this is in the public interest, what is? Parliament should find out the facts and tell us. That is what it's for.

April to May 1992

V

WAR BY OTHER MEANS

THE NEW PROPAGANDA

JOHN MAJOR'S SKILFULLY managed tour of the Far East recalls to mind the anonymous radical song *circa* 1820: 'What land has not seen Britain's crimson flying, the meteor of murder, but justice the plea.' Major's toasting of Li Peng, the accredited mass murderer, was in keeping both with British imperialist tradition and present-day Western Stalinism. True, Major's career has been mostly as an apparatchik, although the keenness with which he engaged in the recolonisation of the Middle East and the slaughter of tens of thousands of Iraqi conscripts and civilians suggested he was made of stronger stuff. His journey to China for the purpose of offering alliance and reassurance to those who ordered the massacre in Tiananmen Square and the crushing of the democracy movement, guarantees his prominent place above the mausoleum of the 'new world order'.

None of this is surprising. The symbiosis of the actions and endorsements of grey men with bloody repression is well documented. Chamberlain fawned over Hitler; Kissinger unleashed the equivalent of five Hiroshimas on Cambodia; Bush dispatched several thousand Panamanians as the precursor of his 'famous victory' in the Gulf. And all were attended by a fellow-travelling media. Major's Chinese exercise, amoral by any normal standards of human behaviour, was routinely misrepresented as an heroic 'bullying stand' on behalf of human rights. That Major's concern for human rights did not extend to Hong Kong, where he has the power directly to influence policy on democratisation, was not considered important and was widely suppressed. The posturing of the old Soviet Stalinists was celebrated within similar fixed boundaries of public discourse.

Western Stalinism is by far the most insidious variety. In a democracy, manipulation of public perception and opinion is, by necessity, more subtle and thorough than in a tyranny. Major's China trip is a case in point. Contrary to the managed headlines, its aim was to reassure the Beijing regime that the Western imperialist powers had no intention of disturbing the state of capitalism in Hong Kong by allowing genuine democracy to take root. China, after all, is the paragon of what the dissident Russian writer Boris Kagarlitsky has called 'market Stalinism'; that is, an economic state in which there are consumer goods in the shop windows, growing unemployment, depleted public services and a totalitarian regime. Even that most inspirational of China's revolutionary achievements – its system of barefoot doctors – is being swept aside by privatisation drawn from the same Thatcherite model that is undermining the National Health Service in Britain.

The new propaganda differs from the old only in the technology of its conveyance. It says that, following events in the Soviet Union, a market economy and democracy are indivisible and that the unrestrained forces of Western (and Japanese) capitalism equal freedom and life. This supersedes the Cold War refrain of the Russian Threat, which allowed the United States to construct its economic and strategic empire following 1945.

As Paul Flewers wrote in the *Guardian*: 'People really believed that unless they backed their capitalist rulers, Soviet troops would be marching down the street . . . Classic inter-imperialist rivalries which caused two world wars were suppressed, and war was mainly confined to the Third World. Socialism has largely been defined as Stalinism, and consequently capitalism has to a large extent been legitimised.'[1]

Like my generation, the young today are being subjected to the same old routine in a different guise. The crumbling of Stalinism in the Soviet Union will increasingly be used, as the repressive nature of Stalinism itself was used, as a propaganda weapon against those who seek social change – principally, an end to the scourge of poverty.

This works on two levels. In the tracts exalting the 'freedoms' of the market, much is made of the violent history of communism. Nothing is said about the victims of expansionist capitalism. While millions died at the hands of Stalin and his successors within the Soviet Union, millions more were blood sacrifices in wars of imperialist competition. Several million died in a 'small war' in Indo-China. The blood-letting of apartheid in South Africa was underwritten by Western capital. In the Middle East, Anglo-American interests demanded the retention of feudalism and the dispossession of a whole people, the Palestinians.

The Soviet Stalinists were never in this league; they were lousy imperialists beyond the sphere of influence that Churchill and Roosevelt granted Stalin at Yalta. The West and Japan, on the other hand, have capital and debt as their levers of control.

Never before in history have the poor financed the rich on such a scale and paid so dearly for their servitude. During the 1980s, the Third World sent to the West $220 billion *more* than was sent to them in any form.[2] At the current rates of interest, it is a mathematical impossibility for most countries to pay off their debt. Many had to agree to 'structural adjustment' by the World Bank and the International Monetary Fund (IMF). This has often meant the end of uncertain protection for the old, young and sick and 'wage restraint' in countries where the difference between wage and peonage is slight.

Debt and 'market Stalinism' are to be capitalism's greeting to the new Soviet Union. Capital will flow at such a pace that the IMF is already having to 'structurally adjust' Yeltsin's democracy. At the weekend I phoned Boris Kagarlitsky in Moscow and asked him about this. 'Listen,' he said, 'you can invest $1,000 here now and get $10,000 back immediately. And that's just the exchange rate. We are the new Brazil, just waiting to be Latin Americanised.'

On this side of the Atlantic, the new propaganda concentrates on fortress Europe. The EC is the 'new world', with open borders and markets, a hive of prosperous, liberal energy – as long as you can get in. It is a fine illusion, for in the wider world, economic inequality has reached the highest point in human history; during the 1980s the number of countries catching up the industrialised states, in per capita terms, fell by three quarters. In other words, poverty has never risen as fast.[3]

The truth is quite simple: the rhetoric of Thatcher and Reagan was false, the literal opposite of the truth. Thatcher and her ideologues were brilliant propagandists and social destroyers – as those in Third World Britain and in structurally adjusted Africa, Chile and elsewhere bear silent witness. It is, of course, not necessary to look at the world through such a distorted prism. Socialism was never Stalinism: socialist struggles gave liberal democracy much of its gloss. The ignorant certainties are no less venal today than they ever were, whatever their disguise.

September 15, 1991

THE WAR AGAINST
DEMOCRACY

THE WAR AGAINST democracy, which replaced the Cold War, had a notable success in Moscow this week. The promoters of the totalitarian 'market' accelerated their assault on the lives of millions with the destruction of the second freely elected parliament in 1,000 years of Russian history. Boris Yeltsin, the former Communist Party boss of Sverdlovsk, a position he used to oppose basic democratic rights, brought troops and tanks into the heart of his Russian 'democracy' and allowed them to murder the elected representatives of the people. He could have been a Pinochet or a Somoza. John Major, for his part, said he admired Yeltsin's 'restraint'.

The Orwellian cover given these events in the west is astonishing even by the standards of previous propaganda models, such as the Gulf War, in which the slaughter of 200,000 people was dispatched down the media's memory hole. It would be illuminating to see a comparative study of *Pravda*'s reporting of the pre-Gorbachev Soviet Union and western reporting of Yeltsin's Russia. The similarities of systematic, ideological distortion would say much about the propaganda that we in the west often call news.

The BBC, ever conscious of its 'impartiality', has led the propaganda barrage, constantly referring to Yeltsin's draconian methods as 'reforms' and his parliamentary opponents as 'hardliners' and 'extremists'. Boris the Good, on the other hand, is 'the democrat whose patience finally snapped': such a generous description of a man whose troops had just burned the nation's parliament.[4] (Imagine a BBC report from Berlin in 1933, 'The Reichstag was burned down only after Herr Hitler's patience snapped.')

Since Yeltsin discovered 'democracy' under Gorbachev, he has played to the western media gallery, whose reporting of his rise has helped to sustain him in power. With his American advisers and with American presidents propping him up, here, after 75 years, was a dictator who could deliver the Russian hinterland to foreign capital.

The necessary media mythology quickly followed. This summer, it has been Yeltsin versus the 'hardline communist' parliament. In fact, the parliament was neither undemocratic nor run by so-called hardliners. All the deputies were democratically elected in multi-candidate contests. Like Yeltsin himself, the majority were ex-communists; but most of them were, until recently, Yeltsin supporters. They elected him as the parliament's first chairman, passed the constitutional amendments that launched his presidency and stood by him during the abortive coup in 1991 when the White House and its parliament were the very symbol of Russian democracy.

'Far from defending democracy,' wrote Renfrey Clarke, a Russian specialist not published in Britain, 'Yeltsin's coup was launched because democratic institutions were beginning to work. The system of checks and balances was functioning as intended, with the legislature and the judiciary curbing the ability of the president to continue implementing policies that had failed and lost popular support. But instead of accepting that the other branches of government had the right to insist on a change of course, Yeltsin responded as a committed totalitarian.'[5]

Renfrey Clarke writes for Australia's *Green Left Weekly*. Together with another freelance, Fred Weir of the *Morning Star*, and Jonathan Steele of the *Guardian*, his reports are rare in a coverage that has served the expectations of Western economic interests – just as the Western press did before and after the 1917 revolution (with the honourable exception of Morgan Philips Price of the *Manchester Guardian*).

The largely untold truth in the West is that Yeltsin has

returned Russia to military Stalinism, that *he* is the hardliner, and that the blood spilt this week is the direct result of ruthlessly applied 'market reforms' – the same 'reforms' that have caused so much suffering in Britain. 'Yeltsin's policies have met opposition,' wrote Clarke, 'not because the Russian parliament is dominated by bloody-minded conservatives – an absurd claim – but because these policies are both contrary to the interests of most Russians and deeply flawed. Few economic programmes have been so ill suited, and few have failed so comprehensively.'[6]

Under Yeltsin, Russian industrial output has collapsed to 60 per cent of the level of January 1990. Price rises amount to 2,600 per cent. Real *per capita* incomes have dropped to Third World proportions, placing many Russians, who once enjoyed a certain social security, on a par with Mexicans. The obsessiveness of Yeltsin's 'shock therapy' – prescribed by Thatcherite advisers using discredited models – has been accompanied by a campaign against pluralism reminiscent of Thatcher.

In decree after decree, Yeltsin has undermined the new democratic institutions. In Decree No. 1400, he suspended the constitutional court, Russia's third arm of government. When the chairman of the court, Valery Zorkin, challenged the legality of this, his telephone was cut off on the personal order of the president. During the referendum campaign in April 1993, the national television service was hijacked by Yeltsin, then refused all but token airtime to opposition candidates.

This week, he has banned a swathe of opposition parties and newspapers with hardly a word of protest from Washington and London. When the Sandinistas briefly suspended an opposition newspaper, funded by the CIA, the American press made this a *cause célèbre*. The Sandinistas were not approved by Washington; Yeltsin is. Adding to the Orwellian lexicon, the *New York Times* describes his thuggery as a 'democratic coup'.[7] He has now drained future elections of democratic substance; the millions who suffer from and oppose his 'reforms' will have no one to vote for. His crime, this week, is to have crossed a threshold of violence beyond which lies an abyss well documented in Russian history.

What has happened in Russia is a vivid example of the war against democracy being waged all over the world in the name of the 'global economy' and 'development', the euphemisms for market imperialism. Of course, a Boris Yeltsin is not always available; and when democratically elected leaders dare to place the interests of their country before those of the rulers of the world, they become the target of economic warfare. This happened in Chile under Salvador Allende, in Jamaica during Michael Manley's first term and in Nicaragua under the Sandinistas. ('We got rid of the communists in Nicaragua,' boasted former President Carter recently.)[8] When the Guatemalan human-rights activist Ramiro de Leon was elected president last June, he pledged to make his 'first priority' the ending of the poverty that afflicts almost 90 per cent of his people. Within a month, the pressure from Washington was such that de Leon bowed to IMF demands for an 'open market' and economic austerity for the majority. Had he not complied, he said, his country would have been 'destabilised'.

Such honest nuggets are rare. Last January, the *Wall Street Journal* published an article entitled 'Why Global Investors Bet on Autocrats, Not Democrats'.[9] Shortly afterwards, the head of the American bankers Morgan Stanley and Company told *Business Week*: 'There is a saying on Wall Street that you buy when there is blood on the streets.'[10]

October 8, 1993

THE SILENT WAR

Manila

IT IS MORNING and the sun is like a burning branch, but not here. Just as night consumes winter days in the far northern hemisphere, so dusk is permanent here. Silhouettes drift up the main street, through the smoke and haze. The ashen rain, like the stench, is constant; it stiffens your hair; your eyes weep with it and your throat is coated with it. There are two dominant sounds: the thud-thud of the dump trucks, and coughing. The children hack and spit as they descend on the trucks like crows waiting for the clod to turn.

Much of the road is the texture of bracken. It is the same on the embankments, where fire crackles. There is a shop with a fire smouldering next to it; the people in it are unconcerned; they are from Hogarth's London. A truck from the markets arrives. 'This stuff won't sell,' says Eddie. 'They'll keep it and eat it.' Each dragging a hessian bag and an iron hook, the children haul away their rotting catch. They are beaming.

This is Smoky Mountain, a massive rubbish tip that rises out of Manila Bay above the slum at Tonda. Eddie, Teresita and their four surviving children live in the *barrio* at the foot of Smoky Mountain. Eddie was a fisherman on one of the Philippines' southern islands until cash cropping, most of it prawns for restaurant tables in America and Europe, forced him to take his chance in Manila.

Teresita was a 'domestic' who, unable to feed herself, began scavenging on Smoky Mountain on her twentieth birthday, eleven years ago. 'We are here', she says, 'because

201

every day we can get money; this is work and *life*.' Only
Eddie is working now, as Teresita has been told she has heart
disease. From collecting pieces of glass, tin and plastic for
six hours, he makes fifty pesos, the equivalent of £1.10: just
enough to supply the next meal. They live from meal to meal
with only a breakfast of leftover rice assured. 'I used to like
scavenging,' says Teresita, 'because you had to concentrate
on the search, and you forgot about eating.'

Their shack is made from plywood, which is as precious
here as pesos; it is the currency of barter and increases in
value. In order to pay a midwife to deliver baby Mary Grace
two weeks ago, Eddie borrowed half from a neighbour and
paid her the rest in plywood. They so treasure the wood that
none of it is spared for the roof over their second room,
which is open to the ash. When the monsoon rain comes,
the six of them huddle in a corner two feet by two feet
beneath the only piece of corrugated iron.

There is no running water. Water is paid for and carried
in. There is no sewer, of course; they wrap their waste in
plastic and take it up to Smoky Mountain. Almost every
child is sickening; a strain of dengue fever is the latest. Yet
the children stepping over stagnant pools on their way to
school wear clothes that are neat and scrubbed, white collars
for the boys and big bows in the girls' hair, exercise books
under their arms, encased in plastic wallets. If the treatment
of and affection for children indicates the degree of civilisation, this is a profoundly civilised place. Not once did they
or their parents ask me for anything. That people here are
frustrated in their attempts to extend survival to the pursuit
of a decent life says much about the nature of the forces
ranged against them.

The people of Smoky Mountain are the face workers of
modern poverty. Their lives are a metaphor for the condition
of most of humanity, whose accelerating impoverishment in
the 1990s is allowed only fleeting intrusion upon Western
consciousness. Seventy per cent of the population of the
Philippines, or about forty-five million people, live in a poverty that has been defined here as 'that income level below

which people cannot buy for their families recommended nutrient requirements, cannot provide two changes of garments, cannot permit grade-six schooling for their children, cannot cover minimal costs of medical care and cannot pay for fuel and rent'.[11]

There are numerous, complex factors causing this, all of them overshadowed and compounded by debt and its silent war. It is a war whose jargon speaks of 'low level violence': that is, of children dying often unseen and slowly.[12] According to UNICEF, it causes the deaths of 650,000 children every year.[13] 'In the Philippines', says John Cavanagh, of the Institute of Policy Studies in Washington, 'we have calculated that one child dies every hour because debt repayments consume vital services like health care.'[14]

It is, however, a cost-effective war: indeed the profits to date have surpassed all expectations. In the period 1983–90, the poor countries paid £98,000 million to the rich countries. That's a net figure, after taking into account new loans and all aid. It works out at about £1.4 million per hour. Put another way: by the end of Red Nose Day this year the equivalent of all the money that Comic Relief raised in Britain – about £12 million – had come back to the rich countries in interest payments on loans that most people in poor countries never knew existed.[15] British high-street banks have done nicely, having collected more than £1 billion in tax relief on loans that are still current.[16]

Perhaps this will surprise those who have been long persuaded that we 'haves' have given limitless 'aid' to the 'have-nots'. Capitalism is even said to be suffering from 'compassion fatigue'! Such a perspective may now be changing as well-informed dissident groups, notably the World Development Movement and Christian Aid, force a public debate. The oldest human rights organisation in the world, the Anti-Slavery Society, is in no doubt: debt is 'contemporary slavery' and interest payments a form of 'national bondage'.[17] In the twenty-first century, debt and so-called 'free trade' will discipline the 'new world order'. Britain, says Douglas Hurd, will not give 'aid' to any country unless 'the market' dominates its economy.[18] Recolonisation has begun: official.

Since 1972, the Philippines' national debt has risen from $2.7 billion to $29 billion. Much of this is the result of secret and often fraudulent deals by the dictator Ferdinand Marcos. The World Bank and the International Monetary Fund quietly approved of Marcos and worked to keep him in power. According to internal World Bank documents, the martial law imposed by Marcos in 1972 made possible the 'economic reforms' that 'opened up the economy to the inflow of foreign capital'.[19] Within two years, during which the country's democratic institutions were muzzled, World Bank loans to the Philippines had increased fivefold. After more than a century of debilitating struggle for their independence, Filipinos were watching their sovereignty again slip away.

The centrepiece of World Bank strategy – formulated within an institution based in Washington, headed by an American and funded principally by the United States and its allies – was Rural Development, known as 'RD'. 'Rural Development', wrote the Filipino economist Walden Bello and his colleagues in their exposé of the World Bank, 'was counter-insurgency. And its targets were obvious: the independent peasant movements and armed rural-based revolutionary forces like the New People's Army.' As in its other client states, the World Bank set out to undermine an economy that had the capacity to feed the population. The instrument was a strategy called 'export-led industrialisation', which was ideologically based and of minimal economic worth. This, wrote Bello, 'virtually abandoned the domestic market as the basis for industrial advance and tied the fate of economic growth almost completely to favourable external factors . . . '[20]

Since 1972, the World Bank has poured more than $7.5 billion into the Philippines.[21] During that time the growth rate has fallen and poverty has risen by a third; and rural people – like Eddie – have been dispossessed by an economy addicted to earning more and more foreign exchange to pay off the interest on foreign loans.[22]

The feudal oligarchies – from which Cory Aquino comes – have done well; and those who played golf with Ferdinand Marcos at Manila's Wack Wack Country Club have done wonderfully. Marcos is now believed to have looted some $15 billion. In 1981, Vice-president George Bush raised his glass to Marcos and said, 'We love you, sir . . . we love your adherence to democratic principles and democratic processes.'[23]

Filipinos threw out Marcos in 1986. The heroine of the moment, Cory Aquino, was handed an opportunity unparalleled in recent colonial history. She could have demanded that the debts incurred by Marcos be wiped out so as to allow her people to benefit from the deeds of their civilised uprising. Instead, she pledged to 'vigorously seek to renegotiate the terms of our foreign debt'.[24] She did nothing of the kind and is now often reminded of her earlier description of the Philippines as 'a land of broken promises'.[25]

'People power,' as Manila's lively columnists write, was really 'some people power'. Aquino has given priority to paying back every dollar and cent. She has held on to several of Marcos's decrees, including the notorious Presidential Decree 1177, which appropriates whatever funds are necessary from the budget to meet debt repayments. This violates the post-Marcos constitution guaranteeing that education must command the highest proportion of the national budget.[26] Education is currently 15 per cent of the budget; 'debt service' accounts for 44 per cent.[27]

None of this will be on the agenda of the annual binge of the World Bank and International Monetary Fund in Bangkok. To the IMF, the Philippines has been 'structurally adjusted'. This has meant the establishment of 'Export Processing Zones' in areas where food was once grown in abundance. It has meant that almost all the forests will be lost by the end of the century. It has meant that those Filipino workers who go abroad to work, and who provide the main source of foreign exchange, must compete for fewer low-paid jobs in the recession-hit developed world. I once interviewed a married couple in London, he a hospital porter and she a child-minder. They had not seen their own children for four years and worked solely to keep them going. They tried to put aside enough for a phone call home every month.

The current demands of the IMF are for further reductions in public spending, a freeze on wages and new taxes. The Philippines' National Economic Development Authority estimates that, as a result of IMF policies, 500,000 workers will lose their jobs this year.[28] According to an internal voluntary agency memorandum, 'an increase in child labour is anticipated as opportunities for adult labour contract and children are forced to contribute to the family income'. In 1989, the Department of Health said that IMF demands would mean that 399,000 children would be denied milk and vitamins, and 103,000 tuberculosis sufferers medical treatment.[29] The implication is clear: tens of thousands of children will die 'silently' and unnecessarily.[30]

Elizabeth, aged three, and Lito, aged two, were two of these children. Eddie took Elizabeth to the local hospital when her diarrhoea 'would not stop'. The hospital said they would take the child, but Eddie would have to buy the medicines in the market. Health care accounts for 3 per cent of the national budget.

The cheapest he could find cost forty pesos. So he scavenged for a day and got it. But Elizabeth was now seriously ill; and so, too, was Lito whose stomach had distended in a matter of days. Teresita told me how she watched horrified as worms emerged from the mouth of her skeletal child. On the day they buried Elizabeth, in a cemetery occupied mostly by the unmarked graves of children, Lito died too.

October 18, 1991

BANGKOK LAMENT

Bangkok

ON ARRIVAL IN Bangkok, we were tagged and assigned seats in a fleet of new Volvos driven by men in white ice-cream suits, white shoes and white peak caps. In the back of my Volvo were two men in pinstripes; one of them arranged debt equity swaps, the other owned a third of a bank in Ecuador. With lights flashing and police outriders going ahead – and looking terrific in their ice-cream suits, reflecting sunglasses, parachutist's wings and decorative holsters – we headed into Bangkok's famous traffic, which had vanished, past Bangkok's famous street vendors, most of whom had vanished, through an underpass where people have scratched for a living since I have been coming here; and they, too, had gone. In their place were teams of women in blue smocks waiting to catch anything, a leaf, before it sullied the ground.

Along the way Coke, Pepsi, IBM, Nissan and a large massage parlour welcomed us to the World Bank/International Monetary Fund conference '... everything 50 per cent off for you delegates and participants'. On arrival at the Holiday Inn, people in white coats and tails ran at us, bowing low. We were thanked for everything; one of them got into the lift and thanked us for going up and down. Thais are polite and gracious people but do not normally engage in the sort of spectacular deference for which the door-openers of Tokyo department stores are famous.

Once in room 2436, things were becoming clearer. There was much to look at, including a picture of Margaret Thatcher and the words: 'You don't have to be rich and

207

powerful ... When the daughter of a humble grocery shop owner went on to become prime minister of Britain, she proved it! Now we are proving it *again*!' The 'we' is a computer firm.[31]

Next to this was a profile of World Bank President Lewis T. Preston. 'He is, first of all, a Marine,' it said. 'However, an intimate family friend swore that he and his wife are warm and hospitable ... *but* no one fails to mention that Lew Preston is one tough *hombre*!'[32]

Next to Lewis T. Preston was a form for me to fill in my blood group. A Thailand health guide advised against sharing a toothbrush, due to the prevalence of Aids. Under 'Emotional Health' it warned that some of us World Bankers might have difficulty adapting to our new environment and find ourselves feeling depressed. 'This stage is not unusual,' it reassured us, 'nor is it a sign of failure.'

Do tough *hombres* like Lewis T. Preston get these depressions too? Surely not. The World Bank seldom has a surplus of less than a billion dollars and everyone wants to borrow from it – everyone being those very poor countries whose economies have been 'structurally adjusted' by the World Bank and the IMF so that they can compete with other very poor countries for ever-diminishing export markets in order to acquire hard currency, in order to pay back the World Bank and the IMF the interest charges on loans they have repaid several times over.

The consequences of this system bring to mind Tolstoy: 'I sit on a man's back, choking him and making him carry me, and yet assure myself and others that I am very sorry for him and wish to ease his lot by all possible means – except by getting off his back.'

In Senegal, 40 per cent of the fertile land is given over to growing peanuts for Western margarine; in Ghana half the arable land is devoted to cocoa for Western chocolate bars; and in Colombia cut flowers are grown on farmland for export to the American rich. In these countries, the corollary is widespread, increasing malnutrition.

Remember Live Aid? In 1985, the twenty-nine poorest

countries of sub-Saharan Africa paid back to the World Bank, the IMF and Western commercial banks a total of $6.7 billion – more than twice as much as they received in emergency aid from governments and the good-hearted.[33]

These facts are known here as 'unmentionables'. The original aim of the World Bank, says Lewis T. Preston, 'was and remains the reduction of poverty'. The original aim as enshrined in the 1947 Bretton Woods charter was, in so many words, to provide markets for the rich world and to control the resources of the poor. Understandably, in these triumphant days, it is difficult for the corporate do-gooders to restrain themselves. 'We should not be afraid', Norman Lamont told the conference, 'to say that what we are extolling here are the virtues of *capitalism*! And the driving force of capitalism is the pursuit of *profit*!' There, he said it: no blah about eradicating poverty from Norman, whom a Bangkok radio station persists in calling 'Chancellor of the Excesser, Norm Lament'.[34]

The World Bank usually holds its annual conference in Washington. The last conference held in Asia was in Manila in 1976 soon after the IMF had given the dictator Ferdinand Marcos $4.5 billion, or about a third of the amount he is now believed to have had stashed away when he died.[35] In return for this largesse, Marcos built a number of luxury hotels to accommodate the World Bankers in the manner to which they are accustomed when deliberating about the poor. The poor, of course, were kept well away. Marcos sent the bill to the city authorities, who passed it on in municipal taxes; the poor of Manila are still paying it off.

Something similar has happened here. A vast conference centre, with gilded lacquer and other adornments, was completed just in time for the conference, and at great cost. In a country where rural children still die from malnutrition and preventable disease, and where low wages, bonded child labour, prostitution and illegal sweatshops support a 'growing' economy, the poor will end up paying indirectly.

The display of wealth has been unrelenting. A three-star chef has been flown in from Paris, reported the Bangkok

Nation, accompanied by 'succulent turkeys from the famous Bresse region . . . Belgian caviar from Iran, smoked salmon from Norway and prime rib from the US'.[36] Following the seminar on the conversion of socialism to capitalism and 'the lessons learned', delegates headed off to a party where, said the *Nation*, 'they must have been surprised and delighted that something very appropriate to their status was in store for them . . . a display of gems consisting of an 89-karat diamond, a 100-karat emerald and a 336-karat opal.'[37]

'It is just not acceptable', says Lewis T. Preston, 'that so many people in the world have to live on less than a dollar a day.'[38] The 6,000 employees of the World Bank are unlikely to find themselves in such straits. Middle-ranking civil servants earn 300 times the *per capita* income of half of humanity, and their perks include first-class air travel and tenure in deluxe hotels, costing up to $45 million a year.[39]

As part of Bangkok's 'beautification' for the conference, an iron wall was built opposite the convention centre, painted in bright murals and draped with a 'Welcome to Thailand' sign. Alas, during a heavy downpour the sign fell down, revealing to the delegates a large number of poor people hidden behind the wall. These are the slum people of Klong Toey. To most of them 'beautification' has meant eviction to places where it is often impossible for them to resume work as street vendors, or keep their jobs as day labourers and domestics.

For as long as I have been coming to Bangkok, one of the city's landmarks, as you drove in from the airport, was a small town of people living beside the railway tracks. A few weeks before the World Bank conference began, everything was bulldozed: homes, a kindergarten, a school. The people were moved to wasteland well out of sight of the to-ing and fro-ing Volvos, though still beside the railway line. Each was given £90 as 'removal expenses'. They have no electricity and running water, and the army says it wants its tents back once the conference is over. The Miss Universe circus is due next, and another 5,000 people are likely to be evicted.

The beautifiers and bankers have not had it all their way.

Forty-three countries have sent representatives to an International People's Forum at Chulalongkorn University. People who have been both victims and opponents of 'development' have spoken, often movingly, about the effects of World Bank capital projects, and IMF austerity programmes in their countries.

Vandana Shiva from India described how hundreds of thousands of people had been made homeless all over India by flooding caused by World Bank dams and irrigation schemes, which have taken little account of the environmental impact. 'They see only new markets and new investment zones that come with the dams,' she said. 'They cause these environmental disasters because it is assumed that "development" must come from outside. They think they bear a kind of White Man's Burden; but they do not really study life.'[40]

According to American economist Patricia Adams, 'World Bank-sponsored hydro projects have flooded a million and a half people off their land; and another million and a half are about to follow.'[41] One of the themes of the World Bank conference has been the Bank's new 'green' image as it emphasises the need to protect the environment. In selecting Thailand as the venue of its conference this year, the bank is making a point that the Thai economy should serve as an example to others. In fact, Thailand is the model exploitative economy: an environmental disaster, with its great forests wiped out by uncontrolled logging and profiteering.

I put several of these 'unmentionables' to senior officials of the World Bank and the IMF, in particular the conclusions of the UNICEF study that more than half a million children died every year as a result of high growth rate and austerity policies imposed by the institutions.[42] The officials sought to discredit the UNICEF figures. 'Oh, that one's got suspect data,' said Richard Erb, deputy managing director of the IMF. He offered nothing to support his statement.

There have been numerous sideshows. The most demeaning was a press conference called by the Russians to announce that they were more 'pro-market' than anyone. One of them said, 'Comrade Yavlinsky wants to explain his views on . . .'

211

He was interrupted by his colleague, who said, 'What's this comrade stuff?' To which the first Russian replied, 'My God! Sorry. Old habits die hard.'[43]

The saddest are the Vietnamese, who fought for half a century to free their country from colonialism and to establish a national health care system, remarkable by Third World standards, as well as free education and a minimum wage. In Bangkok, the Vietnamese have been promising to do almost anything to get the United States to lift its embargo so that the IMF can 'structurally adjust' them and impose more austerity, if that's possible. They say they have no choice but to sell off much of the forests not destroyed by American defoliants; and they took the opportunity to announce that they had abolished the minimum wage. Their labour force will now be the cheapest in Asia, which means that people must work in 'free-enterprise zones' for a pittance. Yet Washington still says no; the embargo stands; the punishment goes on.

Some things transcend even 'the virtues of capitalism', as Norm Lament surely would agree.

October 25, 1991

THE BETRAYAL OF BOSNIA

IF THE BOSNIAN Serbs fail to implement the latest 'peace plan', the Americans may still bomb the Balkans, with the British in tow. The last time this alliance took to the air in strength, some 200,000 people were slaughtered, many of them the very ethnic minorities whom President Bush claimed he wished to 'protect'. The difference now is that even the turkey-shooting generals know they can't get away with this one. Yet President Clinton – fresh from giving the usual nod to the latest round of Israeli 'ethnic cleansing' – believes that Caesar must make a gesture 'to stop the killing'.

'Political language,' wrote George Orwell, 'is designed to make lies sound truthful and murder respectable, and to give an appearance of solidity to pure wind.' Regardless of what the 'ethnic cleansers' have done to their neighbours in former Yugoslavia, Western governments are also guilty; and the renewed threat of American bombing adds a grotesque dimension to an often secret Western policy of dividing Yugoslavia along ethnic lines, dismantling it and eventually re-colonising it.

The Balkans have many tragic distinctions. Certainly, if ever a single issue has illuminated the difference between expressions of public morality in the West and the 'pure wind' of *realpolitik*, it is the fate of Bosnia. The semantics of Douglas Hurd are now unacceptable to people watching the Balkan horrors unfold on television. Public opinion has become more than a fleeting force. Having been made witnesses to genocide, perhaps for the first time, people want it

213

stopped. But it can only be stopped if its unstated causes, and the West's complicity, are understood.

Western governments are not the hand-wringing bystanders they pretend to be. From the beginning, the West has backed the ethnic warlords and neglected the non-sectarian and anti-war citizenry who represent the ideal of Yugoslavia; and for all its flaws, the old federation offered at least nominal constitutional respect to 'separate identities' and minority rights. The West's support for the regime in Croatia and its encouragement of Croatia's historical fascism is hardly referred to these days; yet Croatia's president, the Hitler apologist Franjo Tudjman, has been openly courted by Western governments, notably the German government, while his soldiers and surrogates have been murdering thousands of Serbs and 'cleansing' their communities, mostly out of sight of the Western media.

Although Serbian forces inflict most casualties now, it was the terrorising and disenfranchising of Serbian minorities in Croatia by Tudjman's HDZ regime that precipitated the conflict. For every Serbian 'chetnik' there is a Croatian 'ustasha'. It is only since the Croatians have begun to murder large numbers of Muslims in the vicinity of British UN troops that the media spotlight has found them and the full disastrous scale of Western clientism has been revealed.

Tudjman's regime has been the beneficiary of European intervention, which has been forced by Germany's new expansionism. Once reunified, Germany began its economic drive east and to dominate *Mitteleuropa*. 'It's our natural market,' said the chairman of the East Committee, the German industrial group promoting German takeovers in the East. 'In the end, this market will perhaps bring us to the same position we were in before the first world war. Why not?'[44]

This 'natural market' extended to the northern republics of Yugoslavia – Croatia and Slovenia. During the Second World War, the Nazis installed a puppet fascist state in Croatia. After the war, half a million Croats moved to Germany, where their *émigré* organisations enjoy great influence.

In 1989, Milovan Djilas warned that 'In some states [of Europe], for example Austria and Germany, there are influential groups that would like to see Yugoslavia disintegrate – from traditional hatred, from expansionist tendencies and vague, unrealistic desires for revenge.'[45]

In February 1991, the Council of Europe promoted Germany's separatist plans by linking economic advantage to the Yugoslav federal government's 'restraint' in dealing with the secessionist movements in Croatia and Slovenia.[46] The Tudjman regime was ready for this; violent anti-Serb demonstrations were held in Split, giving a clear signal to Croat and Serb minorities elsewhere to begin fighting for land and their lives.

The EC then compounded this by openly threatening the federal government that future economic assistance would depend on 'respect for minority rights'. Interpreted in Yugoslavia, this meant that the secessions had tacit EC approval.[47] Indeed, once the Yugoslav army had deployed units throughout the country, with the objective of holding the federation together, the EC secretly threatened to cut off $1 billion in promised aid.[48]

In October 1991, the EC delivered the *coup de grâce* at a special conference on Yugoslavia at The Hague. Behind a rhetorical veil of reasonableness, ministers gave *de facto* recognition to the secessions by effectively abolishing Yugoslavia. In its *Draft Convention on Yugoslavia*, the EC announced that the republics 'are sovereign and independent with [an] international identity'.[49] As a former US ambassador to Yugoslavia, William Zimmerman, told the *New Yorker*: 'We discovered later that [German foreign minister] Genscher had been in daily contact with the Croatian foreign minister. He was encouraging the Croats to leave the federation and declare independence, while we and our allies, including the Germans, were trying to fashion a joint approach.'[50]

Bosnia's leaders pleaded with the West not to recognise the secessionist states, knowing that both Croats and Serbs would then fall on multi-ethnic Bosnia. They argued that whatever had gone before, the worst could be contained without recognition. They were supported by the Macedonians who said that they, like the Bosnians, would have no choice but to seek independence; and that, in turn, would provoke Serbia. No EC minister sounded a warning or reminded his colleague of what was an open secret in Western capitals: that in March of that year, Tudjman and Slobadan Milosevic, the Serb leader, although despising each other, had conspired to carve up Bosnia between them as soon as the time was right. And international recognition would be that time.

The momentum in Germany for recognition was now well under way. Most of the German media concentrated on Serb atrocities. By the time the European leaders met at Maastricht in December 1991, a deal had been done in all but name.

The deal was that Germany would submerge its most exalted postwar achievement, the Deutschmark, into a common European currency if the German Croatia lobby was given its way on recognition. This was never openly linked to the Maastricht treaty itself; however, brokered by the French, it was a major factor. To put a decent interval between Maastricht and the recognition of Croatia and Slovenia, 15 January 1992 was the date set for the announcement. Two days after the Maastricht conference broke up, on 18 December, Germany broke ranks and recognised Croatia.

No EC government publicly objected to this opportunism. Neither Hurd nor Major said anything. Yet, at a stroke, it made a mockery of European strictures to the developing world on human rights and civilised behaviour. Set against what has happened since in Bosnia, and is likely to happen elsewhere as a result, recognition was an act of breathtaking irresponsibility. The Europeans, wrote Sean Gervasi, 'turned a manageable internal conflict into appalling fratricide'.[51]

The West's role in Yugoslavia's suffering is not confined to Germany's *fait accompli*. The fact that the Bush administration waged economic warfare against Yugoslavia has received little attention, yet the effect on ethnic tensions has been devastating. In 1989, when the Berlin Wall fell,

216

pressure was applied by Washington to all the former communist states to follow the 'market' model. The usual 'market reforms' were demanded, notably privatisation and conditions amenable to Western 'investment'.

Having already embraced something of a 'mixed economy' and being dependent on Western capital transfers, trade and tourism, Yugoslavia had already fallen victim to a 'market' recession long before the rest of Europe. Throughout the 1980s, discontent had risen among working people, while those willing to exploit ethnic tensions waited for their opportunity. In 1989, the new federal prime minister, Ante Marcovic, went to Washington and requested $1 billion in loans from the US and $3 billion from the World Bank. When told of the scale of austerity his country would have to accept, he warned that unemployment would increase to 20 per cent and 'there is the threat of increased ethnic and political tensions . . .'[52] The moment the Marcovic Government devalued the currency and began to close 'unprofitable' state enterprises and cut public services, 650,000 Serbian workers went on strike and the plan collapsed.[53] Yugoslavia was now on its own, denied a fraction of the aid Washington gave to ideologically friendly Poland.

However, 'economic reforms' had begun to take hold in separatist republics, as the Germans encouraged Croatia and Slovenia to join the great 'European market' and to 'disassociate' themselves from Yugoslavia. The federation, noted Gervasi, had 'walked a tightrope through the 1980s until economic and political crisis, particularly the fall in the standard of living, broke its balance. As rival ethnic groups shook the rope and the state teetered, EC intervention helped push [it] into the abyss . . .'[54]

When the Western allies recognised Bosnia in 1992, there was no acknowledgement that Bosnia's pluralism did not spring from some imagined independent state but from a federal unit that was an integral part of multi-ethnic Yugoslavia.[55] Moreover, the date chosen for recognition was the anniversary of the Nazi bombing of Serbia – a day when Serbs renew their cherished self-image of heroic resistance against impossible odds. In Serb nationalist eyes, here was the West partitioning their homeland, having not long celebrated the end of the partition of Germany. And now here was the *Luftwaffe* choosing the skies over Bosnia for its first military operation since the Second World War. With such disregard for national sensitivity, the West has smoothed the way for rabid nationalism to exploit a past shared by decent people and for the Serbian peace movement to be condemned as 'unpatriotic'.

In Russia, with its close ties to Serbia, the spectacle of NATO forces, with German participation, bombing Serbian targets, killing and maiming Serbian women and children, might well have the kind of reaction that not even Boris Yeltsin, the West's man, could stop. The First World War began, after all, in Sarajevo.

Even belated attempts by the EC to deter the extremists promoting 'Greater Serbia' have been botched; the policing of sanctions was considered farcical until recently. And if sanctions are applied to Serbia, why are they not also applied to Croatia? Ask any British soldier who has to carry the incinerated corpses of the victims of Croatian fascism. That the multi-ethnic Bosnians, especially those in the towns who have demonstrated no desire to attack anybody, should have been denied the means of defending themselves is absurd, and wrong. They stand defenceless not only against Serbs, whose arms supplies are assured, but against Croats, who through extensive *émigré* connections and powerful foreign friends, continue to move large shipments of weapons from Austria, Slovenia and Hungary.[56]

Just as I believe the Cambodian people should have arms in order to resist the Khmer Rouge, so the Bosnians should have arms to resist those who would visit a version of 'Year Zero' upon them; and they are up against fascism on two fronts. Breaking the Bosnian sieges with massive humanitarian aid is essential; the use of force worse than useless. One turkey shooter could ignite the rest of the Balkan tinderbox. The painful moral and practical dilemmas faced in the region, scarred by the legacies of competing empires, are not solved by Western so-called statesmen, offering 'peace plans' that further provoke and divide, and who seldom see the results of their culpability.

May 7, 1993

OPERATION RESTORE HOPE

ON CHRISTMAS EVE 1992, BBC television news announced that America's 'only purpose' in Somalia was to ensure that hungry people were fed. This was generally agreed throughout the media on both sides of the Atlantic. Congratulations were offered to President Bush for his 'bold' decision to 'send the cavalry to the rescue'. *Time* magazine published a two-page colour photograph showing Somali children reaching out to a marine for 'the gift of hope'. A marine corporal was asked about the danger he faced. 'In a way,' he said wistfully, 'I'm sort of hoping for a little combat.'[57]

Within days of their arrival, two US helicopter gunships fired their missiles at three armed vehicles, killing all nine Somalis in them. The justification for this 'little combat' was that the helicopters had been attacked. In fact, the Somalis were engaged in a private fight, and, according to witnesses, no one fired at the helicopters.

The nine dead equals the number of British soldiers killed by US aircraft during the Gulf War. The difference is that, while the British incident became a much-publicised scandal, the Somali incident barely rated a mention. Last week, on the eve of Bush's triumphant arrival in Somalia, US helicopters dropped leaflets warning people that if they were found merely carrying a weapon they would be shot. Many of the weapons were supplied originally by Washington; no irony was noted.

Operation Restore Hope, as this model of media manipulation is called, is not just a public relations stunt staged by a beaten and discredited president who, in the wake of his 'bold' decision on Somalia, pardoned those who almost certainly would have blown the whistle on his role in the Iran-Contra crimes. Bush is not engaged in a humanitarian mission to restore hope to the starving. He has sent guns and bombs to skeletal children to restore order: the 'new world order'. It took a lone letter writer to the *Guardian*, Andy Abel, to state the obvious, which professional commentators apparently could not. 'We are invited', he wrote, 'to believe that there is starvation in Somalia because armed gangs loot food stocks. There is looting because there is not enough food.'[58]

The severity of the drought in Somalia was known to the US and other Western governments as long ago as mid-1991, when satellite evidence left no doubt about what was coming. They, and the international organisations they effectively control, did nothing until, as with Ethiopia in the 1980s, disturbing television images exposed their culpable inaction. Until then, according to the Congressional watchdog, the General Accounting Office, the US government had allowed its client regime in Somalia, the murderous dictatorship of Mohammed Siad Barre, to steal American-donated food and divert it from the starving to the army and profiteers. Once Barre had fled Mogadishu, the US, according to the last American ambassador, 'turned out the light, closed the door and forgot about Somalia'.[59]

Not quite. The Bush administration ran a 'rat line' for the war criminals of Siad Barre's regime. According to a Canadian Broadcasting Corporation report, Washington dispensed tourist visas and easy passages to Canada for Somali officers who had trained at Fort Leavenworth in the mid-1980s, including one who allegedly ordered the execution of 120 villagers.

At the same time, Bush administration officials vigorously discouraged donors from helping Somalia, regardless of reports that up to 2,000 Somalis were dying every day. In 1992, Bush withheld American food aid for two straight months – right to August 13 when, as the underdog in a presidential election campaign, he mounted the podium at the Republican Party convention and announced to his prime-time audience that 'starvation in Somalia is a major human tragedy' and he, George Bush, would ensure that the US 'overcame the obstacles' in getting food to 'those who desperately need it'.[60]

Within weeks of a US food airlift getting underway, most of its cargo planes were grounded after the wing of one of them was hit by a bullet: a relatively minor occupational hazard that did not deter private donors. In any case, it was now September 18; the last phase of the presidential campaign was underway and, to no one's surprise, the 'major human tragedy' in Somalia was no longer an issue. Somalis could go on starving until it was time to use them again.

When the time came, just before Christmas, the media images of Operation Restore Hope were almost perfect. The marines were greeted by massed television cameras and satellite dishes and looked every bit like the cavalry coming to the rescue. They were, as one American TV commentator put it, 'a sight for sore eyes back home'. This was also true in this country, notably among liberal opinion. The American intervention, argued an editorial in the *New Statesman*, had 'proved remarkably successful . . . for once, the US did not permit either free-market prejudices or "strategic" interests to determine its foreign policy.'[61] Thus, the 'good guys' and their 'new world order' were back on the road to redemption, regardless of the historical truth of every American intervention in the developing world this century.

In Somalia, the marines and the media have no ideal enemy. Like the British in pith helmets, they are facing amorphous 'gangs' of natives led by 'warlords'. On the television screen, Somalis are dehumanised. There are no good Somalis, no wise Somalis, no professional and organised Somalis. There are only those 'warlords' and their 'gunmen' and their pathetic victims.

There have been few serious attempts to explain that the divisions and hatred between Somalis are largely the product of European colonialism and of the Cold War battlefield imposed on Somalia by the superpowers. Somalis share a common language and religion and have much more in common than most peoples of Africa. In the nineteenth century, they were divided between British Somaliland, Italian Somalia, French Djibouti and Ethiopian Ogaden. Others were incorporated into the British colony of Kenya. Tens of thousands of people were handed from one power to another. 'They may be made', wrote a British colonial official, 'to hate each other and thereby good governance is ensured.'[62] Siad Barre was the beneficiary of this, playing one group against another with the backing first of the Soviet Union, then of the United States, which flooded the country with modern weapons.

Rakiya Omaar and Alex de Waal, formerly of the human rights organisation Africa Watch, wrote recently in the *Guardian*: 'US military intervention in Somalia has followed a gross misrepresentation of the situation in the country.' They reported that 'three-quarters of the country is relatively peaceful, with civil structures in place', and the famine confined to scattered rural pockets. 'Most of the food is not looted,' they wrote. 'Save the Children Fund has distributed 4,000 tons in Mogadishu without losing a single bag. Other agencies that work closely with Somalia suffer rates of 2–10 per cent, because they consult closely with Somali elders and humanitarian workers.'[63]

Omaar and de Waal wrote that where there was a major problem with starvation is Bardera, which the forces of General Mohammed Siad Hersi Morgan controlled. Morgan is the son-in-law of Siad Barre. His forces are armed and trained by Kenya, another US client. Had Bush been serious about getting supplies through, he had only to intervene with Daniel Arap Moi in Nairobi. 'There has been nothing in the way of attempts to negotiate settlements in comparison with, say, Yugoslavia,' wrote Omaar and de Waal. 'The one serious attempt – by the former UN special envoy Mohammed Sahnoun – was meeting with remarkable success. Sahnoun was forced to resign in October because of his outspoken criticism of the UN's dismal failure in Somalia.'[64]

As for Operation Restore Hope, reported Mark Hubard

in the *Guardian*, no American food has arrived 'to date' and ORH 'is a farce which has cost the American taxpayer $400 million', and requires 'media complicity' in order to 'replace the Somali nightmare with a new array of fantasies to keep reality at bay'.[65]

Last week the Economic Commission on Africa reported on the reality. The growing impoverishment of Africans was of only 'marginal interest' to the West, said the report; and African countries still gave more hard currency to the West, in debt service, than they received in aid.[66]

In the meantime, the stated justification for the United States remaining in Somalia is the pursuit of General Mohammed Farah Aidid, the 'warlord' elevated to international demon status. (Previous such demons include Noriega, Gaddafi and Saddam Hussein.) 'A man may smile and be a villain,' offered the *Observer*, in a profile of Aidid. 'Soft-spoken, courteous, balding, with greying hair and a pot belly, Aidid looks and sounds more like a successful businessman than the man the United Nations accuses of crimes against humanity.' According to the *Observer*, this demon 'is responsible for the deaths of hundreds of thousands of people, through murder or as a result of the famine he helped to create'.[67]

The wonderful thing about accredited demons is that you can say virtually anything about them and it is unlikely you will hear from Sue, Grabbit and Run. Inexplicably, Aidid's unique 'war crimes' were not mentioned in March 1992 when, in Addis Ababa, he signed a UN-sponsored plan for peace and the reconstruction of Somalia. He was then merely 'one of the leaders of Somalia's fifteen factions'. Why is he now being singled out for disarmament and trial before the world? And what is to become of the other 'warlords'? Will they also be pursued by American 'gunships' firing missiles at hospitals and spraying 18,000 rounds a minute at ungrateful natives, including women and children?

Almost certainly not. Demonology is made for one at a time. And spreading the blame can only make difficult the task of the public relations managers. Facts may emerge that those 'hundreds of thousands of people' died for reasons other than the crimes of General Aidid – such as the actions of the imperial power, already outlined, and its hold over the United Nations.

There was a glimpse of this recently when a British aid worker in Somalia, Susan Quick, described how the UN had pushed aside the voluntary workers, in 'blatant violation of all the principles of relief assistance'. She wrote: 'The UN has distributed food in only a handful of sites in a manner likely to increase tension.' She also pointed out that most Somalis being disarmed by the UN were those guarding aid agencies and food supplies.[68]

Of course George Bush's 'humanitarian intervention' has a significance that goes far beyond a media stunt and is in keeping with radical policy and organisational changes at the United Nations that have seen the Security Council become an instrument of American power since the end of the Cold War. The term 'humanitarian intervention' is merely the latest, preferred euphemism for foreign intervention, without regard to the fact that the UN Charter specifically forbids any violation of national sovereignty. Secretary-General Boutros Boutros-Ghali, who is Washington-approved, has allowed the White House to dictate the reorganisation of the world body down to the appointment of its most senior executives. He appointed Ronald Reagan's attorney-general, Richard Thornburgh, as head of administration. It was Thornburgh who gave the US the 'legal right' to kidnap foreign nationals and who is in charge of a programme of 'reform' at the UN, inspired by the extreme right-wing Heritage Foundation. Thus, it now matters not what the UN Charter says, but what Augustus in Washington wants.

The bloody coup ending democracy in Haiti in 1991 demonstrated this. In the Security Council, the French argued that Haiti deserved 'humanitarian intervention' by the UN. They won considerable support, though not from the US. 'The nature of the discussion', wrote the UN specialist Phyllis Bennis, 'made clear that potential targets were more likely to be those already demonised by the west: Gaddafi's Libya,

Saddam Hussein's Iraq, Kim Il Sung's North Korea, Fidel Castro's Cuba, etc. The coup in Haiti was not on the agenda.'[69] So the US would decide.

The French later proposed a multinational command for the UN's Military Staff Committee, who would carry out future 'humanitarian interventions'. They were told firmly that US forces, when playing a major part, would be answerable only to the Pentagon. The point had been made dramatically at the start of the Gulf War. When the bombing of Baghdad began on January 16, 1991, members of the Security Council emerged from the chamber unaware of what had been unleashed in their name.

Elsewhere in the developing world, there is an unmistakable pattern of American intervention, legitimised by the UN. In Cambodia, the UN's biggest operation, described as a 'model for the world', the US has reimposed its will on Indo-China, using the Khmer Rouge and its US-funded allies as a means of creating an acceptable regime and continuing to destabilise Vietnam, despite lifting the trade embargo.

In Angola, UN-monitored elections produced the 'wrong' winner in the MPLA, which is not forgiven for its ties with the former communist bloc. The MPLA won in spite of American and tacit UN support for Jonas Savimbi, Washington's oldest Cold War client in Africa, who lost the election. Now, Washington is withholding diplomatic recognition, while Boutros-Ghali pressures the democratically elected former rebel leader José Eduardo dos Santos to accommodate Savimbi and Unita in his government. Described by US officials as 'power sharing' and an 'acceptable solution', this is the equivalent of Clinton being forced to bring Bush into his cabinet.[70] Perhaps it is a glimpse of future events in South Africa, should the African National Congress win outright power at the ballot box. Watch as 'power sharing' with the Nationalists and Inkatha is promoted as the only 'acceptable solution' following elections that do not bring instant 'peace' to the country.

Europe is quite a different matter. The United States has minimal interest in a small, weak Balkan state like Bosnia, whose birth it did not attend or approve. Secretary of State Eagleburger's call for a UN tribunal to punish Serbia's 'war criminals' should be set against its silence on the punishment of Pol Pot and his fellow genocidists, who have enjoyed UN (and US) protection.

A rare dissenting voice from within the UN was heard recently when Erskine Childers visited London. Until his retirement in 1989, Childers was senior adviser to the director-general for development and economic co-operation. He described 'the dishonesty, the intimidation and the horrifying military force used against Iraq'. In calling for 'an end to the double standards and hypocrisy with which powerful governments have invoked UN principles', he said it was 'beyond tolerance to allow Israel to invade, annex, carry out mass deportations, violate Geneva conventions and refuse to comply with hundreds of UN resolutions without even a threat of sanctions'.[71]

Not surprisingly, none of this has provoked official or media interest. Parliament has held only one debate on the United Nations in twenty years; and in the public 'debate' about 'humanitarian intervention' the facts about the American takeover at the UN are beyond the pale.

President Clinton has been quick to make use of the Americanised United Nations that Bush left him. His first bold foreign policy decision was to ignore the UN charter and break international law by denying thousands of Haitians free passage on the open seas. Instead, US ships will return them to a vicious regime that, having overthrown democracy, is about to get £50 million from Washington. The victims are those who took to their boats only after Clinton promised in his election campaign to help and protect them. Clinton now says his decision to send them back is to prevent a 'humanitarian tragedy' – a term that comes from the same Orwellian glossary as 'humanitarian intervention'.[72]

Clinton also wants to 'institutionalise' the UN's success in the Gulf War. He says he likes the idea, for example, of a 'UN rapid deployment force, that could be used for purposes beyond traditional peacekeeping, such as standing guard at the borders of countries threatened by aggression, preventing attacks on civilians, providing humanitarian relief'.[73]

It was this last category of 'humanitarian relief' that moved Henry Kissinger to write some remarkable words recently, which the *Guardian* published. The 'objective' in Somalia is 'noble', he began. 'In fact, moral purpose has motivated every American war this century . . . The new approach [in Somalia] claims an extension in the reach of morality . . . "Humanitarian intervention" asserts that moral and humane concerns are so much a part of American life that not only treasure but lives must be risked to vindicate them; in their absence, American life would have lost some meaning. No other nation has ever put forward such a set of propositions . . .'[74]

The author of this tripe was responsible for the 'secret bombing' of Cambodia during which American pilots falsified their logs in order to fly B52 bombers, in defiance of Congress, over a small, neutral peasant country and drop the greatest tonnage of bombs in the history of modern bombardment. Between 1969 and 1975, three-quarters of a million people were killed. Kissinger was also deeply involved in the overthrow of the democratically elected Allende government in Chile.

That Kissinger's views should have been sought at all demonstrates the extent to which the hagiographers of the old imperialism and the apologists of the new retain credibility, using and twisting the words of life, words like 'morality' and 'humanitarianism'. Just as there is now virtually no mainstream debate of difference between 'democracy' and the 'free market', there may be soon no debate of difference between 'intervention', whatever its semantic mask, and imperialism, a non-word in today's vocabulary of control.

In the *Observer* last week, Michael Ignatieff introduced his readers to what he called 'liberal intervention'. 'We are moving towards a new world,' he wrote, 'in which the international community engages itself to protect minorities from majorities, to feed the starving and to enforce peace in case of civil strife.'[75]

This is the same American-driven and bribed 'international community' that oversaw the slaughter of some 200,000 people in Iraq, of whom many, if not most, were the very minorities whom the interventionists claimed they were 'helping'. That aside, the 'we' is important here, for it assumes and emphasises the artificial division in humanity that was always and remains the essence of imperialism, and the antithesis of true internationalism.

January – August 1993

VI
EAST TIMOR

BORN IN TEARS

AT STANFORDS IN London's Covent Garden, reputedly the best map shop in the world, I asked for a map of the island of Timor. 'Timor?' said a hesitant sales assistant. 'Would you please come with me?' We crossed the floor and stood staring at shelves marked 'South East Asia'. 'Forgive me,' he said, 'where exactly is it?'

'Just north of Australia.'

'Oh yes, of course.' After a search, all he could find was an aeronautical map with large blank areas stamped 'Relief Data Incomplete'. More apologies. 'I have never been asked for Timor,' he said. 'Isn't that extraordinary?'

Such is the depth of the silence that has enveloped Timor, or specifically East Timor, the part of the island under an illegal Indonesian occupation since 1975. Other places on the planet may seem more remote; none has been as defiled and abused by murderous forces or as abandoned by the 'international community', whose principals are complicit in one of the great, unrecognised crimes of the twentieth century. I write that carefully; not even Pol Pot succeeded in killing, proportionally, as many Cambodians as the Indonesian dictator, Suharto, and his fellow generals have killed in East Timor.

James Dunn, the former Australian consul in East Timor and adviser to the Australian Parliament, has made a study of census statistics since the Indonesians invaded. 'Before the invasion,' he told me, 'East Timor had a population of 688,000, which was growing at just on 2 per cent per annum. Assuming it didn't grow any faster, the population today ought to be 980,000 or more, almost a million people. If you look at the recent Indonesian census, the Timorese population is probably 650,000. That means it's actually less than it was eighteen years ago. I don't think there is any case in post-World War Two history where such a decline of population has occurred in these circumstances. It's quite incredible; it's worse than Cambodia and Ethiopia.'[1]

Where are all these missing Timorese? The facts ought to be well known, but are not. As a direct result of the Indonesian invasion and occupation, which continues, some 200,000 people, or a third of the population, have died. This estimate was first made in 1983, by the head of the Roman Catholic Church in East Timor, following an admission by the Indonesian Department of Defence and Security that the civilian population of East Timor had halved since the invasion.[2] In 1993 the Foreign Affairs Committee of the Australian Parliament reported that 'at least 200,000' had died under the Indonesian occupation.[3]

Moreover, this figure has been secretly accepted by Western governments, as the CIA operations officer in Indonesia at the time of the invasion confirmed to me in 1993.[4] What in other countries would have been condemned and punished as an act of barbarism and a crime against humanity has, it seems, been quietly deemed acceptable. When pressed in an interview Gareth Evans, the Australian foreign affairs minister, whose policies have supported the Suharto regime, admitted that the number of East Timorese dead 'is horrifyingly large'.[5]

How they died has been Indonesia's and its allies' great secret. Western intelligence has documented the unfolding of the genocide since the first Indonesian paratroopers landed in the capital, Dili, on December 7, 1975 – less than two months after two Australian television crews were murdered by the Indonesian military, leaving just one foreign reporter, Roger East, to witness the invasion. He became the sixth journalist to die there, shot through the head with his hands tied behind his back, his body thrown into the sea.

As a result, in the age of television few images and reported words reached the outside world. There was just one radio voice, picked up in Darwin, Australia, 300 miles to the south, rising and falling in the static. 'The soldiers are killing indiscriminately,' it said. 'Women and children are being shot in the streets. We are all going to be killed. I repeat, we are all going to be killed . . . This is an appeal for international help. This is an SOS. We appeal to the Australian people. Please help us . . .'[6]

No help came. Tens of thousands of people died resisting the invasion, or were slaughtered without reason.[7] Or they died in concentration camps where Indonesian troops herded peasants whose villages were razed. Or they starved. 'I was the CIA desk officer in Jakarta at that time,' Philip Liechty told me, 'I saw the intelligence that came from hard, firm sources in East Timor. There were people being herded into school buildings by Indonesian soldiers and the buildings set on fire; anyone trying to get out was shot. There were people herded into fields and machine-gunned, and hunted in the mountains simply because they were there. We knew the place was a free fire zone. None of that got out.'

The Indonesian military all but closed East Timor to the outside world, making it extremely difficult to verify what was happening there and relatively easy for Jakarta and its defenders to plead ignorance of the atrocities. However, information from credible sources did get out. In 1977, two nuns in Lisbon received a letter from a priest in hiding in East Timor. 'The invaders', he wrote, 'have intensified their attacks from land, sea and air. The bombers do not stop all day. Hundreds die every day. The bodies of the victims become food for carnivorous birds. Villages have been completely destroyed. The barbarities, understandable in the Middle Ages, justifiable in the Stone Age, all the organised evil have spread deep roots in Timor. The terror of arbitrary imprisonment is our daily bread. I am on the *persona non grata* list and any day I could disappear. Genocide will come soon . . .'[8] Another survivor wrote, 'The luck of the Timorese is to be born in tears, to live in tears and to die in tears.'[9]

'Anyone can come to East Timor,' say the Indonesians.

According to Amnesty International, at least 33,000 people remain on an official government blacklist restricting entry to and exit from the country.[10] Those who are granted visas are shepherded, restricted and watched. Journalists who attempt to enter as tourists are generally discovered and deported. In the week I left London for Sydney, en route to East Timor, an Australian film maker, David Bradbury, was arrested in Dili and his videotape confiscated. In the preceding month, correspondents of the *Washington Post, Frankfurter Allgemeine* and the *Sydney Morning Herald* had applied for visas simply to travel to Indonesia; all were refused. In 1994, as the UN Human Rights Commission again considered East Timor and my film, *Death of a Nation*, was shown in a number of countries, two brief, highly restricted press tours were arranged.

The regime, understandably, is frightened of the media, especially television. On November 12, 1991 a British cameraman, Max Stahl (a pseudonym), recorded Indonesian troops shooting and beating to death scores of young people in the Santa Cruz cemetery in Dili. His videotape, which he buried among the graves before he himself was arrested, was shown around the world. When some, like Foreign Affairs Minister Evans, sought to explain away the massacre – which had left more than 450 people dead and 'disappeared'[11] – as an 'aberration',[12] their apologetics were undermined not only by the reaction of the Indonesian regime, whose senior military officer said he wished to shoot and 'wipe out' more 'delinquents',[13] but by international revulsion at the pictures of wounded youngsters dying among the gravestones.

If British television ever reclaimed the power of its documentary tradition it was in Max Stahl's report, made with such skill and bravery. I regret I cannot use his own name; that would identify those of the East Timorese resistance who helped him, and have since helped me.

Max had got in touch with me earlier that year and suggested we go to East Timor together, but events had conspired against my going. For years I had been listening to friends in Australia vent their frustration at not being able to travel freely in East Timor and to film unhindered. Gil Scrine's *Buried Alive* and Mandy King's and James Kesteven's *Shadow over Timor* were both fine films that documented the collusive role played by the West, notably Australia, in the suffering of the Timorese. However, the wall that Suharto and his generals had built around Indonesia's '27th province' remained the obstacle it was intended to be.

For me, the Australian dimension to the genocide in East Timor is especially disturbing. In the Sydney street where I grew up in the years following the Second World War were several 'diggers' (veterans) who had fought the Japanese in Asia. One of them, the father of one of my earliest friends, would display a ceremonial sword he had taken from a Japanese he had killed during an ambush on the 'Portuguese island'. It was common to describe Australia's neighbours in racist terms; and to him, the Timorese were 'boongs' and 'fuzzy wuzzies'; but he also spoke of them with unusual affection and admiration, and would point in a school atlas to where he had served as a commando and talk of the people he had 'left behind'. He had regrets.

It was many years before I understood the importance of these regrets. In December 1941, Australian commandos invaded the neutral Portuguese colony of East Timor in an attempt to prevent the Japanese building airfields from which they could launch an invasion of northern Australia. The arrival of the Australians had the effect of drawing the Japanese to island communities they might otherwise have spared. The Australians fought a classic guerrilla campaign, disrupting a numerically superior Japanese force, and their exploits passed into popular legend, dramatised by Damien Parer's 1942 film, *Men of Timor*. They were able to achieve this only because of a remarkably close relationship forged with the Timorese, who supplied and protected them and who themselves fought like lions.

As a result of this succour, the Australians lost only forty men. The Timorese, however, paid a dreadful price. As many as 60,000 were killed, or 14 per cent of the population. Many died under torture after the Australians hurriedly withdrew, having promised to take people with them; they took no one.

'We shared their homes,' recalled John ('Paddy') Kenneally, then a young commando private. 'You found Australian soldiers sleeping on one side, the fire in the middle, and on the other side would be a granddad and grandmother and all the children and a spare dog or two ... The night on the beach when we left was heart-breaking. [The Timorese] were crying their eyes out ... We went to Timor and brought nothing but misery on those poor people. That is all they got out of helping us – misery.'[14]

In 1943, the Royal Australian Airforce dropped leaflets which began, *Os vossos amigos não vos esquecem* – your friends do not forget you. When the war ended, the government sent the Timorese a wreath of roses and bougainvillea, then promptly forgot about them for twenty years when the foreign affairs minister was moved to describe their country as 'an anachronism, not capable of independence'.[15]

In 1987 I interviewed Arthur ('Steve') Stevenson, a former commando. He told the story of Celestino dos Anjos, a Timorese trained by the Australians, whose ingenuity and courage had saved his life, and other Australian lives, behind Japanese lines. Steve Stevenson returned to Timor in 1970 and had an emotional reunion with Celestino. 'I went to his village,' he said. 'We had a son the same age. The bond between us was wonderful. I owed the man the debt of life. When I got back to Australia I tried to get him the military recognition he deserved, but this wasn't possible as the Timorese were not officially part of the Australian army. I eventually got him one of those loyalty medals they handed out around the islands. To make it special, I arranged for the Governor of Timor to pin it on Celestino. That was 1972. I was there, beside him.'

In 1975 Steve Stevenson heard that Celestino had survived the Indonesian invasion, then heard nothing for almost eleven years. In 1986 he received a letter from Celestino's son, Virgilio, dated two years earlier. Written in Portuguese, it told of Celestino's murder. The son wrote that in August

1983 Indonesian forces entered their village of Kraras . . .
'They looted, burned and devastated everything and massacred over 200 people inside their huts, including old people,
the sick and babies . . . four battalions encircled Bibileo and
fighter aircraft bombed the area intensively during the following weeks.' The Indonesians, he wrote, 'captured about 800
people' who were 'massacred by machine-gun fire . . . on
27/9/83 they called my father and my wife, and not far from
the camp, they told my father to dig his own grave and when
they saw it was deep enough to receive him, they machine-
gunned him into the grave. They next told my pregnant wife
to dig her own grave but she insisted that she preferred to
share my father's grave. They then pushed her into the grave
and killed her in the same manner as my father.'[16]

Vigilio and his brother, who escaped, joined the Fretilin
guerrillas. In 1991 Steve Stevenson learned of their deaths.
'When Celestino and I were reunited in 1970,' he said, 'he
didn't ask me why Australia let him and his people down,
why we deserted them. He felt that was a consequence of
war. It was as if the Japanese reprisals hadn't happened! But
for us, a free people, to let the Timorese down, to watch while
the Indonesians mark their boots on them is intolerable. I
dream about that man and his family, all gone . . .' At the
end of our conversation, he turned away and wept. He died
in 1992.

The history of East Timor is very different from that of
the other islands that make up the volcanic stepping stones,
rising from clear deep seas, east of Bali. The Suharto regime
has tried to justify its illegal occupation on the grounds of
what it calls 'deeply felt and longstanding ties . . . of common
brotherhood'. In fact, the East Timorese have little in
common with Indonesia and especially the Javanese who rule
it. Descended from the Atoni people of the highlands, Malay
and Melanesian immigrants and Chinese, Arab and Gujerati
traders, they have over the centuries developed strikingly
different languages and culture from what is now Indonesia.
Whereas most Indonesians are Muslim or Hindu, the East
Timorese are animist or Roman Catholic. Even their colonial

experience was different, with the Portuguese 'latinising' the eastern half of the island and insulating it from the upheavals of the Dutch colonies, including West Timor, that became Indonesia in 1949.

Unlike the Dutch, the Portuguese were interested in trade, not settlement. They made no attempt to disrupt a civilisation that was divided into kingdoms, or *rais*, ruled by a king or *liurai*. The *rais* were made up of tribal groups which divided into clans, or village units. The thread was kinship; few places on earth have such strong ties of family. Today, exiled Timorese, with feats of memory, can name their hundreds of 'close' relatives.

While they competed with the Dutch for the white aromatic sandalwood of the small trees that covered the mountains and which they sold at great profit in India and Persia, the Portuguese adapted their administrative system to the village units. Their rule was benign, neglectful and, as in other Portuguese colonies, multi-racial. 'What did stick out like a thumb', recalled Paddy Kenneally, 'was the lack of racism. The Anglo-Saxons or the Dutch or the Germans would take native mistresses and they might do something for the children without admitting to them openly, but the Portuguese just didn't seem to have that gulf. It was usual to see a Portuguese properly married to a native wife ... At gatherings you'd see the full range of mixtures in the colours and looks all talking away happily. Some were a mixture of Chinese, Portuguese, Timorese and there were some Portuguese African and Goan Indian troops ... So in one family some would be black, some white and everything in between, and you'd get some attractive combinations with a dash of this or a dash of that. I found the Timorese very attractive, with beautiful eyes and teeth, unless they got into the betel nut. It's a kind of drug. They use lime with it and it can wear their teeth away ...'[17]

Not even the Catholic Church, it seems, resorted to forced conversion, which perhaps explains why Christian and animist beliefs and prejudices coexist in harmony. However, the church, as elsewhere, ran the schools and created an elite that was indebted to its liturgy of power. This changed dramatically with the Indonesian invasion. An East Timorese church emerged, similar to that of the popular 'political' church of Central America. Its priesthood became more Timorese, and for the first time mass was said not in Portuguese but in Tetum, the Timorese *lingua franca*. This represented a direct challenge to the Indonesian ban on the institutional use of all languages except that of the state, *Bahasa Indonesia*. Thus the church forged a solidarity with the people and with the resistance and became, as Peter Carey has written, 'the only institution capable of communicating independently with the outside world and of articulating the pain of the East Timorese people'.[18] In under two decades (from 1975) the proportion of nominal Catholics has shot up from less than 30 per cent to over 80 per cent of the population.

In 1989, Bishop Carlos Felipe Ximenes Belo, the head of the Catholic Church in East Timor and himself a Timorese, appealed directly to the world in a letter to the United Nations Secretary-General. 'We are dying as a people and as a nation,' he wrote.[19] He received no reply.

In April 1974, Portugal's old fascist order, established by Antonio de Oliveira Salazar, was swept aside by the *Revolucão dos Cravos*, the 'Carnation Revolution'. Events in Lisbon moved quickly and chaotically. The new government, drawn from the left-wing Armed Forces Movement, began to decolonise the last of Europe's great empires by offering almost immediate independence to the African colonies of Angola, Mozambique and Guinea-Bisseau, which were already in revolt, and to the Cape Verde islands, São Tomé and Principe. The tiny 'overseas province' of East Timor, 'asleep at the end of the earth', as one Portuguese commentator later wrote, 'was on no one's list of priorities'.

However, within a month of the revolution in Lisbon, three political groups had formed in East Timor. The Timorese Democratic Union (UDT), led by members of the colonial administrative elite and coffee plantation owners, called for federation with Portugal and eventually independence. The

Timorese Social Democratic Association (ASDT), which later became the Revolutionary Front for an Independent East Timor, or Fretilin, comprised most of the younger nationalist opposition who wanted genuine economic reforms. A third party, the Timorese Popular Democratic Association (Apodeti) drew its tiny membership from the border with West Timor and wanted integration with Indonesia.

During the campaign, 'We criss-crossed the country,' wrote José Ramos Horta,* who is today Fretilin's foreign minister in exile. 'Our theme was simple. We spoke the language of the people: "Are we human beings or a sack of potatoes to be sold to another country?" The Timorese, proud and independent, responded enthusiastically to the cry for independence. A literacy campaign was launched; student brigades taught children and adults to read and write in their own language for the first time ever. They helped the people build schools and health centres, where they taught nutrition and hygiene; paramedics were mobilised for a vaccination campaign . . . Nicolau Lobato [a Fretilin leader who was later killed] inaugurated the co-operative schemes that became so popular . . .'[20]

In June 1974, José Ramos Horta travelled to Jakarta, where he met the Indonesian foreign minister, Adam Malik. 'He told me he sympathised "whole-heartedly" with the East Timorese desire for independence,' said Ramos Horta. 'He said that Indonesia respected "the right of every nation [to independence] with no exception for the people of Timor". The Government of Indonesia had "no intention to increase or expand their territory, or to occupy territories other than what is stipulated in the Constitution . . . Whoever will govern East Timor in the future after independence can be assured that the Government of Indonesia will always strive

* José Ramos Horta is today the Special Representative of the National Council of Maubere Resistance, an umbrella organisation based inside East Timor. It represents the political organisations, guerrilla army and civilian resistance. It describes itself as 'non-ideological, the equivalent of a coalition government'.

to maintain good relations for the benefit of both countries".'21

As a piece of deception this has few equals. As James Dunn has pointed out, the conspiracy to integrate East Timor forcibly had already begun when Malik was issuing his reassurances. The Indonesian military dictatorship believed that Fretilin would turn East Timor into a base for communist insurgency, 'another Cuba', which was absurd. Although Fretilin included students recently returned from Lisbon with Marxist views, most of the leaders were Catholic socialists who looked to the Cape Verde philosopher Amical Cabral and the Brazilian priest and educator Paulo Friere; or, like José Ramos Horta, they took Swedish social democracy as their model. Above all, they were nationalists who wanted their people to control their own destinies, trade and resources. This was no more than the Indonesian nationalists had demanded for themselves when they threw the Dutch out of their country. The Fretilin leaders had also made clear that they wanted to live at peace with their huge neighbour, the fifth largest nation on earth.

Like all small nations living in the shadow of a regional power, the East Timorese looked to another likely guarantor of their right to independence. Many of Fretilin's leaders were the sons of Timorese who had fought for the Australians against the Japanese in the Second World War and were confident that their former allies would discharge their moral debt, especially now that the inspiring anti-colonialist Gough Whitlam was prime minister. His government would surely support the rights of the people of East Timor, as it had supported those of other colonised or subjugated nations. The Whitlam government had been among the first to recognise the former Portuguese colony of Guinea-Bisseau; and Whitlam's personal relationship with Suharto suggested that his views would be taken seriously in Jakarta.

What Fretilin's leaders could not possibly measure was the depth and complexity of the Australian establishment's obsession with Indonesia. In recent years deference to Jakarta has become an article of faith second only in importance to a veiled obedience to Washington among the makers of Australian foreign policy. By calling into question the latter Whitlam eventually hastened his own political demise; by acquiescing in a 'special relationship' with Jakarta, he appeared to obey the instincts that have dominated Australia's post-Second World War view of the world, which – and it is a great irony – he had pledged to change.[22]

Since the Japanese bombed Darwin in 1942 and terrified those of us clinging to the southern seaboard, there has been a fear of Asia: that one day the brown and yellow 'hordes' to the north will fall down on under-populated white Australia as if by the force of gravity. This is seldom admitted, of course, and perhaps these days it is no longer widely believed. Strategic studies regularly assure the Australian people that they have nothing to fear from anyone. Yet 'Asia' lies deep within the political psyche; and 'living with Asia' is often the excuse for some astonishing acts of appeasement, known as *realpolitik*.

Long before he became prime minister, Gough Whitlam, already an outspoken champion of the rights of small nations, made it clear that the Indonesian archipelago was an exception. In 1963 he said that, although the East Timorese had the right to self-determination, 'we must not get bogged down in another futile argument over sovereignty'.[23] He was referring to West New Guinea, which Indonesia had swallowed in the early 1960s, after a long dispute with Australia and the United Nations. But there were no grounds for a dispute over East Timor. This was a Portuguese colony whose people had the same rights, under the UN Charter, as any other colonial people. Yet, wrote James Dunn, 'No thought was given to what the East Timorese might want . . . The attitude that this ugly relic of old-world colonialism should not be allowed to get in the way of the urgent task of improving Australia–Indonesian relations came to dominate.'[24]

By 1966, after the populist Indonesian president Sukarno had been effectively deposed by Suharto, Australian politicians rushed to reward the new regime with their support for a consortium of Western aid. An influential Australian Indonesia specialist, Professor J. A. C. Mackie, expressed this enthusiasm in a eulogy for the Suharto regime's 'moderate' character. The new government, he declared, was 'clearly anti-communist and committed to a low-key, unassertive foreign policy, with a new stress on regionalism and "good neighbourly" relations with nearby countries. The stage was set for the working out of a new and more constructive, enduring set of links.'[25]

The fact that Suharto and his generals had, in seizing power, killed between 300,000 and a million Indonesians was not mentioned, as if this was irrelevant to the 'new and constructive set of links'; and indeed it was.

The United States, to which Australia deferred in strategic matters in its region, had no time for Suharto's predecessor, 'Bung' Sukarno. Under the non-aligned Sukarno, mass trade union, peasant, women's and cultural movements had flourished. Between 1959 and 1965, more than 15 million people joined political parties or affiliated mass organisations that were encouraged to challenge British and American influence in South East Asia.[26] Indonesia had one of the largest communist parties in the world.

None of this was acceptable to Washington which, in 1949, had declared that the 'major function of the region was as a source of raw materials and a market for Japan and Western Europe', in an emerging global system managed by the United States and ultimately subordinated to American interests.[27] In 1967 Richard Nixon wrote, 'With its 100 million people and its 300-mile arc of islands containing the region's richest hoard of natural resources, Indonesia is the greatest prize in South East Asia.'[28]

A 'new and constructive set of links' between the United States and the Indonesian military had long been forged, allowing the generals to receive US equipment in spite of Sukarno's hostility. In 1965, following rumours of a coup against Sukarno, six generals were murdered in what is often described as a 'communist coup'. If it was that, it had unique features. None of the middle-ranking military officers who took part was a communist; and the US embassy denied that the Indonesian Communist Party (PKI) had any reason to take part.[29]

As Noam Chomsky has pointed out, the coup 'miraculously spared the pro-US Suharto, while targeting elements of the military considered anti-American' and allowing Suharto to carry out 'an actual military coup which led to the slaughter of half a million people in a few months, mostly landless peasants, and crushed the popular-based Communist Party; at the same time, incidentally, turning Indonesia into a "paradise for investors".'[30]

Declassified American documents have since revealed that the United States not only supported the slaughter but helped the generals to plan and execute it. The CIA gave them a 'hit list' of 5,000 Communist Party supporters including party leaders, regional committee members and heads of trade unions and women's and youth groups, who were hunted down and killed.

In 1990 a former US embassy official in Jakarta disclosed that he had spent two years drawing up the hit list, which was 'a big help to the army'. 'I probably have a lot of blood on my hands,' he said, 'but that's not all bad. There's a time when you have to strike hard at a decisive moment.' The list had been approved by the US Ambassador, who stated that the US had 'a lot more information' on the PKI than the Indonesian army. As people on the list were murdered, their names were crossed off by American officials.[31]

With the slaughter under way, US Secretary of State Dean Rusk cabled the Jakarta embassy that the 'campaign against [the] PKI' must continue and that the military 'are [the] only force capable of creating order in Indonesia.' The United States, he said, was prepared to back a 'major military campaign against [the] PKI'. The US Ambassador passed this on to the generals, making it clear 'that the Embassy and the US Government are generally sympathetic with and admiring of what the army is doing'. When the military replied that they needed more American weapons to sustain the slaughter, they were told that 'carefully placed assistance' – covert aid – would 'help the army cope . . .'

'No single American action in the period after 1945', wrote the historian Gabriel Kolko, 'was as bloodthirsty as its role in Indonesia, for it tried to initiate the massacre, and it did everything in its power to encourage Suharto.'[32]

The Congress and the mainstream American press welcomed the bloody events as the 'gleam of light in Asia' . . . 'the West's best news for years in Asia' . . . 'hope where there once was none'. The American land invasion of Vietnam in March of that year, 1965, was now justified as providing a 'shield' behind which the Indonesian generals were encouraged to carry out their important anti-communist work.[33]

The British Labour government did not stand in their way. A year after the extermination campaign, Foreign Secretary Michael Stewart visited Indonesia and reported 'reach[ing] a good understanding' with the Foreign Secretary, Adam Malik, a 'remarkable man' who was 'resolved to keep his country at peace'.[34] This remarkable man was to play a key role in the events that led to the second great slaughter, in East Timor.

In September 1974 Australia's prime minister, Gough Whitlam, met President Suharto at the village of Wonosobo in Java. According to well-informed journalists travelling with him, Whitlam's clear signal to Suharto was that East Timor was his for the taking. Under the headline, 'Canberra aim for Timor: go Indonesian', Hugh Armfield of the Melbourne *Age* conveyed the background briefing he was given by Australian officials. 'Australia is expected to take a significant step in the next few weeks', he wrote, 'towards ensuring that the tiny enclave on Timor becomes part of Indonesia. Australia and Indonesia are likely to make a joint approach to Portugal, urging that this is the only practical solution for its 450-year-old colony . . . Mr. Whitlam and President Suharto agreed last weekend that the best and most realistic future for Timor was association with Indonesia'.[35]

Peter Hastings of the *Sydney Morning Herald*, who was close to the Whitlam entourage, reported, 'Mr. Whitlam went much further, one suspects, than his Indonesian hosts required in publicly announcing, by means of a Foreign Affairs official press briefing, that "an independent Timor would be an unviable state and a potential threat to the area", even though the AAP report added that the Prime Minister is thought to have made clear that the people of the colony should have the ultimate decision on their future'.[36]

Some have argued that Whitlam's extraordinary, contradictory statements stemmed from disinterest, even ignorance. Certainly, applying his reasoning, it could be said that the small independent Pacific states of Nauru, Tonga, Samoa and Papua New Guinea were also 'unviable'. Peter Hastings later blamed Whitlam's advisers who, he wrote, 'furnished the Prime Minister with such an unsophisticated briefing before he left for Central Java to give away, without being asked, what was not his to give away.'[37]

Yet Gough Whitlam had built a reputation as a politician who did not rely on advisers. His actions remain a puzzle. Here was a man who defended even the right of the Baltic states to independence from the Soviet Union. He was the champion of the weak against the strong: of the Vietnamese against Nixon and Kissinger, of draft resisters at home, of the Palestinians and Cubans, and Polynesians suffering under France's nuclear tests. He was the first Australian prime minister to give land back to the Aborigines. His breadth of vision and determination to open up new horizons to the Australian people were, to my generation, without precedent; and perhaps here lies part of the explanation.

Whitlam wanted to lead Australia away from its Eurocentricity and give it a new, vital role in its own region. He wanted the great nations of Asia – China and Indonesia – to take white Australia seriously; and he was impatient to achieve this in what he must have known would be only a relatively brief period in office. 'Perhaps he perceived', wrote James Dunn who, like me, admired Whitlam, 'that [Australia] would have become bogged down in an acrimonious and confrontational dispute with Indonesia, which may have revived all the "yellow peril" fears of the past, forcing us back, as it were, into our isolationist and racist shell'.[38]

Whatever his motives, tiny East Timor became, to paraphrase a remark by the present Indonesian foreign minister, 'grit in his shoe'. What makes Whitlam even more of an enigma to his admirers is that, as the evidence of his misjudgement has mounted year upon year, he has taken a combative line, even flying to the United Nations in an attempt to get it to drop East Timor as an issue. In an article in the *Sydney Morning Herald* in 1991 he accused the Australian media of conducting a 'vendetta against Indonesia since the deaths of two television teams' and Fretilin of 'massacres' and general 'brutality' while not once referring to Indonesia's genocide. On the contrary, he heaped praise upon the Indonesian dictator. 'President Suharto is a reasonable and honourable man', he wrote. 'Every Australian ambassador will confirm that. It is outrageous what Australian newspapers and persons in public positions say about him and his Government ... In due course our correspondence and the records of our conversations will reveal the range and depth of our relationship'.[39] Did this 'range and depth' include discussion of Australia's responsibility towards a small and vulnerable neighbour and the predictable consequences of Indonesian aggression?

Within weeks of the Whitlam/Suharto meeting in Java, a clutch of generals close to Suharto launched a secret intelligence operation, code-named *Operasi Komodo*, aimed at destroying the East Timorese independence movement, which, far from being 'unviable', was then making significant progress.

In January 1975 Fretilin and its main opponent, UDT, established a united front to demand independence. This was short-lived. Agents of *Operasi Komodo* influenced UDT, creating divisions, distrust and eventually conflict. The UDT leaders were told independence was only possible if the 'communists' of Fretilin were 'neutralised'. Backed by Jakarta, UDT mounted a coup attempt with the Portuguese stepping aside and creating a political vacuum. This led to civil war and between 1,500 and 2,000 deaths. (When Indonesian officials and their foreign supporters attempt to explain the years of slaughter that followed the Indonesian invasion, they often blame the 'civil war' that lasted less than a month.)

During the coup attempt the Portuguese governor and administration left Dili for the nearby Atauro Island, to avoid being directly involved in the fighting. Fretilin had recently won a victory in local elections and was now firmly in control. Its popularity was confirmed by two Australian delegations that travelled widely in East Timor following the civil war. James Dunn was a member of a group from the Australian Council for Overseas Aid (ACOA). 'Whatever the shortcomings of the Fretilin administration', he reported, 'it clearly enjoyed widespread support from the population, including many hitherto UDT supporters . . . Australian relief workers visited most parts of Timor and, without exception, they reported that there was no evidence of any insecurity or any hostility towards Fretilin. Indeed, Fretilin leaders were welcomed warmly and spontaneously in all main centres by crowds of Timorese. In my long association with Portuguese Timor, which goes back fourteen years, I had never before witnessed such demonstrations of spontaneous warmth and support from the indigenous population.'[40]

With Portugal distracted by political upheaval at home and Fretilin the *de facto* government in East Timor, Western governments became alarmed. In July, the British Ambassador in Jakarta, Sir John Archibald Ford, sent his Head of Chancery to East Timor. 'The people of Portuguese Timor are in no condition to exercise the right of self-determination,' he reported. 'If it comes to the crunch and there is a row in the United Nations we should keep our heads down and avoid siding against the Indonesian Government.'[41] Ford recommended to the Foreign Office that it was in Britain's interests that Indonesia should 'absorb the territory as soon as and as unobtrusively as possible'.[42]

The US Secretary of State, Henry Kissinger, having recently watched American power and his own ambitions humiliated in the 'fall' of Saigon, signalled to Jakarta that the United States would not object if Indonesia invaded East Timor.[43] Within weeks a clandestine invasion began. On September 4, the CIA reported that 'two Indonesian special forces groups entered Portuguese Timor'. On September 17 the CIA reported, 'Jakarta is now sending guerrilla units into the Portuguese half of the island in order to engage Fretilin forces, encourage pro-Indonesian elements, and provoke incidents that would provide the Indonesians with an excuse to invade . . .'[44]

The CIA and other American intelligence agencies intercepted much of Indonesia's military and intelligence communications at a secret base run by the Australian Defence Signals Directorate (DSD) near Darwin. The information gathered was shared under treaty arrangements with Canberra and London and summarised in the *National Intelligence Daily*, published by the CIA, which was on President Ford's desk early each morning in 1975. Thus, Western governments knew well in advance Indonesia's intentions and the day-by-day detail of its covert operations. Moreover, leaked diplomatic cables from Jakarta, notably those sent by the Australian Ambassador Richard Woolcott, confirmed this.

Ambassador Woolcott reported that two of the principal conspirators, including Suharto's crony General Benny Murdani, had 'assured' him that when Indonesia decided to launch a full-scale invasion, Australia would get 'not less than two hours' notice'.[45] In one remarkable cable sent to Canberra in August 1975, Woolcott argued Indonesia's case and how Australian public opinion might be 'assisted'. 'What Indonesia now looks to from Australia, in the present situation,' he wrote, 'is some understanding of their attitude and possible action to assist public understanding in Australia rather than action on our part which could contribute to criticism of Indonesia'. The government could say publicly, Woolcott advised, that 'Australia cannot condone the use of force in Timor, nor could we accept the principle that a country can intervene in a neighbouring territory because of concern, however well based that concern might be, over the situation there. At the same time [we] could concede that Indonesia has had a prolonged struggle for national unity and could not be expected to take lightly a breakdown in law and order in Portuguese Timor . . .'

Woolcott proposed that '[we] leave events to take their course . . . and act in a way which would be designed to minimise the public impact in Australia and show private understanding to Indonesia of their problems . . . although', he added, 'we do not want to become apologists for Indonesia'. He concluded, 'I know I am recommending a pragmatic rather than a principled stand but that is what national interest and foreign policy is all about . . .'[46] There was not a word of concern for the interests or the fate of the East Timorese, who were, it was apparent, expendable.

On November 28, 1975, Fretilin leaders unilaterally declared independence, establishing the Democratic Republic of East Timor. Ministers were sworn in before a cheering crowd in Dili, the Portuguese flag was lowered after 450 years, and a new flag, red, black and yellow with a white star, was raised. Across the border in Indonesian West Timor, foreign minister Adam Malik, the author of 'whole-hearted' assurances that Indonesia had no designs on East Timor, said, 'Diplomacy is finished. The solution to the East Timor problem is now at the front line of battle.'[47] There had, of course, been no diplomacy; Indonesian troops were already inside East Timor.

By December 4, foreign aid workers, journalists and some Fretilin members and their families had been evacuated from Dili; the invasion was expected the following day. But that was also the day President Ford and Henry Kissinger were due to arrive in Jakarta on a visit described by a State Department official as 'the big wink'.[48] The Americans demanded that the Indonesians wait to invade until after the President had left; and on December 7, as Air Force One climbed out of Indonesian airspace, the bloodbath began.

CLEANING THE FIELD

THE INVASION FORCE was led by Ambassador Woolcott's confidant, General Benny Murdani. The inhabitants of Dili were subjected to what the historian John Taylor has described as 'systematic killing, gratuitous violence and primitive plunder'.[49] The former Bishop of Dili, Costa Lopez, said, 'The soldiers who landed started killing everyone they could find. There were many dead bodies in the street – all we could see were the soldiers killing, killing, killing.'[50] At 2 pm on December 9, fifty-nine men were brought on to the wharf at Dili harbour and shot one by one, with the crowd ordered to count. The victims were forced to stand on the edge of the pier facing the sea, so that when they were shot their bodies fell into the water. Earlier in the day, women and children had been executed in a similar way. An eye-witness reported, 'The Indonesians tore the crying children from their mothers and passed them back to the crowd. The women were shot one by one, with the onlookers being ordered by the Indonesians to count.'[51]

As in Pol Pot's Cambodia, the first to die were often minorities. The Chinese population was singled out. Five hundred were reportedly killed on the first day of the attack.[52] An eye-witness described how he and others were ordered to 'tie the bodies to iron poles, attach bricks and throw the bodies in the sea'.[53] In Maubara and Luiquica, on the north-west coast, the Chinese population was decimated.[54] The killing of whole families, and especially children, appeared to be systematic. Soldiers were described swinging infants in the air and smashing their heads on rocks, with an officer explaining, 'When you clean the field, don't you kill all the snakes, the small and large alike?'[55] 'Indonesian troops', wrote John Taylor, 'had been given orders to crush all opposition ruthlessly, and were told they were fighting communists in the cause of *Jihad* [Holy War], just as they had done in Indonesia in 1965.'[56]

When President Ford's plane touched down in Hawaii from Jakarta, he was asked for a reaction to the Indonesian invasion. He smiled and said, 'We'll talk about that later.' His press secretary added, 'The President always deplores violence, wherever it occurs.'[57] Returning to Washington, Kissinger summoned his senior staff to an emergency meeting at the State Department. According to the minutes of that meeting (marked 'Secret/Sensitive'), Kissinger was furious that he had been sent two cables reminding him that the Indonesians were breaking American law by using American weapons in the invasion. His fear was that the cables would be leaked and that Congress and the public would find out about his 'big wink' to the Suharto regime.

KISSINGER: On the Timor thing, that will leak in three months and it will come out that Kissinger overruled his pristine bureaucrats and violated the law. How many people . . . know about this?

STAFF MEMBER: Three.

KISSINGER: Plus everybody in this meeting, so you're talking about not less than 15 or 20. You have a responsibility to recognise that we are living in a revolutionary situation. Everything on paper will be used against me.[58]

Although clearly aware that the use of American arms was illegal, Kissinger sought to justify continuing to supply them by making the victim the aggressor. 'Can't we construe a Communist government in the middle of Indonesia as self-defence?' he asked. Told that this would not work, Kissinger gave orders that he wanted arms shipments 'stopped quietly', but secretly 'start[ed] again in January'.[59] In fact, as the killings increased, American arms shipments doubled.

Five days after the invasion, the United Nations General Assembly passed a resolution that 'strongly deplore[d]' Indonesia's aggression and called on it to withdraw its troops 'without delay'. The governments of the US, Britain, Australia, Germany and France abstained. Japan, the biggest investor in Indonesia, voted against the resolution. Ten days later, as Western intelligence agencies informed their governments of the scale of the massacres in East Timor, the Security Council unanimously called on 'all States to respect the territorial integrity of East Timor'. Again, Indonesia was ordered to withdraw its troops 'without delay'. This time the US, Britain and France voted in favour, not wanting to side publicly with the aggressor in such a public forum.[60]

This resolution authorised the Secretary-General, Kurt Waldheim, to send an envoy to East Timor to make an 'assessment'. But East Timor was quickly relegated by the Permanent Five – US, the Soviet Union, France, Britain and China – which showed no interest in backing the authority of the UN envoy, Winspeare Guicciardi. Six weeks after the invasion Guicciardi was allowed by the Indonesian military to visit Dili, but was so restricted and misled that his visit was worthless.

In a document prepared for Guicciardi's visit, the Indonesian military laid down guidelines to its battalion commanders and administrative officials, which became the model for subsequent visits by delegations of foreign officials. 'All members of the armed forces', the document read, 'must wear civilian dress so that it should appear to the delegation that they are unarmed civilians . . . Roads must be cleaned and free of military equipment'. Answers to questions such as 'What treatment is given to prisoners-of-war?' were to be rehearsed, with 'sensible soldiers playing the role of prisoners-of-war who are being well-treated . . . To ensure realism rations should be improved and those playing the part of prisoners must fulfil their role scrupulously.'

The document concluded: 'Banners of protest against UN

interference should be prepared, such as the following [in English in the original] – "United Nations hands off Timor! We are already integrated with Indonesia! United Nations we do not want your intervention here!" ' (This document was held in secret for twelve years by an official in the East Timorese civil service, and was finally smuggled into West Timor under the floor carpet of a car.)[61]

On February 4, 1976, the CIA reported the success of the charade: 'Jakarta has managed, during the UN representative's visit, to conceal all signs of Indonesian military forces...' The Portuguese offered the Secretary-General a warship so that his envoy could be landed in Fretilin-held areas. The CIA reported, 'The Indonesians are considering whether to sink the vessel before it reaches Darwin...'[62] This was enough to frighten away the United Nations. In striking contrast to action taken against Iraq in 1991, neither the Secretary-General nor the Western powers uttered a word in condemnation of Indonesia for failing to comply with a Security Council resolution, and for violating almost every human rights provision in the UN Charter. On the contrary, the US Government lent diplomatic support to the invasion.

In a secret cable to Kissinger on January 23, 1976, the United States Ambassador to the UN, Daniel Patrick Moynihan, boasted about the 'considerable progress' he had made in blocking UN action on a number of issues related to the developing world, and he mentioned East Timor. This, he explained, was part of 'a basic foreign policy goal, that of breaking up the massive blocs of nations, mostly new nations, which for so long had been arrayed against us in international forums'.[63] Later Moynihan wrote, 'The United States wished things to turn out as they did [in East Timor], and worked to bring this about. The Department of State desired that the United Nations prove utterly ineffective in whatever measures it undertook. This task was given to me, and I carried it forward with no inconsiderable success.'[64]

Moynihan also made clear that he understood the nature of his achievement. He referred to an admission by the Indonesian puppet 'deputy governor' of East Timor, Francisco Lopez de Cruz, that 60,000 people had already died by February 1976 and acknowledged that this was '10 per cent of the population, almost the proportion of casualties experienced by the Soviet Union during the Second World War'.[65] In 1980 Moynihan was the keynote speaker at a conference organised by the Committee for United Nations Integrity, which denounced the United Nations as 'no longer the guardian of social justice, human rights and equality among nations' because it is 'perverted by irrelevant political machinations' and is 'in danger of becoming a force against peace itself'.

In the week of the Indonesian invasion, while he was carrying out his assignment to undermine UN efforts on behalf of the people of East Timor, Moynihan was awarded the highest honour of the International League for the Rights of Man (now the International League for Human Rights) for his role as 'one of the most forthright advocates of human rights on the national and international scene'.[66]

America's support for Indonesia also had strategic Cold War motives. In August 1976, US Defence Department officials met the Australian prime minister, Malcolm Fraser, and cautioned him against straying from the position of his predecessor, Gough Whitlam. American 'security interests', reported the Melbourne *Age*, required the continuing 'goodwill' of the Suharto regime.[67] The Pentagon's uppermost concern was that American nuclear submarines should retain right of passage through the Ombai-Wetar deep-water channels that pass by East Timor. This was essential if the submarines were to continue to move undetected between the Indian and Pacific Oceans.[68]

Australia's compliance was nothing short of enthusiastic. In October of that year, Fraser flew to Jakarta and, in a speech to Indonesia's parliament, gave the first public recognition of the occupation of East Timor. At a press conference, he said his government now 'acknowledged the merger', but 'only for purely humanitarian reasons'.[69] Fraser was accompanied by J. B. Reid, managing director of the Broken Hill Proprietary Company (BHP), Australia's largest corporation. BHP had recently acquired a controlling share in the Woodside-Burmah company, which had been drilling for oil on and offshore from East Timor before the invasion. It was estimated that the seabed between East Timor and Australia, the 'Timor Gap', contained one of the richest oil and natural gas fields in the world.[70]

Ambassador Woolcott, in his cable the previous year recommending 'a pragmatic rather than a principled stand', had written, 'It would seem to me the Department [of Minerals and Energy] might well have an interest in closing the present gap in the agreed sea border and this could be much more readily negotiated with Indonesia . . . than with Portugal or independent Portuguese Timor'.[71]

Other Western governments vied with each other to 'sympathise with Indonesia's problems' by selling Jakarta arms – which, not surprisingly, were used in East Timor. The leading sympathiser was France, which supplied the Indonesian army with tanks and armoured cars and the air force with Alouette attack helicopters, ideal for low-flying 'counter-insurgency' in the mountainous interior of East Timor. In announcing the arms sale, reported *Le Monde* in September 1978, the French Government declared that it would abstain from any discussion in the United Nations about East Timor so as to avoid placing 'Indonesia in an embarrassing position'.[72]

At the same time, the British Labour Government signed a deal with Indonesia for four Hawk ground-attack aircraft. When asked about the implications for East Timor, the Foreign Secretary, David Owen, said that the estimates of the killings had been 'exaggerated' and that 'the most reliable estimates [are] at around 10,000, probably less [and] this includes the civil war . . .' He went on, 'Such a total is, in all conscience, tragic enough, but foreign observers, whom the Indonesians have allowed to visit East Timor, have reported that the scale of fighting since then has been greatly reduced.'[73]

The opposite was true. Owen's 'reliable estimates' of deaths merely reflected Indonesian propaganda, and, far from the scale of fighting being 'greatly reduced', the genocide was then actually reaching its height. Moreover, Western – mainly American – military equipment was now the main instrument of terror. Eye-witnesses to the onslaughts in East Timor spoke of scenes reminiscent of Dante's *Inferno*. 'After September [1978],' wrote a priest, 'the war intensified. Military aircraft were in action all day long. Hundreds of human beings die daily, their bodies left as food for the vultures. If bullets don't kill us, we die from epidemic disease; villages are being completely destroyed.'[74]

Canada, one of the leading Western investors in Indonesia, broke its own laws barring the export of weapons to areas of conflict simply by pretending that there was no fighting in East Timor. The Canadian Government claimed that 'groups opposed to the Fretilin political faction requested the assistance of Indonesia [and] made a formal request for the integration of East Timor, and Timor is now an integral part of Indonesia'.[75] Indonesia was also backed by its partners in the Association of South-East Asian Nations (ASEAN) and by most Islamic countries, by India, which had annexed Portuguese Goa in 1963, and by Japan, which looked to Indonesia for both commerce and vital oil supplies. The Soviet Union and its Eastern bloc allies split their votes in the UN over East Timor rather than upset their own burgeoning *realpolitik* with Indonesia.

As for Portugal, since the Governor's humiliating withdrawal to Atauro Island (the aptly named 'Isle of Goats'), the ineptitude of its handling of its responsibilities might have been excused by the enduring confusion in Lisbon. But the Portuguese appear to have taken, in secret, quite deliberate steps to 'solve the problem' of their colony.

In September 1974, the Portuguese foreign minister, Mário Soares, met his Indonesian counterpart, Adam Malik, and reportedly agreed that Portugal would not discourage support for East Timor's 'integration' with Indonesia. This led the deputy security chief in the Jakarta regime, Ali Murtopo, to remark that 'the problem of Portuguese Timor is now clear'.[76] The Indonesians may have distorted Soares' 'agreement'; certainly, in public Soares maintained that Portugal had a moral obligation to abide by the wishes of the East Timorese. However, when Ali Murtopo made an unpublicised visit to Lisbon a few weeks later, and described to Portuguese leaders Australia's accommodating attitude, he was, according to one account, told that full independence was 'unrealistic' and 'nonsense'.[77]

Six years later the ghosts of East Timor returned Hamlet-like to Portugal. A 1,000-page secret government report on East Timor was ordered declassified by President Antonio Eanes. It described a series of clandestine meetings between Portuguese and Indonesian officials in which Lisbon's left-wing government accommodated Jakarta. At the last of these meetings, in Hong Kong in June 1975, the Portuguese told the Indonesians they had drafted East Timor's decolonisation statute in such a way that it would give them a year to try to persuade the population to accept integration with Indonesia. If this was rejected, and Indonesia chose to use force, 'the Portuguese Government is not prepared to create problems, and could easily send a ship to Timor to evacuate all Portuguese'.[78]

David Munro and I had planned a documentary film about East Timor for more than a year. We wanted to pick up where Max Stahl's exposé had left off and to find out what had happened to those who had 'disappeared' following the massacre in the Santa Cruz cemetery in November 1991; and we wanted to ask why other atrocities and injustices had remained unchallenged for so many years. We intended to film in Portugal, Australia, the United States, Britain and in East Timor, if that was possible. An eye-witness report was crucial; and whether we could get into East Timor with cameras, and get our film out, would determine whether or not the project went ahead. It would be a relatively expensive operation; and although Central Television was prepared to stand most of the cost, another backer was needed.

Australia seemed the most likely place to look for funding.

For geographical and historical reasons there is perhaps a greater awareness of East Timor's suffering in Australia than in any Western country, apart from Portugal. In 1992 I approached the Australian Film and Finance Corporation in Sydney for co-production money. The AFFC at first welcomed my application, while reminding me that final approval rested on a 'pre-sale' commitment by an Australian broadcaster to air the film on Australian television. All my films have been shown in Australia. Curiously, there were no takers for this one. Cost was given as the reason. Shortly afterwards an AFFC official phoned me in London. 'Timor', she said, 'is too much of a political hot potato in Australia while there is a Labor Government in power.'[79]

The 'special relationship' the Australian establishment believes it has with Jakarta involves communications and the profitable commercial sharing of satellite 'footprints'.[80] In 1993 the Australian Broadcasting Corporation (ABC) began transmitting programmes to Asia via an Indonesian satellite, the 'Palapa', to broadcast programmes to Asia. This 'packaging' venture is to include a reciprocal deal with Indonesia's TPI network, which is controlled by Suharto's eldest daughter. It has been described as a 'showcase for Australia'. According to the *Sydney Morning Herald*, the Australian programmes will need to be 'encoded to meet the requirements of the [Indonesian] Ministry of Information . . . Many Asian governments . . . are very concerned about unwelcome political messages raining on viewers from satellites . . . Given the Australian media's touchy relationship with Jakarta, the prospect of the ABC using an Indonesian satellite to broadcast current affairs must be questionable'.[81]

Editorial guidelines for the ABC's satellite signal are laid down in a document drawn up by Radio Australia management, which is headed by a career diplomat. While insisting that journalists should not 'distort or censor' material in order to avoid offending Asian governments, the managers say that material critical of regimes should be broadcast in 'circumspect' language. 'Discreet understatement', said the document, 'is better than melodramatic embellishment' and it warns against the portrayal of 'fanatical separatists . . . freedom fighter terrorists'.[82] How the genocide in East Timor can be reported with 'discreet understatement' is not explained, neither is it made clear which 'freedom fighters' the officials consider 'fanatical' and 'terrorist'.

In 1977 the Indonesian regime threatened to close down the ABC's bureau in Jakarta after its correspondent in Washington, Ray Martin, reported that the Indonesians were using Napalm in East Timor. The threat was relayed to Martin personally by the director general of the ABC, who demanded to know why his scoop had not been verified by other media coverage. (It was.) In 1981 the ABC office in Jakarta was closed down after Radio Australia's reporting of the famine in East Timor, which was the direct result of the Indonesian occupation. It was re-opened in 1990 only after 'careful negotiations'. In future, reported the *Sydney Morning Herald*, 'officials of the Department of Foreign Affairs and Trade are to have regular meetings with the corporation [the ABC], as it has already done with Radio Australia, to discuss where problems with the service might arise'.[83] No problems have arisen. ABC correspondents in Jakarta dutifully report the pronouncements and denials of the regime. After rare videotape of the East Timorese resistance leader, Koni Santana, was made available to the new satellite service, it was 'lost' en route to the Darwin studios.

In November 1991 British photographer Steve Cox, who was a witness to the Santa Cruz massacre, was the only passenger on a flight from Timor to be body-searched by Australian Customs officials when it landed at Darwin. 'They looked at every passport and picked me out,' he said. 'It was clear they had been tipped off and were looking for my film. They were disappointed. I had given it to another passenger, who hid it in her clothing.'[84]

We planned to enter East Timor in three 'teams'. David and

I would go first, followed by Ben Richards,* a voluntary aid worker, and Max Stahl. Each of us would have a Hi–8 video camera, which is not much bigger than a professional stills camera. David had designed a bag with concealed compartments in which the camera operated through a gauze screen. We had started out with a number of eccentric ideas for disguises – priests was one rejected early, followed by ornithologists, although we did acquire the latest volume of *Birds of Borneo, Java and Bali* in preparation for a period of study.

This, however, was overtaken by 'Adventure Tours', which, according to a draft brochure I wrote, offered 'a new concept in developing third world tourism' that promised 'hard currency of the kind only tourism brings'. In 1989, when it was thought that Fretilin was beaten, the Jakarta regime decided to lift the 'batik curtain' around East Timor just enough, it hoped, to improve its international image and to be able to say that its '27th province' was not closed to the outside world. A policy of 'openness' was declared and a few tourists were permitted to travel to Dili, where they were restricted and watched. Tourism, believed the generals, would legitimise their hold on East Timor.

Although the massacre in the Santa Cruz cemetery had set back 'openness', we believed we stood a reasonable chance of success disguised as 'travel consultants'. A London travel agency provided us with documents which lauded our business acumen and which we had translated into *Bahasa Indonesia*. (Of course, if all else failed, we could talk authoritatively about the *Lorico*, Timor's 'curiously small parrot'.) In the meantime, Ben would be travelling on 'aid business'; and Max would acquire yet another identity. We expected one or two of us to be caught, probably David and myself. One successful camera would be enough. We agreed to meet again in six weeks.

Ben and Max flew direct to Indonesia; David and I flew to Australia. In the warm, late southern winter, Sydney, my hometown, was welcoming. I had arranged to meet former

* Like Max Stahl, Ben Richards is a pseudonym.

Ambassador Richard Woolcott, now retired as head of the Department of Foreign Affairs. Standing in front of a spectacular Javanese painting in the dining-room of his flat overlooking Sydney Harbour, he seemed the embodiment of a career diplomat, courteous, with a constant faint smile.

I reminded him of his leaked 1975 cable recommending a 'pragmatic rather than a principled approach' to East Timor. He said that what had happened since had been 'rather disappointing and rather tragic'. 'At that time', he said, 'I saw no intrinsic reason why the East Timorese would not be as comfortable within the Republic of Indonesia as were the rest of the Timorese.'

I suggested that what the Indonesians had done to them amounted to genocide. He disagreed; neither did he believe the figure of 200,000 dead. 'There was a civil war raging,' he said. I replied that it was generally accepted that no more than 2,000 people had died in the civil war. 'I don't know that figure,' he replied.

He said that Australians did not have 'the luxury' of Europeans 'to read moral lectures' to Indonesia, and that the Suharto regime was 'moderate, tolerant and stable'. He said it was 'a myth' that journalists could not visit East Timor, that 'thirty Australian journalists' had been there since 1976. As for the two Australian television crews murdered by the Indonesian army, they were 'unwise to be where they were'.

'The Indonesians', he said, 'are highly sensitive and feel that journalists may well cause further trouble, as happened of course after the massacre of 1991.' I suggested that the 'trouble' had been caused by the Indonesian troops who murdered several hundred people. 'I don't know the truth of this,' he said. 'Some of the journalists were there on tourist visas and had played a part in the stirring up of the trouble.' He added, 'That doesn't justify what happened.'

I asked him if he was seriously suggesting that the action of journalists had led to the massacre in the Santa Cruz cemetery. He replied no, but that was what the Indonesians had put forward. 'The trouble with the world we live in,' he said, '[is that] there has been a very substantial focus on East

Timor [and] it's not the only trouble spot on earth by any manner of means.'[85]

James Dunn also looked the diplomat he once was, as Australia's consul in Dili, though he will be remembered for his tireless personal campaign to break the international silence on East Timor. His book, *Timor: A People Betrayed*, published in 1983 by the tiny Jacaranda Press in Queensland and long out of print, is one of the finest documents of human tragedy, struggle and betrayal I have read. 'I think it is incredible', he told me, 'that the resistance continues with no outside help. It is such a tribute to the East Timorese. I recall one of them saying to me, "Although we have to work with the Indonesians we all support the armed resistance, because it's a spark . . . a spark that shows it isn't over, that somewhere out there some of us are saying, "You can't get away with this".'[86]

'You can't get away with this' could be the title of Shirley Shackleton's autobiography, should she ever decide to write it. I hope she does. The murder of her husband Greg and of his five Australian television colleagues, the cover-up that followed and Shirley's odyssey to find the truth say much about what has happened to the Timorese themselves. When we met in Canberra she spoke only about the Timorese, their courage and ingenuity, and about a recent meeting at the Department of Foreign Affairs between herself, the minister, Gareth Evans, and Amelia Gusmao, wife of the Fretilin leader given a twenty-year prison sentence by an Indonesian kangaroo court.

'Evans didn't want this meeting,' she said. 'But we wouldn't be put off. When he saw us, he put his hand over his heart, looked sorrowful and said, "We can't endanger our relations with the Indonesians. What little influence we have we want to keep." I said, "Are you going to take on Xanana as a special case?" He said nothing. Well, I did it, I broke down, I said, "My husband's dead, but this woman's husband is still alive. You can do something for him." I didn't want to cry, I tell you I didn't want to cry, not there, not in front of him.

Because then they have me typed; I'm the widow, you see, and I can be dismissed. But I won't be . . .'[87]

When the Indonesians launched their secret invasion in September 1975 no proof had been produced that they were operating inside East Timor. So they could continue to lie that the 'instability' in the island was due entirely to the civil war. At 4 am on October 16, Indonesian special forces came ashore on the north coast, near Balibo. The defending Fretilin troops had between them only one machine-gun and quickly withdrew, leaving the two Australian crews. They were Greg Shackleton, aged 29, a television reporter, and Tony Stewart, 21, a sound recordist, both Australians with Channel 7, Melbourne; Malcolm Rennie, 28, a British citizen and a reporter with Channel 9 in Melbourne; Brian Peters, 29, also British, who was the cameraman accompanying Rennie; and Gary Cunningham, 27, a New Zealander and the second cameraman.

Greg Shackleton and the others knew the risks they were taking. From the battlements of the old Portuguese fort they had filmed the Indonesian warships approaching. They must have expected to be captured, but they also had reason to believe they would be released quickly, given the 'special relationship' between Indonesia and Australia. They went to some lengths to demonstrate that they were non-combatants. They were unarmed and dressed in non-military clothing, and Greg Shackleton had painted a large 'Australia' sign and an Australian flag on the whitewashed wall of the house where they were based.

But staying on was very dangerous and demonstrated a real commitment to getting the evidence they had come for. As Greg Shackleton's last recorded words indicated, he felt deeply about helping the East Timorese. This is his last 'camera piece', filmed on the eve of his death:

'Something happened here last night that moved us very deeply. It was so far outside our experience as Australians, and so inextricably interwoven with the atmosphere of this place, that we find it very difficult to convey to you watching in an Australian living-room; but we'll try. We were brought

to this tiny native village from Maliana because we were tor
that Maliana was not safe at night. When we arrived the
second in charge, who speaks very little English, came to us
and in a haunting but urgent way said the commander
wanted to speak to us. And then for the next hour, sitting
on woven mats under a thatched roof in a hut with no walls
we were the target of a barrage of questioning from men
who know they may die tomorrow and cannot understand
why the rest of the world does not care. Why, they ask, are
the Indonesians invading us? Why, they ask, if the Indonesians believe that Fretilin is communist do they not send a
delegation to Dili to find out? Why, they ask, are the Australians not helping us?

'My main answer was that Australia would not send forces
here – that's impossible. However, I said, we could ask that
Australia raise this fighting at the United Nations. That was
possible. At that the second in charge rose to his feet,
exclaimed, "*Commerado* journalist", and shook my hand,
the rest shook my hand and we were applauded because we
were Australians. That's all they want – for the United
Nations to care about what is happening here.

'The emotion here last night was so strong that we, all
three of us, felt we should be able to reach out into the warm
air and touch it. This is Greg Shackleton at an unnamed
village which we'll remember forever, in Portuguese Timor.'[88]

The next day, one of the cameramen filmed the Indonesians
entering the village. He was shot. The others pointed franti-
cally to the 'Australia' sign, and they were shot and stabbed.
A retreating Fretilin soldier who saw this was interviewed by
the Australian journalist Roger East, who himself met the
same fate less than two months later. He told East, 'The
Australians were screaming, "Australians, Australians!" with
their hands up. The soldiers circled them and made them
turn their backs and face the wall of the house. The firing
died down and we crawled away through the undergrowth.
We heard the Australians screaming and then there was a
burst of automatic fire.'[89]

Shirley Shackleton has also spoken to eye-witnesses. 'What

..appened', she said, 'was that most of them were strung up by their feet, their sexual organs were removed and stuffed into their mouths, and they were stabbed with the short throwing knives that the Indonesian soldiers carry. Nobody knows for sure whether they choked to death or whether they choked on their own blood, or whether they just died from their wounds or whether they bled to death.'[90]

The bodies were dragged into the house, where one was found to be still alive. This may have been young Tony Stewart, the sound recordist. Although terribly wounded, he tried to say something into his tape recorder. According to one report, a Timorese reached out to him but was ordered back by an Indonesian officer, who then shot dead the wounded man.[91] The bodies were stripped and dressed in Portuguese uniforms, of the kind used by Fretilin, and the corpses propped up behind a captured machine-gun in front of the 'Australia' sign. An Indonesian soldier took photographs which were intended to 'prove' that the journalists had been fighting for Fretilin. The bodies were then burned.

There is little doubt that the journalists were killed not out of any misunderstanding in the heat of battle, but because they would have exposed Indonesia's conspiracy to invade and to which their own governments were privy. The news reports of Greg Shackleton and Malcolm Rennie would have almost certainly forced the Australian Government to modify its appeasement of Jakarta. 'What is particularly disturbing', wrote James Dunn, 'is that the Whitlam Government knew about the impending attack [on Balibo] some days before it took place. [I] was warned about it by a sensitively placed senior official ... Five days later US intelligence analysts, using information to which Australia had access, advised their government that the attack would be launched in a few days. Thus, the government had at its disposal enough information – and enough time – to warn Australians in East Timor of the impending risks at the border. More importantly, they could have advised the Indonesians of the presence of journalists in the area, and stressed that they should be afforded protection appropriate to their status.'[92]

According to Australian journalist Jill Jolliffe, on the ⟨
the journalists were murdered, the Australian Associate
Press bureau in Darwin was informed by telephone by the
Department of Foreign Affairs that 'something big' was
about to happen in East Timor that day. The 'something big'
had already happened that very morning. When the call
came, the journalists had been dead for four hours.[93]

The Australian Government made no formal, public protest to Jakarta. Two of the dead were Britons; the British
Government said nothing. The official Australian response
was first to try to blame the victims, then to feign that 'no
definitive information' had 'yet come to hand'.[94] According
to the then Foreign Affairs Minister, Senator Don Willesee,
the journalists were 'missing' at 'the scene of heavy fighting
between rival factions'.[95] Willesee referred to a Fretilin soldier
who had 'described the entry of anti-Fretilin forces into
Balibo'.[96] James Dunn, who was present at the interview with
the soldier, wrote that what he 'actually described was the
entry of *Indonesian* troops' into the village where the television teams were.[97]

More than two weeks elapsed before Prime Minister Whitlam took action. This was in the form of a letter to Suharto
in which he sought his friend's co-operation in determining
the fate of the newsmen. Six months later the government of
Malcolm Fraser agreed to participate in an Indonesian
enquiry, which was stage-managed to the point of farce.
'Despite its knowledge of the true facts,' wrote Dunn, the
government 'agreed to this futile exercise in a deliberate
attempt to dispose of an obstacle to the normalisation of
relations between Jakarta and Canberra.'[98]

On April 28, 1976, Australian embassy officials flew from
Jakarta to East Timor. Witnesses to the killings had already
been moved out of Balibo by the army; and the 'Timorese' the
Australian officials met were Indonesian soldiers 'specially
selected from among the troops originating from neighbouring islands where the people resemble the Quemac of
the Balibo area'.[99] Others were trusted agents working for
Operasi Komodo, the Indonesians' subversion campaign, and

ell-known collaborators who went on to occupy high positions in the puppet administration of East Timor, including
the 'governor' and 'vice-governor'.

Unsurprisingly, the official report submitted to the Australian Parliament was inconclusive on just how the journalists
were killed and who killed them. A funeral service was held at
a cemetery in Jakarta with a wreath sent from the Australian
embassy and a card, which read, 'They stayed because they
saw the search for truth and the need to report at first hand
as a necessary task'.[100] Shirley Shackleton's response to this
platitude was understandable outrage. The Department of
Foreign Affairs in Canberra told her that if she wanted her
husband's body brought back to Australia, she would have
to pay for it.

Shirley travelled to East Timor in 1989, at the time of the
Pope's visit to Dili. In the Hotel Turismo she confronted
General Murdani, who commanded the invasion and whose
troops had killed her husband and his colleagues. 'He was
having breakfast in the dining-room,' she told me. 'People
were genuflecting and grovelling to him. After drinking a
double-strength coffee I walked over to his table and said,
"General, my name is Shirley Shackleton. I've always wanted
to ask you what exactly happened to my husband and his
colleagues." He said, "I wouldn't know; we weren't there." I
said to come off it, that Greg had filmed his ships arriving
at Balibo before he had been killed.

'At this he stood up to go; and I realised that for once in
my life I had absolute power over this man, because everyone
was watching and he wouldn't dare be rude to me. So I put
my hand on his elbow and said, "*Sit down*, because we're
not going to get anywhere with that, but I'd like to tell you
what I've seen in the time I've been in Timor." He sat and
he listened as I told him about the atrocities committed by
his troops. I told him that a lot of young men they were now
torturing had Indonesian fathers and were the result of the
rapes of Timorese women. I said the Timorese would never
accept the Indonesians under any circumstances. He said
nothing. He knows who I am now.'

A LAND OF CROSSES

DAVID AND I flew from Sydney to Bali with a plane-load of happy Australian tourists. We caught an internal flight to Kupang in Indonesian West Timor. Not far from where Captain Bligh had sought refuge after the mutiny on the *Bounty*, we found 'Teddy's Bar'. We explained to Teddy about 'Adventure Tours', that we needed a four-wheel drive vehicle and a driver who knew the mountains in the east. He could provide both, but reminded us that foreigners needed special documentation to cross the border. We paid him and left.

It was early Sunday morning as the road reached down to the sea, and the border came into view. The bags with the cameras were beneath the seats. We wound up the tinted windows, and I lay down in the back. Ahead of us was a minibus spilling out its occupants for inspection of their papers. 'Don't stop,' we directed the Timorese driver. 'Drive around it.' The police on duty had walked back to their cabin. We accelerated and were through.

Now the faces changed. In the west of the island people had smiled and waved; here, they almost never did. On the roadside they invariably looked away. The young and the old did not stare; young men consciously turned their backs.

Working with the aeronautical map and its blank spaces, we turned inland to get away from the main military route. On the horizon was a line of black smoke and fire. This was the traditional method of agriculture known as slash-and-burn, wherein the burnt scrub temporarily enriches the soil. The effect was three-dimensional, a harsh, almost menacing landscape. Yet we had only just climbed away from the

271

ɔastal belt, with its lines of sugar palms. Ahead was a plateau of savannah that looked like the vast outback of Australia. Ghost gums rose out of grass almost as tall, then this changed without notice to a forest of dead, petrified trees: black needles through which skeins of fine white sand drifted, like mist. On the edge of this stood the surreal crosses.

They are almost everywhere; great black crosses etched against the sky, crosses on peaks, crosses in tiers on the hillsides, crosses beside the road, overlooking white slabs. I have seen graves and crosses like these in the north of Portugal, where they are stark symbols of the rhythm of life and death in an impoverished corner of Europe. There, you pass them without comment. In East Timor they litter the earth and crowd the eye. Walk into the scrub and they are there, always it seems, on the edge, a riverbank, an escarpment, commanding all before them.

The inscriptions on some are normal: those of generations departed in proper time and sequence. But look at the dates of these, and you see that they are all prior to 1975, when proper time and sequence ended. Look at the dates on most of them and they reveal the extinction of whole families, wiped out in the space of a year, a month, a day. 'R.I.P. Mendonca, Crismina, 7.6.77 ... Mendonca, Filismina, 7.6.77 ... Mendonca, Adalino, 7.6.77 ... Mendonca, Alisa, 7.6.77 ... Mendonca, Rosa, 7.6.77 ... Mendonca, Anita, 7.6.77 ...'

I had with me a hand-drawn map of where to find a mass grave where some of the murdered of the 1991 massacre in the Santa Cruz cemetery had been dumped; I had no idea that much of the country was a mass grave, marked by paths that end abruptly, and fields inexplicably bulldozed, and earth inexplicably covered with tarmac; and by the legions of crosses that march all the way from Tata Mai Lau, the highest peak, 10,000 feet above sea level, down to Lake Tacitolu where a Calvary line of crosses looks across to where the Pope said mass in 1989 in full view of a crescent of hard, salt sand beneath which, say local people, lie human remains.

We approached Balibo, where the Australian television teams had died. We could not see the whitewashed house on which Greg Shackleton had painted 'Australia' before the murders. Shirley also had been unable to find it and believes it has been demolished. The main road wound past the church where Shirley had planted a tree for Greg in 1989. She had struggled to get permission for this, with the Indonesians saying no as it would, they said, admit liability for the murders. Finally, a priest offered the yard behind his church, and prepared a plot; and Shirley was allowed to plant the sapling with Indonesian troops surrounding her, sealing off the vicinity.

'They had not allowed any Timorese to be there,' she said. 'But as I kneeled, saying a few words to Greg, the most wonderful singing washed over me. On the other side of the road, a young people's choir had timed its practice to my being there. I shall never forget those beautiful voices. They came through the barrier the Indonesians had set up between us, and they comforted me. You see, that's how the resistance works; everything is pre-arranged but never appears to be. They will never be defeated.'

The road out of Balibo snaked up through the mountains, with the four-wheel drive easing us around the strewn tree trunks with inches to spare and boulders suspended above as if on invisible wire. 'Gerry', our driver, pumped the brake pedal and leaned back on the handbrake like you do on the oars of a dinghy. It was becoming clear why the untried Indonesian army had taken years to get the better of Fretilin. This was guerrilla terrain, as difficult for outsiders to negotiate as any I have known.

Coming down the spine of the mountains, we were swallowed by folds of baked eroded red earth and by the silence. People seemed absent; but they were there. From the highest crest the road plunged into a ravine that led us to a river bed, then deserted us. The four-wheel drive forded the river and heaved out on the other side, where a boy sat motionless and mute, his eyes following us. Behind him was a village, overlooked by the now familiar rows of whitewashed slabs and black crosses. We were probably the first outsiders the people here had seen for a very long time. The diffident expressions, long cultivated for the Indonesians, changed to astonishment. We had entered, without knowing, a kind of prison.

The village straddled the road, laid out like a military barracks with a parade ground and a police post at either end. Unusually, the militia were trusted Timorese. The remoteness might explain this; the Indonesians remain terrified of Fretilin. That week a patrol of nine Indonesian soldiers had been ambushed and killed. People were moved here from their homes so they could be easily controlled. The village was a 'resettlement centre', similar to the 'strategic hamlets' invented by the Americans in Vietnam as a means of separating the population from the guerrillas. To the Timorese, the 'control areas', as the army calls them, are little better than concentration camps, which they cannot leave without a 'travel pass'. As a consequence, their ability to grow food is extremely limited. In the late 1970s and early 1980s famine claimed many thousands of lives, on a scale likened by international relief officials to the war-related cataclysms that had hit Biafra in the mid-1960s and Cambodia in 1979–80.

Although we saw no starvation, many people were terribly malnourished.[101] Camps such as this are also known as 'model plantations' and produce mostly cash crops for an export trade controlled by an Indonesian company, P. T. Denok, which was set up by generals close to Suharto. P. T. Denok monopolises the trade in sandalwood, cumin, copra and cloves; all the coffee grown in Timor, one of the finest Arabica coffees in the world, is controlled by the generals' front company.[102]

After we had turned south, towards Suai, we saw other camps where many of the faces were Javanese: the product of the 'transmigration programme' designed to unravel the fabric of Timorese life and culture and eventually to reduce the indigenous population to a minority. Meanwhile, the East Timorese are themselves encouraged to 'migrate' to Irian Jaya, Sumatra and West Kalimantan, where there is work and where they remain permanently displaced. From a distance watched a flag-raising ceremony in one of these 'villages Javanese cheer-leaders led a motley group of farmers, who were forced to stand to attention and cry out their allegiance in *Bahasa Indonesia*, a foreign language.

In Suai, the centre for oil drilling on the south coast, militarism seemed to invade all life. Traffic stopped for marching schoolgirls, jogging teachers and anthem-singing postmen ('*Tanah Airku*: My Fatherland Indonesia'). Billboards announced the 'correct' way to live each day 'in the spirit of Moral Training'. In an Orwellian affront to the Timorese, one billboard told them, 'Freedom is the right of all nations', quoting Indonesia's own declaration of independence. This is known as the 'New Order'.

'It is the Indonesian civilisation we are bringing [to East Timor],' said the Indonesian military commander in 1982. 'And it is not easy to civilise backward people.'[103] 'Feeble mentality is still very evident among the Timorese,' explained the Indonesian Armed Forces' magazine. '[Such] low social, economic, mental conditions are the source of many negative features because they result in extremely inappropriate thought processes and experiences. The *Binpolda* [a kind of military brainwashing squad] have a great role to play in building village society if this is to proceed in accord with the programmes that have been decided upon. All the more is this so in East Timor where society so greatly yearns to be guided and directed in all spheres of life. Guiding the people is a process of communication whereas communication means conveying ideas or concepts for the purpose of creating uniformity.'[104]

Timorese occupy few jobs other than as drivers, waitresses and broom-pushers. In a café in Suai the Javanese owner, a portly young woman, flirted with lonely Javanese soldiers while a Timorese girl cooked, served and swept. As the Javanese emptied their bowls of noodles, they snapped their fingers and the girl cleaned around them, giggling nervously. On the wall was a gallery of posters of the Indonesian generals shot in the 1965 'communist coup'. They are the official

artyrs of the New Order. 'If President Suharto hadn't res-
ued the nation, and beaten the communists', we were told,
'Indonesia would have broken up into many pieces.' This
is the state's line, repeated incessantly on television and in
schools.

That the 'martyred' generals died in factional fighting
within the military, leaving Suharto to mount a real coup
and the extermination campaign that was the precursor to
East Timor's agony, is a truth uttered only at great personal
risk. In the New Order, Fretilin guerrillas are 'separatist delinquents' who 'threaten the break-up of the fatherland' and
must be 'wiped out' by the 'heroic people's army'.

Thousands were massacred in Suai in the late 1970s, their
bodies dumped on the oil-blackened coastline. The few Timorese who spoke to us publicly, drifting by the parked four-
wheel drive and muttering snatches of Portuguese and English out of the sides of their mouths, were terrified and, of
course, extraordinarily brave. Every street has a military
façade, with a variety of units, mostly special forces, housed
in former Portuguese villas or prefabricated houses,
announced by large signs and military insignia. Next to the
hostel where we stayed were the 'red berets', whose record
of slaughter is documented. In the heat I slept very little,
covered in an insect repellent so strong it melted the plastic
case of my watch. The sound of the night was the soldiers
next door playing country and western tapes, accompanied
by the melodic humming of mosquitoes that carried the *falci-
parum* strain of malaria, which can be fatal.

'Before the invasion we lived a typical island life, very peaceful,' said Abel.* 'People were always very hospitable to for-

* The identities of most Timorese interviewed inside and outside East Timor
are disguised, including those who insisted they could be identified, saying
they had 'nothing to lose'. The interviews were conducted by myself, and
by Max Stahl and Ben Richards.

eigners. Villagers would go about their daily lives, wor
in rice fields without constantly looking over their shoulde
worrying about the military or guns. I could get up at an
time and come back home at any time, go down to the river,
catch prawns or go hunting without any restriction. I had to
go to school to learn Portuguese. We had to learn to lead
a double life; you go to school to communicate with the
Portuguese, but once you are in a village you are totally
within the traditional village life. But if the Portuguese had
done what the Indonesians have done, the whole of East
Timor would have been populated by white Portuguese.
That's not to say there was no brutality from the Portuguese. Of course any colonial situation is always brutal. But
I think we were happy, yes I think so.

'It is difficult to describe the change since then, the darkness over us. Of fifteen in my immediate family only three
are left: myself, my mother and a brother who was shot and
crippled. My village was the last Fretilin base to fall to the
Indonesians in 1979. There was a massive bombardment.
People said that all the trees were blown off the rocks, whole
rocks became white. Because the land was very fertile; I mean
you can grow almost anything there; lots of people from
the lowlands went up there for protection. So it was over-
populated and very soon there wasn't enough to sustain the
number of people that were hiding there. Disease, and slow
starvation, also took a lot of people. I told you about my
family, but the estimate is that our clan has been reduced
from 5,000 to 500.

'Up until 1985 or 1986 most of our people were concentrated in what they called the central control areas, we lived
in concentration camps for a long, long time. Only in the
last three or four years have some of us been allowed to
return home, but we can be moved again at any time. We
are only allowed to go to specific areas to grow food. We have
to go there at a certain time in the morning and come back
at a certain time in the afternoon.

'Any step away from those guidelines is considered suspect.
Indonesians use local people to spy on the others. So there's

onstant fear of somebody always looking over your oulder. People usually know who the spies are and they earn to deal with it. Certain things are not to be said widely even within the family. People have to be careful what they say about the Indonesians, they have got to pretend that everything is okay, just accept what the Indonesians are doing to them. That is part of finding a way to survive for the next day. But a human body and mind have limitations and can only take so much. Once it boils over, people just come out and protest and say things which mean they will find themselves dead the next day. I suppose you can compare us to animals. When animals are put in a cage they always try to escape. In human beings it's much worse. I mean, we the people in East Timor call it the biggest prison island in the world. You must understand that. For us who live here, it's hell.'

Was it Primo Levi who said that the worst moment in the Nazi death camps was the recurring fear that people would not believe him when he told them what had happened, that they would turn away, shaking their heads? This 'radical gap' between victim and listener, as psychiatrists call it, is suffered *en masse* by the East Timorese, especially the exiled communities. 'Who knows about our country?' they ask constantly. 'Who can imagine the enormity of what has happened to us?'

'I was born in Timor in 1963,' said Constancio. 'When Indonesia invaded I was twelve years old, and I went to the jungle. I was on the run all the time. Then I crept back to Dili to see my family, and I was caught. I was only fourteen. I was tortured, but I survived. In 1990 I helped an Australian lawyer, Robert Domm, meet Xanana Gusmao, our resistance leader. After that they caught me again. It was my birthday; and they tortured me all over my body, so that blood came out from my mouth and my nose and my ears. There were so many of them, hitting me, in front and in the back, and down here in my genitals, many times, so many times. They'd start at nine o'clock in the morning and did not finish until midnight. They let me go; but I heard that I was supposed

to be arrested again, at two o'clock in the afternoon. I ha
no chance to say goodbye to my wife. That was over two
years ago.'

'Have you seen her since?' I asked.

'No, not once.'

'Do you have children?'

'When I went into hiding, my wife was six months pregnant. I have a son. But I have never seen him, except this
one photo I have just received. I look at it all the time . . .'

'What makes you keep on fighting?'

'Because of our *right* to independence. This is a universal
right; and a third of us have died for this right. Don't pity
me. Think of my wife. They keep on interrogating her, torturing her psychologically. This is her daily bread, and the daily
bread of our people, and it is mine, too.'

From the day of the invasion Fretilin gave the Indonesians a
shock. For two years those whom Jakarta had dismissed as
'primitives' held the interior to which most of the people had
fled. It was only the arrival of Western military equipment,
chiefly low-flying aircraft, that changed the course of the
war. Otherwise Fretilin might have forced the Indonesians to
negotiate their way out of East Timor.

Indeed, in 1983 Fretilin forces were in such command of
most areas outside the towns that the Indonesians agreed to
a ceasefire. Today, there are probably no more than 400
guerrillas under arms, yet they ensure that four Indonesian
battalions do nothing but pursue them. Moreover, they are
capable of multiplying themselves within a few days, for they
are the locus of a clandestine resistance that reaches into
every district and has actually grown in strength over the
years. In this way they continue to deny the fact of *integrasi*
– integration – with Indonesia.

Domingos is 40 years old and has been in the jungle since
1983. 'My wife was tortured and burnt with cigarettes,' he
said. 'She was also raped many times. She is now in Kraras.

In September this year [1993] the Indonesians sent the whole population of the village to find us. My wife came to me and said, "I don't want to see your face because I have been suffering too much . . ." At first I thought she was rejecting me, but it was the opposite; she was asking me to fight on, to stay out of the village and not to be captured and never to surrender. She said to me, "You get yourself killed and I shall grieve for you, but I don't want to see you in their hands. I'll never accept you giving up!" I looked at her, and she was sad. I asked her if we could live together after the war, and she said softly, "Yes, we can." She then walked away, back to Kraras.'

Kraras is known by the Timorese as the 'village of the widows' because of the slaughter that took place there. During the summer of 1983 a whole community of 287 people was massacred here. One of them was the man who saved Steve Stevenson's life, Celestino dos Anjos, who, like most of them, was forced with his family to dig his own grave, then shot. I found Celestino's name on a list compiled in Portuguese by a priest who had passed it to Max Stahl. In a meticulous hand he recorded the name, age, cause of death and date and place of death of every one of these people murdered by the Indonesian army in the district of Bilbeo. In the last column he identified the battalion responsible for every murder.

Every time I pick up this list, I find it difficult to put down, as if each death is fresh on the page. Like the ubiquitous crosses, it records the Calvary of whole families, and bears witness to genocide . . . Feliciano Gomes, aged 50, Jacob Gomes, aged 50, Antonio Gomes, aged 37, Marcelino Gomes, aged 29, Joao Gomes, aged 33, Miguel Gomes, aged 51, Domingos Gomes, aged 30 . . . Domingos Gomes, aged 2 . . . 'shot'.

So far I have counted forty families, including many children: Kai and Olo Bosi, aged 6 and 4 . . . 'shot' . . . Marito Soares, aged one year . . . 'shot' . . . Cacildo dos Anjos, aged 2 . . . 'shot'. He must have been Celestino's grandson. There are babies on the list as young as three months. At the end

of each page, the priest imprinted his name with a rub
stamp, which he asked not to be publicised 'in the interes
of personal security'. Using a typewriter whose ribbon had
seen better days, he addressed this eloquent, angry appeal to
the world:

'The international community continues to miss the point
in the case of East Timor. There is only one crime, only
one criminal. To the capitalist governors, Timor's petroleum
smells better than Timorese blood and tears. How long do
the Indonesians think they can imprison, torture and kill?
This is what the Timorese people in their concentration
camps have asked themselves since 1975. It has always been
a question without an answer.

'It even seems as if it is the United Nations itself that is
easing the path of the aggressor, giving it the time and conditions necessary to execute the ethnic and cultural genocide
of the Timorese people and, finally, declare that East Timor
is definitely integrated into the Indonesian Republic. Unfortunately the UN and the international community are the only
viable solution for this tragedy but they have to be consistent
with their condemnation of the 1975 invasion, and not leave
it to the following year, since each year the level of extermination increases.

'So who will take the truth to the world? Sometimes the
press and even the international leaders give the impression
that it is not human rights, justice and truth that are para-
mount in international relations, but the power behind a
crime that has the privilege and the power of decision. It
is evident that the invading government would never have
committed such a crime, if it had not received favourable
guarantees from governments that should have a more
mature sense of international responsibility. Governments
must now urgently consider the case of East Timor, with
seriousness and truth. They must insist and advocate full
Human Rights: the right of the Timorese people to independence.'

*

e drove into Dili in the early afternoon. It was quiet: not ne quiet of a town asleep in the sun but of a place where something cataclysmic had happened and which was not immediately evident. Fine white colonial buildings faced a waterfront lined with trees and a promenade fitted with ancient stone benches. At first the beauty of this seemed uninterrupted. From the lighthouse, past Timor's oldest church, the Motael, to the long-arched façade of the governor's offices and the four ancient cannon with the Portuguese royal seal, the sea was polished all the way to Atauro Island where the Portuguese administration had fled in 1975. Then, just beyond a marble statue of the Virgin Mary, the eye collided with rusting landing craft strewn along the beach. They had been left as a reminder of the day Indonesian marines came ashore and killed the first people they saw: women and children running down the beach, offering them food and water, as frightened people do.

At dawn the next day we walked the length of the beach to the stone pier where people were brought to be shot and their families and friends ordered to count as each body fell into the water. I wanted to record a tribute to Roger East, the Australian journalist who went to East Timor early in November 1975, and stayed to his death. East had been outraged at the killing of Greg Shackleton and his colleagues and sympathetic to Fretilin. Before leaving Darwin he told his sister, 'The people have been betrayed. Someone's got to go and get the truth out.'[105] His brother urged him to get a weapon, but East replied that he was 'too old for that' and had 'lived too long with just a typewriter'.[106]

Arriving in Dili he set up an East Timor news agency and made many friends among the Timorese, who appreciated his dry humour. When the Australian government urged its nationals to leave Dili, he was the only one to stay, in spite of the fact that Indonesian propaganda had called him a 'communist' and promised that he would 'share the fate' of the television crews. As the invasion began and Fretilin withdrew to the east of the city, East remained in the Hotel Turismo, on the seafront, typing a dispatch which he sent to

Australian Associated Press-Reuter in Darwin. Inexplicab
it was never used.

Roger East was caught in the street by Indonesian troops,
bound with wire and dragged to the pier where he could
hear the executions taking place. According to two eye-
witnesses, he kept up a stream of rich, Australian abuse until
the point of his death. He was told to face the sea; he refused
and was shot in the face. His body fell, with all the others,
into the 'sea of blood'. An Indonesian report later claimed
East was an armed revolutionary. After that, all knowledge
of him was denied. Like the aftermath of the Balibo murders,
an enquiry by the Australian Department of Foreign Affairs
came to nothing, and not a word of protest was lodged
publicly with Jakarta.

Staying at the Hotel Turismo, I could not get Roger East
out of my mind. My room was a haven for cockroaches and
spiders, and clearing a path through them was a prerequisite
for a trip to the cesspit of a bathroom. I thought about him
in this squalid and menacing place as he weighed up whether
to stay or go. What would I have done? I would have got out.
Roger East's memory deserves more than his government's
wretched obsequiousness to his killers.

Today, the Turismo is where Indonesian officers, their
hangers-on and local informers can be found. 'Who are you?'
we were asked at the reception. 'I see you are a company
director. What is your company?'

'Adventure Tours,' I replied.

When I recorded a 'camera piece' that morning on the
beach near the pier, under the noses of a group of Indonesian
soldiers and with the camera only partly concealed, I could
hear an echo of my words and felt deep inside me a cold fear
I had not previously known.

We were now being watched constantly and decided to
drive back into the mountains. Climbing the steep road out
of Dili, we passed a war memorial built by the Australian
veterans of the Timor campaign against the Japanese. Its
dedication read, 'To the Portuguese from Minho [a northern
Portuguese province] to Timor'. The memorial was intended

native Timorese who gave their lives for the Australians, but the inscription does not mention the word 'Timorese', because all Timorese were supposed to be Portuguese citizens.

Low cloud engulfed us, with crosses marking every bend, it seemed, all the way to Aileu. 'When they finally forced Fretilin to withdraw from Aileu in 1975', wrote James Dunn, 'Indonesian troops, in a brutal public spectacle, machine-gunned the remaining population of the town, except for children under the age of four, who were sent back to Dili in trucks. These infant survivors were ultimately to be placed in an orphanage near Jakarta, where the "poor victims of the Fretilin terror" were to become the subject of the charitable indulgence of Tien Harto (Suharto's wife) and her coterie of bored wives of the affluent and powerful in the Indonesian capital.'[107]

In the centre of Aileu is the mass grave of victims of the Japanese in 1942. On the hill above are statues depicting God and Jesus, smiling and surreal, and more crosses leading to yet another Calvary. There is no sign of the Indonesian massacre. From behind the tombs of the 1942 memorial, we attempted to evade local spies while filming marching students; once again, a whole town seemed to be marching and honouring the flag of its executioners. I had yet to become accustomed to this irony; it was as if prisoners were taking their exercise in a prison yard hung with bunting and accompanied by a brass band. 'Welcome to Timor,' said an old Timorese man in English sitting on the steps of a café. He stood and lunged for my hand. 'Welcome to the land of *free* people!' At this, he gave out a fine, false laugh, like a cackle. The Javanese owner of the café tapped his finger to his head and said, 'He's okay, just a little mad.'

None of the shops in Aileu is owned by a Timorese; all seemed to be Javanese. As one of the principal sponsors of the 'transmigration programme', the World Bank should be pleased with its success in transforming towns like Aileu. The World Bank is also the main backer of Indonesia's 'family planning programme' in East Timor. According to a senior bank official, 'There is no inherent contradiction between

284

the Indonesian government's population and transmigration programme. We believe that family planning is capable of providing important economic and social benefits to all concerned.'[108]

When the World Bank opened its 'family planning' headquarters in Dili in 1980 the puppet governor of East Timor, Mario Carrascalao, was more to the point. The aim of the programme, he said, was 'to prevent an increase in the population of the province'.[109] For the regime, there is, of course, no 'inherent contradiction' in reducing the East Timorese population while increasing the immigrant population. A senior Indonesian officer told Bishop Belo, 'We only need your land. We don't need people like you Timorese.'[110]

'In the village clinics,' said Christina, 'anything is possible. You have to do what the Indonesian doctors say. Many of the women are injected with *Depo Provera* without knowing what it is. Women have been sterilised when they come to the clinic for something else, even for medicine for their babies. They don't know what is happening, or they are told that it's okay by the *babinses* [the 'guidance officials', or brainwashers, in the resettlement camps]. We have lost so many people killed by the Indonesians, we must give birth in order to compensate or our population will fade away. We are not like any developing country. It's a mistake to think of us that way. We need to *increase* our population, just to survive ... Yes, we know what they are doing to us; we can't fight this kind of attack on us with guns.'

In 1989, General Suharto received the United Nations Fund for Population Activities Prize, which praised his 'support for family planning'.

We drove east, towards Baucau. It was here in 1981 that *Operasi Keamanan* ('Operation Security') had its most devastating effects. Timorese between the ages of eight and fifty were recruited to form human chains across the island, known as the 'fence of legs'. The object was to flush out Fretilin guerrillas, with Indonesian troops following on behind and pursuing them into 'human corrals' where they could be captured or killed. A man who survived one of these 'corrals' reported, 'It was a ghastly sight. There were a great many bodies, men, women, little children strewn everywhere, unburied, along the river banks, on the mountain slopes. I would estimate that about 10,000 people were killed in that operation.'[111] Two years later a 'scorched earth' policy brought repeated bombing raids. This was known as *Operasi Persatuan*, or 'Operation Unity'.

I was struck by the similarity of the landscape to parts of central Vietnam, between Quang Ngai and Song Tra, where the Americans dropped huge quantities of chemical defoliants, poisoning the soil and food chain and radically altering the environment. Indonesians also used chemical defoliants, most of which they made themselves. Today, as in Vietnam, the trees are twisted into grotesque shapes and there is no cultivation. This is known in East Timor as the 'dead earth', a place whose former inhabitants are either dead or 'relocated'.

We reached Baucau in darkness. Baucau is a former Portuguese resort that once proclaimed a certain melancholy style and where holiday flights used to arrive from Australia. ('Come and get a whiff of the Mediterranean!' invited a 1960 Trans Australia Airways brochure.) Today the airport is an Indonesian airforce base and Baucau a military 'company town', surrounded by barracks. In the town square are two enormous statues of Timorese in 'native costume', their hands raised towards an Indonesian flag. The statues, made from reinforced concrete, are crumbling in the tropical climate, their expressions unsmiling and wan.

Behind them stands the Hotel Flamboyant. We climbed the long staircase in darkness and called out. A Timorese man emerged from the shadows, limping and coughing terribly. 'What do you want?' he asked. 'A room?' we said. He turned and struggled along a deserted colonnade, and flung open two doors. There was no water, a fan that turned now and then, a mattress coated with fungus and a window without glass. 'There are no mosquitoes in Baucau,' he said mysteriously. He left us with our echoes. The Hotel Flamboyant was, until recently, a torture centre.

'I was arrested by the military command in Baucau,

KODIM 1628,' said Julio. 'They used electric shocks on me. They attached a wire at the top of my feet, toes, fingers and ears, then started operating the current. I passed out. Then they attached negative and positive wires at the top of my toe, finger and actually inside my ear. I passed out again.'

'My father was arrested several times,' said Alberto. 'He refused to join the new administration. They took him to the police headquarters, then sent for me and my sisters and brothers to see him being tortured. They said to us that if we followed our father's example, this is what would happen to us. They beat him with iron bars at first, then they did something to him that you learn in karate. They put their hands on his stomach and manipulated his organs and intestines. Indonesian soldiers are trained in these methods. They did this to him in four sessions. Then he got a disease in his stomach and vomited a lot of blood. I saw all this happen. He died when he lost all the blood. That was 1983.'

'When I was young', said Agio, 'the military came to my house, and killed my two brothers in front of my eyes. Before they killed them, they prepared a hole and persecuted them. When they did it, they pulled out a heart from one of them and showed it to us. "That's a guilty, dirty, filthy heart", they said to us. "You cannot be like this because this is the heart of a communist..."'

Torture appears to have been systematic throughout East Timor. The Indonesian military publishes an erudite manual on the subject, entitled 'Established Procedure for the Interrogation of Prisoners'. Section 13 reads, 'Hopefully, interrogation will not take place except in certain circumstances when the person being interrogated is having difficulty telling the truth ... If it proves necessary to use violence, make sure that there are no people around ... to see what is happening ... Avoid taking photographs showing torture in progress [such as when] people are being subjected to electric current, when they have been stripped naked etc. Remember do not have such photographic documentation developed outside East Timor which could then be made available to the public by irresponsible elements. It is better to make attractive photographs, such as shots taken while eating together with the prisoner, or shaking hands with those who have just come down from the bush, showing them in front of a home, and so on ... If necessary, the interrogation should be repeated over and over again using a variety of questions, so that, eventually, the correct conclusion can be drawn from all these different replies.'[112]

As John Taylor has pointed out, the torture manual's definition of interrogation, of drawing a 'correct conclusion' from replies which constantly denied this conclusion's inversion of reality, could also have been taken as a guide for the Indonesian military's relations with its Western backers.[113] Foreign 'fact finding' delegations have occasionally visited East Timor under military sponsorship and have been accommodated in the Hotel Flamboyant, presumably in a wing undisturbed by the activities of its torturers. One such delegation was led by Bill Morrison, former defence minister in the Whitlam Government and later Australian Ambassador to Indonesia. The Indonesians allowed the Morrison visit mostly on their terms, including the use of military interpreters. 'The delegation', wrote John Taylor, 'duly recorded that the military had invaded East Timor to quell chaos, that Suharto was reluctant to intervene, that the vast majority of people voted for the military in the elections, that food shortages were due to the long dry seasons and even that malnutrition was due to "a lack of variety in diet".'[114]

Morrison arrived during the ceasefire in 1983, which allowed him to meet a group of Fretilin representatives who had flagged down his convoy. The Indonesian interpreters so distorted his conversation with the guerrillas that all references to atrocities and a nearby concentration camp were omitted. That night the delegation stayed at the Hotel Flamboyant and recorded in their report: 'Back in Baucau the delegation leader informed other members of the delegation of the meeting [with Fretilin] before settling down to a night of bridge.'[115]

Morrison had promised the Fretilin group, 'Somehow we will get a message to you . . .'[116] No message was ever sent; Morrison's report claimed that 'the [Indonesian] administration in East Timor appears to be in effective control of all settled areas';[117] yet his own encounter with Fretilin had contradicted that. On his return to Australia, Morrison was asked to comment on a report from Fretilin that the Indonesians were about to break the ceasefire and attack the population. 'We have just been there', he said, 'and seen with our own eyes, and we have discussed with the military commander . . . Certainly nothing we saw, nothing we were told there, gives any credence to that report.'[118]

A few days later, the Indonesian chief-of-staff, Benny Murdani, launched a new terror campaign, using American and British aircraft. 'This time no fooling around,' he said, 'we're going to hit them without mercy.'[119]

When David and I returned to Dili it was evident that our cover was wearing thin. At the New Resende Inn the same spook was waiting for us as we came and left. Perhaps it was David's highly convincing public conversation with a Javanese travel agent about the 'tourist potential of East Timor' that bought us extra time. Talking to any Timorese was extremely risky. A group of American Congressional aides had been and gone, aware that the streets had been 'cleaned' for their visit, as the Timorese say, with some 3,000 arrests and expulsions from Dili. The nights now belonged to truck-loads of black-helmeted troops.

When an old man approached me in the hotel courtyard, asking me in a whisper to contact his family in exile in Australia, I walked away at first, then turned back and drew him into a passageway. 'All my children are in Darwin,' he said, 'I sent them out. It cost a lot in bribes. Now I long to see them.' I asked him if he had ever tried to leave. He shook his head and ran a finger across his throat. 'Will you take a letter for me?' he asked. 'Post it anywhere but here. They ɔpen everything. I have not had a letter for eight years.' I agreed to collect the letter that evening.

Across the road from the Roman Catholic cathedral three security policemen stopped a woman as she opened the gate, and demanded her name. She kept going to the bishop's door. Brave woman. The church in East Timor is, to the generals, a greater enemy than Fretilin, in spite of the Pope's apparent silence on the genocide during his visit to East Timor in 1989. According to members of the East Timorese church, the Pope was 'poorly briefed' prior to his visit. Once there, they said, he spoke generally about human rights and has since maintained the independence of the East Timorese church by not recognising it as part of the Indonesian Bishops' Conference. Yet he also gave public communion to General Murdani, who led the invasion and whose troops did much of the killing.

The massacre of hundreds of young people who marched peacefully to the Santa Cruz cemetery on November 12, 1991, remains like a presence in Dili. They had set out to place flowers on the grave of a student, Sebastiao Gomes, who had been shot dead at the church two weeks earlier. When they reached the cemetery, they were shot down by waiting troops, or they were stabbed or battered to death. There was no provocation. What was different about this massacre was that foreigners were present, including one with a video camera. However, it was after the foreigners had been arrested and expelled from East Timor (one, a New Zealander, was murdered; several others were badly beaten) that a more typical, unreported massacre took place.

'After the killings in the cemetery,' said Mário, 'I escaped being hit. So I pretended to be dead. The soldiers came and searched all the bodies and me, and hit me on the head so that I bled. They threw me with the other bodies on to a pick-up truck. They took us to the mortuary, locked the door and went upstairs. Some of my friends were still alive, crying. They were calling out for water. I told them the only water was dirty, so we must pray together. I saw with my very eyes that among the bodies were children and old people. Suddenly I heard steps approaching and I lay down again, pretending to be dead. Two soldiers came in. One of them picked up a big stone, and the other got a tablet from a jar. They then said out loud that if anyone was able to walk they had to stand up.

'When some of my friends got up, one of them was hit on the head by the soldier with the stone; he died later. I heard the blows, and it sounded like coconuts cracking as they fall from a tree on the ground. As they got close to me I stood up so suddenly that the soldiers were taken aback. I told them I was an informer, that I really worked for them. I didn't want to lie, but this saved my life. The soldier with the jar of tablets was making the injured take them, and he gave me one; I think it was yellow; it made me vomit.' (We passed several of these tablets to Scotland Yard's forensic laboratories in London, which found them to be paraformaldehyde. When vaporised this is a powerful disinfectant and must not, under any circumstances, be ingested.)

José, a Timorese orderly at the military hospital in Dili, took up the story. 'I was at the hospital receiving the dead and wounded,' he said. 'Most of them were dead, but some were pretending to be. The soldiers didn't unload the bodies one by one; they just pushed them down on the ground. If they spotted one that was alive they killed him by running the van over him. Some of the soldiers were afraid of killing more. So they ordered the Timorese who were there to kill them. People said no, or they ran and hid in the toilets. The Indonesians then tried to inject them with sulphuric acid. But the soldiers stopped doing this as the people screamed too loudly. Instead they gave each of them two pills and they got very ill.'

The hospital orderly described how Indonesian military doctors took part in killing the wounded. 'The doctors themselves went to get poison liquid', he said, 'and they gave it to people to drink. I don't know if the higher ranks in Indonesia knew about this; anyway, they would deny it. This information is not hearsay; it was given to me by someone who was actually told to kill some survivors. We were forced by e Indonesians to do this job. If people didn't take the poison, they were stoned or beaten with sticks. One effect of the poison was that people started passing out one by one. You could see them struggling with their breathing. There was one soldier, a corporal; he was the most ferocious. He gave poison to people. Then he stoned them till they died. Up until now I have not told this to any foreigner. I am worried about my safety. The Indonesian intelligence follows everyone. That is why I have had to keep it secret.'*

While Indonesian officers and spooks sang maudlin songs backed by the Karaoke in the hotel dining-room downstairs, I attempted to shred my notes and stuff them down the lavatory. This succeeded in blocking it, and it then had to be unblocked; the rest David and I burned, almost setting the bathroom curtain on fire. An element of black farce, which had underpinned 'Adventure Tours', was now reasserting itself. With the small videotape cassettes strapped to our legs, bellies and crotches, we said farewell to Gerry, our driver, and set out to leave the country from Dili airport. Swathed in Timorese cloth and nursing a large wooden statue sold to me by a village *liurai* (king), we hoped we looked as 'travel consultants' might, although I doubt if this made as much difference to our fortunes as the wonderfully chaotic distractions at the airport caused by the mêlée of Indonesians desperate to escape from a posting most had come to dread.

I had met the old man who wanted to give me a letter to post. After all the years of separation, he said, with tears in his eyes, he had not been able to compose his thoughts and put them on paper in time for my departure. Instead he gave me a telephone number in Darwin for Isabella, his eldest

---

* This man and the other witnesses to the 'second massacre' in November 1991 are now safely out of East Timor. In February 1994 they gave testimony to the United Nations Human Rights Commission sitting in Geneva.

daughter. I telephoned the number when I got to Bang
A recorded voice said it had been disconnected.

ARMS FOR THE GENERALS

ON OUR RETURN to London I tried to make an appointment to see Ali Alatas, the Indonesian foreign minister of whom former Ambassador Woolcott had spoken admiringly and who has a reputation as a 'diplomatic intellectual' willing to discuss the 'human rights issue' in East Timor. At the World Conference on Human Rights in Vienna in June 1993, Alatas's 'collected speeches on human rights' were distributed in a glossy white folder, including four pages of 'principles of human rights in Indonesian law'. He quoted Hobbes, Locke, Montesquieu, Rousseau and Mill to show that human rights were largely of Western origin and that the West should understand the 'cultural differences' and seek 'balance' and 'co-operation'. He got away with this; no delegate confronted him with evidence of his regime's well-documented genocide.

It is on this theme that Alatas's skill as a propagandist is amply demonstrated. He constantly implies that Suharto's Indonesia, like the rest of the developing world, is a victim of the Western media's colonial mentality and that any criticism of Jakarta's brutality in East Timor is 'condescending'. For this he is often rewarded, not with derision or even scepticism, but with legitimising headlines such as: 'East Timor groups cause image problem, says Alatas' and 'Alatas scorns Timor death toll claim'.[120]

For years the Suharto regime paid America's largest public relations firm, Hill and Knowlton, to promote a respectable image in economic and trade matters, especially on Capitol Hill. This was a Hill and Knowlton speciality, having turned out expensive propaganda for the governments of Kuwait,

China, Turkey, Peru and Israel. However, in the afterma
the 1991 Dili massacre, the Indonesian regime turnea
Burson-Marsteller, which had overtaken Hill and Knowltc
as the giant of American public relations. According to
officials in Jakarta, Indonesia would now take 'a more
aggressive line in defending its East Timor policies' and there
would be 'a change from a passive posture to a more forceful,
sophisticated approach'.[121] The *Far Eastern Economic
Review* reported that the Burson-Marsteller contract was
worth $5 million.[122]

I telephoned the executive vice-president of Burson-Marsteller, Michael Claes, whose signature appears on the contract
with Indonesia. He denied all knowledge of an East Timor
account. I asked if he was being secretive because the government retaining his firm's services was responsible for genocide. He laughed. 'Look,' he said, 'if you're going to ask me
a serious question . . . then why don't we just keep it at that
level, okay? I mean, those amateur techniques are not going
to work with me, okay?' He asked me for my sources for
the genocide. I said, 'The President of Portugal, the Roman
Catholic Church . . .' He interrupted. 'The Roman Catholic
Church, eh? You mean, you talked to a building?'[123]

If this was an example of its new 'sophisticated approach',
the Suharto regime was in difficulty. Of course, my conversation with Claes merely reflected the nervousness of those
who pick up Jakarta's chalice. Under the Foreign Agents
Registration Act, Burson-Marsteller must lodge all documents relating to a foreign client with the Justice Department.
Copies of these documents show intense lobbying by the
public relations firm on behalf of the Suharto regime. In
one letter to Congress, Burson-Marsteller's 'vice president,
government relations' described the Indonesian response to
the Dili massacre, in which more than 400 people were
murdered or wounded, as 'that unfortunate incident'.[124]

Foreign Minister Alatas had left the United Nations in
New York by the time I arrived. However, Indonesia's
Ambassador to the UN, Nugroho Wisnumurti, agreed to
see me. In the mould of Alatas and other senior Jakarta

ɔmats who can claim much success in explaining away
. bloody record of the regime, Wisnumurti is an urbane
ɹan whose unctuous fluency reminded me, for a brief
moment, of Douglas Hurd. Indeed, I began by asking him if
the regime valued the support of those like Hurd who had
praised Indonesia for its 'recognition of basic freedom' and
said that Western countries could not 'export Western values
[on human rights] to developing nations'.[125]

'We welcome that kind of approach on human rights,' said
the ambassador. 'Britain's position towards Indonesia has
been quite consistent . . . Of course, Indonesia does not claim
to be the angel of the international community. We have
made some mistakes . . .'

I asked what these mistakes were. 'Oh, it happens everywhere, including Western countries,' he replied. 'You know
what I am referring to. There are sometimes abuses of military authority . . . some personalities use firearms without
authority . . .'

I said the President of Portugal and numerous others had
accused his government of genocide.[126] He denied this, saying
that Indonesia had promoted only 'development and human
rights'. To prove his point, he said, the East Timorese had
actually voted in a referendum to join Indonesia. Moreover
it was 'completely untrue' that the survivors of the Santa
Cruz cemetery 'incident' had been murdered.

'Why are you asking these questions?' he admonished me.
'I only appreciate those who really want to get some information in order to promote a better understanding of the
situation . . .'

It seemed that the ambassador had never been really challenged about East Timor. As I left he handed me a dossier of
papers entitled *East Timor: Building for the Future*. These
claimed that 'the East Timorese people had rightly assumed
their inherent right to decolonise themselves . . . by choosing
independence through integration with Indonesia', and that
this had been achieved within 'the letter and spirit of the
United Nations'.[127] I showed the documents to Professor
Roger Clark, a world authority in international law at Rut-

gers University in New Jersey. 'A total distortion,' he s⸱
'The Indonesian invasion and occupation were and a⸱
illegal, brutal and can be compared to Iraq's invasion o⸱
Kuwait. Only the world's reaction was different.'

However, in the United States, where East Timor is little
known, Indonesian propaganda has entered the canon of
mainstream reporting. The *New York Times* has referred to
'the former Portuguese colony' that is 'now Indonesia's 27th
province'. It has used the dateline, 'Dili, Indonesia' – which
is comparable to 'Kuwait City, Iraq'. In 1988 the long
New York Times report, headlined 'Jakarta's Human Rights
Record Is Said to Improve', made no mention of the genocide
in East Timor.[128] However, these distortions are in contrast
with *New York Times* editorials on East Timor that have
appeared since 1979, many of them reasonably good
responses to Indonesian propaganda.

In January 1992 the *Washington Post* published an article
by C. Philip Liechty, a former senior CIA operations officer
based in Jakarta at the time of the invasion. Liechty accused
the Indonesians of lying to the world and getting away with
it. 'There is not a shred of truth in the Indonesian version of
events,' he wrote. 'East Timor was an undefended sitting
duck for the expansionist Indonesian generals. A slaughter
of tens of thousands followed, but little factual reporting on
the bloodiest atrocities left the island; the Indonesians made
sure of that, effectively blockading East Timor, cutting off
communications, turning back journalists and Western
observers, terrorising the population and lying to the world
about it, as now.'[129]

When I met Philip Liechty in Washington, he reminded me
of other former CIA officers I have known, who joined during
the early 1960s with a sense of idealism, based on 'service
to my country', and subsequently spent much of their careers
disenchanted.[130] He told me, 'Suharto was given the green
light [by the US] to do what he did. There was discussion in
the Embassy and in traffic with the State Department about
the problems that would be created for us if the public and
Congress became aware of the level and type of military

stance that was going to Indonesia at that time. It was covered under the justification that it was "for training purposes"; but there was concern that this might wear thin after a while, so the decision was taken to get the stuff flowing from San Francisco as fast as possible, to get it on the high seas before someone pulled the chain. As long as the Indonesians continued to certify that they were only using the equipment "for training", then we could get it through the bureaucracy.'[131]

I asked him what kind of equipment was sent. 'Everything', he replied, 'that you need to fight a major war against somebody who doesn't have any guns . . . M16 rifles, ammunition, mortars, grenades, food, helicopters. You name it; they got it. And they got it direct. The normal course would have been for the stuff to be distributed through the Indonesian supply system in Java. But most of the equipment was now going straight into Timor.

'Without continued heavy US logistical military support the Indonesians might not have been able to pull it off. [Instead] they were able to stay there at no real cost to them; it didn't put any pressure on their economy and on their military forces because American taxpayers were footing the bill for the killing of all those people and for the acquisition of that territory to which they had no right whatsoever. It is something that I will be forever ashamed of . . . The only interest that I ever saw expressed, the only justification I ever heard for what we were doing there was concern that East Timor was on the verge of being accepted as a new member of the United Nations and that there was an excellent chance that the country was going to be either leftist or neutralist and not likely to vote [with the United States] at the United Nations.

'For extinguishing that one vote, maybe 200,000 people, almost all of them non-combatants, died. President Ford was very much aware of what was happening; it was brought to his attention in official reports. He can never make the case that he was misled.'

I asked Liechty how he felt as he saw the evidence of

genocide and its cover-up unfold before him in Jaka.
'When the atrocity stories began to appear in the CIA repor
ing', he said, 'the way they dealt with these was to cover
them up as long as possible; and when they couldn't be
covered up any longer, they were reported in a watered down,
very generalised way, so that even their own sourcing was
sabotaged. In intelligence, sourcing is the most important
thing. At that time my disillusion was already low. I continued to do what I was supposed to do on my tour. I
certainly didn't feel like being the Lone Ranger. There certainly were others who felt as badly as I did.' I asked him
what would have happened had anyone spoken out. 'Your
career would end,' he replied.

With the inauguration of President Clinton, American
policy on East Timor seemed to change. During his election
campaign, Clinton had referred to the Indonesian occupation
as 'unconscionable'. In March 1993 the United States supported a resolution of the United Nations Human Rights
Commission expressing 'deep concern' over Indonesia's
behaviour in East Timor. Under Presidents Reagan and Bush,
the United States had helped to block similar resolutions. In
July, in Tokyo, Clinton handed Suharto a letter signed by 43
Senators protesting at the Indonesian occupation. (In
response, Suharto told Clinton that it was 'out of respect for
the human rights of East Timor's people' that Indonesia had
invaded.)[132]

Clinton also supported an amendment to the Foreign Aid
Bill which, in its original wording, demanded 'immediate and
unrestricted access' for humanitarian groups to East Timor
and 'withdrawal of Indonesian armed forces' and 'the right
of self-determination' for the East Timorese. Unless Indonesia
complied, all American arms sales would cease.

As a result of vigorous lobbying of Congress by the Suharto
regime, its American advisers and front organisations, and
with the State and Defence departments reportedly 'working
together to neutralise the amendment',[133] the wording was
diluted so that the President would be required only to 'consider' the human rights situation in East Timor before

roving major weapons sales. By the end of 1993 the
reign Aid Bill still had not reached the floor of Congress.
At the time of writing it seems likely to be postponed for up
to a year, or indefinitely. The sound and fury of the American
system had promised much and delivered little. Even a
modest ruling by Congress in the aftermath of the Santa Cruz
massacre – that Indonesian military officers were no longer
to receive training in the United States – was ignored. 'Congress's action', said a State Department official, 'did not ban
Indonesia's purchase of training with its own funds . . .'[134]

It is ironic that one of the obstacles to bringing pressure
on a Western-backed tyranny like Indonesia is the very concept of 'human rights', which has become part of the language of post-Cold War politics. Clinton's expressions of
concern for 'human rights' are reminiscent of those of President Carter, who described 'human rights' as 'the soul of
[American] foreign policy'[135] while increasing American arms
supplies to Indonesia at the height of the slaughter in East
Timor. Under Clinton a change in policy *seems* possible. But
the rhetoric goes on, while American military and economic
support for Suharto goes on (as it does, of course, for other
acceptable dictatorships).

In other words, while the impression is given that 'human
rights' are integral to American and all of Western policy-
making, the opposite is the functional truth; 'human rights'
are a useful cosmetic but otherwise irrelevant. As the
historian Mark Curtis has pointed out, 'The justification for
supporting bloodthirsty dictatorships and mass murderers
can no longer be made by referring to the evils of the other
side [in the Cold War]. The excuse that still worse atrocities
would be committed if favoured states fell into the Soviet bloc
is no longer available . . . Another formulation is currently
popular: that Third World states conducting mass repression
and who happen to pursue economic policies favourable to
Western business interests are somehow unable, because of
cultural reasons, to safeguard human rights. Western
attempts to impose our high standards might be viewed as
interference in their internal affairs (something which surely

we could not contemplate) and therefore business sh[...]
continue as normal ...

'In the extremely unlikely event that Indonesia adopted
economic policies preferential to its poor – thus threatening
the right of international capitalism to exploit the nation's
resources – the historical record suggests that Western leaders
would suddenly discover human rights as a relevant issue in
their relations with Jakarta and start condemning Indonesia's
brutal aggression as an outrageous act intolerable by any
civilised standards.'[136]

In the meantime, the US Department of Commerce says
that Indonesia offers 'excellent trade and investment opportunities for US companies [that are] too good to be
ignored'.[137] The British government has been one of the first
to seize these 'opportunities'. A few months before the
Indonesian invasion the Confederation of British Industry
(CBI) announced that Indonesia presented 'enormous potential for the foreign investor'.[138] Since then British companies
have made huge profits in the 'favourable political climate'
offered by General Suharto and by a labour market in which
the better paid workers receive some 20 pence an hour.

Shortly before the Santa Cruz massacre Douglas Hurd
urged the European Community to 'cut aid to countries that
violate human rights'.[139] Shortly after the massacre the British
government increased its aid to the Suharto regime by 250
per cent to £81 million, the largest percentage rise of any
donor country.[140] A government minister, Baroness Chalker,
claimed in Parliament that this was 'helping the poor in
Indonesia'.[141] In fact, half of British aid to Indonesia is made
up of Aid for Trade Provisions (ATP), which ensures con-
cessionary loans and highly favourable credits for British
goods and investment. Rio Tinto Zinc, British Petroleum,
British Gas, Britoil, Rolls-Royce and British Aerospace are
among the British conglomerates helping Indonesia's poor.

The British war industry has provided a vital prop for
Suharto since 1978 when Foreign Secretary David Owen
dismissed estimates of East Timorese dead as 'exaggerated'
and sold the Indonesian generals eight Hawk ground-attack

raft worth £25 million each. By the end of 1994 Britain il have sold, or agreed to sell, a further 40 Hawks, and nore are 'in the pipeline'. These are in addition to Wasp helicopters, Sea Wolf and Rapier SAM missiles, Tribal Class frigates, battlefield communications systems, seabed mine disposal equipment, Saladin, Saracen and Fernet armoured vehicles, a fully-equipped Institute of Technology for the Indonesian army and training for Indonesian officers in Britain.

When a Foreign Office minister, Baroness Trumpington, was asked about the military potential of Land Rovers sold to the Indonesian army, she said, derisively, 'My farmer friends would laugh . . . to think that they were offensive weapons!' British Aerospace manufactures the Land Rover, which it describes as one of 'the world's most successful pieces of defence hardware'.[142] I saw Land Rovers used widely in East Timor by the occupying forces. It is very likely that the bodies of the young people murdered or wounded in the Santa Cruz massacre were thrown into the back of British Land Rovers.

In Washington a line often heard is that it doesn't matter what the US does to withhold arms from Indonesia, because Jakarta will simply get what it needs from Britain. A great deal of British mendacity has been deployed in justifying its underpinning of one of the world's most barbarous regimes. This has concentrated on the Hawk aircraft, an especially efficient weapon. 'The point of selling Hawk aircraft to Indonesia', the armed services minister, Archie Hamilton, told Parliament in 1993, 'is to give jobs to people in this country. There is no doubt in my mind that a Hawk aircraft can do nothing to suppress the people of East Timor. The aircraft is not suitable for that purpose and we have guarantees from the Indonesians that the aircraft would not be used for internal suppression.'[143]

This was an extraordinary statement even by modern parliamentary standards. Since Hamilton uttered it, British Aerospace have sacked more than 4,000 workers. It is, however, constantly echoed. 'There is no evidence', said Baroness Chalker, 'that aircraft sold in the past to Indonesia have been

used for internal security purposes.'[144] When the def
minister, Jonathan Aitken, was asked in Parliament 'h
many dead or tortured East Timorese are acceptable to th
government in exchange for a defence contract with Indonesia', he replied, 'That is a ridiculous question.'[145] But of
course it was not.

The government has promoted the Hawk as a mere 'trainer'. British Aerospace, however, say that it 'has been designed
from the outset with a significant ground attack capability'.[146]
The Indonesians appear to be in no doubt. According to the
Research and Technology minister, B. J. Habibie, the Hawks
'will be used not only to train pilots but for ground attack'.[147]

The independent Center for Defense Information in Washington is even more explicit. Its director, retired US Rear
Admiral Eugene J. Carroll, told me, 'These British aircraft
are ideal counter-insurgency aircraft, designed to be used
against guerrillas who come from and move among civilian
populations and have no adequate means of response to air
attack. In other words, they are there to shoot high velocity
cannon and deliver ordnance at low levels against unprotec-
ted human beings.'[148]

As for there being 'no evidence' that the Hawks are used
in East Timor, there are plenty of eye-witnesses. In interviews
with myself and Max Stahl, Timorese have described in detail
Hawks attacking civilian areas.

José Gusmao, a Timorese now exiled in Australia, said, 'I
watched a Hawk attack on a village in the mountains. It
used its machine-guns and dropped incendiary bombs. The
Hawk is quite different from the American planes; it has a
particular nose. You can tell it anywhere.' Another Timorese
eye-witness, José Amorin, told me, 'I first saw the Hawks in
action in 1984. They were standing at the airport at Baucau,
where they are based. They are a small aircraft, not at all
like the OV–10 Bronco and the Skyhawk from the US. They
are perfect for moving in and out of the mountains. They
have a terrible sound when they are coming in to bomb, like
a voice wailing. We immediately go to the caves, into the
deepest ones, because their bombs are so powerful. They fly

ow . . . and attack civilians, because the people hiding in
e mountains are civilians. Four of my cousins were killed
a Hawk attacks near Los Palos. They were hiding in caves
as the Hawks bombed every day for almost a week. On the
sixth day they bombed the mountain so that stones covered
the cave entrance, and my cousins were trapped. They died
in the cave. Most people in East Timor know about the
British Hawks. Why doesn't the British government send a
fact-finding mission and ask the people?'

José Amorin came to London in November 1993 and
presented his evidence at the Foreign Office. He told me, 'I
met a senior official and gave him a lot of information. I told
him where the Hawks were based in East Java and East
Timor. He said they were only trainers. I replied that if they
were used for training, it was on live targets in East Timor.
I described to him everything. He said he would take
seriously my points and pass them to the Minister. He could
give me no categorical assurance that the Hawks were not
being used in East Timor.' (Later, this official denied that he
had been given any such evidence.)

In 1992 a spokesman for the East Timorese independence
movement described Britain as 'the single worst obstruction-
ist of any industrialised country' in promoting international
action on East Timor.[149] The British Foreign Office has played
a leading, some would say traditional, role in this process.

Following the murder of the two television crews by the
Indonesian army in October 1975, the Foreign Office refused
to give out details of the two Britons killed, Malcolm Rennie
and Brian Peters. An official said that the families did not
wish to be 'disturbed by the media'. This was a lie. Brian
Peters' sister, Maureen Tolfree, told me she had had no contact with the Foreign Office and had not even been notified
that Brian had been killed, and that all their mother knew
was what she had read in the press. 'It was as if he never
existed,' she said. Certainly, no public protest was made to
the Jakarta regime. When she flew to Jakarta to attempt
to collect Brian's remains she was taken to a room in the
airport where a British or Australian embassy official – she

cannot say which – telephoned her and told her it would ɛ unwise for her to stay in Indonesia.

When *The Times* published a report in 1977, headlined 'Indonesia Accused of Mass Murder in East Timor',[150] the journalist responsible was called to the Foreign Office and asked to explain his interest in East Timor. 'It was obvious', said David Watts, a South East Asia specialist, 'that I was being warned off the story. It had the opposite effect.'[151]

When people write to the government or their MP about East Timor, they receive replies that not only deny any British complicity, but attempt to devalue the scale of suffering of the East Timorese. J. L. Wilkins of the South East Asia Department of the Foreign Office is the author of a number of these replies. 'No one really knows the truth' about the death toll is his message, because some estimates 'are sometimes so dramatically different' from the British government's that they 'cannot help but suspect them to be exaggerated'.[152] The same devotion to historical accuracy was shown by a Foreign Office official who, when asked about the large death toll, said, 'Yes, but it didn't happen in one year.'[153]

When the United Nations Human Rights Commission met in Geneva in April 1993, a posse of Foreign Office officials allied themselves with representatives of the Jakarta regime in an attempt to divide the European Community vote and prevent a resolution condemning Indonesia. Only when this 'disgraceful bullying role', as one observer called it, was clearly failing did Britain fall in with its EC partners and vote for the resolution.[154]

Two months later the same officials, reported the *Guardian*, 'deliberately misled critics of Indonesia into thinking that the British government was pushing for International Red Cross access to political prisoners in East Timor'. A 'restricted access' Telex from the British Embassy in Jakarta said, 'Pont [Pierre Pont, the ICRC delegate to East Timor] judges, and I agree, that for the moment the military and civilian authorities will be fighting this out behind the scenes and that pressure from outside would contribute little.'[155]

The Telex was dated June 24. On June 30 a Foreign Office

...nister, Alastair Goodlad, wrote to Labour MP Greg Pope ...aying that Britain was urging Indonesia to allow access to the resistance leader, Xanana Gusmao, and other political prisoners. A later version of the same letter, signed by the head of the Indonesia section at the Foreign Office, Richard Sands, emphasised that 'we are currently pressing the Indonesians to allow resumed ICRC access to Xanana Gusmao and others'. This was entirely false. An internal Foreign Office memorandum, which accompanied both the Telex and the second letter, read, 'Attached for infn/edification. The letter is for stonewalling.'[156]

British closeness to the Indonesian tyranny was nurtured by Margaret Thatcher. As with arms deals she personally promoted in the Gulf and elsewhere, it was Thatcher who pushed the most recent sale of Hawks when she visited Jakarta in 1985. In 1992 she became the first foreigner to receive the annual award from the Association of Indonesian Engineers: a reward for 'a decade of enhancing UK-Indonesian cooperation in technology'. She told the assembled chiefs of Indonesia's weapons industry, 'I am proud to be one of you.'[157]

One of Thatcher's staunchest admirers is Alan Clark, the Tory multi-millionaire MP who lives in a castle in Kent and has a reputation for speaking his mind. As 'defence procurement minister' under Thatcher, Clark was responsible for the sale of the latest batch of Hawk aircraft to Indonesia for £500 million. I interviewed him in November 1993, in his London *pied à terre* in Albany, off Piccadilly. The following has been slightly abridged:

J.P. When the sale of Hawk aircraft was being finalised with Indonesia you told Parliament, 'We do not allow the export of arms and equipment lightly to be used for oppressive purposes against civilians'. How does that work? How does the government not allow that?

A.C. Well, you scrutinise every military report. [The] equipment we're talking about is police-type equipment. I mean, riot guns, CS gas, anti-personnel stuff and obviously instruments of torture, gallows, that kind of thing [and]

perhaps a water cannon, armoured cars, sort of heavy-r~~
control kit. But once you get into military equipment, you're
into a different category of decision.

J.P. But can't military equipment be used as police
equipment?

A.C. Oh yes.

J.P. I mean, Hawk low-flying attack aircraft are very effective at policing people on the ground, I would have thought.

A.C. No, they're not, because policing means one thing.
In this case it means repression by an authoritarian regime
of domestic incidents . . . riots, protests, that sort of thing. I
mean, aircraft are used in the context of a civil war.

J.P. But East Timor isn't a civil war. The civil war has been
over for eighteen years. This is an illegal occupation, which
the British government acknowledges to be an illegal occupation.

A.C. I'm not into that. I don't know anything about that.

J.P. Well, you were the minister.

A.C. Yeah, but I'm not interested in illegal occupations or
anything like that . . . I mean *you* call it illegal . . .

J.P. No, the United Nations does.

A.C. Okay, well, anyway, there is this distinction between
police equipment which covers riot control, the instruments
of torture, the low-grade stuff, the military equipment which
is also subject to very high-level scrutiny.

J.P. Your colleagues in government have talked about getting guarantees from the Indonesians so that the Hawks
won't be used for oppressive purposes in East Timor. What
exactly are these guarantees?

A.C. Well, I never asked for a guarantee. That must have
been something that the Foreign Office did . . . a guarantee
is worthless from any government as far as I'm concerned.

J.P. Shouldn't the public be cynical about all this after what
happened over Iraq? Shouldn't the public be cynical about
assurances, guidelines and denials from government about
the sale of arms?

A.C. Well, I don't know what you mean by the public, but
I don't think the majority of people give a damn about it . . .

...less those weapons are going to be used against our own troops.

J.P. But it's the assumption that the public doesn't give a damn that allows ministers and officials to deceive; isn't that correct?

A.C. Why should they want to deceive if the public doesn't give a damn?

J.P. You say they don't give a damn, but that's an assumption that has yet to be tested scientifically ... I would have thought that ministers are public servants, are they not?

A.C. Certainly, but you measure public opinion by dining-rooms in Hampstead.

J.P. I've never been in a dining-room in Hampstead.

A.C. Haven't you?

J.P. No.

A.C. Well, I'll accept your assurance. You see, there's a concept known as the chattering classes, and they get tearful about different issues, and talk to each other about them. I hold them in complete contempt. They tend to regard themselves in some way as being 'the public'. They get a lot of coverage in the *Guardian* and the *Independent*.

J.P. Should a government lie to its people?

A.C. No, certainly not ... One must take very great care not to.

J.P. Mislead its people, deceive?

A.C. Well, deceive is the same thing. But misleading ... you get into a very grey area of definition here. Misleading gets you into the territory of both semantics and gullibility. People often don't want to believe things. They feel more comfortable if they don't focus their attention on things ...

J.P. The fact remains that British aircraft kill and maim people in East Timor, and the government allows the sale of these aircraft on flimsy assurances that they won't be used there.

A.C. Flimsy, no. I mean, they are given in a proper diplomatic context. I attach very little value to such assurances.

J.P. Isn't all this, in broad terms, about the right of a small country not to be invaded by a large neighbour?

A.C. Yeah, but they weren't British, were they?

J.P. That makes a difference?

A.C. Of course it makes a difference.

J.P. So if they're not British, you can then sell them aircraft to help a powerful neighbour get on with occupying the territory that it's invaded?

A.C. I must caution you. In the way you express things [you] are constantly foreshortening these arguments and giving them a particular colouring . . .

J.P. This is a regime that has perhaps one of the bloodiest records of the twentieth century.

A.C. Well, that's a very competitive sphere.

J.P. This regime has competed well in that league.

A.C. Has it? There's Stalin, Pol Pot and others.

J.P. In East Timor it has killed more people proportionately than Pol Pot killed in Cambodia. By all credible accounts it's killed a third of the population. Isn't that ever a consideration for the British government?

A.C. It's not something that often enters my . . . thinking, I must admit.

J.P. Why is that?

A.C. My responsibility is to my own people. I don't really fill my mind much with what one set of foreigners is doing to another.

J.P. Did it bother you personally when you were the minister responsible [and] that British equipment was causing such mayhem and human suffering, albeit to a set of foreigners?

A.C. No, not in the slightest. It never entered my head.

J.P. You don't lose sleep over it?

A.C. No.

J.P. I ask the question because I read that you were a vegetarian and you are seriously concerned about the way animals are killed.

A.C. Yeah.

J.P. Doesn't that concern extend to the way humans, albeit foreigners, are killed?

A.C. Curiously not.

J.P. Why not?

A.C. Well, it's a philosophic field. I suppose there is a relationship with the doctrine of original sin and innocence and so on . . .

J.P. In your view, are there categories of arms that should never be sold?

A.C. Yes. Nuclear, ballistic missile technology, chemical biological precursors, things like that. But in the conventional arms marketplace, as far as I'm concerned, it's open season.

J.P. You have said that where a regime is oppressively outrageous, as the gassing of children is, an army supplier should back off. Do you consider the mass slaughter of children in East Timor oppressively outrageous?

A.C. Do you mean, lined up in front of a ditch?

J.P. Yes. One of the examples used is of children and their mothers being burnt alive in a house, trapped there and burnt by the Indonesians. What's the difference?

A.C. I think gassing is dreadful. It's one of those techniques that actually breaks through one's protective indifference and is upsetting. But the other things that you mentioned . . . they just occur in combat or violent occupation situations.

J.P. I'm still not sure of the difference. Why is gassing any worse than shooting, burning, torturing?

A.C. I can't tell. There's something about it that deeply offends one's natural instinct, I suppose. It's a different threshold of violence. The other things, the examples you've given . . . I'm not familiar with the situation in East Timor . . .

J.P. You once asked a television audience, 'Does anyone know where East Timor is?' Am I right in taking from that rather contemptuous dismissal, that [East Timor] is simply expendable?

A.C. I don't understand the use of the word expendable.

J.P. Of no consequence?

A.C. If you want to get worked up about something I can steer you in all sorts of directions, if that's your hobby, bleeding . . .

J.P. Well, no, the bleeding has been done in East Timor . . . often because of British military equipment.

A.C. I mean you can look anywhere, so what's all this

310

about East Timor suddenly? ... I mean, how many people are there in the world? A billion or something? I mean, if you want to rush round and say gosh, look how dreadful this is, whatever it is, you won't have any problems. British military equipment is being used in Kashmir, and British military equipment is being used in Sri Lanka. We don't live in an ideal world.

In my film *Death of a Nation* there is a sequence filmed on board an aircraft flying between northern Australia and Timor. A party is in progress; bottles of champagne are being uncorked. There is much false laughter as two men in suits toast each other. The larger man is uneasy and deferential as he raises his glass. 'This is an historically unique moment', he says, '... that is truly uniquely historical.' This is Gareth Evans, Australia's foreign affairs minister since 1988. The other man is Ali Alatas, the Indonesian foreign minister. It is 1989 and the two are making a symbolic flight to celebrate the signing of the Timor Gap Treaty, which will allow Australian and international oil companies to exploit the seabed off East Timor. The ultimate prize could amount to seven billion barrels of oil or, as Gareth Evans put it, 'zillions' of dollars.[158]

Declared by Prime Minister Whitlam in 1975 to be too poor for a 'viable' independence, the East Timorese were now being denied any profit from their own natural wealth. When in 1979 the Australian government gave *de jure* recognition to Indonesia's occupation, negotiations for the spoils were already under way. In 1985 Australia became the first Western country formally to recognise Indonesia's sovereignty over East Timor with a blunt statement by Prime Minister Bob Hawke that the Timor Gap Treaty 'can in practice be concluded only with the Indonesian government'.[159] Asked about the international principle of not recognising territory acquired by force, Gareth Evans said, 'What I can say is simply that the world is a pretty unfair place.'[160]

311

According to Professor Roger Clark, the Timor Gap Treaty also has a simple analogy in law. 'It is acquiring stuff from a thief,' he said. 'If you acquire property from someone who stole it, you're a receiver. As far as I'm concerned, the Indonesians are in the position of someone who stole territory, and the Australians are dealing with them as though they had some kind of legitimacy. I find that is complicity. The fact is that they have neither historical, nor legal, nor moral claim to East Timor and its resources.

'Moreover, the obligation *not* to recognise the acquisition of territory acquired illegally is reflected in a very significant 1970 resolution of the General Assembly that was co-sponsored by Australia on the twenty-fifth anniversary of the United Nations. This spelt out in detail some of the legal principles that are stated broadly in the UN Charter. Australians were members of the committee that laboured for seven years to draft the language that was adopted unanimously and is a flat prohibition.'[161]

On a visit to Indonesia in February 1991 to finalise the treaty, Evans said, 'I have taken the view that Australia does have a duty as an international good citizen to go on raising [human rights] issues ... The truth of the matter is that the human rights situation [in East Timor] has, in our judgement, conspicuously improved, particularly under the present military arrangements ...'[162] Nine months later the Indonesian military killed or wounded more than 450 people in the Santa Cruz massacre. Evans described this as 'an aberration, not an act of state policy'.[163]

The Indonesians agreed. A 'special commission of enquiry', set up by Suharto, blamed a few soldiers and said that the ultimate responsibility lay with the 'provocations' of the unarmed victims. Evans described the Indonesian reaction as 'positive and helpful' and 'very encouraging'. He said he was 'reasonably happy' with the enquiry's findings, adding that the victims unaccounted for 'might simply have gone bush'.[164] Within two months of the massacre, the joint Australian-Indonesian board overseeing exploitation of the Timor Gap awarded eleven contracts to Australian oil and gas compan-

312

ies.[165] On the day that Australian Resources Minister Alan Griffiths signed a further part of the treaty with his Indonesian counterpart, Amnesty International described the massacre as probably a planned military operation and the Indonesian enquiry as totally lacking in credibility and 'principally directed at the appeasement of domestic and international critics and the suppression of further political dissent in the territory'.[166] An Indonesian court subsequently sentenced ten low-ranking officers mostly to a few months' prison, including one who served his time on holiday in Bali. In contrast, eight Timorese demonstrators were given sentences ranging from five years to life.

When protesters planted crosses in front of the Indonesian Embassy in Canberra, one for each of the murdered, Gareth Evans had them removed. When a federal court ruled that Australia's diplomatic regulations did not give him this power and ordered the crosses restored, Evans quickly changed the regulations. A spokesman for Evans explained that the Indonesians had complained that the 'dignity of its embassy had been impaired by the crosses'.[167]

In September 1993, Australian Prime Minister Paul Keating arrived in Washington. It was the week following the US Senate Foreign Relations Committee's unanimous vote to propose a bill banning arms sales to Indonesia unless it improved its human rights record in East Timor. Keating objected to this, and called on the Congress and the President to take a more 'balanced' view of human rights in Indonesia and to allow Suharto to have his say. Referring to 'the East Timor thing' he said, 'You want to stay positively engaged with [the Indonesians] so you can still talk about the things that worry you as well as giving both sides an incentive for co-operation in economic areas where your interests do clearly line up.'[168] The Indonesians were ecstatic. 'What he has done', said Jakarta's ambassador in Canberra, 'is walk right into the lion's den and make our case. Keating is our comrade in arms.'[169] Jakarta's weapons chief, B. J. Habibie, said, 'This is music to my ears.'[170]

Keating, who is proud of his pugnacious, often abusive

313

style in Parliament – he has called his opponents 'harlots', 'sleazebags', 'boxheads', 'loopy crims', 'pieces of criminal garbage', 'scumbags' and 'piss-ants' – ordered a video to be made of his more theatrical performances and sent it to Suharto. According to the *Sydney Morning Herald*, the Indonesian dictator 'showed the video to his entire cabinet, who were reportedly mightily impressed'.[171]

Two weeks before *Death of a Nation* was due to be shown on television in Britain, its disclosures about a second massacre in Dili, in November 1991, were published in the Australian press. This caused near-panic among Indonesia's backers. Without having seen a frame of the film, Paul Keating, Jakarta's 'comrade in arms', angrily condemned it, and me. My 'credibility', he said, was 'under a cloud' because of my work in Cambodia. This was a remarkable statement by the leader of a government whose 'peace plan' in Cambodia was the direct result of public response to my film, *Cambodia Year Ten*.[172]

Keating's attack was inspired by Gareth Evans, whose dismissal of corroborated evidence he, too, had not seen was published under headlines such as 'No evidence to back Pilger claims'.[173] I doubt if there has been another time when an Australian prime minister and his foreign affairs minister have used their high office to vehemently deny evidence, unseen, of murderous violence carried out by a ruthless dictatorship in an illegally occupied territory. When *Death of a Nation* opened in Perth, federal police, who take their orders direct from Canberra, were sent to the Lumiere Cinema and demanded to know 'who had told the cinema to put it on'.[174]

In their panic, Keating and Evans even cast doubt on the original Dili massacre. Keating said it had happened in a 'murky period' during which 'it isn't clear what happened'. Furthermore, said Evans, there were 'a number of witnesses who have said nothing like what is claimed to have happened'.[175]

314

There were no such 'witnesses'. Evans was referring to a priest presented to foreign journalists by Indonesian officials during a controlled visit to Dili – hurriedly arranged by the regime in order to pre-empt the worldwide showing of *Death of a Nation* and the UN Human Rights Commission hearings on East Timor. This was Marcus Wanandi, an Indonesian-Chinese priest installed in Dili by Suharto to 'assist' Bishop Belo, the outspoken Timorese who heads the Catholic Church and has never accepted Indonesian rule. Wanandi and his powerful family are close to Suharto; one brother runs a multi-million-dollar business with Suharto's daughter, 'developing' East Timor; the other runs a 'strategic institute' in Jakarta that helped plan the invasion in 1975. Wanandi told a senior Australian bishop, Hilton Deakin, that talking to the Timorese was a waste of time because 'they have just come out of the trees'.[176]

Wanandi's 'evidence' that there was no second massacre contradicted Bishop Belo, who told Max Stahl of his trust in the statements of eye-witnesses. He said he had informed the Indonesian 'special commission of enquiry' about the unreported killings. 'Twice', he said, 'I told them that not only have they to investigate the massacre in the Santa Cruz cemetery, but also in other places where people were killed . . . for example, in the [military] hospital. They showed no interest. The military authorities [wanted] to give the Timorese people these extreme lessons. We think there is no justice . . . no justice.'

Bishop Belo was silenced during the two restricted press tours in 1994. Only Wanandi was interviewed by foreign reporters, who paid little notice to his ties to the regime and the obvious set-up his 'evidence' represented. In the meantime, the regime made much use of the Keating/Evans denials and abuse, which were quoted in press releases distributed by Indonesian embassies around the world. My film, said Ali Alatas, having not seen it, 'is entirely fictitious'.

Rupert Murdoch's *Australian*, Australia's only national newspaper, took a keen interest in my film. The paper's foreign editor, Greg Sheridan, had previously attacked both the Clinton administration for raising human rights with the Suharto regime, and the Foreign Affairs Committee of the Australian Parliament for its estimate that 'at least 200,000' people had died under Indonesian rule in East Timor. Now he attacked my film, having not seen it. Referring to eye-witness accounts of a second massacre in the Santa Cruz cemetery, he wrote, 'The sad truth is that even genuine vic-tims frequently concoct stories . . .'. He went on to accuse me of 'extreme tendentiousness'.[177] I sent a message to the editor-in-chief, Paul Kelly, requesting the right of reply. This was eventually agreed and I submitted an article that answered Sheridan and outlined the Australian Government's complicity in the genocide. I heard nothing for more than two weeks.

In the meantime, the *Australian* sent its Jakarta corre-spondent, Patrick Walters, on the first shepherded press tour of Dili, accompanied by Indonesian officials. Walters pro-duced a memorable series of disgraceful pieces. Jakarta's 'eco-nomic achievements' in East Timor were 'impressive', he wrote, giving official statistics of Jakarta's generous 'develop-ment' of the territory. As for the resistance, it was 'leaderless' and beaten. Indeed, you wondered what the fuss was all about as 'no one was now arrested without proper legal procedures'. 'The situation regarding human rights', the puppet governor told him, 'is very good at the moment'.[178]

Walters' next dispatch, written on his return to Jakarta, made the symmetry clear. Under the headline, 'Murdoch tunes into Indonesia', he wrote, 'Mr. Rupert Murdoch left Jakarta yesterday after a two-day visit, optimistic about the prospects of his Hong Kong-based Star TV network for further expansion in South-East Asia.' Murdoch told his man, 'I'm here to learn about Indonesia and learn about the market. We are looking at the prospects for Star TV.' A new Indonesian satellite, Indostar, explained Walters, 'is of considerable interest' to Murdoch, who plans to expand Star TV's coverage of Asia.[179]

With Murdoch just arrived from Jakarta and Walters' reporting of Jakarta's 'achievements' in East Timor still fresh, editor-in-chief Kelly rescinded my right-of-reply. He said I had written the 'wrong' article, which, anyway, did not meet 'that standard of accuracy required by this paper'.[180] Twice I asked him to substantiate this charge; I suggested that, as an editor, he had an obligation to detail my alleged inaccuracies. He failed to reply. In December 1993 Paul Kelly was appointed by Gareth Evans to the Australia-Indonesia Institute, a body funded by the Australian Government to promote Indonesia's and Australia's 'common interests'.

In the week that Kelly rejected my article Prime Minister Keating launched an unprecedented 'trade and cultural promotion' with Indonesia. The attacks on my film now made perfect sense. Surrounded by businessmen and representatives of the arts, Keating made an extraordinary speech in which he announced a 'partnership' with Jakarta that would 'stand as a model for co-operation between developed and developing countries'. He described the 'stability' of the Suharto regime as 'the single most beneficial development to have affected Australia and its region in the past thirty years'.[181] He made not a single reference to East Timor, let alone to the fact that the Suharto regime had one of the most barbarous records of the twentieth century. All reference to the tens of thousands of deaths that had helped to pay for this great 'benefit' to Australia was excluded from press reports of Keating's speech – in the same way that all reference to Stalin's crimes was excluded from the Soviet and East European press. Keating's speech was lauded as 'mature'.

On the same day that Keating spoke, Dr George Aditjondro, a leading Indonesian academic, released in Australia two papers on East Timor based on twenty years' research. In so doing, he risked his livelihood, and possibly his life; a few days later his house in Central Java was attacked by stone-throwing thugs. 'I wanted to take off the veil of secrecy around East Timor,' he told me. The Aditjondro papers describe a 'culture of violence' imposed on the territory, with systematic atrocities, such as mass rape, amounting to an assault on the very fabric of East Timorese society. The estimate of 200,000 deaths, he said, was 'moderate'.[182]

This was ignored by Keating and other Western leaders and by most of the media. Paul Kelly's *Australian* published only Jakarta's denials. The Jakarta regime, said an editorial in the *Australian*, 'can be declared moderate'.[183]

Amnesty International has said of the Indonesian regime: 'If those who violate human rights can do so with impunity, they come to believe they are beyond the reach of the law.'[184] Western politicians who speak of a 'pragmatism' and 'realism' in relation to East Timor not only give support to a lawless bully, but condemn an entire nation to a slow cultural and physical death. They may not yet have their way.

The United States has, as ever, pivotal power. Even if the proposed congressional action to ban arms sales is not quite 'historic', as its supporters claim, it represents a perceptible change in American outlook and understanding, and the emergence of the East Timorese, and the great crime committed against them, from the shadows of imperial geo-politics. In 1993 the UN Human Rights Commission called on Indonesia to allow international experts on torture, executions and disappearances to investigate freely in East Timor. At the time of writing, the UN Commission has again summoned Indonesia into its dock. In 1994, in an action brought by Portugal against Australia, the World Court will decide whether the Timor Gap Treaty is legal or not. (Indonesia does not recognise the World Court.) According to Roger Clark, the Australian government will probably comply with the decision. In a parallel case brought by the Timorese themselves, the Australian High Court will also decide on the treaty's legality. There is every likelihood that both courts will find against it.

It is one of recent history's more melancholy ironies that

the Timorese place most hope in the actions of their former colonial masters, the Portuguese, who so ignominiously abandoned them. Public opinion in Portugal feels strongly about East Timor. People constantly write to the government and to newspapers, demanding justice for the Timorese. There is a sense of guilt, as if the nation's honour was sullied in the retreat to Atauro Island in 1975. The politicians are acutely aware of this, especially the President, Mário Soares, who has also been prime minister and foreign secretary since the revolution in 1974. Under the constitution, he has personal responsibility for the remaining overseas territories: Macau and East Timor.

I flew to Lisbon and interviewed President Soares in the magnificent eighteenth-century Palacio Belém (the 'Pink Palace') overlooking the Tagus River. He is an interesting anti-fascist; during the Salazarist years he was an outspoken opponent in exile. For a head of state, he spoke with undiplomatic passion about the Timorese. 'They have never submitted to the power of Indonesia,' he said. 'Even isolated in the mountains, they make sure we never forget; one feels a wind of silence that heroically accuses . . . There has been a real genocide, a cold destruction of a people, their complete identity, destroying their habits, their traditions, language and religion . . . over 200,000.'

I asked him how much blame should lie with Portugal. 'After our own dictator fell on April 25, 1974,' he said, 'there was a revolutionary period in which the state was practically in the street. We had a million Portuguese from the former colonies returned to Portugal without work, without money, with nothing. Perhaps this explains a bit of what happened over East Timor. I don't exclude there was guilt, and incompetence and lies over our role there.'

I said, 'Your EC partner, Britain, is now the biggest arms supplier to Indonesia. What's your view of this, in the light of evidence that British Hawk aircraft are being used in East Timor?'

He replied, 'I was in England recently and spoke to John

Major and Douglas Hurd about Timor. The Foreign Secretary said that dictators could usefully provide certain guarantees. He defended what he called the "realistic policy" that England often follows in defending its own interests, while forgetting a bit about international law and moral values. I replied that the English had thought like this at the end of the Second World War in relation to the dictators of Portugal and Spain. And because of this so-called "realistic policy" we Portuguese were held back for more than thirty years. I said, "We can never forgive you for this. It's also possible the Timorese will never forgive you, either." '

I asked Soares if he could give an unambiguous assurance that Portugal would stand by the Timorese until they won independence. 'I give it', he said, 'without a doubt. We are very proud of them.'

By all accounts the Timorese resistance should have been wiped out years ago; but it lives on, as I found, in the hearts and eyes of almost everyone: eyes that reflect a defiance and courage of a kind I have not experienced anywhere else.

Recent opposition has come most vociferously from the young generation, raised during Indonesian rule. This has particularly angered the generals, who had anticipated that the second generation would have been 'resocialised', to use a favourite word of the regime. It is the young who keep alive the nationalism minted in the early 1970s and its union with a spiritual, traditional love of country and language, in spite of the ban on all Timorese languages; it is they who bury the flags and maps and draw the subtle graffiti of a sleeping face resembling the tranquil figure in Matisse's *The Dream*, reminding the Indonesians that, whatever they do, they must one day reckon with a Timorese reawakening.

When Amelia Gusmao, wife of the resistance leader, Xanana, was forced into exile, young people materialised along her route to the airport and stood in tribute to her, then slipped away. And when Xanana himself was brought before a kangaroo court in 1993, he gave the regime a glimpse of its 'problem'.

Although he was prevented from speaking from the dock,

his statement of defiance was released all over the world. 'The Indonesian generals', he wrote, 'should be made to realise that they have been defeated politically in East Timor. I acknowledge military defeat on the ground. I am not ashamed to say so. On the contrary, I am proud of the fact that a small guerrilla army was able to resist a large nation like Indonesia, a regional power which in a cowardly fashion invaded us and sought to dominate us by the law of terror and crime. As a political prisoner in the hands of the occupiers of my country, it is of no consequence at all to me if they pass a death sentence here today. They are killing my people and I am not worth more than their heroic struggle . . .'[185]

Among the Timorese in exile and their supporters all over the world those who have not allowed the world to forget about East Timor are Constancio Pinto, Abel Guterres, José and Fatima Gusmao, Ines Almeida, José Amorin Dias, Agio Pereira, George Aditjondro, Carmel Budiardjo, Arnold Kohen, Shirley Shackleton, Gil Scrine, Noam Chomsky, Jim Dunn, John Taylor, Pat Walsh, Peter Carey, Michele Turner, Jill Jolliffe, Max Lane, Robert Domm, Mark Aarons, Steve Cox, Margherita Tracanelli, Mark Curtis, Steve Alton, Will McMahon, Jonathan Humphreys and Tom Hyland.

José Ramos Horta's personal struggle stands out. Sometimes without the money to pay his telephone bill in New York, he has helped keep the name of his people alive in the corridors of the United Nations, and of governments in Washington, Brussels, London, Tokyo and Canberra. 'I am their biggest embarrassment,' he told me. 'They are often patronising to me, sometimes hostile; but they are never allowed to forget.' His two brothers and sister were killed by the Indonesians; he is often desperately homesick for a country he has not seen since he escaped in 1975. He once put to me a plan to hire a small aircraft and fly home. I helped to talk him out of it, as 'home' would have been an Indonesian cell.

I asked José if he ever felt defeated. 'Yes,' he replied, 'but then I think about those in the mountains, the women, the

321

old people, the kids as young as seven years old, who have the courage to smuggle information out, to travel from one resistance group to another, to monitor the international radio, to pass on hope and encouragement to the villages. My mother kept going this way; I remember receiving a message from her asking *me* not to give up. "Your comrades", she wrote, "are still fighting." My mother's name is Natalina.'

José Ramos Horta has met the Indonesians abroad and put forward, with Xanana Gusmao, a three-phased peace plan. In phase one, lasting about two years, the Timorese, Portuguese and Indonesians would work under the auspices of the United Nations to implement a range of 'confidence building measures' that would include 'a drastic reduction in Indonesian troops and weaponry in East Timor and a significant UN presence'. Phase two would last five to ten years, with political autonomy and a democratically elected People's Assembly. Finally, a referendum would determine the sovereign status of the territory. 'Indonesia should seize the olive branch we are now offering,' said José. 'Only withdrawal from East Timor will help it regain its international reputation.'

Perhaps East Timor's greatest hope lies in public opinion around the world. When *Death of a Nation* went to air in Britain, British Telecom registered 4,000 calls a minute to the number displayed at the end. When I showed the film in the Palais des Nations in Geneva, where the UN Human Rights Commission was sitting, the positive response, I was told by several members of the Commission, was unprecedented and led directly to a majority vote by the Commission authorising a Special Rapporteur on Extrajudicial Executions to go to East Timor to investigate the Santa Cruz massacre and others.

There is also hope in the waning power of Suharto and his generals. For all the West's promotion of Indonesia as the 'next Tiger' about to emulate the 'market take-off' of Singapore and Taiwan, Suharto's dictatorship is stagnant. Like Marcos and Somoza, the tentacles of his family, cronies and loyalists reach into almost every corner of economic life.

In a list compiled by an Indonesian business magazine, the richest man in Indonesia is named as the former head of the state oil monopoly. Three of Suharto's six offspring are among the ten wealthiest, including a son with a fortune of more than $220 million; and most of them control monopolies.[186]

For Indonesia, the result is a sapped, indebted economy and disparities of wealth that are quite unacceptable to a society once proud of its political energy and vision. Discontent is growing. 'Since the beginning of the twentieth century', wrote the Indonesia specialist Max Lane, 'a fundamental aspect of Indonesian history has been the struggle for freedom and human rights. At first the struggle was against colonial oppression ... Thousands of Indonesians, especially workers, entered colonial prisons as payment for the assertion of their rights. Their movements had visions of what Indonesia might be like after independence, none of which accord with the political system that prevails in Indonesia today.'[187]

The Indonesian mass movements fought for and expected political democracy and social justice, regardless of whether they were Islamic or communist. Between 1945 and 1959 Indonesia had one of the freest parliamentary democracies in the world. In 1955 there were general elections with more than thirty parties competing. The oppression at home and in East Timor is unworthy of such a nation; and a great many Indonesians understand this. They are silent out of necessity; but for how long? Who would have imagined, a few years ago, that Eritrea and Namibia would be independent, and that South Africa would have majority rule?

The enduring heroism of the people of East Timor, who continue to resist the invaders even as the crosses multiply on the hillsides, is a reminder of the fallibility of brute power and of the cynicism of others.

VII

TRIBUTES

ELSIE AND CLAUDE

THIS WEEK HAS been the anniversary of Elsie's death. Such has been my distraction lately that it has arrived and almost taken me unawares. The living make their demands, but the dead have rights too, especially those whose memory remains a source of strength in difficult times; in that way, they live on. 'How'sitgoingluv?' her telephone voice would say in the days when voices from afar sounded far away; when an imperious official would interrupt to say, 'Nine minutes up. Are you extending?'

The last time I saw her in her natural habitat was that last day on the beach before Claude's funeral. It was late autumn in the southern hemisphere. We sat in the place where we usually sat whenever I came home: in a saddle of sand against the promenade wall touched by the first spokes of early morning sun. 'Now listen,' I said to her almost as a ritual, 'you may wear that hat [it was a wonderful straw sombrero] but you still have a lot of freckles.' To which she gave her standard reply, 'Do me a favour, love. Swim behind the shark net, will you?'

We had sat in that place for a few days during almost every one of the twenty-seven years since I had left Australia. My return meant much to her. For the first day, she would speak non-stop about Claude and the past, without ever saying his name. Then she would listen, her sunglasses on her nose. I would talk about perhaps coming back to Australia to live, to which she would say with due solemnity, 'I think it's too late, John.' Year after year I would fly down from Southeast Asia and tell her what I had seen and what had moved and shaken me. Her listening, during my divorce, saw me through it.

One of our rituals, on the beach, was to stare at those great gateposts to the South Pacific, Sydney Heads, and try to imagine the thoughts and fears of our Irish great-grand-parents, Francis McCarthy and Mary Palmer, who arrived in leg-irons in the 1820s. Francis had been sentenced to fourteen years' 'penal servitude' in New South Wales for 'uttering unlawful oaths' and 'making political agitation'. Mary was an Irish scullery maid who was sentenced to death for stealing. This was commuted to 'transportation for life'. They both belonged to what Queen Victoria called 'the inflammable matter of Ireland': *animae viles*, as Robert Hughes wrote, that had to be disposed of along with the 'swinish multitude' of the English lower orders.[1]

Most of Elsie's large family – she was the fifth of nine children – did not wish it to be known publicly that 'the Stain' was upon them: that is, they had convict blood. (It is now fashionable to admit it.) In order to obliterate all evidence of this congenital flaw, her siblings embraced certain sub-Thatcherite poses, such as attempts (often hilarious) to eradicate the nasal sound from their speaking voice and the adoption of 'English ways', including an obligatory xenophobia towards all non-British elements: that is, Tykes, Yids, Refos, Krauts and Abos, to name but a few. Once in my presence, when a sister questioned the veracity of our criminal pedigree, Elsie managed to silence the room by saying, 'I'm proud of the McCarthys. They didn't belong to some false respectable deity. They had guts. Give 'em a break.'

She met Claude when she was sixteen and he was eighteen. I have a sepia photograph of them swooning beside a lake: she was a few inches taller than he. She was always self-conscious about this; and I would thank her for giving her height to me. Although she spoke fondly about a medical student, and later on there was a shadowy character called Lex, Claude was her life-long love; and I hope she will forgive me for saying that out loud. This piece is a tribute to them both.[2]

They had grown up in the Kurri Kurri, New South Wales, where Claude was an apprentice coal miner, having left school at fourteen during the First World War, when his father, an old clipper sailor, was forced out of the pits for being of German birth, even though he was one of the first naturalised Australians. This was wine-growing country; and Claude became famous as the boy who beat Ebenezer Mitchell's record by tying four acres of vines in a single day. With the proceeds, he supported his impoverished family.

Elsie didn't meet him until both had come to Sydney, where she was one of the first 'scholarship girls' at Sydney University. Claude was then an 'artisan in training' at the Sydney Mechanics Institute, where he read avidly for the first time: Dumas, Dickens, Shakespeare, Marx and his favourite, the American writer, O. Henry. Elsie would smuggle him into the university library, which was still being built. He was one of the early members of the Australian Socialist Party, which was an offshoot of the American 'Wobblies' and in the new world radical tradition. Long ago he told me, in his cautious way, that he and Elsie shared 'decent politics'.

When in 1922 she took him home to her family it was just as well she asked him to wait at the railway station, because they made it clear to her they didn't want a Bolshie carpenter with a German name for a son-in-law. Her response to this was to marry the Bolshie carpenter. On the morning of her wedding, she sent her family a one-word telegram, 'GOING'. That afternoon she followed it with another, 'GONE'.

She claimed it was pure coincidence that they got married within sight of the Female Factory, where Mary, her great-grandmother, had been interned, and which was now the Parramatta lunatic asylum. 'During the ceremony,' said Elsie, 'I remember the wailing from the imbeciles' yard. I said to your father, "God, I hope this isn't a bad omen!" '

They moved into a room overlooking the surf at Bondi, and she began to teach Latin and French, almost losing her first job when her headmistress found a copy of *The Socialist* in her locker. She was accused of 'bending young minds'. Her students at this school so loved and admired her that every year until her death, they held a dinner in her honour – and often in her absence: she had long lost confidence in herself.

She lost it perhaps because, as she wrote in her letter of resignation, there were 'domestic considerations'. That meant that she and Claude were coming apart. I cannot remember when it happened; there was shouting in the night and she seemed to grieve constantly; and I resented her tears. It doesn't matter who was to 'blame'. In truth, neither was. She made her demands, and he found another.

Suddenly, she changed her life. She went to work in factories, on assembly lines making fake leather handbags and model aeroplanes; she cherished many friends there and her rumbustiousness returned from time to time. Claude now had a government job driving in the Outback; and he relished those dawn mornings when he would strap a canvas water bag to the front bumper of his Vauxhall Velox and head west, where his freedom was.

In 1962, on the wharf at Circular Quay, she told me she knew I was 'going for good'. Something happened then. In her sixties, with little more than her state pension, she set off around the world. She would disappear from view occasionally, turning up once in the Solomon Islands. In London, she stayed in my eight foot by six foot garret in Old Compton Street, Soho, where I would find her on the doorstep laughing with the prostitutes from the club next door. 'Do you know my son *very well*?' she would ask them as I approached.

And when we went to Paris that weekend she distinguished herself by ordering, in her fluent Aussie French, a brute of a taxi driver to open the door for her; and he did. When a stroke took most of her language, she continued to speak in French, as sometimes happens with stroke victims who are bilingual. Our discussions on the beach, joke-telling and family bitching included, were now conducted in fractured French, with slabs of Latin. *Nil illegitimi carborundum!*

She and Claude had not seen each other for thirty years, though they had spoken once on the phone, accidentally.

330

That last day on the beach I told her he had died. She stared out at the Heads, then said, 'Well, he was getting on . . .' The next morning she watched me put on a dark suit and tie and go off to his funeral; she waved from the balcony. Something made me turn back, and I found her on the floor of the kitchen.

August 2, 1991

CURT GUNTHER

WALKING ALONG BROADWAY, navigating the hustlers and beggars, I came upon a familiar New York event. A hospital truck, which takes away the dead, had just made another call; someone had collapsed and died on the street. No one knew who it was. No one had seen it. A human tide had washed over him, or her, before a cop had arrived; and New Yorkers will tell you why. Helping someone can be an invitation to a mugger, whose accomplice may be the 'victim'. So, in this case, as in most, the treadwheel of the city did not stop. And when the body had gone, Santa Claus selling gold watches took its place. This made me think about Curt.

Curt died like that the other day. He suffered a heart attack on Sixth Avenue near the corner of 50th Street and lay on the sidewalk for how long we do not know. Whether or not he was still alive, and frightened, we do not know; he was dead when the truck came. His name was Curt Gunther and he was both an old friend and a remarkable man.

Lizette, who married Curt in his sixties and gave him what some call 'stability' and others call happiness, had been waiting for him in their hotel room and was beside herself when he didn't come back. She knew that trouble used to stalk Curt and she intended to take him home safely to California the next day. 'We have him,' said a Manhattan hospital and no more: that is the rule.

At his funeral in a Catholic church, she looked on in amazement at a huge floral tribute shaped like a 35-milli-metre camera. Jewish like Curt, she had never been inside a church and wondered if this spectacular offering was a

Christian icon. It had come from his oldest colleagues and friends, and especially Ken Regan, with whom he started 'Camera 5', the great New York picture agency that has recorded contemporary history, and America, with few professional equals. Curt's is an American story that Damon Runyon or Woody Allen might have written. Indeed, he was in real life the character Woody Allen likes to play: a brilliant calamity.

I knew Curt was different when we first met on assignment in Calexico, in the vineyards of California, twenty-three years ago. Robert Kennedy, then a candidate for president, was due the next morning. We put up in a fleapit with a Coke machine beneath the staircase. When the machine took Curt's money and gave no Coke, he pushed it sideways to investigate and the staircase collapsed.

The next day, flying with Kennedy on his campaign plane, I had arranged an interview with the candidate. Only one of us was allowed to join him. As Kennedy and I talked, there was a piercing 'Owww!' A bony hand extending from the lavatory had been snapping Kennedy's picture when someone slammed the door on it. Later, the same extraterrestrial periscope with a camera perched on the end appeared next to our seat. 'What's this?' asked Kennedy. 'Curt Gunther,' I said. A face that tried to see through often shattered pebble glasses, a face that never smiled, appeared at our elbow. 'How do you do?' said Curt, as always overdoing the formality. He then took arguably the finest, final pictures of the man who would have been president and who the next day was shot in front of me.

Curt, more than all of my American friends, embodied immigrant America: the huddled mass. He was born and grew up in Berlin and, at the age of thirteen, acquired his first Leica camera; photography became his obsession. His photographs of Berlin under the Nazis were through the eyes of someone watching the approach of his own violent death. During a parade of SS stormtroopers he was thrown into a doorway and arrested. He struggled free and escaped from Germany; his family died in the death camps. When he arrived in New York he was eighteen, broke and spoke no English. He remained broke. He also bore throughout his life that melancholia and *chutzpah*, that audacity and sense of irony, that distinguished so many in a generation of refugees from Jewish Germany, who became America's greatest scientists, musicians, film-makers and comics. Milton Berle, Jack Benny and Curt Gunther could have been triplets. Curt was, above all, a supreme photographer.

He loved to photograph boxing, and not only because people used to hit him from time to time. Straight off the ship in 1938, he headed for Joe Louis's training camp in upstate New York where the world heavy-weight champion was preparing to defend his title. Curt slipped past the guards and managed to confront Louis and, with no English, asked if he could take his picture. Taken aback by this unusual person, Louis not only agreed, but handed Curt $100. *Life* magazine published Curt's pictures of the champion. They are now classics.

Disaster, of course, beckoned. Hitch-hiking back to the Louis camp, Curt fell asleep and found himself in Canada from where he was deported back to Germany. He escaped again, returned to America, met Maggie, a devout Catholic from Texas, and moved to California, where they had six children. Hollywood claimed him. He knew most of the major studio stars and several were his close friends: Elizabeth Taylor, Rock Hudson, Ava Gardner among them. Rhonda Fleming had a serious crush on him, as did numerous women. When the Beatles arrived in America in the early sixties, Curt was the only photographer they asked to stay with them, partly because he could match John Lennon at poker and partly because they found it difficult to believe that Curt could fall off a ladder or horse at the very moment he was taking a picture.

For a while, to make a dollar, Curt specialised in 'Americana'. He photographed a waterskiing elephant. He photographed a funeral parlour where they built 'dream coffins', such as one shaped like a Rolls-Royce. He found an organisation in Atlanta, Georgia, that hired out an embalmed body under the slogan: 'Have dinner with Mike. He's 115 years old.' Whenever Curt said. 'Lissen, you're not gonna believe this . . . ' he was invariably right.

In 1969 we went to Las Vegas on serious business and were temporarily distracted by an Elvis Presley concert, during which Curt sang 'Blue Suede Shoes'. The next day he persuaded the billionaire recluse Howard Hughes to lend the two of us an aircraft and a pilot who would fly as close as possible to the Nevada nuclear test site (Hughes, who owned a lot of Las Vegas, was opposed to nuclear testing). As a result, we were able to land in places where the contamination threatened the food chain and people and to describe a nuclear wasteland and peril in the heart of America. This, like many of the stories I did with Curt and his partner Ken Regan, appeared in a *Daily Mirror* that was pre-Maxwell and a very different newspaper than it is today.

During the early Ronald Reagan years, Curt and I traced the journey in John Steinbeck's *The Grapes of Wrath* as much of America went back on the road in search of work. We found the new unemployed in caravan parks and tents, in cardboard shacks and under bridges. They were small farmers forced off their land by rising interest rates, and skilled workers for whom there was no longer anything on offer in an economy increasingly polarised between high-paying new technology and low-paying service industries. They represented a new breed of American 'loser' and the beginning of a depression that now impoverishes almost one American child in four. From Oklahoma to Arizona to California, Curt's camera engraved them brilliantly on metal-grey February skies.

Not surprisingly, he had a house built right on the San Andreas fault in California, and he phoned once to say there was a tidal wave in his backyard and his house was disappearing into the earth. It almost did. He was the only photographer to cover the British Open Golf Tournament wearing carpet slippers: his only shoes having been stolen from his Blackpool hotel the night before. During a brief affair in the 1960s with a very tall woman, her even taller husband would appear on cue to break Curt's cameras and ribs. When a drunk driver smashed into Curt's old Chevvy on the California freeway, he survived and Maggie did not.

The way Curt finally went, lying on the Manhattan pavement, with people walking round him, was simply inappropriate.

December 6, 1991

NOAM CHOMSKY

'TO CONFRONT A mind that radically alters our perception of the world', wrote James Peck in his introduction to *The Chomsky Reader*, 'is one of life's most unsettling yet liberating experiences. Unsettling because it can undercut carefully constructed rationales and liberating because at last the obvious is seen for what it is.'[3]

For me, Noam Chomsky has been liberating the 'obvious' since I read him while reporting from the United States on the American war in Vietnam. Without Chomsky's rigorous marshalling of evidence, his critique of American power and his courage, the truth, the 'obvious' about that war, would not have been told: nor the truth about so many 'small wars' and human upheavals in our time. His pursuit of truth is unquestionably heroic; and I, along with millions who have been informed by him, owe him much. For only Chomsky has consistently breached the walls of Orwellian 'truth' that conceal so much about our 'free' society and the suffering of those throughout the world who pay for our 'freedom'.

In his essays, books and speeches he has demolished authorised myth upon myth, relentlessly, with facts and documentation drawn mostly from official sources. His disclosures and clarity exemplify Kundera's aphorism that the 'struggle of people [against power] is the struggle of memory against forgetting'. He has shown that the war in Vietnam, far from being a 'tragic mistake', as it is so often misrepresented, was a logical exercise in imperial power, and that the United States, in furthering its strategic interests in the region, invaded a small peasant country, systematically devastating

337

its environment and killing its people, communist and non-communist. Without a significant body of opposition in the United States, owing much to Noam Chomsky's intellect and pen, President Reagan might well have invaded Nicaragua with American troops.

I first read Noam Chomsky's *The Backroom Boys* on a flight to Vietnam in 1974. 'Peace with honour', the pledge upon which Richard Nixon and Henry Kissinger had been returned to power, was well under way. American ground troops had been withdrawn and American bombers were dropping a greater tonnage of bombs on Indo-China than had been dropped during all of the Second World War.

The Asian war was no longer news.

In *The Backroom Boys*, Chomsky quoted an American pilot explaining the 'finer selling points' of Napalm: 'We sure are pleased with those backroom boys at Dow [Chemical]. The original product wasn't so hot [sic] – if the gooks were quick enough they could scrape it off. So the boys started adding polystyrene – now it sticks like shit to a blanket. It'll even burn under water now.'[4]

I knew this to be true; I once touched a Napalm victim and her skin came away in my hand. What Chomsky did in that and other books, and in his speeches and papers, was not simply to chronicle modern savagery, but to place it within a systematic 'division of labour'. One group of back-room boys had approved the development of Napalm and another had refined it 'so it'll keep on burning right down to the bone'. The pilots merely delivered it. Meanwhile, the media ensured that the whole unthinkable process remained virtually invisible, and acceptable.

In this way, political leaders, whose 'moderation' contained not a hint of totalitarianism, could, at great remove in physical and cultural distance, execute and maim people on a scale comparable with the accredited monsters of our time. Thus, John Kennedy terror-bombed Vietnam; and Gerald Ford and Henry Kissinger backed genocide in East Timor; and George Bush, with John Major in tow, conducted last year's slaughter in the Gulf and called it a 'moral crusade'.

In identifying such truths, Chomsky has got himself into a great deal of trouble. One of the roots of the hostility towards him is that he strikes at the heart of America's libertarian self-image, distinguishing between liberals and conservatives only to illuminate their common ground. Indeed, his first two books, *The Responsibility of Intellectuals* (1967) and *American Power and the New Mandarins* (1969), were frontal assaults on American intellectuals and journalists whose liberalism, he maintained, served to mask their role as 'ideological managers' of a lawless, imperial system that caused death and destruction around the world.

Like the dissident writers of the former Soviet empire, he returns in most of his work to a fundamental theme of morality: that Americans, and by implication those of us living within the American orbit, are subject to 'an ideological system dedicated to the service of power' which has no notion of conscience, and demands of the people 'apathy and obedience [so as] to bar any serious challenge to elite rule'.[5]

Alternative views are marginalised by a 'device of historical amnesia and tunnel vision cultivated in intellectual circles'.[6] He refers to American academics and journalists as a 'secular priesthood' to whom America's 'manifest destiny', its 'right' to attack and coerce small nations, is seemingly God-given.[7]

For this he has been frequently denied publication, notably in the great liberal newspapers which he unnerves and shames; for, in his analysis of imperial power, he has achieved the intellectual independence so often claimed by liberal journalists and his critics. What is often forgotten in recalling the scandals of Watergate, Irangate, the secret bombing of Cambodia and the endemic corruption of the Reagan years is that so few journalists tried or were allowed to expose them. On Zionism – still one of the great American taboos – Chomsky wrote in *The Culture of Terrorism* that the relationship of American liberal intellectuals with Israel compares with their predecessors' flirtation with the Soviet Union in the 1930s. They are fellow-travellers, he wrote, with 'protective attitudes towards the Holy State and the effort to downplay its repression and violence, to provide apologetics for it . . .'⁸

What has infuriated Chomsky's enemies is that he is almost impossible to pigeon-hole. He was against the manipulations of both sides in the Cold War, believing that the superpowers were actually united in suppressing the aspirations of small nations. It is characteristic of this brilliant maverick that, while many chose to celebrate the end of the Cold War, he was cautious. He describes as an American nightmare 'the dominance of the Eurasian land mass by one unified power' – Europe; and that what we are seeing today 'is a gradual restoration of the trade and colonial relationship of Western Europe with the East'. He says, 'The big growing conflict in world affairs is between Europe and the United States. It's been true for years, and it's now becoming pretty serious . . . They [the US establishment] really want to stick it to the Europeans.'⁹

Although Chomsky describes himself as a libertarian socialist, he supports no ideology. Indeed, his political stands seem oddly untheoretical for one who made his name as a theorist, in linguistics. He believes revolutions bring violence and suffering and he argues that 'one who pays some attention to history will not be surprised if those who cry most loudly that we must smash and destroy are later found among the administrators of some new system of repression'. If he has a faith it is in 'the commonsense of ordinary people . . . ever since I had any political awareness I was always on the side of the loser.' The essayist Brian Morton recently wrote that 'many Americans are no longer convinced that our government has the right to destroy any country it wants to – and Chomsky deserves much of the credit.'¹⁰ The late Francis Hope wrote of him: 'Such men are dangerous; the lack of them is disastrous.'¹¹

I have corresponded with Noam Chomsky for years, but had not met him until recently. In 1989 I went to hear him speak in a packed hall in Battersea in London and, to my surprise, found not an accomplished orator but a gentle, self-effacing man with an endearing dash of anarchy about him.

He could barely be heard past the third row and was much concerned with responding to the convoluted interruption of a heckler. His commitment to the principle of free expression, 'the voice of all the people being heard', has often got him into difficulty; the man haranguing him, and whose right to be heard Chomsky defended, had neo-fascist views. He struck me as a humane and thoroughly moral man; and I liked him.

Certainly, his gentleness belies the hell-raiser, reminding me of Norman Mailer's description of him in his book, *The Armies of the Night* (they shared a prison cell in 1967 following the march on the Pentagon), as 'a slim, sharp-featured man with an ascetic expression, and an air of gentle but absolute moral integrity'.[12] He is also very funny; his use of farce and irony, often miscast as sarcasm, allows him to turn officialspeak around.

When we met, I asked him about this, specifically the power of common political shorthand like 'moderates' and 'extremists'.

He said, 'In educated circles they're taken very seriously. No journalist, no intellectual, no writer can simply express the truth about the Vietnam war that the United States *attacked* South Vietnam. That isn't being moderate ... In the 1930s, the American government described Hitler as a moderate, standing between the extremists of the left and right; therefore we had to support him. Mussolini was a moderate. In the mid-1980s Saddam Hussein was a moderate, contributing "stability" to the region. General Suharto of Indonesia is described regularly as a moderate. From 1965, when he came to power, slaughtering maybe 700,000 people, the *New York Times* and other journals described him as the leader of the Indonesian moderates.'

I said, 'But they often describe you as an extremist.'

'Sure, I *am* an extremist, because a moderate is anyone who supports Western power and an extremist is anyone who objects to it. Take for example, George Kennan [the post-war American Cold War strategist]. He was one of the leading architects of the modern world and is at the soft or dovish end of the US planning spectrum. When he was head of the policy planning staff he quite explicitly said – in internal documents, not publicly of course – that we must put aside vague and idealistic slogans about human rights, democratisation and the raising of living standards and deal in straight power concepts if we want to maintain the disparity between our enormous wealth and the poverty of everyone else. But it's rare that someone is that honest.'

I said, 'You've had some spectacular rows. Arthur Schlesinger accused you of betraying the intellectual tradition.'

'That's true, I agree with him. The intellectual tradition is one of servility to power, and if I didn't betray it I'd be ashamed of myself.'

I reminded him that he had accused Schlesinger and other liberals of being a 'secular priesthood' in league with the US government in some vicious policies abroad. Could that ever be substantiated?

'Well yes, I've documented it. Actually the term "secular priesthood" I borrowed from Isaiah Berlin who applied it to the Russian commissar class; and of course we have one, too. "Commissar" is an accurate and useful term. In any country there is the dominance of the respected and respectable intellectuals who serve external power. We may honour Soviet dissidents but internally they were not honoured; they were reviled. The people who were honoured were the commissars, and this goes back in history. The people who were honoured in the Bible were the false prophets. It was the ones we call the prophets who were jailed and driven into the desert, and so on. If a British intellectual writes vulgar apologetics for US government atrocities, that's no different from the vulgar apologetics of any American intellectual for Stalin.'

I said, 'Your books are almost never reviewed in the American mainstream press and you're never asked to write for them. Have they made you, in established circles, a nonperson?'

'Oh sure. In fact, if that wasn't the case I would wonder what I was doing wrong ... Take the city where I live, Boston. The *Boston Globe* is probably the most liberal newspaper in the United States. I have many friends in the *Globe*. They not only can't review my books, they can't list them in a listing of books by local authors! In fact, the book review editor has said that none of my books would be reviewed and no book by South End Press, the local collective, would ever be reviewed as long as they were publishing anything of mine.'

I said that his attacks were mainly aimed at the United States and he often referred to the 'dark side of America'. And yet he acknowledged that America was probably the freest society in history. Wasn't there a fundamental contradiction there?

'No. The United States is, in fact, the freest society in the world. The level of freedom and protection of freedom of speech has no parallel anywhere. This was not a gift; it's not because it was written in the Constitution. Up to the 1920s, the United States was very repressive, probably more so than England. The great breakthrough was in 1964 when the law of seditious libel was eliminated. This, in effect, made it a crime to condemn authority. It was finally declared unconstitutional in the course of the civil rights struggle. Only popular struggle protects freedom.'

'But if America is the freest society on earth, where is the systematic oppression you so often attack?'

'Britain was one of the freest countries in the world in the nineteenth century and had a horrendous record of atrocities. There's simply no correlation between internal freedom and external violence. In fact, things are even more complex in the United States, which probably has the most sophisticated system of doctrinaire management in the world. You see, the basic idea which runs right through modern history and modern liberalism is that the public has got to be marginalised.

'The general public are viewed as no more than ignorant and meddlesome outsiders, a bewildered herd. And it's the responsible men who have to make decisions and to protect society from the trampling and rage of the bewildered herd. Now since it's a democracy they – the herd, that is – are permitted occasionally to lend their weight to one or another member of the responsible class. That's called an election.'

I mentioned the incident at Battersea Town Hall when he defended the right of a neo-fascist to heckle him. 'Does that right extend to everybody?' I asked him.

'Yes. If we don't believe in free expression for people we despise, we don't believe in it at all.'

'But does a racist speaking in an ethnic community, using provocative, violent language, have that same right?'

'Sure. Let's take an actual case. There is a largely Jewish town in Illinois with plenty of Holocaust survivors. A group of Nazis asked to have a march – very provocative. The American Civil Liberties Union defended their right and I agreed.'

I asked him if he would support the right of 'free speech' for those calling for the death of Salman Rushdie.

'To speak, yes . . . [but] you have to ask whether it's incitement to imminent violent action. There's no precise litmus test that tells you where to draw the line. [With Rushdie] I agree we're getting near the border. I mean if we got to the point where someone said, "Shoot!" and there's Rushdie standing over there, that's *not* protected [free speech]. If it's somebody making a speech saying I think he ought to be killed, I don't think they ought to be stopped from making that speech. Now how exactly you make these decisions is a subtle matter, but it seems to me protection of the right of freedom of speech is extremely important.'

Chomsky clearly pays a personal price for his dissidence. 'It makes me infuriated,' he has said. 'I get angry. I'm a pretty mild guy. I don't throw plates around, but internally I am seething all the time . . . A lot of my friends have burned out and I can understand that. It's very wearing and it's very frustrating.'

I asked him how he kept going. 'I don't think you should underestimate the compensations. The United States is a very different country than it was thirty years ago. It's a much more civilised country, outside of educated circles . . . Today we have to revive the understanding of the eighteenth and nineteenth century that autocratic control of the economic system is intolerable. There's a major attack on democracy going on in the world [with] a kind of world government being established which involves the IMF and the World Bank and the GATT. This has to be understood . . . and it has to be struggled against.'

June 1990 – December 1992

345

OLIVER STONE

FIVE YEARS AFTER the assassination of John Kennedy, I had dinner in New Orleans with Jim Garrison, then the city's district attorney. Garrison had gathered enough evidence to persuade three judges and a grand jury to indict a New Orleans businessman called Clay Shaw for conspiring with at least two others to murder the president.

Garrison's case contradicted the findings of the official Warren Commission, which in 1964 handed down twenty-six volumes of patently inconclusive reassurance that Lee Harvey Oswald, the accredited assassin, had acted alone. The Commission's report has since been largely discredited, not least by Congress, whose House Assassinations Committee in 1978 found, after a year-long investigation, that 'President John F. Kennedy was probably assassinated as a result of a conspiracy.'

This is what Garrison concluded a decade earlier. He was a lone voice then, and a courageous one. Established forces, including Kennedy's successor Lyndon Johnson, had backed the Warren Commission; and Garrison himself was a prominent public official in a conservative southern city whose burghers did not mourn Kennedy. His life was threatened as a matter of routine; yet he was respected as an investigator; and he was incorruptible.

Garrison believed that Oswald was telling the truth when he announced to the world's press, shortly before his own assassination in the Dallas police headquarters, that he was a 'patsy'. 'Actually,' Garrison told me, 'Oswald was a decoy who never knew the true nature of his job. He never expected to die. There were about seven men involved in an old-fashioned ambush of the president. Shots came from the three directions and the assassination team didn't leave the scene until well after they had done the job. They were fanatical anti-Castro Cubans and other far-right elements with connections to the Central Intelligence Agency.'

Garrison's theory was that Kennedy had been working for a peaceful détente with Castro and the Soviet Union and had been already thinking ahead to an American withdrawal from Vietnam. Carl Oglesby, whose lobby group successfully urged the setting up of the Congressional Select Committee on Assassinations, recently wrote that Garrison, now a judge, believed that Kennedy was killed and Oswald framed 'by a right-wing "parallel government" seemingly much like "the Enterprise" discovered in the Iran–Contra scandal in the 1980s and currently being rediscovered in the emerging BCCI scandal'.[13]

Twenty-eight years after Kennedy was shot, Jim Garrison is back on the American stage: put there by the Hollywood director Oliver Stone, whose latest film, *JFK*, is based on Garrison's 1988 memoir, *On the Trail of the Assassins*.[14] Even before he had finished filming, Stone found himself under attack. The established press, which greeted the Warren Commission's report and barely acknowledged the congressional findings that undermined it, let fly at Stone on the basis of a leaked first-draft script, and less.

Stone's film, raged the *Chicago Tribune*, was an insult to 'decency' itself. Indeed, there comes a point 'at which intellectual myopia becomes morally repugnant. Mr Stone's new movie proves that he has passed that point.'[15] The writer had not seen even the script.

According to the *Los Angeles Times*, the '*JFK* knocking business has thus far consumed 1.2 million words'. It has filled 27 columns in the *New York Times* alone. It has produced a Big Brother cover on *Newsweek* warning the world 'not to trust this movie'.[16] Stone has been accused of almost everything bar mother molestation: he has a war neurosis, he is homophobic, he has 'fascist yearnings'.[17]

The few who have defended the film have themselves been attacked. Pat Dowell, film critic of the *Washingtonian* magazine, wrote one laudatory paragraph and ended up having to resign after her editor killed it 'on principle'. 'My job', said the principled editor, 'is to protect the magazine's reputation.' These are the words that threatened his magazine's reputation: 'If you didn't already doubt the Warren Commission report, you will after seeing Oliver Stone's brilliantly crafted indictment of history as an official story. Is it the truth? Stone says you be the judge.'[18]

In the *Washington Post*, the reporter who covered the Warren Commission, George Lardner, was given a page to mock Stone and Garrison. Referring to Garrison's suggestion that as many as five or six shots might have been fired at Kennedy, Lardner wrote, 'Is this the Kennedy assassination or the Charge of the Light Brigade?'[19] The Congressional Assassinations Committee found that at least four shots and perhaps as many as six were fired. Two-thirds of the eyewitnesses reported a number of shots that came from in front of Kennedy and not from behind, where Oswald was hiding.

When I first went to Dallas in 1968, I interviewed five people who clearly remembered hearing shots that came from the bridge under which Kennedy's motorcade was about to pass. The trajectory of a bullet was still engraved in the pavement in Dealey Plaza; it could not have been fired by Oswald from behind.

One of the witnesses I spoke to was Roger Craig, a Dallas deputy sheriff on duty in Dealey Plaza as Kennedy's motorcade approached. He said that not only did the shots come from in front of Kennedy, but he saw Oswald getting into a waiting station wagon in Dealey Plaza fifteen minutes after the shooting. Craig later identified Oswald at Dallas police headquarters. He said Oswald remarked, 'Everybody will know who I am now.' According to the Warren Commission, Oswald was nowhere near the police station when Craig saw him. After he repeated his evidence to Garrison, Craig was shot at in a Dallas parking lot. When I met him, he and his family were being constantly followed and watched. He was subsequently 'retired' from the Dallas police.

That was five years after the assassination, during which an estimated 35 to 47 people connected with it had died in unbelievable circumstances. Two Dallas reporters, who were at a meeting with nightclub owner Jack Ruby the night before he killed Oswald, died violently: one when a revolver 'went off' in a police station, the other by a 'karate chop' in the shower at his Dallas apartment. The columnist Dorothy Kilgallen, the only journalist to have a private interview with Jack Ruby during his trial, was found dead in her New York apartment after telling friends that she was going to Washington 'to bust the whole thing open'. A CIA agent, who had also told friends he could no longer keep quiet about the assassination, was found shot in the back in his Washington apartment. David Ferrie, a pilot, was found dead in his New Orleans home with two suicide notes beside him. Four days earlier Ferrie had told reporters that Garrison had him 'pegged as the get-away pilot in an elaborate plot to kill Kennedy'.

Midlothian is down the road from Dallas. When I met Penn Jones, the editor of the *Midlothian Mirror*, his offices had just been fire-bombed. Every week Penn Jones devoted space in his paper to evidence that the Warren Commission had ignored or dismissed out of hand. He showed me a pirated copy of the 'Zapruder film', shot by Abraham Zapruder, a passerby in Dealey Plaza, and the only detailed record of Kennedy being shot. It shows Kennedy and Texas Governor John Connolly, who was seated in front of Kennedy, clearly being struck by separate bullets – once again, contradicting the Warren Commission. Time-Life bought the film for $25,000 but refused to release it for public viewing until Garrison subpoenaed it.

Garrison's efforts to build a case were frequently sabotaged. The extradition of witnesses from other states was refused; the FBI refused to co-operate. Garrison failed to convict Clay Shaw, because he could not prove Shaw's CIA connection. In 1975, a year after Shaw died, a senior

CIA officer, Victor Marchetti, claimed that both Shaw and Ferrie had worked for the CIA, and that the CIA had secretly backed Shaw against Garrison, who had been right all along.[20]

Perhaps this cannot now be proved; and Shaw, after all, was acquitted by a jury. But whether or not Garrison's version of events is 'correct', none of the evidence he assembled deserves the orchestrated disclaimers that *JFK* has attracted.

Having now seen *JFK*, I understand the nature and gravity of Oliver Stone's crime. He has built a convincing version of the conspiracy to kill John Kennedy, and the conspiracy to cover it up. Worse, he is in danger of persuading the masses, especially the young who don't remember where they were on the assassination day. Worse still, he has told them through America's principal propaganda medium, Hollywood, and they are packing in to see his film. It is, wrote Andrew Kopkind in the *Nation*, an 'historic achievement'.[21]

You get a flavour of the achievement and the heresy from several of Stone's attackers, notably those who miss the irony of their own words. A *Washington Post* columnist, Charles Krauthammer, reminded his readers that 'early in the days of *glasnost*, a formerly suppressed anti-Stalinist movie, *Repentance*, caused a sensation when shown in Moscow. It helped begin a revolution in political consciousness that ultimately brought down the Soviet Union. That is what happens in a serious political culture.'

What he is saying is that the custodians of American Stalinism can rest easy: that although '*JFK*'s message is at least as disturbing as that of *Repentance* ... it is received by a citizenry so overwhelmed with cultural messages, and so anaesthetised to them, that a message as explosive as Stone's might raise an eyebrow, but never a fist.' Therefore: 'The shallowness of our political culture has a saving grace.'[22]

Stone's film *is* an American version of *Repentance*; and you sense the fear of it from the Krauthammers as they deride unconvincingly the notion that the conspiracy 'has remained airtight for 28 years'. It has not remained airtight; there is an abundance of available, documented evidence that demolishes the official version, points to a co-ordinated operation in Dallas on November 22, 1963 and to a cover-up worthy of the crime.

For all the flaws in his film – and they are the usual Hollywood gratuities – Stone's unpardonable sin is that he has shamed a system that has not brought a single prosecution following the assassination (except Garrison's), and he has shamed journalism and journalists. 'Where were *Newsweek*, the *New York Times . . . NBC et al.* for the last twenty-eight years?' wrote Kopkind in one of the few pieces to go against the tide. 'Why didn't they scream from the commanding heights of the media that the government's most powerful agencies were covering up the US crime of the century? How can they blame Stone for doing what they should have done long ago?'[23]

Stone's film suggests that the assassination of Kennedy allowed Lyndon Johnson to escalate the Vietnam War. After winning the presidency in 1964 as a 'peace' candidate, Johnson staged the 'Gulf of Tonkin Incident', a wholly fraudulent tale about North Vietnam attacking American ships, and began to bomb North Vietnam in 1965. The marines were soon on their way.[24] The suggestion that the United States did not 'stumble' into Vietnam 'naively' or 'by mistake' is itself enough to enrage those who police the Authorised Truth.

However, Garrison has always been cautious about directly implicating the US government, in the form of the CIA, and agrees with the congressional committee's chief counsel who argued that the conspiracy originated in the Mafia. But he sees no logic in leaving it there. The Mafia and the CIA have long had close ties, such as in 'Operation Mongoose', a CIA plot to kill Fidel Castro using Mafia assassins. If the Mafia killed Kennedy on its own, Garrison said recently, 'Why did the government so hastily abandon the investigation? Why did it become so eagerly the chief artist of the cover-up?'[25]

This and other outstanding questions are raised brilliantly by Stone. Why was Alan Dulles, head of the CIA, left virtually in charge of the Warren Commission? Why did Chief

Justice Earl Warren – whom columnist Krauthammer lauds as a 'principled liberal' – allow himself to be so manipulated that much of the report that bears his name borders on the farcical? Take, for example, the 'magic bullet' which managed to make a couple of U-turns on its journey from Oswald's bolt-action rifle. Why were photographs of the dead Kennedy doctored? Why did Kennedy's brain go missing after a Washington autopsy report contradicted that of the Dallas doctor who received the body and was in no doubt that Kennedy had been shot from the front? And so on.

Thousands of the 1.2 million words attacking Stone have concentrated on his portrayal of Kennedy as a 'lost leader'. Kennedy was hardly that; but in any case, Stone devotes very little of *JFK* to his misguided admiration for Kennedy; and it is hardly relevant whether or not Kennedy was actually planning to take America out of Vietnam or to make peace with Fidel Castro. The point is, Kennedy was *perceived* in those days as a dangerous Catholic liberal who might.

I well remember the furore when Kennedy proposed using the anti-trust laws to break up the steel industry. For that alone, it was seriously suggested that he was a closet socialist. Stone has described this 'blind hatred' of Kennedy by the far right. 'My father hated him,' he said. 'They hated him like they hated Franklin Roosevelt.'[26]

Like Stone and Garrison, the two reporters who pursued the Watergate affair were often dismissed as 'paranoid' and 'conspiracy-theorists'. Watergate *was* a conspiracy. The Iran–Contra scandal was a conspiracy. The 'Gulf of Tonkin Incident' was a conspiracy. The secret bombing of Laos and Cambodia was a conspiracy. The overthrow of Salvador Allende was a conspiracy. Far from requiring 'protection' from film directors like Oliver Stone, Americans have apparently never been in any doubt about the Kennedy assassination. Year after year, more than two-thirds of those polled say they believe there was a conspiracy to kill him.[27] These are the people the critics dismiss contemptuously. 'They'll forget it by the time they reach the car park,' wrote one of them.

I don't think they will forget it. Video-leasing has helped some fine films endure, among them Stone's *Salvador* and Costa-Gavras's *Missing*. Both, like *JFK*, offered a perspective on the secret or 'parallel' government in Washington – which, long before the Kennedy assassination, has helped to engineer the fall of numerous regimes. More recently, it ran America's illegal war against Nicaragua, and was responsible for the Iran–Contra scandals. When Colonel Oliver North was acquitted the other day on a technicality, George Bush spoke the truth when he said, 'It sounds like the system worked real well.'[28]

Bush has played an important part in the 'system'. With Bush as director, the CIA intervened illegally in Angola and Jamaica, spending $10 million to get rid of Prime Minister Michael Manley, the dangerous socialist. Under Bush, a secret group called 'Team B' doctored facts and statistics in order to exaggerate the 'Soviet Threat'.[29]

Bush's friend, Robert Gates, the new director of the CIA, promises that the CIA will grow, regardless of the Soviet collapse.[30] Perhaps the difference these days is that the secret government is secret no more. Bush is president; CIA men are now ambassadors; American covert operations are now overt. Whereas pilots' logs once had to be falsified, this is no longer necessary – as 200,000 dead Iraqis bear silent witness. All this is now called the 'new world order'; and 'preserving order' and 'encouraging democracy' are euphemisms used every day on both big and small screens. Clearly, when *Hollywood* departs from the script, something must be done.

October 4, 1991 to May 1992

FARZAD BAZOFT

IT IS THE second anniversary of the death of Farzad Bazoft, the *Observer* journalist hanged by Saddam Hussein for doing his job. I believe this is an important anniversary, not least as an opportunity to pay tribute to a reporter who died pursuing his craft with the kind of independence and courage that is rare. But there is much more to remember than his murder. There is the behaviour of the British Government and of much of the British press in relation to his murder, which has wider implications for free journalism.

Just before he was hanged, Bazoft told a British diplomat: 'I was just a journalist going after a scoop.'[31] And quite a scoop it might have been, too. On the day Bazoft left London for Iraq, to report elections in Kurdistan, there was a huge explosion in a factory near Baghdad, where Iraq was thought to be developing missile technology. Some 700 people were reported killed.[32] Bazoft, on the spot, did what a good reporter should have done: he headed for the site to find out what exactly had happened, and why. When he got there, he took soil samples as evidence. He was arrested, tortured and sentenced to death in a kangaroo court.

Few believed Saddam Hussein would hang him; and at first the press reflected our shock and anger. Britain had to break off diplomatic relations with this 'stupid and brutal regime', said the *Evening Standard*. 'To do less would be to suggest that there might have been some justice in taking the life of Mr Bazoft.'[33] But this tone was to change.

Within 24 hours of the hanging, the *Sun* led the way with its 'exclusive', headlined 'Hanged Man Was a Robber'.[34] The facts were not in dispute; Bazoft had stolen £500 from a building society when he was a student ten years earlier. What was significant was that the story had been provided by a 'security source': in this case, MI5 acting on behalf of the Thatcher Government, apparently seeking any excuse not to suspend its lucrative business and arms deals with Saddam Hussein.

During the 1980s Baghdad had been a favourite jaunt for Thatcher's boys. Among the unframed travel souvenirs of David Mellor, then chief secretary to the Treasury, is a photograph of himself with Saddam Hussein, their paunches extended from the comfort of the Old Torturer's sofa, with Mellor beaming at the Old Torturer himself.[35] Five of his ministerial pals had sat on the same sofa.

Indeed, such was the extent of Britain's support for and complicity with Saddam Hussein that Bazoft's hanging was the gravest inconvenience. Something had to be done. He would be smeared. The *Sun*, *Daily Mail* and *Daily Express* relegated the hanging and featured the ten-year-old robbery.

This had the desired trigger effect. The *Mail* the next day carried the headline, 'Bazoft "A Perfect Spy for Israel" says MP'.[36] *Today* refined this to 'Bazoft "Was an Israeli Agent" '.[37] The quotes were from the Tory MP Rupert Allason, who writes spy books under the name Nigel West.

That was enough to silence earlier demands for sanctions against Iraq. Those newspapers that had published allegations about Bazoft's 'spying' now called for 'caution' and 'a cool head' in dealing with Iraq. A leading article in *Today* spoke for them all. 'Withdrawing our ambassador and sending home a few students will hardly rock the Hussein regime . . . ' said the paper.[38] Woodrow Wyatt, who usually spoke for Thatcher, told readers of the *News of the World*: 'It's ridiculous to reduce or cut off our trade'. His solution to the 'whole incident' was 'maximising trade and saying nothing more about Bazoft'.[39]

The smear came to a head with an infamous editorial in the *Sunday Telegraph*, which demands inclusion in journalism studies courses. For no finer example exists, not even in the *Sun*, of journalism's sewer. Under the headline 'How Innocence Can Equal Guilt', there were these words:

> A group of journalists were to have visited the [explosion] site with the permission of the Iraqi government. Permission was then withdrawn. Mr Bazoft decided to go anyway. He took photographs and soil samples. How was this different from spying? True, Farzad Bazoft would have passed on his information to a British newspaper rather than to the British government. But that would have still been spying. In these circumstances the investigative journalist takes on the role of spy.[40]

Hugo Young of the *Guardian* was one of the few to reply. He described the *Sunday Telegraph*'s 'scorn for investigative journalism' as 'matched by the extreme infrequency with which any of them has been known to insert a new fact into the public realm. Investigating nothing, save that which will confirm their unbreakable political prejudices ... the pride of Tory journalism produced the most weaselling and morally insensate explanation that the Iraqi Government can ever hope to read ... with a subtext for Western eyes which says that investigative journalism is a punishable offence against the state.'[41]

That a principal function of the press (and the rest of the media) is to limit news and public debate within an established 'consensus' seems, to me, beyond doubt. For many journalists, Macaulay's notion of a 'fourth estate of the realm' simply does not apply. But these days there is an added element. It is smear of an especially malicious, spiteful and ruthless strain that varies from tabloid to 'quality' broadsheet only in presentation. Perhaps Jack Jones was right when in 1984 he warned of a 'new wave of Goebbels-type methods beginning to spread in our country'.[42] The campaigns against *Death on the Rock*, Arthur Scargill, Salman Rushdie and Farzad Bazoft, to name just a few, were to follow.

Of course, for those newspapers that have no qualms about

their role as state protector and propagandist, smear is a form of censorship; and the aim, if not the method, is the same as it was in Soviet Russia. In this way Thatcher's censorship laws, like the Kremlin's, are promoted and guarded by journalists. In its smear against Farzad Bazoft, the *Sunday Telegraph* likened investigative journalism to an offence against the state. Sadly, it has become just that.

Among belongings of Farzad Bazoft released by Iraq some months after his hanging were several books he had read in prison in Baghdad. One of them was my book, *Heroes*. At the bottom of a page on which I had listed journalists noted for their bravery and sacrifice he had added his own name, and this: 'Farzad Bazoft of the *Observer*, who tried to tell the truth about a "big explosion" that killed so many people in Iraq, was arrested. Under pressure and fear, he gave a "false confession" and was accused of spying. He's a journalist, too.'[43]

March 20, 1992

357

JOHN MERRITT

I FIRST KNEW John Merritt when we were both on the *Daily Mirror* and he was in his twenties. I remember overhearing an argument John was having with a clutch of editorial executives; he was objecting to a special 'drugs issue' of the paper, which, by highlighting the victims of heroin rather than those who controlled the trade, came close to voyeurism. He had just returned from Pakistan and knew that the untold story lay with powerful international forces. He put his case with passion and fluency. As a serious popular journalist, he loved his craft and loathed its trivialisation.

This is not to suggest that John was without a sense of fun. The mystery remains, for example, as to who planted the plastic turd that greeted Robert Maxwell and James Callaghan as they stepped out of the *Mirror*'s executive lift, causing Maxwell to boom, 'Who did *this*?' A corporate inquiry, though inconclusive, produced only one suspect.

Certainly the *Mirror* was at its best when it published a John Merritt investigation, whether it was about homelessness or the links between the Tories and the British National Party and other groups on the extreme right. When I was helping to start up *News on Sunday*, I tried to poach him as chief reporter; but he was then on his way to the *Observer*, which became his journalistic home and where he was distinguished as, in my view, the finest reporter of his generation.

His exposé in 1989 of the horrific psychiatric colony on the Greek island of Leros – a political prison during the years of the Greek junta that became a dumping ground for the seriously ill and inadequate alike – was a classic of its kind. For this, John took the expected fire; he was denounced in the Greek Parliament as 'a tool of the CIA wanting to keep Greece out of the EC'. After European Community grants to Greece were frozen as a consequence, the worst units were closed down.[44] In this business such triumphs are too infrequent.

John then reported on the suffering of refugees seeking asylum in Britain, who were routinely bundled back to places of great danger, sometimes to torture and even death.[45] They were Kurds and people from the Horn of Africa and Latin America. Almost all the refugees he wrote about were eventually allowed in. That the Home Office was an accessory to the crimes of their tormentors angered him greatly; it was this edge to his humanity that was reflected in so much of his work.

Take John's piece written from his hospital bed.[46] Those who read it will not, I believe, easily forget it. In a sense, it was a typical Merritt investigation, in which he rooted out truths about two areas of medical care in Britain: the Bristol Cancer Help Centre, where complementary methods of cancer treatment have been pioneered; and a general medical ward at Hammersmith Hospital in London, with its overworked nurses and junior doctors, its drug addicts with collapsed veins, its alcoholics from the streets and its cancer patients undergoing chemotherapy.

John was one of the latter group. He had leukaemia: and the quotations from his diary written in a Hammersmith ward last autumn – written, I hasten to say, with none of the self-indulgence he accused himself of – ought to be read by every member of the government directly responsible for dismantling the NHS. Here are a few extracts:

Wednesday, 7 November: 'Hooked up' to chemo and antibiotics for 18 hours. Shaky, emaciated old lunatic, Mr Moody, in bed opposite takes his pyjamas off and pees over floor, hobbles towards me and tries to climb in my bed . . . Night-time: Mr Moody is swearing and yelling, 'They are trying to kill me.' Man in bed behind is being sick. Old man in next bed is sitting on his bed, covered in excrement. The smell is appalling. This is a madhouse ...

Wednesday, 14 November: 2am: My curtains are torn apart and semi-clad lunatic, like King Lear, crashes on my bed, yelling, 'Why won't you help me? I haven't done anything wrong.' Nurse takes him away. 2.30am: Old man tries to get in my bed, says I'm his father. 3am: Old man who has dirtied himself comes through my curtains; he is going to urinate on my bed; he pulls my chemotherapy stand over. I grab him by the throat and tell him I will kill him if he comes back. He starts to cry.

John described in the piece how he was first told that he would develop leukaemia 'sooner or later ... A professor called Goldstone told me, "Don't torture yourself with any ideas of self-help; it will only make things worse." He was not only arrogant, he was dead wrong.' John turned to the Bristol Cancer Help Centre where cancer patients are treated very differently and where he found decency, calm and hope. Much of his *Observer* article was devoted to answering distorted criticism of the centre, whose existence has been threatened by falsehoods recycled in the media.

John was 33. When we met for lunch the other day we talked about the swimming and sunshine that are balm to us both. He told me he had decided to stop chemotherapy and take a more holistic approach to fighting his cancer. His wife, Lindsay, supports him in all of this. Leukaemia sufferers become anaemic and vulnerable to infections and the risk of bleeding. In many cases this can be stopped by chemotherapy, but John is one of those for whom a bone marrow transplant is the only hope. Chemotherapy can force the leukaemia into remission, but side-effects are often extremely unpleasant and can undermine the quality of everyday life.

John described his decision to stop chemotherapy as no

more than realistic. It was typical of the man that he asked that anything I write about him had a wider focus. John was one of a little-known group of people who go about their lives as normally as they can while awaiting a life-saving bone marrow transplant. For many, the odds are against them finding a perfect tissue-type match. This was especially true of John, whose tissue-type was extremely rare. However, someone, somewhere, had John's tissue-type; and the search for that person, and for people with all the other combinations of tissue-types, was made by the Anthony Nolan Research Centre, based at London's Royal Free Hospital, which has the second largest register of potential bone marrow donors in the world.

The centre was established in 1974 and named after Anthony Nolan, then aged two, who was born in Australia and whose parents brought him to Britain in search of a bone marrow transplant. No tissue-type match was found; and Anthony died at the age of seven. The centre gets no support from the government; in 1989, a grant of £11,000 – one technician's wages – was abolished. In the age of cutbacks, resources in this field of medicine are severely limited. One transplant costs an estimated £80,000. Last year, 341 transplants were carried out in Britain, compared with 537 in France, where the government takes all responsibility for funding. There is a smaller NHS-funded donor scheme, which is tied to the National Blood Transfusion Service; unlike the Anthony Nolan Centre, its 'search' for tissue-types does not extend abroad.

Linda Hartwell, manager of the Anthony Nolan Centre's operations department told me,

We are linked to registers in the United States, Australia, France and Germany; and this will soon be conducted by computer. Owing to the hundreds of thousands of combinations of tissue-types, we constantly need to add donors to our register. At present, we urgently need new donors. We are able to tissue-type 500 new donors every week. In spite of the publicity from time to time, many people are still unaware of the form of treatment. Some believe only the dead can donate. But that's not so. You can live *and* give life to someone else. It's wonderful.

Andy Burgess, an engineer from Redhill in Surrey, literally saved the life of Lloyd Scott, an Essex fireman. Bank manager Neil Singleton gave bone marrow tissue that matched with a patient in Denmark. Sarah Furber did the same for an American girl. The centre has a large file of such stories; in the haystack there are many needles that *are* found.

No more than a drop of blood can start the process of saving a life; a routine blood test is enough to indicate the bone marrow type of a potential donor. If a match is found, the donor undergoes a straightforward surgical procedure lasting about an hour and a half. There is no incision, no stitching: the marrow is taken from the hip bone using hollow needles. Apart from the temporary effects of a general anaesthetic, a healthy person should suffer no after-effects. I recommend it, for the sake of those like John, for whom a 'match' was not found in time.*

July 29, 1991

---

* As a potential donor you need to be between 18 and 40 (unless you are already on the list). By writing to, or phoning, the Anthony Nolan Centre, you will receive an information pack. After you have completed the registration form and returned it, you will be sent a simple blood sample kit. You take this to your GP, give a sample and post it back. This is where you write or phone: The Anthony Nolan Research Centre, PO Box 1767, London NW3 4YR. Telephone: (071) 284 1234.

BABY HERMES

THERE IS A scene in my favourite movie, *The Blues Brothers*, in which lovable muso-crooks Jake and Elwood finally reach the centre of Chicago on their 'mission from God'. Pursued by hordes of police cars and a posse of vicious Country and Western types, the pair manage to stay ahead of the game (and play some great rhythm and blues along the way) thanks to the Bluesmobile, a 1970s former police car, which can turn cartwheels and, if necessary, fly.

On reaching Chicago, however, the Bluesmobile dies. The tyres deflate, the doors and bumpers fall off, the mighty V8 engine gives one last gasp. No matter the approaching sirens, Jake and Elwood stand, heads bowed, in tribute to a faithful friend. Behind those sunglasses there are tears.

Such a moment happened to me the other day. Having been driven at indecent speed all its life and most of mine, my thirty-year-old Baby Hermes typewriter died. Well, almost. This is a sad story with a happy ending.

First, let me describe the machine. It is about twelve inches square, light green and made of steel. Whatever has been said uncharitably about the Swiss, I maintain a respect for those mountain folk, for they made it. Moreover, it has unique features. It has every letter of the alphabet, except 'k', which fell off in Phnom Penh. It has both pound and dollar sign keys (an exciting innovation at the time) and an exclamation mark (unheard of in a portable). It also has a 'Sh' key. I don't know what 'Sh' is, and this is the first time I have hit that key in thirty years. And it has a lid, like a steel trap. Getting the lid off is often impossible due to a dent received when it was thrown downstairs during a riot at Richard Nixon's nomination in Miami in 1972.

Here I should explain that in the world of technology, I am an alien. I have only just mastered a banker's card. My fax is in the local sweet shop. The owner, Mr Mohammed Afzal, rings me when a fax arrives; we are a smooth team. The truth is I have an affection for ancient belongings and am inclined to venerate them. If belongings define the person, this is a bit worrying. My own Bluesmobile, for example, has been described as the 'last of the sit-up-and-beg cars' by one of its regular passengers; and while I concede it is a Zephyr of rust, a Zephyr it is. But I digress.

The other day, having completed the ritual shaking in order to get my typewriter's lid off, *everything* came off: the back, the sides, the roller. Every screw popped. This had never happened before.

It had not happened at the Allenby Bridge crossing between Jordan and Israel when an Israeli customs official, having cheerfully snapped each of my cigars and squeezed my tooth-paste, ordered me to 'open that!' When I couldn't, and he couldn't, he picked it up and threw it down on the floor. If he suspected it of being a dangerous device, this was eccentric behaviour. Still, it worked; the lid came off, and not a screw stirred.

The Baby Hermes has survived many such incidents. Since I paid £12 for it in Aden – it was marked down from £15 as a 'superseded model' – it has sat in my shoulder bag as I have made my way to places of instability and war. Eric Piper, the photographer and dear friend with whom I worked for many years, claimed it saved our skins in El Salvador.

Our car had been stopped by government troops at the foot of the Guazapa volcano. This was not uncommon and always unpleasant. With our legs and arms spread against the car, a jackboot amused himself by slamming the door on Eric's fingers, while another searched the car.

'What is *this*?' enquired Jackboot No. 2.

'A typewriter,' I replied.

'*This*?' he laughed. 'Open it!'

Eric, who knew the problem of the lid, said, 'Christ, he'll go crazy.'

When I failed to open it, both jackboots tried and failed. One of them pounded it with his fist, as I have done on occasions. Such was the diversion caused by the mugging of my Baby Hermes, not to mention the general derision arising from the fact that this was the sole equipment of a foreign correspondent, that Eric had time to slip $50 into the palm of Jackboot No. 1; and we were on our way.

I lost it only once: in Shanghai. It was returned to me anonymously two days later in Peking, polished, with my missing laundry attached.

In Mali, in a place called Kayes, said to be the hottest on earth, it was taken hostage by Monsieur Lamez. A bulbous, stone-like figure with almost nothing to say, he was one of six Europeans left behind when the French abandoned this regional centre of their west African empire. He owned the only hotel. In the early morning, between six and seven, Monsieur Lamez would talk to his monkeys. At dusk, he would sit facing his great prison gate and stare through the bars at nothing. When it was time for me to leave, Monsieur Lamez charged me ten times the tariff posted on his wall. I objected, put the correct amount on his desk and left.

When I returned to my room to collect my things, it was empty. The Baby Hermes was missing. 'I have put it in with the monkeys,' said Monsieur Lamez. 'When you wish to pay me what I ask, you will get it back.' It was true: the Baby Hermes was nestling in the straw of the monkey cage, with a monkey urinating close by. The mad Lamez laughed. 'Is my offer not reasonable?' he said. I thanked him for his reasonableness, and paid up.

My friend A. U. M. Fakhruddin loved the Baby Hermes, especially the sound it made: the marvellous resonance, as the key hit the page. (Remingtons sound similar, but not as urgent.) In 1970, Fakhruddin was cultural editor of *Chitrali*, a mass circulation weekly in what was then Dacca. I knew him during the Bengali liberation period that led to the demise of West Pakistan and the birth of Bangladesh.

Journalism is a Bengali tradition. Bengali reporters are among the most tirelessly inquisitive news-gatherers in the world. Their reports have a purple eloquence whose origins might be part-Raj and part-Tagore, the Bengali Byron. They are incorrigible romantics; and brave. *Chitrali* had shouted 'Joi Bangla!' (free Bengal) at the Punjabi occupiers, and its leading lights, like Fakhruddin, lived in constant fear of arrest, and worse. He sometimes hid in my hotel room, where I would return to find him gently tinkering on the Baby Hermes. I wanted to give it to him. The last word I had from him was a page in the roller on which he had typed this from Hamlet's soliloquy:

Whether 'tis nobler in the mind to suffer
The slings and arrows of outrageous fortune,
Or to take arms against a sea of troubles,
And by opposing end them?

On the day the Baby Hermes collapsed, I was bereft. So, I'm sure, was Daisy (my cat) who sleeps in the lid as I work. I took it to Dave Smith and Don Large, who run S & L Typewriters in Raynes Park, south London, and whose fine craftsmanship keeps antiques like mine on the road. 'You realise,' said Dave with due solemnity, 'unless we can find another like it, its days are numbered.' I asked him to spare nothing in his search, though I could feel a major life change coming on.

For some years, I have listened to my friends and colleagues who have long been computerised. Until recently, they sounded like Moonies or Scientologists, devoted to their new cult. 'It's so *easy*,' they say. 'You'll *never* want to go back to (chortle) *that*.' I would point out that the occasional word had been written before Alan Sugar claimed Thatcherite sainthood by selling lots of Amstrads. But my resistance is fragile. My entry into the New Age is imminent; I have consulted a computer doctor who is used to dealing with technological primitives. Also, he runs a rhythm and blues band. Jake and Elwood would surely approve.

Stop press: Dave and Don have found another Baby Hermes, circa 1960. Its best parts have been transplanted to mine, which has been completely restored. The lid, though, still won't come off without a thump. Some things are just timeless.

August 21, 1992

VIII

ON THE ROAD

TWO RUSSIAS

I FIRST WENT to Russia almost thirty years ago, going overland from Brest, along empty rutted roads through Minsk and Smolensk. This was the 'age of shadows', as the scientist Valentyn Turchin described it to me. I returned on several occasions and met many dissidents who were not protected to some extent by fame abroad. I met musicians, actors, miners, Volga Germans, Tartars, trade unionists and Christians. They shared an abiding bravery. During the mid-1970s, shortly after Leonid Brezhnev had signed the Helsinki agreement 'to respect human rights and fundamental freedom', there was a brief period of tolerating dissidents, if tolerance it was. By 1977 this was past.

To meet Vladimir and Maria Slepak I had to leave my hotel at dawn, before the KGB shift took up position on their stairs. They lived just off Gorky Street; after a withering climb by torchlight to Apartment 77, I was greeted by Vladimir's great bearded head, beaming from the door ajar. He and Maria were scientists. Vladimir came from a family of devoted communists and was named after Vladimir Ilyich Lenin. They both served short prison terms for 'anti-Soviet activities'. It was clear they had been singled out because of the help they had given others and specifically for Vladimir's work as an adviser to the beleaguered committee set up to monitor the Soviet commitment at Helsinki on human rights.

The day before I met them their telephone had been disconnected and their flat raided, and books and letters, even writing paper, confiscated. 'What is bizarre', said Maria, 'is that those of us who call on the state not to break laws

371

guaranteed by the Soviet Constitution are known as law breakers!'

As all their files had been taken away, they now drew on formidable memories. Case after case of discrimination, wrongful imprisonment and torture came out of their heads. 'I run through the list every morning so I won't forget it,' said Maria. 'It is very tiring.' That morning they had been trying to find writing paper to put down what they could remember of Vladimir Klebanov's case. He was a miner in the Ukraine, who had refused to demand overtime from his men and to send them down pits when he believed that safety regulations were being ignored. He had been imprisoned for 'slandering the Soviet State'. His crime was that he had objected to twelve deaths and 700 injuries at one colliery and he had tried to form a free trade union. The Slepaks believed he had been moved to a mental hospital. 'He is now an "untouchable",' said Vladimir. 'If we try to find out about him, the authorities will say he doesn't exist.' Maria nodded. 'But we shall find him,' she said.

They gave me lunch, apologising for the stale bread and cheese, which was all they had. I contributed a bottle of brandy. 'Oh my God, what will happen to the lists up here?' said Maria, tapping her head. We parted as old friends, and on the way out I got a taste of what they had to go through every time they entered and left their home. At the bottom of the stairs was a pack of KGB men. They all had apparent curvature of the spine, and an air of studied sullenness. They stared, blew cigarette smoke in my face and lunged at my briefcase. One of them cleared his throat in my path.

The next day I interviewed a senior editor at *Pravda*, who made a remark to be relished. 'You must understand,' he said, 'there would be no Russian dissidents if the Western press ignored them.' Did this mean, I asked, that if people and events could be ignored then they did not exist or they did not happen? 'If you like,' he replied.

On the day before I left Moscow a friend and I set out to say goodbye to the Slepaks. As we turned into the courtyard of their block of flats, two men walked straight at us. '*Nyet*,' said one of them as we started for the stairs. We kept going. A pincer of arms shot out, spun us around and ejected us back into the courtyard. And there we stood, looking up into the vicinity of the eighth floor, hoping to catch sight of Vladimir and Maria. We were about to leave when an object fell out of the sky. It was a tin mug and taped inside it was a note, which read, 'Good voyage to you! Please remember us.'

Shortly afterwards the Slepaks were arrested for displaying an 'anti-Soviet' banner on their balcony. Vladimir was given a five-year sentence of exile for 'malicious hooliganism' and was sent to a camp in the Buryat republic on the Mongolian border. Maria was given a three-year suspended sentence and joined him in exile. In 1982 Vladimir completed his sentence and returned to Moscow, his health impaired. In his absence both his sons had been allowed to leave the country. When Mikhail Gorbachev came to power in 1985, he let Vladimir and Maria go. Shortly afterwards they emigrated to Israel.

In the summer of 1990 I returned to the Soviet Union with my son, Sam. The 'age of shadows' was no more. Almost everything seemed to have changed; it was the height of *perestroika* and *glasnost*. This was my diary:

Saturday. It is almost midnight on arrival at Leningrad. The silver twilight of one of Leningrad's 'white nights' is accompanied by a silence unheard in any other large city I know. The poetess Olga Bergolts described wartime 'white nights' in a broadcast to the world from Radio Leningrad in 1941. 'The silence', she said, 'lasts for long intervals of twenty to thirty minutes. Then the German shelling is like a mad squall of fire . . . '

It is good to be a tourist. As a journalist, too often you don't have time for the past. I am reminded that during the 900 days of the German siege of Leningrad, perhaps a million people died, most of them from starvation. The silhouettes we pass in the half-light were witnesses; Pyotr Klodt's four bronze horses, which were buried as the Germans reached the edge of the city, are back on their pedestals on Anichkov Bridge. Outside our hotel are the four funnels of the cruiser *Aurora* which fired the blank shot that signalled the storming of the Winter Palace and the October Revolution. It is partly obscured by a sign: 'Levi Jeans – Duty Free', and in scribbled ballpoint: 'No Russian money please'.

Sunday. It is Navy Day. Warships, bedecked with flags, stand with the *Aurora* against the baroque façades of Peter the Great's city, still in the yellow that Peter ordered as a relief from the metallic sky over the Gulf of Finland. On the embankment are groups of dishevelled young men in camouflage jackets. Several are drunk and are shouting at the ships. They are veterans of the war in Afghanistan. To come upon such open, anti-state belligerence is a shock. The young men move across to the huge statue of Lenin at the Finland Station; the police eye them like cats, but leave them alone.

A fisherman watching this puts down his rod and greets me in German, then English. He was a draughtsman who has spent his retirement learning languages. 'Soviet people have been ghosts,' he says, 'not wishing to see or be seen, not wishing to know, just hoping to survive. But many of us have kept faith with language. It has been our secret act.' He produces a much-used copy of *How to Win Friends and Influence People* by Dale Carnegie. 'With *this*,' he laughs, 'I began to learn English.'

As a teenager during the German siege he was pressed into carrying food supplies across Lake Lagoda, which became known as 'the Road of Life'. When the spring ice could no longer withstand the weight of lorries, even horses and sleds, the city turned to its young to trek twenty miles across the ice. 'Each step was uncertain,' he says. 'If you fell down, you died quickly.'

His uncle was a member of the Philharmonic Orchestra which on the night of August 9, 1942, played Shostakovich's Seventh (or Leningrad) Symphony. Like orchestral artillery, this was broadcast on all wavelengths and heard in London and Berlin. 'That,' he says, 'was our last glory.'

Later, at Piskarevskoye cemetery Sam and I are much moved as both Shostakovich and Tchaikovsky are played across a landscape of graves and trees bound with red scarves. People come and go with single red flowers; many are young. I can think of no other city where the pain of war remains such a lasting presence.

'Good day,' says a young man. 'I have complete Soviet uniforms for you to buy. I have a soldier's suit and a sailor's suit. I have a Red Army belt and I have many Red Army watches. Everything in the Soviet military I have – a big bargain for you. You pay me in Marlboro.'

Monday. Today, the first anniversary of my mother's death, reminds me of my first visit to the Soviet Union. She wrote to me here, describing the excitement in the mining town of Kurri Kurri, New South Wales, where she grew up, on the day in 1917 they heard about the revolution in Russia.

'The miners were in the middle of a long strike,' she wrote. 'Families were hungry. But that morning, when red flags were hoisted over the lodges, people were cheered up and couldn't give a damn about the war [against Germany].' I replied in a different mood, that people in the Soviet Union seemed 'furtive and frightened'. 'They look through you,' I wrote. '1917 might have happened somewhere else.'

'Mr Gorbachev', says the Intourist guide, 'has done good things. But we've had too many icons and saints in this country and we're fed up . . . ' This anti-establishment tirade is delivered in front of the Winter Palace, whose storming she denounces as 'no more than a *coup d'état*'. Would a tourist guide in London mount such an onslaught on the national mythology? 'We don't have a history any more,' she says. 'We had to throw it away when *glasnost* showed up the lies.'

She describes how the Soviet education system is being decentralised, and is intrigued when told that education in Britain is going the other way. 'A national curriculum?' she says. 'That's how you order minds, not educate them. Are you *objecting* to this?'

Tuesday. In the shops on Nevsky Prospekt the leaves of cabbages lie on bare shelves. People do not shop, they forage, and the foragers are mostly women. A dozen of them are asleep in our Underground carriage, gripping their bags of bruised apples and plastic sandals. A survey published the other day says that two-thirds of girls aged sixteen and seventeen would rather consider prostitution than face a life as hard as their mothers'.

Of course, if you have the right sort of money you do not queue. At the restaurant in our hotel, the head waiter's greeting is: 'What money you got, Mister? You got dollars, marks, pounds . . .?' When I reply that we have Russian money we are almost thrown out. Sam says I must not play that joke again if we are to eat.

Money power, never before known in the Soviet Union, is the other side of *perestroika*. Western propaganda, that money power equals democracy, has become Soviet propaganda. The new economic order has made the rouble the currency of the poor and people will do almost anything to get hard currency. There are hard-currency prostitutes, who are said to be 'safe', and soft-currency prostitutes, with whom you take your chances.

Wednesday. The train to Moscow bounces along, with the passengers contriving an adventurous spirit. The restaurant car is Fawlty Towers transferred to rolling stock, run by a local Manuel. 'Pssst,' he says, 'Russian champagne, only five funts . . . '

'What's a funt?'

'You know, funts . . . English funts. Also caviar. Only ten funts.'

'Excuse me,' he is asked by an elderly Englishwoman, 'where is the toilet?'

'Next carriage, Madam.'

'You'd better hang on, dear,' whispers her husband. 'It's full of Russians.'

Thursday. Moscow is warm and not at all as I remember it,

a wan city seen through a curtain of rain. Tanya, the Moscow Intourist guide, is another subversive, funny and dry. 'This week,' she announces, 'Moscow has run out of umbrellas, even though there's no rain. When we ran out of alcohol, people started making moonshine. But they needed sugar; then sugar ran out ... Over there is the statue of Uri the Long Armed. God knows why they call him that.

'Now condoms are running out ... and soap. You try living without condoms and soap! Of course, it's not too bad if you have five children. Then they make you a Hero of the Motherland and give you free cream ...

'Over there is the Soviet Union's first McDonald's where a Big Mac costs half a day's wages and you stand for an hour waiting to get it. In the West you call this fast food. In front of us is the new American Embassy, which is empty because the Americans refuse to move in. They say it's full of bugs. What do they expect?

'Over there is where they're showing *Rambo* ... And that's where Gorbachev works. You call him Gorby. I call him ... ' She puts her hand over the microphone. Gorby is everyone's target, though there is grudging respect for him, perhaps even pride. In the museums there are 'Gorbachev rooms' which apply *glasnost* to the displays and tableaux. The independence movements in the Baltic states are described almost objectively; ethnic problems are not minimised. 'We are correcting the mistakes of the past,' says a curator in a monotone that gives rise to the suspicion that only the 'line' has changed. This is a suspicion widely shared: that 'the centre' is merely protecting itself by painting on a new face while, say the cynics, 'the old heart beats unerringly'.

Friday. Today the front page of the *Moscow News* has sensational news: the lifting of state censorship on the press for the first time since the revolution. 'Human thought and word have at last been liberated,' says the paper, 'so why aren't we celebrating? Why don't we journalists congratulate each other? The answer is simple: the manager has been sacked, but the master has remained in place . . . '

'No, they haven't repented', says a headline over a fine, angry piece by Lev Razgon, who asks: 'Why is it so difficult to believe them – both the government and the KGB? To this day there has been no state recognition of the fact that the eviction of millions of peasants to meet their death . . . were criminal acts. Oh, how moving are the short items in newspapers to the effect that the surviving "victims of unlawful repression" can now use municipal transport free of charge and receive a few tins of canned food in special food parcels.'

Sitting in the sun in Pushkin Square, I find it difficult to believe I am reading this. I recall the comment of the *Pravda* editor thirteen years earlier, implying that as long as state laws were ignored, they did not exist. When I repeated this to Valentyn Turchin, he said, 'We are the society of the Two Truths. When we embrace only one of them, we shall be free.' This 'embracing', now well under way, is an achievement that is difficult to overstate.

Saturday. On the fringe of Red Square an old man holds up a placard which reads: 'All power to the Soviets.' After seventy-three years the irony is almost indigestible. This was Lenin's call: the original ideal. In devolving power, is the new Soviet Union seeking the original ideal? Power in Moscow and Leningrad no longer belongs to 'the centre' but to 'Soviets' headed by democratically elected mayors, Gavril Popov and Anatoly Sobchak, who are not members of the Communist Party. In Britain 'the centre' has long abolished popular local government.

Today is brides' day. There are brides on every street and dozens of them in Red Square. They flock from the Palace of Weddings, a McDonald's of marriage, to lay flowers at Lenin's mausoleum and the eternal flame. They then range Moscow looking for a party, sitting in the vestibules of vast Gothic, smoky restaurants renowned for their knees-ups. There are brides in the Kremlin Armoury, gazing upon Catherine the Great's wedding gown, woven with gold and silver thread. And there are brides in Gorky Park pedalling pedaloes, their lace veils trailing in the water. And there are brides listening to jazz bands in the subways and catching the Underground to the football.

Today's match is at Dynamo, Moscow's premier club. Six of us pay the equivalent of sixty pence. There are no FA-approved urinal conditions, no terraced cages. The stadium is modern and spacious and only a quarter full. But there seem to be almost as many militia as fans, and whenever a goal is scored an officer stands, almost ceremoniously, and orders his men to face the crowd. This has a comforting familiarity for the English. We leave through lines of troops, trailing a Dynamo supporter, happily drunk and conducting a conversation with his one English word: 'Liverpool'.

The sun has moved to the other side of Pushkin Square. I wait for Sam, who is in the McDonald's queue. He has been made more offers for his Levis and trainers and says he can make a good profit. I point out that the original capital investment was mine.

As we set out for Moscow airport the impression I have is of a society taking remarkable risks, and vulnerable. The apocalyptic reporting of events here did not prepare me for the *extent* of the changes, and their creative force. In Britain there is no hint of an equivalent departure from the 'established order', whose accelerating concentration of executive power, secrecy and supine parliamentary opposition demand, at the very least, a 'Gorbachev solution'.

Of course, the vulnerability here derives from within, and from those who cannot wait to get their hands on this resource-rich giant. There was always a synthesis between both sides in the Cold War. Nixon and many of America's leading capitalists recognised this. Both sides knew that 'communism' was a myth in the Soviet empire and that state capitalism was a not so distant relative of monopoly capitalism. Both sides knew that a move across the divide required no serious ideological loss. At the same time both sides used – in very different ways, of course – the notion of 'communism' as a propaganda ploy against the rise of genuine democratic socialism.

When Ralph Nader, the American consumer protector, was here recently he expressed shock at the naive Soviet view of 'the market'. 'They are moving', he said, 'from being hypercritical of everything Western to hypersycophantic towards everything Western . . . They will create an internal corps of minions for the multinationals and an imitative economy. It's the Third World all over again.'

As the East Germans realised, 'naivety' is a passing phase. One of McDonald's Moscow managers resigned recently, saying she did not see the point of yet another treadwheel turned by cheap labour. How the Soviet people deal with their brave new illusions may prove to be their greatest challenge since the *Aurora* fired its blank shot that shook the world.

June 1977 to August 18, 1990

TERMINATOR IN BIFOCALS

WHEN I LIVED in America I would drive from New Orleans through the night to Florida. In those days, the Deep South could be menacing to a nosey outsider; and reaching Florida, just as a flamingo-pink sky burst over ragged silhouettes of telegraph poles and palms, was a joy.

I have an affection for Florida, partly because of the weather, but also because Florida is the state that doesn't quite fit. It is not Dixie; if anything, it is an extension of Bolivar's America, certainly of Cuba. It also has remarkable tribes: poor whites who missed the turning to California, including those from New York's huddled mass who live as if Ellis Island was yesterday, in faded art deco hotels converted to nursing homes.

The most opulent ghetto on the east coast of America is also here, at Palm Beach. But Palm Beach, dripping with diamonds and scandal, is in the same county as Belle Glade, the heart of the sugar-cane fields where the newest, mostly illegal immigrants do arguably the dirtiest and hardest job in America. They live in compounds run by the American Sugar Corporation, and little has changed since Edward Murrow's documentary, *Harvest of Shame*, exposed 'the middle of hell'. Many of the workers suffer from a disease spread by rats that breed in the cane; and if they complain they are likely to be packed off back to the West Indies. The State Department used to send its fresh-out-of-college diplomats down to Belle Glade to get a taste of the underdeveloped world, though anywhere within a few blocks of the White House would have sufficed.

I would drive down the Gulf of Mexico road which, in the Sixties, was barely two lanes. A seam of ash-white sand and gentle breakers was interrupted by tackle kiosks and fishing villages: from Pensacola to Indian Rocks. A town called St Petersburg was motels and white clapboard houses, a Rotary and a square dance club. That's where Zoë and I are now; she's my six-year-old, who is also a swimmer and a beach-comber, though she can't wait to get to Disneyworld.

There are still fishermen on the beach, but now they com-pete for space with lobster-red Brummies and massive couples from Middle America under sail in puce shellsuits. 'Where you all from?' almost everyone says; the answer is unimport-ant. I was once asked this on a Florida beach, having just emerged from the surf where a hovering police helicopter had teargassed me: part of the festivities to celebrate the renomination in Miami of President Nixon. For me, America has always been a blend of the lovable and the lethal.

The Knights of Lithuania arrived this week. They are pool-side and Sam, the guitarist at the bar, says to them: 'You people are the Now Generation. You did it over there: you showed the world what freedom is.' He adds, 'Say, any of you knights *been* to Lithuania? . . . no? . . . Any of you know where it *is*?' Giggles poolside, though the question is not unreasonable.

On the large screen in the Activities Room, a television commentator announces the first anniversary of Iraq's invasion of Kuwait with the suggestion that, a year ago, the Now Generation did not know where in the world Iraq and Kuwait were. 'Eggsactly one year ago today,' says the television man in his regulation voice-of-history baritone, 'the world's status quo took a direct hit . . . America was poised for war, but praying for a diplomatic breakthrough. But it was not to be . . . Sure, it wasn't much of a contest, but America found itself.'

Cue on the big screen Secretary of Defense Dick Cheney, speaking for the Now Generation. 'Mr Secretary,' says Mr Baritone. 'I'd like to ask you a personal reflection. What's going through your heart on this anniversary day?'

'Pride, sir, *real* pride.'

'Thank you so much, Mr Secretary.' Now back to Barbie in the studio.

The victory parades have been run again, in between the Alka Seltzer ads and the child abuse hot lines. 'We could have easily done it without the British and French,' wrote the foreign editor of the *St Petersburg Times*. ' . . . You can call this America assuming its God-given role as leader of the forces of light and right. You can even call it America as Head Honcho. Big Kahuna. Numero Uno . . . '[1]

The fluent inanities are now virtually unopposed. Power is unabashed, and celebrated with all the ignorant certainties that echo the totalitarianism over which the Now Generation claims to have triumphed.

Forty million Americans have no medical care; yet power triumphant has been reason enough for the Congress to approve $2 billion for a weapon called a Superconducting Supercollider. And the Pentagon confidently expects much more: $500 billion for weapons for which an enemy is still pending, including $24 billion for Ronald Reagan's Star Wars fantasy.

The Now Generation's very own will be a C17 military transport aircraft, so huge, wrote Tom Wicker of the *New York Times*, that it will make 'it easier to carry US troops here and there, to police up those little wars that may be part of the new world order'.[2] Ironically, although this is a society whose economy is based largely on war industry, there is no concept of war on its own soil; the consciousness of war remains the preserve of Hollywood.

The continuing obsession with soldiers 'missing in action' in South-east Asia is a variant of this. In striking, silent contrast, there is nothing about the hundreds of thousands of Vietnamese who are 'missing' and the devastation done to their country, both during the American war and the current American-led embargo.

Here on the beach, at St Petersburg, the lovable side is exemplified in the boundless grace and enthusiasm of the college youngsters who look after Zoë and her friends in the hotel's 'kids' club'. The lethal side is, as ever, on the omnipresent news. So far this year, more than 23,000 people have been murdered in America, the highest number ever.

In the *St Petersburg Times*, Jacquin Sanders writes a column called 'Faces'. 'All right,' he tells us, 'maybe I'd never fired a trendy assault weapon before. But Clearwater Firearms and Indoor Gun Range was making an offer I couldn't refuse: rent an Uzi and fire two clips for $19.75 ...

I took off my bifocals. Terminators don't wear bifocals ... I fired a few single shots [and] shifted to automatic and cut loose three or four barrages. They were noisy and jerky and satisfied the soul ... 'Killed him dead,' I said with satisfaction.

Tom Falone, the former police officer who has owned the place for 15 years, is a big man with a belly and untrusting eyes. His son and daughter are in college. Each has a handgun and a rifle. 'They aren't flag-waving nuts,' said Tom, 'but neither would hesitate to use their weapons if they had to.' The rent-an-Uzi special is advertised on a board across the street from Clearwater High School ... but this is Florida in the 1990s.[3]

August 9, 1991

THE MAGIC OF DISNEY

AMONG THE FUNNIEST American movies of recent years is a series called *National Lampoon's Vacation*. They include black farce that is rare for Hollywood. Actually, I have long identified with the central character, one Clark W. Griswald, played to bemused perfection by Chevy Chase.

Clark Griswald's manic enthusiasm for pleasing his kids will be familiar to many fathers at this time of year. In his first escapade, Griswald takes his offspring to Wallyworld. (Dare they call it Disneyworld, lest the heirs of kindly old Walt sue them to death?)

What immediately endeared Griswald to me was his disastrous odyssey to the juvenile Heaven on Earth. At an overnight stop, he tied the family dog to the back of the car and forgot about it. Further on, he was persuaded to pick up an unloved aunt who, once on board, expired. Thinking this one through, Griswald tied the body to the luggage rack, finally depositing it on the doorstep of an equally unloved cousin. 'Nothing can stop us now, kids!' he declared. 'Wallyworld, here we come!'

When he finally reached Wallyworld, it was closed for repairs. Griswald, being American, pulled a gun and demanded that the security guard open it up. (I won't tell you what happened then; you'll have to get out the video.)

None of this was necessary when Zoë and I arrived at the gates of the real Wallyworld the other day. As a precaution, I had had my hair cut. Long before Zoë was born, in the days when the length of your hair was as hot a political issue as trees are today, I sought entry into Wallyworld, only to be stopped by a man shaped like a cigar-store Indian with 'MARVIN' on his lapel.

'Sir,' said Marvin, 'you have a Factor Ten problem.' Factor Ten turned out to be 'undesirable facial hair' and hair that overlapped your collar. (Factor Seven, mysteriously, was feet.) The Magic Kingdom was then an oasis in an America said to be in turmoil. Disneyland in California, and later Disney-world in Florida, were places where all those threatening images of long-haired youth, and an unwinnable war in Asia, dissolved into Mickey, Donald *et al.*, and Prince Charming's castle lit up every night with 'Honor America'.

Much has, and hasn't, changed. Facial hair is still an issue, but only for those who work at Disneyworld. They must have none; and their teeth must be white and straight. If you want a 'life with Disney', you must wait six months while your background back to childhood is scrutinised. If accepted, you become a Disney Person, relatively well paid and with privileges otherwise regarded as the thin edge of socialism in America: medical cover for you and your family.

Zoë and I are not doing anything by half measures here. We are staying *in* Disneyworld – actually, on the corner of North Dopey Drive. The street signs have ears and the buses say 'MK' (Magic Kingdom). There are Mickey and Goofy dollars that are legal tender; and people are so *nice* that the trial of an all-American serial killer on the news (*not* the Disney Channel) comes almost as a relief.

This is not to say there are no ripples here at Disneyworld. The other day as Zoë and I, together with a wedge of other Griswalds and their kids, ran to get Snow White's autograph, a scrum developed. 'Please children, please parents,' implored Snow White, 'one at a time ... Oh dear, oh dear, oh shi ... ' There was no hulking Marvin to protect her. Only 'new men' with a pure past now guard the kingdom. They wear pink-striped shirts and they broadcast just the one tape: 'Have a nice day ... have a nice evening ... have a nice day ... have a nice evening ... '

Alas, the Griswald pack was soon out of control as small people were thrust forward to be photographed, videotaped and otherwise authenticated by the hand of a Disney star. *'Please,'* said one of the Nice Days, 'let's have some order here.'

'Assholes,' mouthed Snow White, her smile intact. Fortunately, several of the Seven Dwarfs were not far behind and were able to create a diversion. The Griswald pack now fanned out to seek the attention of Grumpy, Sleepy and Sneezy. Zoë and I, of course, hung in there.

Something similar occurred in the Hall of Presidents. A huge Griswald in red-striped calf-length shorts and multiple-zoom lens burst in. There were two small Griswalds, one of them armed with a Super Soaker 100, which is a neon-coloured imitation machine gun that spurts water for up to fifty feet. (It's the current rage here.)

'Look, you guys,' said the huge Griswald, 'they're all here . . . Jefferson, Lincoln, Roosevelt . . . '

'This one was a crook wasn't he, Dad?'

They were standing next to a picture of Richard Nixon that looks like John the Baptist.

'He was,' came the reply, *'our president!'*

What is striking is the number of adults here without children. For many, Disneyworld is the logical extension of America itself: a vast shopping mall, albeit with cars and trolleys provided in which to load children instead of groceries. Above all, Disneyworld is brilliant child's play; and all attempts at deeper analysis usually founder there. America's two enduring gifts to modern civilised life are its music, based on black culture, and Walt Disney.

Certainly, Disney has given to millions of children all over the world a joy that his best imitators have never quite matched. A friend of mine, Peter Brown, who works for British Airways at Heathrow and helps to organise 'Dream-flights' to Florida for seriously ill children, can vouch for the positive effects of that first glimpse of the Magic Kingdom.

Why is Disney different? For one thing, Walt and his original draughtsmen and animators knew about kids. They almost never patronised them. There is a cinema just inside the main gates that shows some of Disney's earliest, vintage cartoons that are both funny and wry to the point of irony. The story of Goofy as a suburban man who changes personality behind the wheel of his car is unsentimental social comment. I clearly remember seeing it at a Saturday matinee; I must have been only a year or two older than Zoë, who laughed out loud when we saw it together.

The highlight here is the electric parade at night. It was all going magically, as we say, until a great eagle appeared, lit up in incandescent white, its imperial beak spotlighted. 'HONOR AMERICA!' the eagle commanded yet again, thereupon the *Star Spangled Banner* boomed forth in super-fantastic Disneyworld stereo. Missing were Stormin' Norman as Peter Pan and Saddam Hussein as Captain Hook. Then I read that General Schwarzkopf – whose child victims still suffer in Iraq – has been signed up to tape an 'I'm going to Disneyworld!' TV commercial.

He is in good company. According to the porter in my hotel, two US Army helicopters use a clearing near North Dopey Drive and a big, stooped guy with broad shoulder pads can be seen stepping out of one of them. 'Mr Reagan,' said the porter, 'comes down to Disneyworld at least twice a year.'

August 16, 1991

HAVE A NICE WAR

ON VETERANS' DAY last week, the Walt Disney company announced it was building a new theme park near Washington, devoted to a 'serious fun celebration' of American history. 'This won't be a Pollyanna view of America,' said Disney vice-president Robert Weiss. 'We want to make you feel what it was like to be a slave. We want to make you a Civil War soldier. We're going for virtual reality. And, look, we'll be sensitive about the Vietnam War.'[4]

The Vietnam War, which was America's longest war, will be part of a permanent exhibition entitled 'Victory Field'. Just how the war will be 'sensitively' depicted is not explained in Disney's handouts. Neither is there reference to other colonial wars and invasions, such as the assaults on civilian populations in Latin America, the Caribbean and the Philippines. These events are largely eradicated from primary and secondary education in the US, while the Vietnam 'experience' is taught, if at all, as a costly, well-intentioned 'mistake', even a 'noble crusade'.

The 'cost' is frequently represented in mawkish, self-serving terms that concentrate on America as victim and the relatively few American casualties of the war (compared with the Vietnamese) and the fraudulent saga of Americans missing in action, which was the device for maintaining an 18-year embargo against Vietnam. Hollywood, thankfully, has tired of Vietnam angst and moved on to other box office concerns, leaving the sustenance of myths to others.

Last Friday, the *Washington Post* devoted almost all of its front page to the Disney announcement and to a story headlined: 'Our place for healing'. This was the unveiling of a $4 million Vietnam War women's memorial by Vice President Al Gore. 'We never listened to the women's story,' said Gore, 'and we never properly thanked them. This memorial does that.'[5]

The bronze memorial shows three American women helping a wounded soldier. In fact, most of the women who served in Vietnam were seldom near the fighting, contrary to what is now being suggested. They were nurses, secretaries, clerks, air traffic controllers and intelligence analysts. Eight were killed in fifteen years of war.

During the same period more than five million Vietnamese died, a disproportionate number of them women. These women died beneath a rain of American bombs and 'anti-personnel' devices that made Vietnam a laboratory for the new technology of 'civilian wars'. They died in the paddies and fields, in fragile bunkers, trying to protect their children from the Napalm that struck their villages in great blood-red bursts. In North Vietnam, they died in all-woman militias, courageously putting up a curtain of small-arms fire as American F105s and Phantoms came in at 200 feet; and they died on hillsides such as Dong Loc, where I found the graves of an entire anti-aircraft battery, of young women . . . Vo Thi Than, aged 22, Duong Thi Than, aged 19. And they died in prison 'tiger cages', tortured to death, and from drug overdoses in brothels and bars that served the invader.

And they are still dying from the effects of the American programme of defoliation, which was known as Operation Hades until it was changed to the friendlier Operation Ranch Hand, and which destroyed almost half the forests, and poisoned the earth and food chain. As a result of the chemicals used, countless Vietnamese women continue to give birth to babies without eyes and brains.

So Gore is right when he says 'we never listened to the women's story'. In America there is no 'place for healing' for the women of Vietnam, just another reminder of how the historical truth can be manipulated in an open society. President Bush may have been right when he announced in 1991 that his 'victory' in the Gulf had extinguished the 'Vietnam syndrome', which is the euphemism for the deep misgivings of many Americans for what their government did in Vietnam.

I happened to be interviewing a former US government official, who served in South East Asia, the day after the Disney announcement and the memorial unveiling. A troubled man, he spoke about the killing of a third of the population of East Timor by the Indonesian dictatorship, which was armed and encouraged by the same Washington group responsible for the devastation of Vietnam; he mentioned Henry Kissinger's name a great deal. Looking out at the falling leaves in Connecticut Avenue, he said, 'You know, I walk past these memorials and I think it's a real shame people are not aware that our dead are a fraction of those we killed or whose deaths we oversaw. This distance between myth, the big lie, and truth, is amazing to me, even after all these years.'

There will be no tableau for East Timor in Disney's 'Victory Field'. And I doubt if El Salvador will be represented, even though the truth of what happened there – and is still happening – made a brief public appearance last week. Some 12,000 official documents, released under pressure from Congress, revealed that Presidents Reagan and Bush conspired with the tyrants running the death squads in El Salvador. Some 75,000 people were killed between 1980 and 1991, most of them murdered by death squads and by government 'security forces', equipped, funded and often trained by the US. Today, El Salvador is said to be a United Nations 'peace triumph'. In fact, friends of Reagan and Bush are still running the death squads. In August, they killed 271 'suspected leftists'.[6] This is their contribution to the election next month, in which the left and popular forces have been persuaded by the UN to take part. President Clinton has promised to restore $11 million in aid to the new El Salvador regime.

And will the 'sensitive' treatment of Vietnam by Disney extend to Operation Restore Hope in Somalia? The similarities are striking. The American 'gunship' attacks on civilians are little different from Vietnam, where the helicopter 'gunship' was developed as an effective means of 'pacifying' people on the ground. And Clinton, who is said to have opposed the war in Vietnam, has strongly backed its rapacious echo in Somalia. Most of the dead are, of course, 'local' – a Washington term. In Vietnam, they were known as 'merelies', short for 'merely gooks'.

In the second half of the twentieth century, the Vietnam War provides us with a unique historical context; it remains the touchstone for understanding modern imperialism. Those who were seduced into believing that George Bush sent the marines to Somalia for charitable purposes would have been spared their present disillusionment had they referred to the 'saviour' role of the marines in Vietnam in 1965. The places, personalities and immediate goals may change; the presumptions of power do not.

I think Disney should not be too 'sensitive' in its approach to Vietnam. It should proclaim that the war was at least a partial victory for America. Most of the American objectives were met. Vietnam was physically ruined and the 'virus' of its alternative development model stopped from spreading to the region. An American-led blockade forced the Vietnamese to all but abandon the gains of their system, such as universal health care and education, and to welcome the IMF and the World Bank, which are presently busy 'restructuring' the country to fit into the 'global economy'. After a half century of repelling invaders, the Vietnamese now advertise themselves as 'the cheapest labour in Asia'.[7] I have never quite understood why Hollywood failed to acknowledge this achievement. Surely, in the 'virtual reality' of Disney's Victory Field, the time is right.

November 19, 1993

THE SECRET VALLEY

IT SITS LIKE Picasso's horseman in a terraced field of maize. Around the rider's neck is a blue saddlebag, which is quiet now. For a while Bruno stood there, like a condemned man beneath a tree, grieving the silence.

I have known Bruno for almost as long as I have known Italy. He is one of the last to make charcoal in an earthen kiln, *La Carbonaia*, a natural source of energy that goes back millennia. He is as thin as a grasshopper and has worked his Tuscan farm since *Il Duce*'s day. This is not classic Tuscany; the terrain is rugged and harsh. Umbria is just over the ridge, and the spurs of the mountains interlock in such a way that their sweep and acoustics are dramatic. When the late summer storms come, bringing swollen thunderheads and great arches of lightning, the echo is similar to that of heavy artillery. When Mita, who is Bruno's wife, delivers her early morning monologue, all of us in the valley are informed of her wishes.

Bruno's father, Agostino, whom I met when I first came here twenty years ago, was a commanding presence in what he called *la valle segreta*: the secret valley. His snap brim hat was always straight, his collarless shirt buttoned to the neck. He bought his farm with his demob money following the First World War and got it for a good price, he claimed, because he agreed to marry the daughter of the owner, a priest. He and Mario Rossi, the great accordion player, and the young Gianfranco Valli, were the *patroni* then – although Gianfranco was a part-time *patrone*. He was a veterinarian who served Cine Città, the movie studios in Rome, and who was described as 'the vet to the stars'. He had a wonderfully dry wit, delivered imperiously; he would declare, 'It was I who saved the life of Elizabeth Taylor's poodle!'

But I digress. Gianfranco is dead, crushed in his small vineyard when his jeep rolled over him three years ago this week. So too is Mario Rossi, who played the Mexican Hat Dance through the night at the *festa* that welcomed my friends and me, and our families, into the valley; so too is Agostino Antolini. And so is Diamanta, Agostino's widow.

Bruno is *patrone* now. He is not a model farmer of the kind approved in Brussels. He has a confusion of wheat, olive trees and trellised vines, with tobacco as the only cash crop. In 1974, the year the electricity came, he and Mita were still living by barter. In 1981, the year they got the phone on and the bathroom with bidet was built above the stables, they were fully fledged consumers. I remember seeing for the first time the strange, flickering blue light of television in the silhouette of their fifteenth-century house. Directly behind and above them is the Monte Maggio, with its forest wall of beech, oak and chestnut. It was on these slopes that Mita's family, who were landless peasants, worked as share-croppers. So it is not surprising that she, not Bruno, is the most ambitious consumer; there is a second bathroom downstairs now, with gold taps and lights around the mirror.

As for Bruno, well, these days he is under siege from *i cinghiali*, the wild boar that come down from the Monte Maggio. They come when he leaves the fields and they eat the maize until he reappears at sunrise. They respect his authority, clearly. He carries only his ancient *zappa*, a heavy steel mattock balanced on a long wooden handle. So it made sense that he should make the scarecrow look like himself, or how he wished to look. It is mounted on a wooden steed, ever vigilant, an heroic figure. It even wears his best blue cap.

But the wild boar don't give a damn. They come and eat the maize anyway. I doubt if they would be as bold were Diamanta, Bruno's mother, alive. Like the boar, she would prowl the fields in the pre-dawn light, appearing in doorways and windows, motionless, hollow-eyed and swathed in black, scaring the wits out of *bambini* and unsuspecting foreigners.

So Bruno thought of something new. On my first night back in the valley, just before midnight, when all sound is limited to the plop of falling fruit, Bruno brought up his own artillery. For seven straight sleepless hours the valley was blasted by rap, heavy metal, Motown, Madonna, Kylie Minogue, Elvis and none other than Richie Benaud. Now Richie is normally a soft-spoken bloke; but here he was at four in the morning bellowing an old Test score to non-cricketing fans from Teverina to Seano. Richie, inexplicably, was on the tape that Bruno had made and which was broadcast at multi-decibel level from an outsized speaker in the saddlebag of his wooden Don Quixote. When I pleaded for a respite the next morning, he said, 'Wild boars hate music,' though he failed to explain why they should have it in for cricket.

Had I not realised this was a Bruno plot, I might have taken action similar to that of the miscreants who, in under-standable desperation, shot out the speakers of the Miracle Nun of Teverina. The Miracle Nun lived nearby, in a hilltop fortress guarded by Filipinos. She claimed to have been blind and to have had her sight restored by a vision of the Virgin. This was fine; but there was a sinister and pecuniary air about her sect, like that of the Moonies; and she herself was seldom seen. But she was heard. At night three-foot speakers dispensed her diatribe to a local population that, while respectful of the Church, has a history of anti-clericism. One night there were four shotgun blasts and silence was restored. The Miracle Nun has now gone, owing, it is said, many millions of lire in unpaid tax.

Italy was the first country I came to from Australia thirty years ago. I got off the ship at Genoa and lived here for most of that year; and the civilisation, kindness and sardonic way of the Italians have enriched my life ever since, and once again offer a future. In the early days, I travelled with two compatriots, one of whom bore the fine name of Bernardo Giuliano and was a distant relative of the Sicilian gunman,

Salvatore Giuliano. Bernie, a gentle taciturn man who spoke with an Australian country drawl, managed to perplex everyone he met by not understanding a word of Italian. We three ran a small freelance organisation, grandly called INTEREP. Our offices were in numerous *pensioni*, youth hostels and fields. We wrote about pasta, opera and cars; and no one paid us.

My favourite city then was Siena in Tuscany; and some years later I was introduced to the rib of mountains that runs eastward from the vast plain of the Val Di Chiana to the upper valley of the Tiber. This is where the hill tribes are; the Antolinis and Rossis and Vallis. The beauty of the place is announced by Cortona, an Etruscan town that, inside its walls, is Renaissance Italy in every modern sense. For as long as I can remember, the *comune* at Cortona has routinely provided art and music, scholarship and politics from all over the world, as a public service. The municipal library is world renowned. Last week, in the Piazza della Repubblica, the mayor, Ilio Pasqui, made Alexander Dubček an honorary citizen; almost everybody came.

Like most of Tuscany, Cortona has been communist-run for years, and the Italian Communist Party (PCI) emblem is fixed to the wall opposite the clock tower. The PCI, which recently changed its name to the Democratic Party of the Left (PDS), today holds half the thirty seats in the *comune*, with the Socialists providing a majority. Those at present issuing blanket inanities about communism might reflect upon the achievements of this decidedly non-Stalinist variant in Italy, where mass support for 'Eurocommunism' has helped modern democracy to flourish where it matters most to people: not in central government but in the regions, cities and towns.

An American writer and friend, Nancy Jenkins, who used to live here, once described the time of year when the Tuscan summer 'seems to turn and settle on itself like a tawny country cat curling in the warmth of the sun . . . ' That is the time now. Along from Cortona, just before you come to the Miracle Nun's place, the swimming pool owned by the local parish sits deserted in a saddle of the mountains like a Hockney painting superimposed on countryside. The last of the Rossi brothers, Guido, stands on his balcony at Teverina, a handkerchief around his throat where he had an operation for cancer, rendering him silent. Beneath him is the Virgin lit up in her place on his facing stone wall. His wife, a jolly woman, died last year; and I sometimes think about him alone in that cavernous place.

This is the time when assorted feuds come to a head as the grapes ripen; and much of the wine will be terrible as usual. (Once, I said to a visitor, 'See that wine you're drinking; it comes from the vines just over there.' To which he replied, 'Doesn't really travel, does it?')

As for Bruno, he is inspecting the threshing machine, whose duplicate is in the museum of folklore in Cortona. He'll soon hitch it to his old tractor and will it into action. But now it is Sunday, and he is sitting with his cronies outside the local *bottega*, where they are fixtures every week. He is wearing his new brown suit; his shoes are polished, his jacket over his shoulders, a glass in his hand. 'Wild boars', he mumbles as a greeting, 'hate music.'

September 6, 1991

IX
CAMBODIA

RETURN TO YEAR ZERO

'IT IS MY duty', wrote the correspondent of *The Times* at the liberation of the Nazi death camp at Belsen, 'to describe something beyond the imagination of mankind.' That was how I felt in the summer of 1979. During twenty-two years as a journalist, most of them spent in transit at places of uncertainty and upheaval, I had not seen anything to compare with what I saw then in Cambodia.[1]

My aircraft flew low, following the unravelling of the Mekong River west from Vietnam. Once over Cambodia, there appeared to be no one, no movement, not even an animal, as if the great population of Asia had stopped at the border. Nothing seemed to have been planted nor was growing, except the forest, and mangrove, and lines of tall wild grass. On the edge of towns this grass would follow straight lines, as though planned. Fertilised by human compost – by the remains of thousands upon thousands of men, women and children – these lines marked common graves in a nation where as many as a million-and-a-half people, one-fifth of the population, were 'missing'.

We made our approach into what had been the international airport at Phnom Penh. At the edge of the forest there appeared a pyramid of rusting cars like objects in a mirage. The pile included ambulances, a fire engine, police cars, refrigerators, washing-machines, generators, television sets, telephones and typewriters. 'Here lies the modern age,' a headstone might have read, 'abandoned April 17, 1975, Year Zero.' From that date, anybody who had owned such 'luxuries', anybody who had lived in a city or town, anybody

401

with more than a basic education or who had acquired a modern skill, anybody who knew or worked for foreigners, was in danger. Many would die.

Year Zero was the dawn of an age in which, *in extremis*, there would be no families, no sentiment, no expression of love or grief, no medicines, no hospitals, no schools, no books, no learning, no holidays, no music: only work and death. 'If our people can build Angkor Wat,' said Pol Pot in 1977, 'they can do anything.'[2] In that year he killed probably more of his people than during all of his reign. Xenophobic and racist, he might have modelled himself on one of the despotic kings who ruled Angkor, the Khmer empire, between the tenth and thirteenth centuries. He was an admirer of Mao Tse-tung and the Gang of Four; and it is not improbable that much as Mao had seen himself as the greatest emperor of China, so Pol Pot saw himself as another Mao, directing his own red guard to purify all elites, subversives and revisionists. In the end he created little more than a slave state.

In my first hours in Phnom Penh I took no photographs; incredulity saw to that. I had no sense of people, of even the remnants of a population; the few human shapes I glimpsed seemed incoherent images, detached from the city itself. On catching sight of me, they would flit into the refuge of a courtyard or a cinema or a filling station. Only when I pursued several, and watched them forage, did I see that they were children. One child about ten years old – although age was difficult to judge – ran into a wardrobe lying on its side which was his or her shelter. In an abandoned Esso station an old woman and three emaciated children squatted around a pot containing a mixture of roots and leaves, which bubbled over a fire fuelled with paper money: thousands of snapping, crackling, brand-new banknotes lay in the gutters, sluiced there by the afternoon rains, from the destroyed Bank of Cambodia.

During the coming weeks one sound remained in my consciousness day and night: the soft, almost lilting sound of starving, sick children approaching death. In the eight months since the Vietnamese liberation, only three relief planes had come from the West – none had been sent by Western governments, the International Red Cross or the United Nations – in spite of appeals from the new regime in Phnom Penh. By the end of October, the tenth month, UNICEF and the Red Cross had sent 100 tons of relief; or as the Red Cross in Geneva preferred to call it, 'more than' 100 tons. In effect, nothing. Few geopolitical games have been as cynical and bereft of civilised behaviour as that which isolated and punished the people of Cambodia, and continues to do so in 1992. It is a game that beckons a second holocaust in Asia.

David Munro and I go back to Cambodia as often as we can. David and I have together made five documentary films about Cambodia; and our long friendship is committed to telling Cambodia's story until the world repays its blood debt, and there is peace. During each visit I sleep only a few hours every night. Lying bathed in sweat, waiting for sunrise, listening to the hammer blows of rain, I fall in and out of a dream-state which has assumed an unwelcome familiarity. In the passageway outside there is the sound of something being dragged on flagstones, like a bundle. This is followed by the urgent flip-flop of rubber sandals and by indistinct voices, as if conferring; then by the sound of a voice that soon becomes recognisable as the rise and fall of sobbing. The dream moves on to a setting in the countryside, which is lush and green as the sun burns away skeins of mist, revealing pieces of cloth fluttering from earth that is speckled white.

I have talked to my friend, Chay Song Heng, about this. Heng spent three and a half years as a prisoner of the Khmer Rouge, pretending to be an idiot so that the guards would not suspect him of being educated and kill him. Confined to a rice-growing 'co-operative' and banned from speaking all but compliances, he imagined he was 'a friend of the moon'. He studied the lunar phases and kept a mental record of the hours, days, months and years. 'When liberation came on December 25, 1978,' he said, 'can you imagine, I was only two days wrong!'

Heng is a translator and interpreter of English. His weekly government salary is enough to buy one can of Coca-Cola, so he takes classes in one of Phnom Penh's 'England-language streets'. He is a diminutive man, who walks with a bounce, although I have now and then seen him tremble and his eyes reflect acute anxiety. 'In the Pol Pot years,' he said, 'I used to walk to the corner of the paddy in the evening. There I would practise my English. I would say to myself – well, mumble actually, in case I was overheard – "Good morning, Heng, and how are you this morning?" and I'd reply, "I'm quite well, thank you, apart from the difficulty of living. I am a captive in my own country, and I am condemned for nothing. But they have neither my brain, nor my soul." By the way, do you know "The Cat and the Moon" by W. B. Yeats? I recited that to myself many times.'

> The cat went here and there
> and the moon spun round like a top,
> And the nearest kin of the moon,
> The creeping cat, looked up . . .

On my return in 1989, I drove into Phnom Penh with Heng. Every bridge leading into the city had been destroyed by the Khmer Rouge, except one which is now the city's artery and its monument to Year Zero. 'On the morning of April 17, 1975,' said Heng, 'the Khmer Rouge came down our street, banging on the doors, ordering us to get out. The whole city was being evacuated, pushed out. My mother, father and I got to the bridge at five o'clock, and it took us two hours to cross it with guns in our backs. During the night a woman gave birth to twins; when the guards told us to get up and move on, the new babies were left in the grass to die. The mother died later, I was told.'

Heng is one of the few people to have retained his real name. Most people have a number of aliases, or entirely new identities. Everybody remembers the moment when a list of names was read out by the Khmer Rouge. You waited for your name, and to hear it was to prepare for death. Heng is a government servant. As we spoke, he had just heard the news that fifty people had been taken off two trains by the Khmer Rouge. A list was compiled on the spot and government servants were shot dead.

Fear is a presence in Cambodia. Once, as I set out from London for Cambodia, I was told that Vietnamese intelligence had intercepted a Khmer Rouge death list and that my name was on it. Three weeks later, returning on an empty road to Phnom Penh, David and I ran into a Khmer Rouge ambush. We narrowly escaped, and the snapshot I carry in my mind is that of armed men in black lying on their bellies, motionless beneath a truck, aiming point blank at us.

It was a glimpse, no more, of what people in Cambodia continually live with; and it is contagious. Addressing the puzzle of my dream as we sat together in the frayed foyer of the Monorom Hotel, Heng said, 'You are beginning to dream as we do. You are touched by what we fear is coming. You see, we are a people walking around like sleepwalkers in a world shaped by the shadows of the past and by forces from outside, *never* by ourselves.' Visitors are often struck by the apparent normality of Phnom Penh, the spectacle of people trading, building and repairing, thronging at a cinema, waiting for a bus. But this, too, is part of the dream-state. Watch the eddies of panic when masonry falls from a building denied renovation since the first American bomb fell twenty-one years ago; or people immobilised when a burst of automatic fire is heard in the distance; or the traffic stopped by legless people demonstrating for food.

In Cambodia the surreal and the real merge. A few miles from Phnom Penh are the green hillocks of my dream, in which the bodies of as many as 20,000 people were dumped after they had been tortured and murdered, usually by skull fracture. Many were photographed at the point of death by members of Pol Pot's gestapo, S-21. Many were small children. It is their bone fragments that speckle the earth white.

Further east is Kandal Stung, a market town that was 'carpet-bombed', where protruding stone foundations resemble an excavation of antiquity. There is nobody there now. At the provincial hospital at Kampong Cham, where children die because an international embargo proscribes life-saving equipment and drugs, one ward appears about to collapse. According to a doctor, it was hit by an American bomb in the early 1970s.

At the ferry town of Neak Loeung the main street is comprised almost entirely of façades, although people have come back. The bombing of Neak Loeung was described by the US Defense Department as a 'mistake'. To rectify it the then American ambassador to Cambodia, Emory Swank, drove to the ruins in a large car and passed out $100 bills to relatives of the dead and missing: that sum apparently being the going rate in Washington for a Cambodian life.[3]

New evidence from US government documents, declassified in 1987, leaves no doubt that the bombing of Cambodia caused such widespread death and devastation that it was critical in Pol Pot's drive for power. 'They are using damage caused by B52 strikes as the main theme of their propaganda,' the CIA director of operations reported on May 2, 1973. 'This approach has resulted in the successful recruitment of a number of young men. Residents [. . .] say the propaganda campaign has been effective with refugees in areas that have been subject to B52 strikes.'[4] What Nixon and Kissinger began, Pol Pot completed.

Thousands of those who had survived the bombing were force-marched west. They were singled out as 'Vietnamese in Khmer bodies' – because they lived in the eastern zone, close to Vietnam. Like the Jews who were made to wear yellow stars, they had to wear special blue scarves and became known as the 'blue-scarves people'. Like the Jews they were decimated.[5]

Svay Toeu is one of the poorest villages, where people live in houses of mud and straw. Several led me to a cigar-shaped object the length of a man, on which children were playing. It was a bomb from a B52, which had lain there for sixteen years with only its detonator removed. Beyond it a necklace of craters extended to the horizon. At dusk we walked back through the village to a shrine made entirely with human skulls. About five hundred were arranged in wooden tiers, and there was a separate pile of tiny skulls. The moonlight caught a line of watching faces, as still and silent as the trees in which there are no birds. They were children and women; in areas such as this, where the killing was unrelenting, up to 70 per cent of adults are women.

Many of the widows still describe, obsessively, their husbands' violent deaths and the cries of their smallest children denied food; and how they were then forced to marry a man they did not know. Such traumas are said to have caused an epidemic of genital herpes and stopped menstruation.

I first visited Kompong Speu in 1979, as famine swept much of Cambodia. Since then the hospital has been rebuilt and schools reopened; and there are pictures of tranquillity, as saffron-robed monks stroll along the edge of a paddy, past playing children and their bullock. And yet, in the great shadows that follow the afternoon rain, the 'men in black' are back; and the night is theirs for the taking.

Here people who have resisted have had their villages burned down. Others now live in 'zones of free Kampuchea', where men and women are separated and forced into marriage, and the able-bodied are marched to Thailand and back, carrying boxes of ammunition. Those who have tried to escape have been shot. Others have stepped on land-mines. Beside the road, old men dig First World War-style trenches. They stop and watch, standing shoulder-deep, as if marking their own graves.

I know of no one in Cambodia who has doubts about what Pol Pot will do if, or when, he returns in the Trojan Horse the West, and the United Nations, is building for him. What he commands is not significant support, as some commentators have suggested, but significant fear. Certainly, as Western diplomacy has worked to accommodate the Khmer Rouge, Pol Pot has been laying his plans in his secret enclave in southern Thailand. We hear little about his strategy, which is surprising as most of the reporting of Indo-China originates in Thailand. It is as if the phantom persona the Khmer Rouge have contrived for the 'Great Master' has been accepted by the outside world, especially its media.

Roger Normand, fieldwork editor of the *Harvard Human Rights Journal*, has interviewed numerous senior Khmer Rouge cadre and battlefield commanders. Thanks to his patient researches, it is possible to understand the essence of Pol Pot's strategy; this is, above all, to fool Western governments and to take power in whatever guise and however long it takes. In 1990 Normand obtained the briefing notes of Pol Pot's clandestine speeches and lectures to his leadership, in the barracks of Zone 87. They show Pol Pot's conscious use of the veto the West has given him over the 'peace process'. In one speech he outlined his plans to 'delay the elections' until his forces controlled the countryside, and he warned of the danger of accepting a political settlement before his cadre had 'prepared' the people and could 'lead the balloting'.

Pol Pot's public face, Khieu Samphan – who was his president during the genocide, and who in pinstriped suit has since smiled his way around the world at the 'peace conferences' that have been crucial to the tactic of delay – dropped in on one of these briefing sessions. 'I am so busy I have no time to eat,' he said, 'because the outside world keeps demanding a political end to the war in Kampuchea. I could end the war now if I wanted, because the outside world is waiting for me, but I am buying time to give you comrades the opportunity to carry out all your [military] tasks.'

At this point Pol Pot interrupted and said that 'to end the war politically' would make his 'movement fade away' and 'we must prevent this from happening. . . . We shall push a liberal capitalist line,' he said, 'but we are not changing our true nature.'[6]

This 'true nature' was demonstrated during Pol Pot's reign when, in pursuit of a 'pure, agrarian nation', he wiped out more than a million-and-a-half people, including 15 per cent of the rural population whose interests he glorified.[7] The Khmer Rouge slogan was: 'Preserve them – no profit. Exterminate them – no loss. We will burn the old grass and the new will grow.' When Khieu Samphan was asked what 'mistakes' the Khmer Rouge had made, he replied, 'We were too slow to move against our enemies.'[8] That is, they failed to kill enough people. Ben Kiernan, associate professor of South-East Asian history at Yale, has examined the Normand papers as part of his study of Pol Pot's preparations for the reconquest of Cambodia. 'Pol Pot', he says, 'is playing the international community for suckers.'[9]

The United Nations has provided Pol Pot's vehicle of return. Although the Khmer Rouge government ceased to exist in January 1979, its representatives continued to occupy Cambodia's seat at the United Nations. Their right to do so was defended and promoted by the United States as part of their new alliance with China (Pol Pot's principal underwriter and Vietnam's ancient foe), their cold war with the Soviet Union and their revenge on Vietnam. In 1981 President Carter's national security adviser, Zbigniew Brzezinski, said, 'I encouraged the Chinese to support Pol Pot.' The United States, he added, 'winked publicly' as China sent arms to the Khmer Rouge through Thailand.[10]

By January 1980, the United States had begun secretly funding Pol Pot. The extent of this support – $85 million from 1980 to 1986 – was revealed six years later in correspondence between Congressional lawyer Jonathan Winer, counsel to a member of the Senate Foreign Relations Committee, and the Vietnam Veterans of America Foundation. Winer said the information had come from the Congressional Research Service. When copies of his letter were circulated the Reagan Administration was furious. Then, without adequately explaining why, Winer repudiated the statistics, while not disputing that they had come from the Congressional Research Service. However, in a second letter to Noam Chomsky, Winer repeated the original charge, which, he told me, was 'absolutely correct'.[11]

As a cover for its secret war against Cambodia, Washington set up the Kampuchean Emergency Group, known as KEG, in the American embassy in Bangkok and on the border. KEG's job was to 'monitor' the distribution of Western humanitarian supplies sent to the refugee camps in

Thailand and to ensure that Khmer Rouge bases were fed. Although ostensibly a State Department operation, its principals were intelligence officers with long experience in Indo-China.

Two American relief aid workers, Linda Mason and Roger Brown, later wrote, 'The US Government insisted that the Khmer Rouge be fed ... the US preferred that the Khmer Rouge operation benefit from the credibility of an internationally known relief operation.'[12] Under American pressure, the World Food Programme handed over $12 million worth of food to the Thai Army to pass on to the Khmer Rouge. '20,000 to 40,000 Pol Pot guerrillas benefited,' according to former Assistant Secretary of State Richard Holbrooke.[13]

I witnessed this. In 1980 a film crew and I travelled in a UN convoy of forty trucks, seventeen loaded with food, seventeen with seed and the rest with 'goodies', which was the term UN people used for their assorted largesse. We headed for Phnom Chat, a Khmer Rouge operations base set in forest just inside Cambodia and bunkered with land-mines. The UN official leading the convoy, Phyllis Gestrin, a University of Texas psychology professor, was worried and clearly disliked what she was doing. 'I don't want to think what this aid is doing,' she said. 'I don't trust these blackshirts.' She could barely suppress her fear and demonstrated it by driving her Land Rover across a suspected minefield and into a tree. 'Oh man,' she said, 'this place gives me the creeps. Let's get it over with.' At that, she turned the Land Rover around and pointed it back along the track. 'We always position it so we can get out fast,' she said.

After the trucks had dropped their 'goodies' in a clearing Phyllis solicited the signature of a man who had watched in bemused silence from a thatched shelter. 'Well, I guess what I've got here is a receipt,' she said, with a nervous laugh. 'Not bad, from a butcher like him ... ' The 'butcher' was the base commander, who demanded that the foreign aid people address him as 'Monsieur le Président'. They also knew him as 'Pol Pot's Himmler'.

In 1979 I had seen in Siem Reap province the mass grave of several thousand people shortly after it was unearthed. Many of the corpses had been beaten to death, as their splintered skulls clearly showed. Now, smiling before me was Pol Pot's governor of the province at the time of that mass murder. His name, he told me, was Nam Phann, which was a military alias. He was eager to confirm that Western aid had nourished and restored the Khmer Rouge. 'Thank you very much,' he said, 'and we wish for more.' I asked him whom he regarded as his allies in the world. 'Oh,' he replied, 'China, the ASEAN* nations . . . and the United States.'

The Kampuchean Emergency Group maintained close contact with bases like Phnom Chat. Working through 'Task Force 80' of the Thai Army, which has liaison officers with the Khmer Rouge, the Americans ensured a constant flow of UN supplies. KEG was run by Michael Eiland, whose career underscored the continuity of American intervention in Indo-China. In 1969–70 he was operations officer of a clandestine Special Forces group code-named 'Daniel Boone', which was responsible for the reconnaissance of the American bombing of Cambodia.[14] By 1980 Colonel Eiland was running KEG from the American embassy in Bangkok, where it was described as a 'humanitarian' organisation. He was also responsible for interpreting satellite surveillance pictures of Cambodia and in that capacity was a valued informant of a number of resident members of Bangkok's Western press corps, who referred to him in their reports as a 'Western analyst'. Eiland's 'humanitarian' duties led to his appointment as Defense Intelligence Agency (DIA) chief in charge of the South-east Asia Region, one of the most important positions in American espionage.

In November 1980 direct contact was made between the Reagan White House and the Khmer Rouge when Dr Ray Cline, a former deputy director of the CIA, made a secret visit to a Khmer Rouge operational headquarters inside Cambodia. Cline was then a foreign policy adviser on President-

* Association of South-East Asian Nations

elect Reagan's transitional team. Within a year, according to Washington sources, fifty CIA agents were running America's Cambodia operation from Thailand.

The dividing line between the international relief operation and the American war became more and more confused. For example, a Defense Intelligence Agency colonel was appointed 'security liaison officer' between the United Nations Border Relief Operation (UNBRO) and the Displaced Persons Protection Unit (DPPU). In Washington he was revealed as a link between the US Government and the Khmer Rouge.[15]

By 1981 a number of governments had become decidedly uneasy about the charade of the United Nations' continued recognition of Pol Pot. This was dramatically demonstrated when a colleague of mine, Nicholas Claxton, entered a bar at the United Nations in New York with Thaoun Prasith, Pol Pot's representative. 'Within minutes,' said Claxton, 'the bar had emptied.'

Clearly, something had to be done. In 1982 the United States and China, supported by Singapore, invented the Coalition of the Democratic Government of Kampuchea, which was, as Ben Kiernan pointed out, neither a coalition, nor democratic, nor a government, nor in Kampuchea.[16] It was what the CIA calls 'a master illusion'. Prince Norodom Sihanouk was appointed its head; otherwise little had changed. The two 'non-communist' members, the Sihanouk-ists and the Khmer People's National Liberation Front (KPNLF), were dominated by the Khmer Rouge. The urbane Thaoun Prasith – a personal friend of Pol Pot, he had called on Khmer expatriates to return home in 1975, whereupon many of them 'disappeared' – continued to speak for Cambodia.

The United Nations was now the instrument of Cambodia's punishment. Not only was the government in Phnom Penh denied the UN seat, but Cambodia was barred from all international agreements on trade and communications, even from the World Health Organisation. The United Nations has withheld development aid from only one Third World country: Cambodia. In the United States, religious groups were refused export licences for books and toys for orphans. A law dating from the First World War, the Trading with the Enemy Act, was applied to Cambodia and, of course, Vietnam. Not even Cuba and the Soviet Union were treated in this way.

By 1987 KEG had been reincarnated as the Kampuchea Working Group, run by the same Colonel Eiland of the Defense Intelligence Agency. The Working Group's brief was to provide battle plans, war material and satellite intelligence to the so-called 'non-communist' members of the 'resistance forces'. The non-communist fig leaf allowed Congress, spurred on by an anti-Vietnamese zealot, Stephen Solarz, to approve both 'overt' and 'covert' aid estimated at $24 million to the 'resistance'. Until 1990 Congress accepted Solarz's specious argument that US aid did not end up with or even help Pol Pot and that the mass murderer's American-supplied allies 'are not even in close proximity with them [the Khmer Rouge]'.[17]

While Washington has paid the bills and the Thai Army provided logistics support, Singapore, as middle man, has been the main 'conduit' for Western arms. Former Prime Minister Lee Kuan Yew is a major backer of American and Chinese insistence that the Khmer Rouge be part of a settlement in Cambodia. 'It is journalists', he said, 'who have made them into demons.'

Weapons from Germany, the United States and Sweden are passed on directly by Singapore or made under licence by Chartered Industries, which is owned by the Singapore Government. The same weapons have been captured from the Khmer Rouge. The Singapore connection has allowed the Bush administration to continue its secret aid to the 'resistance', even though this breaks a law passed by Congress in 1989 banning even indirect 'lethal aid' to Pol Pot.[18] In August 1990, a former member of the US Special Forces disclosed that he had been ordered to destroy records that showed American munitions in Thailand ending up with the Khmer

Rouge. The records, he said, implicated the National Security Council, the President's advisory body.[19]

Until 1989 the British role in Cambodia remained secret. The first reports appeared in the *Sunday Telegraph*, written by their diplomatic and defence correspondent, Simon O'Dwyer-Russell, who had close professional and family contacts with the highly secretive Special Air Services, the SAS. O'Dwyer-Russell disclosed that the SAS were training Cambodian guerrillas allied to Pol Pot.[20] Oddly, for such a major story, it was buried in the paper. 'I could never understand why,' O'Dwyer-Russell told me. 'When I filed the copy, I had the clear impression I had a page one lead. I never received an adequate explanation.' Shortly afterwards, *Jane's Defence Weekly*, the 'military bible', published a long article alleging that Britain had been training Cambodian guerrillas 'at secret bases in Thailand for more than four years'. The instructors were from the SAS, ' . . . all serving military personnel, all veterans of the Falklands conflict, led by a captain'.

One result of the British training, reported *Jane's*, was 'the creation of a 250-man KPNLF sabotage battalion [whose] members were taught how to attack installations such as bridges, railway lines, power lines and sub-stations. Their first operations were conducted in Cambodia's Siem Reap province in August, 1986.'[21]

Other diplomatic correspondents were able to confirm the *Jane's* report; but little appeared in print. In November 1989, after the showing of *Cambodia Year Ten*, a film made by David Munro and myself, British complicity in Cambodia's international isolation and civil war became a public issue.[22] Some 16,000 people wrote to Prime Minister Thatcher, seeking an explanation.

The film repeated the allegations about the SAS and drew attention to an interview the Prime Minister had given shortly before Christmas 1988 to the BBC children's programme, *Blue Peter* (which had raised large sums for Cambodia). Thatcher was asked what her government could do to help stop Pol Pot coming back to power. 'Most people agree', she said, 'that Pol Pot himself could not go back, nor some of his supporters, who were very active in some of the terrible things that happened.' She then said, 'Some of the Khmer Rouge of course are *very* different. I think there are probably two parts to the Khmer Rouge: those who supported Pol Pot and then there is a much, much more *reasonable* group with the Khmer Rouge.'

At this, the interviewer was taken aback. 'Do you really think so?' she asked, to which Thatcher replied, 'Well, that is what I am assured by people who know ... so that you will find that the more *reasonable* ones in the Khmer Rouge will have to play some part in a future government ... '[23]

This raised urgent questions, several of which I put to a Foreign Office minister, Lord Brabazon of Tara, in a filmed interview for *Year Ten*. I asked him to explain Thatcher's statement that there were 'reasonable' Khmer Rouge. Who were they? I asked. 'Um,' he replied, 'the ones that Prince Sihanouk can work with.' When I asked for their names, a Foreign Office minder stepped in and said, 'Stop this *now*. This is *not* the way that we were led to believe the line of questioning would go.'

The minder, Ian Whitehead, had earlier taken me aside and urged me to 'go easy on him'. Now he refused to allow the interview to proceed until he had approved the questions. As for the minister, he had left the interviewing chair and could not be persuaded to return. The head of the Foreign Office News Department later claimed that David Munro had given an 'assurance' that Whitehead's intervention in front of the camera would not be shown. No such assurance had ever been given. This was a taste of Foreign Office disinformation, of which a great deal more was to come. What the episode demonstrated was that the government was keenly aware that its policy on Cambodia was indefensible.

British special military forces have been in South-east Asia since the Second World War. Britain has supplied advisers to the Royal Thai Army since the 1970s, along with the Americans, in what is known as Operation Badge Torch. In 1982, when the American, Chinese and ASEAN governments contrived the 'coalition' that enabled Pol Pot to retain Cambodia's UN seat, the United States set about training and equipping the 'non-communist' factions in the 'resistance' army. These were the followers of Prince Sihanouk and his former minister, Son Sann, the leader of the KPNLF, who were mostly irregulars and bandits. The resistance was nothing without Pol Pot's 25,000 well-trained, armed and motivated guerrillas, whose leadership was acknowledged by Prince Sihanouk's military commander, his son, Norodom Ranariddh. 'The Khmer Rouge', he said, are the 'major attacking forces' whose victories were 'celebrated as our own'.[24]

The guerrillas' tactic, like the Contras in Nicaragua, was to terrorise the countryside by setting up ambushes and the seeding of minefields. In this way the government in Phnom Penh would be destabilised and the Vietnamese trapped in an untenable war: their own 'Vietnam'. For the Americans, in Bangkok and Washington, the fate of Cambodia was tied to a war they had technically lost seven years earlier. 'Bleeding the Vietnamese white on the battlefields of Cambodia' was an expression popular with the US policy-making establishment. Of course, overturning the government in Hanoi was the ultimate goal.

The British provided jungle training camps in Malaysia and in Thailand; one of them, in Phitsanulok province, is known as 'Falklands camp'. In 1991 David Munro and I filmed an interview with a Cambodian guerrilla who had been trained by the British in Malaysia. Although a member of the KPNLF, he had worked under cover as a Khmer Rouge. He described a journey by train and covered truck from Thailand to an unknown destination. He was one among troops from all three Cambodian groups, including the Khmer Rouge. 'The Khmer Rouge were much more experienced and older,' he said. 'We eventually arrived in a camp in Malaysia, run by the Malaysian Army, where the instructors were British and Americans in uniform. Although we slept and ate separately from the Khmer Rouge, we wore the same uniforms and trained together with the same equipment as one army. We were all taught exactly the same. The British taught us about laying mines and setting booby traps.'

The Cambodian training became an exclusively British operation after the 'Irangate' arms-for-hostages scandal broke in Washington in 1986. 'If Congress had found out that Americans were mixed up in clandestine training in Indo-China, let alone with Pol Pot,' a Whitehall source told Simon O'Dwyer-Russell, 'the balloon would have gone right up. It was one of those classic Thatcher–Reagan arrangements. It was put to her that the SAS should take over the Cambodia show, and she agreed.'

Shortly after seven-man SAS teams arrived from Hong Kong and the SAS base in Hereford, a new British ambassador took up his post in Bangkok. This was Derek Tonkin, who had previously been at the embassy in Hanoi. During his time as ambassador the British operation in Thailand remained secret.

This was extraordinary, but not surprising. Western correspondents based in Bangkok have long relied upon 'intelligence sources' and 'Western analysts' for stories about communist Indo-China, and have accepted the constraints of official advice. This partly explains why so much reporting of Indo-China has reflected the attitudes of Western governments or, more precisely, of Washington. Bangkok is a convivial place for cold warriors and for those seeking what the journalist Paul Quinn Judge once described as a 'better result in Indochina'.[25] It is also a 'place of mirrors', as a Thai friend calls it, in which an ostensibly free press is tolerated within a fixed 'consensus'. Journalists who step outside this are intimidated or even murdered, and transgressing foreigners are often told quietly to leave.[26] The bloody events that stripped away Thailand's mask in May 1992 left a number of journalists among the dead and injured.

For whatever reason, there was little reporting of the activities of KEG and the true nature of its successor, the Working Group. The fact that British soldiers were training Cambodians to kill and maim each other was not known, or covered up. Similarly, Operation Badge Torch was not considered newsworthy. Neither was Pol Pot himself, who could commute from his headquarters at Trat to his beach house at Bang Saen without hindrance from curious Western journalists. The military hospital in Bangkok where he was treated regularly for haemorrhoids was but a few minutes from the bar of the Foreign Correspondents Club. When Pol Pot slipped into the beach resort of Pattaya in June 1991, to direct the Khmer Rouge delegation attending a major peace conference, his presence was not reported until much later.[27]

Thailand is run by a paddle wheel of beribboned generals. Although untested in battle (apart from 'battles' against unarmed students) they have made a multi-million-dollar 'killing' out of the international aid programme for Cambodian refugees. This is an extension of the graft that consumes much of the Thai economy, whose staples are child labour and tourism based on prostitution. For many years this subject was taboo. For apologetic Western eyes – investors, bankers and journalists – its vast underbelly did not exist; Thailand was 'booming', an 'economic tiger' and a 'model' for the rest of Asia.

Cambodia Year Ten was shown in thirty-six countries in 1989. The Swedish foreign minister phoned me to say that such was the public response in Sweden that his Government would change its stance at the forthcoming vote on Cambodia at the United Nations. 'We shall no longer support the seating of the coalition,' he said. (Sweden abstained.) The day after the film was shown in Australia, the Hawke Government abandoned its support for a direct Khmer Rouge role in a future Cambodian government and announced an Australian plan to have the United Nations temporarily administer Cambodia and hold elections. This became the United Nations 'peace plan'.[28] In Britain the Government told Parliament that British diplomats would visit Cambodia for the first time in fifteen years and promised £250,000 in humanitarian aid. This significant movement in Western policy-making came as historic changes were taking place in the communist world. In September 1989 the Vietnamese withdrew unconditionally from Cambodia.

The revelation of Britain's training of Pol Pot's allies caused an uproar in Parliament and the Government's embarrassment was acute. Copies of a parliamentary statement by Foreign Secretary Douglas Hurd were sent to people who wrote to the prime minister or to their MP. 'We have never given', it said, 'and will never give support of any kind to the Khmer Rouge.'[29] This was false. From 1979 to 1982 the British Government voted in the United Nations for Pol Pot's defunct regime to occupy Cambodia's seat. Moreover, Britain voted with the Khmer Rouge in the agencies of the UN, and not once did it challenge the credentials of Pol Pot's representative.

The Hurd statement failed to satisfy a great many people and caused one of those curious disturbances in the House of Commons when Tory MPs have to deal with postbags overflowing with letters on a subject they wish would go away. Several debates on Cambodia ensued, minister after minister denied that Britain was indirectly backing the Khmer Rouge – until William Waldegrave, then a Foreign Office minister, made a slip and gave what the opposition interpreted as a 'tacit admission' that the SAS were indeed in Cambodia.[30]

Labour MPs now demanded the government withdraw the SAS, and threatened to identify the Secret Intelligence Service (MI6) official who ran the British operation from the embassy in Bangkok. He was assigned to Thailand around the time that Derek Tonkin was appointed ambassador.

As a result of publicity, and the parliamentary exposure, the SAS operation was hurriedly invested with greater secrecy or, as they say in Whitehall, given 'total deniability'. The official at the embassy was withdrawn (he was a close friend and tennis partner of Tonkin) and the training was 'privatised'; that is, the instructors were no longer to be serving personnel. In operational terms that made no difference whatsoever, as SAS personnel normally 'disappear' from army records whenever they go on secret missions. What was important was that the Government could now deny that British servicemen were involved. 'Britain', announced

Foreign Office minister Tim Sainsbury, 'does not give military aid *in any form* to the Cambodian factions'.[31] 'I confirm', Margaret Thatcher wrote to Neil Kinnock, 'that there is no British Government involvement of any kind in training, equipping or co-operating with Khmer Rouge forces *or those allied to them.*'[32] (My italics.) Parliament and the British people were misled, repeatedly.

There is a curiously fervent edge to the expression of Britain's Cambodia policy. This is perhaps surprising as Cambodia belongs to a part of the world that the empire did not reach. Much of this passion flowed from the civil servant responsible, David Colvin, the long-serving head of the South-east Asia Department at the Foreign Office. Until his transfer in late 1991 Colvin was in complete command, writing and overseeing pronouncements of the secretary of state, as well as keeping a close eye on the Bertie Wooster figures who come and go as Foreign Office ministers – those like Lord Brabazon and his successor, the Earl of Caithness, whose signatures appear on Commons written replies and standard fob-off letters sent to the public.

Colvin served at the British embassy in Thailand during the American war in Vietnam. He was strongly pro-Washington and could be observed at public meetings on Cambodia, displaying his impatience with speakers who opposed British policy. Once, during a Commons debate, he made his objections from the public gallery so obvious that he was identified by Chris Mullin, MP.[33] His scribbled handwriting – 'rubbish' and 'fatuous' – appears on the pages of a study by the Cambodia specialist, Raoul Jennar, who has argued against the inclusion of the Khmer Rouge in the peace process.[34] In the margin next to where Jennar warns against giving advantage to Pol Pot, Colvin has scrawled that Jennar 'must be a socialist'.[35] Colvin made clear he wanted the Khmer Rouge included.[36] 'When I met Mr Colvin,' the former foreign policy adviser to the Thai prime minister, Kraisak Choonhaven, told me, 'I informed him that supporting the so-called non-communists in the coalition was the same as supporting Pol Pot. I got the distinct impression he did not believe this.'[37]

For most of 1990 David Munro and I – together with Simon O'Dwyer-Russell of the *Sunday Telegraph* – pursued an investigation into Western support for the Khmer Rouge in Europe, the United States and South-east Asia. By the summer we believed we had accumulated sound evidence that the SAS was directly training the Khmer Rouge. Our sources were in the Ministry of Defence and in 'R' (reserve) Squadron of the SAS. One of them, himself a former SAS trainer in Thailand, told us,

We first went to Thailand in 1984. Since then we have worked in teams of four and eight and have been attached to the Thai Army. The Yanks [Special Forces] and us worked together; we're close like brothers. We trained the Khmer Rouge in a lot of technical stuff – a lot about mines. We used mines that came originally from Royal Ordnance in Britain, which we got by way of Egypt, with markings changed. They are the latest; one type goes up in a rocket and comes down on a parachute and hangs in the bushes until someone brushes it. Then it can blow their head off, or an arm. We trained them in Mark 5 rocket launchers and all sorts of weapons. We even gave them psychological training. At first they wanted to go into the villages and just chop people up. We told them how to go easy . . .

Some of us went up to 100 miles inside Cambodia with them on missions. There are about 250 of us on the border at any one time and a lot of those would change sides given half the chance. That's how pissed off we are. We hate being mixed up with Pol Pot. I tell you: we are soldiers, not child murderers. It costs half a million quid to train one of us. Putting us in the service of a lunatic like Pol Pot makes no sense. There is no insurgency in Cambodia that threatens us.

O'Dwyer-Russell interviewed two SAS trainers whose

military background he knew well. They described in detail how they had taught Khmer Rouge troops mine-laying and mines technology. None could be interviewed on film; the Official Secrets Act – 'reformed' by Douglas Hurd when he was home secretary – prevented them from speaking publicly and Central Television from broadcasting their words. In any case, the SAS is a small, tight regiment and dissenters are not welcomed. O'Dwyer-Russell proposed that he speak on behalf of the men.

I didn't have to remind him that, as a senior correspondent of a high Tory newspaper, he was risking not only his relationship with Whitehall, upon which his present job largely depended, but also his career. 'That's not the point,' he said curtly, unravelling to his full six feet six and a half inches. 'The point is, this whole thing has gone too damn far. We're training bloody mass murderers. And that's not what the British Army should be about. And those of us who know should speak out, *regardless*!'

Simon O'Dwyer-Russell appeared to have been carved out of the British establishment. He wore a navy-blue blazer, usually a bright polka-dot silk tie with glittering tie-pin and highly polished size-15 brogues, custom made. His voice boomed. He enjoyed the social life around hunting, while disapproving of the sport itself. He came from a service family – his father was a senior RAF officer and his brother a Harrier pilot – and he went to King's College, London, where he took a degree in war studies.

Although his own military career was limited to the Territorials, Simon had many close friends in the elite regiments, and rode regularly in Hyde Park on horses of the Household Cavalry. He had especially strong personal and family contacts in the SAS. A senior colleague on the *Sunday Telegraph* wrote that he had achieved 'unrivalled access to both the Armed Forces and the security services at all levels', which enabled him to produce 'a series of notable exclusives' along with 'apoplexy at the Ministry of Defence'.[38]

During 1989 and 1990 David Munro and I got to know Simon well and to regard him as a maverick whose professional honesty was matched by a sense of moral outrage, and courage. He had three conditions for appearing in our film. He would need the approval of his principal informants, as he would be speaking for them and there was a risk that they might be identified by their association with him. He would require the permission of his editor, Trevor Grove; and his paper should publish the story first on the Sunday prior to transmission. David and I agreed. On the morning after meeting Grove, he phoned to say that he had been given the go-ahead.

The following is part of the interview I conducted with Simon, which was broadcast in David's and my film *Cambodia: The Betrayal* on October 9, 1990. He used 'my understanding' as the words agreed with his informants in the Ministry of Defence.

JP: 'What is the nature of British assistance to the Khmer Rouge now?'

SO-R: 'Well my understanding is that following the row that erupted last autumn as a result of partly your programme, and partly because of my own newspaper, the government put the word out that support from that date onward was to be very much more covert in its nature, so that it was passed very clearly to being an MI6 operation. The result of that has been that there are a number of former SAS people who are now out of the service and who are private individuals but that are working to some form of contract to provide training and mines technology to the Khmer Rouge.'

JP: 'What exactly do you mean by mines technology?'

SO-R: 'One can lay anti-personnel and off-route mines which can be detonated automatically by the sound of people moving along the track. There are an increasing number of anti-personnel mines which fire thousands of pellets into the air and once they bed themselves in people's bodies are incredibly difficult to find, for doctors working with fairly rudimentary field equipment.'

JP: 'So these are the kind of mines that are being supplied by the British?'

SO-R: 'My understanding is that the British are still involved in supplying those sorts of mines, yes.'

JP: 'Are they British-made mines?'

SO-R: 'The mines themselves need not necessarily be British because there are a series of licensing agreements that obviously exist worldwide, bringing with it the element of deniability ... We are not laying mines with "Made in the UK" on them.'

The British Government's response was swift. In the *Independent* of October 12, a front-page headline said, 'Hurd rejects Pilger's Cambodia allegations'. Inside, half a page was devoted to a long riposte under Hurd's name, an unusual step for a foreign secretary. 'The brutality and murder of the Pol Pot regime shocked the world,' wrote Hurd. 'The British Government took the lead in denouncing it at the UN.'

In fact, the opposite was true. The government of which Hurd was a foreign office minister took the lead in *supporting* Pol Pot's claim on Cambodia's seat at the United Nations. 'Interestingly enough,' wrote Hurd, 'some of those who are now loudest in denouncing the Khmer Rouge, at the time acted as their apologists.'

Nothing was offered to substantiate this slur. My stated admiration for Noam Chomsky was cited and Chomsky was also smeared as one who had 'condemned reports of Khmer Rouge atrocities as Western, anti-communist, propaganda'. Considering its baselessness, this was a remarkable claim for a serving foreign secretary to make and one which reflected the government's anxiety that the cover on its most secret military adventure had been lifted. In a letter to the *Independent* on October 22, Chomsky refuted Hurd's smear with reference to his own condemnation of the Khmer Rouge for 'major atrocities and oppression' and 'a grisly record of barbarity'.[39]

The rest of Hurd's article was a blanket denial of any British link with the Khmer Rouge. He dismissed O'Dwyer-Russell's disclosures as 'ruminations', and praised the Government's 'commitment' to bringing peace to Cambodia. He also lauded the 'effectiveness' of British 'humanitarian' aid to Cambodia: an astonishing remark.

The day after the Hurd article appeared a dismayed senior official of the Overseas Development Ministry disclosed that a request for British funding specifically for the repair of a water filtration plant in Cambodia had been turned down 'on ministerial direction' because it was regarded as 'developing aid' that might assist Phnom Penh.[40] Cambodia has one of the highest death rates in the world from preventable water-borne diseases.

Following Hurd's denial, Chris Mullin, MP tabled a written parliamentary question asking Defence Secretary Tom King, 'if British servicemen or any other employees of his Department have been involved in providing military training for Cambodians in Malaysia, Thailand, or Singapore . . . ' The question was returned to Mullin by the Commons Table Office, which refused to accept it. The Table Office clerk had written the word 'blocked' on it.[41]

Shortly after the start of the Gulf War in January 1991 President Bush described Saddam Hussein as 'Adolf Hitler revisited'.[42] Bush also expressed his support for 'another Nuremberg'; and the call to try Saddam Hussein under the Genocide Convention was echoed in Congress and across the Atlantic in Whitehall.

This was an ironic distraction. Since the original Hitler expired in his bunker, the United States has maintained a network of dictators with Hitlerian tendencies – from Saddam Hussein to Suharto in Indonesia, Mobutu in Zaire and a variety of Latin American mobsters, many of them graduates of an American school of terrorism in the US-run Canal Zone in Panama. But only one has been identified by the world community as a genuine 'Adolf Hitler revisited', whose crimes are documented in a 1979 report of the UN Human Rights Commission as 'the worst to have occurred anywhere in the world since Nazism'.[43] He is, of course, Pol Pot, who must surely wonder at his good fortune. Not only is he cosseted, his troops fed, supplied and trained, his envoys afforded all diplomatic privileges, but – unlike Saddam Hussein – he has been assured by his patrons that he will never be brought to justice for his crimes.

These assurances were given publicly in 1991 when the UN Human Rights Sub-commission dropped from its agenda a draft resolution on Cambodia that referred to 'the atrocities reaching the level of genocide committed in particular during the period of Khmer Rouge rule'.[44] No more, the UN body decided, should member governments seek to 'detect, arrest, extradite or bring to trial those who have been responsible for crimes against humanity in Cambodia'. No more are governments called upon to 'prevent the return to government positions of those who were responsible for genocidal actions during the period 1975 to 1978'.[45]

These assurances were also given as part of the UN 'peace plan' which was drafted by the permanent members of the Security Council: that is, by the United States. So as not to offend Pol Pot's principal backers, the Chinese, the plan has dropped all mention of 'genocide', replacing it with the euphemism: 'policies and practices of the recent past'.[46] On this, Henry Kissinger, who played a leading part in the mass bombing of Cambodia in the early 1970s, has been an important influence; it was Kissinger who in July 1989 urged Bush to give the Peking regime 'most favoured nation' trading status in spite of the bloody events in Tiananmen Square only weeks earlier. Kissinger regards the Chinese leadership as a moderating influence in South-East Asia and supports China's 'present course'.[47]

At the first Cambodian 'peace conference' in Paris in August 1989, American delegates demonstrated their desire to rehabilitate China and, if necessary, its Khmer Rouge client. American and other Western diplomats entertained

Chinese and Khmer Rouge representatives in private; and it was in this atmosphere that the word 'genocide' was declared 'impolitic'. In a briefing document bearing the handwriting of the Australian minister for foreign affairs, Gareth Evans, a 'specific stumbling block' is 'identified' as 'whether it is appropriate or not to refer specifically to the non-return of the "genocidal" practices of the past'.[48]

It is difficult to imagine Herbert Vere Evatt, Australia's minister for external affairs at the birth of the United Nations, similarly wondering whether or not it was 'appropriate' to refer to the 'genocidal practice' of Hitler's Third Reich. Evatt was the first president of the United Nations and played a significant part in the formation of the world body, which arose from the commitment of all nations that 'never again' would the Holocaust be allowed to happen. But it did happen again, in Asia; and it could happen yet again.

The attitude of the Australian Government was salutary. In announcing his 'UN plan' for Cambodia in November 1989, Senator Evans said his aim was to exclude the Khmer Rouge. And yet the plan called on the Hun Sen Government to step aside. Evans described this as 'even-handed'.[49] In its 153 pages the Australian Government's 'working paper' made no mention of Khmer Rouge atrocities, which were all but dismissed as 'human rights abuses of a recent past'.[50]

In the UN General Assembly, the Australian representative, Peter Wilenski, used this euphemism to describe the killing of more than a million-and-a-half people, or a fifth of Cambodia's population.[51] As Ben Kiernan has pointed out, 'The plan soon degenerated into a refusal to take any action without Khmer Rouge acceptance – not at all a means to exclude them.'[52] As for bringing Pol Pot before the 'Nuremberg' proposed by President Bush for Saddam Hussein, this was proposed in 1988 by Gareth Evans's predecessor, Bill Hayden, and rejected by US Secretary of State George Schultz.[53]

The lesson for Saddam Hussein here was patience. Just as Pol Pot has been restored, if not completely absolved, so the

Iraqi 'Hitler' could reasonably expect to be left alone. And just as those who have politically and militarily opposed the return to power of Pol Pot have been undermined by Western governments and the United Nations, so have those, like the Kurds, who have fought Saddam. This is the order of the world, both old and new.

The UN 'peace plan' for Cambodia, part of which grew out of the Evans plan, was an essential part of this order. Few such documents, proclaiming peace as its aim, have been as vague and sinister. The new, cleansing jargon was deployed throughout; the Khmer Rouge were reclassified as a 'faction' and given equity with the three other 'factions'. Their distinction as genocidists was not considered relevant. Each 'faction' was to regroup in 'cantonments' where 70 per cent of their weapons would be surrendered 'under UN supervision'. Disarming the conventional Phnom Penh Army would be relatively simple; disarming the Khmer Rouge would be virtually impossible, as most of their arms flowed across the Thai border and were held in secret caches.

The Khmer Rouge, said the plan, 'will have the same rights, freedoms and opportunities to take part in the electoral process' as any other Cambodians and specifically to 'prohibit the retroactive application of criminal law'. So not only did the mass murderers have the same rights as those who survived the pogroms but they were granted immunity from prosecution. There would be 'free and fair elections', regardless of the fear and coercion that were Pol Pot's stated strategy in a country that had never known elections. Never mind, said the UN plan, a 'neutral political environment' was the way forward. Here the informed reader struggled not to break into demonic laughter. Proportional representation, the chosen electoral method, would apparently produce a 'neutral' coalition, headed by Prince Sihanouk.[54]

Norodom Sihanouk is much romanticised by Westerners, who describe his rule as *la belle époque*. On his throne Sihanouk knew how to patronise and manipulate foreigners; he was the reassuring face of feudal colonialism, a colourful relic of the French Empire, a 'god-king' who was his country's leading jazz musician, film director and football coach.

But there was another Cambodia beneath the lotus-eating surface of which foreigners were either unaware or chose to ignore. Sihanouk was a capricious autocrat whose thugs dispensed arbitrary terror. His dictatorial ways contributed to the growth of the communist party, which he called the Khmer Rouge. His own 'Popular Socialist Community' had nothing to do with socialism and everything to do with creating suitably benign conditions for the spread and enrichment of a corrupt and powerful mandarinate in the towns and of ethnic Chinese usurers in the countryside.

It was at first puzzling that the United States should now see in Sihanouk 'the hopes for a decent and democratic Cambodia',[55] because the Cambodia he ran was anything but democratic. The prince regarded himself as semi-divine and the people as his 'children'. Members of the Cambodian Parliament were chosen by him, or their seats were bought and sold. There was no freedom to challenge him. His secret police were feared and ubiquitous; and when an organised opposition arose seeking an end to corruption and poverty, many of its leading members were forced to flee for their lives into the jungle, from which cauldron emerged Pol Pot and his revolutionaries.[56]

Although a number of his relatives were murdered by the Khmer Rouge, Sihanouk retains the distinction of being one of the first to support them and one of the last to condemn them. After he was overthrown in 1970 and replaced by General Lon Nol, he called on his people to join Pol Pot's *maquis*. During this time he was said to be a prisoner of the Khmer Rouge in Phnom Penh. Yet, during his 'imprisonment', he flew to New York and addressed the United Nations General Assembly as Pol Pot's head of state. He misled the world about the true nature of the Khmer Rouge, saying that 'a genuinely popular democracy and a new society have been born in Kampuchea – a society without the exploitation of man by man...'[57] This inspired many expatriate Cambodians to return to a fate of torture and death.

Sihanouk's closeness to the Khmer Rouge provided a challenge for his Western backers. In 1979 the British journalist William Shawcross, a personal friend of Sihanouk, claimed the prince had 'roundly denounced the brutality of the Khmer Rouge' from exile in Peking. As the transcript of Sihanouk's press conference showed, he said nothing of the kind, referring only vaguely to 'violations of human rights'. In fact, he gushed with praise for the Khmer Rouge regime: 'The whole country [was] well-fed,' he said, ' . . . the conditions were good . . . Our people . . . had more than enough to eat. And suppose there is a reign of terror. How could they laugh? How could they sing? And how could they be gay? And they are very gay.' Sihanouk went on to say that his people were so 'happy' that 'my conscience is in tranquility . . . it seems [there was] better social justice . . . I confess that the people seem to be quite happy with Pol Pot.'[58]

In 1990 Sihanouk said he 'would agree to anything the Khmer Rouge wanted'.[59] He was equally blunt on American television: 'The Khmer Rouge', he said, 'are not criminals. They are true patriots.'[60] He told the American journalist T. D. Allman, who has known him for many years, that he personally was not opposed to genocide.[61] To some observers of the 'mercurial' prince, he is unstable; to others he is a fox. A former Foreign Office diplomat, John Pedler, who has known Sihanouk since the 1960s, believes the prince remains in awe of his former jailer during the Pol Pot years, the Khmer Rouge leader, Khieu Samphan. 'It is a psychological attachment,' wrote Pedler in 1989. 'They are like the rabbit and the snake. One of his actual jailers, Chhorn Hay, a hardcore Khmer Rouge who oversaw his imprisonment in the Royal Palace, is often among his entourage, a constant reminder to him that his life is still in the hands of "Angkar" [Pol Pot's mythical organisation]. The West – and indeed, he himself – still has not recognised how much of what he purveys is Khmer Rouge propaganda.'[62]

One of Sihanouk's most ardent promoters in the United

States was Congressman Stephen Solarz, chair of the House of Representatives' Asia and Pacific Affairs Committee. In 1989, out of 535 Senators and representatives, only Solarz had visited Cambodia since the overthrow of Pol Pot. This indicated the depth of understanding about a country upon which the United States has rained the greatest tonnage of bombs in the history of aerial bombardment. Solarz was responsible for building support for the Bush Administration's backdoor support for the Khmer Rouge, which he called 'covert lethal aid' to the 'non-communist resistance'.[63]

Solarz's claim – that 'non-communist resistance forces do not train or fight with the Khmer Rouge and are not even in close proximity with them' – was breathtaking.[64] There was abundant evidence to the contrary, including film of Sihanoukists and Khmer Rouge troops attacking a village and looting it, even videotaping each other in the act.[65] There was voluminous detail of their joint operations in *The Cambodia Report on Collaborative Battles*.[66] 'Sihanouk's forces carry out joint military operations with the Khmer Rouge,' wrote John Pedler in 1991, 'as I was personally able to confirm when I visited Kompong Thom in central Cambodia. I was in that province when the last remnant of the Sihanoukist forces involved in a joint operation with the Khmer Rouge against the provincial capital were ousted from their positions in Pre Satalan.'[67]

On February 28, 1991 the White House issued a statement on Cambodia which it clearly hoped would be ignored or lost by a media overwhelmed by the day's other news: 'victory' in the Gulf. President Bush, it said, had admitted to Congress that there had been 'tactical military co-operation' between the 'non-communist' Cambodian forces and Pol Pot's Khmer Rouge.[68] The statement was a condition demanded by Congress for its final approval of $20 million for the 'non-communists'.

Writing in New York's *Newsday*, the former Indo-China war correspondent Sidney Schanberg (whose epic story was dramatised in the film *The Killing Fields*) scornfully referred to the 'disingenuous semantic game' that 'Solarz and his

White House pals have played with life and death in Cambodia'. This 'magnificently weasel-worded' announcement, he wrote, was confirmation that the White House had been lying on Cambodia.[69]

August 1979 to June 1992

THROUGH THE LOOKING GLASS

ALTHOUGH THERE ARE several close contenders, the *Sunday Times* can justifiably claim to be Britain's premier newspaper of smear. Since Rupert Murdoch was permitted by his friend, Margaret Thatcher, to buy Times Newspapers without regard to the rules restricting monopoly ownership, smear has been almost as regular a feature of the *Sunday Times* as the vacuities of 'style' journalism that bring in much of its profitable advertising.[70] Unlike the unpretentious *Sun*, with which it shares offices in the Murdoch fortress at Wapping, East London, the *Sunday Times* suggests to its readers that it is a 'quality' newspaper; and from time to time it does publish work of a proper professional standard. But the smearing and pillorying of its 'enemies', together with the crude promotion of the interests of its owner and of sections of the British establishment – notably the Ministry of Defence and the security services – now characterise and distinguish the paper.

The *Sunday Times*'s attacks on British television are famous. These spring from Murdoch's original alliance with Thatcher, which deepened following his 'victory' over the print unions at Wapping in 1986. 'Wapping' was crucial to Thatcher's strategy to emasculate the trade unions and to further her ideological aims of 'deregulating' British society. Three years later Murdoch was rewarded when the Government's deregulation of broadcasting allowed him to launch Britain's first satellite television network, Sky Channel.

Murdoch had long used the editorial pages of his papers to attack and undermine the BBC and ITV, which he saw as obstacles to his own expansion in television.

Thatcher shared his view of these institutions – it is fair to say she loathed them – and devoted herself as prime minister to trying to break them up. These efforts resulted in the 1991 Broadcasting Act, which sought to end the 'cartel' of ITV, but instead produced a farcical 'auction' that cost the industry heavily in resources while leaving most of the network in place. It did, however, achieve one goal dear to Thatcher's heart: it got rid of Thames Television, whose franchise is not to be renewed in 1993.

Just as the *Sunday Times* faithfully expressed Thatcher's spleen against television, so it played by few rules when attacking her opponents. In 1988 the paper conducted a smear campaign against Thames and the producers of its current affairs investigation, *Death on the Rock*. This report was significant in television journalism because it lifted a veil on the British secret state and revealed something of its ruthlessness – specifically, its willingness to use death squads abroad. The report described how an SAS team had gone to Gibraltar and carefully assassinated an IRA sabotage squad.

The *Sunday Times* attack on *Death on the Rock* served to marshal the Thatcher forces against Thames – from the usual vocal backbench Tories to the then foreign secretary, Sir Geoffrey Howe, and Thatcher herself; and, of course, numerous 'government sources'. One of the *Sunday Times* reporters assigned to the Thames story, Rosie Waterhouse, accused her own paper of being 'wide open to accusations that we had set out to prove one point of view and misrepresented and misquoted interviews to fit – the very accusations we were levelling at Thames'.[71] She later resigned. An enquiry conducted by a former Tory minister, Lord Windlesham, vindicated the programme's accuracy and integrity. The *Sunday Times* branch of the National Union of Journalists called for an enquiry into the paper's role in the affair. There was none.

On reading a book on the episode by Roger Bolton, the Thames executive producer, I recognised much of my own experience and feelings during the orchestrated attack on my documentary film, *Cambodia: The Betrayal*.[72] In its issue of March 24, 1991 the *Sunday Times* brought to a climax its smear campaign against the film and myself. Occupying much of a broadsheet page was a huge photograph of me holding the Richard Dimbleby Award presented to me the previous Sunday by the British Academy of Film and Television Arts (BAFTA) for a lifetime's work as a broadcast journalist. In place of the BAFTA gold mask was my head with the eyes taken out. Phillip Knightley, who twice won Journalist of the Year for the *Sunday Times*, described this as one of the most 'shocking things' he had seen in a newspaper.[73]

Under a black banner headline, the illustration and article covered the whole page: the sort of treatment a major Mafia figure might expect. I was represented as a disreputable person, who had no right to the numerous professional awards my colleagues had given me over a quarter of a century in journalism. I was certainly not worthy of the 'Oscar' which the full council of BAFTA had voted to award me.

The smear was malicious and almost all the 'facts' were wrong, right down to the trivia. Joe Haines, Robert Maxwell's hagiographer, was quoted as the source of an assessment of my worth during my 'early days' on the *Daily Mirror*. In the 1960s, he recalled, I had 'long got up the noses' of those working near me . Haines was not on the *Mirror* during the 1960s; he was Harold Wilson's press secretary until the mid 1970s. There was much else like that.

The attack was a model of McCarthyism. I was not a journalist, I was not even a polemicist; I simply falsified. No evidence was produced to justify this grave charge. Worse, I covered for communists. Three examples were given.

First, I had reported in 1979 that the only substantial relief reaching Cambodia in the first nine months following the defeat of Pol Pot came from communist Vietnam. This was wholly true, if unpalatable. Up until August of that year Vietnam had sent to Cambodia 30,000 tons of rice and rice seed and 5,000 tons of other goods, such as condensed milk.

With others, I witnessed and filmed the Vietnamese convoys arriving from Saigon. In striking contrast, the International Red Cross and UNICEF had sent to Cambodia 100 tons of relief during all of ten months.[74]

Second, I had not reported 'as other journalists reported, [that] Vietnam had placed huge obstacles in the way of an international relief programme'. I had not reported it because it was false. It was propaganda that had originated in a bogus CIA report which, as the *Guardian* reported, was central to 'an international propaganda offensive' conducted by the White House and the State Department to spread derogatory stories about Vietnamese behaviour in Cambodia.[75] The campaign was propagated by US Government officials and journalists based in Washington, London and Bangkok. Western journalists who did go to Cambodia specifically refuted the stories about 'obstacles'.[76] Even the American ambassador to Thailand refuted them.[77]

Third, I was a dupe, because I had been 'invited' to Cambodia by the Vietnamese Government. I have never accepted an invitation from any government of any stripe: I got into Cambodia, as others did, by journalistic nous and with the help and encouragement of a number of indefatigable individuals who care about helping the Cambodian people.*

Indeed, so vile had been my reporting from Cambodia, according to the *Sunday Times*, that I had even failed to recognise America's 'humanitarian motives' in Indo-China and the 'tireless work' of the American ambassador in Bangkok on behalf of the Cambodian people. This 'tireless work' was apparently undertaken in 1980, the year the Kampuchean Emergency Group (KEG) was set up in the US embassy in Bangkok, from where it tirelessly ensured that humanitarian supplies reached the Khmer Rouge.

---

* In his 1980 report to Oxfam, Jim Howard, who began Oxfam's Cambodia operation, wrote, 'It was made clear by Pilger that they wished to film where they liked on the aid programmes and the general situation, and they would not work to a pre-planned schedule as this was too limiting and they would decide daily what to film and where. The arrangement was partly ... to avoid "set pieces" arranged by the authorities.'[77]

Here the serious purpose of the smear was made clear. My crime was to have accused the West of aiding the Khmer Rouge and the British Government of secretly contributing to Cambodia's suffering. For this the *Sunday Times* produced one of its principal informants, another Western ambassador who had 'worked tirelessly' for Cambodia. It was none other than Derek Tonkin, HM Ambassador to Thailand during the build-up of SAS trainers in that country, where they taught Cambodians to lay mines that blew off the limbs of countless people. The *Sunday Times* did not mention this fact at all. The article presented Tonkin as an aggrieved 'retired diplomat'. This is an excerpt:

> Watching the [BAFTA] ceremony on television last Sunday, Derek Tonkin, a retired British diplomat, murmured with dismay, as Pilger accepted his prize from Melvyn Bragg, the television arts guru, who described him as an outstanding journalist . . . 'When I was British Ambassador to Thailand,' he said, 'I worked very hard to get a solution to the Cambodian problem. So had other members of the international community. So many people had worked so hard and Pilger just wrote the entire effort off.'

Tonkin denied everything. He denied the presence of the SAS. He denied that Margaret Thatcher had said that some Khmer Rouge were 'reasonable people' who 'will have to play a part in a future government . . . '

The ex-ambassador was supported by William Shawcross, who told the *Sunday Times* that 'Tonkin's analysis seems to me to be cool and precisely correct'. Shawcross made no mention of Britain's secret Cambodia operation, and did not explain why the 'analysis' of a top government official should be deemed 'cool and precisely correct'.

Before the *Sunday Times* piece appeared, I was phoned by one of its reporters, Andrew Alderson, who asked me to trust him. 'We are *not* doing a hatchet job,' he said. 'We are doing a profile following your BAFTA award.' He referred to Tonkin's attack on me in that week's *Spectator*. I replied that the SAS operation had been run from the British embassy in Bangkok. 'This has clearly got to go in,' he said. Almost nothing of what I told Alderson was published.

The following week, when I enquired indirectly about a right of reply, I was told that this might be considered 'if it is put through a lawyer'. On five Sundays in March and April I was the subject of smear and abuse in the *Sunday Times*, including a suggestion by Derek Tonkin that I was unhinged.[78] A friend with contacts in senior management at the *Sunday Times* was told that the decision to smear me 'came right from the top'.

Of course, journalists must accept that criticism is an occupational hazard, and that those who dispense it have to take it – as long as it is fair. When it is character assassination, baseless in fact and part of an orchestrated political assault, it requires exposure. For me, this is especially true when it has to do with an issue about which I care deeply.

Copies of the *Sunday Times* smear were distributed by the Foreign Office as part of a 'Pilger package' sent to people who wrote to enquire or protest about government policy in Cambodia. When one was forwarded to me, I sought an explanation from David Colvin. He replied that the government had distributed ten 'pro' and 'anti' articles 'to demonstrate your mixed reputation'.[79] I wrote to him that the great majority were 'not only "anti" but riddled with recycled falsehood, distortion and inaccuracy'.[80] These were mostly from the *Sunday Times* and the *Spectator* and drew on two principal sources: Derek Tonkin and William Shawcross.

Tonkin's interest was self-evident. He had been a senior government official at the time of a secret British military intervention in Cambodia's civil war. Shawcross's interest was not quite so obvious – although others have described his previous attacks on my work as both a 'vendetta' and an 'obsession'.[81] Whatever his motives, I had no interest in that which distracted from Cambodia's struggle. In a published reply to one of his attacks, I asked him not to work against, but with me for the benefit of Cambodia.[82]

Shawcross is best known as the author of *Sideshow*, a book about the 'secret' bombing of Cambodia ordered by President Nixon and Henry Kissinger. I praised *Sideshow* in my films *Year Zero* and *Year One*; and I have personally and publicly defended his work to Kissinger. I believe that in a world where serious journalists are under attack – the fate of Farzad Bazoft is an extreme example – we should support each other; for the wider political significance of such attacks ought never to be underestimated.

To many of its readers, *Sideshow* represented a trenchant criticism of the American political establishment and its military conduct in Indo-China. But this was not the case, nor was it the reputation sought by Shawcross, who was embarrassed by his 'adoption' by the anti-war movement. His prime target was not the system that had underwritten the war – and was now doing business with Pol Pot – but Nixon and Kissinger, whom the Eastern establishment held in contempt.

Indeed, in his second book on Cambodia, *The Quality of Mercy*, Shawcross paid fulsome tribute to those US Government and other Western officials who were among his principal sources. At the same time he cleared up any misunderstanding of his purpose by exonerating the American crusade in Indo-China.[83] He is a staunch defender of America's 'humanitarian motives'. He believes the government of Vietnam is responsible for most of Cambodia's recent suffering. As Grant Evans has pointed out, a theme of Shawcross's 'Cambodia campaign' is that it is always the communists who allow 'politics' to thwart the 'humanitarianism' of the West and the converse is apparently unthinkable.[84]

Ironically, in seeking to redeem the West, he denies not only recent history – such as the killing of more than half a million Cambodian peasants by American bombs[85] – but also the undisputed message of his own book, *Sideshow*: that the bombing provided a catalyst for the rise of the Khmer Rouge. In *The Quality of Mercy* he appeared to go out of his way to invest one of those indirectly involved with the US bombing campaign, Colonel Michael Eiland, with humane motives. Acknowledging that Eiland had previously 'taken part in secret, illegal intelligence-gathering missions into Cambodia', Shawcross wrote, 'Inevitably, his work made some journalists and relief officials suspicious of his new task on Cambodia's west flank' (that is, running KEG). 'Others', wrote Shawcross, 'found him a diligent and effective official concerned above all with the efficacy of the relief operation. Eiland himself later said that his work and his views during the 1979–80 Cambodia crisis were dominated ... by his first posting in the US Army – to a base near Dachau. In 1983 he returned to the Pentagon to work in the Defense Intelligence Agency.'[86] Such apologetics help to explain Shawcross's attacks on those who identify the other side of America's 'humanitarian motives', its complicity with and restoration of the genocidists.

In his paper, *The Cambodian Genocide, 1975–1979: A Critical Review*, Ben Kiernan, the world-renowned Khmer-speaking scholar at Yale, who has worked with Shawcross, wrote,

Not a single Western country has ever voted against the right of the Khmer Rouge government-in-exile to represent its former victims in international forums. International commentators often followed suit. An interesting example is the British journalist William Shawcross [who] chose to hang the label of 'genocide' on the Khmer Rouge's *opponents*. He alleged that Hanoi's invasion to topple Pol Pot meant 'subtle genocide' by enforced starvation ... Fortunately, he was very wrong ... but he remains preoccupied with opponents of the Khmer Rouge.[87]

In an article published in the *Observer* on the day I was to receive the Richard Dimbleby Award (Headline: 'The Trouble with John Pilger'), Shawcross wrote, 'Cambodia's travails arouse passions'.[88] Indeed. But the reason he gave for writing the piece was erroneous; he claimed to object to my receiving the award for *Cambodia: The Betrayal* when, in fact, it was awarded to me for a lifetime in broadcast journalism, spanning some thirty-six documentary films. The rest of his article echoed familiar official denials, including the foreign secretary's. He complained that I had 'constantly compared' the Khmer Rouge with Hitler's Nazis while ignoring the historical examples of communism. This too was false. I had likened Pol Pot's reign both to Maoism and to 'Stalin's terror'[89] and had described the Khmer Rouge as 'the most fanatical, extreme left-wing regime'.[90] I pointed these out to Shawcross, but the inaccuracies remain uncorrected and are constantly recycled. Clearly, to deny the historical truth is to cut one of Cambodia's lifelines.

The year Shawcross completed *Sideshow*, 1979, was the year of the defeat of Pol Pot by the Vietnamese. Those of us who went there and reported at first hand the suffering of the Khmer people and the part played by our own governments in prolonging their suffering, found to our surprise significant parts of our eyewitness accounts contradicted by Shawcross – who had not been to see for himself. Writing from London and Washington, Shawcross endorsed and promoted a series of hearsay stories that the Vietnamese were committing 'subtle genocide' in Cambodia. In the *Washington Post* he wrote that 'one-half of all the international aid reaching the port of Kompong Som [in Cambodia] ... was being trucked into Vietnam'. His sources for this damaging and, as it turned out, entirely false charge was a 'defector' who had been immediately shipped off to Paris and 'put under wraps'.[91] In a sensational and widely quoted article entitled 'The End of Cambodia', Shawcross gave credence to an unsubstantiated story that the Vietnamese were behaving in a barbarous way in Cambodia: mining ricefields and shooting farmers.

The effect of Shawcross's 'exposé' was to blur the difference between Cambodia under Pol Pot and Cambodia liberated by the Vietnamese: a difference of night and day. Shawcross wrote that 'it seemed possible that they [the Vietnamese] were a lesser enemy of the Cambodian people than the Khmer Rouge. Now the awful possibility arises that they may not be. Indeed, there have been reports that they are

441

treating the Cambodians with almost as much contempt as the previous regime did ... if there is a famine in Cambodia today it is principally the Vietnamese that must bear the immediate responsibility.'[92]

More puzzling than this allegation was its similarity to the message coming from official Washington sources. On January 8, 1980 John Gittings reported in the *Guardian* that State Department sources had revealed 'their intention of mounting an international propaganda offensive to spread atrocity stories about Vietnamese behaviour in Kampuchea. Within days, presumably on White House instructions, US journalists in Bangkok and Singapore were shown the appropriate 'refugee stories ... '

They were also shown 'the latest US intelligence report', which claimed that humanitarian aid was being diverted 'into the hands of pro-Soviet Vietnamese and the Heng Samrin military'.[93] At that time the UN under-secretary general in charge of the humanitarian operations in Cambodia and Thailand was Sir Robert Jackson, a distinguished civil servant and veteran of many disaster emergencies. When asked about the stories of diversion of aid, he replied, 'In terms of the Vietnamese Army living in, say, Kampuchea, we have never had one complaint from anywhere nor have any of our people. There's been all these allegations ... and we've said, "Look, for heaven's sake, will you give us the time, date and place and we'll follow through." We've never had one response when we've asked that question.'[94]

Journalists in Cambodia in 1979 and 1980, at the height of the emergency, found nothing to confirm the 'subtle genocide' story. Jim Laurie, the prize-winning producer of American ABC News, who travelled extensively in Cambodia, wrote in the *Far Eastern Economic Review*:

At no time during 26 days in Kampuchea did this correspondent find any indication of wilful obstruction in the delivery of international relief supplies. Nor did there appear to be any basis for allegations that food was being diverted to either Vietnam or Vietnamese troops . . . Interviews revealed no complaints of Vietnamese troops preventing the harvest of rice as alleged in some Bangkok reports.[95]

In reply to a letter I wrote to Shawcross in 1983 he retracted the 'genocide' story. He wrote that the retraction had already been published and he gave me a reference, which proved inaccurate.[96] If this was a professional difficulty for one journalist, it was a human disaster for the people of Cambodia. That most emotive and evocative of words, 'genocide', united conservatives and liberals in America. Communists could be damned and lumped together again – Pol Pot with Ho Chi Minh. And now that there was 'evidence' that the Vietnamese communists were practising 'genocide' (the 'subtle' soon fell away), surely America's war against them had been justified.

During these rites of absolution, the truth about Cambodia expired in the United States. The documentary films David Munro and I had made, *Year Zero* and *Year One*, were shown throughout the world, but not in America where they were virtually banned. An assistant to the director of news and current affairs programming at the Public Broadcast Service (PBS), Wayne Godwin, explained, 'John, we're into difficult political days in Washington. Your films would have given us problems with the Reagan Administration. Sorry.'[97]

With the Vietnamese now demonised as marauding invaders, the United States reinforced its total blockade against Cambodia, a country with which it had no quarrel. Like Vietnam, Cambodia now bore a 'Category Z' in the US Commerce Department, which meant that not even parts of water pumps supplied by the foreign subsidiaries of US corporations could be exported. In the United Nations the Khmer Rouge were soon concealed behind the façade of a 'coalition', invented by the US and China, while Pol Pot's red and yellow flag continued to fly in United Nations Plaza.

*

443

On June 25, 1991 the British Government admitted that the SAS had been secretly training the allies of Pol Pot since 1983.[98] For almost two years ministers had denied the allegations that Simon O'Dwyer-Russell, David Munro and I had made in films and articles. Twice in the *Spectator* Derek Tonkin had categorically denied that Britain was training Khmer terrorists. 'I deny it,' he replied, when challenged by Chris Mullin, MP.[99] The Government had never before made such an admission. On questions about the SAS and the security services, ministers either issued a blanket denial or refused to comment. The Cambodia operation involved both the SAS and MI6. What made it different was the risk of the whole truth coming out in court.

Shortly after *Cambodia: The Betrayal* was transmitted in October 1990, two former British Army officers, Christopher Mackenzie Geidt and Anthony de Normann sued Central Television and myself for libel. The two men were named in the film as witnesses to the final withdrawal of Vietnamese troops from Cambodia in September 1989. Also in Phnom Penh, as a British parliamentary observer, was the shadow overseas development minister, Ann Clwyd, who was surprised to find the men officially listed as representatives of the Ministry of Defence.

To my astonishment, the two men claimed the film had accused them of training the Khmer Rouge to lay mines. My initial response was straightforward: nowhere in the film was there any such accusation, nor was any intended; and I was prepared to say so. But libel actions are not that simple.

At a preliminary hearing, counsel for both sides put the legal argument about whether or not the film could be construed as defamatory. In other words, could it be interpreted to mean something it was not intended to mean? The judge decided that only a jury could decide, and it was put down for trial. In more than thirty years as an investigative journalist this was the first time I had been sued: a record, I believe, with few equals.

As we accepted that the two men had *not* trained Khmer Rouge guerrillas, or indeed any Cambodian guerrillas, we obviously could not justify an allegation we did not intend to make and did not believe we had made. The basis of our case was that the words I had used did not carry the meaning the plaintiffs put on them and that, in any event, the film was honestly commenting on a matter of public interest, namely British Government intervention in Cambodia. Our defence had crucial questions to put to three ministers – Mark Lennox-Boyd of the Foreign Office, William Waldegrave, formerly of the Foreign Office, and Archie Hamilton of the Ministry of Defence – all of whom had made misleading statements to Parliament about the SAS operation in Cambodia. We subpoenaed these ministers. We also subpoenaed the commanding officer of the SAS, Lieutenant-Colonel John Holmes, and his predecessor, Brigadier Cedric Delves. Both of them had a great deal to tell the court about Britain's 'non-existent' support for those in alliance with Pol Pot.

Most important for our case, our questions to them would be based on information we had been receiving from a 'Deep Throat' source within the British intelligence world. David and I had numerous meetings with this person, who cannot be described in any way. What he told us proved highly reliable. He supplied precise details, which we were able to confirm with official and other sources. He informed us that the SAS operation had not ceased in 1989, as the Government had claimed; on the contrary, it had become 'the principal direct Western military involvement in Indo-China'.

On June 25, the Government delivered a bundle of government documents to our solicitors. These were covered by a letter from the Treasury solicitor, J. A. D. Jackson, who wrote, 'Let me say at once that it is not the desire nor the intention of HM Government to interfere with a fair and proper hearing of the issues in the present litigation. Nevertheless the Crown, and indeed the court itself, has an obligation to consider the public interest in relation to the disclosure of information falling within certain categories.' He went on to say that this 'public interest' demanded that 'only certain information be disclosed in court'.

The threat was close behind. The Government, he warned,

'is prepared to intervene in the proceedings at any stage . . . in respect of documents and/or oral evidence from *any* witness'. Attached to this was a statement by Archie Hamilton, in the form of a written parliamentary reply to a stooge question in which the Government admitted for the first time that which he and his ministerial colleagues had worked so hard to suppress: the existence of an SAS Cambodia operation.

As a damage-control measure, it was neat. Training had ended in 1989, according to Hamilton, and its purpose had been 'to strengthen the position of those forces [the Sihanoukists and the KPNLF] in relation to the more powerful forces of the Khmer Rouge and in their struggle against the Vietnamese-imposed regime in Phnom Penh'. No mention was made that the Khmer Rouge effectively led this noble 'struggle'. Neither were we told anything about the excluded information, which fell into these 'certain categories'.[100] Could this be that the training was still going on? Could it be that the Khmer Rouge were the direct beneficiaries?

Our five subpoenas were stopped, meaning that our main witnesses could not be called. When the trial began, the authority for this gagging order – a 'Public Interest Immunity Certificate' signed by Tom King – was presented to the judge.[101] The promised 'intervention in the proceedings' was now underway, and in a most spectacular fashion. Acting for the Government, John Laws, QC, spelt out the catch-all provisions of the 'certificate'. For example, evidence regarding the SAS and the security services, such as MI6, which might have been produced as evidence by our defence counsel, would be challenged and the judge would be asked to rule it out of court.

We looked on almost incredulously as much of our evidence was pored over by Laws and his junior, Philip Havers, and up to six officials from the Ministry of Defence, the Foreign Office and MI6. An affidavit by a former Foreign Office official submitted in our defence was censored as this scrum of Government officials leaned over Laws's shoulder and directed his pencil in moments of high farce. (They were especially concerned about a passage which said it was 'common knowledge' that both the SAS and the American Special Forces were involved in Cambodia.) 'Is it OK to leave in the Americans?' said one of them, to which another replied, 'No, take them out.'[102]

Laws told the judge that 'national security' might be at stake with the disclosure of evidence that 'travels into the area that the secretary of state would protect'. He did not explain what events in Cambodia had to do with Britain's national security. The judge asked what he had in mind. Alas, it was not possible to be precise as he did not know what else the defence might produce. The judge accepted this restriction. This meant that if we called a Ministry of Defence witness he would not even be allowed to confirm or deny anything about the SAS; and we would not be allowed to challenge this.

The Government had effectively tied a gag on the whole trial. Our defence counsel, Desmond Browne, QC, described this 'considerable injustice' as 'grossly unfair'. He said it was reminiscent of the *Spycatcher* case four years before when the Government had intervened in a trial in an uncannily similar way – then, as here, in the name of 'national security'.

With all our principal witnesses silenced, we withdrew and Central Television paid damages to the men who insisted they had been libelled. Central had been prepared to see the trial through to its conclusion, and had left the final decision to me.[103] The backing of the company – especially that of Andy Allan, Colin Campbell and Roger James – was exemplary at a time of real political pressure on ITV, not least given the auction of franchises that saw off one ITV company, Thames, which had challenged the Government on another matter involving the 'national security' and the SAS.

In many respects ITV and Channel 4 have taken over the traditional, often mythologised, newspaper role as whistle-blower. It is a tenuous responsibility for broadcasters, who are bound both by commercial and a plethora of legal constraints. Overshadowing them all, of course, are the libel laws; and until Parliament empowers the courts to accept the public interest as a defence and to reject political intervention in the conduct of justice, the British judicial system will continue on its steady, downward path.

On the day the case was settled, David and I began making our sixth documentary on Cambodia by placing on film the statements of witnesses whose evidence would have been ruled inadmissible under the Government's gagging order. With Noel Smart and Mel Marr, the cameraman and sound recordist who had worked with us on *Cambodia: The Betrayal*, we drove from the High Court to Heathrow and caught a plane to a European city, where we had arranged a clandestine meeting with a former Cambodian guerrilla. This is the man referred to on page 416, who had been trained by the British in Malaysia and had worked under cover with the Khmer Rouge.

Back in London, we filmed an interview with General Tea Banh, minister of defence in the Phnom Penh Government, who had flown from Cambodia to give evidence in the libel case. He had brought with him intelligence documents and other evidence, which described the training of Khmer Rouge by six British officers at Nong Nhai camp on the Thai border.[104] 'The main source is a senior Khmer Rouge,' he said. 'Nong Nhai is a well-known Khmer Rouge training camp.'

Of course, a representative of the Phnom Penh regime would have a vested interest. Yet in this instance, Tea Banh and Hun Sen's closest adviser, Uch Kiman, who had accompanied him, were deeply concerned about offending the British Government. They believed they needed British goodwill if they were to gain anything from the UN peace plan, with which they said they had no choice but to comply. They also believed that *Cambodia: The Betrayal* had told an important truth about how the Khmer Rouge had been kept going by the West, and they were prepared to take a calculated risk and back us.

The same could be said of our 'Deep Throat' source who, at the end of the libel case, agreed to be interviewed on film as long as his face was hidden and his voice altered. In the interview he described his career 'in British intelligence working on the operational side overseas'. (David and I, and executives of Central Television, know who he is.) He said that not only was the British training of Cambodians continuing, but that there was now an even 'greater commitment' by the Government. I asked why. He replied,

The situation in that part of the world is becoming increasingly *more* sensitive. We have the problems of an imminent destabilisation within the People's Republic of China. We have Vietnam, which is quietly making overtures to the West ... We have a power vacuum in Cambodia itself. At the same time, the lessons of Americans in Vietnam have been well learned and what is being done now is to provide a greater degree of on-the-ground support and training [than] the American old-style of going in heavy and high.

Shortly before Christmas Simon O'Dwyer-Russell died. David and I were stunned. He was twenty-nine. He had suffered a heart complaint and undergone a by-pass operation in October. He was recovering well when he suddenly relapsed. The *Sunday Telegraph* published an obituary that warmly celebrated his memory, describing his 'series of notable exclusives' and his 'unrivalled access to both the Armed Forces and the security forces at all levels.'[105] Incredibly, there was no mention of his biggest scoop: the secret British operation in Cambodia.

Simon would have been arguably our most important witness in the libel case. Before the case was due to be heard, I had a meeting with the editor of the *Sunday Telegraph*, Trevor Grove. I asked him if he would repeat in court some of the praise that his newspaper had showered upon Simon at the time of his death. It was, I pointed out, Simon who had broken the SAS in Cambodia story and appeared as a witness in *Cambodia: The Betrayal*. It seemed reasonable

449

that his editor should now speak out for his memory, as a character witness.

Grove was clearly discomfited by this. 'I'm afraid', he said, 'there were problems with Simon . . . ' Without elaborating on this, he went on to cast doubt on Simon's professionalism, capping it with: 'You know, the MoD even had a file on him.' I suggested that a Ministry of Defence 'file' might be regarded as recognition of Simon's independence and worth as a journalist. I recounted his paper's proud recall of Simon's 'series of notable exclusives' and his 'unrivalled access' to the military and the security services 'at all levels'. And there was the Simon O'Dwyer-Russell Prize that King's College was soon to inaugurate for War Studies essays, which had been funded by his colleagues as a lasting tribute. 'Yes,' he said, 'but I'm afraid I'm not in a position to speak for him. I'm so sorry.'

In the week after the case was settled the *Sunday Telegraph* published a prominent article in which I was accused, by clear implication, of once supporting the Khmer Rouge. 'It must not be forgotten', said the paper, that the Khmer Rouge 'publicly thanked people like him [that is, me] for their help.'[106]

I phoned Trevor Grove and told him he had published lies. I said I had never supported the Khmer Rouge and that, far from thanking me, they had set out to kill me. His response was to blame his staff. 'You see, I don't really have charge of that page,' he said. 'I'm so sorry.'

Like the *Sunday Times*, the *Sunday Telegraph* had relied on the same two ubiquitous sources, Derek Tonkin and William Shawcross. After I had written a reply to the paper, I was phoned by the letters editor and told I could not mention Shawcross's name, or correct his allegations.[107] When David Munro wrote to the *Evening Standard* to explain Tonkin's involvement, his letter was not published.[108] When Chris Mullin wrote to the *Spectator*, following a poisonous tirade by Paul Johnson, his letter was not published.[109]

I recount these episodes not merely as further examples of how a section of the British press routinely plays the part of medieval witchhunter, but of the important function of the Western media in sidetracking the issues of life and death in Cambodia. The most urgent issue today remains the prospect of the return of the Khmer Rouge in some form. But as the Khmer Rouge role was central to American policy, critics of this policy, who oppose the return of the genocidists, were to be targeted, rather than those who supported their return. This was the point Ben Kiernan made. At times it had a 'looking glass' quality; but the logic was there.

The struggle to eradicate public memory was most crucial. 'Public opinion' had proven a potent force in the defence of Cambodia's human rights, as thousands of letters to Downing Street had demonstrated. Moreover, the three stages of Cambodia's holocaust were all within public memory: the American bombing, the Pol Pot period and the American-led blockade against the survivors of stages one and two, which had maintained Cambodia in a state of physical ruin, disease and trauma. Public awareness of how the Khmer Rouge had been rehabilitated – diplomatically, politically and militarily – could not be tolerated.[110]

Diminishing Western culpability is, of course, standard media practice in most global matters. However, support for those who put to death a fifth of the Cambodian population presented a challenge. In this, Pol Pot provided a lead. 'We must', he said in 1988, 'focus attention on the Vietnamese aggression and divert attention from our past mistakes.'[111]

The discrediting of Cambodia's liberators was an essential first step. As already noted, this began with an act of self-defence described as an 'invasion',[112] false accusations of Vietnamese 'atrocities' and 'subtle genocide'. Once Pol Pot's communists could be equated with Vietnam's communists, regardless of the fact that one group was guilty of genocide and the other was not, in propaganda terms almost anything was possible.

Numerous initiatives by the Vietnamese to extricate themselves from Cambodia were dismissed or went unreported, and the attempts by others to broker peace derided. When the Australian foreign affairs minister, Bill Hayden, tried to develop contacts in the region in 1983, he was vilified in the press as a 'communist dupe' and his efforts dismissed as 'stupid' by the US secretary of state, George Schultz.[113]

By 1985 Vietnam's only condition for the withdrawal of its troops was that the Khmer Rouge be prevented from returning to power.[114] This was welcomed by several Southeast Asian governments, and rejected by the United States.[115] On July 13, 1985 the *Bangkok Post* reported, 'A senior US official said that [Secretary of State] Schultz cautioned ASEAN to be extremely careful in formulating peace proposals for Kampuchea because Vietnam might one day accept them.' When the Vietnamese withdrew unconditionally from Cambodia in 1989, Western support for the Khmer Rouge – justified as necessary *realpolitik* as long as Vietnamese troops remained in Cambodia – did not cease; it increased.

While the Vietnamese were fulfilling their 'aggressor' function in Western eyes, the Khmer Rouge were being regarded very differently. From 1979 the American far right began to rehabilitate Pol Pot. Douglas Pike, a prominent Indo-China specialist, described Pol Pot as a 'charismatic' and 'popular' leader under whom 'most' Cambodian peasants 'did not experience much in the way of brutality'.[116] Pike argued that the Khmer Rouge should share political power in Cambodia: the essence of the UN 'peace plan'.[117]

In 1980 the CIA produced a 'demographic report' on Cambodia, which softened Pol Pot's reputation by denying that he had carried out any executions during the last two years of his regime. In fact, in 1977–8 more than half a million people were executed.[118] During Congressional hearings in November 1989 Assistant Secretary of State Richard Solomon repeatedly refused to describe Pol Pot's crimes as genocidal – thus denying his own department's earlier unequivocal position.[119]

Journalists whose reporting reflected the US Administration line received the highest commendation. Nate Thayer, an Associated Press reporter, was described as 'brilliant' by Congressman Stephen Solarz, one of the architects of US policy.[120] Richard Solomon called the following Thayer commentary 'the most sober-minded and well-informed assessment of that issue I've seen'.[121]

In Thayer's view the 'good news' in Cambodia struggled to be heard above the din of the 'tales of terror'. Writing in the influential *Washington Quarterly*, he described the one-and-a-half million people who died during the Khmer Rouge years as 'displaced'. Using the official euphemism, Thayer distinguished 'the policies and practices of the Khmer Rouge' from what he called the 'violence and misery that preceded and succeeded them'. He wrote that, while Pol Pot did implement some 'objectionable policies' these were 'largely perpetrated only on a certain section of the population ... to which journalists, scholars and other foreign observers have had access'. Thayer claimed that 'perhaps 20 per cent of Cambodians support the Khmer Rouge'. The source for this? Why, Pol Pot himself! The author made no further mention of the 20 per cent Pol Pot had already 'displaced' somewhere.[122]

It is difficult to imagine a *New York Times* headline: 'Hitler Brutal, Yes, But No Mass Murderer'. Inserting 'Pol Pot' for 'Hitler', this announced a major article which dismissed Pol Pot as 'a bit paranoid', and claimed there was 'no genocide'.[123] (The author, Richard Dudman, had earlier credited the Khmer Rouge with 'one of the world's great housing programmes'.[124]) Just prior to publication of this, two Cambodia specialists, Roger Normand and Ben Kiernan, separately offered the *New York Times* articles that spelt out Pol Pot's genocidal past and plans for the future. These were rejected.[125] The *Nation* was the only American journal to accept Normand's landmark exposé of Pol Pot's secret speeches, which made mockery of Washington's insistence that the Khmer Rouge could be included in the 'peace process'.[126]

In Britain, the rehabilitation was similar. In June 1990, the *Independent* published a major report by its South-east Asia correspondent, Terry McCarthy, headlined: 'Whatever the crimes committed by Pol Pot's men, they are on the road to power. The West must stop moralising and learn to deal with them.'[127] McCarthy called on the West to 'reach out' to the Khmer Rouge. The 'genocide issue', as he put it, had been 'exploited to the full'. The point was, the Khmer Rouge had changed. They were now 'respected' for their 'discipline' and 'honesty' and 'admired' for having 'qualities that most spheres of Cambodian society lack'. Moreover, they had 'considerable support' in the countryside because 'many' peasants 'do not have particularly bad memories' of Pol Pot. He offered no real evidence of this 'support' among a rural population of which 15 per cent had perished during the Pol Pot years. He advocated increased aid to the Khmer Rouge to 'entice them back into the real world of human politics'. It is time, he wrote, 'to face up to the fact that the Khmer Rouge embodies some deeply entrenched traits of the Cambodian people . . . '[128]

These mysterious 'traits' became a popular theme in the revised explanation for Cambodia's suffering. Forget the actions of Pol Pot, Washington and Beijing; the ordinary people of Cambodia had allowed these horrors to happen because that was the way they are. According to Michael Fathers in the *Independent*, 'Cambodians are a neurotic people with an intense persecution complex . . . '[129]

Meanwhile, reported *The Times*, Pol Pot had ordered the Khmer Rouge 'to protect the country's wildlife'. Cambodians were 'not to poach birds and animals, and to refrain from killing them for any reason' because they were 'an important part of Cambodia's heritage'. And the source for this nonsense? 'Western intelligence sources' no less, inviting us to believe that Pol Pot had ordered his most trusted general to 'sentence' anyone found poaching rare birds. This general, according to the same disinformation, was himself 'hot on ecology issues and protection of endangered species'. And who might this 'green' Khmer Rouge general be? He was the notorious Mok, who between 1975 and 1979 was credited with the deaths of thousands of members of the human species. In Cambodia today he is still known as 'The Butcher', though Western journalists prefer to call him 'Ta Mok'. *Ta* gives him the affectionate sobriquet of 'Grandfather'.[130]

In the same spirit, *The Times* announced: 'Khmer Rouge asks for another chance.' (The temptation, again, is to conjure the headline: 'Nazis ask for another chance.') The redemption seeker in this case was Mok's boss, Son Sen, who is Pol Pot's defence minister. He explained to *The Times* that he 'did not deny the past [but] we have to think about the present and the future'.[131] Son Sen stands accused of the murder of 30,000 Vietnamese villagers in 1977. Under his authority, Tuol Sleng extermination centre in Phnom Penh tortured and murdered at least 20,000 people and, like the Gestapo, recorded all details.[132]

On November 28, 1991, the leader writer of the *Independent* proffered the following memorable advice to the people of Cambodia: 'The promise of a return to respectability of the Khmer Rouge is the wormwood baked into the cake. It makes it hard to swallow for those who will always be haunted by the horrors of that regime. If Cambodia is to find peace, then swallowed it must be, *and in its entirety*.' (My italics.)

Few dissenting voices were heard above this. In Britain, one of the most informed and courageous voices belonged to Oxfam, which in 1979 defied Government pressure and went to help stricken Cambodia. That was the year Margaret Thatcher came to power and one of her first acts as prime minister was to join the American boycott of Vietnam and suspend all food aid there, specifically powdered milk for Vietnamese children. She gave Vietnam's 'invasion' of Cambodia as the reason.

In June 1979 representatives of the main British voluntary agencies were called to the Foreign Office, where they were told that the British boycott of Vietnam now applied to Cambodia. They were warned that the Vietnamese were 'obstructing' aid and that if they attempted to fly into Phnom Penh, they might be fired upon. This was official deception on a grand scale, setting the tone for British policy to the present day.

At the meeting was Jim Howard, an engineer and Oxfam's senior 'fireman', a veteran of disaster relief in Biafra, India, the Sahel, Latin America and Asia. Howard embodies Oxfam, which was set up in 1942 by Quakers with the aim of arousing public interest in the suffering of civilians in Europe, especially children, who were denied food because of the Allied blockade. What struck me about Jim Howard when we first met in Phnom Penh, was that he saw every problem he was sent to solve unfailingly from the point of view of the people in need.

Oxfam ignored the Foreign Office 'warning'. Howard flew to Paris with £20,000 in cash and got in touch with an air charter company, based in Luxembourg, whose Icelandic and Danish pilots had a reputation for flying 'anything anywhere'. They were prepared to fly a DC8 to Phnom Penh; Howard set about loading it with drugs, vitamins and powdered milk. On August 19 he sent his passport to the Vietnamese embassy in Paris, where it was stamped and returned to him that afternoon. A few hours later he was airborne.

When the aircraft landed at Bangkok to refuel, a source of obstruction which the Foreign Office had neglected to mention, the Thai regime refused to allow it to fly on to Phnom Penh. 'We told them "OK",' said Howard, ' "We'll fly somewhere else; we'll fly to Saigon instead." So they finally let us take off and we circled out over the South China Sea and indeed flew overhead Saigon, before heading for Phnom Penh. The pilot couldn't believe his eyes. There was nothing at Phnom Penh airport. We did one low run and went in. There wasn't even a fork lift. We lifted the supplies down by hand. All the skilled people were dead, or in hiding. But there was willingness and gratitude. We landed at eleven in the morning; by four o'clock that afternoon, the milk and antibiotics were being given to the children.'

Jim Howard's aircraft was only the second Western relief aircraft to arrive in Cambodia in the eight months since the end of Asia's holocaust.

I was already in Phnom Penh, working by candle-light in my room at the old Hotel Royale. The afternoon monsoon had been so insistent that rain had poured through the louvres of the french windows and two rats scampered to

456

and fro, across the puddles. When Jim Howard walked in, I was endeavouring to compile a list of urgently needed items – the very things he had brought – which I intended to give to the Australian ambassador in Bangkok. To illustrate the enormity of what had happened, I told him that, down the road, one man was struggling to care for fifty starving orphans. 'Where do I start?' he said: words that would make for him, and others at Oxfam, a fitting epitaph.

The following day his first cable to Oxford read: '50 to 80 per cent human material destruction is the terrible reality. One hundred tons of milk per week needed by air and sea for the next two months starting now, repeat now.' So began one of the boldest rescue operations in history. Shortly afterwards, a barge left Singapore, sailing into the north-eastern monsoon, with 1,500 tons of Oxfam seed on board. Guy Stringer had put the whole remarkable venture together in a few weeks and with just £50,000.

Like Jim Howard, he had already navigated his way through a political storm. Singapore was, and still is, supporting those allied with Pol Pot. Back in London, Oxfam's director, Brian Walker, stood his ground calmly against press charges of 'aiding communists'. Indeed, Oxfam's strength has been not to be deterred. But its very presence in Cambodia and the success of its schemes have made it enemies from London to Washington to Bangkok. An American ambassador in Bangkok would berate visitors with his views on 'those communists at Oxfam'.

Cambodia had a profound influence on the way Oxfam saw its responsibilities. Many Oxfam workers believed it was no longer enough to dispense 'Band Aid charity' and that the organisation should take more literally its stated obligation 'to educate the public concerning the nature, causes and effects of poverty, distress and suffering'.

In 1988 Oxfam published *Punishing the Poor: The International Isolation of Kampuchea*, by Eva Mysliwiec, Oxfam's American chief representative in Phnom Penh and the doyenne of voluntary aid workers in Cambodia.[133] Marshalling her facts, most of them gained at first hand, she presented a picture of a people who had suffered more than most and were now being punished by so-called civilised governments for being on the 'wrong side'; she identified the roots of their suffering in the American invasion of Indo-China. Her book was distributed throughout the world.

The reaction became an assault in 1990. An American-funded extreme right-wing lobby group, the International Freedom Foundation, presented an 'Oxfam file' to the Charity Commission in London. Its author was a young Tory activist, Marc Gordon, who had made his name a few years earlier by 'joining' the Nicaraguan Contras. His complaint of 'political bias' was supported by several back-bench Conservative MPs. Gordon told me, 'All the incidents we cited in our submission to the inquiry were upheld.' I asked an official at the Commission if this was true and he would neither confirm nor deny it. 'A fact is a fact,' he said boldly. Oxfam was never told officially who its accusers were, or the precise nature of the evidence against them.

In 1991 the Charity Commission censured Oxfam for having 'prosecuted with too much vigour' its public education campaign about Pol Pot's return. Threatened with a loss of its charity status, Oxfam no longer speaks out as it used to and has withdrawn from sale a number of its most popular publications, including *Punishing the Poor*.

It seemed to me that those who were meant to keep the record straight had two choices. They could blow the whistle and alert the world to the betrayal of Cambodia, as Oxfam did, and risk incurring a penalty, be it smear or sanction. Or they could follow the advice of Son Sen's wife, Yun Yat, who was minister of information during the years of genocide. In boasting that Buddhism had been virtually eradicated from Cambodia and that the monks had 'stopped believing' (most of them had been murdered), she said, 'The problem becomes extinguished. Hence there is no problem.'[134]

August 1979 to June 1992

458

A FAUSTIAN PACT

AS EACH OF the principal speakers rose from his chair in the ornate Quai d'Orsay, a silver-headed man a dozen feet away watched them carefully. His face remained unchanged; he wore a fixed, almost petrified smile. When Secretary of State James Baker declared that Cambodia should never again return to 'the policies and practices of the past', the silver head nodded. When Prince Sihanouk acknowledged the role of Western governments in the 'accords', the silver head nodded. Khieu Samphan, Pol Pot's face to the world, is a statesman now, a peacemaker; and this was as much his moment as Sihanouk's; for without his agreement – that is, Pol Pot's agreement – there would be no 'accords'. When a French official offered him his hand, the statesman stood, respectful, fluent in diplomatic small-talk and effusive in his gratitude – the same gratitude he had expressed in the two letters he had written to Douglas Hurd congratulating the British Government on its policy on Cambodia.[135] It was Khieu Samphan who, at one of Pol Pot's briefing sessions for his military commanders in Thailand, described his diplomatic role as 'buying time in order to give you comrades the opportunity to carry out all your [military] tasks'.[136] In Paris, on October 23, 1991, he had the look of a man who could not believe his luck.

Some 6,000 miles away, on the Thai side of the border with Cambodia, the Khmer people of Site 8 had a different view of the world being shaped for them. Although supplied by the United Nations Border Relief Operation (UNBRO), this camp had long been a Khmer Rouge operations base and, since 1988, had been made into a showcase by Pol Pot. Its leadership was elected; the Red Cross and selected journalists were allowed in. Whisky was produced. Faces smiled, much as Khieu Samphan smiled. The object of this image-building exercise was clear: to persuade Western governments that the Khmer Rouge have 'changed', are now following a 'liberal capitalist line' and could be legitimised as part of a 'comprehensive settlement'.

As Khieu Samphan raised his glass in Paris, a nightmare began for the people of Site 8. The gates were closed, and foreigners told to stay away. A few days earlier the camp's leaders had been called to a 'meeting' with senior Khmer Rouge officials and were not seen again. The camp library, central to the showpiece, was closed and people were told they must no longer be 'poisoned by foreign ideas' as they prepared to return to the 'zones'. From here and in the 'closed camps' run by the Khmer Rouge along the border, the forcible, secret repatriation of hundreds, perhaps thousands of refugees had begun.

They crossed minefields at night and were herded into 'zones of free Kampuchea' in malarial jungles without UN protection, food or medicine. Even as the UN High Commission for Refugees announced that an orderly return of all 370,000 refugees was underway, there were as many as 100,000 refugees in Khmer Rouge border camps and more were trapped in the 'zones', to which UN inspectors had only limited access or none at all.

If the 'peace process' was proving a theatre of the macabre, Prince Sihanouk provided his own theatre of the absurd. As decided in Paris, he returned to Phnom Penh in November 1991 to head the transitional 'supreme national council', made up of representatives of his followers, the KPNLF, the Hun Sen Government and the Khmer Rouge. 'I am returning to protect my children,' he said. 'There is *joie de vivre* again. Nightclubs have reopened with taxi dancers. I am sure soon there will be massage parlours. It is our way of life: it is a good life.'[137] He brought with him four chefs, supplies of pâté de foie gras hurriedly acquired from Fauchon, one of Paris's most famous gourmet shops, a caravan of body-guards and hangers-on, including two sons with dynastic ambitions. (With their father ensconced in his old palace, Prince Ranariddh and Prince Chakrapong have set their private armies on each other. 'Anyway,' said Ranariddh, 'my brother has run out of troops.' Prince Sihanouk described this as 'just a small clash ... they are good boys, but as brothers there is bickering. They never got on as children.'[138])

Many Cambodians were pleased to see the 'god-king', and the elderly struggled to kiss his hand. It seemed the world had again located Cambodia on the map. The cry, 'Sihanouk is back' seemed to signal a return to the days before the inferno of the American bombing and the rise of the Khmer Rouge. Sihanouk's presence even suggested to some that the Khmer Rouge had surrendered. For them the Paris 'accords' meant that the United Nations would protect them. They could be pardoned for failing to comprehend the perversity of an agreement which empowered the United Nations to protect the right of the genocidists to roam the cities and countryside free from harm and retribution, and which had appointed two of Pol Pot's henchmen to a body, the Supreme National Council, on which they could not be outvoted. This was described by Congressman Chet Atkins, one of the few American politicians to speak for the Cambodian people, as 'the consequence of a Faustian pact' with Pol Pot.[139]

At one of his many press conferences, Sihanouk was asked about the Khmer Rouge. 'In their hearts', he said, 'they remain very cruel, very Maoist, very Cultural Revolution, very Robespierre, very French Revolution, very *bloody* revolution. They are monsters, it is true ... *but* since they decided to behave as normal human beings, we have to accept them ... naughty dogs and naughty Khmer Rouge, they need to be caressed.' At this, he laughed, and most of the foreign press laughed with him. His most important statement, however, caused hardly a ripple. 'Cambodians', he said, 'were forced by the five permanent members of the UN Security Council ... to accept the return of the Khmer Rouge'.[140]

The following day Khieu Samphan arrived to join the

461

prince on the Supreme National Council. Suddenly, the gap between private pain and public fury closed, and the people of Phnom Penh broke their silence.[141] The near-lynching of Khieu Samphan might have been influenced by the Hun Sen Government, but there could be no doubt that it was heartfelt. Within a few hours of landing at Pochentong Airport, Pol Pot's emissary was besieged on the top floor of his villa. Crouched in a cupboard, with blood streaming from a head wound, he listened to hundreds of people shouting, 'Kill him, kill him, kill him.' They smashed down the doors and advanced up the stairs, armed with hatchets. Many of them had lost members of their families during the years that he was in power, at Pol Pot's side. One woman called out the names of her dead children, her dead sister, her dead mother – all of them murdered by the Khmer Rouge. The mob dispersed after Hun Sen arrived and spoke to them. Khieu Samphan and Son Sen (who had escaped the attack) were bundled into an armoured personnel carrier and taken to the airport, and flown back to Bangkok.

On April 17, 1975, the first day of Year Zero, the Khmer Rouge entered Phnom Penh and marched the entire population into the countryside, many of them to their death. Generally, people did as they were told. The sick and wounded were dragged at gunpoint from their hospital beds; surgeons were forced to leave patients in mid-operation. On the road, a procession of mobile beds could be seen, with their drip-bottles swinging at the bedposts. The old and crippled soon fell away and their families were forced to go on. Ill and dying children were carried in plastic bags. Women barely out of childbirth staggered forward, supported by parents. Orphaned babies, forty-one by one estimate, were left in their cradles at the National Paediatric Hospital without anyone to care for them. The Khmer Rouge said that the Americans were about to bomb the city. Many believed this, but even among those who did not, defeatism, fear and exhaustion seemed to make them powerless. The haemorrhage of people lasted two days and two nights, then Cambodia fell into shadow.

What happened to Khieu Samphan more than sixteen years later, in the streets he helped to terrorise and empty, was a catharsis, and only the beginning.

Now, when Khieu Samphan and Son Sen were in Phnom Penh, their stays were brief and secret, and they were guarded behind the walls of a UN compound, 'the protected wards of the international community', as Chet Atkins has described them.[142] Western ambassadors presented their credentials to Prince Sihanouk. The French ambassador was first; Cambodia, after all, used to be theirs, and they look forward once more to the fruits of 'trade'. The American ambassador, Charles H. Twining Jr, followed. 'It seems to me', he announced, 'that if we [that is, the United States] neglect the countryside, then the Khmer Rouge can come back again.' The ambassador assured the people of Cambodia that he and his staff would refuse to meet any Khmer Rouge official. 'We'll refuse even to shake hands with them,' he said. 'That's the bottom line.'[143]

His remarks brought to mind a meeting of the UN Credentials Committee in September 1979. The United States strongly supported a Chinese motion that Pol Pot's defunct regime continue to be recognised as the only government of Cambodia and to occupy Cambodia's seat in the General Assembly. As the American representative, Robert Rosenstock, gathered his papers after voting for Pol Pot, somebody grabbed his hand and congratulated him. 'I looked up,' he recalled, 'and saw it was Ieng Sary [Pol Pot's foreign minister]. I felt like washing my hands.'[144]

The people of Phnom Penh now saw a procession of Western notables, among them those who pointedly did not visit the country following their liberation from Pol Pot, not even to pay respect at the shrines to the victims of their holocaust. Lord Caithness of the Foreign Office has been through, lauding the peace plan and telling Cambodians: 'Look here, it's now up to you.'[145] (Lord Caithness later gave his private view to an ex-aid agency official. 'It's falling apart,' he said.)[146]

One visiting notable to receive much media attention was Gareth Evans, the Australian foreign affairs minister credited with thinking up the 'peace plan' and who promised to be 'even handed' in his treatment of the Khmer Rouge.[147] Evans had made a series of assertions which left little room for doubt about the future. 'I think it's pretty well obviously clearly decided', he said, 'that [the Khmer Rouge] has no military future ...' Indeed, the danger of the Khmer Rouge regaining power was 'negligible'.[148]

Evans apparently based this confidence on 'personal assurances' given to him by the Beijing regime. He said that when he told the Chinese foreign minister that the Khmer Rouge would be 'totally internationally isolated' if they caused the peace plan to break down, the foreign minister 'agreed absolutely'.[149] Remarkably, Evans then declared the 'genocide issue and all the emotion that's associated with that' over and done with and 'resolved'.[150] One wondered if he had asked ordinary Cambodians during his visit if the 'genocide issue and all the emotion associated with that' was 'resolved'. And had he considered that the regime handing out 'reassurances' was the same regime that had reassured the world that it was no longer arming Pol Pot when it was, and the same regime that had massacred hundreds of Chinese students when it said it wouldn't? And how did he explain China's 'two approaches' to Cambodia – seeking international respectability by backing the UN plan, while its ambassador in Phnom Penh secretly sided with Pol Pot?

From Gareth Evans we at least could understand the scale of risk being taken in the name of the Cambodian people by those who came and went. No doubt to demonstrate its faith in Evans's certainties, the Australian Government committed itself to sending back terrified Cambodian refugees. In 1992 Evans was nominated for the Nobel Peace Prize by Congressman Solarz, who had been largely responsible for maintaining the Khmer Rouge's position at the centre of US policy. Indeed, it was Solarz who had ensured that the US plan for Cambodia was largely concealed behind the façade of the 'Evans Plan'. Not for the first time was an Australian foreign affairs minister successfully used by Washington, and Australian 'initiatives' defined by Washington.

'If Cambodia's peace process remains on course', wrote Colin Smith in the *Observer*, ' . . . it will be because of Khmer Rouge restraint'.[151] In January 1992 the Khmer Rouge launched a major offensive, attacking government positions in Kompong Thom, in the hinterland around Kampot and Siem Reap. What was striking about these attacks was their smooth co-ordination and the fact that troops appeared to materialise from base camps the UN inspectors knew nothing about and to bring up firepower – including artillery – from a network of secret dumps. All of this was in violation of the 'accords'.

When a clearly marked UN helicopter flew over the area, it was attacked and an Australian UN commander wounded. 'You must realise', said the Khmer Rouge commander in Pailin, 'the country is still at war.'[152] The absurdity of the UN position was demonstrated by the fact that UN personnel were barred from moving more than 400 yards from Khmer Rouge military headquarters in Pailin, while the UN commander, Lieutenant-General John Sanderson, confirmed that UN forces had 'prevented the Phnom Penh army from significantly building up the counter-offensive'.[153]

Indeed, some accused the UN of having 'two sets of rules'. While the Phnom Penh Government opened its territory and prisons to the UN Transitional Authority in Cambodia (UNTAC), as agreed at Paris, the Khmer Rouge would not even talk about it. While the UN intervened in Phnom Penh to stop a law limiting press freedom, it did nothing to stop the restriction of a whole range of freedoms in Khmer Rouge zones. While the UN allowed the Khmer Rouge to build its headquarters in Phnom Penh, next to the Royal Palace and surrounded by a high security fence, it never authorised the Phnom Penh Government to open offices in any of the Khmer Rouge towns. And while the UN began to disarm the Phnom Penh Army, it stood by while the Khmer Rouge fortified their positions and conducted a pogrom against the ethnic Vietnamese population.

According to the Cambodia specialist Raoul Jennar, the Khmer Rouge were given 'the perfect ally . . . time'. 'They are not prisoners of a calendar they would impose on themselves,' he wrote. 'They have succeeded in eight months of "peace" in reinforcing their military positions without having conceded anything, while the other parties, respecting their promise [at Paris], have begun a process which puts them, a little more each day, in a position of weakness. This is, to date, the real result of the UN operation in Cambodia.'[154] As Jennar and others pointed out, those running the UN operation in Cambodia were so committed to the 'peace plan' working, they 'hide the truth'.[155]

The truth is that the Paris agreement gave the Khmer Rouge a long-term advantage, having already caused 'Lebanonisation' of the country. Although a principal sponsor of the 'accords', the United States continued to give unilateral aid to the so-called 'non-communist' factions. The US government aid agency, USAID, spent several million dollars building a strategic road and facilities across the Thai border into the KPNLF headquarters at Thmar Pouk.[156] The Thai Army were, as ever, zealous collaborators in such ventures. At one crossing, Thai soldiers escorted Thais to work in the gem mines controlled by the Khmer Rouge: the source of great wealth for both the Khmer Rouge and the Thai generals.

In Phnom Penh under the UN unreality persisted. Echoing Neville Chamberlain, the head of UNTAC, Japanese diplomat Yasushi Akashi, 'publicly rebuked' the Khmer Rouge for their lack of co-operation.[157] General Sanderson said, 'It's outrageous ... them stopping our people'.[158] One of his officers, a Dutch colonel, complained about dealing with the Khmer Rouge, 'One day a nobody is a somebody,' he said, 'then a somebody is a nobody. A corporal becomes a colonel. They are friendly one day and unfriendly the next.'[159] A Western diplomat said he 'hoped' the Khmer Rouge 'will take a pragmatic approach'.[160]

In the meantime, the Khmer Rouge stepped up their attacks. During the first half of 1992 their immediate aim was to gain control of two strategic highways leading to Phnom Penh and so cut off the northern provinces from the capital. But Khmer Rouge commanders were also securing and expanding their 'zones'. They did this by laying mine-fields around villages so as to deter people from leaving the areas they control. This is known as 'population control'. People who try to escape or stray into a mine-infested paddy, as children frequently do, become a 'strategic drain on the community': that is, a burden on the Government in Phnom Penh.

Cambodia has long been a war of mines; all sides use them, and refer to them as 'eternal sentinels, never sleeping, always ready to attack'. In September 1991 the leading American human rights organisation, Asia Watch, published a report entitled 'Land Mines in Cambodia: The Coward's War'. Even for those who have known Cambodia's suffering it is a shock-ing document – all the more so for its expert attention to the aims and techniques of mine-laying and its effect on an impoverished peasant people.

One of the authors is Rae McGrath, a former British serviceman who is director of the Mines Advisory Group. What McGrath and his colleagues found was 'the highest percentage of physically disabled inhabitants of any country in the world . . . the highest percentage of mine amputees of any country . . . Surgeons in Cambodia perform between 300 and 700 amputations a month because of mine injuries . . . for every victim who makes it to hospital, another will die in the fields.' 'These grim statistics', says their report, 'mean that the Cambodian war may be the first in history in which land mines have gained more victims than any other weapons.'[161]

I have seen many of the victims. They are usually civilians, such as 23-year-old Rong, a beautiful young woman lying in the hospital at Kompong Spen with her three-year-old infant beside her. When she stepped on a mine she fell into water and lay for three hours, bleeding. When her father found her, he applied a tourniquet, carried her to the road and flagged down a motorcycle taxi. He took her to a first-aid post; it was seven hours before she reached hospital. In Cambodia direct transport is always difficult to come by; a twenty-mile excursion by bicycle, motorcycle taxi and horse may take a day. The mine that Rong stepped on had driven dirt and bacteria deep into the wound, causing infection to spread fast. The blood vessels had coagulated and there was thrombosis high up her leg. Had she been able to get to the hospital quickly, her leg might have been saved. 'I knew there were mines around,' she said. 'Every day I was in fear of them. But the work has to be done.'

Her story is typical. There is little hope for her future. Describing the after-effects of amputation, the Asia Watch researchers wrote:

Nearly every aspect of a Cambodian's life is set to the rhythm of rice cultivation – the flooding, the planting, the re-planting and harvesting. It is very labour intensive ... And a person who is physically disabled can become a burden. There are no rehabilitation centres, and Cambodia has no laws to protect amputees against discrimination or exploitation. Female amputees are less desirable as wives because they cannot work in the fields, and male amputees are now allowed to become Buddhist monks. Many amputees drift to Phnom Penh and become beggars or petty criminals.[162]

The laying of mines in Cambodia, said Colonel Alan Beaver, the first UN officer responsible for mines clearance, 'is probably one of the worst modern, man-made environmental disasters of the century'.[163] The United Nations repatriated tens of thousands of refugees back to countryside made uninhabitable by mines and without even a strategy for a major mine-clearing operation. The Khmer Rouge refused to allow UN cartographers to assess the extent of their minefields, and the UN said it could not begin large-scale mine clearance 'until the necessary cash resources become available'. In 1991–2 the UN was $800 million in arrears, half of which was owed by the United States. Cambodia would be cleared of mines, said the sceptics, by people stepping on them.

This attitude was not reflected in the work of certain American and other Western volunteers in Cambodia. 'NGOs' (Non-Government Organisations) were the country's lifeline, their work cherished by Cambodians, not least that of the American Quakers and Mennonites and, more recently, a group of Vietnam War veterans. Encouraged by our 1989 film, *Cambodia Year Ten*, they set up a prosthetics programme which for the first two months of 1992 fitted 300 'Jaipur limbs' to the amputee victims of mines. This is the simple, aluminium limb developed by Dr P. K. Sethi in Jaipur in India, specifically for Third World conditions. Ron Podlaski, a big, rumbustious, endearing man, who carries his wounds from the American war in Indo-China, runs the project in Phnom Penh, picking up the pieces of lives devastated by governments that now balk at spending a fraction of what they spent on backing war.*

In its report Asia Watch named two foreign powers that 'are or have been involved in training Cambodian resistance factions in the use of mines and explosives against civilian as well as military targets'. They are China and Britain. Coming three months after the British Government's admission that it had trained the allies of the Khmer Rouge, the Asia Watch study provided evidence of the terrorist techniques on offer from the British instructors. The SAS, said Asia Watch, taught 'mines warfare' and 'the use of improvised explosive devices, booby traps and the manufacture and use of time-delay fuses'. The training 'was conducted in strict secrecy: students were not told where they were being taken and were only allowed outside the camp during training exercises'.

Although the report did not say the British were involved

---

* The limb programme is run by the Indo-China Project, an offshoot of the Vietnam Veterans of America Foundation. Donations can be sent to Suite 740, 2001 'S' Street NW, Washington DC 20009, USA. Phone: (202) 483 9222.

directly with the Khmer Rouge, it revealed that many of the mines and other terror weapons in the SAS training programme were standardised among all three resistance groups. For example: the Five-way Switch – a booby trap that rips off legs – is used by the Sihanoukists and the Khmer Rouge. The British trainers, the report noted, carried sidearms and wore the 'winged dagger', the SAS cloth badge, and the SAS fawn-coloured beret.

Such a swashbuckling image of Her Majesty's special forces must be set against the impact of their work. The SAS trained the KPNLF. On February 19, 1991, said Asia Watch, the KPNLF attacked a displaced persons' camp at Sala Kran, killing nine civilians, including two children aged four and ten, a pregnant woman and a 75-year-old man. Days after the raid, 'camp residents, terrified that their attackers would return, sent a young boy back to their village to see if it was safe to return. But he stepped on a mine and was killed. When residents learned of the boy's fate, they dispatched two older boys to the village. They, two, were killed by land mines' – mines laid presumably with skills passed on by British soldiers wearing winged-dagger patches.[164]

In January 1992 Amnesty International published its report, *Repression Trade UK Limited: How the UK Makes Torture and Death its Business*.[165] Amnesty used as one of its main examples the secret training of Cambodian terrorists by the SAS. When asked about the Amnesty report, Lord Caithness said, 'Oh, that's old hat. We didn't lay any mines.'[166] In a letter to the *Guardian*, Rae McGrath of the Mines Advisory Group wrote,

> Claims by Lord Caithness or anyone else that Cambodians were not taught to lay mines are simply untrue. They were not only taught how to lay mines, but also how to booby-trap them. In addition, they were shown where to lay mines in such a manner that ensured, in the context of Cambodia, maximum casualties among rural farmers and their families. It is important to recognise that these were, as one would expect from the SAS, high-

calibre courses lasting six months with fifty students of platoon to company commander level. Three of those months were devoted exclusively to training in the use and manufacture of explosives ... and the use and dissemination of landmines ... the SAS training was a criminally irresponsible and cynical policy.[167]

On March 5, 1992 former ambassador Derek Tonkin disclosed that he was one of the principals of a company, the Vietnam Trading Corporation, that was 'very anxious to assist' in clearing mines in Cambodia.[168] Tonkin later revealed that his partner, Neil Shrimpton, was negotiating with Royal Ordnance for a mine-clearing contract in Cambodia. 'I like to keep my hand in,' said Tonkin.[169] The senior British representative in Thailand at the time British troops were teaching Cambodians to lay mines was now hoping to be in business clearing them.

From 1979 to 1992 UN Development Programme (UNDP) in New York withheld development aid from Cambodia as a result of pressure from the United States, China, Britain and Singapore. Development aid comes in the form of tools, materials and expertise, with which poor countries can make a start at developing themselves. It provides such essentials as a clean water supply and decent sanitation. Cambodia has neither. Jim Howard of Oxfam estimated that less than 5 per cent of the country's drinking water was uncontaminated. In 1988 Thames Water sent a team to Phnom Penh and found that as the level of water in the city's pipes rose and fell, it spilled into the streets and drew in drainage and raw sewage. They recommended that an entirely new system be installed urgently. This has not happened, of course. There are still no resources and most of Cambodia's engineers were killed. In any other Third World country, the UNDP would fund such a priority project.*

---

* In June 1992 an international conference in Tokyo 'pledged' $880 million towards reconstruction of Cambodia. The largest pledge of $200 million came from Japan.

471

In 1988 a senior diplomat at the British embassy in Bangkok told Oxfam's Eva Mysliwiec: 'Cambodia is a country of about seven million people. It's of no real strategic value. As far as Britain is concerned, it's expendable.'[170] Cambodia's expendability, and punishment, are exemplified by its children. Whenever I went back, I visited the National Paediatrics Hospital in Phnom Penh, the most modern hospital in the country, and I invariably found seriously ill children lying on the floors of corridors so narrow there was barely room to step over them. A relative would hold a drip; if the child was lucky, he or she would have a straw mat. Most of them suffered from, and many would die from, common diarrhoea and other intestinal ailments carried by parasites in the water supply. In hospital after hospital children died like that, needlessly and for political reasons; and they are still dying.

The international embargo ensured that hospital drug cupboards were depleted or bare; there were no vaccines; sterilisation equipment was broken; X-ray film unobtainable. At Battambang Hospital in the north-west I watched the death of an eleven-month-old baby, while her mother looked on. 'Her name is Ratanak,' she cried. Had there been a respirator and plasma, the child would have lived. A light was kept shining on her face to keep her temperature up. Then the hospital's power went down and she died.*

In the north-west most of the children fall prey to epidemics of mosquito-carried diseases – cerebral malaria, Japanese encephalitis and dengue fever. 'Our particular tragedy', Dr Choun Noothorl, director of Battambang Hospital, told me, 'is that we had malaria beaten here before 1975. In the 1970s the World Health Organisation assisted us with training, medicines and funding. I remember the statistics for April 1975; we had only a handful of malaria cases; it was a triumph.'

---

* After seeing Ratanak's death in our film, *Cambodia Year Ten*, Brian McConaghy, a forensics expert with the Royal Canadian Mounted Police, established a network of health centres throughout Cambodia. He called it 'The Ratanak Project'.

In April 1975, when Pol Pot came to power, Battambang Hospital was abandoned, its equipment and research files destroyed and most of its staff murdered. When the Vietnamese drove out the Khmer Rouge, the World Health Organisation refused to return to Cambodia. Malaria and dengue fever did return, along with new strains which the few surviving Cambodian doctors were unable to identify because they no longer had laboratories. Today two-and-a-half million people, or a quarter of the population, are believed to have malaria. The same estimate applies to tuberculosis, which was also beaten in 1975. Most are children.[171]

During the 1980s former senior Foreign Office official John Pedler met many of the world's foreign-policy makers in his capacity as representative of the Cambodia Trust. He later wrote to me: 'Specifically, I was told in Washington at the top career level that "the President has made it clear that the US will not accept the Hun Sen Government" and "we are working for a messy sort of situation with a non-Hun Sen government, but without the Khmer Rouge, who will continue to lurk in the jungles" i.e. for a state of affairs which will favour the destabilisation of Hanoi.'[172] This is the 'better result' that Washington's ideologues have sought in Indo-China.

Their hope is Sihanouk, who can no longer afford to trust his own people and moves among them behind a phalanx of ten North Korean bodyguards. It is Sihanouk who personifies the gap between extreme rural poverty and the better-off in the towns. As Catherine Lumby reported, 'It is a class distinction which the Khmer Rouge has traditionally been quick to exploit – paying the peasants double for their rice crop and often feeding villages in return for shelter during the civil war.'[173]

According to William Shawcross, only Sihanouk and 'a huge foreign presence and dollars in the countryside' can provide 'the best guarantee' against the return of the Khmer Rouge to power.[174] But what will happen when there is no longer a foreign presence? Who will catch the fluttering dollars as they fall upon the villages and hamlets? And how will the dollars get further than other, deeper pockets? Such an exquisite colonial solution brings to mind again Emory Swank, the American ambassador who passed out $100 bills to relatives of those killed by American bombs – $100 then being the going rate for a Cambodian life.[175]

These days, the Khmer Rouge would not object to such a raw show of capitalism. After all, they now advocate a 'liberal capitalist line'. Neither are they insincere, according to the historian Michael Vickery. 'They consider it [free-market capitalism],' he wrote, 'the fastest route to the type of destabilisation which will most favour their return to power.'[176]

As for Sihanouk, now astride the Trojan Horse, he is seventy-one years old; if necessary the Khmer Rouge will wait for him to die on his throne, or dispose of him quietly. They are not rushed. Everything is going to plan. Pol Pot has told his commanders to 'remain in the jungle' until they 'control all the country'. And then they will be ready.[177]

All of this was preventable. Had the great powers kept their distance following the defeat of Pol Pot in 1978, there is little doubt that a solution could have been found in the region. In 1980 the Indonesian and Malaysian Governments – fearful of Pol Pot's chief backer, China – acknowledged that the Vietnamese had 'legitimate concerns' about the return of Pol Pot and the threat from China. In 1985 Australian Foreign Affairs Minister Bill Hayden was told by Hun Sen, 'We are ready to make concessions to Prince Sihanouk and other people if they agree to join with us to eliminate Pol Pot.'[178] Four years later, reported *The Economist* from Paris, a Sihanouk–Hun Sen alliance against the Khmer Rouge was 'torpedoed' by the US State Department.[179]

Perhaps the most alluring promise of peace came when Thailand's elected prime minister, Chatichai Choonhaven, invited Hun Sen to Bangkok, and Thai officials secretly visited Phnom Penh with offers of development aid and trade. Defying their own generals, the reformist Thais proposed a regional conference that would exclude the great powers. Prime Minister Chatichai's son and chief policy adviser, Kraisak Choonhaven, told me in 1990, 'We want to see the Khmer Rouge kicked out of their bases on Thai soil.' He called on 'all Western powers and China to stop arming the Cambodian guerrillas'.[180]

This represented an extraordinary about-turn for America's most reliable client in South-east Asia. In response, Washington warned the Chatichai Government that if it persisted with its new policy it would 'have to pay a price' and threatened to withdraw Thailand's trade privileges under the Generalised Special Preferences.[181] The regional conference never took place. In March 1991 the Chatichai Government was overthrown and the new military strongman in Bangkok, Suchinda Krapayoon, described Pol Pot as a 'nice guy', who should be treated 'fairly'.[182] (It was Suchinda who turned the army on pro-democracy demonstrators in Bangkok, killing hundreds. He was forced to resign.)

At the same time Japan proposed that the United Nations exclude from a settlement any group that violated a ceasefire. Japan also proposed the establishment of a special commission to investigate the crimes of the Khmer Rouge.[183] US Assistant Secretary of State Richard Solomon rejected the proposals as 'likely to introduce confusion in international peace efforts'.[184]

'Listen,' said David Munro as we drove into Phnom Penh in June 1980, the year after the end of the holocaust. The tinkling of bells on hundreds of pony traps carrying people and food and goods was a new, rich sound. Compared with the emptiness of the year before, Phnom Penh was a city transformed. There were two bus routes, restaurants, raucous markets, reopened pagodas, telephones, a jazz band, a football team and currency. And there were freedoms, uncoerced labour, freedom of movement and freedom of worship. I had never seen so many weddings, neither had I ever received as many wedding invitations – four in one day. Marriage had become a mark of resilience, of freedom restored, and was celebrated with as much extravagance as was possible in the circumstances, with long skirts and brocade tops and hair piled high with flowers, and the men bearing gifts of precious food arranged on leaves, their necks craning from unaccustomed collars and ties. There were electricity and reopened factories – some of them paid for by the British viewers of our film *Year Zero*. An estimated 900,000 children had been enrolled in rudimentary schools and 19,000 new teachers given a two-month crash course: an historic achievement.

The tenuous nature of this 'normality' was demonstrated to me during a 'disco night' I attended one Saturday at the Monorom Hotel. The women and children sat on one side of the room, *palais*-style, the men on the other. It was a lot of fun, especially when a competing jazz band next door struck up with 'Stompin' at the Savoy'. But when a cassette of the much-loved Khmer singer, Sin Sisamouth, was played, people stopped dancing and walked to the windows and wept. He had been forced to dig his own grave and to sing the Khmer Rouge anthem, which is about blood and death. After that, he was beaten to death. It brought home to me that the efforts of the Cambodian people to recover from their nightmare of bombs and genocide ought to be the object of our lasting admiration; at the very least the willingness of our representatives to help them, not hurt them.

By any standards the efforts of the regime led by 42-year-old Hun Sen were remarkable. It attempted to secure and reconstruct a country without the basic means and skills which in Britain would be considered essential to run a local council. In the late 1980s the nation was self-sufficient in rice, and the *riel*, the currency, was stabilised by basing its worth on a national resource: the cotton that makes the scarves everyone wears. In its relationship with Vietnam, the Hun Sen Government was not unlike the West German Government after the Second World War. Just as the Federal Republic outgrew the tutelage by the Allies, Phnom Penh shed its subservience to Hanoi. Although described as communist, it was a government of Khmer nationalists: of survivors. Despite disinformation that sought to smear them as

'Pol Potists', only a minority were defectors from the Khmer Rouge and these came mostly from a dissident group that bore comparison with the 1944 Movement in the German Army that sought to overthrow Hitler.[185]

However, the isolation and privations had their effect. Corruption became a cancer, especially during the time of uncertainty and precarious transition. While Hun Sen was forced to disband the 200,000 militia because there was no public money to pay their wages, a number of his top officials grew wealthy by selling public properties to foreigners. The issue caused anger and dismay among people who were prepared to go into the streets and stand up to the Khmer Rouge. Having failed for a decade to overthrow the Hun Sen Government by force, its enemies now pinned their hopes on the United Nations to dismantle it and on intolerable internal pressures to destroy it.

August 1979 to April 1994

KING SIHANOUK'S
DEMOCRACY

I RETURNED TO Cambodia in October 1992, in time for
Ron Podlaski's wedding. After the monks had left and everyone had been garlanded in jasmine, Ron and Bo Pha, his
Khmer bride, stood in the narrow street most of the day and
night, clasping hands with hundreds of people. Many were
guests; many were street people. All were invited. I shall not
easily forget them.

At a table of honour were six young men, none of
them more than twenty-one years old, who had lost one or
both legs in Cambodia's minefields. Recognising each other,
we raised our beers in a boisterous toast; I had met them a
few days earlier at Kien Khlang, on the banks of the Mekong,
where Ron runs the Vietnam Project's Limb Centre. One of
them, a cherubic boy of eighteen, had strapped on to his
uneven stumps two new legs, made from beaten tin and
rubber, and heaved himself on to the parallel bars. He walked
for the first time since a small 'anti-personnel' mine had left
him a bleeding ruin.

He walked at his first try, with the other amputees encouraging him in the soft, tonal lilt of the Khmer language. The
next day he set off without the aid of the bars. 'Didn't you
fall down at all?' I asked him at the wedding. 'No, not once,'
he said; and when I asked him why he and his friends had
not worn their new legs, he said, 'Tonight we intend to drink
a lot of beer. Legs aren't necessary for that; they get in the
way.' The interpreter could barely tell me this over their

laughter. They had come from Kien Khlang on a fleet of motorcycles, riding pillion, each with bouquets of gifts for Ron and Bo Pha.

To walk the streets of Phnom Penh now was to run a gauntlet of limbless people, phantoms they seemed at night, some of them in threadbare uniforms, many of them children. One night a teenager without hands came at me from a doorway. He had touched a mine.

It is this that makes the work of Ron Podlaski and the other American Vietnam veterans who run the limb centre such an important counterweight, however small, to the foreign forces that still beleaguer this nation. At the very least they provide a glimpse of the human resources, both Khmer and foreign, that could begin to restore Cambodia. There is another connection. Cambodia is, according to some of Washington's ideologues, 'the last battle of America's war in Vietnam'. Ron Podlaski, Dave Evans, Bobby Muller and Ed Miles see themselves on the other side of this battle – 'this time on the right side', says Ron.

Ron is a big, rumbustious man in his forties who was hauled before a judge in New York in 1968 and told he was a 'menace to civilisation'. 'I had hit a cop on the head,' he said. 'This was normal behaviour where I grew up. The judge said, "I'll give you a choice: Vietnam or jail." I said, "Where's Vietnam?" He said, "Across the George Washington bridge." '

Ron joined the Special Forces, running secret missions into Laos and Cambodia. 'We were told to use amphetamines to keep from falling asleep,' he said, 'because we couldn't trust the local people not to kill us in our beds. These were the people we were meant to be fighting for. They hated us. I learned quickly.'

Like many veterans, Ron came home an addict and angry, believing he had been conned. I didn't meet him at the Lincoln Memorial in 1971 when he and other veterans threw back their medals; but I think I remember his larger-than-life presence. I certainly remember Bobby Muller at the Republican Party's convention in Miami the following year. I remember his booming eloquence reaching the candidate, Richard Nixon, over the cat-calls of the faithful. He shouted to Nixon that he was lying when he promised 'peace with honour' to Indo-China. For that, he was thrown out in his wheelchair.

Bobby was a marine who had been shot in the spine, losing the use of his legs. He and Ron and Ed Miles and others formed Vietnam Veterans Against the War, bringing to America a political awareness that could not be ignored; for they were ordained American heroes. Ed Miles is a double amputee who stepped on a mine during an ambush. Years later he went back to the Vietnamese village where he fell and did not recognise it. A woman, however, recognised him: not his face, just as the young American who had lost his legs. She remembered, because the next day other Americans came and razed the village.

On their return home these veterans spoke about atrocities that were not reported. They described how half of those who had carried America's battle colours were now unemployed or beset by drugs and alcohol. As many servicemen, they said, had come home and killed themselves as had died in the war. They proposed that such an adventure never happen again, anywhere.

In 1978, they formed the Vietnam Veterans of America Foundation and have since devoted themselves to preventing a repeat of such an adventure. They have funded a curriculum for schools and colleges on the Vietnam war, seeking to end the 'historical amnesia' that has allowed the same people in Washington to pursue 'other Vietnams'. They have initiated projects in Vietnam for children orphaned by the war. In Cambodia they have produced their most remarkable achievement.

At their prosthetics centre at Kien Khlang they use the 'Jaipur limb', a simple aluminium leg with a latex foot that requires no high-tech components. The foot moves almost naturally from side to side and using the limb requires minimal training, because of the confidence it gives.

The prosthetist is Dave Evans who went to Vietnam at the age of eighteen and lost both his legs before his nineteenth birthday. Back home, he retrained as a nurse and went to El Salvador where he became the director of a prosthetics programme helping the *Frente Farabundo Martí Liberación Nacional*, the FMLN. 'When I came to Indo-China as a US marine,' he said, 'we were told we were "ambassadors in green". I believed that junk. I guess I was determined to come back as another kind of ambassador; and here I am.' He walks and runs like a very fit man. The centre employs three Indian trainers from the Jaipur centre and soon Khmer trainers, most of them amputees, will begin to take over. They fit some 150 limbs a month.

The United Nations now deployed seven military units to train Khmers to clear mines. In one area of Kompong Thom province, fewer than 52 out of 4,000 mines were cleared in six months. In Battambang province not a single mine was cleared. Instead, the people were clearing the mines: farmers with spades, children with sling shots; and by stepping on them. 'We have done virtually nothing,' a UN Dutch army mine clearer told me. 'What are we here for?'

At Ron Podlaski's wedding, the Khmer band played rock 'n' roll; and the Indian trainers from the limb centre – Roddy, Than and Abdul – danced to the sitar; and Bo Pha wore several magnificent dresses of incandescent brightness. Like most Khmers who knew the Pol Pot era, her eyes have a wistfulness, a distance and a deep sadness. Bo Pha's father, two brothers and brother-in-law were all murdered by the Khmer Rouge. 'I have a boat and weapons ready,' said Ron, 'if they look like coming back. We'll get everybody out that we have to . . .'

The day after the wedding Ron, Dave, Bobby and Ed were at Phnom Penh airport, on their way to Vietnam where they plan another limbs centre. It is one of their many current projects, including a worldwide campaign to ban the use and production of land mines. Watching the four of them cross the tarmac to the aircraft – only one of them, Ron, has the use of his legs – I recalled Martha Gellhorn's tribute to that 'life-saving minority of Americans who judge their government in moral terms, who are the people with a wakeful conscience and can be counted upon ... they are always there.'[186]

A month later Ron was captured by Khmer Rouge troops while on a river journey to a new project in the north-east. They discussed in front of him whether or not to kill him, deciding finally to let him go. 'We'll kill you next time,' they told him.

I had not been to Cambodia for two years and was not prepared for the astonishing transformation. Two years earlier the sun had beaten down on a languid Phnom Penh decaying after fifteen years of international isolation. There was no 'peace process' then; there were no UN blue berets and white vehicles. This was a city of gentle anarchy, of bicycles and mopeds and silhouettes strolling at night down the centre of a road, backlit by a single headlight.

Now the streets were a cataract of white vehicles, jeeps with flashing lights, Mercedes with brocade seat covers, Suzukis with whores on call, bicycles with filing cabinets on delivery, elephants announcing Cambodia's first takeaway pizza and, at the margin, the limbless like crabs awaiting their chance.

Watching them reminded me of the dream-like quality of Cambodia, a society whose very fabric was torn apart and never repaired, whose trauma endures just beneath the surface. Suddenly, and for no apparent reason, the traffic swelled like an engulfing wave, spilling on to the pavement, a clutch of motorcycles and Toyotas abreast, sweeping aside pedestrians and vendors. One of the human crabs was struck by a bicycle and raised his only fist. Someone screamed. Open in their sorrow, the Cambodian people are often oblique in their fear; it is this internal bleeding that foreigners cannot see.

On my first day back, I walked to the Khmer Rouge compound, just behind the Royal Palace. Surrounded by a high wall, it had air-conditioned flats and offices, including a boardroom with comfortable sofas where UN officials, diplomats and journalists waited their turn to see Pol Pot's men. I met a man called Chhorn Hay, who had a fixed smile and opaque eyes and spoke perfect English. Lining up with others, I found myself shaking hands and regretting it. 'So nice to see you again,' he said to us all. 'Yes, of course, we shall consider your request for an interview. Please leave your hotel room number in the visitors' book . . . thank you so much for coming to see us.' As we left, their grey Mercedes was being dusted down. Chhorn Hay called out, 'Be careful. You may need an umbrella. Bye, bye, *bonsoir*!'

Did this happen? Were the Khmer Rouge really here, wearing suits and saying 'Bye, bye, *bonsoir*'? For me, standing at their gates, all the disingenuous semantic games and the contortions of intellect and morality that have tried to give them respectability and make the 'peace process' appear to work took on a vivid obscenity. I realised I had walked down this road on the day I arrived in Phnom Penh in 1979, in the aftermath of the holocaust.

There is a grassy area in front of the Royal Palace in Phnom Penh, where people gather on Sundays to look at the Mekong, have their photograph taken and watch their children play in safety. I have often come here to catch the breeze and enjoy the normality. When the UN chose to hold a military parade here, it did more than disturb the peace. Ordinary Cambodians were barred from attending: that is, until a UN official was reminded that some might be necessary for the purposes of public relations. 'Get a few of those people over here,' he said into the public address system. A few dozen were pushed to the edge of a crowd of foreigners in time to hear a Ghanaian band strike up 'Onward Christian Soldiers'. Prince Sihanouk arrived with his North Korean bodyguards and was met by the Head of the UN mission, Yasushi Akashi, and the UN military commander, General Sanderson. Beside them as a guest of honour stood a smiling Khieu Samphan, Pol Pot's man.

I had never seen him in the flesh and I was struck by his relaxed, almost jovial demeanour and by my own reaction. The sense of nightmare returned. Here was the Khmer Goebbels standing to attention as the 'Christian soldiers' marched by: the British, the Australians, the Americans. Here he was being fêted by other 'dignitaries'. A senior UN officer bowed his head to him. And when an international choir sang some mawkish rubbish about saving the world, he clapped, and he clapped. 'Thank you all for coming,' said the voice on the public address: 'and a reminder about the fun run tomorrow. The winner gets $200 in cash!'

The next day I interviewed General Sanderson and I asked him how he felt to be in such company. He replied that he was 'neutral'. I asked him how you went about creating a 'neutral political environment' when one of the 'factions' was guilty of genocide. 'They are *your* words,' he said. I quoted to him the report of the UN Special Rapporteur who described the Khmer Rouge as guilty of genocide 'even under the most restricted definition'. I said, 'General, he was speaking for the body you represent and he described them as genocidists.'

'He may well have, but I'm not going to.'[187]

The UN spokesman, Eric Falt, a Frenchman, was more to the point. 'The peace process', he told me, with a fixed smile, 'was aimed at allowing [the Khmer Rouge] to gain respectability.'[188] UN officials were now reluctant to use the term 'Khmer Rouge', preferring the acronym, NADK, for National Army of Democratic Kampuchea. On a visit to Pol Pot's heartland in the north-west, Australian foreign affairs minister Gareth Evans pinned a gold kangaroo on the uniform of a Khmer Rouge soldier. 'Congratulations,' he said, shaking the incredulous man's hand. When asked about this, Evans said, 'The young Khmer Rouge cannot be blamed for what happened in the mid-1970s.'[189]

The 21,000 UN troops and officials, their 8,000 vehicles, their villas and their camp followers gave me a sense of *déjà vu*. Was this the honky-tonk Phnom Penh of the early 1970s, just before the Khmer Rouge took power? According to a report by the UN Children's Fund, there were 20,000 child prostitutes, and 3,000 UN personnel had contracted sexually transmitted diseases.[190] Before the UN arrived, Aids was unknown; now 14 per cent of prostitutes were believed to be HIV-positive. A memo distributed to UN personnel said, 'Please try not to park your Landcruiser outside brothels.'[191]

UN personnel had their own generators and clean water, while nothing was done about the water supply, which was fed by the sewers and left tens of thousands of children dying from intestinal diseases. (Drugs are available, but only at a price, on the 'free market'.) There was little work for people who could not serve foreigners. Young men were blinded with flash burns from welding iron gates for UN villas. They lay on bamboo mats in agony, with damp rags on their faces, until their next shift.

Every UN 'peacekeeper' received a 'hardship fee' of $145 a day on top of salary and perks. This was more than most Cambodians earned in a year and twice the monthly wage of a Cambodian risking his life to clear the landmines that many UN personnel would not touch. Such was the process of recolonisation, which was evident even among the voluntary aid agencies. I visited an aid official in his air-conditioned office, which was cold and obsessively tidy; the only sound was that of his computer printer. We could have been in London or Los Angeles; and I was struck by the distance between him and the precarious life outside the tinted windows. He spoke about 'data', 'mechanisms' and 'impacting' and used the sanitising terms that are a lingua franca among foreigners. The Khmer Rouge, to him, were now a 'faction' with political and moral equity with the other 'factions'.

At the Cambodiana Hotel, a 'luxurious' monstrosity on the banks of the Mekong, opened since I was last there, this distancing was complete. Ordinary Cambodians were not allowed in. The Austrian manager was fastidious; no beer cans on the table, please. There were photographs of dignitaries in the foyer, including Lord Caithness, former Minister of State at the Foreign Office and promoter of the Khmer Rouge's place in the 'peace process'. A man from the International Monetary Fund had set up an office in one of the rooms. True to its skills, the IMF had unearthed a 'debt' of $65 million incurred by the Lon Nol regime in 1971. Interest had apparently been ticking over for twenty-two years. A foreign 'consortium' would pay this off, I was assured unofficially, in return for the 'appropriate trade concessions'. At a cocktail party, overlooking the pool, the talk was about the corruption that is 'a way of life here'. No irony was noted.

At a special UN conference in Tokyo in 1992 the world community pledged $880 million to 'rehabilitate services' in Cambodia. This was hailed as the 'foundation' of the 'peace process'. The aid would be delivered as an 'emergency'. Flicking on his air conditioner with a remote control, the Phnom Penh representative of the UN Development Fund, Edouard Wattez, assured me, 'The money is coming in quite significantly.' I asked him which government had given the most. 'The United States,' he said. 'They have pledged $60 million.' I asked him how much of this had arrived. 'Two million,' he winced, 'for road repair.' And this 'road repair' has, in fact, restored a network of strategic highways from Thailand into Cambodia along which the Khmer Rouge mount checkpoints and move ammunition and supplies.

The Cambodia specialist Raoul Jennar has described the commitment of UN resources to Cambodia as a deception, 'a real myth'. The real figure was not $880 million, he says, but $660 million, of which most is not 'new money' and only 20 per cent will be distributed in the foreseeable future.[192]

Although the United Nations operation was given an international face in Cambodia, only those who adhered to 'Western' (i.e. American) policy were given key positions. The UN financial adviser, Roger Lawrence, a US official, ran the Central Bank of Cambodia and 'represented' Cambodia at meetings of the Washington-dominated World Bank and the IMF. Thus, Cambodia was being eased into the world of 'structural adjustment programmes' (SAPS), which would ensure that it had a deregulated, low wage 'growth' economy favouring foreign investors, such as the Thais, Singaporeans and, of course, Japanese, who were already 'investing' in the country with the finesse of pirates falling on buried treasure.

The UN 'information and education department' in Phnom Penh was given to Timothy Carney, described by his friend

William Shawcross as 'a dedicated and skilled American diplomat'.[193] Indeed Carney was an important official in the US embassy in Phnom Penh in the 1970s when his government was devastating Cambodia. He is the author of books that mention the bombing only in passing; like most from that era, he has never expressed public regret for his service to an administration that killed and maimed perhaps 500,000 Cambodians. Carney went on to become Asia Director of the National Security Council, America's top policy-making body, based in the White House. He was one of those largely responsible for US insistence that the Khmer Rouge be part of the 'peace process'. Not surprisingly, he then turned up in a top UN job in Cambodia, effectively running propaganda.

Stephen Heder was appointed Carney's deputy. Heder is an American researcher who used to sympathise with the Khmer Rouge.[194] In 1979 he went to work for the US State Department in Thailand – an unexplained switch of loyalties. In his UN job, he produced a number of reports damning the Hun Sen Government which were publicised, but nothing on the Khmer Rouge infiltration of the US-backed royalists.

According to the Cambodian writer Chanthou Boua, who lost all her family in the holocaust, UN Khmer staff were used to investigate the family backgrounds of the Hun Sen leadership, looking for Vietnamese antecedents. The aim of this 'was to appease the Khmer Rouge'. UN staff, she said, were also being directed 'to comb the villages looking for ethnic Vietnamese. Those subject to allegations of illegal immigration which are proved "correct" are deported within 24 hours. Ethnic cleansing is not mentioned in the Paris Agreement.'[195] The UN also made public the names of three former Vietnamese soldiers. This was picked up by the media as 'evidence' that Vietnamese troops remained in Cambodia – a long discredited claim that the Khmer Rouge have used as effective propaganda. One of the Vietnamese turned out to be an ethnic Khmer from southern Vietnam; the others were demobilised veterans who had married local women. Pol Pot would have approved this tactic. 'We must focus attention on the Vietnamese,' he told his cadres in 1988, 'and divert attention from our past mistakes.'[196]

Media propaganda played a vital part in imposing the essentially American 'peace process'. In the run-up to the elections in early 1993 the UN was generally depicted as an oasis of order in a country where mass killing was somehow unique to and congenital in the Cambodian race. 'Imagine a country where people have been killing each other without mercy for 20 years and more . . .' wrote Robert McCrum in the *Guardian* magazine.[197] Imagine 'a country that does not have a national will for peace' (the *Independent*).[198] 'You see,' Yasushi Akashi, UN chief in Cambodia, told the BBC, 'violence is deep-rooted in the Cambodian tradition'. And this from a Japanese!

Devaluing the truth of the past – that no society had been so brutalised by foreigners – was essential. Cambodia, lamented William Shawcross, who had supported the inclusion of the Khmer Rouge in the Paris 'accords', was too often described 'like many other crises' with 'quick-fix clichés [such as] piles of skulls and "Asian Hitlers" overlaid in the outdated rhetoric of the Vietnam war'. This was a country that was little more than an 'amoral state' which the Paris accords offered 'a chance to change'.[199]

The 'good news' was that the Khmer Rouge were 'isolated' and 'finished'. Nate Thayer of the Associated Press wrote that, according to 'analysts', the Khmer Rouge were waiting for the 'final blow' that would 'destroy or marginalise the group'. Buried at the end of Thayer's piece was this: 'Large areas of the countryside remain firmly under Khmer Rouge control, including areas rich in rice, gems and safe supply lines . . .'[200]

'And what of the Khmer Rouge?' asked William Shawcross in the *New York Times*. 'For them, the election was like holding a Crucifix to Dracula.' In December 1992, Shawcross wrote that there were 27,000 Khmer Rouge; seven months later he had reduced this to 10,000 – which meant that half of Pol Pot's army had miraculously disappeared.[201] Before the Paris 'accords' Western 'intelligence analysts' estimated there were as many as 30,000 Khmer Rouge troops in the field. Clearly, argued Western governments, they were so strong they could not be excluded from the 'peace process'. Now the figure was put at half that, with the same 'analysts' contending that the Khmer Rouge were so weak they could now be dismissed and the UN operation declared an 'historic success'.

The opposite was true. In the three and a half years from the signing of the 'peace accords' to the elections in May 1993, Pol Pot had actually quadrupled his area of operation and was in a more commanding position than at any time since the 1970s.

The Khmer Rouge now represented a pincer movement extending from the south to the east and north along the borders with Thailand and Laos, all the way east to Vietnam. One of the pincers was less than fifty miles from Phnom Penh. The UN almost disclosed the gravity of these Khmer Rouge gains when its own evacuation orders leaked out shortly before the elections. UN officials quickly rescinded them, so as to 'lessen any unnecessary climate of fear'.[202]

Shortly before the elections, the Washington Cambodia specialist Craig Etcheson secretly photographed UN military situation maps in battalion headquarters across the country. 'Some people might argue,' Etcheson said, 'that the term "operation" doesn't mean that the Khmer Rouge completely control these areas, but that's hardly relevant if you happen to be a villager living there, who is under Khmer Rouge coercion and forced to pay them taxes. In many of these villages, Khmer Rouge cadres are actually present – this means control. The UN maps show that the Khmer Rouge operate with varying degrees of impunity in 25 per cent of the country; and in another 25 per cent of the country they are operating freely by day and in control by night. That's half of Cambodia in which they have a military advantage they did not have before the UN arrived in October 1991.'[203]

The elections were won by the Funcinpec party, commonly known as the 'royalists'. Their leader is Prince Norodom Ranariddh, Sihanouk's son. He won 58 seats in a constituent assembly, and the Cambodian People's Party (CPP), the former Hun Sen Government, won 52 seats. This 'triumph for democracy' was in fact a triumph for the United States, similar to the American 'win' in the Nicaraguan elections in 1990 that got rid of the Sandinistas.

Like the UNO coalition that won in Nicaragua, the Cambodian royalists were part of a coalition built and nurtured by US intelligence agencies while a US-led economic boycott impoverished the government.[204] The Khmer Rouge, while not wanted as a regime, were used to achieve this. They dominated the coalition and today remain Cambodia's hidden hand of power. In a comparative article about Angola, the *New York Times* quoted a senior State Department official as saying, 'UNITA is exactly like the Khmer Rouge. Elections and negotiations are just one more method of fighting a war. Power is all.'[205]

As the Indo-China writer Paul Shannon has observed, the elections were a 'victory for racism, taking place in an atmosphere in which racial hatred was stirred up against ethnic Vietnamese citizens of Cambodia [by] both right-wing and Khmer Rouge political forces ... Funcinpec encouraged and benefited from this [and from] UN policies of disarming ethnic Vietnamese [which] made some of these atrocities possible'.[206] Such was the UN's 'neutral political environment' that was its own prerequisite for 'free and fair' elections.

At first, the Khmer Rouge called the elections a 'theatrical farce'. Then they appeared to change course. The masters of deception now campaigned for Prince Ranariddh's party. According to foreign electoral observers, many Cambodians thought they were voting for Prince Sihanouk, who still commanded loyalty. Few were aware that Sihanouk had described his son's 'royalists' as infiltrated by 'a large number of Khmer Rouge ... tasked with eliminating true royalists'. Pol Pot's men, said Sihanouk, held the 'important positions' and had become 'chiefs of bureaus, heads of provincial organisations'. The Khmer Rouge takeover of Funcinpec, he said, was 'almost complete'.[207] Shortly before the elections almost the entire royalist military command defected to the Phnom Penh

Government. One of them, General Kim Hang, said, 'The Khmer Rouge have been employing [the royalists] only for a cosmetic.'[208]

This will not surprise those who have read recent Cambodian history. Pol Pot did not come to power suddenly. On the contrary, he did as he is doing now; and the echo today is of the early 1970s, when he built a united front of the Khmer Rouge and Cambodian royalty. Over the following years, Khmer Rouge agents infiltrated, liquidated and replaced the majority royalists. By 1975, 'Year Zero', Pol Pot had complete power.

A captured Khmer Rouge document, dated January 10, 1992, indicated that a similar process was under way. It said, 'We must concentrate first on accelerating the infiltration of category one forces in order to gradually establish in advance the prerequisites'[209] for the takeover of the royalists. In 1988, Pol Pot said: 'The fruit remains the same; only the skin has changed.'[210]

The UN's undoubted achievement was the work of its electoral volunteers; and the spectacle of the Cambodian people voting was moving. But the 'democracy' this represented was undermined long before people went to the polls by the advantage the Western powers gave to the Khmer Rouge. During the pomp that saw Norodom Sihanouk crowned king in September 1993, little was said about the ethnocentric, secretive regime over which he now holds sweeping powers – just as he did in the 1960s when his volatile, dictatorial ways led to the rise of the Khmer Rouge. Since then, he has had a relationship with the Khmer Rouge, described by his friend, John Pedler, as that of 'a rabbit with a snake'.[211] This is why the Khmer Rouge supported the royalists during the election, demanding that Sihanouk be given 'full power as the king'. Only Sihanouk, they said, would enjoy the support of Pol Pot's 'military might': and only he could resolve the issue of 'national reconciliation'. By that, they meant a subversive foothold in the regime. In October 1993, Sihanouk announced an 'advisory role' for the Khmer Rouge in the new government. The

Khmer Rouge replied by demanding a role for themselves in the army.[212]

Prince Ranariddh has played this down, appearing even to 'overrule' his father. However, in December 1993 the *Sydney Morning Herald* disclosed that 'secret talks are being arranged to negotiate a controversial plan' to bring the Khmer Rouge into the government. One of the promoters of this is China, which, according to the accredited 'good news', long ago abandoned its former client, Pol Pot. At the 'secret talks' the Chinese are expected to offer sanctuary to Pol Pot and his principal cohorts while 'allowing the more acceptable members to go to Phnom Penh'.[213]

In the same week that these machinations saw light, the *New York Times* documented, from classified diplomatic messages, the clandestine alliance of the Khmer Rouge and the Thai military – who between them make some $500 million a year in timber and gems. Chinese weapons for Pol Pot's army fill Thai military warehouses. Thai military units transport arms and escort Khmer Rouge troops. In August 1993 Thai troops looked on while the Khmer Rouge held twenty-one UN officials hostage on Thai soil. 'The Thais remain the lifeline for the Khmer Rouge,' reported a Western diplomat, stationed in Phnom Penh. 'Unless the Thais shut them off, the Khmer Rouge could be around forever.'[214]

Anything is possible now that the greatest obstacles to Pol Pot's return have been swept away. In early 1994 the Western press made much of Khmer Rouge 'defectors', many of whom turned out to be boys recently recruited, and of the 'fall' of Pailin, the Khmer Rouge 'headquarters'. In fact, Pailin never fell; the Khmer Rouge withdrew and surrounded the government forces. 'The Khmer Rouge are in the midst of their biggest offensive for five years,' reported the Mines Advisory Group from Battambang in April, 1994. 'Government forces are collapsing in the face of this onslaught . . .'[215]

Indeed, wrote Craig Etcheson in the *Phnom Penh Post*, 'Pol Pot is better positioned today than at any time since 1979. The Vietnamese are gone. The "puppet regime" is defeated, replaced by an unstable conglomeration. Pol Pot still has his army and still has highly placed friends in China and Thailand. He is wealthy. He has hugely expanded his territory and population. He has deeply infiltrated the opposing parties, and once again he has both overt and covert operatives in Phnom Penh. And he has convinced most of the world that the Khmer Rouge threat is no more. Nearly 3,000 years ago, the Chinese General Sun Tzu wrote in his classic treatise, *The Art of War*: "All warfare is based on deception . . . He who lacks foresight and underestimates his enemy will surely be captured by him." '216

On the eve of the elections the Khmer Rouge slaughtered thirty-three ethnic Vietnamese in a village south of Siem Reap. Among the dead were eight children. It was an indication that the killing fields had returned; and the US chief of mission, Charles Twining, said he was worried history might repeat itself. Khieu Samphan replied by threatening a pogrom. 'Twining's nightmare', he said, 'might repeat itself.'217 The writer Chanthou Boua described the fear of speaking out among Cambodians embroiled in the 'peace process'. And yet, she wrote, 'the UN should take responsibility for such atrocities, because it is the UN Security Council that legitimised the Khmer Rouge.'218

She is right and those who believed in a Faustian pact with the Khmer Rouge were wrong, and have been proven wrong. The Western-imposed 'peace process' has been, to paraphrase the Vietnamese independence fighter Huu Ngon, 'a silver bullet, more deadly than the real one. It does not kill you instantly, but step by step'. If the pro-Washington urban-dominated coalition does not survive, and Pol Pot appears some time in the future, those responsible ought not to be allowed to wash their hands and say they tried their best to bring peace to this 'impossible country'.

'The main thing', says Australian Foreign Affairs Minister Gareth Evans, one of the architects, 'is to accentuate the positive . . . to keep our fingers crossed.'219 No, the main thing is to tear down completely the Berlin Wall that the West built around Cambodia; and Thailand should be cast as an international pariah if its military continues to back Pol Pot.

Of course only the Cambodians can beat Pol Pot on the battlefield; and their national army should not want for the kind of resources that were so generously provided to the genocidists and their allies.

In the meantime, the leaders of the Khmer Rouge should be tried *in absentia* before a special commission of the International Court of Justice. In this way their crimes can be fully acknowledged, making appeasement a crime. If the United Nations Secretary-General can agree to set up an 'international criminal court' in the Balkans to try those accused of crimes 'reminiscent of genocide', he can do the same for a country where genocide, according to the UN's Special Rapporteur, has already happened '. . . even under the most restricted definition'.[220] Among those Western governments that are signatories to the Genocide Convention, there must be one prepared to summon the skills of its jurists, if not the moral force of its public opinion, and take the overdue action.

But they should hurry. While Cambodia is declared 'solved' and slips back into media oblivion, the Khmer Rouge demand that King Sihanouk close the Tuol Sleng extermination centre in Phnom Penh, which has stood, like the edifice at Auschwitz, as a reminder of the thousands of men, women and children who were tortured and died there. 'Not only is this the symbol of the evil of the Khmer Rouge,' as Chet Atkins wrote, 'it is also a repository for records and evidence to be used for an eventual prosecution.'[221] Pol Pot, Khieu Samphan, Son Sen and the others are looking ahead, as they tend to do, and thinking what can be done now to destroy the evidence.

'If understanding is impossible,' wrote Primo Levi of the Nazi holocaust, 'knowing is imperative, because what happened could happen again.'[222] The simple truth is that no peace was ever built on unrepudiated genocide; and the words 'Never again' remain the cry of civilisation.

August 1979 to April 1994

X
UNDER THE VOLCANO

A LAND OF BROKEN
PROMISES

Manila

AS YOU FLY into Manila the silhouette of Mount Pinatubo rises like the sharpest of jagged teeth. All around it is a carpet of grey. This is lava from the eruption of last July, still moving like sticky sand, sinking ever deeper into the earth, petrifying forests and putting rivers to flood.

Pinatubo is part of a chain of recent disasters; two weeks ago a typhoon killed some 6,000 people in Leyte. These are vulnerable islands; but if it is true that nature strives to compensate, it has done so here with fertility of land and foreshores and sea that should sustain a large population, especially one as resourceful as that of the Philippines.

This has not happened. Children die easily here. Last week a study published in Manila revealed that a third of the population was so impoverished they could not get enough to eat, and that overall poverty was now 70 per cent: a rise of more than 10 per cent since Corazon Aquino became the 'people's president' in 1986.[1] Of course, the reasons are complex; Filipinos have a long history of colonial exploitation; yet Aquino's failure, and unwillingness, to give anything but tokens to the people in return for the civilised uprising that saw off Marcos is widely regarded both as a betrayal and a potential catalyst. '1986 was our finest hour in the eyes of the world,' said J. P. Arroya, Aquino's first executive secretary, in a moving speech the other day. 'We had blazed an historic trail in mankind's long struggle for freedom.

President Aquino walked in a sea of praise. Why, then, receiving so many compliments herself, did she not ask something for the rest of the people?'[2]

He was referring to the interest payments that consume almost half the national budget and to Aquino's decision, announced in an emotional speech before the US Congress, that 'the Philippines will pay every penny of its debt'.[3] That much of the foreign debt is based on fraudulent loans, negotiated secretly by Marcos and his cronies, was not allowed to intrude upon her standing ovation. 'She did not simply campaign for office,' wrote the journalist James Goodno in his fine book, *The Philippines: Land of Broken Promises*, 'she led a national crusade for liberation. She symbolised hope . . . '[4]

But no more. When Imelda Marcos returned home the other day, her lawyer expressed the new mood when he said, 'Listen, it's ridiculous: it's absurd! Every Tom, Dick and Harry here in the Philippines has this problem. No one is ever prosecuted.'[5] The 'problem' was the charge that his client had pilfered $5 billion from the national treasury. Whether or not corruption is greater now than under Marcos is debatable: and no one suggests that Cory Aquino indulged in Imelda's famous habits. Rather, with the hope invested in her, she put a liberal face on an illiberal system and so legitimised and refined the feudal enrichment of the few at the expense of the majority.

This is vividly demonstrated by her 'land reform'. Land reform is what rural people have dreamt about since the Peasants' Revolt. It was Aquino's first promise; and in 1988 the Comprehensive Agrarian Reform Law was passed, allowing the government to buy land and distribute it to tenants and agricultural workers with long-term, low-interest loans. Instead, the law's 'loopholes' have turned it into a bonanza for landowners. It allows land to be transferred to family members; landowners can choose the best lands to keep and corporate farms need only give tenants nominal 'shares'. All coffee, cocoa and rubber plantations are exempt.

Aquino offered to use her own, vast estate, *Hacienda Luis-*

ita, as a model for the reformers to emulate. As a *haciendero*, a member of one of the landed oligarchies, she and her brothers own a 60,000 hectare sugar plantation north of Manila. It is run strictly on class lines, with the Cojuangcos (her family) and their managers living in a village of mansions with a country club and a golf course.

Most of the cane cutters and the *sacadas*, the very poor migrant workers, pay for water and electricity, and in the tradition of the *peon*, supplement their low income by borrowing from the Cojuangcos. Their debt, plus interest, is subtracted from their wages: a microcosm of the nation. Aquino's workers, wrote James Goodno, 'are on the whole willing to concede the management a good life so long as they are treated with dignity. This is not always the case. The president's brother, Congressman José "Peping" Cojuangco, pampers his race horses and roosters. His horses live in cool, comfortable stables and the fighting cocks occupy individual shelters. Extra care protects them from disease.'[6] No such care and protection is extended to the *sacadas* and their children.

In 1989, with much fanfare, the Cojuangco family sold shares to a third of its workers. They kept control of 67 per cent and the most profitable sugar mill. The dividends amount to about seventy pesos a month, which, as Goodno points out, 'is hardly enough to feed an average family for one day'.[7]

The centrepiece of the Aquino Government's 'economic restoration' is a vast export zone, known as the Calabarzon 'superproject'. It exemplifies the most discredited kind of imposed 'development'. Dreamt up in Washington and funded mostly by Japan, it has been one of the 'economic reforms' demanded by the International Monetary Fund, along with higher taxes, public spending cuts, mass sackings and other wonders of 'structural adjustment'. The head of the National Economic Development Agency has described the scheme as 'a giant fabrication'. In resigning, she said the last thing the country needed was more debt.[8]

The 'superproject' will destroy about 6 per cent of all food-growing land – land on which more than eight million people live and depend. Japanese, American and other Western factories will rise from the former paddies and fields. Most of the farmers have been given little or no notice; bulldozers have arrived; compensation is minimal. 'When all this is gone,' Teresita Vallez, a farmer, told me, 'how will we ever compensate for the farmland destroyed by Pinatubo? Our children will end up as squatters in Manila.'

Many of the sons have already joined 'the groups', meaning the resistance. 'A big fight is coming,' people say matter-of-factly. I spent the early morning and night with a police unit who scour Manila for homeless children. The lieutenant in charge shook his head and said, 'It's not something I would have believed possible a few years ago. But now the poverty is too terrible. My men pick up kids in a van that doesn't have lights because we can't afford to replace them. We can't afford to be policemen unless we drive a taxi or sell ice-cream cones.'

We drove along Roxas Boulevard, with squatters' shanties on one side, and the high walls of 'forbidden cities' on the other. These are where the rich, the politicians and many foreigners live. They have their own water supply; the lawns are lush and rubbish is collected. No one gets in without 'screening', which means fingerprinting for maids and nannies. 'Why do they need all those men with pump-action shotguns at the gates?' said the lieutenant. 'Maybe the politicians in there are feeling guilty. Or maybe they are afraid of those people and their kids that tap-tap on the windows of their cars at traffic lights.'

What Aquino has demonstrated is that presidential elections are irrelevant contests between the same 'trapo' (traditional) groups. Foreign journalists tend to write about Philippine politics as a freak show, preferring the stereotypical Filipino immersed in religion and an attitude of *bahala na* ('What the heck'). The *Daily Globe*, one of Manila's lively papers, ran a finely ironic front page which had pictures of Cory Aquino and Imelda side by side, showing both of them giving away charity, 'food and promises' to the poor.[9] Cory continues to play the ordinary housewife she is not and Imelda attempts to reincarnate Evita Peron. Imelda is still making statements like, 'The only wealth is in my heart.' (Recently she said of her late husband, whose mummified remains have been brought back from Honolulu: 'He looks even better now.')

Filipino journalists travelling with them say that neither appears to comprehend the degree of bitterness and anger that lie just beneath the surface of the courtesy and tolerance that greet them. If 'people power' took the Marcoses, and the world, by surprise in 1986, it is likely to do so again. The truth is that Filipinos have fought back in spite of their colonial past; yet each time real independence has seemed within grasp, a reformist elite, promising 'freedom', 'land reform' and 'democracy', has been entrusted with power.

By attacking the mass organisations that spearheaded 'people power', the Aquino Government wasted no time in reinforcing the historical pattern. Many of Marcos's repressive labour laws were retained. Vigilante groups, or 'anticommunist associations', were given a free hand. Called *Tadtad* (literally 'chop chop') and MACHO ('Mobile Anti-Crime Hit Operatives'), they have intimidated the mildest opposition in the slums and the countryside, where they have close ties with the Army. This is similar to the 'low-intensity conflict', or organised terror, that has plagued Central America. Less than two years after the euphoric days of Aquino's coming to power, Amnesty International reported, 'Political killings carried out by the government and government-backed forces in violation of the law have become the most serious human rights problem in the Philippines.'[10]

In the face of this, the 'open mass movement', as the resistance is known, has mobilised – carefully avoiding peripheral confrontation. The leading trade union federation, *Kilusang Mayo Uno* (KMU), which can claim much of the credit for getting rid of Marcos, now has 700,000 active members. Added to this is the civilian force of the Peasant Movement of the Philippines, the KMP; and the million activists of the National Democratic Front. The NDF is a Philip-

501

pines phenomenon. Whereas all over the world the student movement faded in the 1970s, here it went from strength to strength. The NDF's groups range from Christians for National Liberation, to the communist New People's Army.

The NPA, which has never been defeated, has about 22,000 members, of whom half are guerrillas. According to James Goodno, 'the NPA influences 20 to 25 per cent of the population . . . But the revolutionary movement is far larger . . . An extensive underground network stretches from southern Mindanao to northern Luzon. And, for the first time in Philippine history, radical mass movements actually exist in most provinces and cities.'[11]

However, many in the resistance are careful not to under-rate the power of the army, or the willingness of the United States to be 'invited' to put down a popular uprising. It used to be said that the Philippines was 'another Vietnam waiting to happen'. I was never persuaded of this; the analogy seemed too pat. Now, as the distant rumbling of another kind of volcano grows, the signals are familiar.

November 22, 1991

NICARAGUA

WHEN BRECHT WROTE, 'By chance I was spared. If my luck leaves me, I am lost,' he might well have been referring to Nicaragua. In 1979, it was because President Carter was preoccupied with the American hostages in Iran that Nicaragua was spared the usual intervention when its people rose up against the tyrant Anastasio Somoza, of whom Richard Nixon had said: 'Now that's the kind of anti-communist we like to see down there.'

Exploiting their luck, the Nicaraguans went on, precariously, to lay the foundations of a decent society unheard of in most countries of the region. Indeed, they smashed the stereotype; no more did they work on 'Somoza's farm'; no longer were they victims, accepting passively their predicament.

The depth of the Nicaraguan revolution struck me when I stayed in a frontier community, El Regadio, in the north of the country. Like everywhere in Nicaragua, it is very poor and its isolation has made change all the more difficult. However, within a few years of deposing Somoza, the Sandinistas had established a 'well baby clinic', including a rehydration unit which prevents infants from dying from diarrhoea, the most virulent Third World killer.

When I was there no baby had died for a year, which was unprecedented. The production and consumption of basic foods had risen by as much as 100 per cent, which meant that serious malnutrition had disappeared. There was a new school attended by children who, before 1979, would have laboured in the fields; and a total of eighty-seven people, mostly middle-aged *campesino* women, had learned to read and write. One of them, a large mixture of jolliness and shyness called Petrona Cruz, mentioned to me the word, *pobreterria*, for which there is no precise translation. 'It's the equivalent of people calling themselves the scum of the earth,' she said. 'It was a view of ourselves based on shame, on believing that things could never change. The word doesn't exist *now*.'

Many in the West may have forgotten, if they ever knew, the political subtlety of the Nicaraguan revolution. In the early days there were Stalinists, Maoists, liberals and even conservatives among the Sandinistas, but the dominant strain were genuinely non-aligned radicals and visionaries, who were probably closer to Mexico than Havana, and to 'liberation theology' than Marx. A friend of mine, Xavier Gorostiaga, a Jesuit economist, told me, 'When the North Americans reduce our uniqueness to a jargon they themselves do not understand, they deny the power of our nationalism. For example, the most powerful influence on Marxism here is Christianity and our Indian heritage. In Nicaragua today to be a Christian can *mean* you have a real option for the poor.'

Unlike the Cubans, the Sandinistas left most of the economy in private hands (and were attacked from the left for doing so). They held the country's first democratic elections in 1984; and in all their programmes designed to end hunger, preventable sickness and literacy, they maintained an 'option for the poor'.

They offered to their neighbours, all of them suffering under murderous Washington-sponsored tyrannies, a clear demonstration of regional nationalism at last succeeding in abolishing *pobreterria*. Consequently, they represented a threat. During the second half of the 1980s, they were attacked by the United States, using a Contra army funded, equipped and trained by the CIA, often secretly and illegally, whose speciality was the terrorising and murder of civilians. Today, only the United States stands condemned by the World Court for the 'unlawful use of force' against another, sovereign state – Nicaragua.

The result was the devastation of the frail Nicaraguan economy. Last year, the Sandinistas narrowly lost the country's second election (they remain the largest single party). In hindsight, one can view that as inevitable. They were much too confident of their base and some had become arrogant; above all, people wanted the blockade to end and Washington off their backs; many queued to receive their $40 each for voting for Violetta Chamorra – an irresistible bribe if you have an income of less than $200 a year.

I was reminded of this last Saturday evening when I was invited to the celebration of a remarkable project in London. More than seven years ago a young man called Robert Todd – Todd to his friends – was moved by a documentary film *Nicaragua*, made by Alan Lowery, Elizabeth Nash and myself and shown on ITV. Todd decided to 'do something'. He began by buying for £18,000 a derelict house – actually little more than a shopfront – in Vauxhall. He then drew together a network of craftsmen and women, artisans, carpenters, electricians, most of them amateurs.

They set about building a house, which would be sold and the money given to Nicaragua. The house is mostly of wood, the result of inspired scrounging: the stairs are of mahogany and there are magnificent handmade parquet floors; doors are from the floor of Battersea power station; window frames from the laboratory desks at local schools; stairs from British Rail desks, much of it acquired during judicious raids on skips. There are fine skylights, stained-glass windows, and murals drawn by local children.

It is not just a beautiful house, but a symbol of the conversion of the obsolete and the abandoned to new life, and of the energy of commitment. Less than £9,000 was spent on materials, and all the labour was given free. A year ago the house may have been worth a quarter of a million pounds. 'It's been a race against the collapse of capitalism!' says Todd, now with an anxious eye to the falling property market. Certainly the house is worth a great deal of money and, when it is sold, this will help restore Nicaragua: perhaps to

505

build again well-baby clinics and to restore agricultural co-operatives now bereft of resources.

For me, the achievement represented by the house built by Todd and Sarah, Mick and Tim, and many others, reinforces the notion that while luck, always ephemeral and capricious, will depart, people will wait, their hope never lost. Nicaragua's revolution, and its 'threat', remain pending.

March 29, 1991

CHILDREN OF PALESTINE

WHEN THE MIDDLE East peace conference opened in Madrid last week, I remembered Ahmed Hamzeh, a street entertainer, and his young son. I met them in a Palestinian refugee camp on the occupied West Bank twenty-three years ago. It was a bitterly cold and wet Easter and the wind spun off the bare side of the valley and carried the stench of a sewer that overflowed and merged with mud.

Some 3,000 Palestinians lived in huts here, prisoners in their own land. Water trickled brown, if at all, from communal taps; and there were communal illnesses, such as gastroenteritis, blindness and madness. There was no *intifada* then. The young were simply sick and passive. They went to a United Nations school; but mostly, like the adults, they went nowhere. They ambled up and down the camp's one street, through dust or mud. Or they huddled outside the administration block, where the melancholic voice of Oum Kalhoum, the beloved 'Star of the Orient', washed over them.

Ahmed Hamzeh had been born in Haifa and his son in Jerusalem. Their Haifa home had long been appropriated by the State of Israel. In the stampcde during the 1967 Six Day War the family had lost each other; the mother had been killed accidentally and a daughter had died from untreated pneumonia. Ahmed Hamzeh, who spoke good English, bought a monkey to survive. 'You will forgive me,' he said, 'if after all these years ... 20 years I have been in this place ... if I look like a peasant. I used to think I was an artist, not a beggar. Maybe I am not even a peasant now.'

When I walked away from him, I noticed he was leading

his son, who was about eight years old. I asked a UN man why the boy stumbled. 'It's trachoma,' he said. 'In the early days it blinded hundreds of children in the camps.' I remembered this moment when I read President Bush's opening remarks to the Madrid conference. 'We have seen too many generations of children', he said, 'whose haunted eyes show only fear ... too many funerals for brothers and sisters, the mothers and fathers who died too soon; too much hatred.'[12] Here was the President of the United States seeking to touch those of us who regard children as a precious resource and who believe that the interests and rights of children ought to lie beyond cynical manipulation. And here was the president at the same time demonstrating his benign neutrality, speaking of hope, not complicity. Unfortunately, the former was absent from this hymn of statesmanship.

The Palestinian writer Edward Said got it right. 'US policies', he wrote,

> are on trial at Madrid. The US has supported Israel politically and financially for the past two decades in complete violation not only of UN resolutions, but also of US laws and political principles. The US sent 650,000 troops to restore a corrupt and medieval Kuwaiti royal family, and has subsidised the Israeli military occupation of Arab territories to the tune of over $4 billion a year, and a total since 1967 of £77 billion.[13]

The Madrid conference is not as it is being represented: a coming together of intractables, with George Bush and his secretary of state in the middle 'knocking heads together'. The United States, regardless of James Baker's much publicised 'impatience' with the Shamir regime, is firmly on one side – the side of American, Israeli and Saudi power in the region. Edward Said is close to the truth when he says, 'My fear is that the US wishes to produce a cosmetic and "pragmatic" track of negotiating proposals that will either give us nothing real or force us to abandon the forum.'[14]

The other night the BBC showed a remarkable film, *Do*

They Feel My Shadow? made by Nicholas Claxton and Cherry Farrow.[15] It was set in Gaza where the *intifada* began in December 1987. A sliver of land between Israel and Egypt, Gaza is home to 750,000 Palestinians, none of whom, says Claxton in his commentary, 'can have an identity . . . where to sing a Palestinian song or to raise a Palestinian flag can lead to arrest and imprisonment.'

And a great deal more. Mahoud Al-Ashkar is 11 years old. He was shot in the eye with an Israeli plastic bullet. His eye came out in his hand. Another eleven-year-old, Mahmoud Al-Hissi, was beaten so badly by Israeli soldiers that both his wrists sustained multiple fractures and an elbow was dislocated. The boy told UN relief officials he was stripped and hung up by his feet and clubbed. He was then taken to the roof of the building where the soldiers threatened to throw him to his death.

These are common cases. An official of the Swedish Save the Children Fund describes research conducted over two years with 14,000 cases of child injuries. She said the shooting of children was contrary to 'official military orders', but there was a 'second set of orders, understood by the soldiers'. An Israeli colonel replied that the children who threw stones were dangerous in a way 'that is inconceivable to the Western mind'. He said his soldiers never aimed to kill children and, anyway, only shot at them as a last resort.

This was contradicted by the Swedish report, which concluded that only a quarter of the children shot dead were anywhere near a stone-throwing demonstration. Thousands of injured children were under the age of ten; hundreds were under five. 'Most of them', said the Swedish researcher, 'had been beaten on their hands and upper bodies. A third suffered broken bones, including multiple fractures.'

Claxton quoted a UN report that put the number of children shot dead in the past three and a half years at fifty-six. Almost all died as a result of direct fire, *not* of random shots or ricochet. Not a single Israeli soldier had been imprisoned for the killing of a Palestinian child.

A boy called Jihad, who was himself beaten, described

how his father was beaten to death by Israeli soldiers in front of him, his mother and two sisters. On the day the soldiers came to his home, he said, 'My father took us into a room and locked the door ... but they broke it down ... the soldiers would take his head and hit it against the wall ... The other soldier broke his truncheon on him. Then he said, "Bring me a knife ... he has to die." ' Later, Jihad saw his father's body and described it as 'all dissected, his arms and his stomach'. Four soldiers were tried, convicted of manslaughter and pardoned. The family has had no compensation.

Lulu is eight years old. A rubber bullet hit her in the brain. She is now a pretty vegetable whose family hug and kiss her, hoping in vain for a reaction. Apart from rubber and plastic bullets 'like marble', the Israelis also have a stone-throwing machine that hurls 600 stones a minute. 'It's our own *intifada* on wheels,' said an officer.

Children in the Claxton film speak movingly, yet with a curious detachment. 'We no longer fear,' they said; and that life was a simple matter of 'killing or getting killed'. A Palestinian psychiatrist said the effect was that 'the children take authority into their own hands. Their parents try to protect them, but no one can stop them.'

In Gaza there is, as on the West Bank, an illegal Israeli settlement, including recent arrivals from the Soviet Union. Encouraged by the extremist policies of the Shamir Government and funded mostly from abroad, they live behind barbed-wire fences in what is described as 'a location for the rebirth of pioneering Zionism'. One of the children, thirteen-year-old Esther, was asked by Claxton if she had any contact with Palestinian children. 'No,' she replied, 'sometimes when I go on the bus I see them going to school, but I never saw them particularly. I never talk to them.'

June 28, 1991 to November 8, 1991

510

THE FIRE NEXT TIME

WHEN I WENT to report and live in the United States in the sixties, I was fortunate to make friends with some of the finest people I have known. They, and their work, left a lasting impression on me. Martha Gellhorn once described them as 'the people with a wakeful conscience, the best of America's citizens; they can be counted on, they are always there. Though the Government tried viciously, it could not silence them.'[16]

It is often difficult to see these people, and their achievements, through the façades of America today. When I first knew them, their influence was being felt in the political process, the courts and the media. They had pushed American liberalism to its limits and made real change seem possible. Much of this was illusion; but their glory was the Civil Rights Act of 1964 and the Voting Rights Act the following year.

I saw a great deal of America then, especially the old Confederacy. My travelling companion was often Matt Herron, who, with his wife Jeannine, had been on the first 'freedom rides' that brought young people from the North to support the black emancipation movement in the South. Matt was a photo-journalist whose picture essays of struggle and outrage appeared in *Life, Look* and Hugh Cudlipp's *Daily Mirror* and were to become a distinguished chronicle of the decade. Based in Mississippi, the Herrons and their comrades lived in fear of their lives; three of them were murdered. The murder of blacks was, of course, routine.

When President Johnson signed the Civil Rights Bill, it was

a programme devised by Jeannine Herron that brought the first organised pre-schooling to some 5,000 children in Mississippi. Yet she and Matt remained circumspect in their celebration. 'One victory', they wrote to me, 'doesn't mean it can't be taken away by other means.'

A cornerstone of the Civil Rights Act is the statute that makes job discrimination illegal. In 1971, the Supreme Court determined that blacks and other minorities could still be victimised by the imposition of impossible job qualifications. In passing judgement on what became known as the Griggs case, the court placed the burden of responsibility on an employer to demonstrate that the required qualification was an occupational necessity. This decision probably deserves more credit for integrating America's workplace than any other.

During the years that followed, notably the Reagan era, the political character of the Supreme Court changed by design. In 1989, the Supreme Court overruled the Griggs decision and reversed the burden of proof. Employers no longer have to prove that the qualifications they demand have anything to do with the job on offer. This has had, wrote Anthony Lewis in the *New York Times*, 'a drastic effect . . . it made it almost impossible for victims of alleged job discrimination to win lawsuits'.[17] Lewis cited a common case: a fifty-year-old black man who had held a caretaker's job at the same factory for fifteen years. When the factory closed, he applied for the same job elsewhere. He came with references praising his honesty and hard work. He failed to get the job because he did not have a secondary school certificate.

George Bush denies he is a racist. However, as a candidate for the Senate in 1964 he opposed the Civil Rights Act; and he now wants an entirely new civil rights bill that includes 'quotas'. He and his White House coterie are working hard to undermine compromise legislation that has won bipartisan support in Congress. At the same time, Bush has nominated for the Supreme Court a black judge, Clarence Thomas, who has made a name by repudiating almost all the traditional civil rights agenda. His nomination relieves the president of the need to defend his position against charges of racism and makes it likely that, if Congress gives its approval, future Supreme Court decisions will serve to keep blacks in their place. Even the National Association for the Advancement of Colored People, so often accused of Uncle-Tomism, regards Bush's man as repugnant.

The effect of Bush's insidious campaign will be to exacerbate some of the worst poverty in the world. In spite of significant black advances, such as the rise of a black middle class, poverty and degradation in black America has to be seen to be believed; and few white Americans, or visitors to America, see it.

Stepping over beggars on Broadway may leave an impression; but that is nothing to compare with a glimpse of what is now called the 'underclass' in those zones of American cities where the poor blacks and Hispanics are. For students interested in the uncelebrated effects of the doctrine that has brought about 'the end of history', I recommend a trip to the South Bronx in New York. When I was there twenty years ago a taxi would not take me past a safe point. It was worse than many impoverished Third World cities; certainly it was more menacing and its people more despairing. I had not seen anything like it in the Soviet Union, which is upheld as the vanquished model of all economic iniquity.

Today, the South Bronx is worse. One has only to read the reporting of Camilo José Vergara to understand how steep has been the descent of America's blacks under Reagan and Bush, and how ruthless and sinister are the current measures to keep them down. Almost one American child in four is now born into poverty, and the majority of these are minorities who subsist in human rubbish dumps like the South Bronx. 'Before the clock strikes midnight,' wrote Paul Savoy in the *Nation*, 'twenty-seven children in America will have died from poverty, violence and social neglect.'[18]

Twenty years ago black Americans put places like this to the torch. They staged 'poor people's marches' and they and their white allies assembled in front of the White House to demand their rights to 'life, liberty and the pursuit of happiness'. Since then, their communities are petrified by an almost total absence of opportunity for young unqualified blacks, other than the opportunity of drug addiction and crime. Moreover, drugs have usefully depoliticised and contained the poor, thereby complementing the ethos of a system that at once raises expectations and dashes them.

The ghettos have become America's gulags, which do not exist unless you have to live in them. In 1970, George Wallace, governor of Alabama, was right when he said that 'you gonna see this whole country Southernised; and when that happens, we gonna seem like a Sunday School down here.'[19] Reagan 'Southernised' much of America, and Bush is continuing his work.

In March 1991 a gang of uniformed white Los Angeles policemen viciously beat an unarmed black man as he lay on the ground after they had stopped his car. This was nothing unusual for a police force regarded as brutal by even American standards. But a witness had secretly videotaped the attack, which was shown on national television. The four policemen were eventually charged and tried a year later. When they were acquitted by an all-white jury, south Los Angeles and other ghettos across America rose as one. City blocks were razed; gun battles were fought from street to street, tenement to tenement. Only when the army was called out – its previous assignment was Iraq – was 'order' restored.

In June 1992 Amnesty International issued a report on America's 'affront to human rights'. Amnesty's investigation of 40 cases in Los Angeles showed that suspects were shot by the police although they posed no threat, and that officers acted without fear of being disciplined. This represented a national pattern.[20]

So will another white American generation now arise with a 'wakeful conscience'? Or have they been persuaded that only one Berlin Wall was built and one system of apartheid given root? The fire next time will not wait for the answers.

August 1991 to June 1992

LIONS OF JUDAH

THAT OLD FAVOURITE 'Marxism' is having another run through the gauntlet, followed closely by 'Marxism-Leninism'. According to Paul Henze, ideologue of the Rand Corporation in Washington, the defeated regime in Ethiopia was not only Marxist-Leninist but ruled with 'dogmatic rigidity'. Moreover, the Tigrayans, who were among those liberating Addis Ababa last week, are 'more Marxist than Colonel Mengistu'. Indeed, says Henze, if you include their Eritrean allies, 'the political contest in Ethiopia was almost exclusively among Marxists'.[21]

Bad guys, all of them.

Fear not: the victorious Ethiopian People's Revolutionary Democratic Front (EPRDF) leader, Meles Zenawi, has 'disavowed Marxism-Leninism' and now, Henze assures us, supports democracy and a 'free' economy. And, although they 'still have to overcome Marxists in their ranks', the rebels have been 'developing maturity and statesmanship'. In other words, they know the score. 'Herman Cohen, the US assistant secretary of state for African affairs', wrote Henze, 'has made clear to them that Ethiopia will get the international support it needs *only* if they lay the groundwork for a new political system . . . ' (My italics.) The implication is: Starve, you Marxist-Leninists; arise, you free-marketeers!

Regardless of whether Colonel Mengistu wished the world to regard him as a Marxist-Leninist, in reality he was no different from the murderous tyrant preferred by Washington and its imperial tribunes, such as the Rand Corporation. Neither was he seen off by recanting 'Marxists' converted to

515

the 'free' economy. It says much about the influence of Western triumphalism these days that the victory of home-grown socialism in Ethiopia is routinely misrepresented by such pejorative shorthand. The political subtlety of the EPRDF is reminiscent of that of the Sandinistas in Nicaragua, whose dominant strain was closer to that of radical Christianity than to Marxism.

Whether or not the EPRDF survives in its present form, the winner in Ethiopia is a genuine people's movement that has had almost a generation to evolve and to win not only the hearts and minds but the trust of millions betrayed by consecutive regimes and their foreign patrons.

So Ethiopia has a chance: an odds-against, candle-flicker of a chance of recovering from the historical debilitation that has scared it since the Amhara warlords of nineteenth-century Abyssinia did their deals with the European imperialists. It was entirely appropriate that the British Government should greet the changes in Ethiopia by sending in the SAS to protect the remnants of the family of the deposed emperor, Haile Selassie. His savagery against his people is not forgotten, and his mantle of 'Lion of Judah' is now deserved by them.

The hope of Ethiopia's revolution is shared by those of us who trekked across the desert to Tigray and Eritrea when these were places of no consequence in the geo-political game. But now some of us feel we should say to these brave and civilised societies: Beware of 'maturity and statesmanship' and other such code-words; beware when a Bush apparatchik plays a 'peace-making' role.

The Ethiopians, and especially the Eritreans, need only look back to their recent past for the markers. In 1952, a UN decision, engineered by Washington, federated Eritrea with feudal Ethiopia. The Americans had promoted the federated solution as part of their Cold War policies, and with little regard to the merits of the case, as Secretary of State John Foster Dulles made clear when addressing the Security Council. Regardless, he said, 'of the point of view of justice', the strategic interests of the United States in the Red Sea basin and considerations of world peace 'make it necessary that the country [Eritrea] has to be linked with our ally, Ethiopia'.[22] Haile Selassie had dutifully supplied an Ethiopian brigade to fight in the Korean War, and the Americans supported him as he systematically crushed the Eritreans, subverting their parliament, banning their language, murdering their leading partisans and imprisoning thousands. Washington was rewarded with the Kagnew communication station in the Eritrean capital of Asmara.

The strength of the Eritrean movement, the EPLF, an Eritrean friend once told me, is that, 'we are ourselves; we have no political debts'. Eritrea's enemies have come at her from over every ideological horizon, from both imperial and 'revolutionary' Ethiopia, from both the United States and the Soviet Union and their respective clients, Israel and Cuba. The cluster bombs used against Eritrea were made in the United States, supplied by Israel and dropped by Soviet aircraft which were piloted by Ethiopians and occasionally by Cubans.

Since 1961, in spite of a poverty harsh even by the standards of the poor world, the Eritreans have begun to build – in isolation – a self-reliant, humane and literate society. They have achieved this unaided, except for a modicum of Arab cash and a right of way through Sudan. Most of their arms, trucks, machines and tools either have been captured from the Ethiopians or are the products of their own ingenuity.

In northern Eritrea, I walked through a complete industrial town that had been built underground. At the end of the tunnels and mine shafts were factories and foundries, insulated by Ethiopian parachutes and powered by captured Birmingham-made generators. Here the sons and daughters of nomads and farmers had organised their own industrial revolution. In the 'metal shop', an entire Soviet Mig-21 fighter-bomber, which had crash-landed, almost intact, had been recycled into guns, buckets, ovens, kitchen utensils, ploughs, X-ray equipment. In the 'electronics plant', copies of Sony radios were produced on an assembly line. In the 'woodwork factory' school desks were laid out with rows of crutches and artificial limbs.

One of their greatest achievements is the emancipation of women in a conservative society that is devoutly and equally Muslim and Christian. The traditional system of land tenure in Eritrea used to be known as *diesa*, whereby heads of families in the villages had equal rights to the land, which was redistributed every seven years. This had long been corrupted by private landlords. In the sixties, the EPLF abolished large private holdings and reformed the *diesa* system. Women were given the right to own their own plots. Indeed, women previously had neither political nor social rights; female circumcision was universal, as it still is in much of Africa. All of that has been reversed by EPLF legislation: and although traditional attitudes remain, women now are mechanics, teachers and engineers and make up a third of the army.

Here a bleak irony intrudes. 'We have no use of birth control,' a young woman told me some years ago. 'We cannot get enough children to replace those who die too soon [from malnourishment-related diseases] or are killed.' Her school was a cave. One notebook and two pencils were shared among a class of fifty; crayons and toys were unknown. The children were taught that if caught in an air-raid in the open they must squat in single file, so only some in the line would be hit.

The price these people have paid for their independence has never been properly reported. Getting there was always a long and dangerous journey; we would travel at night for fear of strafing and on the roads dug by hand that coiled around the mountains into mist. On either side, on spilling terraces, were circles of raised stones; the headlights never lost them and the deeper we went into Eritrea the more commonplace they became. They were the graves of thousands of people killed from the sky and those who died during the great famines. For years only driblets of relief reached here. The British agency War on Want deserves credit for standing by the Eritreans.

The EPRDF Government will depend on goodwill between

the Eritreans and the Tigrayans. The two leaderships have their disagreements. The Tigrayans never wanted to secede; the Eritreans always regarded themselves as an independent nation. There is every indication that they will resolve their differences. 'One should not abandon democracy to achieve socialism,' Meles Zenawi said last week, 'because we are convinced that if socialism is not democratic, it's not going to be socialism at all.'[23]

It was significant that he pointedly denied the story put out in London that the Americans had 'invited' the EPRDF to enter Addis and take power. 'It was our decision to go in,' he said, 'and we would have done so with or without the consent of the United States . . . we will not allow any foreign country to invite us into our capital.'[24] We shall see if this spirit is perceived as 'mature' and 'statesmanlike' and we shall hope that it is Ethiopia's time to live, at last.

In the meantime the Eritreans have voted to become an independent state. The Ethiopians have accepted this fact, even though it means they have lost their only route to the sea. After more than thirty years of war and of national heroism – there is no other description – the Eritreans have run up their flag and sent their representative to the United Nations. That deserves our celebration.

June 1991 – June 1993

XI

AUSTRALIA

DOWN AT BONDI

BEHIND THE AQUAMARINE perfection of postcard Australia, the volatility never fails to reassure. On my first day back in Sydney, it was typically February: a flaming dawn, hard rain alternating with hot sun, and winds bringing in the sticky salt of the South Pacific. My mother used to stand on her back steps above Joe's Armenian laundry and watch bush fires licking the horizon, and curse the ash on her washing. February marks the end of a long summer. It is, according to an unreliable source, when most people have their 'nevers sprike down'.

Zoë, my seven-year-old, and I did what I have done for years on the first day. We headed for Bondi, where I grew up. Hindus making for the Ganges will understand. Under wild skies, the bay was running an even, rolling surf, with the great waves rising like blue-green pyramids. These days the boys and girls on their boards have Vietnamese and Greek names.

On the beach, though, are those who have surfed almost every day for half the century: Cec and Phyllis, in their seventies, who greet me as if a day, not a year, has passed. They were friends of Jack Platt, the Bondi shark catcher, who died last year, remarkably, in his bed. 'You remember that huge Grey Nurse he caught off the rocks?' says Phyllis. 'Well, we've got its teeth.' 'Looks like rain,' says Cec, as it lashes down on us.

Zoë is mystified as to why so many Australians speak with 'accents'. In my lifetime, Australia has changed from a second-hand Britain and Ireland to the world's second most culturally diverse society (after Israel). The predominant voices now are from Chile, Iran, Lebanon, Vietnam, Turkey and less and less from the 'Old Dart' (Britain). The sycophancy to English royalty is confined to municipal politicians and the media; the newspapers wrapped themselves in the Queen, who was here last week, and informed us 'where to watch Her Majesty'.

If you want to become an Australian citizen – and pride of citizenship has a particular resonance in this immigrant society – you must swear allegiance to the ridiculous Windsors. This helps to explain why a million non-Anglo-Australians have not taken out citizenship. Like many, a friend of mine, an Italian, took the oath in private ' . . . because the ceremony is so shaming'.

This will change. Australia's leading authority on ethnic populations, Dr Charles Price, says that, by the year 2052, Australians will consist of 'some northern European types with fair hair, some Middle East types, some Asian types, some southern European types [and] a sizeable number of mixtures . . . ' The largest proportion of new immigrants is from Asia; and they are 'marrying out'.[1] What this says is that the Anglo-Irish establishment, which has maintained Australia as an imperial lighthouse, first for Britain and now for the United States, may eventually fade away. The nostalgia that pervades so much of Australian popular culture is part of its farewell.

Yet the promise and excitement that derives from these momentous and admirably peaceful changes has been set back in recent years; so much so, it seems, that even those who used to bear their optimism almost as a deity wonder if the nation will recover. It will, of course; but only after hardship unexpected and unimagined.

In the old mythology, youth and Australia were synonymous. Yet nowhere in the West has youth been so discarded and betrayed. In 1992 one in three young Australians was unemployed, many of them fending for themselves in the inner cities.[2] According to OECD figures of the late 1980s, a higher proportion of Australian children are born into poverty than British.[3] I ran into a friend the other day who said he had discovered an 'emergency feeding programme' at a local primary school. 'We don't see it,' he said, 'because of this . . . ' He pointed at the sun.

The sun is Australia's gloss. It has allowed politicians to deny the severity of poverty, in the same way that they have denied the extent of Aboriginal suffering. In the first five years of the Hawke Labor Government, the former trade union boss oversaw, in a predominantly wage-earning society, the transfer of $A30 billion from wages to profits.[4] For a country that could boast the most equitable spread of personal income in the world, Australia now has walls separating the rich and poor as high as those in Britain and America.

There are historical reasons for this; the vulnerability of Australia's wool- and wheat-based prosperity is one; but the policies of a Labor Government have provided the catalyst. And those in the British Labour Party who wish to replace political vision altogether would do well to study the Australian Labor 'model'. Nine years of Labor in power has yielded Thatcherism without Thatcher; far-right ideology served up as economic necessity and the cult of market forces entrenched: known as 'economic rationalism'.

Even some of Australia's traditional conservatives are uneasy. 'At the beginning of the 1980s,' wrote Malcolm Fraser, the former conservative prime minister, 'the top 1 per cent of the population owned as much as the bottom 10 per cent. Now that 1 per cent owns as much as the bottom 20 per cent.'[5] Under Labor, the political ground has moved so far to the right that the current opposition derives from the stone-age wing of Australian politics.

Tax avoidance – made legal – became the growth industry under Labor, whose rich 'mates' could not believe their luck. In the 1980s, Alan Bond, Rupert Murdoch, Kerry Packer and other 'mates' of Bob Hawke's regime seldom paid corporate tax of more than 13 cents in the dollar, even though the official rate stood at 49 cents.[6] Only in Australia could the rich claim tax relief on interest paid on their foreign debts.

Only in Australia could 'Bondy', owner of gold mines, pay no tax on gold profits. Before they collapsed, Bond's companies accounted for an incredible 10 per cent of the Australian national debt of more than $A100 billion, which is behind only that of Brazil and Mexico. This has to be paid back by the nation in earned export income. Meanwhile, Bond is serving two and a half years in prison, convicted of dishonestly concealing a $A16 million 'fee' in relation to a failed merchant bank in Perth. The bank's former chairman, Laurie ('Last Resort') Connell, is awaiting trial. Like Bondy, Connell is, or was, a close mate of 'Hawkie'.

Hawkie (a.k.a. 'The Silver Bodgie') retired from politics last week, dumped by his party in the manner of Thatcher's going. Unlike her, he cultivated a populist image. He was the ordinary bloke's ordinary bloke, who would 'always stand shoulder to shoulder with my mates'. He didn't specify which mates. 'This stuff about the meek inheriting the earth', he once said, 'is a lot of bullshit. The weak need the strong to look after 'em.'[7]

The strong are Hawke's 'big mates', who ran 'the big end of town'. They include Kerry Packer, who owns tracts of Australia, the only national commercial TV network, most of the magazines Australians read, resorts and so on. When Hawke's Labor Government came to power in 1983, Packer's wealth was estimated at about $A150 million. He is now a billionaire many times over. Last week Packer's Channel Nine paid Hawke an undisclosed sum for the exclusive rights to televise the Silver Bodgie's announcement of his retirement from politics. The Australian Broadcasting Corporation had asked Hawke for his 'last free interview' and was told, 'You've had it.' The ABC responded by playing a Hawke voice over the 1960s song, 'I'm leaving on a jet plane', replacing the words with, 'I'm leaving on a gravy train.'

The former Labor prime minister has been signed up by International Management, which hustles for tennis players and pop stars. Although guaranteed a pension of $A100,000 a year, an office, a car, a chauffeur, free first-class travel, free postage, free telephone and much more, Hawke is demanding large amounts for much of what he does and says as a public person. He is to be paid a reputed $A100,000 for each of a series of interviews with 'world statesmen'. One of Sydney's luxury hotels was approached by his agents for a suite of rooms for six months as part of a 'special deal'. The suite would be gratis and the Silver Bodgie would put in a number of 'celebrity appearances'. The hotel said no.[8] Hawke leaves the highest unemployment Australia has known for sixty years. Officially it is almost 11 per cent; unofficially it is more than 15 per cent: something of a record in the capitalist world.[9]

Such is one of the sources of a cynicism that is like a presence in working-class Australia. Moreover, Hawke's successor, and one-time heir apparent, Paul Keating, is the architect of the economic disaster that resource-rich, energetic, talented, sunny Australia should never be. One of Keating's first acts as treasurer was to abolish the Reserve Bank's authority to monitor money leaving the country. This allowed the 'big mates' to avoid tax on a previously unheard-of scale. In 1983, Keating suddenly lifted all banking controls and floated the Australian dollar in a highly unstable speculators' market. Farmers were forced to pay interest rates of up to 30 per cent; many went bankrupt.

Australia belongs to no trading bloc; it is on its own and, unless it maintains much of the protection claimed as a right by Japan, America and the European Community, it can never 'compete' in the 'free market'. Hawke once described the consequences of Keating's policies – chaotic by any standards – as an 'historic transformation', wrought by the 'world's greatest treasurer'. More than one million unemployed Australians would doubtless agree with the former, if not the latter.

The title of Donald Horne's path-breaking book, *The Lucky Country*, written in the 1960s, is often misunderstood; it was meant to be ironic. Lucky with its climate and beauty and, at times, opportunity, Australia has always been a nation of wage-earners and 'battlers'. The great depressions of the

1890s and 1930s were felt here more deeply than anywhere; and this is true of many features of the current recession.

It was this history of harsh economic experience, and struggle, that produced many of the world's first gains for working people: pensions, child benefits, a basic wage and (with New Zealand) the vote for women. In 1920, the zinc and silver mines of Broken Hill, in the far Outback, fought for and won a 35-hour week and safety conditions at the workplace, half a century ahead of Britain and America. It is hardly surprising that the most potent Australian myth is that of a society priding itself on 'a fair go for all'.

Most Australians – those who do not own banks or junk bonds, or land, or newspapers, or resorts, or ride on gravy trains – deserve better, if not 'a fair go for all'. When fires were lit on Bondi beach for unemployed and homeless youngsters, the fact the surf ran true and the sun shone made no difference to the shadow over this extraordinary country.

February to June 1992

528

WILD COLONIAL BOYS

OCCASIONALLY, FROM BENEATH a surface of colonial fidelity, Australia's anger has broken through. Surrounded by Australian war graves in France, the poet Geoff Page wrote: 'The dead at Villers-Bretonneux rise gently on a slope towards the sky . . . Headstones speak a dry consensus. Just one breaks free: "Lives Lost, Hearts Broken – And For What?" '[10]

During the First World War, Australia, with a population of fewer than five million, sustained more than 211,000 dead and wounded young men. As a percentage, more Australians died than Americans in both that war and in the years of the Vietnam War. No army suffered losses in the proportions of that which came dutifully from farthest away.

The British used Australians, and their own, as 'shock troops': cannon fodder. On Gallipoli peninsula, for every 500 yards gained, at least 1,000 Australians were lost. And For What? The Kaiser offered no threat of invasion to the Antipodes. It is a painful irony that Australians have shed more battlefield blood than most, and that so much of this sacrifice has not been in the cause of independence, but in the service of an imperial master. Australians fought in China's Boxer Rebellion so that British mercantile interests could continue trading in opium; and in New Zealand so that British imperial interests could exploit that country and destroy the resistance of the Maori people; and in South Africa so that the same class could subdue the Boers and dominate the Cape of Good Hope.

529

And when Australia itself was threatened in 1942 – and a last line of defence was drawn across the continent from Brisbane, and young children, myself included, were evacuated to the Outback – the Australian prime minister, John Curtin, was told by Churchill that his troops were needed elsewhere and not told, deliberately, that Singapore and Australia had been abandoned.[11]

In denying this momentous treachery last week, and declaring that 'Australia was not attacked by Japan', those like Sir John Stokes, MP expressed the ignorance, trivialisation and condescension that have marked the ruling British view of Australia. In fact, the Japanese attacked Australia in 1942, destroying Darwin in fifty-nine bombing raids and shelling Sydney, while Australia's defence forces were far away under imperial command.

The remarks by Paul Keating about these matters were long overdue. He was, of course, using nationalism to create the illusion of difference between Labor and the conservative opposition. However, the importance of his 'republican stand' cannot be overstated, both for what it meant for many Australians and what it concealed.

Australia's bloodied and often secret past is not, I believe, much understood in Britain: nor is its struggle for independence. The old bromides and stereotypes are preferred: Barry Humphries' Les Patterson *et al.* For Keating merely to describe his country as 'necessarily independent', and to predict that it would 'one day' become a republic, was bold enough. To attack the British establishment by illuminating one of its sacrificial disasters (Singapore), and the duplicity of its greatest hero, was to reach into forbidden parts, including Australia's own complicity.

The truth is that Australians are one of the most profoundly colonised peoples on earth. Governments in Canberra may claim a voice of their own and that Australia is an independent and vigorous member of the world community. But this is not so. And when it has been so, the moment has been brief.

Most young Australians know of the Whitlam years

(1972–75), when an Australian government in 100 days laid the ground for the civilised, democratic society Australia was meant to be. Few will know of Ben Chifley's and Herbert Vere Evatt's 'New World' (1945–49), in which Australia was to be non-aligned, prosperous and absent from other people's wars. Evatt, the foreign minister, was one of those who framed the UN Charter and, as first president of the UN, announced the Declaration of Human Rights. In 1948 Washington declared his government a 'security risk' and began to undermine it: a prototype for a process later known as 'destabilisation'.[12]

Today, Australia's place in the world is defined by the interests of its Western 'protectors': the United States having long replaced Britain in this role. Australia at the United Nations has voted predominantly with what is known as the 'Western European and Other Group'. Australia is part of the 'other': an appendage. This has helped to refine an official obsequiousness, the 'cringe' of which Keating spoke. Until a few years ago, what ought to have been Australia's proud national day was hardly recognised. On New Year's Day, 1901, when the states federated and became the 'Commonwealth of Australia', the first governor-general, the Earl of Hopetoun, stood with his plumes limp in the rain in Centennial Park, Sydney, and listened not to rousing declarations of independence but to pleas from the local elite that the Royal Navy not leave its kith and kin to the mercy of the 'yellow hordes' – those who might fall down upon them as if by the force of gravity. 'The whole performance', wrote the historian Manning Clark, 'stank in the nostrils. Australians had once again grovelled before the English.'[13]

In place of this national stillbirth, we have had April 25, 'Anzac Day', an often drunken commemoration of hopeless hours in 1915 when Australians achieved 'glory' in the charnel house at Gallipoli: one of Churchill's earlier 'triumphs'. The Anzac 'heritage' not only led us into other wars, it wedded us to a wrong view of history and ourselves.

This was the British connection to which Keating referred. It gave us King and Country and a viceroy empowered to get rid of an elected government; and who did. Australian politics has never recovered from the coup against Whitlam, the circumstances of which remain part of a national pact of silence. As Whitlam himself has pointed out, the governor-general today 'can sack the government, can appoint and sack ministers, can dissolve the House of Representatives'.[14]

The man who sacked Whitlam, Sir John Kerr, had close links with both British and American intelligence. On the day Whitlam was summoned by Kerr to be told he was out, he was threatening to expose the CIA network in Australia and, so the Americans believed, to tear up the treaty that gave the CIA control of one of the most important spy bases in the world: at Pine Gap, near Alice Springs.

Under the UKUSA Treaty, Australia allowed Britain and America to run electronic surveillance bases which are so secret they have 'extra-terrestrial status'. Pine Gap is supplied direct by the US Air Force. It has its own water and power supplies. There is a seven-mile 'buffer-zone' in the bush, and planes cannot fly within a four-kilometre radius of the base. The Australian Parliament and people know little of its function.

From Pine Gap and the base at Nurrungar, the Americans planned much of their nuclear war fighting strategy. This placed Australia on the front line of a potential nuclear war in Europe – without Australians' knowledge or approval. Today, under the same colonial treaty, another satellite base is being built at Geraldton in Western Australia, in keeping with American policy to intercept economic information. It will spy on Australia's neighbours in Asia, whose commercial secrets are likely to end up in London and Washington.[15]

The nuclear desert at Maralinga in South Australia is an enduring example of the colonial state. In 1950, Prime Minister Clement Attlee sent his Australian counterpart, Sir Robert Menzies, a top-secret cable asking for permission to test British nuclear weapons in Australia. James McClelland, the Australian judge who presided over the Royal Commission of Enquiry into the effects of the tests, told me, 'Attlee asked Menzies if he could lend him his country for the atomic tests. Menzies didn't even consult anybody in his cabinet. He just said yes. With anything that came from the British it was ask and you shall receive, as if they were God's anointed.'[16]

Once again, the Australian people knew nothing. Eighteen months later they were told in a one-paragraph announcement that 'an atomic weapon' would be tested in Australia 'in conditions that will ensure that there will be no danger to the health of people or animals'.[17] This, of course, excluded the Aborigines who, unlike sheep, were not counted in the census.

The attitude shared by the British Government and its supplicants in Canberra was similar to that of the first colonisers of Australia in the late eighteenth century. To them, the Aborigines did not exist as human beings; Australia was 'terra nullius': empty land. Today, an area almost the size of south Wales is contaminated with plutonium, scattered like talcum powder across the lands of Aboriginal people. In 1984 the McClelland commission went to London and sought information from British officials. They were, as McClelland recalled, 'often treated contemptuously'. The commission recommended that the British be pressed to clean up their lethal mess. This has not happened and is unlikely to happen.

Nor are Australians likely to know the degree of long-term danger. Both Britain and America routinely censor Australian archives. As the historian Greg Pemberton recently wrote, 'even federal cabinet records, the most precious of all government documents recording the collective decisions of our elected ministerial leaders, are being censored at the insistence of our allies . . . formerly open archival records which show Australia's links with the CIA are now being censored. All references to Britain's spy agencies MI5 and MI6 have long been expunged.'[18]

It was a pity that Keating failed to identify the current source of Australia's 'cringe'. Since the US Navy 'saved Australia' at the Battle of the Coral Sea, following the British rout at Singapore, Australia has provided Washington with unlimited favours: so much so that, according to a former US ambassador to Canberra, President Johnson 'thought that

Australia was the next large rectangular state beyond El Paso and treated it accordingly'.[19]

Like his decision to hand Maralinga over to the British, Menzies kept from Australians his intentions to involve them in the American war in Vietnam. Menzies' emissaries pleaded with Washington to allow him to send troops. In 1962 Australians went as 'advisers'. It was not until 1964 that it was revealed that many of them were members of 'black teams' – death squads. They took orders from the CIA and their reports were kept from the Australian Army and the Australian Government. When the Menzies Government complained to Washington that the British were better informed on the progress of the war than America's Australian comrades-in-arms, the reply was succinct. 'We have to inform the British to keep them on our side,' said George Bundy, the assistant secretary of state. 'You are with us, come what may.'[20]

During the years of the Hawke Labor Government – of which Keating was a member from the outset – Australia's obedience was never in doubt. An electoral pledge to 'without hesitation re-establish aid programmes to Vietnam' was abandoned following a phone call from George Schultz, the US secretary of state, to his 'mate', Bob Hawke.[21]

In 1991 the foreign affairs minister, Gareth Evans, announced that Australia had at last achieved an independent foreign policy.[22] This metamorphosis apparently had taken place since Evans took charge. Such self-congratulation is not unknown in a politician, especially one who used to be known as the 'minister for mates': neither is it insignificant. For Evans and Hawke succeeded in covering Australia's continuing imperial 'cringe' with a specious gloss – a peculiarly Australian deference that Paul Keating failed to acknowledge in his outspokenness.

The 'Evans Plan' for Cambodia is often put forward as an important example. Adopted by the Permanent Five at the United Nations, it reflected American hostility towards Vietnam, rather than any proper assessment of the dangers of the Khmer Rouge. Had Evans gone to the General Assembly with a plan that called not for an accommodation with the Khmer Rouge, but for their prosecution under the Genocide Convention, his claim of a truly independent foreign policy might have been justified. His initiative might have galvanised other governments uneasy about 'toeing the American line on Cambodia', as one diplomat disclosed, and produced a result in Cambodia with the Khmer Rouge truly isolated, instead of biding their time, as they are.[23]

In the build-up to the Gulf War Prime Minister Hawke, like Menzies before him, lobbied Washington for permission to send Australian troops. In one speech he used the 'commanding moral authority of the UN' thirty-three times, concluding, 'So now we must fight!'[24] Driving home the point, he declared, 'Big countries cannot invade small countries and get away with it.'[25]

Contrast that with Hawke's reaction to the Santa Cruz cemetery massacre in East Timor in 1991. Hawke *asked* Indonesia for 'genuine contrition, a dinkum enquiry ... '[26] When the Indonesian Army attempted to cover up the massacres by announcing that it had found six officers guilty of 'errors and negligence', Gareth Evans was among the first to 'welcome' the 'appropriate recognition that the military's behaviour was excessive ... ' and ordered federal police to remove East Timorese and Australian protesters from outside the Indonesian Embassy in Canberra. In 1989 Australia signed the Timor Gap Treaty with Indonesia, allowing Australian companies to exploit the petroleum resources in East Timor's waters. At the time Evans said, 'There is no binding legal obligation not to recognise acquisition of territory that was acquired by force.'[27]

Evans has described Australia's sub-imperial role in Asia by using Secretary of State James Baker's metaphor of American power as 'a balancing wheel'. The 'central support' was the United States–Japan alliance; the southern spoke extended to Australia, 'an important, staunch, economic, political and security partner'.[28] When George Bush arrived in Australia in 1991 – the first visit by an American president for a quarter of a century – he was on his way to the 'central support' of the 'balancing wheel'. The stop-over in Australia was, as the Washington press corps travelling with him knew, of little significance other than as a place to acclimatise to the eastern hemisphere. Australia, they were told, was 'on the team'. He would play golf with his 'old mate', Bob Hawke, and he would say a few words.

Every member of both houses of the Australian Parliament was flown back to Canberra, at the government's expense, to hear Bush speak. 'We won't let you down,' he reassured them, 'and we will stay involved right up to the very end of eternity because we know it's fundamentally in our interests and hope like hell it's in yours!'[29] The Earl of Hopetoun, in presiding over Australia's 'independence day' in 1901, delivered a similar assurance from Queen Victoria.

Paul Keating's political hero is Jack Lang, the 'Big Fella', who was premier of New South Wales during the Great Depression. In 1930, the British banks, to which Australia was deeply in debt, sent an imperial bailiff, Sir Otto Niemeyer, to all but foreclose on the state's economy. Sir Otto demanded interest payments of £10 million a year. With a third of the workforce unemployed, he said Australians were 'living luxuriously' and that wages and the dole would have to be cut. Lang promised, 'No cuts in wages, no cuts in public services' and, if necessary, the debt would be repudiated.[30]

The 'Big Fella' was sacked by Sir Philip Game, the governor of New South Wales, a British viceroy acting in the name of the King of England. Forty years later, uppity Gough Whitlam was got rid of in similar circumstances.

It is ironic that Keating looks back to Lang; for no Treasurer surrendered as much of Australia's economic independence and security as Keating. Throughout the 1980s, Keating and his 'economic rationalists' paid court to the New York financial world, which could withhold credit ratings and turn its collective thumbs down on the Australian economy as effectively as Sir Otto Niemeyer had done half a century before.

With the rise of Alan Bond and the other 'mates', the cult of the 'markets' became an obsession of the Hawke–Keating partnership; and sovereignty was exchanged for debt. Australia is the most foreign-owned developed country in the world, next to Canada. How can Keating speak of Australia 'breaking free', having just announced legislation that will allow Japanese loggers to exploit almost 90 per cent of Australia's remaining tropical and temperate forests – in the cause of 'investment'?[31]

I am of Keating's generation. We glued cotton wool to our Christmas cards, sang imperial hymns and memorised a catalogue of regal, violent events on the other side of the world; this was known as 'history'. Some – like my mother's family – denied those of our forebears transported to 'penal servitude' for 'uttering unlawful oaths', rather than disclose 'bad stock': the words Churchill used during the Second World War.[32]

Keating is right to deride such a 'golden age', presided over by an Anglophile *ad absurdum* (Menzies) who wrote secretly in his diary: 'A sick feeling of repugnance grows in me as I near Australia' and who was later promoted to be Lord Warden of the Cinque Ports.[33]

But how, I wonder, does Paul Keating intend to prevent other Gallipolis, other Vietnams, other Maralingas? How does he intend to get back Australia's secrets and resources from the United States, Britain and Japan and its newspapers from Murdoch? How will he stop the haemorrhage of capital and find jobs for the young? Only in the answers to these questions will he, and the rest of us, find that 'necessary independence'.

March 6, 1992

IN THE HEART OF THE COUNTRY

Sydney

WALKING FROM THE Opera House to the ferry jetties of Circular Quay, one of the most spectacular short journeys on earth, I came upon a white man playing a didgeridoo: the long Aboriginal instrument whose haunting woodwind sound speaks for black Australians in a way that some whites understand. That is to say, it reminds them that their country is not quite theirs: that it has a rapacious, secret past; that it is half won and its story half told.

Even the inept playing of a white busker surrounded by tourists had this effect on me, especially as tangible evidence was close at hand. Standing in the busker's audience you had only to raise your eyes to see the figure on the street corner opposite: that of a black man slumped in the gutter, around whom people walked, as if he was a hole in the ground. The irony would be searing were it not an everyday matter.

In Australia, such matters are 'everyday' once again. For almost four years, following the setting up in 1987 of a Royal Commission of Enquiry into black deaths in custody, the condition and rights of Aboriginal people were issues. Newspapers published stories of atrocities against blacks as if they represented a phenomenon, rather than an historical pattern of events. In particular, the frequent, violent death of black Australians in prisons and police custody at last became news; and the news was shocking to many white Australians who will tell you that they seldom lay eyes on their black compatriots.

When the Royal Commission was appointed by the then prime minister, Bob Hawke, the former chief psychiatrist at Bargwanarth Hospital in Soweto wrote to the *Sydney Morning Herald* to point out that the rate of black deaths in custody in Australia was thirteen times higher than in South Africa.[34]

Comparison with South Africa is beyond the pale in Australia; it offends the nation's self-image of 'fair go'; and the Royal Commission was undoubtedly meant to deal with that. Royal Commissions are common in Australia. One of them is almost always in progress. They are like the teams that paint the Sydney Harbour bridge; once they finish one end, they must start again. Asked to describe the purpose of a typical Australian Royal Commission, the former judge and Royal Commissioner James McClelland called it 'a device employed by governments to sweep under the rug a problem which they either could not or did not want to solve'.[35]

Because there is guilt about the Aborigines, and because Australian governments have sought to persuade their Asian and Pacific trading partners that racism is no longer condoned, as it was under the White Australia Policy, there was some hope that the Royal Commission enquiring into the deaths of black people in custody would take a high moral stand and make its recommendations so tough they were unsweepable. The chief commissioner, Elliott Johnston, declared his shock at what he found. 'Until I examined the files of the people who died [in police custody],' he said, 'I had no conception of the degree of pin-pricking domination, abuse of personal power, utter paternalism, open contempt and total indifference with which so many Aboriginal people were visited on a day-to-day basis.'[36]

The Commission spent almost four years and $A30 million in its investigations and deliberations. When it reported last year, it made 339 recommendations. Not one of them was a call for criminal charges against police or prison officers or a conclusion of foul play, regardless of overwhelming evidence to the contrary. Instead, changes in policing and custodial methods, education and poverty, were to be left to the same state authorities that have been the main oppressors of black Australians. In the case of John Pat, who died in a police cell after a 'fight' with four police officers (who were subsequently acquitted of his manslaughter), Commissioner Johnston commented, 'I do not accept as necessarily true much of the evidence of the officers relating to this incident.'[37] Yet he proposed no action.

One of the Commission's main recommendations was that Aborigines – a small minority who in many towns make up the majority of prisoners – should be jailed only as a last resort. This statement of the obvious had been the Commission's theme since its inception. The response of state governments has been equally clear: more Aborigines have been sent to prison than ever before. A study last month by the Institute of Criminology at Sydney University found that the number of Aborigines jailed during and since the Royal Commission had risen by a quarter. In New South Wales – regarded as the most progressive state in its treatment of Aborigines – the increase was by 80 per cent. The author of the report, Chris Cunneen, said, 'This shatters the illusion that New South Wales is a more civilised state. It is now a leading "redneck state" – second only to Western Australia in its imprisonment of Aborigines.'[38] In July 1992 the Queensland Government announced, apparently with pride, that Aboriginal prisoners who tore up blankets in a bid to hang themselves would no longer be charged with 'wilful damage'.

In the meantime, according to a report by the Human Rights Commission, police systematically torture young Aborigines to get them to confess to crimes.[39] Another report concludes that if you are black and seriously ill, you are unlikely to get an ambulance to come and get you. Aboriginal health levels are described as 'shameful'. The death rate of black children is two and a half times that of white children; for adults, the rate is three times higher. Diseases considered preventable in white Australia ravage Aboriginal communities; tuberculosis is an epidemic.[40]

As if this wasn't enough, a study by the World Council of Churches says the impact of such manifest racism is 'genocidal' and accuses the Australian Government of finding an 'institutionalised way of underdeveloping Aborigines'. For me, the Council's most telling observation was that a 'conspiracy of silence surrounds the plight of Australia's Aborigines . . . '[41]

This is both true and remarkable – remarkable because the reports mentioned above, and numerous others, were all published widely. And there will be more of them, filling columns of space in the Melbourne *Age* and the *Sydney Morning Herald*. It is as if they are part of the veneer of civilised behaviour: to be accepted with due solemnity, then disregarded.

This has not always been the case. Twenty-five years ago a national referendum was held in which more than 90 per cent of the Australian electorate voted to give the federal government the constitutional right to legislate justice for the Aboriginal people. No referendum anywhere in modern times had produced such an overwhelming, positive result. The prime minster and his ministers could override the states on all questions relating to Aborigines; they had been handed an 'historic mandate'. The Whitlam Government drew up comprehensive land-rights legislation, part of which was made law in 1976 by the Fraser Government – but only in the Northern Territory, which the federal government administered. Redneck states were allowed to proceed with redneck policies.

When the Hawke Labor Government came to power in 1983, the minister for Aboriginal affairs, Clyde Holding, said that a national land-rights policy was 'the only restitution' for crimes that he compared with Hitler's persecution of the Jews.[42] Nothing happened. Bob Hawke dropped land rights from his government's agenda. He cried in public for the victims of Tiananmen Square in China and he damned apartheid; Australia led the campaign for sanctions against South Africa.

Such familiar hypocrisy has, however, met a modern resistance. This springs from an Aboriginal renaissance that has yet to receive the historical recognition it deserves; I can think of no equivalent. It began in 1966 when the Gurindji people went on strike at the world's biggest cattle station at Wave Hill, near Alice Springs. They were protesting against subsistence wages and poor conditions. Instead of returning to work, as expected, they camped on what they regarded as their land and in defiance of their employers, the English pastoral conglomerate headed by Lord Vestey.

It came as something of an embarrassment to white trade unions, proud of their legal minimum wage, to learn that highly skilled stockmen were paid a few dollars a week, plus a few sacks of flour, sugar and tea, and suffered living conditions no better than those provided for the station's dogs. A national campaign formed behind the Gurindji; but Vestey refused to acknowledge their grievances. As the strike endured, Aboriginal demands changed radically, so that the call was no longer for improved pay and working conditions but for land rights and self-determination.

The Gurindji's stand had a chain reaction. The Yirrkala people instructed lawyers to challenge the British common law interpretation of *terra nullius*. It failed; but Aboriginal activism now grew quickly. In 1972 Aborigines set up a 'tent embassy' outside Parliament House in Canberra and flew a flag of red, yellow and black, denoting earth, sun and people. For the first time world attention was drawn to a cause few outside Australia had known about. Gough Whitlam, then leader of the opposition Labor Party, was invited into the tent by Aboriginal representatives and joined them in an historic meeting to negotiate terms for national land rights and human rights.

Shortly after he became prime minister in December of that year, Whitlam commissioned a land rights enquiry by a judge, Justice A. E. Woodward. The Woodward Commission recommended legislation to give back to Aboriginal people those parts of Australia where they now lived and had traditionally lived and which for them had spiritual importance.

In 1975 an Aboriginal Land Rights Act was drafted by the Whitlam Government. It was to be applied at first in the Northern Territory, which did not have statehood and was run directly by the federal government. In August of that year Whitlam took a handful of soil and slowly poured the grains into the hands of Vincent Lingiari, a leader of the Gurindji people. The Government gave back to the Gurindji some 1,250 square miles. 'The people of Australia', said Whitlam, 'are finally restoring this land to you and your children for ever.'[43]

Three months later the Governor-General, Sir John Kerr, dismissed the Whitlam Government in a 'constitutional coup'. The following year a conservative coalition government, led by Malcolm Fraser, introduced only a shadow of Labor's land rights legislation. The Act gave freehold, 'inalienable' title to the land to Aboriginal communities living on 'reserves' in the Northern Territory. A Supreme Court judge was appointed as Land Commissioner to hear Aboriginal claims. It was a beginning, even if virtually all the 'inalienable' land handed back was arid wilderness. The richest, most productive land, amounting to more than half the land of the Northern Territory, was leased to cattle owners, who represent 0.1 per cent of the population.

At the same time black Australia began to produce its first renaissance men and women. They were teachers, historians, writers, artists and playwrights. Kevin Gilbert became the first Aboriginal playwright to be acknowledged by white Australia at a time when the national census included sheep, but not him. I last saw him standing at the back of a literary event in Canberra, shouting, 'Killing and indifference are the same thing: don't you people understand that?' Born in 1933 on the banks of the great Lachlan river at Condolobin in New South Wales, his mother was a Wiradjuri-Kamilaroi woman, his father Irish. Like most children of mixed parentage he was taken from his mother at the age of seven and sent as an 'orphan' to a 'reserve' where Christianity was meant to strip him of his Aboriginality: that was the theory. Like so many, he grew up with little education, and with violence and alcoholism. In a drinking bout he murdered his wife, for which he was imprisoned for fourteen years. At Bathurst jail, one of Australia's toughest, he spent years in the 'intractable yards' and was regularly beaten senseless.

Yet he came back from the abyss; he taught himself to paint and to read and write; and his appetite for books became voracious. His first play, *The Cherry Pickers*, was performed in 1971 while he was still in prison. On his release he became one of the most eloquent of the land rights activists, who time and again called upon white Australia to face the truth of its past.

Typically, he once read out loud his poem, *Memorials*, facing a country town's cenotaph on Anzac Day. All around him were veterans. His was the only Aboriginal face. He read:

> Our history is carved
> in the heart of the country
> our milestone memorials
> named Slaughter House creek
> the Coniston Massacre, Death
> Gully and Durranurrijah
> the place on the clifftops called
> Massacre Leap
> where the mouth of the valley
> filled up with
> our murdered dead bodies
> the place where our blood flowed
> the river ran red
> all the way to the sea . . .

When he had finished, there was an incredulous silence, 'almost a hurt', he told me. Then, in his rasping voice, he reminded his captive audience that in a country littered with cenotaphs to the white dead in foreign wars, not one stood for those who fought and fell in their own country. Then he walked away.

Kevin Gilbert died last year, leaving plays, books and poetry that are not quite what Europeans might describe as the work of a literary man; they were angry. In his 1973 book, *Because a White Man'll Never Do It*, he gave a new breed of black activists the nourishment they had lacked. He called on them to abandon 'the mentality of the victim and of acquiescence' and, 'having faced the facts of our degradation, to fight . . .'[44]

The suppression of Aboriginality has relied on white Australia's stereotypes, especially the patronising distinction drawn between full-blooded Aborigines and those of mixed parentage. It is still said there are few 'true' Aborigines and that the tribal minority and the urban dispossessed 'have nothing in common'. In 1985, in an event hardly reported, thousands of tribal Aborigines came to wintry Canberra to join up with their paler cousins from the cities. They assembled on the steps of the Federal Parliament and demanded land rights. 'As I stood with them,' wrote the author Stewart Harris, 'I sensed that an Aboriginal nation was being born. The tribes and clans of the people who owned Australia before 1788 have become united in the past decade as never before. For the first time I saw tribal elders and old women from the Centre and North confidently using hand microphones to speak their minds in their own language and also in English. They were sharing the opportunity with Aborigines from the south and east, whom they used to call "yeller fellers" . . .'[45]

On the day of the 1988 'Bicentenary' more than 30,000 Aborigines converged on Sydney – 'yeller fellers' from the urban and country slums and tribal people from Alice Springs and as far away as the Piebara, in the north-west. They travelled in 'freedom buses', painted in the Aboriginal colours of red, gold and black, and in cattle trucks and old Toyotas. The temperature passed 100 degrees. Radiators blocked, head gaskets cracked. Eight buses broke down but only one was abandoned. The hum of the didgeridoo and the resonance of clapping sticks generated new energy; but the old people, who had insisted on going, were severely tested. One of them died on the road to Adelaide, and the convoy faltered, consumed with grief.

When the buses arrived in Sydney, in Belmore Park, traditionally a resting place for the homeless, they were met by thousands of white Australians, young and old, in that universal solidarity that transcends nation, language and race. As a tall ship emblazoned with a Coca-Cola advertisement led the Bicentennial spectacular on Sydney Harbour, black and white threw wreaths into the water.

In December 1992 Prime Minister Paul Keating addressed several thousand people in the largely Aboriginal suburb of Redfern. It was the eve of the International Year for the World's Indigenous Peoples, the sort of contrivance that attracts rhetoric and little else. But Keating went further than any Australian leader ever had; he described vividly the genocide that is still often denied. 'We took the traditional lands and smashed the traditional way of life,' he said. 'We brought the diseases and the alcohol. We committed the murders. We practised discrimination and exclusion. It was our ignorance and our prejudice – and our failure to imagine these things done to us.'[46] Whatever the scepticism one felt about the utterances of a consummate politician like Keating, there was no doubt that his damning, shaming words reinforced a landmark decision by the Australian High Court six months earlier.

This was the 'Mabo judgment', named after Eddie Mabo, a leader of the Meriam people of tiny Murray Island in Torres Strait in the far north. With four others, he began a High Court action in 1982, seeking legal recognition of their traditional land rights. They argued that Murray Island had been 'continuously inhabited by our people despite the coming of the Europeans'. The High Court agreed and in recognising native title, ended the fiction of *terra nullius*. To say that shock waves have since rolled across the Australian establishment is to understate white reaction to a judgment that appears to grant Aboriginal people ownership of large tracts of Australia. The mining industry in Western Australia – a state with a shameful record towards Aborigines – seems to be suffering a sort of corporate hysteria. 'If this decision stands,' said one mining analyst, 'Australia could go back to being a stone age culture of 200,000 people living on witchetty grubs!'[47]

That is not likely. On the contrary, the real danger is that the historical trend will continue and the Aborigines will be subjected to a new, liberal tokenism. Assurances to white Australia that freehold land and the backyard barbie are safe have far outnumbered those to black Australia. Within days of another fine speech by Paul Keating, in which he said that white Australians could never live in peace until they had achieved reconciliation with the indigenous people, he supported a bill introduced by the Northern Territory government aimed at forestalling Aboriginal land claims over silver and zinc deposits in Arnhem Land. Sadly, more of this tactic can be expected.

Paul Coe, an Aboriginal barrister who runs the Aboriginal Legal Services in Sydney, believes the Mabo decision will give little to the majority of Aborigines and that only the imposition of international law can right the historic wrong. Under international law, a territory can be acquired by another country only if the inhabitants cede ownership or if all of them are dead. 'Australia was stolen,' he said. 'There was genocide, but we survived and we voluntarily ceded nothing. The Mabo decision makes it quite clear that there will be no compensation for acts of extinguishment; it legitimises the white hold over us.'[48]

Shortly before Christmas 1993 Parliament passed the Native Title Bill, described by Keating as an 'ungrudging and unambiguous recognition of native title' as defined by the High Court.[49] Opponents of the bill believe it fails to guarantee more for the Aboriginal people than it takes away from them and that its 'other aim' is to 're-stabilise' the economic positions of the mining and pastoral industries, which represented the Mabo decision as a threat.

'The base line for Aborigines', wrote Pat O'Shane, an

Aboriginal magistrate, 'is control of their land. Yet the purpose of the act is to protect and preserve big capitalist interests, with only some token gesture of recognition of the moral issues underlying the High Court's decision. Its primary provisions are designed to validate (read: protect and preserve) any land grants that may be invalid because of native title. These provisions legitimise the dispossession which has continued from January 26, 1788 to this day.'[50]

Aboriginal supporters of the legislation echo a guarded optimism not dissimilar to that expressed by many Palestinians following the signing of the accords with Israel. They say that this is the 'best offer' to date from white Australia and that only by testing it will it demonstrate value, or not.

Certainly, we white Australians are finding out that, until we finally give back to black Australians their nationhood, we can never claim our own. 'Only those', wrote Kevin Gilbert, 'who love the land and love justice will ultimately hold the land.'[51] His words, wrought from such pain and struggle, deserve a just reply.

March 1992 to January 1994

NOTES

Introduction

1 *Heroes,* published originally by Jonathan Cape, London in 1986, has since been reissued by Pan in two editions (1987 and 1989).
2 The *Guardian,* February 12, 1990.
3 *The Late Show,* BBC Television, June 6, 1991.
4 The *Observer,* May 3, 1991.
5 *Clive James on 1991,* BBC Television, December 31, 1991.
6 The *Guardian,* October 23, 1991.
7 Ibid., September 23, 1991.
8 Ibid., October 23, 1991.
9 *Z Magazine,* April 1991.
10 The *Guardian,* May 6, 1992.
11 Ibid., May 18, 1992.
12 The *Australian,* May 28, 1992.
13 *Heroes,* p. 532.
14 Liz Curtis, *Ireland, the Propaganda War: The British Media and the 'battle for hearts and minds',* Pluto Press, London, 1984, pp. 279–90.
15 The *Guardian,* March 9, 1991.
16 *Socialist,* March 25–April 2, 1991.
17 The *Sunday Telegraph,* March 18, 1990.
18 The *Guardian,* April 4, 1992.
19 John Pilger, *A Secret Country,* Vintage Books, London, 1992, pp. 286, 290.
20 Ibid., pp. 4–5.
21 Ibid., p. 320; OECD figures researched by Carole Sklan for *The Last Dream,* Central Television, 1988; Radio 2UE Sydney economic analysis, February 4, 1992.
22 Analysis by David Bowman, former editor-in-chief of the *Sydney Morning Herald,* March 1994.

23 *A Secret Country*, pp. 239–326.
24 Private communication.
25 The *Guardian*, July 4, 1991.
26 *The Truth Game*, Central Television, 1988.
27 Johnson's remark quoted by Stanley Karnow in *Vietnam: A History*, Viking Press, New York, 1983. See also *International Herald Tribune*, November 21, 1991.
28 Edward S. Herman and Noam Chomsky, *Manufacturing Consent: The Political Economy of the Mass Media*, Pantheon, New York, 1988, p. 184.
29 The *Independent*, March 1, 1991; also, commentators on the BBC FM's war report noted the 'light casualties'.
30 *International Herald Tribune*, June 4, 1992; also Denis McShane, *Peace and Democracy News*, winter 1992.
31 *Los Angeles Times*, February 18, 1991.
32 The *Nation*, March 5, 1990, cited by Noam Chomsky in *Deterring Democracy*, Vintage Books, London, 1992, pp. 355–6.
33 The *Guardian*, May 16 and July 2, 1992.
34 *State of the World's Children*, UNICEF, New York, 1989, p. 1.
35 *Human Development Report*, United Nations Development Programme and Oxford University Press, 1992.
36 *Poor Britain: Poverty, inequality and low pay in the nineties*, Low Pay Unit, March 30, 1992; the *Guardian*, July 16, 1992.
37 The *Guardian*, August 12, 1988.
38 As told to Karl Jacobson, 'The Studs you like', *Weekend Guardian*, May 9–10, 1992.
39 *War by Other Means*, Central Television, 1992.
40 Cited in *New Statesman and Society*, October 11, 1991, from *Nicaragua: A Decade of Revolution*, edited by Lou Dematteis, W. W. Norton, London.

I INVISIBLE BRITAIN

1 Rough Sleepers Report, London Housing Unit, May 17, 1991. See also *London Housing News*, May 1992.
2 The *Guardian*, June 4, 1991.
3 The *Guardian*, June 12, 1991.
4 'Inner City Deprivation and Premature Deaths in Greater Manchester', Tameside Metropolitan Borough Policy Research Unit, 1988.
5 As confirmed to the author.

6 *Poor Britain: Poverty, inequality and low pay in the nineties*, Low Pay Unit, March 1992. See also LPU reports 1991.
7 The *Guardian*, September 11, 1991.
8 The *Daily Mirror*, September 13, 1991.
9 Cited by Brian Simon in *Marxism Today*, September 1984. It comes from Stewart Benson's 'Towards a Tertiary Tripartism: new codes of Social Control and the 17+', in Patricia Broadfoot (ed.), *Selection, Certification and Control*, Falmer Press, London, 1984.
10 Cited by Shelter, 1990.
11 Analysis by Michael Meacher of government statistics supplied in a parliamentary written answer, *Hansard*, March 6, 1991; also *Poor Britain*, Low Pay Unit, 1992.
12 The *Guardian*, September 13, 1991.
13 *Hansard*, March 29, 1983.
14 *World in Action*, Granada Television, 1978.
15 *Race Attacks*, Home Office report, 1981.
16 The *Sunday Telegraph*, October 6, 1991.
17 The *Daily Telegraph*, July 2, 1991.
18 The *Daily Mail*, July 10, 1991.
19 The *Daily Star*, May 24, 25, 27, 29 and 31, 1991; June 15, 1991.
20 The *Daily Mail*, October 3, 1991.
21 The *Sun*, October 3, 1991.
22 The *Guardian*, May 15, 1982.
23 Commentary on London Broadcasting (LBC).
24 The *Independent*, December 14, 1991.
25 Cited in *CARF*, Campaign Against Racism and Fascism, no. 8, May–June 1992.
26 The *Evening Standard*, March 26, 1992; the *Daily Mail*, April 2, 1992.
27 The *Sun*, April 7, 1992.
28 Cited by Michael Ignatieff, the *Observer*, October 13, 1991.
29 Letter from Julian Nettel to Harriet Harman, MP, September 23, 1991.
30 As told to the author.
31 Ibid.
32 Ibid.
33 Camberwell Community Health Council 'Casualty watch' report, May 1991.
34 *South London Press*, March 13, 1992.

35 As told to the author.
36 Ibid.
37 Ibid.
38 *Today,* April 22 and 23, 1991.
39 The *Guardian,* April 7, 1990.
40 Letter from Malcolm Alexander to William Waldegrave, December 20, 1990; radio interview with Malcolm Alexander, LBC, January 3, 1991.
41 George Orwell, *The Road to Wigan Pier,* Penguin, London, 1989.
42 Report of Department of Health and Social Security appeals tribunal, cited in the *Daily Mirror,* July 31, 1984.
43 The *Sunderland Echo,* October 17, 1992.
44 Correspondence with the National Union of Mineworkers.
45 Cited by Easington District Council, correspondence, February 11, 1993.
46 *Easington Colliery,* a brochure produced by North East Coal, Sunderland.
47 The advertisements, featuring several miners, appeared in the national press in January, February and March, 1992. Arnie Makinson's photograph was published in the northern editions of the *Daily Mirror.*
48 '*Safety of British Nuclear Weapons Designs: US Nuclear Weapon Safety: The implications for the United Kingdom?*' BASIC Report 91.2, 1991.
49 *Washington Post* 1990 report, cited in the *Guardian,* April 22, 1992.
50 The *Guardian,* April 23, 1991.
51 *The Problems of the Trident Programme,* Greenpeace, July 1991.
52 With thanks to John Ross.
53 Poll carried out by On-Line Telephone Surveys, London, between February 24 and March 1, 1992. 1,405 people were asked: 'Currently the UK is proposing to increase its sea-based nuclear weapons capabilities with the Trident nuclear missile system, at a cost of £10.5 billion. How strongly do you agree with this proposal?' Agreed: 28%. Neither agreed nor disagreed: 8%. Disagreed: 56%. Didn't know: 8%.

II DISTANT VOICES OF DISSENT

1 Walter Lippmann, *Public Opinion*, 1921; cited by Edward S. Herman and Noam Chomsky in *Manufacturing Consent*, Pantheon Books, New York, 1988, p. xi. See also *Manufacturing Consent* for Chomsky's analysis, repeated and amplified in his many other works.

2 John Pilger, *Heroes*, Jonathan Cape, London, 1986, p. xv.

3 Paul Gordon and David Rosenburg, *Daily Racism: The Press and Black People in Britain*, Runnymede Trust, London, 1989, p. 69.

4 *Independent on Sunday*, February 4, 1990.

5 The *Observer*, February 4, 1990.

6 *Channel 4 News*, London, during the week January 28–February 4, 1990.

7 Edwin R. Bayley, *Joe McCarthy and the Press*, University of Wisconsin Press, Madison, 1981.

8 Cited in the *Independent*, October 28, 1988.

9 Milan Kundera, *The Book of Laughter and Forgetting*, Penguin, London, 1983, p. 5.

10 The *Guardian*, November 8, 1991.

11 John Clark, *For Richer for Poorer*, Oxfam, Oxford, 1986, Appendix 1, pp. 90–1.

12 *Third World Resurgence*, published by Third World network, Penang, Malaysia, Issue no. 12, 'Manufacturing Truth. The Western Media and the Third World'.

13 Study cited in *Third World Resurgence*, Issue no. 12.

14 Ibid.

15 Ibid.

16 Ibid.

17 Ibid.

18 See *Heroes*, Chapter 15, 'History as Illusion'.

19 Cited by Michael Albert, *Z Magazine*, April 1991.

20 *Third World Resurgence*, Issue no. 12.

21 The *Daily Mail*, July 15, 1984.

22 Maurice Edelman, *The Mirror: a political history*, Hamish Hamilton, London, 1966, p. 1.

23 This account is from *Heroes*, Chapter 42, 'You Write. We Publish'.

24 Audit Bureau of Circulation figures cited in *Media Week*, July 19, 1985; and the *Guardian*, October 28, 1985 and January 27, 1986.

25 *Marketing Week*, January 31, 1986.

26 Richard Belfield, Christopher Hird and Sharon Kelly, *Murdoch: The Decline of an Empire*, Macdonald, London.

27 The *Sunday Mirror*, December 5, 1991.

28 See Roger Bolton, *Death on the Rock and other stories*, W. H. Allen, London, 1990.

29 The *Guardian*, September 5, 1990.

30 The *Independent on Sunday*, March 4, 1990.

31 See *Heroes*, pp. 535–7.

32 Ibid., pp. 526–31.

33 Ibid., pp. 517–20.

34 Edward Said, *Culture and Imperialism*, Chatto & Windus, London, 1993.

35 Letter from Deirdre English, editor of *Mother Jones*, cited by Christopher Hitchens, *New Statesman* Diary, April 17, 1981.

36 Noam Chomsky, *Year 501: The Conquest Continues*, South End Press, Boston, 1993.

37 The *Independent*, May 15, 1989.

38 Letter to the *Guardian*, 1987.

39 Reagan used this term many times, perhaps for the first time at a veterans' rally during the election campaign in 1979. Bush used the second term on the eve of the Gulf War, January 1991.

40 Susan George, *The Debt Boomerang*, Pluto Press, London, 1993.

III THE QUIET DEATH OF THE LABOUR PARTY

1 Labour Party, Breaches of Constitutional Rules III (4); also Constituency Rules Clause IV (5).

2 Letters from Jean Calder to the author and the *New Statesman*, August 1, 1992 and September 28, 1992.

3 Ibid.; also Report by Joyce Gould to the NEC on The Friends of Brighton, September 25, 1991.

4 Letter from Jean Calder to John Smith, August 21, 1992.

5 Report cited in the *Guardian* and correspondence with the author.

6 Correspondence with the author.

7 Richard Heffernan and Mike Marqusee, *Defeat from the Jaws of Victory*, Verso, London, 1993.

8 Ibid.

9 The *Socialist Worker* (from the *Financial Times*), September 1993.

10 The *Green Left Weekly*, Sydney, November 17, 1993.

11 The *Independent on Sunday*, March 28, 1993.

12 Ibid.

13 Ibid.

14 I am grateful to Chris Lamb for this analysis in the *Guardian* (letters), March 31, 1994.

15 The *New Statesman and Society*, January 21, 1994.

16 The *Daily Telegraph*, February 4, 1994.

17 *Panorama*, BBC Television, September 20, 1993.

18 The *Guardian*, October 1, 1993.

19 Ibid., January 28, 1993.

IV MYTHMAKERS OF THE GULF WAR

1 Cited by Phillip Knightley, *The First Casualty: From the Crimea to the Falklands: The War Correspondent as Hero, Propagandist and Myth Maker*, Pan Books, London, 1989, p. 109.

2 Ibid., p. 81.

3 BBC Radio 4, December 30, 1990.

4 These press comments appeared during the second half of December, 1990.

5 The *Observer*, November 30, 1990.

6 Ian Lee, *War in the Gulf: A Medical, Environmental and Psychological Assessment*, Medical Campaign Against Nuclear Weapons, December 14, 1990.

7 As told to the author.

8 Ibid.

9 Ibid.

10 The *Independent*, December 28, 1991.

11 Michael Klare, the *Nation*, June 8 and October 15, 1990 and February 11, 1991; United States Army, *A Strategic Force for 1990/2 and Beyond*, January 1990.

12 Christopher Hitchens, *Harpers Magazine*, January 1991.

13 Ralph Schoenman, *Iraq and Kuwait: A History Suppressed*, October 1990, p. 12.

14 *Santa Barbara News-Press*, September 24, 1990 and Philip Agee, *Z Magazine*, November 1990.

15 Philip Agee, as above.

16 *New York Daily News*, September 29, 1990.

17 Ralph Schoenman, *Iraq and Kuwait*, p. 13.

18 See Knut Royce, *Newsday*, August 29 and 30, 1990 and January 3 and 21, 1991.

19   The *Observer*, December 30, 1990.
20   Cited by Phillip Knightley, p. 7.
21   The *Guardian*, January 24, 1991.
22   *Arming Saddam: The Supply of British Military Equipment to Iraq 1979–1990*, Campaign Against the Arms Trade, February 1991.
23   The *Guardian*, January 24, 1991.
24   See *Ropes of Sand*, by former CIA operations officer Wilbur Crane Evelard, cited by Jeff McConnell, *Boston Sunday Globe*, September 9, 1990.
25   The *Independent*, February 6, 1991.
26   The *Independent*, February 11, 1991.
27   The *Observer*, February 10, 1991.
28   BBC Television News, February 11, 1991.
29   Ibid.
30   *Vietnam Veterans of America Foundation Gulf Digest*, February 1991.
31   The *Guardian*, February 5, 1991.
32   John Pilger, *Heroes*, p. 263.
33   The *Daily Mirror*, February 8, 1991.
34   *Vietnam Veterans of America Foundation Gulf Digest*, February 1991.
35   As told to the author.
36   The *Weekend Guardian*, January 12–13, 1991.
37   *Vietnam Veterans of America Foundation Gulf Digest*, February 1991.
38   Ibid.
39   The *Observer*, February 10, 1991.
40   *Vietnam Veterans of America Foundation Gulf Digest*, February 1991.
41   *Heroes*, pp. 113–14.
42   As told to the author.
43   Martha Gellhorn, *The Face of War*, Virago, London, 1986, p. 254.
44   'The South Supplement', *New Statesman and Society*, October 11, 1991.
45   Ibid. I am grateful to Carlos Gabetta for his analysis.
46   The *Independent*, February 28, 1991.
47   Ibid.
48   Ibid.
49   Ibid.

50 The *Guardian*, March 1, 1991; *The Times* and *Daily Telegraph*, March 1, 1991.

51 The *Daily Telegraph*, March 2, 1991.

52 The *Daily Mirror*, March 2, 1991.

53 BBC Radio 4, FM 'Gulf reports' frequency, March 1, 1991.

54 BBC Television News, March 1, 1991.

55 Jeremy Bowen was questioned by Peter Sissons on BBC Television News, February 14, 1991.

56 The *Observer*, March 3, 1991.

57 The *Sunday Times*, March 3, 1991. Robert Harris subsequently wrote to me, enclosing what he described as 'a letter of apology' to be forwarded to Bobby Muller. Muller found no apology; Harris merely regretted not using his words differently.

58 The *Guardian*, February 21, 1991.

59 Stanley Karnow, *Vietnam: A History*, Viking Press, New York, 1983. Cited by Noam Chomsky in *Manifesto: Vietnam Retrospectives*, April 21, 1985.

60 Neal Acherson, the *Independent on Sunday*, March 10, 1991.

61 The *Observer*, March 10, 1991.

62 The *International Herald Tribune*, February 23–24, 1991.

63 *Into the Media War*, a study by the Glasgow University Media Group: Greg Philo, Frank Masson, Greg McLaughlin, March 1991.

64 BBC and Independent Television News, January 15, 1991.

65 BBC Television Gulf War coverage, January 18, 1991.

66 Michael Ignatieff, the *Observer*, March 31, 1991.

67 The *Independent*, March 28, 1991.

68 See William Blum, *The CIA, A Forgotten History*, pp. 275–8.

69 The *Guardian*, May 16, 1991.

70 The *New York Times*, March 26, 1991.

71 BBC and ITN, March 13, 1991.

72 The *Boston Globe*, January 18, 1991.

73 The *International Herald Tribune*, February 23–24, 1991 and the *Washington Post*, March 18, 1981, cited in the *Independent* the following day.

74 The *New York Times*, cited by the *Guardian*, January 16, 1992.

75 I am indebted to Noam Chomsky for this observation. In the *Guardian* of July 22, 1985 he wrote, 'The weaker the country, the greater the threat [to US policy], because the greater the adversity under which success is rendered, the more significant the result'.

76 Cited by Paul Rogers, the *Observer*, June 28, 1992.
77 Ibid.
78 The *Guardian*, March 23, 1991.
79 Commission of Inquiry for the International War Crimes Tribunal, New York hearing, May 11, 1991.
80 The *Guardian*, March 23, 1991.
81 The *Observer*, May 3, 1991.
82 The *Guardian*, May 18, 1991.
83 The *Independent*, May 9, 1991.
84 Letter from M. V. Cooligan, Head of Export Control and Embargo, Department of Trade and Industry, to R. Turner, Oxfam, September 1990. This letter was sent again in March 1991.
85 Report to UN Secretary-General by Nicholas Hunton, Director-General, Save the Children Fund and Frank Judd, Director, Oxfam, 1991.
86 Report by Dr Eric Hoskins, Gulf Peace Team, received May 21, 1991.
87 *Vietnam Veterans of America Foundation Gulf Digest*, May 1991.
88 *The Economic Impact of the Gulf Crisis on Third World Countries*. Memorandum to The Foreign Affairs Select Committee, March 1991.
89 Private communication.
90 Comparisons from 'The War Dividend', *Guardian*, January 25, 1991.
91 Ibid.
92 Ian Lee, *Continuing Health Cost of the Gulf War*, The Medical Educational Trust, London, 1991.
93 *The Economic Impact of the Gulf Crisis on Third World Countries*, see Note 88.
94 The *New York Times*, December 2, 1990; *Covert Action*, No. 37, summer 1991.
95 *US News and World Report*, December 10, 1990.
96 *BBC Short Wave Broadcasts Summary*, November 1991.
97 *Middle East International*, October 12, 1990; also, as told to Richard McKerrow by Steve Sherman.
98 *BBC Short Wave Broadcasts Summary* and *Middle East International*; Turkish press review, July 22, 1991.
99 World Bank and OECD figures from Nexus.

100 *US News and World Report*, December 19, 1990; the *Nation*, December 7, 1990.

101 The *Nation*, December 24, 1990; also Geoffrey Aronson, Institute for Policy Studies, Washington, Background Paper, October 1991.

102 *The Times*, September 19, 1990; also *War by Other Means*, Central Television, 1992.

103 *Middle East Report*, November and December 1991.

104 The *New York Times*, December 2, 1990; Carl Zaisser, *US Bribery and Arm-twisting of Security Council Members during the November 29 Vote on the resolution allowing the use of force in ousting Iraq from Kuwait*, 1991.

105 Carl Zaisser.

106 Phyllis Bennis, *Covert Action*, No. 37, summer 1991.

107 World Bank statement, Nexus.

108 Carl Zaisser.

109 Phyllis Bennis; *BBC Short Wave Broadcasts Summary*; *Village Voice*, February 26, 1991.

110 The *New York Times*, December 2, 1990; also Phyllis Bennis.

111 Phyllis Bennis; also Nexus.

112 Private communication of source material.

113 The *Guardian*, February 21, 1991.

114 BBC Television Gulf War coverage, January 18, 1991.

115 Richard Norton-Taylor and David Pallister, the *Guardian*, March 7, 1992; Paul Foot, *Daily Mirror*, March 6, 1992; David Hellier and Rosie Waterhouse, the *Independent*, March 14, 1992.

116 The *Guardian*, May 3, 1992.

117 *Scotland on Sunday*, November 17, 1991; also *BBC Short Wave Broadcasts Summary*.

118 Statement by Iraq Trade Minister, Mehdi Saleh, New York, March 12, 1991.

119 The *Guardian* (letters), April 4, 1992.

120 *Lies of Our Times*, 'Down the memory hole', June 1991.

121 *TV Guide*, June 12, 1986.

122 See Note 101.

123 *The Times*, September 19, 1990.

124 *New Statesman and Society*, April 24, 1992.

125 *Socialist*, March 11–24, 1992.

126 The *Daily Mirror*, April 17, 1992.

127 Ibid.

128 The *Observer*, May 10, 1992.

129 Ibid.
130 Ibid.
131 Ibid.

V WAR BY OTHER MEANS

1 The *Guardian*, September 3, 1991.
2 *War by Other Means*, Central Television, 1992.
3 *Socialist Economic Bulletin*, no. 3, December 1990.
4 BBC Radio 4 News and Nine O'Clock Television News bulletins, October 1–5, 1993.
5 The *Green Left Weekly*, September 29, 1993.
6 Ibid.
7 The *New York Times*, published in the *International Herald Tribune*, September 9, 1993.
8 CNN News (South East Asia), September 22, 1993.
9 The *Wall Street Journal*, January 12, 1993.
10 Cited in *Economic Intelligence*, New York, March 1993.
11 Aida Fullers Santos and Lynn F. Lee, *The Debt Crisis: A Treadmill of Poverty for Filipino Women*, Kalayaan, Manila, 1989, p. 22, cited by Dale Hildebrand in *To Pay is to Die*, *The Philippine Foreign Debt Crisis*, Philippine International Forum, 1991.
12 Susan George, *The Debt Boomerang*, Pluto Press, London, 1992.
13 As told to the author.
14 UNICEF, *State of the World's Children*, 1989, p. 1.
15 Official statistics cited in 'Red Noses buy only 8 hours of debt relief', *Socialist*, April 11, 1991.
16 In a written answer in the House of Commons, the Government stated that tax relief to banks on 'doubtful sovereign debt' amounted to 'about £70 million in 1987–8, over £0.5 billion for 1988–89 and about £0.33 billion for 1989–90'. *Hansard*, December 19, 1990, p. 180.
17 *Anti-Slavery Reporter*, published by the Anti-Slavery Society for the Protection of Human Rights, Series VII, Vol. 13, no. 5, 1988, p. 19.
18 The *Guardian*, June 7, 1990.
19 Walden Bello, Band Kinley and Elaine Elinson, *Development Debacle: The World Bank and the Philippines*, Institute for Food and Development Policy, Philippine Solidarity Network, San Francisco, 1982, p. 23.
20 Ibid., p. 25.

21 Statistic supplied to the author by Walden Bello.

22 Poverty statistics from IBON Databank study, Manila; cited in the *Daily Globe*, November 11, 1991.

23 Walden Bello, *Development Debacle*, p. 1.

24 Dale Hildebrand, *To Pay is to Die: The Philippine Foreign Debt Crisis*, Philippine International Forum, 1991, p. 9.

25 James B. Goodno, *The Philippines: Land of Broken Promises*, Zed Books, London, 1991, jacket quotation.

26 Hildebrand, p. 15.

27 Ibid., p. 3.

28 Cited in an internal report for Save the Children Fund, Manila and London.

29 Ibid.

30 See UNICEF, *State of the World's Children*, 1989, p. 1.

31 *Asian Wall Street Journal*, special advertising feature, October 1991.

32 *Annual Meeting News*, Bangkok, 1991, October 14, 1991.

33 John Clark, *For Richer for Poorer*, Oxfam, Oxford, 1986, p. 91.

34 The *Bangkok Post*, October 17, 1991.

35 A total of $12 billion taken by Marcos was estimated by, among others, Morgan Guaranty Trust, *Business Week*, April 21, 1986.

36 The *Nation* (Bangkok), October 14, 1991.

37 The *Nation* (Bangkok), October 16, 1991.

38 Press conference, Bangkok, October 17, 1991.

39 Documentation received. See the *Observer*, April 22, 1990 and *New Internationalist*, December 1990.

40 The *Bangkok Post*, Observer 15 and 17, 1991.

41 Ibid., October 15, 1991.

42 UNICEF, *State of the World's Children*, 1989, p. 1.

43 The *Bangkok Post*, October 15, 1991.

44 The *Washington Post*, February 16, 1992.

45 The *Fletcher Forum of World Affairs*, summer 1992, citing an article by Djilas.

46 *Chronology of the Yugoslav Crisis*, January 1990–May 1992, Institute of International Politics and Economics, Belgrade, 1992, p. 1.

47 *European Community and the Yugoslav Crisis*, Institute of International Politics and Economics, Belgrade, 1992, p. 8.

48 *Facts on File*, May 9, 1991, p. 342, cited by Sean Gervasi in *Covert Action*, No. 43, winter 1992–3. (I am grateful to Sean Gervasi for his enquiry and analysis.)

49 *European Community and the Yugoslav Crisis*, p. 10.

50 The *New Yorker*, August 24, 1992.

51 *Covert Action*, No. 43.

52 The *New York Times*, October 14, 1989.

53 *Facts on File*, December 31, 1989, p. 985, cited by Gervasi.

54 *Covert Action*, No. 43.

55 I am grateful to Misha Gavrilovic for this reminder, and other insights, in a letter to the author.

56 *Covert Action*, No. 43.

57 *Time*, December 28, 1992.

58 The *Guardian*, December 14, 1992

59 *Covert Action*, No. 43.

60 BBC Short Wave Broadcasts, August, 1992.

61 The *New Statesman*, December 18, 1992.

62 Private correspondence collection of J. E. Walsh.

63 The *Guardian*, December 5, 1992.

64 Ibid.

65 The *Guardian* magazine, January 9, 1993.

66 BBC Short Wave Broadcasts, December, 1992.

67 *The Observer*, June 20, 1993.

68 The *Guardian*, June 19, 1993.

69 *Covert Action*, No. 43.

70 See Victoria Brittain, 'West must act or the losers take all', the *Guardian*, March 3, 1993.

71 'Reforming the United Nations', speech at Pax Christi conference, London, January 23, 1993.

72 BBC Shortwave Broadcasts, December, 1992.

73 The *Guardian*, December 29, 1992.

74 Ibid., December 16, 1992.

75 The *Observer*, January 10, 1993.

VI EAST TIMOR

1 Interview with the author, Canberra, August 1993, for *Death of a Nation: The Timor Conspiracy*, Central Television, broadcast on the ITV network, February 22, 1994.

2 The *Irish Times*, September 8, 1983. See also James Dunn, *Timor: A People Betrayed*, Jacaranda Press, Australia, 1983, p. 320.

3 Joint Standing Committee on Foreign Affairs, Defence and Trade, *Australia's Relations with Indonesia*, Australian Government Publishing Service, Canberra, 1993, p. 96.

4   Interview with the author, Washington, November 1993, for *Death of a Nation: The Timor Conspiracy*. In March 1994, Dr George Aditjondro, a leading Indonesian academic with twenty years' research on East Timor, said in an interview that the figure of 200,000 deaths was a 'moderate' estimate. On April 14 1994, the *Sydney Morning Herald* published an admission by Abilio Soares, the Jakarta installed 'governor' of East Timor. 'I think it is true', he said. 'Maybe around 200,000 people have died in East Timor since 1975.'

5   The *7.30 Report*, ABC Television, November 26, 1991.

6   The *Age*, Melbourne, December 8, 1975.

7   Dunn, pp. 282–341.

8   Ibid., p. 313.

9   Ibid.

10   Correspondence with Amnesty International, December 1993.

11   Max Stahl's film was shown in *In Cold Blood*, produced for Yorkshire Television by Peter Gordon, January 7, 1992. For latest figures of the dead and 'disappeared', see report by 'Peace is Possible in East Timor', Lisbon. *Tapol Bulletin*, No. 113, October 1992.

12   Mark Aarons and Robert Domm, *East Timor, A Western Made Tragedy*, Left Book Club, Sydney, 1992, p. 66.

13   *Tapol Bulletin*, No. 108, December 1991. Indonesian armed forces Commander-in-Chief (later vice-president), Try Sutrisno, said, 'These delinquent people have to be shot. And we shall shoot them.'

14   Michele Turner, *Telling East Timor: Personal testimonies 1942–1992*, New South Wales University Press, Sydney, 1992, pp. 13–18.

15   Garfield Barwick, Minister in the Menzies government, said this in 1963, cited in the *Sydney Morning Herald*, January 1, 1984.

16   I am grateful to Michele Turner for this detail of Celestino's death. See *Telling*, pp. 174–6.

17   Ibid., p. 14.

18   Peter Carey, *The Forging of a Nation: East Timor, 1974–93*, paper for the Conference on 'Nationalism and Ethnicity in South East Asia', Berlin, October 1993, pp. 11–12.

19   Letter to UN Secretary-General Perez de Cuellar, February 6, 1989.

20   José Ramos Horta, *Funu, The Unfinished Saga of East Timor*, Red Sea Press, New Jersey, 1987, pp. 38, 39.

21 Ibid., p. 43.

22 For an explanation of the overthrow of Gough Whitlam in November, 1975, see 'The Coup' in John Pilger, *A Secret Country*, Vintage, London, 1992.

23 Dunn, pp. 132–5.

24 Dunn, p. 135.

25 J. A. C. Mackie, 'Australia's Relations with Indonesia: Principles and Policies', part 2, *Australian Outlook* 28, 1974.

26 Max Lane, *New Internationalist*, March 1994.

27 Cited by Noam Chomsky in his preface to José Ramos Horta's *Funu, The Unfinished Saga of East Timor*, Red Sea Press, New Jersey, 1987.

28 Carmel Budiardjo and Liem Soei Liong, *The War against East Timor*, Zed Books, London, 1984, p. 49.

29 Gabriel Kolko, *Confronting the Third World*, Pantheon, New York, 1988 p. 178.

30 Chomsky, 1987.

31 'US Agents "drew up Indonesian hit list" ', the *Guardian*, May 22, 1990.

32 Gabriel Kolko, pp. 180–1. I am indebted to Mark Curtis for the basis of this analysis.

33 Chomsky, 1987.

34 Michael Stewart, *Life and Labour: An Autobiography*, Sidgwick and Jackson, London, 1980, p. 149.

35 The Melbourne *Age*, September 13, 1974.

36 The *Sydney Morning Herald*, September 16, 1974.

37 Ibid., November 19, 1974.

38 Dunn, p. ix.

39 The *Sydney Morning Herald*, December 10, 1991.

40 Dunn, p. 210.

41 The *National Times*, Sydney, May 30 and June 5, 1982.

42 Richard Walsh and George Munster, *Documents on Australian Defence and Foreign Policy 1968–1975*, published by J. R. Walsh and G. J. Munster, Sydney, 1980, p. 216.

43 Mark Hertsgaard, 'The Secret Life of Henry Kissinger', *The Nation*, New York, November 29, 1990. Copy of minutes acquired and authenticated by Victor Navasky, editor of *The Nation*.

44 The monitoring reports of the CIA – to become known as 'The Timor Papers' – were published in the *National Times*, Sydney, May 30 and June 6, 1982. See also 'The Timor Papers' section

in *The Book of Leaks*, by Brian Toohey and Marian Wilkinson, Angus and Robertson, Sydney, pp. 143–95.

45 Ibid.

46 Ibid.

47 The *Canberra Times*, December 3, 1975.

48 John G. Taylor, *Indonesia's Forgotten War: The Hidden History of East Timor*, Zed Books, London, 1991, p. 64.

49 Ibid., p. 68.

50 *Tapol Bulletin*, No. 59, September 1983.

51 Taylor (citing Dunn), p. 68.

52 Ibid., p. 69.

53 Amnesty International testimony, 1985, cited by Taylor, p. 69.

54 Ibid., p. 70.

55 Correspondence with the author. See also Taylor.

56 Taylor, p. 70.

57 The *Boston Globe*, November 8, 1975.

58 Hertsgaard, *The Nation*.

59 Ibid.

60 See Carmel Budiardjo, the *New Internationalist*, March 1994.

61 Cited by Taylor, p. 73. The document was originally published in *Timor Link*, London, No. 12/13, April 1988.

62 *The Timor Papers*.

63 Taylor, pp. 169–70.

64 Daniel Patrick Moynihan, *A Dangerous Place*, Little Brown, New York, 1978, p. 247.

65 Cited by Chomsky. Lopez de Cruz said that 60,000 had died 'in six months of civil war' (which had lasted two weeks from August 11, 1974). He was forced to retract by the Indonesians and claimed he had really meant 'casualties', not all of which were deaths. A close associate of de Cruz told James Dunn that, in his original statement, de Cruz had actually said 'massacred'. See Carmel Budiardjo and Liem Soei Liong, *The War against East Timor*, Zed Books, London, 1984, p. 49.

66 Chomsky, 1987.

67 The Melbourne *Age*, August 3, 1976.

68 Taylor, p. 74.

69 *The Times*, October 12, 1976.

70 Taylor, p. 75.

71 *The Timor Papers*.

72 Chomsky, 1987.

73 Letter from David Owen to Lord Avebury, June 19, 1978.

74 Taylor, pp. 86–7.
75 Chomsky, 1987.
76 Soekanto, ed. *Integrasi*, Jakarta, 1976, cited by Dunn p. 84.
77 Ibid.
78 Jill Jolliffe, 'Lisbon "connived" at Timor annexation', the *Guardian*, October 17, 1981.
79 The official has since left the AFFC.
80 See the *Sydney Morning Herald*, December 1, 1992 and the *Australian*, March 3, 1993.
81 The *Sydney Morning Herald*, August 20, 1992.
82 The *Australian*, January 1, 1993.
83 The *Sydney Morning Herald*, December 1, 1992.
84 As told to the author.
85 Filmed interview with the author, August 1993, for *Death of a Nation*, Central Television, broadcast February 22, 1994.
86 Ibid.
87 Ibid.
88 Channel 7 Melbourne, October 1975.
89 The *Courier-Mail*, Brisbane, April 27, 1983.
90 Interview with the author.
91 Dunn, p. 237.
92 Ibid., p. 239.
93 Jill Jolliffe, *East Timor: Nationalism and Colonialism*, University of Queensland Press, 1978, p. 233.
94 Australian *Hansard*, House of Representatives, October 30, 1975.
95 Ibid., October 21, 1975.
96 Ibid., October 30, 1975.
97 Dunn, p. 245.
98 Ibid., p. 247.
99 Ibid., pp. 247–8.
100 Ibid., p. 246.
101 American journalist Rod Nordland reported the famine. See the *Philadelphia Inquirer*, May 28, 1982.
102 Carmel Budiardjo and Liem Soei Liong, pp. 103–5.
103 Ibid., p. 98.
104 *Angkatan Bersenyata* (Indonesian armed forces newspaper), October 24, 1985, cited by Taylor.
105 *New Journalist*, Sydney, May 1979.
106 Ibid.
107 Dunn, p. 286.

108 Letter from the head of the Indonesia Country Programme Department, East Asia and Pacific Regional Office, World Bank, to Carmel Budiardjo, *Tapol Bulletin*, September 12, 1985.
109 Cited by Taylor, p. 159.
110 The *New York Times*, April 24, 1993.
111 Interview with Christiano Costa by Carmel Budiardjo, Geneva, March 1988.
112 Instruction Manual No. PROTAP/01-B/VIV 1982, 'Established Procedure for Interrogation of Prisoners', Military Report Command, 164 Wira Dama, July 8, 1982, p. 34 in translation.
113 Taylor, p. 144.
114 Ibid., p. 138.
115 Australian Government Printing Service, 1983, Appendix 24B, pp. 157-60.
116 Ibid., p. 160.
117 Ibid., p. 163.
118 Ibid., Appendix 35, pp. 207-13.
119 *Sinar Harapan* (Indonesian press), August 17, 1983.
120 The *Australian*, January 24, 1994.
121 The *Far Eastern Economic Review*, July 30, 1992.
122 Ibid., April 22, 1992.
123 Filmed interview, November 1993.
124 Enclosure with letter to John Lynn, Administrative Assistant, c/o Hon. J. Bennett Johnston, US Senate, from Richard S. Fitzsimmons, Vice President, Government Relations, Burson-Marsteller, August 5, 1992.
125 *BBC Short Wave Broadcasts*, FE/1656,AL/1, April 6, 1993.
126 President Soares interviewed by the author, November 1993.
127 Republic of Indonesia, *East Timor: Building for the Future*, Department of Foreign Affairs, Jakarta, July 1992.
128 See the *New York Times*, July 19, 1985; November 21, 1988.
129 The *Washington Post*, January 6, 1992.
130 Philip Liechty left the CIA in 1979.
131 The interview with Philip Liechty appeared, in part, in *Death of a Nation: the Timor Conspiracy*, Central Television, London, February 1994.
132 The *International Herald Tribune*, July 8, 1993.
133 The *Far Eastern Economic Review*, September 23, 1993.
134 The *New York Times*, December 8, 1993.
135 Chomsky, 1987.

136 Mark Curtis, from the manuscript of a book on British foreign policy to be published 1994.
137 Mark Curtis, the *New Internationalist*, March 1994.
138 Ibid.
139 The *Sunday Times*, August 18, 1991.
140 *Tapol Bulletin*, No. 118, August 1993.
141 *Hansard*, July 21, 1993.
142 Cited in *Tapol Bulletin*, No. 113, October 1992.
143 *Hansard*, January 12, 1993.
144 Ibid., July 26, 1993.
145 Ibid., May 18, 1993.
146 British Aerospace press release, April 5, 1978.
147 *Reuter*, April 7, 1993.
148 Interview with the author, November 1993.
149 Curtis, the *New Internationalist*.
150 The *Times*, February 1, 1977.
151 As told to the author.
152 Letter from J. L. Wilkins to Alex Palmer, February 23, 1993.
153 Letter from Alex Palmer to the author, November 6, 1993.
154 *Tapol Bulletin*, No. 116, April 1993.
155 The *Guardian*, August 13, 1993, by Margaret Coles. Foreign Office documents, including 'restricted' Telex to FO, letter from Alastair Goodlad to Greg Pope MP and memorandum about 'stonewalling' were passed to Margaret Coles by Jonathan Humphreys of the East Timor Coalition, who was the recipient of the 'leak'. Copies of all documents with the author.
156 Ibid.
157 *Tapol Backgrounder*, 'Indonesia: the British Perspective', 1993.
158 Interview with the Australian Broadcasting Corporation, Kuta, Bali, February 9, 1991, cited by *Indonesian News*, Volume 19, No. 2, February 1991.
159 The *Sydney Morning Herald*, August 23, 1985.
160 Aarons and Domm, p. 39.
161 Interview with the author, November 1993.
162 *Indonesia News*, Vol. 10, No. 2, February 1991.
163 Aarons and Domm, p. 66.
164 The *Sydney Morning Herald*, December 28 and 30, 1991.
165 Aarons and Domm, p. 39.
166 The *Sydney Morning Herald*, February 7, 1992. See also Amnesty International, 'in accordance with the law', statement before the

UN Special Committee on decolonisation, July 1992, AI Index: ASA 21/11/92.

167 Ibid., April 18, 1993.
168 Ibid., September 13, 1993.
169 The *Far Eastern Economic Review*, September 30, 1993.
170 The *Sydney Morning Herald*, September 17, 1993.
171 Ibid., October 29, 1993.
172 Keating's remarks cited by the *Sun-Herald*, February 13, 1994. In 1990 Gareth Evans told Kraisak Choonhaven, senior foreign policy adviser to (and son of) the Thai prime minister, that it was my 1989 film, *Cambodia Year Ten*, that had, according to Kraisak, 'undoubtedly put the issue of Cambodia back on the international agenda and regenerated Australia's part in the peace process'.
173 The *Age*, February 21, 1994.
174 The *West Australian*, April 6, 1994.
175 The *Age*, February 22, 1994.
176 Ibid.
177 The *Australian*, February 14, 1994.
178 Ibid., February 18 and 19, 1994.
179 Ibid., February 26, 1994.
180 Fax from Paul Kelly, March 15, 1994.
181 The *Age*, March 17, 1994.
182 George Aditjondro, *From Memo to Tutuala*; and *In the Shadow of Mount Ramelau*, Satya Wacana Christian University, Central Java, 1994. Also, interview with the author, March 31, 1994.
183 The *Australian*, March 18, 1994.
184 Amnesty International, 'Indonesia/East Timor, the suppression of dissent', July 1992, AI Index: ASA 21/09/92.
185 The *Sydney Morning Herald*, May 28, 1993.
186 The list appeared in *Info Bisnis Monthly*, cited by *Australian Associated Press* and *Reuter*, November 10, 1993.
187 The *New Internationalist*, March 1994.

VII TRIBUTES

1 Jeremy Bentham, *Panoptican Versus New South Wales*, p. 7, cited in Robert Hughes, *The Fatal Shore*, Collins Harvill, London, 1987, p. 2.
2 I began this tribute in *Heroes*.

3 Noam Chomsky, *The Chomsky Reader*, edited by James Peck, Serpent's Tail, London, 1987.

4 Noam Chomsky, *The Backroom Boys*, Fontana, London, 1973.

5 This quotation is from an interview similar to that in *Language and Politics*, Black Rose Books, Montreal, 1989, p. 700. (Having mislaid my original Chomsky sources, I am indebted to Carlos Otero for this Note, and the following.)

6 Chomsky, *The Culture of Terrorism*, Pluto Press, London, 1988.

7 Chomsky's extended sense of Isaiah Berlin's term 'secular priesthood' is developed in his major essay, 'Intellectuals and the State', reprinted in *Towards a New Cold War*, Sinclair Brown, London, 1982.

8 Chomsky, *The Culture of Terrorism*, p. 24; also *Language and Politics*, p. 693.

9 *Radical Philosophy*, no. 53, Autumn 1989, pp. 31–40.

10 Cited in *The Late Show*, BBC television, December 1992.

11 Ibid.

12 Norman Mailer, *The Armies of the Night*, Weidenfeld and Nicolson, London, 1968.

13 *Lies of Our Times*, September 1991.

14 Jim Garrison, *On the Trail of the Assassins*, Sheridan Square Press, New York, 1988.

15 The *Chicago Tribune*, May 14, 1991.

16 *Indo-China Project Press Digest*, January 1992.

17 *Newsday*, January 7, 1992.

18 The *Washington Post*, January 24, 1992.

19 Ibid., May 19, 1991.

20 *Lies of Our Times*, September 1991.

21 Cited in *Socialist*, January 29–February 11, 1992.

22 The *Washington Post*, January 24, 1992.

23 Cited in *Socialist*, January 29–February 11, 1992.

24 See *Heroes*, pp. 187–8.

25 *Lies of Our Times*, September 1991.

26 *Behind the Headlines*, BBC Television, January 1992.

27 *Lies of Our Times*, September 1991.

28 The *Guardian*, September 17, 1991.

29 *The Truth Game*, Central Television, 1983; also sourced by Christic Institute, Washington.

30 The *Guardian*, September 21, 1991.

31 The *Evening Standard*, March 15, 1990.

32 The *Independent*, August 6, 1989.

33 The *Evening Standard*, March 15, 1990.
34 The *Sun*, March 16, 1990.
35 See 'Salesman Hurd' and elsewhere in 'Mythmakers of the Gulf War'.
36 The *Daily Mail*, March 17, 1990.
37 *Today*, March 17, 1990.
38 Ibid., March 19, 1990.
39 The *News of the World*, March 18, 1990.
40 The *Sunday Telegraph*, March 18, 1990.
41 The *Guardian*, March 20, 1990.
42 *Tribune*, April 6, 1984.
43 The *Observer*, June 24, 1990.
44 The *Observer*, September 10 & 15, October 15, 1989.
45 Ibid., May 6 & 13, 1990; April 7 & August 4, 1991.
46 Ibid., July 14, 1991.

VIII ON THE ROAD

1 The *St Petersburg Times*, August 1, 1991.
2 The *New York Times*, August 1, 1991.
3 The *St Petersburg Times*, August 1, 1991.
4 The *Washington Post*, November 12, 1993.
5 Ibid.
6 The *New York Times*, November 9, 1993.
7 Vietnam Development Bank circular, 1993.

IX CAMBODIA

1 I have taken the body of this opening account from the 'Year Zero' chapter of *Heroes*, Jonathan Cape, London, 1986; Pan Books, London, 1987 and 1989.
2 Cited by Denis Bloodworth, 'The man who brought death', *Observer* magazine, January 20, 1980.
3 *Vietnam: A Television History*, Programme 9, 'The secret war: Laos and Cambodia', Central Television, 1983.
4 *Efforts of Khmer Insurgents to Exploit for Propaganda Purposes Damage Done by Airstrikes in Kandal Province*, Intelligence Information Cable, May 2, 1973, declassified by the CIA on February 19, 1987.
5 Ben Kiernan, the *Sydney Morning Herald*, January 6, 1989.
6 Roger Normand, *The Nation*, August 27, 1990.

7   Ben Kiernan, *The Cambodian Genocide: Issues and Responses*, Yale paper, 1990, p. 1.

8   Khieu Samphan was interviewed by David Hawk, *Index on Censorship*, January 1986.

9   As told to the author.

10 Elizabeth Becker, *When the War Was Over*, Simon and Schuster, New York, 1986, p. 440.

11 Letters from Jonathan Winer to Larry Chartienes, Vietnam Veterans of America, citing Congressional Research Service, October 22, 1986. Letter from Winer to Noam Chomsky, June 16, 1987. Telephone communication with the author, August 1989.

12 Linda Mason and Roger Brown, *Rice, Rivalry and Politics: Managing Cambodian Relief*, University of Notre Dame Press, Indiana, 1983, pp. 135, 159.

13 William Shawcross, *The Quality of Mercy: Cambodia, Holocaust and Modern Conscience*, Andre Deutsch, London, 1984, pp. 289, 345, 395.

14 William Shawcross, *Sideshow: Nixon, Kissinger and the Destruction of Cambodia*, Andre Deutsch, London, 1979.

15 The colonel's role was 'made plain' at a meeting with staff members of the US Senate Intelligence Committee on February 10, 1990, according to John Pedler, who was at the meeting.

16 *Inside Asia*, February and June 1985.

17 The *New York Times*, May 14, 1989.

18 *Cambodia: The Betrayal*, Central Television, 1990.

19 The *San Francisco Examiner*, August 12 and 15, 1990.

20 The *Sunday Telegraph*, September 24, 1989.

21 *Jane's Defence Weekly*, September 30, 1989.

22 *Cambodia Year Ten*, Central Television, 1989.

23 *Blue Peter*, BBC Television, December 19, 1988.

24 In 1990 Ranariddh said that, in a proposed attack on Siem Reap, 'The Khmer Rouge will be the major attacking forces': *Associated Press*, October 11, 1990; *Indochina Digest*, October 6, 1990. His separate statement that Sihanoukists celebrated Khmer Rouge victories as their own was reported in the *Sunday Correspondent*, November 5, 1989.

25 *Cambodia Year One*, Associated Television, 1980.

26 See report by Committee to Protect Journalists, New York, 1989, 1990, 1991; also *Index on Censorship* file. One recent example was the Thai regime's refusal to renew the resident's permit of Alan Boyd, an Australian correspondent of the *South China*

Morning Post and the *Australian*, following articles critical of the military government.

27 The *New York Times*, August 7, 1991.

28 The *Sydney Morning Herald*, October 20, 1990 and Ben Kiernan, *Cambodia's Missed Chance, Superpower Obstruction of a Viable Path to Peace*, Indo-China newsletter, Issue 72, November–December 1991, p. 5.

29 *Hansard*, November 8, 1989.

30 'Waldegrave makes tacit admission of SAS link to Khmer Rouge', the *Independent*, November 14, 1989.

31 Letter to John Bowis, MP, May 16, 1990.

32 Letter to Neil Kinnock, October 17, 1990.

33 *Hansard*, October 26, 1990, p. 650. See also pp. 640, 641.

34 Colvin's comments, and name, were on a copy of Raoul Jennar's 'A Dangerous Gamble: An analysis of the "Comprehensive political settlement" worked out by the Five Permanent Members of the UN Security Council to end the conflict in Cambodia', Document RMJ/9, December 11, 1990.

35 Ibid.

36 Letter from D. H. Colvin to D. Belfield, May 17, 1991 in which Colvin refers to 'the need to include the Khmer Rouge in the peace process'.

37 As told to the author.

38 Tribute to Simon O'Dwyer-Russell, the *Sunday Telegraph*, December 16, 1991.

39 Letters from Noam Chomsky to the *Independent*, October 22 and November 23, 1990.

40 Private communication with the author.

41 Parliamentary questions for answers, October 18, 1990; note from Chris Mullin to the author, October 16, 1990.

42 The *Guardian*, October 16, 1991.

43 Cited by Penny Edwards, the *Guardian*, November 4, 1989.

44 Agence France Presse report from Geneva, August 30, 1990.

45 Ben Kiernan, *The Cambodian Genocide: Issues and Responses*, p. 28.

46 Ibid., p. 29.

47 On June 5, 1990, *The Times* reported Kissinger as saying, 'I would not be surprised if ten years from now, China, even following its present course, will appear like a freer country than Russia and a more prosperous one.'

48 The *Sydney Morning Herald*, October 20 and December 6, 1990.

After the contents of the Evans briefing document were published in the *Sydney Morning Herald*, Senator Evans replied in a letter to the paper on December 10, 1990. 'The truth is', he wrote, 'that in a statement circulated [at Paris] on August 28, 1989, I described, as one of "five stumbling blocks ... identified in the work of the Committees, and by the Co-presidents" the following: "whether it is appropriate or not to refer specifically to the non-return of genocidal practices of the past". Other "stumbling blocks" I referred to were such matters as "the composition and powers of the transitional administration" and "whether it is appropriate to acknowledge or not the presence of Vietnamese or other settlers in Cambodia". The point is simply that I was making a value-neutral assessment of where we were then at in the negotiating process, identifying controversial words and phrases and issues generally which remained to be addressed ...'

49 The *Sydney Morning Herald*, October 20, 1990.
50 Australian Government, *Informal Meeting on Cambodia, Issues for Negotiations in a Comprehensive Settlement: Working Papers*, Jakarta, February 26–28, 1990.
51 *Cambodia Year Ten Update*, Central Television, 1989.
52 Ben Kiernan, *Cambodia's Missed Chance*, p. 5.
53 Ibid., p. 4.
54 See Raoul M. Jennar, 'Cambodian Chronicles (I), Fourteen Days which shook Cambodia' and 'Cambodian Chronicles (II), The very first steps towards a fragile peace', European Far Eastern Research Center, Brussels, December 5, 1991/March 15, 1992.
55 The *Washington Post*, April 29, 1989.
56 Elizabeth Becker, *When the War Was Over*, Simon and Schuster, New York, 1986.
57 *Official Records*, UN General Assembly Thirteenth Session, October 6, 1975.
58 Transcript of Sihanouk's press conference, January 7, 1979, cited and analysed by Ben Kiernan, *The Cambodian Genocide: Issues and Responses*, pp. 25, 26.
59 Ben Kiernan, *Cambodia's Missed Chance*, p. 9.
60 *Peter Jennings Reporting*, ABC News, April 26, 1990.
61 *Vanity Fair*, April 1990.
62 John Pedler, *Cambodia: A Report on the International and Internal Situation and the Future Outlook*, NGO Forum on Kampuchea, London, April, 1989.
63 The *Washington Post*, April 29, 1989.

64 The *New York Times*, May 14, 1989.

65 *Cambodia Year Ten*, Central Television, 1989.

66 Cambodia Study Group, *Resumé of Selected Collaborative Battles, Cambodia 1988-90*. Copyright Cambodia Study Group 1990.

67 Affidavit sworn by John Pedler at Rome, June 14, 1991.

68 The *Washington Post*, February 28, 1991.

69 *Newsday*, March 7, 1991.

70 See Thomas Kiernan, *Citizen Murdoch: The unexpurgated story of Rupert Murdoch – the world's most powerful and controversial media head*, Dodd, Mead & Company, New York, 1986, pp. 237-50.

71 Memo from Rosie Waterhouse to Robin Morgan, May 1988, cited by Roger Bolton, *Death on the Rock and other stories*, W. H. Allen, London, 1990, p. 29.

72 Ibid.

73 As told to Jane Hill.

74 See *Heroes*, Chapters 35 and 36.

75 The *Guardian*, January 8, 1980.

76 See *Heroes*, Chapters 35 and 36.

77 Ibid., p. 429.

78 'Pottiness of Pilger', letter by Derek Tonkin, *Sunday Times*, March 17, 1991.

79 Letter from David Colvin to the author, May 9, 1991.

80 Letter from the author to David Colvin, May 13, 1991.

81 Letter from David Munro to William Shawcross, May 14, 1991; Ben Kiernan, *The Cambodian Genocide, 1975-1979: A Critical Review*, Yale paper, 1991, p. 19.

82 The *Observer*, March 24, 1991.

83 *The Quality of Mercy: Cambodia, Holocaust and Modern Conscience*, Andre Deutsch, London, 1984.

84 *New Left Review*, no. 152, July–August 1985.

85 Report by Finnish Inquiry commissioners, cited by Edward S. Herman and Noam Chomsky in *Manufacturing Consent: The Political Economy of the Mass Media*, Pantheon, 1988, p. 263.

86 William Shawcross, *The Quality of Mercy*, pp. 181, 182.

87 Ben Kiernan, *The Cambodian Genocide, 1975-1979: A Critical Review*, pp. 16, 19.

88 The *Observer*, March 17, 1991.

89 The *Daily Mirror*, September 12, 1979.

90 *Cambodia Year One*, Associated Television, 1980.

91 The *Washington Post*, March 18, 1980. I have taken this, and following examples, from *Heroes*.

92 *New York Review of Books*, January 24, 1980.

93 James Reston, 'Is there no Pity?' *New York Times*, December 12, 1979.

94 Interview in *The Eagle, The Dragon, The Bear and Kampuchea*, Central Television, 1983.

95 The *Far Eastern Economic Review*, January 4, 1980.

96 Letter from William Shawcross to the author, January 27, 1983.

97 *Heroes*, p. 411.

98 Written parliamentary answer by the Armed Forces Minister, Archie Hamilton; the *Guardian*, June 27, 1991.

99 The *Spectator*, March 23 and May 4, 1991. Chris Mullin wrote to the *Spectator* on July 23, 1991: 'No doubt Mr Tonkin will argue that the KPNLF and the Sihanouk army are not terrorists, a subtlety which will, I imagine, be lost on most Cambodians.' His letter was not published.

100 Letter to Mishcon de Reya, solicitors, from R. A. D. Jackson, Assistant Treasury Solicitor, June 25, 1991, accompanied by High Court documents.

101 High Court Public Immunity Certificate signed by Tom King, Defence Secretary, June 25, 1991.

102 Overheard by David Munro, myself and others.

103 This is the complete text of a statement by Central Television issued following the libel settlement on July 5, 1991: 'Cambodia is a uniquely devastated country. The suffering endured as a result of Pol Pot's reign of terror has been compounded by the wilful isolation of the Cambodian people. Cambodia is the only country in the world to be denied United Nations development aid. This is part of a punitive embargo devised and led by the United States and China, and backed by the British Government.

'Britain's involvement has been crucial. Since late 1989 government ministers have issued a series of denials that British troops have been secretly training Pol Pot's allies on the Thai/Cambodian border. These denials have been in response to allegations, especially allegations made by us in our documentary films.

'Last week the government finally admitted that the SAS had been training the so-called "non-communist resistance" – part of a coalition dominated by Pol Pot's Khmer Rouge – since 1983. In fact, serving and former British soldiers have been instructing Cambodian guerrillas in a range of military skills, including sabotage, the laying of mines and other modern techniques of terrorism. In Central's film last year, *Cambodia: The Betrayal*, it was estimated that eighty Cambodians lose a limb every day as a consequence of stepping on mines.

'In our film Ann Clwyd MP, Shadow Minister for Overseas Development, was interviewed about two men with military connections whom she had encountered in Phnom Penh during the withdrawal of Vietnamese troops from Cambodia in September 1989. The presence of the two men was described as mysterious. It should be made clear that these two, who sued us, played no part in the guerrilla training. In an agreed Statement in the High Court today, we have accepted that and made clear that it was never our intention to suggest that these men were involved in training. The libel case concerning these two men has now been settled.

'Our film was principally concerned not with individuals but with governments – and especially the secret aid given by Western governments, including the British Government, to one side in the Cambodian civil war.

'Not only was Britain's role made clear by the government's admission last week about SAS training – but it was demonstrated again this week in the High Court, where the government was represented by two counsel, and others, who intervened in the libel case in an extraordinary way.

'Indeed, the government dramatically intervened even before the case came to court by stopping five subpoenas issued by our lawyers on three government ministers – Archie Hamilton, Mark Lennox-Boyd and William Waldegrave – and the head and former head of the SAS. The authority for this gagging order was contained in "Public Interest Immunity Orders" signed by the Secretary of State for Defence, Tom King.

'In open court this week the government's representatives made clear that no evidence would be permitted that went beyond the statement last week by the Armed Services Minister, Archie Hamilton, confirming British military training of Cambodian guerrillas.

'The government counsel – John Laws QC and Philip Havers – spelt out the wide-ranging, catch-all provisions of the Secretary of State's order. For example, certain evidence regarding the SAS and the security services, such as MI6, which might be brought by our defence counsel would be challenged and a ruling sought that it not be allowed. The government counsel spoke in open court about "national security" being at stake with the disclosure of evidence that "travels into the area that the Secretary of State would protect".

'The judge accepted this government restriction – which meant that a Ministry of Defence witness would not even be allowed, for example, to confirm or deny anything about the SAS and that counsel acting for the defence would not be allowed to challenge this.

'The defence counsel – Desmond Browne QC – described this as "grossly unfair" and a "considerable injustice". He drew a parallel with the Spycatcher case in 1987 in which the government intervened in a similar way.

'In the meantime, the Cambodian people enter their thirty-third year of war and suffering in which Western governments have played a major part.'

104 Document addressed to David Munro, signed by Long Visalo, deputy foreign minister, State of Cambodia, June 28, 1991, reads: 'Report of Mao Makara (Khmer Rouge defector) ... Nong Nhai Training Camp belonging to the Khmer Rouge, 6 British instructors came here in May, 1987'.

105 The *Sunday Telegraph*, December 16, 1990.

106 Ibid., July 7, 1991.

107 My reply was published in the *Sunday Telegraph*, July 14, 1991.

108 Letter from David Munro to the *Evening Standard*, July 22, 1991 (unpublished), in reply to the *Evening Standard* article, July 19, 1991.

109 Letter from Chris Mullin to the *Spectator*, July 23, 1991, replying to Paul Johnson's article, *Spectator*, July 20, 1991.

110 Noam Chomsky identifies these three stages in *Manufacturing Consent*, written with Edward S. Herman. See Chapter 6, The Indo-China Wars (II): Laos and Cambodia; Pantheon, New York, 1988.

111 Roger Normand, *The Nation*, August 27, 1990.

112 The Vietnamese proposed a mutual pull-back of troops from their border with Cambodia on February 5, 1978. Three days later at the UN they issued a United Nations Circular to members detailing a proposal for a demilitarised zone of five kilometres on either side. The Vietnamese ambassador put this to the Secretary-

General on March 3, 1978. It was subsequently rejected (see UN Circular NV/78/9, February 8, 1978).
113 In 1982 the Vietnamese began official partial withdrawals of their troops. In 1983 Hanoi proposed a timetable for the withdrawal of troops to Indonesia's Foreign Minister, Kusumaatmadja, who· called it a 'significant step forward'. The Thai Foreign Minister Siddhi welcomed 'significant new elements' in Hanoi's proposals.
These elements were clarified in 1985, when Hanoi dropped its demand that the Chinese threat would have to end before any full Vietnamese troop withdrawal from Cambodia. In March 1985, Bill Hayden, visiting Hanoi, announced that the Vietnamese now insisted only that the Khmer Rouge be prevented from returning to power. Hayden called this a 'considerable advance'. Indonesia's Mochter called it 'an advance in substance' on the previous Vietnamese position. *Sydney Morning Herald*, October 20, 1990; see also Ben Kiernan, *Cambodia's Missed Chance*, p. 6.
114 Ben Kiernan, *Cambodia's Missed Chance*, p. 3.
115 Ibid., p. 6.
116 *St Louis Post-Dispatch*, November 29, 1979.
117 The *New York Times*, August 5, 1989.
118 The *Guardian*, October 6–7, 1989.
119 Hearings on Cambodia, the Asian and Pacific Sub-committee of the House Foreign Affairs Committee, Washington D.C., April 10, 1991.
120 Ibid.
121 Ibid.
122 *Washington Quarterly*, Spring 1991, p. 85.
123 The *New York Times*, August 17, 1990.
124 *St Louis Post-Dispatch*, January 15, 1979.
125 *Lies of Our Times*, 'Down the memory hole', June 1991.
126 *The Nation*, August 27, 1990.
127 The *Independent*, June 8, 1990.
128 The *Independent*, to its credit, gave me the same space in which to reply to the McCarthy article: July 6, 1990.
129 The *Independent Magazine*, December 7, 1991.
130 *The Times*, January 31, 1991.
131 *The Times*, November 27, 1991.
132 Source: Cambodia Campaign to oppose the return of the Khmer Rouge, Washington D.C.; also the *Guardian*, November 18, 1991.

133 Eva Mysliwiec, *Punishing the Poor: The International Isolation of Kampuchea*, Oxfam, Oxford, 1988.

134 Ben Kiernan, *The Cambodian Genocide: Issues and Responses*, p. 11.

135 Letter from J. Wilkins, South East Asia Department, Foreign Office, to C. Preece; July 9, 1991.

136 *The Nation*, August 27, 1990.

137 The *Sydney Morning Herald*, *Good Weekend* magazine, December 14, 1991.

138 *Indochina Digest*, February 21, 1992.

139 The *Washington Post*, January 26, 1992.

140 The first quotation is from the *Guardian*, November 20, 1991; the second is from Reuter, November 16, 1991.

141 I am grateful to Catherine Lumby for this, and other observations, in her excellent article in the *Sydney Morning Herald*, November 30, 1991.

142 The *Washington Post*, January 26, 1992; also Ben Kiernan, *Khmer Rouge Strategy in Cambodia: Exploiting and Subverting the UN Agreement*, 1992.

143 The *New York Times*, November 15, 1991.

144 Gareth Porter, *Kampuchea's UN Seat: Cutting the Pol Pot Connection*, Indo-China issue no. 8, July 1980.

145 Private communication following the Caithness meeting in Phnom Penh.

146 As told to the author.

147 The *Sydney Morning Herald*, October 20, 1990.

148 *Sunday*, National Nine Network Australia, September 1, 1991.

149 *Indochina Digest*, June 19, 1992.

150 *Sunday*, cited by Dennis Shoesmith in *Cambodia after the Paris Agreements*, February 17, 1992.

151 The *Observer*, December 1, 1991.

152 The *Sydney Morning Herald*, February 29, 1992.

153 The *Bangkok Post*, citing Agence France Presse, March 28, 1992.

154 Cambodian Chronicles (IV), EFERC 9, July 2, 1992.

155 Cambodian Chronicles (III), EFERC 7, May 11, 1992; and Paul Davies, *Cambodia: Interference is not aid*, May 26, 1992.

156 Paul Davies.

157 Reuter, June 3, 1992.

158 United Press International, May 30, 1992.

159 Reuter, June 10, 1992.

160 Ibid., June 11, 1992.
161 *Land Mines in Cambodia: The Coward's War*, Asia Watch, New York, September 1991, pp. 1, 2.
162 Ibid.
163 *Indochina Digest*, May 1, 1992.
164 Reuter, January 2, 1992.
165 *Repression Trade UK Limited: How the UK makes Torture and Death its Business*, Amnesty International, January 1992.
166 Reuter, January 15, 1992.
167 Letter from Rae McGrath to the *Guardian*, January 20, 1992 (unpublished).
168 Letter from Derek Tonkin to the Editor, *Vietnam Broadsheet*, March 5, 1992, published summer issue 1992.
169 As told to Paul Donovan, April 24, 1992. (Verbatim notes supplied.)

I wrote to Tonkin on May 18, 1992 and advised him I was writing for publication about his latest involvement in Indo-China. My letter said, 'I have a copy of your letter for publication in *Vietnam Broadsheet* (March 5, 1992) in which you state that your firm has plans for mines clearance in Cambodia. Paul Donovan has given me a record of his conversation with you and your associate, Neil Shrimpton, in which you identify Royal Ordnance as the company with which you are seeking contracts for clearing mines. Would you like to comment on this?

'On the question of mine-laying, I note in your letter of 5 March, 1992 that you say "the only detailed account, claiming any authority", about the type of military training given by British troops to Cambodian guerrillas is *Jane's Defence Weekly*. This, of course, is not correct.

'In September, 1991 Asia Watch and the Mines Advisory Group produced a comprehensive and expert report giving details of British instruction in mine-laying to Cambodian guerrillas. Amnesty International subsequently produced a report based upon the Asia Watch and Mines Advisory Group study. I presume you have read this.

'In reviewing your public statements on this matter I note that you have not denied that, during your time as ambassador to Thailand, British troops trained Cambodian guerrillas to lay mines. Is this still your position? Or do you deny it?'

Tonkin replied on May 25, 1992, that he had 'no wish to make any comment'.

170 As told to the author, June 1989, and repeated in part of *Cambodia Year Ten*, Central Television, November 1989.

171 *Cambodia Year Ten.*

172 Letter from John Pedler to the author, February 3, 1992.

173 The *Sydney Morning Herald*, November 30, 1991.

174 The *Spectator*, November 2, 1991.

175 *Vietnam: A Television History*, Programme 9, 'The Secret War: Laos and Cambodia', Central Television, 1983.

176 Michael Vickery, *Cambodia After the Peace*, Samizdat, Penang, December 1991, cited by Jennar, p. 16.

177 Roger Normand, *The Nation*, August 27, 1990.

178 Ben Kiernan, *Cambodia's Missed Chance*, pp. 2–4.

179 *The Economist*, September 30, 1989.

180 *Cambodia: The Betrayal*, Central Television, 1990; also from untransmitted material.

181 The *Far Eastern Economic Review*, March 2, 1989.

182 Senator Bob Kerrey; testimony before the US Senate Foreign Relations Committee, April 11, 1991.

183 Ben Kiernan, *Cambodia's Missed Chance*, p. 10.

184 Ibid.

185 Stephen R. Heder, a Cambodian scholar who was worked both for the US State Department and Amnesty International, found that 'after careful examination of all the available evidence, I have seen no evidence that any of the ex-Khmer Rouge in positions of high political authority in today's Cambodia were involved in large-scale or systematic killing of Cambodian civilians'. *Recent Developments in Cambodia*, a paper presented at the Australian National University on September 5, 1990.

186 Martha Gellhorn, *The Face of War*, Virago, London, 1986, p. 254.

187 Interviewed on film in October 1992 for *Return to Year Zero*, Central Television, March 1993.

188 Ibid.

189 The Melbourne *Age*, cited in the *Bulletin*, May 11, 1993.

190 Report by the Danish-based Child International, sponsored by UNICEF, cited in the *Guardian*, November 11, 1993.

191 Document seen by the author.

192 Correspondence with the author.

193 The *New Statesman and Society* (letters), July 2, 1993.

194 See William Shawcross, the *Washington Post*, March 16, 1980.

195 The *New Statesman and Society*, May 28, 1993; the *National*

Catholic Reporter, May 14, 1993; also communication with the author.

196 Roger Normand, *The Nation*, August 27, 1990.

197 The *Guardian* magazine, May 22, 1993.

198 The *Independent*, May 10, 1993.

199 The *Australian*, June 26, 1993.

200 The *Phnom Penh Post*, June 6–12, 1993.

201 *Time* magazine, December 28, 1992; the *Daily Telegraph*, May 12, 1993; the *New York Times*, October 11, 1993.

202 Private communication.

203 Interviewed by the author, June 1993. See Craig Etcheson, 'The Calm Before the Storm', CORKR Situation Report, March 1993.

204 See *Indochina Newsletter*, Issue 79, 1993, No. 1.

205 Cited in *Indochina Digest*, June 1993.

206 *Indochina Newsletter*, Issue 79, 1993, No. 1.

207 The *Far Eastern Economic Review*, February 4, 1993.

208 Ibid.

209 Nayan Chanda, 'Cambodia in search of an elusive peace', Aspen Institute, Vol. 8, No. 2, February 8, 1993.

210 Roger Normand, *The Nation*, August 27, 1990.

211 John Pedler, *Cambodia: A Report on the International and Internal Situation and the Future Outlook*, NGO Forum on Kampuchea, London, April 1989.

212 *Indochina Digest*, October 1993.

213 The *Sydney Morning Herald*, December 28, 1993.

214 The *Guardian*, December 23, 1993.

215 Report by Paul Davies, MAG South East Asia Desk Officer, April 28, 1994.

216 The *Phnom Penh Post*, August 13–26, 1993.

217 The *Far Eastern Economic Review*, cited in *Indochina Digest*, August 1992.

218 The *National Catholic Reporter*, May 14, 1992.

219 The *Sydney Morning Herald*, cited in *Indochina Digest*, February 1993.

220 Report to the UN Economic and Social Council, July 2, 1985.

221 The *Washington Post*, January 26, 1992.

222 Cited by Penny Edwards, the *Guardian*, November 4, 1989.

X UNDER THE VOLCANO

1   IBON Databank study, cited in the *Daily Globe*, November 11, 1991.
2   The *Daily Globe*, October 9, 1991.
3   *War by Other Means*, Central Television, 1991.
4   James Goodno, *The Philippines: Land of Broken Promises*, pp. 3–7.
5   Letter to the author.
6   James Goodno, *The Philippines*, pp. 5, 6.
7   Ibid., p. 4.
8   *AMPO Japan-Asia Quarterly Review*, Vol. 23, No. 1, 1990.
9   The *Daily Globe*, October 10, 1991.
10 Amnesty International report, cited in *New Statesman and Society*, June 21, 1991.
11 James Goodno, *The Philippines*, p. 287.
12 The *Guardian*, October 31, 1991.
13 The *Guardian*, October 30, 1991.
14 Ibid.
15 *Do They Feel My Shadow?*, made by Goldhawk Films, broadcast BBC 2, July 4, 1991.
16 Martha Gellhorn, *The Face of War*, Virago, London, 1986, p. 254.
17 The *New York Times*, August 5, 1991.
18 *The Nation*, June 17, 1991.
19 *Heroes*, pp. 138, 139.
20 The *Guardian*, June 27, 1992.
21 The *Guardian*, May 29, 1991.
22 Market International Report (Ethiopia summary), January 1979, cited in *Behind the War in Eritrea*, edited by Basil Davidson, Lionel Cliffe and Bereket Hable Selassie, Spokesman, Nottingham, 1980, p. 39.
23 *BBC Short Wave Broadcasts Summary*, June 1991.
24 Ibid.

XI AUSTRALIA

1   The *Sydney Morning Herald*, August 3, 1987.
2   In February 1992 youth unemployment was estimated at 34 per cent. Source: Radio 2UE Sydney economic analysis, February 4, 1992.

3   1986 OECD figures researched by Carole Sklan for *The Last Dream*, Central Television, 1988.

4   *Direct Action*, November 29, 1988.

5   The *Sun-Herald*, December 15, 1991.

6   Statex – *Sydney Morning Herald* study, October 31, 1987.

7   The *Sydney Morning Herald*, February 21, 1992.

8   The *Sydney Morning Herald*, February 15, 1992.

9   The *Sydney Morning Herald*, February 18, 1992; Radio 2UE economic analysis, February 14, 1992.

10 Geoff Page, 'Inscription at Villers-Bretonneux', in *Shadows from Wire: Poems and Photographs of Australia in the Great War*, ed. Geoff Page, Penguin, Sydney, 1983, p. 94.

11 Historian James Rusbridger referred to a secret memo sent by British Chiefs of Staff to Churchill in August 1940 – which maintained that Singapore could not be defended. The memo is one of a number of documents omitted from official histories of the period and which, according to Rusbridger, demonstrate that Churchill withheld the warning on Singapore from the governments of Australia and New Zealand. See the *Sun-Herald*, February 16, 1992; the *Guardian*, February 28, 1992.

12 John Pilger, *A Secret Country*, Vintage Books, London, 1992, p. 159.

13 Manning Clark, *The Quest for an Australian Identity*, James Duhig Memorial Lecture delivered at the University of Queensland in 1979; published by University of Queensland Press, St Lucia, 1980, p. 18.

14 The *Sydney Morning Herald*, November 13, 1978.

15 See Brian Toohey, the *Sun-Herald*, Febuary 2, 1992.

16 *The Last Dream*, Central Television, 1988.

17 *A Secret Country*, p. 169.

18 The *Sydney Morning Herald*, January 9, 1992.

19 *Allies*, documentary film directed by Marian Wilkinson, produced by Sylvie Chezio, Cinema Enterprises Property Ltd, Australia, 1981.

20 Alan Renouf, *The Frightened Country*, Macmillan, Melbourne, 1979, p. 279.

21 *A Secret Country*, p. 267. The original source was from within the prime minister's office, as told to the late William Pinwill.

22 The *Sydney Morning Herald*, November 4, 1991. Evans made the claim in a book written with Bruce Grant, *Australia's Foreign*

Relations in the World of the 1990s, Melbourne University Press, 1991.

23 Private communication with the author.

24 Cited by Catherine Lumby, the *Sydney Morning Herald*, January 9, 1992.

25 Cited by Noam Chomsky, the *Guardian*, January 10, 1991.

26 Cited by Lumby.

27 Australian *Hansard*, November 1, 1989.

28 The *Sydney Morning Herald*, December 28, 1991.

29 *BBC Shortwave Broadcasts Summary*, January 1992.

30 *A Secret Country*, pp. 152, 153.

31 The *Guardian*, January 17, 1992.

32 David Day, *The Great Betrayal: Britain, Australia and the Onset of the Pacific War*, Angus and Robertson, Sydney, 1988, p. 287.

33 The *Sydney Morning Herald*, August 31, 1987.

34 Ibid., October 11, 1986.

35 Ibid., May 22, 1991.

36 Ibid., May 8, 1991.

37 Ibid.

38 Ibid., February 18, 1992.

39 Ibid., April 18, 1992.

40 Ibid., February 12, 1992.

41 Ibid., February 4, 1991.

42 Ibid., March 30, 1985.

43 The *Independent*, January 23, 1988.

44 Kevin Gilbert, *Because a White Man'll Never Do It*, Angus and Robertson, Sydney, 1973.

45 The *Sydney Morning Herald*, May 9, 1985.

46 The *Guardian*, July 17, 1993.

47 Ibid.

48 Ibid.

49 Ibid.

50 The Melbourne *Age*, January 29, 1994.

51 Cited in correspondence.

INDEX

and the Gulf War 128, 138, 176

Hussein, Saddam:
atrocities against Kurds 138, 149, 155, 165, 166, 169
awarded 'Gardener's World award' 3
and Bazoft's murder 354–5
British arms deals with 118, 137–8, 172, 184–5, 355
British support for 355
compared with Hitler 425, 427
and invasion of Kuwait 74, 127, 128, 129, 130, 139, 167, 183, 185
portrayal in media 73–4, 143, 354
Shi'a opposition to 162, 165, 166–7, 168
US support for 162, 165, 185, 341
see also Gulf War, the

Huu Ngon 493

Hyland, Tom 321

IBA 86

Ieng Sary 463

Ignatieff, Michael 145, 228

IMF see International Monetary Fund

immigration (in Britain) 35–7, 38

imperialism 19, 69
American 88–93, 148–50, 161–2, 166, 168, 194, 228, 229, 337–8, 339, 341–2, 392
'information' 70, 72–4, 88–9

In Cold Blood (film) 563 n11

Independent:
coverage of Cambodia 453, 454, 455, 488
coverage of Gulf War 127–8, 140, 151–2, 162
'Hurd rejects Pilger's Cambodia allegations' 424–5

Independent on Sunday 65, 86

India:
Indonesia backed by 259
effect of World Bank dams on 211
as UN Security Council member 181

Indo-China Project 469n

Indonesia 239, 322–3
America and 245–6, 294–5
Australia and 244–5, see also under Australia
and Cambodia 474
Japanese investment in 255, 259
see East Timor; Suharto, General

Indostar (satellite) 316

'information imperialism' 70, 72–4, 88–9

Inge, C. D. 34

Institute of Policy Studies, Washington 203

intelligentsia, American:
Chomsky attacks 339, 341–5

Interception of Communications Act 84

International Freedom Foundation (US) 458

International Herald Tribune 158

International League for Human Rights 257

International Management (Australia) 526–7

International Monetary Fund:
Cambodian debt to 485–6
and Guatemala 200
and 'structural adjustment' of the Philippines 69–70, 205–6
and Yeltsin's democracy 195
see also World Bank

International Red Cross:
aid for Cambodia 403, 436, 460
and East Timor 305–6

Australian support for 12,
244–5, 247, 264, 313–14, 317
British arms sales to 16, 258–9,
301–4, 306–11
his coup against Sukarno 244,
245–6, 275–6, 341
and family members in power
261, 284, 315, 323
and the invasion of East Timor
233, 237, 239, 247, 249, 251,
254, 274, 288, 297, 299
and Paul Keating 12, 313–14,
317
receives UN Fund for
Population Activities Prize
285
and the Santa Cruz massacre
312
and US public relations firms
294–5, 299
US support for 245–7, 299, 300,
425
and Marcus Wanandi 315
his waning power 322–3
Gough Whitlam's relationship
with 243, 247, 269
suicides:
in Britain 110–11
of Vietnam War veterans 146
Sukarno, 'Bung' 244, 245
Sun:
on Bazoft's murder 354, 355,
356
coverage of the Gulf War 126,
159
as market leader 64, 76, 77,
79, 81
and racism 36, 38, 77
Sun Tzu, General: *The Art of
War* 493
Sunday Mirror 80
Sunday Telegraph:
accuses author of supporting
Khmer Rouge 450
smears Bazoft 355–6, 357

on investigative journalism 10
and Simon O'Dwyer-Russell
414, 421, 422, 423, 449–52
Sunday Times 79, 154
smear campaigns 433, 434,
435–8
Sunderland Echo 53
Svay Toeu, Cambodia 406–7
Swallow, Norman 18, 87
Swank, Emory 406, 474
Sweden:
and arms supplies to Khmer
Rouge 413
change of stance at UN 418
freedom of the press in 81
as model for Fretilin leaders
243
Sydney, Australia 523, 538
'Bicentenary' celebrations
545–6
Sydney Morning Herald 236,
247–8, 249, 261, 262, 314, 492,
539, 541, 563 n4
Sydney University 329, 540
Syria: US and Assad regime
179–80, 187–8

Target USA (film) 159
Tawney, R. H. 30
Taylor, A. J. P.: on newspapers 76
Taylor, D. J.: 'While the pen
sleeps' 17
Taylor, Elizabeth 334, 394
Taylor, John G. 253, 288, 321
Tea Banh, General 448
Teachers' Pay Review Body 115
television:
and Broadcasting Bill
amendments (1990) 68,
83–7
and censorship 83–7, 183
current affairs programmes on
6–7, 84–7, 92
coverage of Gulf War 71,